VIOLENCE AND THE FEMALE IMAGINATION

Violence and the Female Imagination

Quebec's Women Writers Re-Frame Gender in North American Cultures

PAULA RUTH GILBERT

McGill-Queen's University Press
Montreal & Kingston · London · Ithaca

ISBN-13: 978-0-7735-3031-7
ISBN-10: 0-7735-3031-2

Legal deposit second quarter 2006
Bibliothèque nationale du Québec

Printed in Canada on acid-free paper that is 100% ancient forest free (100% post-consumer recycled), processed chlorine free.

This book has been published with the help of grants from the International Council for Canadian Studies and George Mason University.

McGill-Queen's University Press acknowledges the support of the Canada Council for the Arts for our publishing program. We also acknowledge the financial support of the Government of Canada through the Book Publishing Industry Development Program (BPIDP) for our publishing activities.

Library and Archives Canada Cataloguing in Publication

Gilbert, Paula Ruth
Violence and the female imagination: Quebec's women writers re-frame gender in North American cultures / Paula Ruth Gilbert.

Includes bibliographical references and index.
ISBN-13: 978-0-7735-3031-7 ISBN-10: 0-7735-3031-2

1. Canadian fiction (French) – Women authors – History and criticism. 2. Canadian fiction (French) – Québec (Province) – History and criticism. 3. Violence in literature. 4. Women in literature. 5. Sex roles in literature. 6. Violence in women – North America. 7. Canadian fiction (French) – 20th century – History and criticism. I. Title.

PS8089.5.W6G54 2006 C843'.54093552'082 C2005-906628-8

This book was typeset by Interscript in 10.5/13 Sabon.

To Randy

Contents

Acknowledgments

When one has been working on a major project like this book for so many years, it is difficult to acknowledge the many people and organizations that have helped in some way during that whole period. And when one has been in the field of Quebec Studies and Women's Studies for decades, it is even harder to include all the wonderful colleagues and mentors along the way. This limited list will have to suffice.

My interest in Quebec, Canada, women, and violence would perhaps not have become so prominent in my intellectual (and professorial) life, had it not been for the wonderful collaboration that I have had over the years with my dear friend Lorna Irvine. I must also follow this acknowledgment with a second one for the productive collaboration with my close colleague and friend Kim Eby, who has taught me so much about the community psychological aspects of violence and gender. More in line with my own training in literature and criticism oriented toward issues of violence and gender is Lori Saint-Martin, whose work has informed mine for years. I can say the same about Mary Jean Green, whose intellectual achievements and friendship have been enormously important for me for several decades. This last acknowledgment brings me to the powerful friendship that I have had since the 1970s with my fellow "Frenchettes": Mary Jean Green, Jane Moss, Karen Gould, and the late Jeanne Kissner. Other compatriots in the fields of Quebec Studies, women's studies, and literature also need to be thanked: Miléna

Santoro, Roseanna Dufault, and Janine Ricouart. And finally I need to acknowledge the work of my two former doctoral students: Jennifer Gauthier, who taught me so much about Canadian and Quebec film, and Molly Dragiewicz, who has made me better understand issues of domestic violence and gendered discourse.

A special thank you is due to my department chair and friend, Jeffrey Chamberlain, whose unfailing encouragement and belief in my project have been extraordinary. Reviewing my translations, consistently expressing his pride in my work, and making me laugh, Jeff has been extremely important to my project during these long years.

I am grateful to the National Endowment for the Humanities, which supported my research with a Faculty Research Fellowship. I acknowledge the support of George Mason University in its award to me of a study leave, the College of Arts and Sciences Dean's Office for supplemental funding during that year on the NEH Fellowship, and the Department of Modern and Classical Languages for its additional financial support toward the production of this book. The program and faculty in Women's Studies have also been wonderfully encouraging.

A warm acknowledgment goes to the professional staff at McGill-Queen's University Press: my editor, Philip Cercone, who never failed in his belief in my work; Joan McGilvray, whose coordinating efforts made the process manageable; Susanne McAdam, who moved along the arrangements for the cover jacket image; and Jane McWhinney, who is, without doubt, the most thorough, intelligent, and sensitive copy editor I have ever worked with. And of course a very special acknowledgment to Bonnie Baxter, whose amazing 1992 woodcut *Chimère* adorns the cover of this book and so beautifully represents its subject matter. As an artist, Bonnie clearly "reads" representation and reality together, as do I.

On a more personal note, I would like to thank my brother, Arthur Gilbert, of the University of Denver, whose common interest in issues of violence and gender has stimulated endless discussions, and whose own disciplinary training has forced me to look more carefully at historical and international perspectives. To my sister, Marian Knapp, whose academic interests in issues of aging in an interdisciplinary context dovetail with many of my own, I also offer my thanks. I have much appreciated the consistent interest and encouragement of Morris and Eleanor Gabel. To Christopher McCoy, who never believed that he would have a mother-in-law interested in such topics, I also send an acknowledgment. And I express my deepest thanks and love to my extraordinary daughter, Meredith Gilbert Lewis, who has always been proud of her mother's areas of research and writing.

I most especially acknowledge Michael Randy Gabel. His tireless work on the figures for the chapters, his frequent resolution of computer problems, his determination to make me place all of this work in the context of a full life and lifestyle, his never-ending sense of humour, encouragement, support, and pride – all of this has me dedicate this book to him.

NOTE ON TRANSLATIONS AND PERMISSIONS

Published translations of the primary and critical texts have been used whenever available and are referenced in the Works Cited and Consulted. All other translations are my own. Generally the English translation appears first in the text, followed by the original French. I would like again to acknowledge the generous help of Jeffrey Chamberlain, who reviewed my translations and made excellent suggestions. My copy editor, Jane McWhinney, also suggested certain changes, which I have accepted.

Certain parts of this book have been previously published in very different forms in the following journals and edited volume. I gratefully acknowledge their respective editors for permission to include these materials in this book:

"'The Killer Awoke before Dawn': The Multiple Mirrors of Hélène Rioux's Eléonore." *Québec Studies* 20 (1995): 56–65.

"Pre and Post-Mortem: Regendering and Serial Killing in Rioux, Dandurand, Dé, and Atwood," with Lorna Irvine. *The American Review of Canadian Studies* 28.1 (1999): 113–33.

"Public and Private Violence: 'Une Mise en discours de la violence' in Aline Chamberland's *La Fissure*." *The American Review of Canadian Studies* 31.1 (2001): 359–83.

"Discourses of Female Criminality: Suzanne Jacob's *L'Obéissance*, A Novel of Infanticide/Filicide." *Québec Studies* 32 (fall 2001/winter 2002): 37–55.

"Discourses of Female Violence and Societal Gender Stereotypes." *Violence against Women Journal* 8.11 (November 2002): 1271–300.

"Section I: Conceptualizing Violence." Pp. 1–2 (Introduction) in *Violence and Gender: An Interdisciplinary Reader*, Ed. with Kimberly K. Eby. Upper Saddle River, New Jersey: Pearson Education/Prentice Hall, 2004.

VIOLENCE AND THE FEMALE IMAGINATION

INTRODUCTION

Regendering Violence and Appropriating Power: Beyond the Binary

In the waning years of the twentieth century and the dawning of the twenty-first, scholars of human behaviour have been rethinking concepts of violence. In *Violence, Identity, and Self-Determination*, for example, Hent de Vries and Samuel Weber state that the question of violence has imposed itself with renewed urgency "with the collapse of the bipolar system of global rivalry." They remark that violence, which had formerly been simplistically construed as a manifestation of binary opposition – the intrusion of an external other/adversary upon the self/same – now needs to be studied more subtly as the attempt to delineate the borders that separate self from other.[1] Furthermore, traditional approaches to this problem need to be brought into question, disparate disciplines broken down, and transdisciplinary methods applied (1–2). Deirdre Lashgari, in *Violence, Silence, and Anger: Women's Writing as Transgression*, similarly underscores several discourses crucial to understanding women's literary responses to violence in particular. She singles out: decentring; refusing to perpetuate systems of binary opposition; celebrating a multiplicity of discourses and voices; exposing contradictions and discrepancies; and crossing over, transgressing, and questioning the unknown ground of the Other and the boundaries of the familiar.

How do these issues and discourses relate to and inform the present work, *Violence and the Female Imagination*, this study of recent violent fiction by women writers of Quebec? I am interested in the literary representation of violence that women do, particularly the violence they do to others rather than to themselves. It is popular opinion that worldwide – both in the "real" world and in literature, film, media, and pop culture – increasing numbers of women are exhibiting outwardly directed violent tendencies and acting on them. I am speaking here not about the violence that women do in reaction to past or current abuse by male or female partners (although one often blames the intrusion of an external other, a patriarchal society that has pushed some women to deviant behaviour and crime); I am speaking, rather, about the increase in the representation of women who harm, maim, torture, and kill, acting, not out of reaction, but on their own initiative. It is here that I find the first link with the rejection of binary causes that is central to this scholarly "problem": I am walking a fine line between seeing the representations of these women either as infantilized and unstable, incapable of "real" violent feelings and actions, or as new renditions of the "classic" evil sister and stepmother, whore, Eve-like temptress, serpent, nymph/vampire, and devouring mother. Are these violent literary female protagonists "really" violent or are they simply postmodern versions of the same old female in the male eye?

Why should one study this literature of Quebec written by women? The literature of this postcolonial, francophone, North American society provides a fruitful case study. At the crossroads of a French theoretical, cultural, and linguistic tradition, an English-Canadian dominance, a British presence, and especially a powerful and sometimes smothering U.S. popular culture and media, Quebec society and the literature that reflects and helps create it constitute an interesting laboratory for broad scholarly investigation. Canada is perceived as, and indeed *is*, a far less violent country than the United States (although not as peaceful as one commonly thinks, according to crime statistics), and within Canada, Quebec is one of the least violent provinces. Quebec, in its own right, is not in an "and/or" polarity, not in a binary opposition – hence my second link. In its own search for identity and self-determination, it is on the decentred margins, at the boundaries, but its form of violence, of revolution, has always been quiet – a war of words and political stances, often in reaction to constitutional experiments by the Canadian federal government. Its literature similarly provides experimental representations that go beyond defined genres, refusing to be limited by the binary.

There has, however, long been a tradition in Québécois literature of violent relationships and situations, much of which has been interpreted as pathological, spilling over from a former "priest-ridden" atmosphere and the consequent stifling of life and creativity in the province. But more recently – in the 1980s, 1990s, and first decade of this century – unlike the more tranquil political and social context from which they arise, some younger feminist women writers of Quebec have been creating a multiplicity of voices whose narratives exude a fascination for eroticism, bold sexual action and language, cruelty, and violence, culminating at times in crimes such as infanticide and serial killing. In other words, while Canada and Quebec continue to "fight it out" in the constitutional, political, and legal arenas, some Québécois fictional women are slashing their way toward non-gendered territories.

In a third link with the effort to go beyond the binary perspective in attempting to understand violence, we must ask whether these narrated women are striking out at an external other or are harming themselves, as women have often done in acts of self-destruction resulting from depression or other such pathologies? Do these fictional women simply reflect a perceived increase of violence in a society where there are higher numbers of female gangs, female serial killers, and women prison inmates? Are the violent media – especially from the United States –affecting writers of Quebec fiction? Are women imitating men in the recent outward direction of their anger and hostility? Some critics have taken the "blame-it-on-feminism" approach: that women are more violent because they are now liberated, free to act like men, taking advantage of the new roles and opportunities now available to them. Given the observation that several of these Quebec women writers use biting irony and parody in their depictions of violent women killers, are such "tough" women mocking men in their "macho" exploits of sexuality and violence? Are they "feminizing" violence, regendering violence, going beyond gender toward the non-binary boundaries between the self and the other, as they attempt to re-envision and re-frame gender in the violent cultures of North America? Such questions are at the core of the research for and the writing of this book. Given the importance of better understanding violence in our societies – both real and representational – and by "reading" both the real and the representational together, this study clearly has deep and wide significance.

Violence and the Female Imagination: Quebec's Women Writers Re-Frame Gender in North American Cultures consists of five chapters. Chapter 1 surveys different approaches to the causes of violence as it relates to gender, conceptualizing and theorizing from fields such as philosophy, psychology, sociology, criminology, history, political science, biology, feminist theory, and cultural studies, as these theories inform literary representations of violence and gender through language, imagery, narrative, and intertextuality. In chapter 2, I begin to discuss the complex interconnectedness of the United States and Canada, focusing primarily on the French-speaking province of Quebec. Basing some of my interpretations on comparative crime statistics, my major emphasis in this chapter is on the concepts of Americanization and *américanité* ("Americanness") as they inform current discussions of Canadian cultural policies and Quebec's self-ascribed identity as a "nation" in North America – often through its culture and literature. The impact on Canada, and Quebec in particular, of American popular culture through the media (news, television, films, music, popular fiction, and magazines) informs my analysis of "cultural and literary violence" as a possible negative effect of either the *américanité* or the Americanization of Quebec.

The major literary focus of this book occurs in its following chapters. In chapter 3, I begin by presenting theories of the sexuality and violence of female representation and of the representation of female sexuality and violence, picking up on issues raised in chapter 1 and introducing, in particular, concepts of the pornography of representation and the female grotesque. Quebec literary critics have remarked that since the early 1980s much Quebec writing has become increasingly postnationalistic in character, as issues of immigrant, plurilingual and hybrid cultures, globalization, international feminist concerns, *américanité*, and continuing explorations of Quebec "nationalism" take their place on literary platforms. The view of these Quebec literary critics and a number of women writers on *américanité*/North American society at the close of the twentieth and the opening of the twenty-first centuries thus continues my discussion, as I begin the analysis of representative texts and focus closely on one major example: the stark influence of U.S. popular culture in Hélène Rioux's novel *Les Miroirs d'Éléonore*. I next discuss theories and narratives of eroticism, pornography, and graphic sexuality in the imagination of female writers, placing them in a global context, investigating the effects of parody, and analysing a number of representative novels and short stories from Quebec.

Chapter 3 then moves into the arena of female sexuality and cruelty/violence – first in examples from the United States, France, and Britain and then in several from Quebec. Finally, I discuss female literary violence – at first briefly in texts by some well known and "older, established" Quebec women writers; then in some powerful and disturbing contemporary texts that reflect the violent popular culture of North America; and eventually in narratives of patricide and castration.

Chapters 4 and 5 focus on specific forms of female criminal activity. Chapter 4 presents a close reading of two novels of infanticide/filicide: *La Fissure* by Aline Chamberland and *L'Obéissance* by the award-winning and widely read Suzanne Jacob. I analyse these extremely dense and complex novels together, since they both underscore the influence of the media and the resulting tension between private and public violence, as read in conjunction with historical and contemporary documents and legal studies related to the killing of one's child.

The novels and short stories of Hélène Rioux, Anne Dandurand, and Claire Dé are at the centre of Chapter 5, where women – again frequently obsessed with popular rock music, television, news, and film – seriously fantasize about, narrate, or actually commit violent crimes and become parodic serial killers in sprees that end in real death, as they bitterly (and often humorously) make a mockery of male power and strength, and ultimately transgress all boundaries that define our genders. In concluding this book I try to understand what this representation of women imitating men, feminizing violence, or regendering violence means in our gendered cultures of violence at the turn of the millennium, and how these contemporary women writers from Quebec are attempting to re-frame such cultures.

Some reviews of recently published books on "real" violent women and female serial killers have labelled these women – the latest focus of late-twentieth and early-twenty-first century feminists – as "new postfeminist icons,"[2] ironically seeing this interest as a fight for women who kill to win access to the criminal (formerly all male) canon. Recently there has been a spate of studies on "tough girls," "bad girls," "wicked women," "Sapphic slashers," "evil sisters," "killer moms" – and most recently "mean girls" – especially as clichés of Hollywood and the wider popular culture of the United States. But little has yet been written about the literary representation of violent women – and certainly not in Quebec fiction. In Quebec literary studies, the works of Lori Saint-Martin, Karen Gould, Luise von Flotow, Kathleen Kellett-Betsos, and Claudine Potvin, in addition to my own published studies, are the most significant scholarly publications to have treated violent literary women. My work has been – and continues to be – an effort to bridge the methodological and disciplinary gaps inherent in such research and writing. Based on broad research in both the social sciences and the humanities, and informed by cultural studies and psychological theory, this work examines the literary representation of female violence in the context of a relatively peaceful and feminist society (with the 1989 Montreal Massacre as an egregious exception) in an attempt to answer the question: why are women writers now creating females "liberated" enough to kill, to take the power of death into their own hands?

1

Conceptualizing and Contextualizing Violence and Gender: From "Real Life" to Theory to Literary Representation

The aim of reflection is to reach a better understanding of the cultural situation by interpreting it in the light of ... works of imagination. In a reversal of familiar procedures, culture takes on the role of a text to be read in the context of representation, expressivity, and fantasy. Such imaginative processes can neither be translated directly into "real" life ... nor be entirely disengaged from it ... They form treasuries of suggestion, nurseries of attitude, that can help produce, sustain, and foster insight into complex cultural realities. When we listen to music or hear the music of language, we resonate with such realities; when we gaze with strained attention at imaginary scenes on the stage or screen, including the screen of the mind's eye, when we read or dream, we are engaged in the making of culture, our making by culture, which includes the mechanism both of sexual violence and, someday perhaps, of its undoing.

Lawrence Kramer, *After the Lovedeath: Sexual Violence and the Making of Culture* (3–4)

Metaphors are the instruments of poetry, beauty, and inner truth. Why blame the tool for how we use it? After all, "guns don't kill people, people do." But we use tools for what we don't want to do with our hands. Metaphors do the dirty work of ideology ... Social paranoia feeds on metaphor, because every image we form rapidly takes on a life and meaning of its own ... Metaphor, by establishing a bridge between image and act, encourages us to bypass common sense and reasonable doubt. Thus it hands us the gun that does our killing ...

Bram Dijkstra, *Evil Sisters: The Threat of Female Sexuality and the Cult of Manhood* (311–12)

APPROACHES TO "REAL LIFE" VIOLENCE

Not all violence is sexual, but it is difficult to imagine any analysis or discussion of violence without a concomitant study of gender. Indeed, definitions of violence, gender, and culture need to underpin any such discussions, especially as one moves from investigations of "real" violence to more philosophical meditations, and finally to its artistic – and here specifically literary – representations.

While there is disagreement within scholarly communities about which theoretical perspectives best explain "real" violence and violent behaviour, there is general agreement on the importance of looking at multiple causal influences (biological, psychological, and socio-cultural/environmental/structural) at multiple levels (individual, community, and societal). It is often mistakenly assumed, however, that all researchers and scholars who study violence and violent behaviour are using the same definitions. Some authors, for example, use the terms "violence" and "aggression" interchangeably and others make a distinction between them. In addition, we must understand the significance of group differences – much discussed in social science research – recognizing that generalities say nothing about the behaviour of specific individuals. The same limitations apply when speaking about risk factors for violence and violent behaviour. While a risk factor indicates that membership in a specific group places one at higher risk for a particular outcome, such as perpetrating violence, it does not imply that any given member of a specific group will actually engage in a violent act.

James Gilligan's "How to Think about Violence" offers a good initial approach to understanding violence and violent behaviour. In this essay Gilligan discusses the role of theory as it relates to our ability to understand and prevent violence. He articulates the need to move away from the tendency to make value judgments about violence and violent behaviour, primarily because such judgments do not help us explain violence or address its potential causes. Gilligan asserts that social and legal institutions, particularly criminal justice systems, have been acting on the "rational self-interest" theory of violence, which assumes that rational self-interest and common sense underlie individuals' engagement in violent behaviour. He, on the other hand, sees violent behaviour as an innate human response to a loss of honour and self-respect. Ultimately, he argues, if we are to prevent violence we must adopt a public health and preventive medicine model in which violence is perceived as a disease that is caused by and affects biological, psychological, and social systems.

Myriam Miedzian's "Boys Will Be Boys" also examines theoretical explanations of violence and violent behaviour. Miedzian, however, is more concrete in her analyses than Gilligan. In reviewing the role of testosterone in aggressive behaviour, for example, she coins the term "masculine mystique" to explore socio-cultural conditions conducive to violence, examines the relationship between abuse, neglect, and aggressive behaviour, and discusses specific risk factors for violent behaviour. More significantly, Miedzian claims that aggression and violent behaviour are primarily male phenomena, and the central focus of her work is to answer the question, "Why are men more violent than women?" This question underlies some of the discussions in this book, as I prepare to analyse female literary characters who challenge such gendered assumptions.

While these approaches argue for multiple levels of causation in theories of violence, others use a more narrowly focused line of inquiry. Elizabeth Susman and Jordan Finkelstein, for example, both of whom work in the area of bio-behavioural health, propose a developmental perspective on biological factors and violence in "Biology, Development, and Dangerousness." They suggest that we consider the dialectical nature of the interactions between physiological and psychological processes, along with the impact of an individual's environment. Although they offer a bio-psycho-social model of "dangerousness" (interestingly using this term rather than "aggression" or "violence"), they focus extensively on biological systems and antisocial behaviour, including the role of the neurotransmitter serotonin.

In "The Tipping Point" Malcolm Gladwell also encourages us to think about violence from the perspective of public health, albeit within a different theoretical framework. Whereas Gilligan advocates a public health approach based on a bio-psycho-social model, and Susman and Finkelstein focus on biological systems within a similar multi-modelled approach, Gladwell takes his lesson from epidemiologists. He uses the notion of a "tipping point" – the point at which ordinary phenomena can turn into public health crises – to address the question of violence. In reviewing research on the non-linearity of social problems, he cites a study that shows that "at the five percent tipping point neighborhoods go from relatively functional to wildly dysfunctional virtually over night. There is no steady decline: a little change has a huge effect" (37). (Interestingly, a cultural critic like René Girard also bases some of his arguments on this same concept of a tipping point, as I point out later in this chapter.)

Additional works by Gilligan, "Shame: The Emotions and Morality of Violence" and "The Deadliest Form of Violence Is Poverty," review two other levels of analysis pertinent to violent behaviour and its causes – levels that are different but intricately related. Gilligan argues that violence is a contagious disease whose pathogen is psychological; social, economic, and cultural factors are consequently more responsible for the spread of this disease than are biological factors. In "Shame," he proposes that – in the absence of love or guilt – feelings of shame are at the heart of violent behaviour and violence is used to replace them with feelings of pride and self-respect. Reflecting some of the socio-cultural issues raised by Miedzian, his work is also relevant to how we socialize boys. Gilligan goes on to discuss the social, economic, and cultural factors that in his view contribute to the spread of violence, specifically in the United States. Structural violence, he says, is a by-product of our social and economic structure. Although hidden, it is the main cause of behavioural violence and causes far more deaths than behavioural violence, demonstrating how the psychological pathogen of shame disproportionately affects those at the lower end of our class system.

Whether measured by suicides, homicides, rapes, gun deaths, or other forms of assault, U.S. society is one of the most violent in the industrialized world (see comparisons with Quebec and Canada in chapter 2). While some of the theories reviewed above might be able to account for this fact, research by Richard Slotkin on the active construction of American frontier mythology and its transformation into history adds an additional dimension. He delves into the creation of Buffalo Bill's Wild West shows, among many manifestations of the violence of the U.S. past, showing that America's frontier history was greatly scripted by William Cody and then reinforced in the public mind as reality. Although Cody strove to present an "authentic" visual representation of the American frontier – prefiguring movies, which began to be popular toward the end of Cody's reign in entertainment – he also presented as "moral truth" a representation of the frontier experience that lauded "violence and savage war [as] the necessary instruments of American progress" (77). Slotkin suggests that the link between violence and progress in the American psyche (not the Canadian) is critical to understanding the United States' current justifications for the use of violence in asserting and preserving dominance at home and abroad – points I consider crucial to any study of violence in today's culture and literature.

In *Demonic Males*, James Wrangham and Dale Peterson go beyond a review of the American past to argue that men have been the more violent sex for millennia, across various cultures – Western and non-Western – and review the ways in which men have dominated women worldwide. Given the consistency of patriarchy, they argue, violence cannot be merely a cultural invention. They hypothesize that patriarchy must be a biological construct, since it is a result of men's temperaments and their evolutionarily derived efforts to control women and work with other men to protect their vested interests.

Each of these approaches – biological, psychological, public health, sociological, and evolutionary – has a role in our understanding of why "real" violence and violent behaviour occur. We need to try to place them within a framework that moves from individual to societal factors as we try to reduce levels of violence throughout the world. We also need to begin to understand more completely how other scholars have treated "real" violence in the world and have attempted to delve into its moral, ethical, philosophical, and cultural causes and meanings.

SCHOLARLY DISCOURSES OF VIOLENCE

Definitions of Violence

In the first volume of *The History of Sexuality*, Michel Foucault develops his concept of "transforming sex into discourse" (20) ["une mise en discours du sexe"] (*Histoire de la sexualité* 29), which began in the seventeenth century. He speaks of the condemnation and denial of sexuality that cause people to seek it out and discuss/confess it in every detail, while the same negative elements and restrictions play into the making of that very discourse (16). In a similar vein, we rightfully abhor violence, and yet we are fascinated by its every detail, as re-enacted in courtroom trials, and reported and depicted in the media. Once again, condemnation and negative elements, linked with voyeuristic public interest and forms of entertainment, play into the transforming of violence into discourse ["une mise en discours de la violence"].

Why are people so fascinated with violence, crime, the criminal? In our times, this fascination takes the form of public obsession with forensic culture, a sort of "forensic noir" fixation on the body of victims, as in the popularity of such American television series as *CSI* and *CSI: Miami* (Doherty, "Cultural Studies and "'Forensic Noir'" B14–15). As Martha Reineke has shown, no rational system can logically respond to evil and horror, and violence often provokes a form of paralysis (occluding woman's agency), an inability to speak, a need for layered "substitutionary violence," and a general investment in soma/the flesh/the body (usually a form of somatophobia against the female body) (1–3). And yet this fascination remains. What does it say about us and our cultures?

Let me first offer some characterizations of the intimate relationship between violence and the culture that produces it. Ann-Louise Shapiro, basing her historical research on the concept of female criminality in late nineteenth-century Paris, has underscored how discourses of crime have become an obsession in society and how crime is a symptom of persistent societal questions, an indicator of cultural anarchy, often celebrated in popular culture (12–15). According to Barbara Whitmer, Western cultural imagination must be viewed as having created what she calls the "violence mythos": "a collection of beliefs that articulates attitudes in Western culture about violence ... defined as injurious or destructive discourse or action of one person or groups toward another" (1). Using Foucault's study on sexuality, she extrapolates the similarities between our views of sex and of violence: Freudian psychoanalytic theory discusses the repression of sexuality in society, and yet that same sexuality is to be found in all aspects of our society. So it is with violence: "Although violence is condemned, at the same time it is represented ubiquitously – in the media, the news, sports, entertainment, advertising – as conflict resolution, with a plethora of inadequate measures for damage control in an age of the victimizer/victim and an addiction to violence" (3).

Some criminologists have shown that our civilian era is far less violent than the civilian past – if one compares, say, current homicide rates in the United States and Western Europe to estimated homicide rates in medieval Europe when personal violence was the order of the day (Rhodes 215–16; see also Stille). Other theorists of violence see present societies as being in a state of perpetual and global civil war (see Hanssen on Enzensberger 180–1): people today live with immense anger and rage (Diamond 7); the increasing instability of gender polarity has increased the incidence of sexual violence (Kramer 261). In sum, for us, violence has become "an unbearable scandal" ["un scandale insupportable"] (Poizat 3), where in effect "violence prevents us from seeing violence" (Perret 41).

Any philosophical discussion of the moral and ethical dimensions of violence to some of the central concerns of many theorists must include a consideration of power and force. In a recent issue of the journal *Le*

Philosophoire dedicated to violence, several essays focus on this issue. Citing Georges Sorel – and, of course Hannah Arendt – on violence, Jean-Claude Poizat, for one, defines violence as the manifestation of force that appears abusive or illegitimate: "Violence designates a situation where the show of force appears to be abnormal in comparison with a certain equilibrium or principle of order, whether natural or social" ["La violence désigne une situation où la manifestation de la force paraît anormale au regard d'un certain équilibre ou d'un principe d'ordre, qu'il soit naturel ou social"] (31). Thus, according to Poizat: violence is the capacity to exert physical constraint upon another, the means by which one restrains another's will, and the instrumental use of force (citing Arendt, once again) (32), essentially moral or political. It remains "the last recourse of power" (Poizat 33). For Yann Renaud, who also bases his arguments on work by Arendt, violence must be seen as action, even though more passive and subtle forms of it are camouflaged in social conventions and rules. Independent of the question of authority, violence is power, the use of force, whether legitimate or not (99–100).

Violence and the Other

A second major concern in attempting to define violence arises when one speaks of power or force against someone else or some other group: its relationship to the "Other," or violence as "the tangible experience of the reality of the other ... the experience of others (Renaud 105). In "Violence et métaphysique" Jacques Derrida discusses the question, initially raised by Emmanuel Levinas and Eric Weil, of whether violence should be ascribed to a philosophical *logos* – a transcendental category – or whether it should be seen as the violation by some Other, some alterity that interrupts or ruptures this philosophical discourse. Leaving aside for the moment a discussion of violence at the level of discourse, for many theorists "the original event where ... violence is anchored is precisely the rapport with the other, since it is first lived as an uprooting from oneself, as a wrenching of the ego and a narcissistic wound, as an intrusion into the damp and somber intimacy of the self. The other looked at me, resulting initially in the experience of embarrassment or even of shame" ["L'évènement originaire où s'ancre cette violence, c'est précisément le rapport à l'autre puisqu'il est d'abord vécu comme un arrachement à soi-même, comme une déchirure de l'ego et une blessure narcissique, comme une intrusion dans la moite et sombre intimité du moi. L'autre me regardait, c'est d'abord l'expérience de la gêne ou même de la honte"] (Poizat 4). Similarly, for Hent de Vries, interpreting Derrida, Levinas, and Weil, violence can be located in any narcissistic strategy used to diminish or annul the other and in which an otherness forces the self to participate or become what it is not (16).

Foucault complicates matters even further in "The Subject and Power," where he distinguishes between a relationship of violence and one of power: "A relationship of violence acts upon a body or upon things; it forces, it bends, it breaks on the wheel, it destroys, or it closes the door on all possibilities. Its opposite pole can only be passivity, and if it comes up against any resistance it has no other option but to try to minimize it. On the other hand, a power relationship can only be articulated on the basis of two elements which are each indispensable if it is really to be a power relationship: that 'the other' (the one over whom power is exercised) be thoroughly recognized and maintained to the very end as a [subject that acts]; and that, faced with a relationship of power, a whole field of responses, reactions, results and possible inventions may open up" (as quoted in Hanssen 153–4).

Although many scholars maintain that poststructuralist feminist theory and Foucauldian theory are incompatible in reference to the consideration of issues such as violence and power, Gail Mason, in *The Spectacle of Violence*, attempts to dispute that assertion and steer a path between the two models. Despite her interpretation of Foucault's work as an argument that violence is not a form of power and her understanding that feminist theory theorizes violence, particularly men's violence toward women, as an expression of (patriarchal) power, Mason argues that for both Foucault and for feminists, "the nexus between violence and power is an *instrumental* one: violence is an instrument of power [and] the instrumental function of violence can be articulated as a question of *knowledge*" (120, 11).

Mason addresses the following questions and considers the answers to each through the work of both Foucault and feminists: Does violence oppress? What is power? Who has power? Is violence power (121–32)? Both models, she responds, agree that violence does oppress and that we need both the feminist definition of patriarchal power and the Foucauldian concept of productive power in order to define what power is. For Mason, although Foucault's suggestion that the question of who has power is ultimately unanswerable may prove to be true, "the productive function of violence is dependent upon the ability of that violence to tell us which subject positions are named as potential perpetrators of violence" (127). As for whether violence is power, an acceptable answer depends upon how much space there is between the two; if both feminist and Foucauldian theory suggest that violence is the outcome of a struggle between power and resistance, then "the idea of an instrumental nexus between violence and power represents a crucial site of convergence" (131). Ultimately Mason considers the definition of an instrument as that site where knowledge becomes the link between violence as a corporeal act and the hierarchies of difference that govern a given power relation: "Violence makes us know things according to the ways in which it makes contact with, or threatens to make contact with, our own bodies and the bodies of others" (132–3). The "deeply visceral knowledge" that we have of violence is the "instrument that connects corporeal injury and emotional harm (the oppression of violence) with the processes of subjectification (the constitutive capacity of power)" (133). For Mason, the path between Foucault and postructuralist feminist theory is thus based on instrumentality, visuality, and knowledge: "The act of violence itself is a spectacle. This is not so much because violence provides us with a striking or eye-catching phenomenon to observe, but, more, because violence is a mechanism through which we distinguish and identify other phenomena. In panoptic terms, then, we can think of the act of violence as a lens, a metaphorical lens through which we see, and come to know, certain things. In this way, violence is not just something to look at. Violence also embodies a way of looking" (134).

Whatever the philosophical stance, the issue at hand is ultimately the outcome of the fear and hatred of the other that characterize violence and our views of violent individuals. Karen Halttunen, in her study of the killer in the American imagination, traces the development of the concept of what she calls "moral otherness" (6), the idea of a monstrous depravity of a criminal or a murderer, which initially appeared in the late eighteenth century in the United States. Previously, all individuals had been seen as *potentially* sinful and capable of committing a crime. But once this inherently monstrous and morally deviant alien (59) made an appearance, evil became seen as an "unnatural perversion" (48), and people became fascinated with "the horror of difference" (236). It is this "horror of difference" (as related to violent women) that will inform much of my subsequent analyses of the representation of violence in literature.

Violence as Innate or Acquired

Who commits these violent acts? Who becomes this monstrous other? People predisposed to violence or people who have acquired the capacity as a result of external factors? Is violence a mediated response to perceived adverse stimuli? Is the motivation an innate and instinctive reaction, or, as Barbara Whitmer asks, is it conditioned by the "cultural context of expectations and acceptability or tolerance for the expression of violent behaviour" (53)? Whitmer reminds us that Freud's belief (and Paul Ricoeur's interpretation of Freudian thought) that the instinct to aggression is an "original self-subsisting instinctual disposition" in humans reflects the "exploitive logos of innate violence in the violence mythos" (100, 111). A belief in the innately violent nature of humans is therefore at the core of the violence mythos, as she defines it: "The cultural transmission of the belief that violence is innate as natural, through tradition and authoritative beliefs, contributes directly to violence being sanctioned and accepted within Western culture and exported to the larger global community" (19).

Other researchers define violence as entirely acquired. Dana Crowley Jack, for instance, distinguishes between anger as an emotion and aggression or violence as an act (43–4). She speaks of the impulse for aggression arising from a sense of disconnection, from the fracture of connection that sets an individual against the external world. Like James Gilligan, Jack sees destructive aggression as the outcome of a disconnection associated with shame (47, 55, 156).

Violence as a Symptom of Trauma

The question of whether violence is acquired or innate (that is, biologically inborn, or a genetically predisposed behaviour as Darwin believed) thus remains hotly debated. The role of trauma perhaps bridges this divide. Whitmer sees violence as a symptom of trauma, and trauma as the problem in the violence mythos: "The tentacles of the violence mythos are varied discourses that radiate from a central cultural belief in innate violence that masks unresolved trauma" (236–7). The recognized authority on trauma and recovery is Judith Lewis Herman, a clinical professor of psychiatry at Harvard Medical School and director of training at the Victims of Violence Program at Cambridge Hospital. Her initial definitions of trauma are particularly helpful. For Herman, "to study psychological trauma is to come face to face both with human vulnerability in the natural world and with the capacity for evil in human nature. To study psychological trauma means bearing witness to horrible events ... When the traumatic events are of human design, those who bear witness are caught in the conflict between victim and perpetrator. It is morally impossible to remain neutral in this conflict. The bystander is forced to take sides" (7). Similarly, Richard Rhodes identifies four stages of what he calls "violentization" – his term for trauma – as external, "acquired" prerequisites for someone to commit serious violence: brutalization; violent subjugation; personal horrification; and violent coaching (112, 319).

There is little disagreement that there is a possibility for violence when one experiences anger and rage (Stephen Diamond 9, 29), whether it stems from trauma, "violentization," or a more general sense of powerlessness. With the latter, we are back to Gilligan's theory of shame. This sense of powerlessness has both innate and external causes, as recognized not only by theorists in the field but also, interestingly, in 1984 by the Conseil Supérieur de l'Éducation du Québec: "Human beings are guilty of violence and responsible for wars. This guilt is due to their need for domination over others and to a lack of domination (control) over themselves, since such aggressive disturbances do not come solely from the nature (heredity) of people, nor from their culture (environment), but rather from an interaction between these two which pushes them to 'destroy'" ["L'humain est coupable de violence et responsable de guerres. Cette culpabilité est due à son besoin de domination sur les autres et à un manque de domination (contrôle) de lui-même, ces désordres agressifs ne venant pas seulement de la nature (hérédité) de l'homme, ni de sa culture (environnement), mais d'une interaction entre ces deux accusées, ce qui pousse l'humain à 'détruire'"] (Vasil 335).

Violence and the Sacred

Is it possible to stop this need to destroy on the part of certain individuals, or is violence contagious, as Gladwell proposed in his epidemiological take on violence and as theorists of the sacred such as René Girard have similarly suggested? Even though violence can destroy everything around us, unfortunately the only solution envisioned is often to escalate that very violence in the name of an assumed higher purpose: "The expansion refers to the possibility of reuniting rivals through a common enemy, a surrogate victim upon which all can simultaneously vent their rage and have no fear of revenge from the dead victim ... Thus, this victimage mechanism becomes represented as 'the sacred'" (Whitmer 127). Girard, like Gladwell and his "tipping point," views violence as a microbe and a plague (54) but also links the impurity of sexuality to that of violence, exploring societies' need for sacrificial, ritualistic blood: "The function of ritual is to 'purify' violence" (59) – only the pure blood of the sacred ritual can purify the impure blood of violence, just as one can purify the act of violence by sanctifying it for a sacrificial purpose. He also points out the similarities between sacrifice and the judicial system, since both are associated with political power and both constitute a double-edged sword: oppression and liberation (39). There can be no consideration of violence without speaking of the law and law making.

Violence and the Power of the Law

To Walter Benjamin, the task of any critique of violence must include its relation to law and justice, since "Lawmaking is power making, and, to that extent, an immediate manifestation of violence" (295). As Slotkin has shown, American society, in particular, was paradoxically founded on the primacy of the law, as well as on the allure of the outlaw. De Vries agrees: "This fascination with the business of law and order, which is also a celebration of violence, cannot be disentangled from the fascination with law and order's underside: the violence of criminality"; "[the] shadow of violence ... attaches itself to the law and cannot be shrugged off" (135, 223).

Whitmer's description of the violence mythos is relevant here also, this time in reference to social control, as incorporated within the judicial system. If the core of the violence mythos is the belief that humans are innately violent, then humans need certain societal structures to control them. Those structures can easily be presented as legitimate; the cultural system "thus becomes a self-reinforcing, self-perpetuating structure of using 'violence to prevent violence'"; and the violence mythos becomes a "symbolic constellation of visible and invisible forms of social control" (1, 2).

Whitmer's analysis invites us, of course, to consider the work of Foucault both in his *Histoire de la sexualité*, in which he describes the power of the law as one that demands obeying subjects (112) and, especially, in his ground-breaking *Surveiller et punir* (published in English as *Discipline and Punish*), where the renowned scholar offers his fascinating study of changes in the penal system – the evolution from torture to prison, issues such as trials, the use of expert witnesses, the ritualistic and theatrical nature of public spectacles of punishment and execution, and the popularity of police literature.[1]

But Foucault's work also concerns issues of power – the use of prison as a form of social control through surveillance, discipline, and punishment. Just as Halttunen states that the criminal is seen by society as a monstrous other, Foucault speaks of justice as having formerly treated the outlaw (the "hors-la-loi") inhumanely (with private and public torture, public execution), while more modern (and, I must add, specifically Western) law tends to treat individuals who are "outside nature" in what is considered a "humane" way ("traiter 'humainement' celui qui est 'hors nature,'" 109). Prison, however, in Foucault's view, has developed into an apparatus of knowledge ("appareil de savoir" 149) where constant surveillance becomes what he cleverly calls a "cellular power" ("un pouvoir cellulaire," 175): every action of the prisoner is constantly being watched, and every cell in a prison compound is visible. The model of such surveillance, of course, is the Panopticon, where guards – and by extension all of society – maintain power over prisoners by keeping them visible at all times. This model, for Foucault, assures the "uninterrupted and automatic functioning of power" (201) and ultimately not only the "power to punish" (301) but also, as ironically and exquisitely stated, an "art of punishment" (296). The power to punish – physically or not – is the power of violence inherent in the judicial system, the law, prisons, and – in the United States – in federal and state executions. As an editorial from the National Center for Policy Analysis lauding the declines in crime rates in the United States, thanks to the twenty-year increase in incarceration levels maintains, "In short, punishment works" (Burnett A29).[2]

Violence at the Level of Discourse

No introduction to the scholarly discourses of violence would be complete without mentioning violence at the level of discourse itself. As Derrida famously declared in his *Writing and Difference*, "Violence appears with articulation" (1979, 147–8). Much has been written about this phrase, again based on Derrida's exploration of Levinas and Weil on violence. As de Vries interprets Derrida:

> There is in language an originary violence, a violence not primarily of fact, but of a different order ... the process of the appearing of the appearance. This

violence is at the origin of sense. The face is not merely a glance; it is also speech, and in speech the cry becomes phrase and expression, and from expression moves to determination: "Now, there is no phrase which is indeterminate, that is, which does not pass through the violence of the concept." (Derrida, *Writing and Difference* 147)

For Levinas, this violence of language is historical and secondary. For Derrida ... this violence of language exists in syntax and articulation ... in any making determinate because articulated against the hyperbolic, wordless excess. Derrida argues that this violence of language is not historical, in the sense that it is not localized as a moment of a scholarly class or priestly caste ... This violence is pre-ethical, it is what allows being to appear as difference, thereby making possible the defeat of ... inarticulation ... Articulation and syntax constitute a "violence," but this is an "anguish" ... through which the indeterminate passes into concepts. It is the price of any discourse at all. (de Vries 78–9)

The belief in language and words as action – as violence – has been articulated for some time. One need only think of the works of Stéphane Mallarmé and Arthur Rimbaud, whether in their poetry or in their commentaries and correspondence on language, the poetic word, and the power of literature. For Mallarmé, for example, the literary book and its language resembled bombs, revolution, fireworks, and ultimately apocalyptic fire that would destroy the world in order to effect a rebirth (Lewis 77–8, 80).

More recently Foucault stated: "Discourses are tactical elements or blocks operating in the field of force relations" (*The History of Sexuality* 101–2). A number of the essays that explore the concept of violence in *Le Philosophoire* similarly confront the problem of language and discourse and their relationship to violence. For Poizat, violence is the negation of the world of discourse and of rationality; it tries to misappropriate discourse and to dispossess it of any thought (4–5). Philippe Boisnard,[3] speaks of the "tyranny of the logos" (137), and even of the vampirization of language that sucks out and thereby neutralizes all singularity: "The 'I is an other' appears, in all its cruelty, to be the reflection of 'THEM'" ["Le 'Je est un autre' apparaît, dans toute sa cruauté, être le reflet du 'ON'"] (139), especially as represented by the media. The violence of language will also no longer permit any passivity on the part of the listener: "Language is corporal engagement in a concealed crack. It is violence that brings out the original force of the eruption of language. Violence that indicates a force, breaking the monotony and the neutralization (reductive and violent act) of language in its sole communicative (commercial) conception" ["Le langage est l'engagement corporel dans la fêlure dissimulée. Il est la violence qui fait ressortir la force originaire de l'éruption du langage. Violence qui indique une force, rompant la monotonie et la neutralisation (acte de réduction et de violence) du langage dans sa seule conception communicationnelle (marchande)"] (Boisnard 148).

We clearly hear resonances of poets such as Mallarmé and Rimbaud. As Whitmer, echoing Paul Ricoeur, summarizes: "Violence gains its meaning from language, its opposite, or other. Violence that speaks is already a violence trying to be right, and begins to negate itself as violence ... It is in discourse, the spoken word, the use of language, that the dialectic of violence and meaning is born. Only in discourse will violence confront meaning" (119–20).

Violent Discourse and Trauma

Whitmer also believes, however, that the discourses of violence and the violence mythos have long concealed the unresolved trauma that is at the core of violent language and acts, as well as in the heart of those experiencing trauma as victims and survivors. She states that there are lacunae in our language for talking about trauma, anger, emotion, and vulnerability, lacunae that stem from the long devaluation of body, emotion, and women. The broader discourse of Western culture, therefore, has not well expressed the complexities of these aspects of human existence, since they have been devalued and marginalized in the discourse of the violence mythos (237). Although words and language can represent violence, they can also be therapeutic. As Herman maintains: "The 'action of telling a story' in the safety of a protected relationship can actually produce a change in the abnormal processing of the traumatic memory. With this transformation of memory comes relief of many of the major symptoms of post-traumatic stress disorder. The *physioneurosis* induced by terror can apparently be reversed through the use of words" (183).

Poststructuralist Feminism and Discursive Violence

Asking who tells a story and who uses these words is, of course, relevant both to gender and violence and to representations of violence in literary texts. Such questions also relate to issues that have arisen in contemporary forms of poststructuralist feminism which, informed by discourse analysis, have focused on the inherent violence of discursive and representational registers, as Beatrice Hanssen aptly describes in her *Critique of Violence* (213). Using as her starting point the writings of Elfriede Jelinek on postwar Austria, Hanssen emphasizes the shift in contemporary feminism from a preoccupation with "material" violence to a consideration of epistemic and discursive constructions of violence by means of a language of violence against violence. She asks: "Is it viable to deploy such a 'violence' as an instrument of criticism in the interest of a feminist *critique*?" (213). This question is at the very heart of the texts of some contemporary feminist writers, particularly women fiction writers in Quebec, whose work I examine below.

Calling such approaches "strategic violence," Hanssen goes on to explain that instead of traditional feminism, which was poised to defeat phallogocentric violence supported by the institutions of patriarchy, poststructuralist feminism "has sought to interrogate the discursive constructions of violence and gender" (214). De Lauretis, for example, taking issue with both Foucault's "rhetoric of violence" and Derrida's "violence of rhetoric" ("Violence" 240), implies that discourse analysis can no longer assume a gender-neutral position. As Hanssen notes: "De Lauretis ends up positing that, insofar as both Foucault and Derrida fail to address the 'historical fact of gender' [de Lauretis, "Violence" 245], both must fall short of explaining how 'violence is engendered in representation' [de Lauretis, "Violence" 240]" (Hanssen 215).

Hanssen moves on to a brief analysis of feminist legal studies to demonstrate how various discursive practices are legitimized by violence in the law, how poststructuralist feminism has begun to interrogate "epistemic violence" (a term used by Foucault and cited by Spivak), and how violence is discursively construed (argued by Judith Butler in her *Gender Trouble*). For Hanssen, whether one uses the term "linguistic" or "textual violence" (Butler 161), or perhaps "critical violence" (Hanssen 216), poststructuralist feminism uses "discursive violence" as a strategy to provide critical potential while underscoring its duplicity: "Insofar as such a feminist praxis seeks to take hold of linguistic violence, it also opposes those theories that reduce language to a mere performative force, divorced from agency as well as ends and means. As a consequence, a tension arises between, on the one hand, the noninstrumental, performative force of language and discourse, which poststructuralist feminism has inherited through its Lacanian, Derridean, or Foucauldian perspectives, and, on the other hand, the effective *re*-instrumentalization of violence in the interest of feminist ends or causes" (216).

This raises a fundamental question for my discussion: how are we to interpret the violent language, images, and metaphors used by certain contemporary women writers whose representations of violent women take place in a poststructuralist, postmodern world still dominated by men who, like many women, see "the Other" as a monstrous being, as a moral alien?

DISCOURSES OF FEMALE VIOLENCE AND SOCIETAL GENDER STEREOTYPES

What if this monstrous, moral alien is a woman? On the one hand, most feminist scholars of and researchers on violence define the term "gendered violence" in a unitary perspective: "Gendered violence refers to the main forms of violence that are committed by heterosexual men towards women, particularly domestic violence, rape, and other forms of sexual assault; such violence is commonly called *violence against women* or *men's violence towards women*" (Mason 7). Ann-Louise Shapiro, on the other hand, while recognizing the usefulness of Foucault's observations (in *Discipline and Punish* [*Surveiller et punir*], for example) that the criminal, not the crime, has become "the object of a new disciplinary apparatus of power/knowledge," and acknowledging his attention to the "systems of meaning that underpin institutional practices," believes – like other poststructuralist feminist critics – that Foucault's "failure to consider the implications of gender difference assumes a unitary discourse" (3) of violence – that is, in contrast to his multi-layered discourse of sexuality. Clearly what we need is a multi-layered discourse of violence.

Given a pervasive cultural belief in a virgin-whore duality, do most people believe that women cannot be violent or cannot be as violent as men? It seems so; otherwise, why are we so enthralled by cases of women who are violent? What is the discourse that we use to talk and write about such criminality? What pushes a woman to violence, and against whom? Who is responsible for the violence that women do? A number of feminist theorists, historians, criminologists, sociologists, media experts, and legal scholars have addressed these important questions, in their efforts better to understand what constitutes the discourse of female violence and how it relates to gender stereotypes in our culture at large.

When Women Commit Violent Acts and Kill

Let me first present some of the overall crime statistics and then the findings on when "real" women kill and under what circumstances. It is now commonplace to state that women have become more violent than ever and are committing increasing numbers of crimes – in the United States, in North America, and throughout at least the Western world, not to forget the appearance of female terrorists and suicide bombers. However, it is important to consider these numbers in relation to the overall crime rate and the numbers of crimes committed by men; distinguish among the types of crimes committed by men and by women; review the trends on the arrests, convictions, and sentencing of male and female criminals; and learn why women commit crimes – and, especially, why they kill. For the purposes of this study, we need, in addition, to review crime rates in the United States, in Canada, and in Quebec – broken down by sex in this chapter and comparatively by country/province in the next. And these findings must be placed in the context of the assumptions, myths, and stereotypes of women (and men) in society.

According to the U.S. Department of Justice, FBI Uniform Crime Reports (UCR) for 2003,[4] out of an estimated 2003 population of 204,034,545 (with 10,843 agencies supplying data), a total of 9,581,423 people were reportedly arrested for all crimes. Of that number, 418,964 arrests were for violent crime (murder, forcible rape, robbery, and aggravated assault) and 1,139,360 for property crime (burglary, larceny-theft, motor vehicle theft, and arson).[5] It must be added, however, that negligible arrest data were received from a number of states and jurisdictions (including New York City and the District of Columbia) and are thus not included.[6] Arrest totals for these areas, however, have been estimated for inclusion in the UCR estimated arrests for 2003, yielding 13,639,479 arrests.[7] The total estimated population of the United States on 1 July 2003 was approximately 290,800,000 (U.S. Census Bureau News), and, based on this total, the U.S. arrest rate in 2003 was 4.695 per 100,000 inhabitants.[8] The UCR preliminary data for January to June 2004 indicate a 2.0% decrease in violent crime over 2003, with decreases specifically in murder (−5.7%), robbery (−5.0%), and aggravated assault (−0.9%), but a 1.4% increase in forcible rape. These decreases follow overall annual decreases in violent crime of 3.1% (2003/2002), 1.7% (2002/2001), and 1.3% (2001/2000).[9]

Canada reports its crime statistics according to incidents reported to the police and by persons charged, rather than by arrests. From a total population of 31,629,677 in 2003, the crime statistics indicate a total of 2,572,243 reported incidents, of which 304,515 were for violent crime (homicide, attempted murder, assaults, sexual assaults – a separate category – other sexual offenses, abduction, and robbery) and 1,303,569 for property crime (breaking and entering, motor vehicle theft, theft under and over $5,000, possession of stolen goods, and fraud).[10] As one can see, it is rather difficult to compare American and Canadian statistics, given the fact that the definitions of certain categories of crimes differ.[11] In addition, variations in rates of crime can result from differing survey methods, as well as from factors such as race, culture, and legal systems (Cabrera 139).

Statistics Canada in turn notes that in 2003, out of a population of 7,487,169 in Quebec, 53,373 violent crimes and 244,757 property crimes were reported.[12] Canada as a whole experienced a 6% increase in overall crime,[13] with Quebec reporting a 6.5% increase.[14] Crime rates in the Atlantic provinces, however, are now generally higher than in Quebec and Ontario.[15] Canada had a 0.7% decrease in violent crime[16] with a rate "11% lower than its near peak in 1993, but still 66% higher than 25 years ago."[17] After an 8% increase in violent crime reported for 2000,[18] a 3% decrease for 2001,[19] a 1.5% increase for 2002,[20] and a 0.7% decrease for 2003,[21] for the ninth year in a row, Quebec reported the fewest incidents of violent crime (713) per 100,000 population.[22] Quebec again experienced a large decline (15.7%) in homicide (from 140 in 2001, to 118 in 2002, to 100 in 2003), with its rate of homicide (1.34 per 100,000 population) then the lowest it had been since the 1960s.[23]

Walter DeKeseredy, in his enlightening text *Women, Crime, and the Canadian Criminal Justice System*, writes that in general – and specifically in Canada – conservatives and liberals alike often claim that interpersonal violence is a gender-neutral problem and that women are as violent as men, without studying why *some* women are violent or using reliable measures of motives (4, 17). For DeKeseredy, as for many other feminist criminologists, however, crime is clearly a gendered social problem. Although the bulk of crimes committed by women in Canada (as in the United States) are minor ones, the sensationalized crimes of murder – like that perpetrated by Reena Virk's peers, who viciously murdered this East Indian immigrant girl in 1997 in British Columbia, or Karla Homolka, who, along with her then husband, Paul Bernardo, sexually assaulted and murdered three young women in Ontario in the early 1990s – are best known by the public (DeKeseredy 1–4). Most women who kill do so after a long history of physical and sexual assault by intimate partners (DeKeseredy 10; Jones, *Next Time She'll Be Dead* 101). These incidents – known as "self-help homicides" in the words of Ann Jones in *Next Time She'll Be Dead* – are not always reported to the police and are therefore missing from police statistics, and are thus often known as the "dark figure of crime" (DeKeseredy 10, 11, 14).

No one is saying that violence is restricted to men, although in comparison to males, women, at approximately 52% of the population, commit a much smaller proportion of both violent and property crimes. Dana Crowley Jack reports that in 1993 in the United States, only 13% of all crimes and 8% of homicides were committed by females (19, 20). More recent crime reports illustrate interesting and somewhat unsettling trends. According to the U.S. UCR for 2003, females accounted for 23.2% of arrests for all crimes (23.0% in 2002), 17.8% for violent crime (17.4% in 2002), and 10.3% of arrests for murder and nonnegligent manslaughter (homicide) (10.8% in 2002), a significant increase from 1993 in these categories.[24] The rates for 2003, however, are relatively unchanged from 2002.

DeKeseredy reports that in Canada from 1961 to 1990, 87% of the suspects for murder were male, and 13% were female. Most male Canadian killers kill other men and are slightly more likely to kill strangers than their spouses. During the same time period, 40% of female offenders killed their husband or common-law partner, and 22% killed one of their children.

The most recent Canadian statistics for 2003 report that for adults over the age of 18, males were charged in 81% and women in 19% of all crimes. These figures include respective male/female rates of 78%/22% for property crimes, 84%/16% for violent crimes, and 90%/10% for homicide. For individuals under the age of 18, males were charged in 70% and females in 30% of all crimes, including a male to female breakdown of 75%/25% for property crimes, 74%/26% for violent crime, and 79%/21% for homicide.[25] (See Figure 1.) In every category, the percentage of women charged either stayed the same, slightly decreased, or slightly increased from 2002, with the notable exception of a 20% increase in overall female crime.[26] Between 2002 and 2001 for homicide rates, there was a 21% decrease for female adults over the age of 18 but, disturbingly, a 19% increase for females under the age of 18,[27] and this after a 4% increase for females over 18 and a 5% increase for females under the age of 18 between 2001 and 2000.[28]

Figure 1
2003 Canadian Male/Female Crime Percentages [Within Age Group]

	property crime	homicide	violent crime (including homicide)
M adult	78	90	84
F adult	22	10	16
M<18	75	79	74
F<18	25	21	26

(Data derived from Wallace, *Crime Statistics in Canada 2003*, 25, Table 9)

The criminal justice scholar Coramae Richey Mann[29] states in *When Women Kill* that there is little support "for the notion that women are becoming more violent, *at least as measured by the commission of homicide* [emphasis mine] ... Total arrest trends by sex from 1983 to 1987 reveal an 8.1% *decrease* in female arrests for murder and nonnegligent manslaughter, but an *increase* of 16.4% in arrests for all violent crimes by females ... The most recent UCR figures (1993:224) continue to reflect these trends. While female arrests for murder and nonnegligent manslaughter decreased 9.6 percent from 1988 to 1992, female arrests for violent crimes increased 32.5 percent during this time period" (176).

Using the Justice Department, FBI Uniform Crime Report figures for 2003, as reported in 2004, we can see some of the trends between 1994 and 2003 for women arrested for various crimes. For this period of time, for all females there was a 12.3% increase for all crimes (after a 14.1% increase in 2002 over 1993[30]); a 30.1% decrease for murder and nonnegligent manslaughter (after a 35.5% decrease in 2002 over 1993[31] and a 6.3% decrease in 2001 over 1992[32]); a 12.5% decrease for property crime (after a 13.1% decrease in 2002 over 1993[33]), but a 9.6% increase for violent crime (after a 17.1% increase in 2002 over 1993[34]), virtually all in aggravated assault.[35] Under the age of eighteen, the figures show: an overall 3.0% decrease in female arrests (after a 6.4% increase in 2002 over 1993[36]); a "comforting" 48.7% decrease in arrests for murder and nonnegligent manslaughter (after a 42.8% decrease in 2002 over

Figure 2
Percentage Change in U.S. Crime by Females, 1994–2003

(Data derived from Uniform Crime Reports 2002, Section 4, Table 33 and Uniform Crime Reports 2003, Section 4, Table 33)

1993[37]); a 9.9% decrease in arrests for violent crime, predominantly in murder, robbery, and arson (after a 2.4% decrease as of 2002[38]); and a 21.1% decrease in arrests for property crime (after a 14.3% decrease in 2002).[39] Troubling, however, are large percentage increases for both adult females and for females under 18 for offences such as other assaults (32.1%/35.9%), embezzlement (42.0%/28.1%), drug abuse violations (34.8%/56.3%), driving under the influence (21.1%/83.5%), and liquor laws (45.5%/25.6%).[40] (See Figure 2.) It must also be noted that there was a significant increase in female crime between 1992 and 1993, so that decreases in 2002 and 2003 are not as positive as they might initially seem, and increases may be even more worrisome. There have been, in addition, decreases in all areas of arrests for males.[41]

It is important to consider the raw figures as well, although they appear to vary according to the specific table reviewed. If one looks at the number of male arrests reported in one particular table, with 10,843 agencies reporting, one sees a total of 7,355,693 arrests – with 344,435 of these for violent crime and 788,914 for property crime. The number of female arrests reported totals 2,225,730 – 74,529 for violent crime and 350,446 for property crime.[42] A different table, however, with only 7,592 agencies reporting, lists 5,958,949 total arrests for males (including 910,981 total arrests for males under 18) and 1,828,638 total

Figure 3
2003 U.S. Male/Female Crime Percentages [Within Age Group]

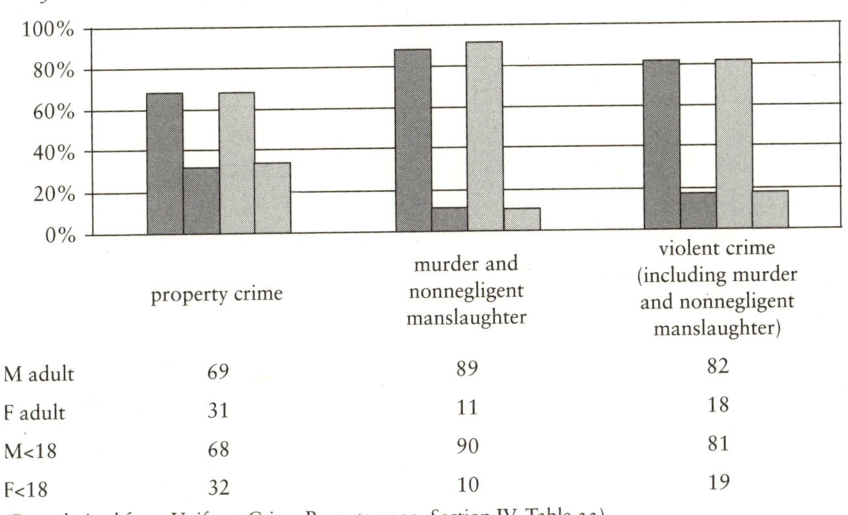

	property crime	murder and nonnegligent manslaughter	violent crime (including murder and nonnegligent manslaughter)
M adult	69	89	82
F adult	31	11	18
M<18	68	90	81
F<18	32	10	19

(Data derived from Uniform Crime Reports 2003, Section IV, Table 33)

arrests for females, including 378,895 total arrests for females under 18.[43] In this same table, under murder and nonnegligent manslaughter, there were 6,268 arrests of males and 747 arrests of females.[44] The differences in the data are of course due to the differing number of FBI agencies reporting for an estimated population of given regions in the United States. But these differences aside, it is clear that substantially more males are arrested than females. (See Figure 3.)

DeKeseredy reports Canadian results: "*Contrary to popular belief, in Canada,* there has *not* been a dramatic increase in violent crimes committed by women [emphases mine]. On the contrary, police data show a slight trend decrease overall" (31). But, like other like-minded researchers, DeKeseredy states that, given the amount of abuse, assault, and violent victimization that women experience at the hands of their intimate partners, it is surprising that the rates of female violence are not higher (32).

Statistics Canada reports the following for 2000: "In recent years, concern has been raised about increasing violence among females, particularly young females. Over the last decade, the increase in the rate of female youths charged with violent crimes (+61%) was more than double that for male youths (+25%) … In 2000, however, the rates of female and male youths charged with violent crimes each increased by about the same amount. The rate of male youths charged with violent crime (1,342 per 100,000 population) is still almost three times that of female youth

(481 per 100,000 population)."[45] Interestingly, there is no corresponding paragraph in the Statistics Canada reports for 2001, 2002, or 2003.

Like Meda Chesney-Lind, who believes that one of the oldest traditions within criminology is the sensationalizing of women's violent crimes (*The Female Offender* 7–8), and Jocelyn Pollock, who writes that popular media accounts depict violent women as more terrible than violent men (25), DeKeseredy believes that the violent crimes of Canadian girls are similarly sensationalized (37), thereby adding to public panic about rising crime rates. Recognizing the work of Schissel on the transformation of Canadian girls into folk devils made of sugar, spice, and evil who inflame emotions over their threat to society, DeKeseredy methodically takes his readers through a study of the nature and extent of crimes committed by Canadian girls. Between 1963 and 1983, 89% of Canadian youth who killed were male, and 11% were female (42). From 1992 to 1996, many more boys than girls were charged with homicide and attempted murder, although the rate has decreased significantly (43). DeKeseredy also shows that girls who kill often come from abusive or negligent families and many have alcoholic or mentally ill parents (44). Boys also outnumber girls in committing physical assault – often revealing their adherence to an "ideology of familial patriarchy" according to which males can abuse females who violate the ideals of male power and control and are justified in demanding obedience, respect, loyalty, and dependency (46).

Rosemary Gartner has done a study of the variation in homicide by gender throughout Canada, tracing the trends in victimization rates and sex-specific offending rates for the period 1921–90. Her findings show that women are much more likely (by a factor of three) to be victims than offenders and that women accounted for 36% of all homicide victims (200). During the 1970s, however, male victimization rose faster than female, suggesting that the most volatile component of the homicide rate was homicide by and against males (200). Noting that "women's risks have not increased relative to men's as their daily activities have become more similar" (210), Gartner reports that female victimization rates are lower than male rates in every category of victim-offender relationships except for intimate-partner killings, where women are four times more likely to be the victims (201).

According to Gartner, the gender gap in offending is much greater than the gap in victimization: women account for 13% of homicide suspects, and their rate of offending is one seventh the male rate. Although both male and female offending rates have increased at similar rates, the absolute difference in female and male offending rates also increased from 1961 to 1990: from 0.26 female and 2.04 male in 1961 to 0.50 female to 3.47 male in 1990 for all homicides (Gartner 201, Table 7.7). In addition, after the 1960s, the character of women's offending changed: in the 1960s, 80% of women offenders were involved in domestic homicides; by the 1980s, only 55% were thus characterized. In other words, while rates of both domestic and nondomestic homicide by women increased, the latter rose more steeply (Gartner 204). With one exception, few regional differences are apparent: "In Quebec, compared to the national average, women are consistently under-represented among both victims and offenders. In the 1970s and 1980s in Quebec, women accounted for only 33% of homicide victims and just under 10% of offenders. In all other provinces women accounted for 36 to 38% of the victims and 13 to 15% of the offenders" (Gartner 204). I provide more data about rates of violence, and especially of homicide in Quebec, in the next chapter. But it already appears that the women writers whose violent female protagonists we shall meet later in this book do not seem to be "reading the reality" of female violence and crime in their own province. Something else must be inciting them.

In its report on homicide for 2003, Statistics Canada reveals that males account for 72% of the victims and 90% of those accused,[46] an interesting increase from 65% of male victims in 2002[47] but similar to that of the 71% figure for 2001.[48] It was reported in 2000 that females accused of homicide tended to kill family members (53% of the time) more often than males accused (31%) of the same crime.[49] No similar data were available for 2001, 2002, and 2003, however. Among youths aged 12 to 17, 48 males and 9 women were accused in 2003 of homicide[50] – 84% male and 16% female – a change from 2002 where the ratio was 79% (33) male and 21% (9) female[51] and from 2001 where the ratio was 83% (25) male and 17% (5) female.[52] (See Figures 4, 5, 6, and 7 for homicide data by sex, 1993–2003.) In 1974, the year of the earliest data reported in this study, those figures were 53 males and 3 females,[53] indicating that 95% of those accused of homicide were male. For 1990 (the same date used in the U.S. figures for comparative purposes) 35 males and 12 females were accused of this violent crime[54] – that is, 74% male and 26% female. These figures therefore represent an increase by a factor of 3.2 between 1974 and 2003, a decrease by a factor of 0.81 between 1990 and 2002, but a decrease by a factor of 0.94 between 2001 and 2003 in the percentage of females between the ages of 12 and 17 accused of homicide.

Figure 4
Trends in Persons Accused of Homicide, by Sex, Canada, 1993–2003 (Numbers)

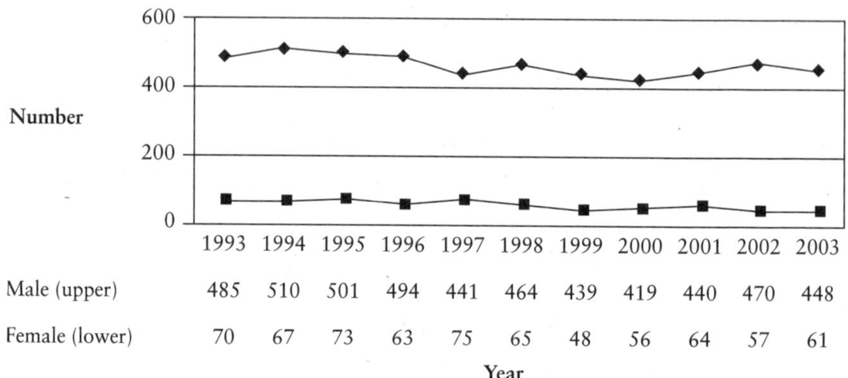

	1993	1994	1995	1996	1997	1998	1999	2000	2001	2002	2003
Male (upper)	485	510	501	494	441	464	439	419	440	470	448
Female (lower)	70	67	73	63	75	65	48	56	64	57	61

Year

(Data derived from Dauvergne, *Homicide in Canada 2003*, Table 11)

Figure 5
Trends in Persons Accused of Homicide, by Sex, Canada, 1993–2003 (Percentages)

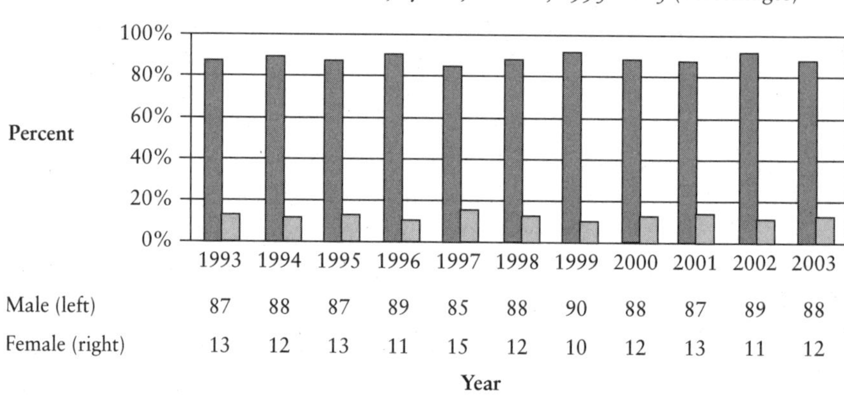

	1993	1994	1995	1996	1997	1998	1999	2000	2001	2002	2003
Male (left)	87	88	87	89	85	88	90	88	87	89	88
Female (right)	13	12	13	11	15	12	10	12	13	11	12

Year

(Data derived from Dauvergne, *Homicide in Canada 2003*, Table 11)

Figure 6
Trends in Youth (12–17) Accused of Homicide, by Sex, Canada, 1993–2003 (Numbers)

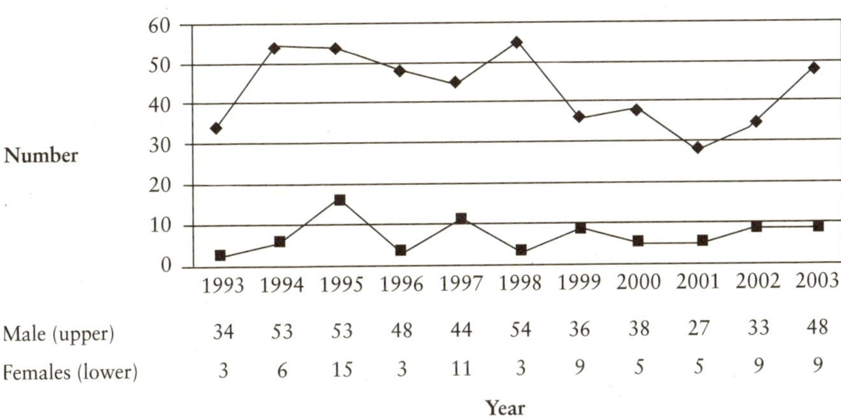

(Data derived from Dauvergne, *Homicide in Canada 2003*, Table 12)

Figure 7
Trends in Youth (12–17) Accused of Homicide, by Sex, Canada, 1993–2003
(Percentages)

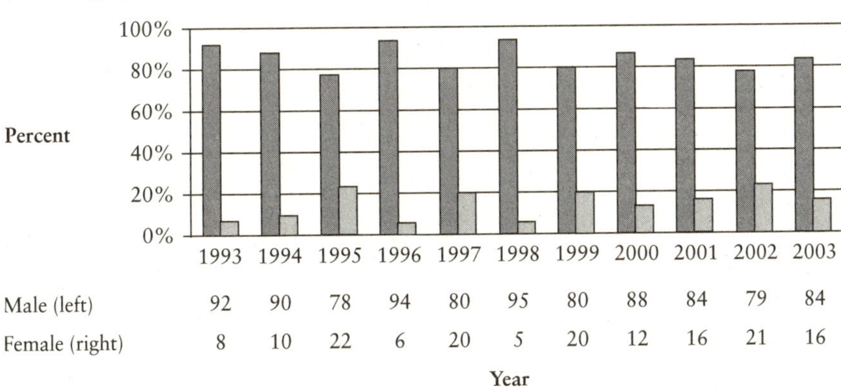

(Data derived from Dauvergne, *Homicide in Canada 2003*, Table 12)

Have there been significant increases in crime among females in the United States and Canada? The figures present mixed results. In both countries, any increases have been levelling off and even decreasing, as has crime in general for both men and women. In the United States, there has been a decrease in homicides among females, but an increase in assault. In Canada, there has been a small increase in female homicide rates (fuelled by an increase for females under the age of 18), along with an increase in violent crime (presumably, therefore, in crimes such as assault), particularly among younger women. The public perception, however, is more alarmist.

Violence and Female Gangs

One cannot mention arrest figures for females under the age of 18 without considering the role of youth gangs in our culture – especially of "girl gangs" and of girls joining male and female gangs – both because increased public awareness of this phenomenon has incited panic over female crime and because a number of the fictional criminals in the texts I shall examine are adolescent girls. Sociologist Irving Spergel presented in 1995 an overview of factors such as age, sex, race, ethnicity, and class and their relation to gang membership, subcultures, and social contexts. He asserted that "the youth gang problem in its violent character is essentially a male problem" (58). But other researchers disagree, and the media echo the supposed changes in gang demographics (see the film *Mi Vida Loca*, for example). Although gang membership is most often associated with masculinity, and some research finds that female gang members are not as violent as their male counterparts, there is clear evidence that young girls and women do join gangs whose repertoire can include violence.

The noted criminologist Anne Campbell, for example, in her *The Girls in the Gang*, presents a historical account that describes female gangs as a recurring social phenomenon. She discusses girls' roles in gangs and how these roles have changed over time. She also raises questions about how cultural constructions of femininity may have influenced scholars, both historical and contemporary, in their interpretations of the roles girls play in gangs and gang culture. She makes interesting observations about the differences between "good girls" and "bad girls" both in male-female gangs and in all-girl gangs. In her *Men, Women, and Aggression*, Campbell makes further important observations. Many young girls join gangs in order to overcome fear and loneliness in their families, communities, and schools, in the hopes that a reputation for violence will ward off opponents. The use of aggression, therefore, becomes a tool for distancing from some and finding intimacy with others: "The girls' gang offers solutions to two fundamental needs: acceptance and safety. It is a sisterhood of like-minded others and an escape from victimization by sheer force of numbers and a tough reputation" (136). Sadly, this entry into a female gang usually involves some sort of an initiation ceremony that perpetrates more violence (the bad girl) and the license to "proclaim herself a 'crazy bitch'" (137). We return to the persistent view of the female as good or bad, as bad or mad.

Meda Chesney-Lind, in *The Female Offender: Girls, Women, and Crime*, states that gang is a code word for race: "A review of the media portrayal of girls in gangs suggests that ... media stories on the youth gang problem can create a political climate in which the victims of racism and sexism can be blamed for their own problems ... As young women are demonized by the media, their genuine problems can be marginalized and ignored. Indeed, the girls have *become* the problem" (57). Similarly, in a review of three recently published books about the new "mean girl," an early twenty-first century variant of the bad girl who has replaced the bad violent girl in gangs of the 1990s, Chesney-Lind reiterates that heavily racialized "media hype and subsequent demonization of girls in gangs and violent girls has led to a 56 percent increase in the detention of girls in the last decade" ("The Meaning of Mean" 21).

Current popular research tends to focus on white, middle-class "mean girls" who engage in non-physical, relational aggression that betrays their powerlessness. Like critics of gender-neutral or sex-symmetrical domestic violence, Chesney-Lind succinctly points out distortions in media reportage that overemphasize the degree of harm in aggression: "Media hype surrounding the discovery of girls' meanness seems to imply that this 'new' attribute makes girls about as violent as boys or worse. This is not the case; virtually all girls' aggression is nonviolent. Boys still constitute over eighty percent of those arrested for serious crimes of violence, and it is boys' violence, not girls' gossip, that gives the US the highest rate of firearm-related deaths among youths in the industrialized world" ("The Meaning of Mean" 22).

Such damaging media hype about bad girls in gangs occurs in Canada as well. DeKeseredy maintains that researchers know very little about the involvement of Canadian girls in youth gangs, since there are as yet no studies comparable to those done in the United States (54). Yet this paucity of research has not prevented public and media outcries concerning this issue. Castigating journalists and researchers who have written about Canadian youth gangs with little accurate data and evidence, DeKeseredy accuses them of helping to generate moral hysteria throughout Canada about crime, female crime, youth crime, and specifically female youth crime (55). Perhaps most interestingly, he cites a "blame-it-on-feminism" statement from NBC News (also cited by Chesney-Lind in 1997, 36) that suggests girls are a threat to U.S. society, maintaining that the situation is similar in Canada: "Gone are the days when girls were strictly sidekicks for male gang members, around merely to provide sex and money and run guns and drugs. Now girls also do the shooting ... the new members, often as young as twelve, are the most violent ... Ironic as it is, just as women are becoming more powerful in business and government, the same thing is happening in gangs" (60).

Acknowledging the research and literature reviews produced by Campbell, and especially by Chesney-Lind and her associates, Sibylle Artz has provided additional findings in her *Sex, Power, and the Violent School Girl*, a study of violent girls in a specific school district in British Columbia. After reviewing the mainstream theories of crime and delinquency (strain, differential association, social control), Artz concludes that few of these sociological theories appear to have dealt with female crime and delinquency. As of the 1970s, however, more researchers became interested in the question: "Why do so *few* girls and women engage in crime and delinquency?" rather than asking, "*Why* do girls and women engage in crime and delinquency?" (Artz 10). Three categories of theories emerged: biological differences; gender role socialization; and "masculinization" of women (Artz 10). Artz quotes statistics that show the considerable rise in crime among young offenders in British Columbia, as well as throughout Canada: from 1986 to 1993, there was a 117% increase in the number of males charged with assault and a 190% increase in the number of female youths charged with the same crime (Artz 15). She neglects, however, to mention changes in the corresponding ratio between males and females charged with assault in Canada between these years: females accounted for 23% of those youth arrested for assault in 1986 and 31% in 1993. So, not only did assault charges increase for both females and males, but females also accounted for a larger percentage in 1993 than in 1986.

What Artz proposes is a different approach to understanding deviance among girls. Like Chesney-Lind and her researchers, she calls for a more qualitative exploration of the lives of deviant girls. She also calls for the study of non-marginalized, violent, working-class and middle-class girls not in youth custody and not members of a gang. Chesney-Lind and Campbell focus on girls from marginalized socio-economical and socio-cultural contexts, including racially mixed girls, girls who came from troubled homes, had experienced physical and sexual abuse, reported feeling lonely and isolated from family members and peers, and – perhaps most significantly – maintained stereotypical notions of gender. They reported a desire to act like a "bad girl" in order to gain status, excitement, and a sense of pride.

Artz's study of girls who were neither in the juvenile justice system nor members of a gang produced interesting emerging patterns: all of her subjects came from families with a long history of violence, alcohol abuse, and generalized dysfunction; they had been exposed to no forms of conflict resolution other than threat, intimidation, and violence; they had internalized their own and others' subordination to hierarchies of power and domination; they were quick to anger and quick to conclude that others "have it in for them" (195–6). But the most interesting of Artz's findings concerns the attitudes of her subjects: "[They] have internalized notions of being female that assign low general worth to women, hold that women achieve their greatest importance when they command the attention of males, and support the entrenchment of the sexual double standard. They have learned to accept the objectification of women and support the monitoring of women's sexuality; thus, they monitor one another's sexual activities closely, and judge any girl or woman harshly if she shows signs of engaging in 'unsanctioned' sex" (195).

Are Women Closing the Gap and Getting Away with Murder?

With the recent concern about girls in gangs, violent school girls, and the fear that women have become more overtly violent (although, as we have seen, not necessarily homicidal), there is also divided opinion on whether females are actually closing the gap between themselves and their violent male counterparts. This concern has usually been voiced in regard to changes (or a lack of change) over time in the extent to which victims have been strangers. In other words, some have expressed the belief that the emergence of a new breed of female killers suggests a trend toward violence against strangers, where the offender has been motivated by the thrill or fun of killing, by a love of violence itself.[55]

Mann, however, found minimal support for this belief (119, 120). What she did find was that the stereotype of the female killer who quietly poisons her victims (often children, the elderly, or people in her care – in a nursing home, for example) has been somewhat modified by the increased female use of firearms. The findings in her own study showed that firearms were used in 46.6% of female-perpetrated homicides, with knives or other cutting implements in 37.8%; the remaining murders were committed with household tools, clubbing weapons, and hands or feet (63).[56]

Women do tend to kill those close to them.[57] They also tend to kill men (as men tend to kill men): "Males are over five times more likely than females to be killed by a female (12 percent compared to 2 to 3 percent). On the other hand ... males are less than twice as likely as females to be the victims of female killers (18.3 percent versus 10.3 percent)"; in other words, both men and women kill men more, but more men kill men (Mann 99; Campbell 77). Interestingly, in Mann's review of the statistics, Canada has the highest proportion (23%) of females killing other females (99).

Some studies charge that "women are getting away with murder," that "there is an open season on men," or that women have been given "a license to kill." Jocelyn Pollock explains these assumptions as manifestations of the "chivalry hypothesis": that women are not arrested as often, that they are convicted less, and that they receive fewer prison sentences than men (87). Such accusations may have been accurate prior to the early 1980s, but since then, as Pollock shows, women are much more likely to be sent to prison, creating what Chesney-Lind and Pollock have called "equality with a vengeance" ("Women's Prisons: Equality with a Vengeance" 155–77). The feminist criminologist Ngaire Naffine also writes that repeatedly "feminists have both rebutted the conventional wisdom about the treatment of women in the courts (that women are the recipients of chivalry) and have identified the continuing presence of discrimination against women ... For example ... girls who are regarded as sexually active have received more punitive treatment than boys by the agents of the law who apparently object to sexual freedom in a young woman" (33).

Mann tackles this question as well. She found that prior to 1983 in the United States, for example, murder charges for women were frequently reduced. After that date, the criminal justice system began to treat men and women more equitably, that is, becoming less lenient toward women than in the past in terms of both prison and probation sentencing (131). Although women who kill tend to be sentenced to less than ten years in prison, a woman who murders a male is slightly more likely to receive harsher treatment from the criminal justice system than a woman whose victim is another female (136, 139).[58] This point relates to the belief by some that the "value" or "worth" of the victim is often taken into consideration when sentencing a perpetrator. In the United States, more women of colour are charged with murder, but once charges are laid, there are only minor differences in further processing. Once convicted, women who have killed strangers are more likely to receive prison sentences (70.6%) than those convicted of killing acquaintances (51.1%) (151). And finally, sentence lengths do vary by gender: in 1991 the average maximum sentence for men convicted of murder was 32.3 years, while for women it was 25.8 years. Mann has found indications, however, that this disparity is changing (159).

As I have mentioned, DeKeseredy has examined the Canadian criminal justice system's response to women and girls in conflict with the law and concludes that adult males and boys constitute the vast majority of cases. Interestingly, he reports a decrease in the number of women processed through the court system in Quebec between 1994 and 1997, a decrease from 6,114 to 5,697 (from 21.3 per 10,000 to 19.5 per 10,000). For female youth processed through the Canadian court system, there was an overall decrease from 1991 to 1995, but an increase in Quebec – from 622 to 685 (21.8 per 10,000 to 23.6 per 10,000) – apparently caused entirely by a rise in drug charges. In addition, far more Canadian men than women are sentenced to federal and provincial/territorial correctional facilities. During the past twenty years, however, the percentage increase in women sent to correctional institutional facilities became much higher than that for men: between 1978/79 and 1995/96, the number of women admitted to provincial/territorial facilities increased by 57% (17% for males); between 1983/84 and 1995/96, the number of women sent to federal institutions increased by 30%, (2% for males) (104–10).[59] In other words, even though fewer Canadian women are showing up in the court system, those who do are being treated more harshly or more "equally" in their prison sentencing.

DeKeseredy has also pointed out that several studies show that women are more likely than men to receive non-prison sentences such as probation. Interestingly, with the exception of the charge for a violent crime, "the severity of an offence is not a major determinant of women being incarcerated; nor is a prior record. Rather, sentence severity is more heavily determined by a woman's 'respectability' ... Those who violate patriarchal gender-role expectations are given more severe dispositions. So, it seems that in addition to enforcing the law, the Canadian criminal justice system, like its United States counterpart, is deeply concerned about enforcing patriarchal or traditional gender-role expectations" (112).

The way we, as a society, speak about women and their use of violence and force has grave implications for social policy and women's experiences in the criminal justice system. Society's cultural stereotypes about women (and gender) affect the way professionals in law enforcement, the legal system, the courts, and social policy agencies treat women who commit violent acts of aggression. As Elizabeth Schneider makes clear in her *Battered Women and Feminist Lawmaking*, for example, law – and, one should add, social policy – "does not exist outside culture but is reflected in popular consciousness, where it takes on a wide range of cultural forms and produces cultural meanings. Law is made, and works, both on the level of 'grand' theory and visionary conceptualization and on the 'ground' level in practice, not only in major law reform litigation but in individual cases" (8).

Gender Construction

The evolving disparity in sentencing to which Pollock, Chesney-Lind, Naffine, and Mann refer, and the growing percentage of women being sent to correctional facilities, which DeKeseredy underscores, begs the question of male and female aggression and violence and the potential differences between them. In making a distinction between sex (a biological construct), and gender (a social construct, the form of which depends on a multitude of societal influences and messages), it is essential that we take into account the range of types of masculinities and femininities in our cultures and the way they inform and are informed by our notions of gender hierarchy and power.

Why are we often uncomfortable with others until we have successfully placed their gender status, and why do we demand that gender be determined by a dichotomy? To what degree are our choices of gender self-determined; is it possible to resist society's expectations of gender conformity? As Judith Lorber states in *Paradoxes of Gender:* "In the social construction of gender it does not matter what men and women actually do or even if they do the same thing. The social institution insists only that what they do is perceived as different" (26). Carol Tavris continues this line of thinking in discussing the conceptualization of gender as a culture, the idea of male as normalcy/the norm, and the intersection between gender and language. Why do we persist in using language that expresses differences between the sexes when the differences are not consistently demonstrated in research? Do our speech and behaviours change when we are in the company of men, women, and women and men? In what ways does context change one's behaviour, and does that behaviour change in sex-typed ways?

Gender is socially constructed, and people tend to place individuals and groups into specific boxes in order to label and "understand" them. Nancy Chodorow is interested in this tendency, arguing that each of us creates personal emotional meaning throughout life. She explores the idea that "an individual, personal creation and a projective emotional and fantasy animation of cultural categories create the meaning of gender and gender identity for any individual. Each person's sense of gender is an individual creation, and there are thus many masculinities and femininities" (69–70).

I have already referred briefly to the violence of the early violent history of the United States, especially in the exploration and "conquest" of the West and its requisite glorification of the "civilizing" nature of the gun. James William Gibson, in *Warrior Dreams: Violence and Manhood in Post-Vietnam America,* presents a view of current American masculinity based on that very past. For Gibson, U.S. history, as "regeneration through violence" (a term coined by Richard Slotkin) was broken by the defeat in Vietnam and the resulting disruption of cultural identity and self-image crisis in America. Basing his observations on the power of Hollywood films and actors such as John Wayne and Rambo, as well as on the growth of print media, Gibson analyses the relationships between the causes of the Vietnam defeat and the rise of the paramilitary. He discusses what he calls the New Warrior in a New War – a warrior who is hostile to authority, sees women as dangerous creatures, and chooses war as a cleaner alternative to the dirty female. For Susan Jeffords, Vietnam veterans have been "established as victims – of their government, the war, the Vietnamese, American protestors, and the women's movement" – and are "portrayed in contemporary American culture as emblems of an unjustly discriminated masculinity. Through this image of the veteran, American manhood is revived, regenerated principally by a rejection of the feminine and sexuality" (116). Given the differing history of this era in Canada, and Quebec, in particular, the characteristics of contemporary manhood should, at least theoretically and ideally, be more positively constructed there, although "age-old" constructions of gender tend to surpass historical conditioning.

Judith Butler, in her highly regarded *Gender Trouble*, perhaps best sums up this non-biological nature of masculinity and femininity and the possibility that violence and aggression (or what Sherrie Inness calls "toughness") are attached not to sex but to gender:

> To what extent do *regulatory practices* of gender formation and divisions constitute identity, the internal coherence of the subject, indeed, the self-identical status of the person? To what extent is "identity" a normative ideal rather than a descriptive feature of experience? And how do the regulatory practices that govern gender also govern culturally intelligible notions of identity? In other words, the "coherence" and "continuity" of "the person" are not logical or analytic features of personhood, but, rather, socially instituted and maintained norms of intelligibility. Inasmuch as "identity" is assured through the stabilizing concepts of sex, gender, and sexuality, the very notion of "the person" is called into question by the cultural emergence of those "incoherent" or "discontinuous" gendered beings who appear to be persons but who fail to conform to the gendered norms of cultural intelligibility by which persons are defined. (23)

Why Women Kill: Male and Female Aggression and Violence

In her book *Men, Women, and Aggression* Anne Campbell writes convincingly of what she sees as the "double standard of aggression" between men and women (50). Her thesis is clear:

> Maleness and aggression have become linked to the point where it is easy to forget about women's aggression. It takes place far less often than men's, and it rarely makes headlines. It is private, unrecognized, and frequently misunderstood. It looks and feels different from men's ... Both sexes see an intimate connection between aggression and control, but for women aggression is the *failure* of self-control, while for men it is the *imposing* of control over others. Women's aggression emerges from their inability to check the disruptive and frightening force of their own anger. For men, it is a legitimate means of assuming authority over the disruptive and frightening forces in the world around them.[60] (1)

Campbell's work on these "cultural lessons in aggression" (1–18) warrants further citation because it presents a fundamental approach that links with other researchers and theorists on violence and gender distinctions, informs my later analyses, and especially raises questions related to the more recent rise in "real" female violence. She states:

> If, in men's accounts of aggression, we are told what it is like to take control, in women's accounts we hear about what it means to lose control. For women, the threat comes from within; for men, it comes from others. For women, the aim is a cataclysmic release of accumulated tension; for men, the reward is power over another person, a power that can be used to boost self-esteem or to gain social and material benefits. For women, the interpersonal message is a cry for help born out of desperation; for men, it is an announcement of superiority stemming from a challenge to that position. For women, the fear of aggression is a fear of breaking relationships; for men, it is the fear of failure, of fighting and losing, or of not being man enough to fight at all. I call women's approach to their beliefs about their aggression *expressive*, and men's approach *instrumental* ... In the normal course of growing up, girls learn to respond to their aggression not with a sense of being purified and calmed but with a sense of shame. Aggression feels good to men but not to women. (7–8)

These comments recall James Gilligan's theory that "the emotion of shame is the primary or ultimate cause of all violence" (110), that the "purpose of violence is to diminish the intensity of shame and replace it as far as possible with its opposite, pride" (111), and that a "central precondition for committing violence ... is the presence of overwhelming shame in the absence of feelings of either love or guilt" (113). Campbell's comments also remind us of the work by Gibson and others on American masculinity, especially in the aftermath of the "national shame" of the American loss in the Vietnam War, which meant that some men needed (and still need) to obliterate that sense of shame by fighting their own private war, thereby attempting to reinstate their sense of manhood.

Mann echoes these ideas in speaking about the need to "save face" through the use of violence, and states that "saving face does not appear to be very influential for women who commit homicide" (62). We should note, however, that not all researchers on issues of violence have the same perspective. Lori Girshick, for example, in her study of woman-to-woman sexual violence, maintains that "violence is not primarily about gender; it is about power and control, gender socialization, and family and relationship dynamics" (17). For Girshick, power and control/domination are at the source of violence, whether by males or females; both women and men have been socialized to condone violence in our culture, so both are capable of violence and do act violently; power is therefore the organizing principle of social hierarchical structures that forms the basis of human interaction and is the underlying cause of both male and female violence (18).

There are differences, however. The distinction between private and public violence, for one, is a significant factor in trying to understand gendered aggression. Saving face usually involves humiliation and the attempted prevention of it in front of others. However, many women who commit violence, including murder, are alone with their victims. According to Campbell, men tend to express their violence more when there are onlookers; in other words, a male audience can encourage male aggression. But one sees the opposite effect on women: "Same-sex spectators ... seem to remind her of the norms about restraint shared by the community of women" (78).

The male hero in a violent battle is caught in a double bind: "He can rescue the world, but the world cannot rescue him" (Whitmer 146). This is, of course, also an aspect of the portrait of Gibson's "New Warrior." For Gibson, this new violent hero must remain alone, perhaps with his male buddies but not emotionally attached to a woman or to a family. If there were a woman, she would most likely turn out to be a "black widow" who sucks out his energy and destroys him – thereby making the female the perpetrator – and a family would only distract him from his aggressive duty. As Whitmer sees it, however, the male cannot survive in isolation. He needs his family to survive, although he cannot express this feeling. When he returns home, however, traumatized by "battle," it is conceivable that he could begin to see "his" woman as his rescuer – something he cannot allow. She cannot rescue him because she would then become the hero, and he would turn into the victim. He often "displaces the traumatic rage and rescue onto the woman" (147).[61]

Whitmer also makes use of Girard's concept of "lack of being," as she underscores some men's constant need to prove their masculinity. The control dynamic of the hero leads to the exploitation of the perpetrator. Violence becomes internalized in the (male) hero who angrily denies his need to be human, to trust and be trusted, and to rely on others. To Whitmer, "Girard's 'lack of being' stems from this damaged sense or lack of social connectivity and affirmation from the outer world" (155).

An understanding of this lack of connectivity is essential if we are to understand gender differences in violence. Campbell believes that women who experience lives of brutal exploitation that destroy their faith in trust and intimacy, too, can unfortunately also be driven to commit aggressive and violent acts (140) – often in their own defence and in defence of their children. These acts, however, seem quantitatively different from the kinds of violence that males commit. Defensive and protective actions are not necessarily considered "violence" in absolute terms.

Campbell's work thus leads me to consider recent research on women's use of violence and force to defend themselves against acquaintance rape and date rape, and especially to defend themselves and their children in domestic violence cases – research that is not the focus of this study but which needs to be mentioned as a significant part of the "perceived" increase in female arrests and criminal activity. Although some studies have reported that men and women use physical violence at equal rates in intimate relationships, other research has clearly shown that such claims fail to take into consideration the nature of the violence and the level of fear and injury experienced by each party (see Brush; Cantos, Neidig, and O'Leary; Cascardi and Vivian; DeKeseredy and Schwartz; Hamberger; and Stets and Straus). Similarly, although there has been an increase in the number of women arrested for domestic violence, some have attributed this increase to mandatory arrest policies; police must cite evidence that both partners have engaged in some aggressive behaviour and then make a dual arrest (or only arrest the woman), without taking into account which of the two people is primarily responsible for the aggression (See Dasgupta, 2001; Lyon; Martin; and Miller).

Researchers such as Shamita Das Dasgupta (2001) and Susan Miller have also recently pointed out that those who have (erroneously, in their view) attempted to prove gender symmetry in family violence cases have used this increase in arrests of women as further evidence that women are as violent as men (Dasgupta, 2001,1). Dasgupta questions the "appropriateness of law-enforcement and judicial responses to women who have used violence against their heterosexual partners" and demonstrates "why we need to reshape current societal responses to changing notions of violence in intimate relationships" (2001, 1–2). She argues – and I agree – that "a broad theoretical perspective that considers the interactions of social [and socio-economic, racial, and ethnic], historical, institutional, as well as individual variables in women's violence would provide a better understanding of it" (5). Contextualizing women's violence in this way would greatly aid practitioners as they work with women from diverse cultures, some of which do not suppress female violence as strictly as do Judaeo-Christian cultures

(Dasgupta, 2001, 8; See also DeKeseredy and Schwartz, Dobash and Dobash, Hamberger, Hooper, Lyon, Martin, Miller, Renzetti, Saunders, Straus, and White and Kowalski.).[62]

Dana Crowley Jack has also undertaken interesting research into what causes women to commit violent acts. In her fascinating book *Behind the Mask: Destruction and Creativity in Women's Aggression*, she hypothesizes that women's aggression develops within a different social reality than men's: "Throughout history, women have been punished for obvious displays of aggression; they have been forced to camouflage their intent to hurt others, their opposition, and even their positive forcefulness, to deliver their aggression in culturally sanctioned but more hidden ways" (4). Echoing Campbell's statement that boys learn early on that "aggression confers agency" (*Men, Women, and Aggression* 32), Jack emphasizes that boys learn physical force, as girls learn the power and use of words and of manipulation, silencing any feelings of aggression (57–9). Initiating the current research into "mean girls," Patricia Pearson agrees: at around ten or eleven, girls "become aggressors of a different kind. They abandon physical aggression ... and adopt a new set of tactics: they bully, they name call, they set up and frame fellow kids. They become masters of indirection" (17). Basing her own work on that of the Finnish psychologist Kaj Bjorkqvist, Pearson sees this behaviour as what Bjorkqvist calls "a kind of social manipulation" that includes "'gossiping, exchanging nasty notes, trying to win others to one's side, and excluding from groups'" (17). One cannot forget, however, Chesney-Lind's warning that such aggressive behaviour in girls must not be seen as the equivalent of far more dangerous physical aggression in boys.

Many of Phyllis Chesler's comments in her major study, *Woman's Inhumanity to Woman*, are also inspired by Bjorkqvist and Campbell, as well as numerous researchers in other fields. Acknowledging that her work has been challenged for appearing anti-feminist, Chesler takes her readers through myriad research studies and scientific, cultural, literary, anthropological, and psychological examples to convince feminist naysayers that women do exhibit hostility, as well as highly aggressive – even cruel and sadistic behaviour – toward other females and that they experience envy and competition, and participate in gossip and the shunning of women and girls (2, 4, 26, 32). Many people do not recognize this behaviour, however, because it is more covert: "Because male aggression is both so visible and so deadly, it tends to obscure our view of female violence and aggression, which is more often subtle, less visible, but chronic" (35). As Chesler, along with a number of researchers, has remarked, women can maternally enchant and then terrorize or "turn on" other women, but their methods are seen as "indirect aggression" (37). She goes on to present historical and anthropological evidence of mothers' and mothers-in-law's cruelty toward their children in Japan, China, and India – women from different classes, races, and geographical regions – as well as several examples of such cruelty within the same race, class, and country, as reflected in literary texts (40–50). After acknowledging the work of certain primatologists, evolutionary theorists, and comparative psychologists on aggression and violence among female primates, Chesler turns to examples of physical violence between women, but she emphasizes – citing Natalie Angier – that the more common indirect forms of aggression are the more psychological ones that begin early in life with backbiting, gossiping, spreading vicious rumours (76–7). Once again, female violence is shown to be generally far less lethal than violence perpetrated by males.

Jack feels that such female behaviour stems from the cultural message given to young and adolescent girls, as well as to adult women, that they must not depart from the sanctioned cultural script. She sees the celebrated work of Carol Gilligan, for instance, on the greater morality of care, sense of connection with others, and level of empathy on the part of women as too simplistic an explanation for their less frequent displays of aggressive behaviour, "an answer too rooted in stereotype and in the moral virtue society expects of women": "Women do hurt others, at times with clear vision and at other times blindly. Though their aggression differs from men's in socially constructed ways and is often less physical, it causes harm" (112). For Jack, women's acclaimed empathy has been shaped by inequality, by the requirement that they serve as caretakers, and by the threat of violence against them. Women wear a mask that says they do not want to hurt, but that mask both protects and hides: it "configures a woman's appearance to accord with a moral norm that is required of her gender more than of men. From the inside, the mask obscures the wearer's vision of the inequities and myths that work to stop her from taking action in the world" (115). As a substitute for agency, this mask, according to Jack, "most often is fashioned from a cloth of stereotypical feminine behavior such as sweetness, silence, and passivity. This strategic performance of femininity disguises women's intent to hurt, control, or oppose others" (236–7).

Gender Polarity

Related to the cultural masks that both men and women wear is Lawrence Kramer's work on simulated and constructed identities of both sexes in his book of essays/musings, *After the Lovedeath: Sexual Violence and the Making of Culture*, with which I began this chapter. Taking examples from literature and music, Kramer postulates that men and women must both assume a position of femininity in relation to a masculinity that belongs to some "other" if they are to become a subject and acquire an identity. This ideal other social, moral, and cultural authority will allow no men – and especially no women – to identify with this masculine subject-position. Men therefore occupy a position that is masculine in relation to the public feminine position and feminine in relation to the masculine position held by another man. These same men are directed to suppress the knowledge that their own position is masculine in content and feminine in structure.

Clearly basing his comments on Jacques Lacan's fiction of possessing the phallus, Kramer modifies this fiction to be one of self-possession. Men are constantly reminded that masculine identity is simulated (like the mask that women wear, according to Jack). They become anxious about gender boundaries and express that anxiety in misogyny and sexual violence: "The basis of the cultural authority associated with the impossible position of absolute masculinity is precisely the threat of violence" (5–7). That violence is the logical outcome of the recognition that any given man does not really possess the phallus but that it belongs to someone else – not necessarily Lacan's general "Other," but rather to someone hiding behind a symbol, possibly even a woman who could expose his imposture (28–9).

As Kramer defines it, the resulting gender polarity occurs when the masculine-feminine duality is constructed around a rigid boundary. The nineteenth century (as Foucault has shown) formed our modern perception of the polarities of masculinity and femininity – as well as of heterosexuality and homosexuality – and its gender system set our agendas as subjects (10, 15). Modern misogyny, according to Kramer, is more vehement and virulent because of the historical change in the nature of masculine empowerment. With the demise of traditional patriarchy, in which the king/prince held the position of absolute masculinity, "the modern era turns the subject's failure to hold the absolute position into something intolerable. There is suddenly no reason the position should not be held. Thus it becomes the object of masculine quest, the modern form of the holy grail" (177–8).

Some men view sexuality as the conquest of women, who (conveniently) become associated with filth; at the same time men are tortured by the terror of a female sexuality so great that it could dissolve their masculinity (37). As Kramer comments: "The logic of gender polarity is inflexible. Someone must always be castrated: which is to say, someone *else.* The man in an economy of lack needs women to embody that lack" (102), a lack that the woman usually fills with adornments, props, and poses so that "the woman's lack is veiled by making her an eyeful" (102). But ultimately: "Sexual violence is partly the product of the actual instability of gender polarity ... perhaps even more damagingly, a product of a staged, fictitious instability, the aim of which is to enforce and reinforce what only appears to be buckling" (261). In other words, it is all artificial, all constructed, perhaps buckling, perhaps not. Masculinity, femininity, gender, power, control, sexuality, and violence are all based upon assumptions, myths, and stereotypes about men and women and the violence that they do.

ASSUMPTIONS, MYTHS, AND STEREOTYPES ABOUT FEARED VIOLENT WOMEN

General Disciplinary Approaches

As with all discussions of violence and gender, it is critical to include many disciplinary approaches when considering the role that culture and society play in shaping our attitudes toward female violence and aggression. Basing her work on female criminality in fin-de-siècle Paris, historian Ann-Louise Shapiro posits that in order to understand modern assumptions about women and crime, we need to look at the history of an expanded cast of dangerous women in the context of fears of social and gender change: "[The] perceived Otherness of women has, historically, allowed the metaphoric Woman to stand in for a wide and contradictory array of qualities, values, and meaning" (4). The discourse of female criminality has thus betrayed anxiety over woman's traditional role in society (12–15) – and continues to do so. According to Shapiro, "born" female criminals (read: "female nature") can be seen as "careening between myth and misogyny" (66), since they represent both order and disorder (123), with lesbians and feminists, especially, cultural equivalents of criminality (206). In other words, if women's behaviour is treated as a cultural marker and discursive sign (218), then "the criminal woman was [and is] like all women, only more so" (66).

In their introduction to *No Angels: Women Who Commit Violence*, Alice Myers and Sarah Wight, both specialists in British media, speculate that excessive storytelling about women's violence is a symptom of society's anxiety over women's roles and their abandonment of traditional femininity; our reluctance to criminalize women betrays our fear of our social fabric falling apart (xii, xiv). According to our rigid cultural gender polarity (see Kramer), violent women are seen neither as sane nor as women. Society needs to see violent women as different – either as mad or bad – since we would otherwise need new discourses to understand that both men and women can be violent (Grindstaff and McCaughey 150; Ballinger 24): "The fact that social tolerance for aggression is gendered reflects the cultural equation of violence and masculinity ... women's aggression is seen as unnatural and therefore pathological ... aggression is a primary marker of masculine/feminine difference, and construing women's aggression as unnatural helps mask the political character of gender inequality (indeed of gender itself)" (Grindstaff and McCaughey 150).

To journalist and feminist critic Ann Jones, in her landmark *Women Who Kill*, the intimation that women are less violent than men either by nature or by socialization raises disquieting conclusions about the innate moral superiority of the female or the need to improve society by bringing up men to be more like women (5). At the same time, women are seen as insane, hysterical, weaker in every way and at every stage of life (160–1, 170). Murder is therefore, she suggests, often situational, and, given a certain set of circumstances, any one of us might kill: "A murderess is only an ordinary woman in a temper" (14). Concurrently, however, society is afraid of extremes – of the female murderer, who, like the feminist, tests established boundaries (13). If a woman is violent, can she truly be "feminine," or must the female murderer be distinctly male, a masculine, monstrous freak (137)?

How can one take these significant multi-disciplinary comments and begin to make sense of the role that assumptions, myths, and stereotypes about violent women play in the "reality" of female violence and in the transformation of that reality into the arena of representation? As put another way by Lisa Duggan, the researcher's method of analysis and understanding must refuse "the separation of social life ('reality') from representations ('myth,' or 'stereotype')" (4) – as feminist archetypal criticism has attempted to do. In this sense, a discussion of myths and stereotypes of female violence, as part of "reality," needs to blend into that of literary representation. Let me first delve more into these powerful and complex assumptions that have been with us seemingly forever.

The Turn-of-the-Century Female

Jack speaks of aggression as "the bedrock upon which gender dualisms are erected: active/passive, warlike/peaceful, competitive/cooperative, separate/connected, and more. The thought of women's aggression arouses inchoate fears of an unnatural blurring of gender lines that have been drawn by evolution. If women are overtly aggressive, then gender, as our society has defined it, will no longer exist" (30). Jack's comments are made in the context of her discussion of the influence of Darwin and Freud on our more modern fears of angry and violent women (29, 30). One cannot overstate this influence, as it has informed Western society's views of women since the late nineteenth and early twentieth centuries.

In his controversial *Evil Sisters: The Threat of Female Sexuality and the Cult of Manhood,* Bram Dijkstra traces the development of American and western European beliefs about women, particularly as they were influenced by turn-of-the-century medical science – by biology, gynecology, psychology, genetics, and sociology. Dijkstra's inquiry sheds light on how women were increasingly seen as predators and vampires who could destroy men – and civilization as a whole. According to Dijkstra, between 1870 and 1911 a variation of the age-old "vital essence" theory was reactivated by such social Darwinists as Herbert Spencer and William Graham Sumner, by Dr Augustus Kinsley Gardner, and in 1911 by A. Gould and Dr Franklin L. Dubois in *The Science of Sex Regeneration* (56–8). According to this theory, each individual has a carefully measured and modest allotment of "vital essence" (i.e., energy) that he or she can use at will. This energy, or current, is concentrated in the blood, of which sperm is considered the purest form (56–7). For women, the womb is the distillery of "vital essence," but much of its vital fluid is lost during menses, and needs to be replenished. Nineteenth-century physicians renewed, therefore, the medieval belief in women's vicious hunger for men's precious seminal fluids, while men such as the novelist and poet Rémy de Gourmont convinced many English-speaking intellectuals that "every woman ... contained within herself the destructive potential of the woman-vampire, the sexual woman, the woman of death" (64). In other words, "the male was a container filled with vital fluids, and woman, the sexual animal, longed to gather these into her deadly womb" (66).

Gourmont and others also promoted the idea of a link between masculinity and evolutionary progress, between masculinity and the triumph of intellect over feminine nature. By 1910 Darwin's contemporaries, who advocated new and dangerous social variations, and medical researchers were extending the seminal/"vital essence" theory to theories of the brain: women were seen as "brain vampires" who could stop the advancement of men (69–71, 73). A fear of a return to repressed animal instincts and impulses in man became a fairly common obsession. Men could either advance by adding to their intellect or degenerate by squandering their vital essence. Influential thinkers such as Gourmont and Ezra Pound set out to demonize the concept of femininity: "They were determined to show the world that women were 'inherently evil,' that they represented nature's entrance into the cave of primal depredation" (75). Men had to preserve their vital essence, their sperm, since each time they ejaculated, they died a little (as in the French "la petite mort") (87).

Ejaculation into a woman was acceptable if the woman stayed within her prescribed role as mother and nurturer. According to the French surgeon and endocrinologist Serge Voronoff in *The Conquest of Life*, published in an English translation in 1928: "Seminal irrigation would give a woman much more masculine 'strength' than would be good for her ... Ordinarily a civilized woman should promptly ovulate and become pregnant" (as quoted in Dijkstra 199): "Women who diverted man's brain food to nonreproductive uses – women with a masculinized tendency toward primitive bisexuality – would, with each potent seminal infusion, become less motherly and more sexual. This clearly was the sliding scale between the virgin mother and the whore that science had been looking for: excessive appropriation of the masculine orchitic elixir would tip the balance toward a 'perversion of the maternal instinct'" (Dijkstra 199).

If this sexual "black widow" woman (as in Gibson's scenario) went still further and took on even more masculine traits, she could become a criminal. In 1893 Cesare Lombroso, the period's undisputed leader in phrenological research and the controversial father of criminal anthropology, stressed in *The Female Offender* that intellectual activity in a woman was a sign of criminal abnormality, a degenerate reversion to an earlier stage of human evolutionary development (Dijkstra 131). Some of the chapter titles in Lombroso's and his co-author, William Ferrero's influential book indeed offer a fascinating scientific-cultural map of assumptions about the female criminal of the day: "The Skull of the Female Offender," "Pathological Anomalies of the Female Offender," "The Brains of Female Criminals," "Facial and Cephalic Anomalies of Female Criminals," "The Criminal Type in Women and Its Atavistic Origin," "Tattooing," "Acuteness of Sense and Visual Area of Female Criminals," "The Born Criminal," "Hysterical Offenders," "Crimes of Passion," "Criminal Female Lunatics," "Epileptic Delinquents and Moral Insanity" (Lombroso 1895).[63] Masculinism was a sign of the bestial in women, just as effeminacy was a corresponding sign in men. Rigid gender polarity was considered necessary for cultural and medical reasons.

Dijkstra's work can be seen in counterpoint to the work of Pearson who, as indicated, argues that both men and other women treat women as if they live and act in an innocence beneath which they conceal the capacity for aggression and violence. I thus return to Jack's "masks," Butler's "gender as performance," Kramer's "veil." But if everyone wears a mask, performs a gender role, or is in some sense covered by a veil, then why is it that much of society cannot accept these multiple facets of women? Why are women inevitably cast in an either/or role? This duality rests at the heart of any discussion of women's gendered role in society; the denial or horror of it inevitably surfaces when they act violently.[64]

Continuing Assumptions about Women and Violence

Theorists – even feminist theorists – from all disciplines may disagree on causes of women's violence and ways to change perception and beliefs, but they seem to be in agreement on the prevailing assumptions about women – especially violent women – even if they admit that there has been some improvement, especially since the turn of the century. They all offer some variation of what Shapiro, Jones, and Myers and Wight have described, as highlighted above: that female criminality is an indicator of cultural anarchy; that the female murderer is a masculine, monstrous freak; and that storytelling about female violence is a symptom of society's anxiety over women's roles.

Anne Campbell says that since "good girls don't fight" (38), men see violent females as an oddity, comic, insane, or laughable (2, 37, 54).

Aggression is the domain of the male, and since the power of science, the law, and the media are still predominantly in the hands of men, the picture of aggression and violence handed down to us is that of its male "instrumental" use to conquer, control, and humiliate (18). When women aggress and become violent, the system is at a loss as to how to handle them:

> Male judges – both official ones in the law courts and the unofficial moral entrepreneurs in the media – try to place a masculine and instrumental interpretation on women's behaviour ... Her actions are forced into a masculine model of aggression, judged to be male, and the woman is seen as having violated not just the criminal law but the "natural law" of proper female behaviour ... In the minds of many men, female aggression remains shrouded in mystery – capricious, irrational, arbitrary. If it cannot be explained in "rational" instrumental terms, then it cannot be explained at all; violent women must be either trying to be men or just crazy. (144)

Jack finds that the ideology of femininity – the myth that women are not aggressive – intersects with certain ethnic, racial, and class stereotypes; socially marginalized and lower-class women are often punished and caricatured for their more overt and sometimes antisocial and aggressive behaviour (16, 8). Many women simply learn to appear non-aggressive or less aggressive for their own safety, since they have had to come to terms with the cultural message that female aggression is an anomaly, more deviant than a man's (21). They have learned these messages since childhood, when fairy tales inculcated images of beautiful and non-aggressive princesses in contrast to ugly, powerful, and wicked witches. Jack sees aggression as "a set of relations based on force and power," as well as a set of social beliefs (29). She cites recent psychological studies that state that women who are violent are merely acting like men, since "real" women are not violent. Like Dijkstra, she points to beliefs that women are still seen as castrating and dangerous vampires (29). She takes issue with the prevailing view that women are morally superior because of their nurturing and caretaking natures and that when they exhibit violent tendencies, they lose that claim, becoming one of the boys, thus negating "the social contract of chivalry that promises protection for specific types of women" (33). In short, like the other feminist theorists mentioned above, to Jack: "Overt aggression by a woman is also a cultural transgression – threatening not only to the social structure but also to the mythology that separates women into demons and angels. If an angel suddenly turns into a demon, punishment can assume apocalyptic proportions" (141).[65]

Blame It On Feminism

One of the most frequently cited reasons for the increase in violence by female "demons" is what, as of the 1970s, can be called a "blame-it-on-feminism" attitude. According Pollock's research for her *Criminal Women*, in every decade theorists assume that progress in social equality between men and women has caused an increase in criminality among females; their fundamental idea is that "recent" progress leads to a "new" female criminal (146). Meda Chesney-Lind agrees: the argument used during the first wave of feminism in 1921 similarly resurrects the "liberated female crook" by linking efforts to improve women's economic and political positions and levels of crime; in other words, women are supposedly seeking equality in an underworld of male crime (*The Female Offender* 111–15).

During the second wave of feminism, law enforcement officials were among the earliest to attribute changes in the numbers of women arrested to the movement for female liberation and equality (Chesney-Lind, *The Female Offender* 112). Both Pollock and Chesney-Lind cite the influence of Freda Adler's 1975 *Sisters in Crime: The Rise of the New Female Criminal,* in which Adler proposed what has come to be called "emancipation theory," "liberation hypothesis," or "masculinity thesis" (Pollock 81–2; Chesney-Lind, *The Female Offender* 113–14). Adler's theory implied that women were becoming more like men, including taking on a more aggressive and criminal nature, as a result of their push for social and economic equality. Despite wide public agreement with this hypothesis, however, analysis of arrest data in the 1970s did not support such claims: the increase in female arrests was in fact due to increases in crimes such as shoplifting, prostitution, and fraud, precipitated at least in part by authorities' growing willingness to prosecute for such traditionally female crimes (Chesney-Lind, *The Female Offender* 114). Perhaps most significantly, "women offenders of the 1970s were unlikely targets for the messages of the largely middle-class women's movement. Women offenders tend to be poor, members of minority groups, with truncated educations and spotty employment histories. These were precisely the women whose lives were largely unaffected by the gains ... of the then white, middle-class women's rights movement" (Chesney-Lind, *The Female Offender* 115).

The careful research that showed the failure to link changes in women's crime to the women's movement went unnoticed in the press; thus, it was fairly easy for what Chesney-Lind calls a "revival of the 'violent female offender'" to begin in 1990, newly focusing on girls in gangs, minority women, and violent urban, street crime. This time, however, despite media hype to the contrary, some serious studies pointed to the underlying causes for an increase in female violent crime – the same reasons as for men in similar socio-economic situations: "This turns the 'liberation' hypothesis on its head. Now it is not presumed economic gain that promoted 'equality' in crime, but rather it is economic marginalization that causes women to move out of their 'traditional' roles into the role of criminal" (Chesney-Lind, *The Female Offender* 118). Chesney-Lind is still not sure. Neither is Pollock, who maintains that there are still underlying differences between men and women which prevent them from exhibiting similar criminal propensities and behaviour (158–9). If this is accurate, then any attempt by women to disrupt these boundaries will once again result in accusations of masculinization and even monstrosity.

Campbell and Naffine also address the "blame-it-on-feminism" theory and dismiss it on psychological and criminological/economic grounds respectively. As Campbell sees it, in the 1970s "the rise in female crime (particularly violence by young women) was attributed to women's liberation. As women achieved the same rights and responsibilities as men, it was argued, their behavior became more and more masculine. Or to put it another way, if women were taught their proper place they would stop committing crime and violence. Researchers took to the streets to measure the psychological masculinity of bad girls, with disappointing results. A fundamental mistake was made: The assumption that violence equals masculinity" (126).

As a feminist criminologist, Naffine sees this issue somewhat differently:

> Perhaps the most time-consuming and fruitless exercise has been the endeavor to prove (and disprove) the thesis that "women's liberation" causes crime in women. This thesis was based on the assumption that if, as a result of the women's movement, women were acquiring the same opportunities as men, particularly economic opportunities, then one of the opportunities they would seize would be the opportunity to offend. The flaws in this thesis are not difficult to detect. To name but three: it assumed a simple, singular, reductive model of crime causation; it assumed, wrongly, that crimes associated with economic

opportunity were rising dramatically among women; and it assumed that women are now financially emancipated, despite the considerable evidence of the feminization of poverty. (32)

Finally, as I have shown above, Artz's findings relating to violent school girls indicate that in contrast to any "blame it on feminism" cause, "the judgments of women ... do not arise because these girls are becoming more emancipated. Rather, this arises because within their life-worlds, they still apply narrow notions of male-focused behavior as the standard for what is right and good for women" (201).

Unfortunately, this view of feminism/the women's liberation movement as the ultimate cause of an increase in crime and violence among women is alive and well. Chesney-Lind, in her introduction to DeKeseredy's study *Women, Crime, and the Canadian Criminal Justice System*, accuses Patricia Pearson (in her widely cited 1997 text) of being one of several backlash journalists who have "managed to parlay women's crime into national prominence for themselves precisely by avoiding the realities of women's offending – choosing, instead, to sensationalize and sexualize women's violence. The demonization of women accused of crimes serves a number of powerful political interests, particularly when the argument is made that women's participation in crime, especially traditionally 'male' crimes like murder, can be blamed on the women's movement" (v).

A well-meaning academic book published in 1992, *Femmes et criminelles*, by the French professor of criminology Robert Cario is another case in point. The jacket design itself starts the reader on this antifeminist journey: "Women and Criminals? In its non-flashy simplicity, the cover of this work itself comes close to producing a shocking effect" ["Femmes et Criminelles? En sa simplicité nullement tapageuse, la couverture de l'ouvrage que voici n'est pas loin de produire un effet de choc"] (Cario). To his credit, Cario does try to shed light on the issue of female criminality, and he does contextualize his findings in a cultural and social framework. But he falls prey to old assumptions, so that, although trying to be fair and non-condescending, he ends up exposing his own sexist and paternalistic attitudes.

In effect Cario states that the poorer classes are especially prone to criminal behaviour and the development of criminal personality (40, 44–6, 217), whereas the dominant classes do not have the time to resort to crime (265). In the past, since women remained at home, responsible for domestic matters and the education and well-being of children, neither did they have time for crime (147). Cario cites Lambroso and others who believe that in fact some women have long been criminal but, like "feminine icebergs," have been hiding their criminality behind the scenes (52).

More recently, according to Cario, there have been two ways of looking at women's criminality. On the one hand, he suggests that increasing equality between men and women in Western societies has caused a decrease in certain "traditionally observed characteristics" (46). He goes on to cite figures on female crimes in France between 1911 and 1985, emphasizing changes since 1975, in order to show the under-representation of women in crime. But, he states: "The more [women] participate in the professional and social world, the more their criminality increases ... Conversely, their confinement to the home and the rearing of children seems to keep them away from delinquency" ["Plus elles participent à la vie professionnelle et sociale, plus leur criminalité augmente ... A l'inverse, leur confinement au foyer et l'éducation des enfants semblent les écarter de la délinquance"] (176). What we have here is clearly a 1990s' version of "blame it on feminism."

On the other hand, Cario seems to echo the "second shift" theory, in a criminological variation: since women work both outside and inside the home, they have less free time for crime (184). Despite being dominated by men and assigned specific social roles that are repetitive and not gratifying, women are surprisingly under-represented in crime; they appear satisfied with their lot (232). When they do turn to crime, their actions stem from what they see as the only way to act upon their environment (255). In summary, according to Cario: "Women are less represented in criminality because the social roles that have been assigned to them on the one hand impose on them multiple domestic and child-rearing tasks and on the other hand determine the consolidation of a specific personality, such that they are positively kept away from criminality" ["Les femmes sont moins présentées dans la criminalité parce que les rôles sociaux qui leur sont assignés, d'une part leur imposent les tâches domestiques et éducatives multiples et déterminent chez elles, d'autre part, la consolidation d'une personnalité spécifique, d'une manière telle qu'elles se trouvent écartées positivement de la criminalité"] (274). In one study, therefore, we have three arguments – an anti-feminist argument, an imposed cultural argument, and an argument claiming innate nature – for both the increase in female crime and the small numbers of female criminals.

Women Who Kill Are "In"

When the news media announced in the late 1990s that violent women were now "in,"[66] Patricia Pearson's *When She Was Bad: Violent Women and the Myth of Innocence* was cited as primary evidence. Despite, or perhaps because of, Chesney-Lind's critique, it is worth briefly reviewing Pearson's "findings" since they present an alternative argument to explain female violence and its recent increase. Pearson sees violence as the constructed province of the male. Visible physical aggression, she says, is the result of masculine display (similar to Jack's cultural masks) where boys dress-rehearse for gender-posturing (7–12). The more indirect strategies of aggression that girls and women use (as noted above) "bestow upon women ignoble traits: hysteria, duplicitousness, manipulation, cunning ... Female aggressive strategies are never valorous, for they are by necessity underhanded, and partly because of that, they run completely counter to the way women want to view themselves" (21). This statement may ring partially true, but it is also incomplete, for such aggressive strategies of females also run counter to the way many men view women; in addition, there is no single way in which women want to view themselves.

Pearson does aptly state that strategies of violence for both men and women stem from a "shared cultural repertoire," but she bases this point on a more controversial one: unlike the male potential for violence whereby if a man hits his lover, he could one day kill her, Pearson states that it is not clear that a woman who slices her skin or turns her words into weapons would suddenly engage in overt violence against someone else. Given what Pearson sees as the obscurity in any gestural connection to aggression in women, she believes that this is why "criminal women wind up so radically isolated from their own sex, cast out as sexual deviants, dykes, witches. Feminist criminologists have tried to bring them back into the fold by recasting them as victims, arguing their violence away" (24). Pearson accuses feminists of falling into the trap of seeing women as incapable of violence or, if they do become violent, as being victims rather than perpetrators.

Pearson goes on to describe the way much of the public reacts to female violence: they see female aggression either as too threatening or too trivial – points to which I return below. She also attacks academics "who define the terms and interpret the data" for denying female aggression because it would be "too alarmingly 'anti-feminist' to even suggest" (31). Pearson cites figures to show that younger women are the fastest growing group of violent offenders on the continent: between 1960 and 1990, aggravated assault and robbery arrests rose twice as fast for girls as for boys; girls' felony arrest rates increased 124% from 1986 to 1995; in Canada young women now account for 24% of all violent offenses in their age group; in the United States, that figure is 18%; since 1970, suicide rates by teenaged girls have dropped by 50% (32).[67] Her last notation about the change in suicide rates for girls is an interesting one. It suggests that girls, who have long been seen as directing violence inwardly toward themselves, while boys direct their violent aggression outwardly onto others, may be gradually becoming more like boys.[68]

What Pearson is arguing – and it is certainly one argument among others – is that we can't have it both ways. We cannot insist on the strength and competence of women in all other traditionally male arenas and yet see them as powerless in areas of violence: "How do we argue that we can be aggressive on every count ... but never in a manner that does harm? How do we affirm ourselves to be as complex, desirous, and independent as men without conceding the antisocial potential in those qualities?" (32). She feels strongly that insistence on the anti-violent nature of women plays into our pre-existing prejudices about female nature – that women are caring and peace-loving individuals who could never want to do any harm to others. In this view, women themselves tend to equate powerlessness with innocence. Pearson is clearly presenting a view that blames either culturally accepted gender roles – that women are non-violent, that women internalize – or women themselves who use these roles as an excuse.

In concluding, Pearson concedes that women do often act in self-defence but emphasizes that this is not the sole factor to consider when analysing female violence: "Whereas they once described violent women as lesbian man-eaters and perverts, we have simply sailed to the other extreme, from whore to madonna. The old fabric of misogyny blends seamlessly with new threads of feminist essentialism to preserve the myth that women are more susceptible than men to being helpless, crazy, and biddable" (56). Feminists, for Patricia Pearson, are at least partially responsible for maintaining some of the myths that we continue to hold about women.

There are feminist critics who contradict Pearson's contention. Sarah Appleton Aguiar, for example, in *The Bitch Is Back: Wicked Women in Literature*, admits that in reading late twentieth-century fiction by feminist authors, readers would have difficulty finding much feminine wickedness among the new "subjectified" female protagonists: "For all of her ubiquitous presence in every other form of [popular] media, the bitch had been noticeably absent from the feminist literary canon. Until recently" (Aguiar 2). Aguiar goes on to explore the very recent "reclamation of the bitch" (6) or the "textual bitch" (10) by feminist writers such as Toni Morrison (*Paradise)* and Margaret Atwood (*The Robber Bride)*. Phyllis Chesler, in her *Woman's Inhumanity to Woman*, also refers to Morrison and Atwood because by 2000/01 women were seeking her out to talk about this topic of women's inhumanity to one another: "This tabooed theme has become hot: It's on women's tongues and in the air" (27). Despite the potential distance between a "born bitch" (Aguiar 11) and a violent woman, and between an American/Anglo-Canadian and a Quebec literary feminist canon, it does seem accurate to proclaim that at least for certain feminist writers – as I intend to demonstrate in this study – the bitch and the violent woman (violent toward both men and women) are "in."

As Aguiar points out, these "mean women" (precursors to the "mean girls") who fall "below the standards of human decency" (King and McCaughey 2) have been popular for some time in other media, especially in film. According to Neal King and Martha McCaughey in their edited collection *Reel Knockouts: Violent Women in the Movies*, in different eras these filmic women emerge as a result of issues of race and class: "Low-brow movies on the 1960s drive-in circuits featured plenty of white-trash mamas wielding baseball bats, broken bottles, and shotguns. In the early 1970s, blaxploitation movies made a star of prison-movie queen Pam Grier ... while no-budget rape-revenge movies began to square off middle-class white women against hillbilly abusers ... [In] the 1980s ... slashers such as *Halloween* ... introduced us to the teenage 'Final Girl' who could defeat the madman who skewered her friends. Science fiction/fantasy movies introduced big-budget female heroes in *Aliens* and *The Terminator.* In the 1990s the doors opened wider" (King and McCaughey 4).

Neal King and Martha McCaughey see 1991 as a banner year for violent women in film, with the release of films such as *La Femme Nikita*, *The Silence of the Lambs*, *Terminator* 2, and *Thelma and Louise* (5). They divide their volume into studies of film genres in which violent women have appeared: martial arts films; film noir/erotic thrillers; cop movies; and prison movies (6–7). In these films, violent women variously focus on the family; use vandalism, armed robbery, and rebellion against race, class, or sex constraints; discover handguns to subvert their meek white housewife image; or express a politics of rage and terrorist culture (8–9). Some feminist scholars, however, according to King and McCaughey, object to this on-screen violence on the basis that such characterizations of violent women are too unrealistic, too sexy, too emotional, or too co-opted (11–20). Indeed, even when these women are strong, aggressive, and violent in popular culture, they remain "buff" and beautiful: take the violent women of Quentin Tarantino's 2003 film, *Kill Bill: Vol. I*, for example, or the sexy female FBI recruit in the American television series *Line of Fire*. And even if some of these cinematic women are patriarchal pawns, they are also "possible tools in the liberation of women from racial, class, gender, and other political constraints that oppress women and deny them equal chances and equal rights" (20). Without equating violent force with positive images, it appears that at least in popular culture, violent women, in the view of some scholars, not only *are* "in" but also *should* be.

The Violent Lesbian

Perhaps one of the most deeply held myths about violent women relates to assumptions about lesbianism. In her study *Fatal Women: Lesbian Sexuality and the Mark of Aggression*, Lynda Hart also reminds us that violence is associated with men. In the eyes of society, if women exhibit violent tendencies, they are not women, but masculinized, often lesbians. She cites Lombroso's 1893 *The Female Offender* (as all theorists on crime tend to do), as well as Havelock Ellis's 1890 *The Criminal*, which praises Lombroso's earlier work. Both writers maintained that the "born" female offender is really not a woman but belongs more to the male than to the female sex. Hart brings these beliefs up to date: "Masculinity theory pursues its circular reasoning by arguing that women are less likely to engage in criminal activity because they are not men. Boys will be boys, say the masculinity theorists; and girls will be girls, unless they do become criminals, in which case they are likely to be masculinized women" (13).

For Hart, the Freudian "enigma of woman and the riddle of her capacity for violence are interdependent" (17), since the violent woman is not exceptional but a handy construct. Indeed, "in the figure of the woman as criminal the essence of femininity meets the alterity of the feminine. And they turn out to be the *same thing*" (36). But, once again coming full circle to the duality of femininity and violence, even when women may seem dangerous, they are – paradoxically – not considered capable of carrying out aggressive acts (78).[69]

More recently, Janice Ristock has investigated violence in lesbian relationships in her 2002 *No More Secrets*. Refuting the effectiveness of the widely used "power and control" model/constellation for an understanding of same-sex partner abuse, Ristock illustrates "how we rely on white, feminist heteronormative categories and constructs to think about violence" and shows how such normative discourse impedes our ability to see a differing set of gendered relations between women (113, 155). Power is a much more complex issue than the binary distinctions that we make between power and powerlessness in the dominant discourse: "A focus on the relations of power within a specific context could help us to move away from abstract notions of victims and perpetrators toward an exploration of how power operates in particular relationships, where we can examine the complexity of women's lives, and scrutinize the power dynamics in women's intimate relationships and in other areas of their lives. This involves a structural, personal, and relational focus; an analysis that involves both-and constructions of social reality, in which we resist the binary either/or positions" (128).

Ristock reminds us of the extent to which our lives are regulated by language, mentioning how our normative assumptions assert categories that include some women and exclude others, thereby recognizing certain forms of violence and not others (138). In what Marjorie Garber calls "category crisis" with respect to transvestism – "a failure of definitional distinction, a borderline that becomes permeable, that permits of border crossings from one (apparently distinct) category to another" (16) – Ristock brings us back to the need to recognize the complexity of women's lives, the complexity of different forms of violence, and especially the ineffectiveness, and indeed danger, of using binary oppositions.

Escaping the labels inherent in a binary system is difficult. We have woman as innocent, gentle, caring, nurturing, and incapable of violence – the angel, the mother, the virgin, the madonna, and yet still the "other." We also see woman as evil, sexual, dangerous, the vampire, the black widow – the whore, the vamp, the "other." A woman who is capable of aggression and violence becomes, therefore, the masculine female, the lesbian, the "other." As Lindsay Van Gelder has quipped: "In many minds the leap from butch to butcher's knife is but a tiny one" (82). The public is enmeshed in these myths of women, and when they read or hear about a case in which a woman has committed a horrifying crime, many are still shocked and proclaim that it is a "first."

Perhaps the most obvious example of these assumptions can be found in "revelations" about female serial killers.[70] One recent case sheds significant light on attitudes toward lesbianism and accusations that lesbians threaten rigid gender polarity: the case of Aileen Wuornos, most recently "immortalized" through both the critically acclaimed documentaries of her life: *Aileen Wuornos: The Selling of a Serial Killer: The 1992 Interviews*; and *Aileen: Life and Death of a Serial Killer,* and through the highly praised feature film *Monster.* Dubbed "America's First Female Serial Killer" and a "Lesbian Killer" by the press, Wuornos was executed by lethal injection in October 2002 in Florida for the murder of seven men whom she said she had killed in self-defence while working as a prostitute (Scholder 37, 54–7). In branding her as a man-hating, lesbian *femme fatale* who lured men into her lair, the sensationalizing of Wuornos's case reflects the apprehension that women, if released from traditional restraints, could wreak havoc on the world (see Scholder, 169–80). As Hart says, "whereas male serial killers are 'naturally unnatural,' as a woman Wuornos has committed *unnatural unnatural* acts" (142). A woman, by definition, is not violent, and if she exhibits violent tendencies and commits violent acts, then she is not a woman (Hart 143). She must be a lesbian.

Lisa Duggan agrees. In *Sapphic Slashers: Sex, Violence, and American Modernity* she echoes much of what Hart, Ristock, Scholder, Dijkstra, and Shapiro have written. Her compelling account of an 1890s' lesbian love/murder case provides the impetus for a broader study of race, sexuality, gender, news reporting, and violence in America. Duggan begins by claiming that "the black beast rapist and the homicidal lesbian both appeared, in new cultural narratives at the end of the nineteenth century, as threats to white masculinity and to the stability of the white home" (3). Women's crimes of violence raised issues of gender and sexuality more profoundly than those committed by men because violent female criminals were thought to have crossed the line of gender to engage in "masculine" activity (23).

Duggan convincingly writes that "assembled from French novels and Anglo-European sexology ... the lesbian embodied a series of links from gender inversion, through sexual deviance, to violence" (28). From the specific murder case that she investigates – the murder of Freda Ward by Alice Mitchell in Memphis, Tennessee, in 1892 – Duggan extrapolates the proposition, widely accepted at the time, that any "abnormal" female must be a homicidal lesbian and therefore must, in turn, be judged as insane. Insanity, after all, was safer than immorality (86, 114). At the turn of the century in the United States, criminal women were put into the same boxes: either mad or bad. In either case, deviance was the key element, a deviance that threatened gender polarity, boundaries, and the "normal" functioning of society.

From Sapphic Slashers *to* Tough Girls

Let us jump ahead to our present time and look at a newer image of women in popular culture in America, an image that in one sense mimics changing gender definitions and in another sense places women right back in the age-old dichotomy. Sherrie Inness, in her *Tough Girls: Women Warriors and Wonder Women in Popular Culture* (and even more recently in her edited collection *Action Chicks: New Images of Tough Women in Popular Culture*), focuses on media images (in film, television, magazines, and comic books) of what she calls the "New Tough Woman" – tough in body, attitude, action, and authority (24) – and confirms that these images represent "a culture in which real women are re-evaluating what is means to be tough" (6). Like Duggan, Inness refuses "the separation of social life ('reality') from representations ('myth,' or 'stereotype')" (Duggan 4).[71]

Referring to the work of Susan Bordo and Judith Butler among others, Inness examines images of women whose toughness challenges gender stereotypes. According to Inness, women who adopt a persona that is strongly coded as masculine are disturbing because they reveal the artificiality of the manifestations of femininity that are considered "normal" in our society. "Tough" and "toughness" (and, I add, "violent" and "violence") are associated with "man" and "masculine," but they really have little to do with the physical body: "Associating toughness with gender rather than sex is threatening to the social order because it breaks down the essentialist argument that gender and sex are indissolubly linked. Instead, any subject who presents an effective performance of toughness can be tough, despite the body's sex" (22).

Tough women, therefore, show that masculine characteristics are not biologically defined but constitute "a carefully choreographed performance that either a man or a woman might engage in" (179). But, Inness concludes: "If masculine attributes, such as toughness, and feminine attributes, too, are conceived as free-floating signifiers that refer to either a male or a female body, our whole culture is destabilized because it is based on what are perceived as the essential differences between men and women ... What must be considered, however, is whether it is desirable for women – either in the popular media or in reality – to ascribe to the same tough images as men" (180).

If "tough women rewrite the script" in a culture where women are usually considered the "natural" victims of men (Inness 8), they remain caught in the very duality that defines them so simplistically, even as they shake the foundations of our still-standing gender polarity – thereby frightening men and other women. After all, both men and women are raised in similar cultures, and as a result, "as men do, women either idealize or demonize women ... To a woman other women are (supposed to be) Good Fairy Godmothers, and if they are not they may swiftly become their dreaded Evil Stepmothers" (Chesler 5). Is there a way out of this dilemma?

Until a wide spectrum of people, along with the cultural, social, legal, academic, religious, and linguistic "texts" that influence society, become more sensitized to the stereotypes that they are disseminating and upholding about women and violence, and until those cultural norms are expanded and at least partially overturned, there will be no way out of this dilemma of the simplistic duality in which women are caught, no matter how they act or what they do. Both theorists and practitioners will – at times unwittingly – continue to perpetuate such gender myths, and such stereotypical discourses will continue to label women as bad or mad if they commit aggressive acts. We have only to remind ourselves of Elizabeth Schneider's comments on feminist lawmaking: "Biases, myths, misconceptions, and personal experience can have a subtle but powerful impact on a lawyer's judgment" (106). If the legal system, constructed by and for men, is being used as a standard to assess female conduct, as Renzetti and Dasgupta have stated, then women's violence contradicts their gender role as passive and helpless persons (Dasgupta, 2001 8). Further, as has been discussed, one must add that biased, "mythical," and misconceptualized discourses can have an equally subtle but powerful impact on those involved in law enforcement and social policy positions, as well as on the public at large. If the way we talk about women and violence has serious implications for social policy and the way women are treated in the criminal justice system, then we must break down and redefine that discourse and move toward a multi-layered discourse of women and violence that will allow women to present and speak for themselves in such a way as to portray the complexities and realities of their lives. Like men, "women are complex and diverse, capable of both love and hate, good and evil" (Chesler 25), and we need to understand the multiple nuances within these complexities.

Do women writers who create violence and violent women offer any alternatives in their literary representations? Do their characters imitate or parody men? Do they voice a "reality" of woman's condition that could lead to harmful and malicious behaviour? Or do they attempt to go beyond gender "at all costs"? Specifically, do certain women writers in Quebec provide different perspectives and narratively re-frame gendered cultures, since they, perhaps more freely than other writers, can distance themselves from the powerful popular culture and life style of the United States, or are they influenced by that culture and life style? These are questions that I address in the remainder of this study, as I move toward analyses of particular Quebec women writers' texts against the backdrop of a "peaceful" Quebec within the "peaceable kingdom" of Canada, the United States's northern neighbour.

LITERARY REPRESENTATIONS OF VIOLENCE AND GENDER

The Violence of Representation and the Representation of Violence

There is a sense in which any literary or artistic representation of violence and gender is actually the representation of another representation. Artistic representation in this instance "represents" the representations/myths/assumptions/stereotypes of women and their "capacity" for violence in a "real" world in which gender is performative and socially constructed. We "read" women, and we "read" violence in literary texts, for example, in order to find out what the representations created by certain writers say about our representations of the world. We cannot separate reality from representation.

As with discussions about violence at the level of discourse itself, much has been written about the violence of representation.[72] Nancy Armstrong and Leonard Tennenhouse, co-editors of the important collection *The Violence of Representation: Literature and the History of Violence*, for example, speak to these issues in their cogent introduction. They divide their authors into two camps: those who seek an "extra-discursive dimension of culture," and those who consider writing itself to be "not so much about violence as a form of violence in its own right" (2). Having made this distinction between two modalities of violence – "that which is 'out there' in the world, as opposed to that which is exercised through words upon things" – Armstrong and Tennenhouse set out to demonstrate that "the two cannot in fact be distinguished, at least not in writing ... Violent events are not simply so but are called violent because they bring together different concepts of social order. To regard certain practices as violent is never to see them just as they are. It is always to take up a position for or against them" (9); violence, therefore, has become the provenance of the "Other," the material of representation.

Armstrong and Tennenhouse add that our preoccupation with violence as an aspect of crime is fairly recent, displacing (especially in legal discourse) the capacity to perpetrate violence from the state/king onto the lowest and most marginalized members of society. With the government as the "defender of individuals over and against those who would do violence to them, crimes became crimes against persons and against property rather than crimes against the state" (17). Armstrong and Tennenhouse see this shift as a new way of reading society; violence has been relocated within individuals designated as "Other" – individuals outside of culture – thereby marking a "shift in the form of political power from violence to representation" (18).

The co-editors conclude their collection with an essay by Theresa de Lauretis because she is concerned with the ways in which the words chosen to represent the subjects and objects of violence are themselves part of the violent events. As de Lauretis herself writes in her essay "The Violence of Rhetoric": "The very notion of a 'rhetoric of violence' presupposes that some order of language, some kind of discursive representation is at work not only in the concept 'violence' but in the social practices of violence as well. The (semiotic) relation of the social to the discursive is thus posed from the start ... From the Foucauldian notion of a rhetoric of violence, an order of language which speaks violence ... it is easy to slide into the reverse notion of a language which, itself, produces violence. But if violence is in language ... then there is also a violence of rhetoric, or what Derrida has called 'the violence of the letter' [*Of Grammatology* 101–40]" (240).

Focusing on the role of the reader, Laura Tanner, in *Intimate Violence: Reading Rape and Torture in Twentieth-Century Fiction*, agrees that the representation of violence occurs at the intersection of linguistic and material worlds. Citing the work of Armstrong and Tennenhouse, Tanner states that "the act of reading a representation of violence is defined by the reader's suspension between the semiotic and the real, between a representation and the material dynamics of violence which it evokes, reflects, or transforms" (6). Suspended between these semiotic and material worlds, the reader must negotiate a position relative to the victim and the perpetrator, as well as to "the attitudes about violation encoded in representation and experienced through reading. The force of the narrative impulsion that aligns the reader with victim, violator, or observer and the reader's reaction to that force create an interactive power dynamic ... in which the reader's own sense of embodied subjectivity comes to be at risk" (3).

For Tanner, just as literary representations of violence can modify a reader's attitude toward empirical violence, even unbeknownst to the reader, some form of empirical violence always shadows its representational counterpart. Reading violence accurately must thus take into account this negotiation on the part of the reader between the "real" and the representational. The reader enters the fictional world by abandoning part of the material world, thereby experiencing a certain sense of disembodiment or detachment. The seductive power of literary representation is mediated, as it pushes and at times unsettles the reader. Like film, literary representations of violence can often be highly charged and highly visual, imposing themselves on the reader's imagination (9, 10, 12). Through the "aestheticization" of a violent text, however, a reader can be seduced into seeing only textual violence while failing to see either any connection to the real world or any personal complicity with the violence enacted in the text (14). Tanner argues that "representations of violation even in texts that do not explicitly foreground the gap between their narrative and textual functions may be read oppositionally if the *reader* is self-conscious about his or her own role in the construction of textual meaning" (15).

The Verbal Aestheticized Story of Violence as a Talking Cure

It seems at first that Michael Kowalewski's approach in *Deadly Musings: Violence and Verbal Form in American Fiction* runs counter to Tanner's work. Kowalewski initially asks the fundamental question: How do acts of violence exist in literature? (7). His answer is clear: "The only presence violence has in fiction is verbal ... Violence is always verbally mediated in novels and stories; it is not 'there' in language except in the sense that it has been rendered ... out of it. Violence thus appears in fiction like everything else with which it shares the page, as something *styled* (styled, not 'stylized')" (4). For Kowalewski, literary violence depends for its meaning on verbal action, much as acting styles do. He speaks of an epistemology of violence – the ways in which we know what we know about violence and the ways in which it has been "performed" in fiction (8). Words have the power to sicken and disgust us, and yet many present critics have attempted to turn violence into Violence, imbuing it with a metaphysical status that detaches it from its verbal origins. Kowalewski wants to "put violence back into texts, not abstract it out of them" (19).

He makes the interesting point that an author can arrange realistic fictional details in a text so that the reader mistakes verbal interaction for an extratextual aspect of life; we really know that a writer has authored a particular scene, and yet we wince as though the scene were real: "We are invited to mis-take a fabric of contributive verbal events for a more repulsive event beyond it" (56, 323). Kowalewski's "realistic imagining"[73] is prompted by language and verbal features (grammar, syntax, and so on) designed to create the illusion that representation is what it triggers in the reader (35). It is the "idea" of violence, the act of imagining this violence – whether explicit or not – that constitutes the imaginative substance of that violence (Kowalewski 51). In this "syntax of fear," the act of representation becomes more powerful than what we say it represents; "realistic imagining" ends up inventing "reality" (59).

Ultimately, however, Kowalewski seems to come full circle and agree with Tanner: "Literary occurrences of violence are not the result, exclusively, of either actual violence or of verbal representation. They result from fusions of the two, from the specific verbal means by which certain stylistic contexts express something that may or may not appear to resemble nonverbal objects and events. Substituting the idea of 'conveyability' for that of 'representation' may help us begin to describe the verbal conditions that must prevail if a fictional depiction of violence is to seem 'violent' in the way we normally use that term" (60).

Tanner and Kowalewski agree that literary representations of violence are mediated in some way. While Tanner speaks of a certain "aestheticization" of a violent text which can lull a reader into avoiding any extratextual context (7, 14), Kowalewski offers the image of an audience member covering his or her eyes and yet peeping at a violent scene through the fingers (47). Similarly, Katherine Ackley identifies what she calls the "Phalaris syndrome," the phenomenon whereby one deflects the impression of horror from literary violence "by substituting an abstraction, either purposely or inadvertently" (Ackley 175). "Instead of noticing the violence," she says, "we admire the art ... Abstraction and allegory have allowed readers to hustle past a front-line vocabulary of cruelty to hobnob with the lofty sentiments in the background" (176). Ackley then reminds us of the long history of writers who have used a vocabulary of "evil," who have designated poets and novelists as outlaws of society, liberated the text and the word with "exploding" language – as noted above in regard to the texts of poets such as Mallarmé and Rimbaud – and broke the linearity of prose with acts of textual violence (177–9). In other words, as readers, we have long been accustomed to "hobnobbing with lofty sentiments" lurking behind a linguistic and textual representation of violence.

And yet what Whitmer calls "the story of violence" – told within a discursive infrastructure through testimony, analysis, theories, symbolic significance, and paradigms of innate and acquired violence (10) – remains an essential mode of recovery for victims of violent trauma. Judith Herman relates that the action of telling one's story can transform a traumatic memory and integrate it into a survivor's life. Such an account is often repetitious, a sort of "prenarrative" that vacillates in its reconstruction of events but offers the "restorative power of truth-telling" (181, 175): "The *physioneurosis* induced by terror can apparently be reversed through the use of words" (183). The action of telling the story allows the individual to reclaim his or her own history, since, once the story is told, the trauma belongs to the past.

Deborah Horvitz has based much of her *Literary Trauma: Sadism, Memory, and Sexual Violence in American Women's Fiction* on the work of Herman, exploring how trauma and loss (and by extension, any experience of violence) can be narratively presented. She finds a palliative role for narrative in what she calls the "discourse of healing" (10). According to Horvitz, trauma blurs the borders between the "political" and the "psychological." Horwitz explains that a story originates at the site where knowing and not knowing converge, where personal meaning is projected into a text, and where the borders between one's inner and outer worlds dissolve (5).[74] Telling a story about trauma or any past violence allows a person to incorporate that experience into his or her life and thereby to gain control over it. Horvitz describes an analogous process in literature: "Fictional characters experience trauma and, subsequently, as a self-protective response, repress its memories. And, it is within the discourse of healing that the operative dynamics among memory, remembering, and narrative converge. Then they may find both the capacity to remember and 'the words to say it,' making healing possible" (10). For Horvitz, each text mimics a "talking cure," functioning as an analyst (19). (I shall return to these concepts as I explore the "healing" narratives of protagonists who have experienced trauma and violence – albeit as the result of the perpetration rather than the victimization of crime – and who instinctively recognize the benefits of a textual "talking cure.")

Sequencing Violence and Characterizing Crime

Finally, two theories present sociological/media/journalistic approaches to the representation of violence. Karen Cerulo, in *Deciphering Violence: The Cognitive Structure of Right and Wrong*, offers an innovative framework for understanding the storytelling of violence, taking into account that the storyteller can structure the elements in such a way as to create the chosen effect on the reader: "The way in which storytellers sequence a violent account can influence audience assessment of violence as right, wrong, or something in between" (3).

She identifies four distinct sequences, each with a narrative option: "*Victim sequences* present violence from the perspective of the injured party ... *performer sequences* unfold violent events from the perspective of the person who commits the act. *Contextual sequences* prioritize the circumstances surrounding a violent act. Finally, *doublecasting sequences* highlight individuals who play a dual role – both the victim and the perpetrator of violence" (5).

Order and timing matter in presenting and reacting to violence. According to Cerulo, such sequences of violence are not randomly applied; rather, strong cultural conventions lead storytellers to use particular sequences at specific times in order to elicit certain reactions to what she calls deviant/heinous, normal, or ambiguous violence. She shows through her research that journalists, reporters, authors, filmmakers, painters, and photographers are all guided by these cultural conventions, as they organize their material on violence (6). Following Maurice Merleau-Ponty, Cerulo refers to the beginning of a violent event as its "point-horizon" structure: "A story's beginning becomes the point from which the audience members view the dimensions of the broader horizon. Audience members come to inhabit the point, grasping all other elements of a story as they are presented to the point of entry" (7).

Still building on Merleau-Ponty, as well as Gérard Genette and Paul Ricoeur on narration, Cerulo analyses structures of meaning, stressing the importance of the dynamic elements of message structure. She focuses on individuals' point of entry, and follows progressive frames of action, exploring how the temporal ordering is prioritized. She argues that any given sequence operates as a silent narrator, a roadmap, or a directing voice that guides the audience or reader's gaze through any verbal or visual account of violence. Each sequence forms a specific lens on the script, thereby eliciting particular judgments on the part of readers and viewers. As Cerulo concludes: "Public perceptions of violence are shaped not simply by *what* storytellers say; *how* narrators present such accounts – the sequencing of story information – can strongly guide public assessments of violence as right, wrong, or somewhere in between" (137).

In a similar vein, DeKeseredy outlines what he calls the "Techniques of Crime Characterization" used in stories by criminal mythmakers, journalists who use these techniques of myth characterization "to shape the presentation of crimes committed by girls to create images for uncritical audiences, and to promote a punitive societal reaction" (39). He discerns nine techniques:

- *creating criminal stereotypes*, such as using phrases like "bad girl";
- *expressing opinions as fact* by interjecting personal opinion without factual basis – "'Prodded by feminism, today's teenaged girls embrace antisocial male behaviour'" (*Alberta Report* 31 July 1995, 24);
- *masking opinions through sources* by collecting opinions of others that closely match one's own view;
- *using value-loaded terminology and biased language* such as "malicious," "evil," "ruthless monsters," "feminist cults of androgyny" (*Alberta Report* 31 July 1995);
- *using a selective presentation of facts*;
- *managing information* or choosing to present certain stories over others – similar to Cerulo's sequencing of the stories chosen;
- *including undocumented sources* of authority;
- *stripping the fact from its context* – what he calls the "decontexualizing of crime" (see Schissel 1997);
- *interviewing selectively* (DeKeseredy 40–1).

The Violence of Representation as Gendered

Is it at all possible to speak of violence without discussing gender? Is it at all possible to understand any representation of violence without referring to its gendered nature? Theresa de Lauretis certainly does not think so. She makes herself quite clear on the subject: "I ... contend that both views [that of Foucault and that of Derrida] of the relation between rhetoric and violence contain and indeed depend on the same representation of sexual difference, whether they assume the 'fact' of gender or, like Derrida, deny it: and, further, that the representation of violence is inseparable from the notion of gender, even when the latter is explicitly 'deconstructed' or, more exactly, indicated as 'ideology.' I contend, in short, that violence in en-gendered in representation" ("The Violence of Rhetoric" 240).

Luce Irigaray agrees, in principle. If, as she states in *Speculum of the Other Woman*, "We can assume that any theory of the subject has always been appropriated by the 'masculine'" (133) ["Toute théorie du 'sujet' aura toujours été appropriée au 'masculin'"] (*Speculum de l'autre femme 165)*, and if the subjectivity denied to woman in real life becomes objectified in representation and discourse, then, as Irigaray encourages, women must turn language upside down, focus on the blank spaces, the silent plasticity, ellipses, and eclipses of discourse, and shake up syntax in order to find her voice and make it known: "She has yet to feel the need to get free of fabric, reveal her nakedness, her destitution in language, explode in the face of them all, words too" (*Speculum of the Other Woman* 143). In some sense, the writers who will be considered in this study have taken Irigaray's words to heart, as they have "exploded" in the literary text with their creation of violent female protagonists.

Applying Irigaray's thinking, along with theories of Roland Barthes and Maurice Blanchot, to novels from Quebec, France, and England, Karen McPherson, in her *Incriminations: Guilty Women/Telling Stories*, focuses on the female voice as a trope of identity and power; the woman, either as predator or victim, is in control because of the power of her voice. The silent woman is potentially the aggrieved woman, the object of violence ("Silence is indeed a gendered question" [McPherson 8]), whereas the raised voices of women will be the voices of outrage (8). As McPherson poetically states: "When she looks at herself in the mirror that the world holds up to her, a woman sees that she has indeed been *framed*; she has been made to embody the interdiction and its transgressing. Unspeaking, unspoken, unspeakable, she must, in the language of the law, be there to be violated. And if she were herself to violate that law and speak her violation? If she were to dismantle the frame?" (10).

Female Transgression

Dismantling this frame, as McPherson shows, is certainly an act of transgression, a form of "writing beyond the ending," as Rachel Blau du Plessis titled her ground-breaking 1985 book: "Writing beyond the ending means the transgressive invention of narrative strategies, strategies that express critical dissent from dominant narrative. These tactics ... take issue with the mainstays of the social and ideological organization of gender, as these appear in fiction" (5). For McPherson, this feminist postcript or post (modern) script is "always in the process of crossing its own boundaries, the transgression *in* narrative *of* narrative" (167). It is the transgressive violence of writing against the law, as recognized by both Barthes and Blanchot. But in McPherson's view, since women are already outlaws, their transgressive actions are compounded by their gender; they are forever incriminated and guilty, no matter what they do. As I shall illustrate, the violent protagonists in the texts studied here have clearly transgressed, but in their case, the trespass of the law (of society and of narrative) is forever encoded in their gendered roles as women.

Women, in other words, cannot win. As Deirdre Lashgari has pointed out in her introduction to *Violence, Silence, and Anger: Women's Writing as Transgression*: "Whatever is read by the dominant group as alien, rough-edged, jolting, or strident is more likely to offend when it comes from a woman" (2). Undoing any binary structure means destabilizing the master narrative that has been adopted by men and internalized and accepted by many women. The language of creative transgression is a dangerous border crossing that culminates in an aesthetic violence that proves that "language *is* loaded and has the power to kill" (Lashgari 13). As Lashgari later testifies in her essay on the work of Janice Mirikitani, this particular writer creates "an aesthetic counterviolence, violating boundaries, violating patriarchal assumptions, violating the reader's own resistance and silences. By peeling the ceremonial covering off the face of violence, she disrupts the deadly sameness, the status quo imposed by social constructs or literary genre. When she shocks, it is with purpose, a way of daring us past our squeamishness, shaking us into hearing, speech, and action" (291). The beautiful and angry poetry of Mirikitani is undoubtedly a raw depiction of the face of violence, but it in no way places a woman in the position of "acting like man" and causing violence to others. And yet this wonderful image that Lashgari gives us here aptly describes the work of many recent feminist women writers who have been shocking us past our squeamishness as they jolt and perhaps offend some readers with their aggressive and violent textual representations of women. Josephine Gattuso Hendin has recently named it "the heartbreaker effect": "Violence by women is a communication sent like a letter bomb to repudiate ideologies of the left or right ... Its explosive methods use appropriation and revision to script a woman's life in innovative ways ... In fiction and poetry, violence serves to explode stereotypes, rewriting conventional female scripts from the dark side" (2).

Female Violence and the Disruption of Representation

The rampaging female who has already become, in some sense, a cliché of Hollywood is, according to Helen Birch in her introduction to *Moving Targets: Women, Murder, and Representation*, forever shifting boundaries between fact and fiction, reality and representation: "Precisely because she is relatively rare, the woman killer presents a far more dramatic spectacle than her male counterpart. Male violence is, after all, old news" (2). Or, as Lawrence Kramer has put it: "Rape is commonplace; castration is news" (183). Her actions are, in effect, within the "tradition of disruption ... the situation of displacement" (MacKendrick 2). In Birch's view, these killer women are anathema to most people and as a result, are categorized, as we know, either as bad, wicked, and inhuman, or as mad and not like "ordinary" women. But, she asks: "Because women have traditionally internalized their feelings of anger or injustice, does this mean we have to pathologize those who do not?" (5).

But we do just that. It is threatening for some people to see those assumptions, those ways of representing our traditional world, mocked and disrupted. If actual sexual violence is grounded in representation, as Lawrence Kramer believes, perhaps "sexual violence is noteworthy only when it disturbs our habitual way of representing the world": sexual violence against women is still normalized and anesthetized, and becomes news only when it "disrupts the order of representation, the order in which subjectivity is framed and regulated ... Sexual violence against men, however, disturbs representation whenever it happens, with no exceptions. It is, in effect, violence against representation itself" (180–3).

Fantasies of Feminine Evil in Fin-de-Siècle Culture

A decade before Bram Dijkstra's work on the "evil sisters" of the turn of the century appeared (a passage of which introduces this chapter), he published *Idols of Perversity: Fantasies of Feminine Evil in Fin-de-Siècle Culture*. In it he convincingly analyses how scientific advances, economic developments, and the cultural environment of the end of the nineteenth century in Europe and America created a unique set of intellectual conditions that greatly influenced not only the artists and writers of that day but also twentieth-century thinking about issues such as sex, gender, race, and class (vii). Through the iconography and literary texts of that period, Dijkstra paints a broad picture of women through the misogynistic eyes of men: the household nun; the invalid; the collapsing and weightless woman; the narcissist and the nymph; the lesbian; the degenerate; the poison flower, siren, beast, vampire, whore; the priestess of death. His canvas can be summed up in the words of Proudhon: "Art has only one gender, it is masculine" (from Proudhon's *La Pornocratie*, 152, as quoted by Dijkstra 208).

According to Dijkstra, by 1900, the woman was portrayed by many intellectuals and artists not only as empty-headed, but also as one who had become: "a raving, predatory beast, a creature who preyed on men out of sheer sadistic self-indulgence ... a poisonous animal [who twists] herself snakelike around the body of a white-winged golden boy-poet who was just about to soar upward to the ideal ... The struggle between man and woman, the battle of the sexes, was a war between the forces of evolution and the emissaries of degeneration. Woman, the intellectuals wanted the world to know, was the Beast of the Scriptures, evil incarnate, an animal – and, worse, a veritable connoisseur of bestiality" (234).

Citing such renowned authors as Constant, Flaubert, Baudelaire, Huysmans, Laforgue, Mallarmé, Mérimée, Zola, Bram Stoker (*Dracula*), and Wilde, and influential painters such as Delacroix, Courbet, Manet, Cézanne, Degas, Renoir, Moreau, and Munch, along with many popular painters of the late nineteenth century who are less well known today, Dijkstra moves from images of the woman as a "flower of evil" (Baudelaire), a companion of fauns, a cat, a snake, a viper, a serpent, and a cobra who is sexually excited by animals (Darwin), and dangerously seductive as a prostitute (Zola) to the woman who has the power to decapitate a man (Flaubert, Mallarmé, Moreau, and

Wilde and their renditions of the story of Hérodias, Salomé, and St John the Baptist). Dijkstra is speaking here of representations of women in the arts (and in science, medicine, social Darwinism, and the culture at large) of little more than a century ago.[75] Why, then, should we be surprised that when women are violent either in the "real" world or in the representational world, many people are stunned (after all, women are supposed to be gentle and submissive), as some shake their heads in confirmation of what they had known all along (after all, women are animalistic and dangerous harpies who are out to hurt men and even children)?

Pathologizing the Lesbian Killer

Women also can hurt other women, as narratives of the killer lesbian tell us. Duggan informs us that, as Dijkstra has shown, the influence of misogynistic literature on the shaping of social and gender hierarchies in both Europe and North America was profound. As I have indicated, her own study of a lesbian murder and subsequent trial in 1892, read in the context of developing connections among sexuality, gender norms, racial injustice, the medicalization of homosexuality, and the violence of late nineteenth-century America, reveals that the published English translations of French novels and the appearance of medical texts on same-sex love and sexual passion fanned the flames of fear of the "abnormal": "Beginning with the first reports of the murder in 1892 [of Freda Ward by Alice Mitchell in Memphis], both the newspapers and the medical journals noted that this case seemed to echo the plots of novels by Honoré de Balzac, Théophile Gauthier, Gustave Flaubert, Aldolphe Belot, and Émile Zola, which were beginning to appear in widely available U.S. editions during the 1890s. Those plots became resources for the elaboration of the elements of the lesbian love murder story, headlined as 'A Tragedy Equal to the Most Morbid Imaginings of Modern French Fiction'" (Duggan 181).

For Duggan, these narrative technologies of sex and violence worked to marginalize certain populations even further, as the "narrativization of the murder," the "pathologizing narrative of the desire of 'girl lovers' ... was in a sense 'coauthored' by many social interests – always unstable, located in a field of conflict over the authorship, language, and plots of appropriate versus dangerous love and courtship" (47, 119).

From Feminine Evil and Lesbian Murder to Tough Girls, Action Chicks, and Deadly Dolls

As I have pointed out, Sherrie Inness does not accept any distinction between "reality" and "representation," between "social" and "mythic." She confirms that a female hero can rewrite stereotypes of womanhood: "Just by *being*, she suggests that the male stronghold on the heroic can be subverted. The woman hero serves as a bold, new role model for women and girls. Her appearance provides one visual clue to a culture that is gradually becoming more open to nonstereotypical gender roles and to women adopting tough roles" (143). However, Inness is using as an example representations of tough girls and women in comic books. As such, these female roles remain peripheral, since comics are doubly marginalized as popular literature and as a genre marketed especially to children.

But, like others, Inness has also questioned whether women should even desire to be tough – that is, like men: "Do we want female characters who are as brutal as the Terminator? Are we hoping to see women who are as merciless as Dirty Harry? Are we secretly longing to cheer for women who are as violent as Rambo?" (180). As Christine Holmlund reminds us, a number of critics of the immensely popular film *Aliens* referred to the tough female protagonist Ripley as "Rambolina," without even recognizing and questioning the resonance of war that such a reference to Rambo suggests (144).

What Inness shows us, however, is that even when tough and violent women – and even the more recent "action chicks" – are portrayed in that representation of reality, they are often and ultimately shown to be "just" girls and women. Like Inness, and King and McCaughey as well, Christine Holmlund demonstrates that the celluloid female murderers, whom she calls "deadly dolls," in films such as *Black Widow*, *Aliens*, *Fatal Attraction*, *Blue Steel*, *Mortal Thoughts*, and *Thelma and Louise*, are still defined as erotic creatures, as measured by their bodies, costumes, hairstyles, and make-up, and are considered incomplete without a male (135–6). In addition, the violent killer woman is usually "proven" to be mad or bad: an insane or psychotic and murderous harpy or black widow – or perhaps a sex kitten – but in the final analysis, simply not quite as tough as the boys (Inness 65–73).[76] Even the renaming of Ripley in *Aliens* as "Rambolina" betrays a condescending male attitude toward a particularly tough woman – the little Rambo who is, beneath her strength and masculine toughness, just another tiny Thumbelina. Ultimately, therefore, these deviant women must be punished in order to uphold society's binary vision of how a "real" woman should be acting – whether it be in real life, in films, or in novels.

Female "Monsters" – Some with a Sense of Humour

Karen Halttunen has suggested that the speechlessness we experience when we are in the presence of something frightening, of horror itself, in the convention of murder literature indicates "an inability to assign meaning to the transgression. To be suddenly deprived of all language by the sight of a dead body is to be rendered incapable of rationally coming to terms with it. Horror is about the essential meaninglessness of evil within an Enlightenment world view committed to the basic goodness of humankind" (56). As Judith Halberstam has pointed out in *Skin Shows: Gothic Horror and the Technology of Monsters*, these reactions stem from what Jean Baudrillard has called the obscenity of "immediate visibility" ("The Ecstasy of Communication" 130) and what Linda Williams has labelled "the frenzy of the visible" (Williams 36). Examining the concept of the monster as a cultural object – from nineteenth century Gothic fiction to contemporary horror films – Halberstam postulates that the "production of fear in a literary text (as opposed to a cinematic text) emanates from a vertiginous excess of meaning ... Multiple interpretations are embedded in the text and part of the experience of horror comes from the realization that meaning itself runs riot [producing] a symbol for this interpretive mayhem in the body of the monster" (2). Whether it is interpretive mayhem in frenzied visibility or in vertiginous literary meaning, as imagined visibility, the monster or, rather, monstrosity itself, inspires in us a fear (and a desire) for the "Other."

But are monsters evil and violent males, or evil and violent females, gone astray? Are violent females usually seen as more monstrous than males because they have transgressed the "normal" boundaries of acceptable gender roles or simply because, like violent men, they do bad things to good people? Or are such females more monstrous because they have trespassed in both ways – taking on the masks of bad (or mad) people who perform bad (and insane) acts against us, much like Aileen Wuornos of the significantly titled film *Monster*? One issue is clear: as Halberstam tells us, contemporary monstrosity seems to have become an "amalgam of sex and gender" (6) – much like Buffalo Bill in

Silence of the Lambs – of indeterminate gender and sexuality or perhaps all gender (6). No wonder some people are frightened and are asking: Who are these violent women? Are they indeed women? Are they women disguised as men? Both women and men? Of no sex and gender? Are they truly monstrous? To Halberstam: "The monster/phantom ... never stands for a simple or unitary prejudice, it always acts as a 'fantasy screen' upon which viewers and readers inscribe and sexualize meaning" (10).

Halberstam convincingly argues that the body of a literary and filmic monster (or the violent woman) becomes a meaning machine that can represent any horrible trait that the viewer or the reader wants to read into the narrative. The monster (violent woman) produces the negative pole of humanity, or at least according to the way many see humankind (that is, broken into binaries, into gender polarity). Such a depiction "disrupts the logic of genre that essentializes generic categories and stabilizes the production of meaning within them ... [and] produces models of reading ... that allow for multiple interpretations and a plurality of locations of cultural resistance" (23). I would argue that like the Gothic, representations of violent women produce an inability to categorize and mark our continued preoccupation with boundaries and their potential destruction. As Karmen MacKendrick has pointed out: "To transgress is to cross boundaries, but it is boundaries after all that mark places. This is as true epistemologically and ontologically as it is corporeally and topographically" (3).

One method used by the female creators of these violent and monstrous women intent on breaking down our borders of normalcy is humour – a technique that I consider in some detail in studying parody in chapter 3 and female serial killers in chapter 5. Halberstam calls it punning, since puns work on the surface and create or enact forms of cultural remembering, often a web of intertextual references. Puns scramble categories and do not respect opposites; inevitably, without familiar binary codes, meaning itself becomes monstrous. As Halberstam cleverly states: "This tendency ... to slip into its opposite ... makes mincemeat of any notion of binaries" (179). Kowalewski calls this use of humour simply "witty" (16); Tanner calls it "exaggeration" (9); and Armstrong and Tennenhouse refer to Bakhtin's term, the "carnivalesque" (12) – the inversion of hierarchical structures, the subversion of official policies, and the turning upside down of everything that we accept as "normal." In a similarly popular vein, Inness uses the word, "camp": "an over-the-top, tongue-in-cheek attitude toward the world, which pokes fun at social conventions and questions social norms. Camp reveals the artificiality of things we accept as the norm (such as gender roles)" (173).

But humour, puns, witticisms, the "carnivalesque," and "camp" are only some of the narrative strategies used by these feminist writers who have chosen to create violent female women. Negotiating between the representational narrative world and the social reality of our gendered and polarized world, these authors present us with an overflow of meanings through which we must wade. And we, as readers, must make choices, or at least raise questions, about how to view these literary women. As Sherrie Inness asks, in her bemused and yet serious tone: "She can shoot, but can she knit?" (124); "She can kick box, but can she cook?" (131); "She can throw a punch, but can she darn a sock?" (133). And I add: She can hurt and kill, but can she also comfort and nurture?

2

Living Together in North America: Canada, Quebec, and the United States

Canadian popular culture is a relational phenomenon that assumes its significance vis-à-vis a particular Canadian conception of the United States. The relationship is both symbiotic and dialectic. Symbiotically, Canadian popular culture needs its American partner as an ambiguous and reversible opposite. Dialectically, Canadian popular culture imposes a particular construction on the United States and then defines and redefines itself in terms of ambivalently held differences ... As a figure of speech, American popular culture is hyperbole; its Canadian counterpart is oxymoron. Americans are cultural narcissists; Canadians ... are cultural schizophrenics.

Frank Manning, "Reversible Resistance" (9)

... the place of Quebec. That this topic is often omitted from the discussion is due in part, one suspects, to a continuing assumption by progressive opinion in English-speaking Canada that the maintenance of linguistic difference is (or should be) sufficient to prevent a similar process of continental cultural integration from taking place there. A moment's reflection on the importance of audio-visual media is enough to dissipate such an illusion, which, despite Quebec nationalism's preoccupation with English Canadian rather than American domination, has not gone without challenge in Quebec itself ... What is needed, at any rate, is more comparative work on the similarities and differences in the ways American popular culture is received and appropriated on both sides of Canada's internal divide.

Andrew Wernick, "American Popular Culture in Canada" (301)

DIFFERING PERCEPTIONS OF CANADA, QUEBEC, AND THE UNITED STATES: A BRIEF OVERVIEW OF A COMPLEX STORY

In a typically clever and topical tone, a 2002 cartoon in *The New Yorker* depicts a man and a woman at a table in a restaurant. "You seem different, yet somehow familiar," says the man. "Are you perhaps Canadian?" In one image and a few words, the cartoonist captures the general attitude of Americans toward Canadians, English Canadians, at least. Cultural, national, ethnic, racial, and gendered stereotypes abound throughout the world, of course, but in the case of Canada – especially English-speaking Canada – and the United States, essentialist images flare up in the preconceived ideas of the "average" citizen, in the bombardment of popular culture, and in discussion and scholarship regarding political and economic issues. With a familiar pattern of domination (read American) and dependency (read Canadian), "concern among Canadians for their relationship to the United States has been historically a national preoccupation" (Flaherty and Manning xii).

Paul Rutherford points out that three images of Canada have repeatedly appeared and maintained their credibility among the intelligentsia and the public: Canada as peaceable kingdom; Canada as "Nature"; and Canada as victim. The peaceable kingdom motif portrays the country as a land of order, good government, sanity, and tolerance, and as "a country that is less aggressive and more humane than its American neighbor" (Rutherford 278). Canada as "Nature" conjures up images of the Great North, vast empty spaces, and wilderness. For Rutherford, these notions present Canada as "very un-American or other-American" – so different from the image of the United States as a"melting-pot, an industrial dynamo, a land of liberty and license, an imperial power beset by troubles or sins that [it] can induce a certain smugness in Canadians" (279). The image of Canada as a victim, vassal state, perpetual colony, imaginary nation, or non-nation has been variously used: by conservatives and radicals to justify their hostility toward American influence and perceived imperialism; by more moderates (i.e., Margaret Atwood), who have stressed the theme of survival in Canadian life; by those who see Canadian national identity as a fiction; and ultimately by Canadians who see their relational status as "a call to arms, a demand that Canadians resist a culture made in America and seek their own destiny" (Rutherford 279).

If America's cultural hegemony over Canada is different from its sway over other countries and cultures, it is because U.S. influence is so pervasive north of the border that many Canadians believe they are in some sense already American: "The United States does not need to teach us its values; there is always a Canadian ready to do it for them" (Ostry 36). Some cultural critics state that Canadians consistently define themselves in relation to the American Other; others interpret Canadians' self-conscious irony, parody, and satire as an affirmation of their culture; and still others steadfastly refuse to succumb to the power of that Other but use the country's relation with the United States as a means toward self-reflection and understanding. Whatever one's cultural stance, however, certain generalized images and stereotypes have found their way into the scholarly explorations and cultural mindset of both countries: Canada as female and the United States as male, Canada as raw and the United States as cooked, Canada as postmodern and the United States as modern.

Reid Gilbert has investigated many of these attitudinal differences and raises important questions: "How do the images of self that fill Canadian popular entertainments differ from those that present America to Canadians in the entertainments that flood across our long, peaceful, but highly porous border? What has been the effect on a contemporary Canadian sense of self of seeing the strong, urban, and often violent images that fill American film and television?" ("Mounties, Muggings, and Moose" 178). For Gilbert, as long as Canadians measure their culture against foreign (and especially U.S.) norms, they will continue to see themselves as "lacking" – in the female sense of the term, thereby recalling the gender metaphors often used to describe the two countries – as flawed, weak, and inadequate. Atwood's theme of survival and exile – now transformed into a more current postcolonial sense of alienation – finds its way back into the picture throughout Canada: "It [the theme of survival and exile] has also been present in Quebecois literature and in the repetitive images of isolation, harsh weather, and deprivation (physical and spiritual) that have formed recurrent motifs in Canadian novels, plays, and films ... But in all genres it is now clear that the easy assumption of the exiled Canadian may seem entirely true only to those who see Canada from the outside" (Gilbert 181).

Unfortunately, in Gilbert's view, many English Canadians, as in many post-colonial cultures, have internalized those assumptions and see themselves (and their culture) as "white niggers of America" ("Nègres blancs d'Amérique"), as Pierre Vallières once called the Québécois: "It is the more chilling that Canadians should take on 'the terms of reality of U.S. life' as that reality becomes progressively more violent and the images in which that reality portrays itself become images of violence made glamorous, images in which the power grows from the violence and becomes synonymous with it. The Canadian is now faced not only with a measure against which his culture seems to be lacking in power, but a sense that to voice his culture in anything but similarly horrific pictures is to admit to a culture that is impotent" (Gilbert 182).

All this "talk" about the identity/non-identity of English Canadians vis-à-vis the powerful and violent United States becomes rather ironic, however, if one sustains the possibility that "la belle province" has somehow managed better than its English counterparts to withstand the influence of its southern neighbour. Perhaps it is the language difference; perhaps it is Quebec's recent success in spreading its cultural name internationally with the likes of Céline Dion, the Cirque du Soleil, Robert Lepage, and certain successful films; perhaps it is the persistent discussion of the new and embraced multiculturalism of hybridity ["hybridité"], cross-breeding ["métissage] and immigrant ["migrant"] literatures and cultures; perhaps it is the self-awareness and pride in this "distinct society" with its "unique character"; perhaps it is the outpouring of studies on the Quebec "nation" and nationalism, along with the seemingly endless talk of negative Americanization but the more newly accepted *américanité* or Americanness, thanks to which Quebec does not feel impotent in relation to the United States, as it often does in relation to English Canada. Or is it the fact that statistics show that Quebec remains one of the least violent provinces in Canada and has not succumbed to the influence of its more violent North American companion. Or has it?

HAVE U.S. VIOLENCE AND CRIME MOVED NORTH?

In the introduction to his 1995 edited volume, *Violence in Canada: Sociopolitical Perspectives,* Jeffrey Ian Ross challenges the perception that Canada is a "peaceable kingdom," since this term helps to perpetuate what he considers a misconception that Canadians have always been and continue to be a non-violent people (3). Ted Robert Gurr, in his foreword to the same volume, concurs. To call Canada a "peaceable kingdom" is to feed into the "myth" that Canada has less social and interpersonal violence than other Western societies, that Canadians have a greater respect for authority and less tolerance for individual and group deviance, and that they are more disposed to giving the state the primary responsibility for maintaining social order (ix). Gurr points out that the essays in Ross's book show that "Canada does indeed have serious problems of violence: homicide rates higher than most Western societies, high levels of violence in aboriginal communities, frequent victimization of children and women, and instances of police and prison violence ... Nonetheless, the magnitude of the most serious kinds of social and interpersonal violence in Canada [is] distinctly lower than in the United States" (ix).

If, as Rosemary Gartner believes, Canadians kill one another (and, I add, commit other types of violence) for the same reasons that prompt people in other countries to exhibit aggressive tendencies and perpetrate violent acts, then what is the point in studying Canadian violence in particular? For Gartner, the answer is quite clear. Speaking specifically of homicides and homicide rates, she states: "The incidence and characteristics of homicide in a society provide insights into the distinctive features of that society, including its historical development, systems of stratification, institutions, and values. Moreover, changes in the rates and characteristics of homicide convey information about more general processes of change. Homicide rates are indicators of the quality of life that a society provides to its members ... [These rates also reveal] the growing fears of Canadians that patterns of homicide in Canada are coming to resemble those in the United States – not just in levels, but also in some characteristics" (186).

Not only can one apply this concept to all types of violence in any country – as well as in Canada and Quebec – but the concept also expands the thesis of this present study: that the literature to be studied in this text can be read in conjunction not only with issues of gender but also within the context of debunking the myth of the Canadian peaceable kingdom, with the rising tide of violence in Canada, and especially with the *feared resemblance* with what Canadians see as a far more violent United States. More specifically, I am asking how certain Quebec literary texts that depict lethal violence committed by women can be read in conjunction with the society of Quebec, which, as I shall show, is one of the least violent Canadian provinces. Despite Michael Moore's insistence that Canada is far less violent than the United States (see *Bowling for Columbine*), I am interested in discovering whether U.S. violence and crime have moved north, and if so, if that influence – or the fear of that influence – has affected Quebec as well as the rest of Canada.

Before moving to comparisons between Canada and the United States, and between Canada and Quebec in reference to specific areas of violence, it is worth mentioning again that the U.S. arrest rate for 2003 was 4.695 per 100,000 inhabitants, with 9,581,423 arrests, of which 418,964 were for violent crime.[1] In 2003 Canada reported 2,572,243 criminal incidents, among which 304,515 were for violent crime[2] and of which 53,373 occurred in Quebec.[3] Most notably, Quebec reported the lowest rate of violent crime rate in Canada for the ninth year in a row and a large decline in homicide – indeed the lowest homicide rate since the 1960s.[4]

Researchers have noted that Canada does have a high crime rate; in fact in 1992 it had the second highest violent crime rate in the Western world after the United States, although it was still far behind (Ross 1). Official data from 1994 report a Canadian murder rate of 2 per 100,000, with assault at a rate of 850 per 100,000, while the American assault rate in that same year was 2,550 per 100,000 (Ross 4). Statistics Canada reported a homicide rate in Canada for 2003 at 1.73 per 100,000 population, with the comparable rate in the United States at 5.69.[5] (See Figure 8.) Violence against women in Canada is particularly troublesome – it is routinely reported and fictionalized in the news, on television programs, and in feature films, but is little studied by serious scholars (DeKeseredy and Ellis 97–8). Walter DeKeseredy and Desmond Ellis report that "Canadians are equally, if not more, violent in intimate heterosexual contexts," with higher rates even than those in the United States: 12.1% and 11.3% in two 1986 studies in the United States; 18% and 24.5% in two Canadian studies for 1990 and 1988 respectively (115). Canadian rates of dating violence are similar to those in the United States. These two researchers conclude, therefore, that it appears that "separated and divorced Canadian men are more violent than their US counterparts" (115).

When considering homicide, however, Canadian rates do fall far below those of the United States, especially in urban areas, and it is this aspect of violence to which Michael Moore specifically refers when he says that in order for the United States to reduce its frightening current rate of homicide, the only hope is to "Canadianize" (Moore, public lecture at Oxford Union, 2002). Interestingly, homicide rates in Canada increase from east (the lowest) to west (the highest), but when the Yukon and Northwest Territories are included, they increase from south (the lowest) to north (the highest) (Gartner 195). The pattern of overall crime rates, however, has begun to change, with rates in the

Figure 8
Homicide Rates per 100,000 by Country, 2003

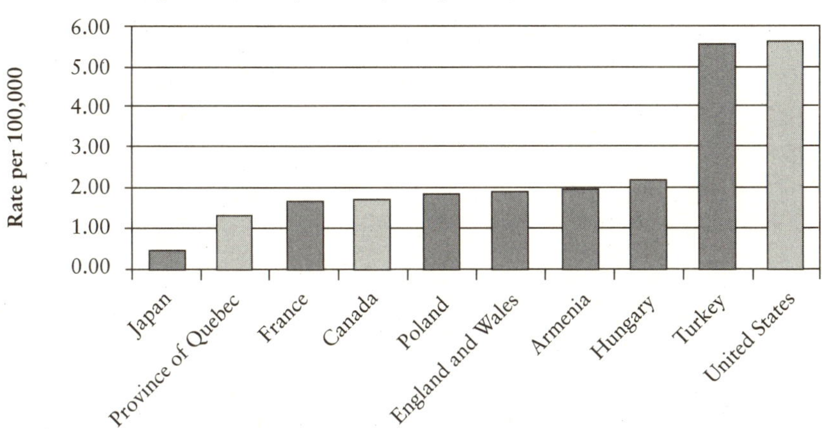

(Data derived from Dauvergne, *Homicide in Canada 2003*, 3, Table 1)

Atlantic provinces now surpassing those in Quebec and Ontario.[6] As in the United States, most homicides in Canada occur in domestic settings and between persons who know one another: "Between 1961 and 1990, intimate partners and other family members were *each* responsible for 17% of all homicides. Another one-third of all homicides were committed by friends or acquaintances of the victims. Only 19% of homicides were committed by strangers, and 15% remained unsolved. Counting only solved homicides, intimate partners and family members accounted for over 40% of the killings" (Gartner 192).

Interestingly, although the fear of crime is much greater in urban areas, and although the largest cities throughout the world have rates of homicide higher than those for any given country as a whole, in Canada these rates do not decline as one goes from large to increasingly smaller communities. The homicide rates for the most rural areas of Canada are only slightly lower than those for the largest cities. In the United States, the homicide rates for the most rural areas are generally even higher than those of small-to-medium cities, but in Canada "the rural contribution to homicide rates is clearly greater and the urban contribution less than is the case in the United States" (Gartner 198).

But I need to talk more specifically about Quebec, where the figures are the most striking. Put simply, until 2000 Quebec had homicide rates at or below the Canadian average since the 1920s – between 1921 and 1989, the national rate per 100,000 persons was 1.56 and that of

Quebec was 1.41, after the four Maritime provinces.[7] Gurr has speculated that the reason for this lower rate perhaps lies "in Quebec's greater homogeneity or in a tendency towards greater stability in social relationships. One could test … by asking whether francophone Canadians outside Quebec are affected by violence in different ways than Québécois" (xii). For 2000, however, with the Canadian rate at 1.76 per 100,000 persons, the comparable homicide rate in Quebec jumped to 2.01, higher than Alberta (1.94), Nova Scotia (1.59), Ontario (1.33), New Brunswick (1.32), and Newfoundland (1.11).[8] As of 2001, homicide rates by province changed again: Canada (1.78 per 100,000); Quebec (1.89), with Quebec higher than Prince Edward Island (1.44), Ontario (1.43), New Brunswick (1.06), Nova Scotia (0.95), and Newfoundland (0.19).[9] For 2002, the Canadian rate for homicide was 1.85 per 100,000 population. As for Quebec and the other provinces, the rates were 1.6 for Quebec (lower than the national statistic), 0.4 for Newfoundland, 0.7 for Prince Edward Island, 1.0 for Nova Scotia, 1.2 for New Brunswick, 1.5 for Ontario, and for Manitoba (the highest rate), 3.1.[10] The spike in the number of homicides at the national level, by the way, was driven by a large increase in British Columbia (up from 84 to 126 homicides, with a 2002 rate of 3.0), partially as a result of 15 homicides in Port Coquitlam in previous years reported by police in 2002 (that is, the murders committed by serial killer, Robert Pickton).[11] Most recently, statistics for 2003 show a Canadian rate for homicide as 1.73 per 100,000 population, with 1.34 for Quebec, lower rates for all of the Atlantic provinces, 1.45 for Ontario, 3.70 for Manitoba, and 4.12 for Saskatchewan.[12] Clearly Quebec had a lower homicide rate than Canada for 68 years, but in 2000 and 2001 its rate was higher. It was lower again for 2002, but the national rate was "skewed" because of British Columbia. In 2003, however, the homicide rate for Quebec was still lower. (See Figure 8) What is one to make of these changes?

Gartner has delved into the regional issue in even greater detail. She reports that Canadian regions differ not only in their homicide rates but also in the types of homicide committed. Data from the Atlantic provinces, Ontario, the Prairie provinces, and the Territories show that over 40% of homicides are between intimate partners or within families, while less than 33% of homicides in British Columbia and less than 25% in Quebec occur between such partners or family members (196–7, Table 7.4). In addition, 30% of homicides in Quebec remain unsolved, the highest in the country, which reports a .32 unsolved rate in contrast to a .68 rate in Quebec (197, Table 7.4). Unsolved homicides are usually those that have been committed by strangers. As Gartner sums up: "In BC and Quebec, then, homicides have a less intimate character than homicides in other provinces. But this does not mean that the *rate* of partner and family killings in these two provinces is necessarily lower than elsewhere. In BC, these rates are actually well above the national average. In Quebec, however, rates of intimate partner and family killings are lower than anywhere else in Canada. Compared to other Canadians, then, Québécois are less likely – both in absolute and in relative terms – to kill intimates or kin" (197). Gartner adds that, to her knowledge, no research has been done to address the reasons why Quebec has lower rates of intimate partner and family killings than the rest of Canada (215).

In 2003, however, Antoine Robitaille tried to understand whether the Québécois are "pacifistes ou pacifiques." He cites evidence that in March 2003 polls showed that Quebecers, at a rate of two to one, wanted peace rather than war even if the United Nations were to sanction the United States' invasion of Iraq, while the rest of Canada, with similar sanctions by the U.N., supported the war with the same margin of two to one (Robitaille 53). In addition, Montreal was seen throughout the world as one of the most "pro-pacificism" cities, in light of the huge public demonstration held there against the war (Robitaille 54). Most significantly, Robitaille suggests what he calls a "French connection": the perception of the United States in Quebec is often mediated through the franco-French media, since those who comment on current news events regularly get their sources from France – perhaps the nation in Europe most notably against the Iraq war (54–5). Robitaille also mentions, however, that the Québécois have a "pacifique" rather than "pacifiste" tradition, both historically and currently, given the power of its Catholicism and the province's minority national status without a real international existence (60–1). Indeed, in matters of power and multilateralism, Canada – with Quebec in the lead – aligns itself more with "Old Europe" than with the United States (Robitaille 61).

Greatly shaped by the claims-making and media hype that propagte myths, misconceptions, and half-truths and, as I have shown in chapter 1, which sensationalize high-profile cases like those of Reena Virk and Karla Homolka, however, there are in Canada "serious discrepancies between public perceptions of violence and the reality suggested by social research" (Gurr xiii). The moral panic that often ensues has caused many Canadians to call for American-style deterents – more prisons, longer and stiffer sentences, harsher treatment of young offenders, and even capital punishment (DeKeseredy 99). Meda Chesney-Lind labels this mood "the imprisonment 'binge' that has been haunting North America for the last two decades." The increase in crimes of women, she says, has particularly signalled "a dangerous and unnecessary mimicking of the United States' pattern of relying on incarceration to manage, but not address, intractable social problems and injustices like racism and economic inequality" (Introduction iv).

Clearly, what many Canadians are reacting to is what Gartner calls a fear of the "Americanization of Canadian Homicide" (209). As she points out – and as I have already stressed – Canadians continue to pride themselves on being law-abiding and non-violent people, especially in comparison with the citizens of the United States "who kill each other at a per capita rate more than three times that of Canadians" (Gartner 209). Although there are suggestions that this difference in rates may be diminishing, evidence still shows that the gap is not closing, especially for homicide rates in large cities. In 1990 homicide rates per 100,000 population for the five largest U.S. and Canadian cities were as follows: New York City: 30.7; Los Angeles: 28.2; Chicago: 30.5; Houston: 34.8; Philadelphia: 31.7; Toronto: 1.9; Montreal: 3.4; Vancouver: 3.5; Ottawa-Hull: 1.5; Edmonton: 3.5.[13] According to the 2001 statistics these rates in Canada were: Toronto: 1.60; Montreal: 2.22; Vancouver: 2.12; Ottawa: 0.36; Edmonton: 2.61[14] – all decreases over the 1990 statistics. The 2002 statistics show the following rates: Toronto: 1.80; Montreal: 1.87 (a significant decrease); Vancouver: 3.26 (with the 15 Port Coquitlam homicides included); Ottawa: 0.93; Edmonton: 2.79.[15] And for 2003, the rates are: Toronto: 1.86; Montréal: 1.59 (again a decrease); Vancouver: 2.07 (no Port Coquitlam homicides); Edmonton: 2.20; Ottawa: 1.15.[16] (See Figure 9 for more comparative data.)

In addition, the proportion of homicides committed with firearms is now lower throughout Canada as a result of gun-control legislation, although, in Gartner's figures, homicides committed with handguns increased.[17] In fact, in 2002 the rate of homicides committed with the use of a firearm reached its lowest level since 1966, at 25.6% of the total number of homicides, down, for example, from 33.7% in 1992, while handguns were used in 65.8% of firearm homicides, as compared with 52.2% in 1992.[18] In 2003, that figure was up to 29.4%.[19] Other types of homicide have either remained stable or have decreased, with the exception of unsolved murders.[20] Although research is scanty,

Figure 9
Homicide Rates per 100,000 by City, 2003

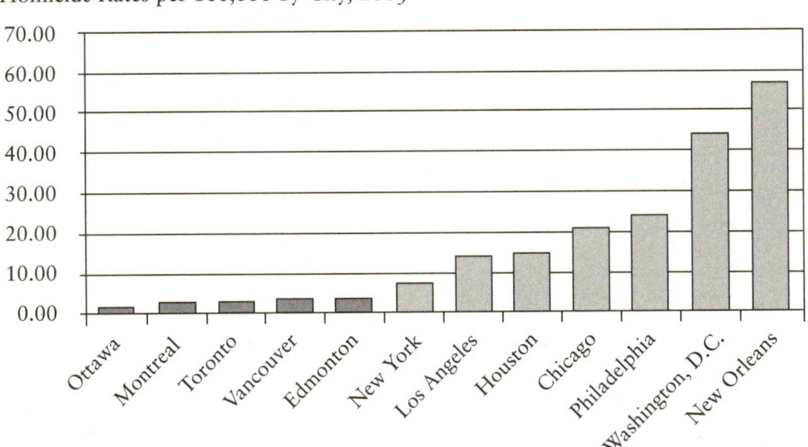

(Data derived from Dauvergne, *Homicide in Canada 2003*, 3, Table 1; Uniform Crime Reports 2003, Table 6; http://www.usatoday.com/news/nation/2004-01-02-city-murders_x.htm)

homicides involving drugs, serial killings, and mass murders seem to have remained at the same levels.[21] According to Gartner, therefore, for the years 1951–84 during which homicide rates were documented, Canada (2.2 per 100,000) placed third among eighteen developed countries behind the United States (8.9 per 100,000) and Finland (2.7 per 100,000) and just ahead of Australia (1.7 per 100,000) (212). In 2001 those figures were per 100,000: Canada (1.78) (just ahead of England and Wales at 1.66); United States (5.64); Finland (2.98); and Russia (19.68).[22] In 2002 those figures were per 100,000: Canada (1.85) (tied with Australia); United States (5.52); Luxembourg (9.01); and Russia (20.54).[23] And in 2003 those figures were per 100,000: Canada (1.73); United States (5.69); Turkey (5.57); Hungary (2.22); Armenia (2.00); England and Wales (1.93); Poland (1.79); France (1.65), with Japan the lowest at 0.51.[24] (See Figure 8.) Still needing research specific to Canada, however, are studies concerning "the east-west regional patterning of homicide rates and the pronounced differences in the characteristics of homicide in Quebec compared to other provinces" (213). According to Gartner, Canadians have been spared the levels of lethal interpersonal violence that plague the United States (213). In other words, in her view, violence and crime – and in particular rates of homicide – have not moved north and most significantly not to Quebec.[25]

More significantly complex for this study, however, is the fact that if one takes seriously Gartner's study for the low rates of homicide in general in Quebec and specifically for the low rates of female homicide-offenders in that province, then how does one "read" the violent female protagonists of the novels and short stories by the Québécois women writers that I study in this text? It remains true that the public perception is that rates of female violence are rising in Quebec, as throughout Canada and the United States. Have these women writers have been influenced by the North American media – Canadian, Quebec, and U.S. – to "buy into" widely held (although false) beliefs, as they reframe issues of gender? In order to understand more fully the Québécois view of their place in this perceived increasingly violent North America of which they are part, therefore, let us review the concepts of *américanisation* and *américanité* (Americanness) as they have been occupying the minds of Québécois – and especially scholars and intellectuals –for the past twenty years or so.

AMÉRICANITÉ AND *AMÉRICANISATION*: HISTORICAL TO CONTEMPORARY

In their beautifully written text *Amériques*, geographers Jean Morisset and Éric Waddell report that the neologism *américanité* (Americanness) – associated in the eyes of Québécois solely with the United States – does not truly have an equivalent in English. In fact it comes from *americanidad*, a word that Hispanics coined in the nineteenth century in order to disassociate themselves from the United States by enhancing the prestige of their constitutive identity (213). James Csipak and Lise Héroux review a history that tells us that the word *américanité* first appeared in print in Quebec in a 1967 article published in *Le Devoir* by Jean-Guy Pilon entitled "Une Réalité issue de l'Amérique" (25). According to Csipak and Héroux (citing Louis Dupont) Quebec playwright Jacques Languirand initiated the questioning of Quebec's *américanité* with a 1971 text called "Le Québec et l'américanité," published at the end of his play *Klondike* (25).

In an essay in *Quebec Studies* Donald Cuccioletta and Albert Desbiens state that the concept of "americanidad" for Latin Americans clearly recognizes their accepted American roots, whereas in Canada and Quebec it evokes the contrary:

> Quebec history is anchored in its colonial past: the French regime first and the British Empire second. We have not tried ... to anchor our historical experiences

to our presence on the continent ... This unwillingness to accept the role of the continent in shaping our culture and identity goes so far as to occlude the first custodians of *américanité*, native peoples. In Latin America they cannot deny this fact because of the process of "métissage" (cross-breeding) that has so characterized the Southern Hemisphere. In our Canadian view of the past, however, we have not placed at the center of our historical imagination this sharing of a new world experience with the native. (11)

Pierre Nepveu maintains that the word is a Québécois neologism that reveals an immense ignorance of America on the part of Quebecers, since it reflects a reduction to stereotypes: primitivism, naturalism, anti-intellectualism, a mythology of wide open spaces, the sanctity of youth and of newness; and, for all of North America, in a "virile" sense, myths of expansion and conquest for fur traders, explorers, pioneers, conquistadors, cowboys, gauchos, and ranchers ["coureur des bois, voyageur, pionnier, conquistador, cowboy, gaucho, fazendeiro"] (Nepveu, *Intérieurs du nouveau monde* 7–8). This concept of virility as a myth for all of the Americas in both the northern and southern hemispheres seems to contradict other thinkers who have long identified the United States as male, and Canada and Quebec as female – both historically and contemporaneously. Myths must have a way of changing gender.

Many scholars who have been and are currently working on the history and the contemporary "status" of *américanité* and *américanisation*, in reference to Quebec in particular, widely cite the definition of these two concepts given in 1996 by Yvan Lamonde: "The Americanization of Quebec, a concept of resistance or refusal, is this process of acculturation by which the culture of the United States influences and dominates both Canadian and Quebec culture – and culture worldwide – while *américanité*, which includes Latin America as much as Anglo-Saxon America, is a concept of openness and movement which affirms Quebec's agreement to its continental belonging" ["L'américanisation du Québec, concept de résistance ou de refus, est ce processus d'acculturation par lequel la culture étatsunienne influence et domine la culture autant canadienne que québécoise – et mondiale – tandis que l'américanité, qui englobe tout autant l'Amérique latine que l'Amérique saxonne, est un concept d'ouverture et de mouvance qui dit le consentement du Quebec à son appartenance continentale"] (11).

Gérard Bouchard and Yvan Lamonde (1995), on the other hand, define *américanité* somewhat differently – in reference to Europe: "By *américanité*, we thus mean new cultural forms that have been put into place since the seventeenth century following migrations from Europe toward the Americas and which reflect the total number of ruptures, processes of differentiation (by means of invention, adaptation), and projects of collective renewal characteristic of several new communities" ["Par américanité, on entend donc ici les nouvelles formes culturelles qui se sont mises en place depuis le XVIIe siècle à la suite des transferts migratoires de l'Europe vers les Amériques et qui reflètent la somme des ruptures, des processus de différenciation (par invention, adaptation) et des projets de recommencement collectif caractéristiques de plusieurs collectivités neuves"] (8). In yet another definition, Louis Balthazar and Alfred Hero (1999) make a distinction between, on the one hand, *américanité* and Americanness, – terms for "what arises from the historical and spatial insertion of Quebec into the American continent" ["ce qui relève de l'insertion historique et spatiale du Quebec dans le continent américain" and, on the other, *américanisation* as "that which values the direct influences of the culture of the United States" ["ce qui tient aux influences directes de la culture des États-Unis"] (182). And finally, Cucciolетta and Desbiens (2000) use these definitions:

> *Américanité* is not a product of domination but one of equality, pluralism, and "métissage." *Américanité* recognizes a specificity related to the Americas while Americanization designates a relationship between a stronger and a weaker partner. To accept *américanité* does not mean to deny the existence of Americanization ... All inhabitants and cultural groups in the Americas have their own *américanité*, their own vision and relationship with the Americas, whether it is perceived consciously or not. Because *américanité* is an active form of culture in constant evolution across the Americas, it is contrary to Americanization, and therefore creates another symbolism, another mythology, another America, many Americas. (7, 10)

But no matter whose neologism or whatever the precise definition, it remains clear that Americanization has been and continues to be seen as a negative influence, while "Americanness" is an identity, a sense of self that has long plagued the Québécois and only fairly recently has provided them with the grist with which they can proclaim themselves more and more proudly as francophone North Americans. For Yvan Lamonde, Quebec now represents a cultural hybridity that integrates French, British, American, and Roman [that is, Vatican] heritages (7; see also Sherry Simon's *L'Hybridité culturelle*). This cultural diversity is what lies at the heart of the Québécois identity that recognizes "a forced feeling of unfamiliarity, a troubling strangeness that makes one say yes to a *relatively* important France, a *newly* important England *in spite of everything*, a *welcoming* America, and a *revised and updated* Rome/Vatican" ["un dépaysement obligé, une étrangeté troublante qui fait dire oui à une France *relativement* importante, à une Angleterre *nouvellement* importante *malgré tout*, à une Amérique *bienvenue* et à une romanité *revue et corrigée*"] (Lamonde, *Ni avec eux ni sans eux* 9).

As a backdrop to this more recently recognized diversity and heritage, however, Lamonde has traced Quebec's historical ambivalence toward its role and place on the North American continent, following its development from 1774 to 1995 ("Ambivalence historique" 61–81): Jules-Paul Tardivel's 1900 decrying of "l'américanisme," distinguishable by a non-religious constitution, criminality, divorce, and atheistic schools (69); Henri Bourassa's (1917) statement that the only way to combat the moral Americanization of Canada was to preserve its distinctive character as an anglo-French, bi-ethnic, and bilingual nation (74); Beaudry Leman's (1928) pronouncement that French-Canadians could not live with or without American civilization – hence the title of Lamonde's *Ni avec eux ni sans eux* (75); and Lionel Groulx's (1941) prophecy that one day people would recognize that one of the most wonderful facts in the history of the northern hemisphere was the resistance of Quebec's "insignificant people" ["notre petit peuple"] to American continentalism and to all other forms of imperialism (as quoted by Lamonde 76).

Perhaps the most interesting aspect of this early history, however, is the developing split between the elite and the people in regard to their acceptance or rejection of American/U.S. culture – a split that has moved well into the twentieth and twenty-first centuries. According to both Lamonde and Bouchard, the elite, educated, and cultured class in Quebec remained consistently turned toward France and its linguistic, cultural, literary, and artistic traditions, while the more "popular" classes – both rural and urban – looked south toward the United States (Lamonde, "L'Ambivalence historique" 80). Bouchard, in his *Genèse des nations et cultures du nouveau monde*, explains this phenomenon eloquently:

For more than a century, [the nation] was forged from above as a culture borrowed, and from below crossbred as a culture of imprint: on one hand a learned culture that denies, by draping itself in its European heritage; on the other, a popular culture that repudiates, by diluting French tradition into a continental look. The educated tried to overcome this antinomy either by idealizing the *people*, denouncing them, or trying to correct them. As for the popular classes, they felt closer to the economic elites with whom they shared the same relationship with the New World, the same "take" on territoriality ... One can see here one of the causes of the political continuity that characterized that period of time (1840–1940): the inability of the educated elite to channel the *américanité* of the popular classes into a plan for rupture, the distrust on the part of the lower classes of those notable people who were too far removed from their daily lives. [Pendant plus d'un siècle, [la nation] s'est tissée par le haut comme culture d'emprunt et métissée par le bas comme culture d'empreinte: d'un côté une culture savante qui nie, en se drapant dans son héritage européen; de l'autre une culture populaire qui renie, en diluant la tradition française dans les airs du continent. Les lettrés ont tenté de surmonter l'antinomie soit en idéalisant le *peuple*, soit en le dénonçant, soit en essayant de le corriger. Quant aux classes populaires, elles se sont senties plus proches des élites économiques avec lesquelles elles partageaient le même rapport au Nouveau Monde, la même prise sur la territorialité ... On peut voir là l'une des causes du continuisme politique qui a caractérisé cette période [1840–1940]: l'incapacité des lettrés à canaliser dans un projet de rupture l'américanité des classes populaires, la méfiance de celles-ci à l'endroit de notables trop éloignés de leur quotidienneté]. (174–5; see also Bouchard, "Québec comme collectivité neuve" 23–4.)

This distinction deepened in the years after the Second World War as Quebec became a non-religious, consumer society, and the "American way of life" moved north – increasingly through the media. According to Lamonde, Jean Le Moyne needs to be acknowledged as the deepest thinker about French-Canadian dualism of this period, for he recognized its double parenthood as European and American, its invention, like all of America, by Europe, and its identity as "almost" European and "almost" American (*Ni avec eux* 91, 75). Bouchard sees in this same period a new vision of the world, as modernity accelerated the decline of old regionalisms, inspired new territorialities, and contributed to an awakening sense of Americanness in all domains (*Genèse* 162). As of the 1960s writers were creating a new Québécois imagery, speaking of *la québécitude* ("Quebecicity") and "naming their country" (Bouchard, *Genèse* 163). In the same decade, the designation "Québécois" took over from the formerly used "French-Canadian" (Bouchard, *Genèse* 169). By 1965 Jacques Godbout was writing about "being oneself" in French, and in 1971 Robert Charlebois was singing his "lament of almost America" ["complainte de presqu'Amérique"], while the journal *Presqu'Amérique* lived a brief life from 1971–1973 (Lamonde, "L'Ambivalence" 77; *Ni avec eux* 78; see also Cuccioletta and Desbiens 6; Dupont 56). In the 1980s and 1990s, literary critics like Benoît Melançon, Jean Morency, and Pierre Nepveu were delving even further into the issue of duality, Quebec's belonging to both the European and the New World spheres, while Nepveu proposed that America could never be the sole key to Quebec's identity, since there will always exist an imaginary space beyond the Atlantic (Lamonde, *Ni avec eux* 78–80). Such an assessment emphasizes the notion that a nostalgia for France and an ambivalence toward America are still alive in the minds of the cultured Québécois, while mass culture ["la culture de masse"] more readily absorbs and occupies its own space in North America.

Current Perspectives on Américanité *and* Américanisation

Since 1995 or so there has been an outpouring of discussions and publications that continue the debate on *américanité* and *américanisation*, Quebec identity, definitions of the Quebec "nation" and the Quebec "people," differences between Canada and Quebec in their views of the United States, and the survival of small "nations" in an increasingly internationalized and globalized world and economy – financial, political, and cultural. A closer look at these current debates will help me study some of the negative aspects of this hybrid North American culture, and its fascination with violence, which, in my view, form the context within which some Quebec women writers are attempting to re-frame gender – in their literary imaginations, at least.

Gérard Bouchard and Yvan Lamonde actively remain at the centre of these discussions on the Québécois and Americans, on Quebec and the United States, and on the "nations" and cultures of the new world, although they have certainly been joined by many others. In their 1995 co-edited collection, Bouchard speaks of *américanité* as a rupture, an appropriation of new territory, and a will for a new beginning, but he also declares that for the Quebecer *américanité* represents both a near and distant problem, both as identity and as alterity, with no equivalent concern in the United States (20–1). Jean Morency in this same collection says that in Quebec *américanité* obsessively defines itself against, or at least in relation to, European cultures (once again "high" culture's nostalgia for the Old World); it evokes a quest for a *certain* (my emphasis) American identity and a transformation or metamorphosis that results from cultural differentiation and reflects the "hybridization" that increasingly characterizes Quebec society and culture (160–1). This search for a certain American identity is therefore intimately linked to the fact that Quebec remains an "*uncertain* country" ["un pays *incertain*"] (my emphasis) in which one is today witnessing "an unprecedented wave of economic and cultural 'Americanophilia,'" ["une vague sans précédent d'américanophilie économique et culturelle"] that has brutally emerged and that could possibly gather strength to the point of "contaminating" high culture (169–71) "[faire] un retour en force, allant jusqu'à 'contaminer' la culture savante" (169–71).

Also in Bouchard and Lamonde's collection, Jean-François Chassay wonders how Quebec – and specifically its literature – can invent its own America when it has to live on a continent with a suffocating giant to its south ("Littérature et américanité" 178): "In an America that people light-heartedly confuse with the country that dominates the continent, thereby crushing other countries, what place remains for these other countries, especially when they speak a diffferent language, when their history and their memory refer back to another culture (French) but participate totally in this North American culture?" ["Dans une Amérique qu'on confond allègrement avec le pays qui la domine, annihilant de ce fait les autres, quelle place reste-t-il pour ces derniers, quand de surcroît ils parlent une langue différente, quand leur histoire et leur mémoire réfèrent à une autre culture (française), mais qu'ils participent entièrement à cette culture nord-américaine?"] (190). As both Bouchard and Lamonde ask in concluding their book, is it possible to find and define a common *américanité* in Quebec, Canada, the United States, and Latin America? ("Conclusion" 392)? Or, as Lamonde asks a year later, can this possibly common Americanness only signify "absorption, integration, and annexation at the end of the day? Agreeing to America, recognizing this belonging as a founding principle, does it necessarily mean renouncing one's distinctive traits or losing this specificity?" ["absorption, intégration, annexion en bout de ligne? Consentir à l'Amérique, reconnaître comme fondatrice cette appartenance a-t-il nécessairement valeur de renoncement à un trait distinct ou de perte probable de cette spécificité?"] (*Ni avec eux* 82).

Bouchard continues this line of questioning in his *Genèse des nations et cultures du nouveau monde* (2000). Having defined itself as of the 1970s in reference to culture and language, the new Quebec "sees itself as a specific francophone nation, crossbred through its former and recent North American history," combining diversity, identity, and interculturalism" ["se donne donc comme une francophonie spécifique, métissée par son histoire nord-américaine ancienne et récente"] (170). Although in Bouchard's eyes Quebec still has a fear of uncertainty, along with its desire for difference, for "distinction" on the North American continent, the anti-American discourse ["le discours anti-étatsunien"] has greatly lost its momentum – rearing its head only in some elitist and leftist rhetoric (171). The genesis ["genèse"] of this contemporary Quebec should thus be seen "not only as the history of a minority culture in America but also as one of the episodes in the creation of the New World" ["non seulement comme l'histoire d'une culture minoritaire en Amérique mais aussi comme l'un des épisodes de la création du Nouveau Monde"] (173). In other words, the *américanité* of Quebec should be celebrated as part of its own history, an ongoing event crucial to the making of the New World.

Not everyone agrees with Bouchard and his like-minded observers. Joseph Yvon Thériault, for example, in his *Critique de l'américanité* (2002), calls *américanité* a "trashy concept" ["un concept-poubelle"] (23). Taking issue especially with Bouchard and Lamonde, Thériault maintains that this concept contradicts the existence in Quebec of a national affirmation that has been attempting since the mid-nineteenth century to propose a social model different from that of Anglo-American America (14). After the failure of the referenda of 1980 and 1995 and the birth of NAFTA, he says, one would have expected the intellectuals of the Quebec "nation" to have abandonned their project of building a unique society in North America, while happily clinging to the American dream. But instead they transformed their desires for autonomy into a continental dream (14–15). *Américanité* thus became "an excessive way of expressing here an uneasiness appropriate to radical modernity and its negation of the subjective dimensions of social life" ["une manière excessive d'exprimer ici un malaise propre à la modernité radicale et sa négation des dimensions subjectives de la vie sociale"] (15). What most surprises and fascinates Thériault is "the permanence of a proposition, persisting ever since the mid-nineteenth century, to create a society in America around a francophone space. Such a proposal, because it is foreign to America, is unthought of and unthinkable for Quebec Americanness" ["la permanence d'une proposition, depuis le mitan du XIXe siècle, de faire société, en Amérique, autour de l'espace francophone. Une telle proposition, parce que étrangère à l'Amérique, est un (im)pensé de l'américanité québécoise"] (20). As one reviewer of Thériault's book states, however, although some proponents of *américanité* will challenge Thériault's analysis, it should lead to a reassessment, or at least to further discussions of this concept as it plays into Quebec's identity (Talbot 1292).

Such discussions have been taking place for some time now – and well before Thériault's entry into the debate. Speaking specifically about the Quebec novel (to which I turn in chapter 3), Chassay sees *américanité*, the "darling word of Quebec vocabulary" ["le mot fétiche du vocabulaire québécois"], as a symptom that reveals and helps makes sense of the cultural space out of which one speaks and writes (*L'Ambiguïté américaine* 18). With the perceived common denominator of Europe – at least for the cultured and artistic classes – this word and concept have come to symbolize the myth of newness and discovery (19). It is not surprising, therefore, that the image that some Québécois have of the United States often comes from France (22), perhaps most significantly from American novels that have been translated into French and published in France, only later making their way into the Quebec market.

Chassy also mentions the influence of essays such as those of the highly respected French sociologist and philosopher of postmodernism, Jean Baudrillard, whose *AMERICA*, originally published in France in 1986, is an enlightening and bold look at the United States. Referring to the "charm and power of American (un)culture" (79), Baudrillard bluntly informs his readers: "There is no culture here, no cultural discourse" (100) His comments on American violence are particularly relevant here. Whether speaking of New York's violence – aimless violence, autistic, reactional, foetal, and gratuitous violence – or the violent mixing of multiple European nationalities and exogenous races (22, 23, 45, 82), Baudrillard emphatically tells his fellow French (and later the Québécois): "America is powerful and original; America is violent and abominable. We should not seek to deny either of these aspects, nor reconcile them" (88). Echoing this rather simplistic view of the United States, Marcel Rioux worries that if the Québécois continue their slide down the slope of forgetfulness, replacing their motto "Je me souviens" [I remember] by "J'oublie vite" [I quickly forget], they will soon become "insipid, uninteresting and insignificant ... a country similar to Baudrillard's America where amnesia and a lack of culture reign" ["insipides, inodores et insignifiants. Un pays semblable à celui de l'*Amérique* de Baudrillard, où règneront l'amnésie et l'inculture!"] (*Une Saison* 39). Amnesia, (un)culture, and violence here appear to be the hallmarks of the United States, by extension of Americanization, and potentially of Americanness, unless the other "nations" on the North American continent assert their own distinctive identities and their own brand of *américanité*.

But while developing, asserting, and indeed publicizing the distinct national brands that will redefine *américanité*, these nations must also deal with the growing phenomenon of Americanization, usually seen as the United States' influence throughout the world, within the context of inevitable globalization and internationalism, the proclaimed death of the nation state, and the unstoppable flow of world mass culture. Although I shall discuss Quebec's search for identity as a "gendered nation" in North America more fully later in this chapter, it still behooves me to mention here one of the theoretical bases upon which many current debates build their argument, the concept of "imagined communities" as defined by Benedict Anderson, especially since it underscores the power of imagination, with which I shall be dealing:

> It is an imagined political community – and imagined as both inherently limited and sovereign. It is *imagined* because the members of even the smallest nations will never know most of their fellow-members, meet them, or even hear of them, yet in the minds of each lives the image of their communion ... The nation is imagined as *limited* because even the largest of them ... has finite, if elastic, boundaries, beyond which lie other nations ... It is imagined as *sovereign* because the concept was born in an age in which Enlightenment and Revolution were destroying the legitimacy of the divinely ordained, hierarchical dynastic realm ... Finally, it is imagined as a *community*, because, regardless of the actual inequality and exploitation that may prevail in each, the nation is always conceived as a deep, horizontal comradeship. Ultimately it is this fraternity that makes it possible, over the past two centuries, for so many millions of people, not so much to kill, as willingly to die for such limited imaginings. (6–7)

During a round table discussion on North American cultures in 2000, Reginald Stuart noted that nation-states are recent creations, formed because of concerns among elites about power rather than culture. Cultures, however, are older than any nation-state. But nation-states create "imagined communities" that attempt to suppress the diversity of local cultures within their political boundaries (433). Almost all scholars of political science and international relations, however, now frame their views on the conjecture that although nation-states may survive for some time to come, their relevance will decrease within the context of increasing globalization (Stuart 438). As Richard Dominic Wiggers asked at this same colloquium: "Are all of us, including those currently living within both Canada and the United States, becoming subsumed into a global culture ...? Is the blending of North American peoples and cultures the harbinger of such a future?" (425).

Scholars who study Quebec in particular focus equally on such questions, as they try to define their "nation's" identity within a North American context. In a collection of essays (1999) on American cultural influence on Quebec – and specifically on the influence of American models and systems in popular culture – for example, a number of contributors concede that this American threat has made most of the world obsessed with the United States and its influence, especially the "American-USA way of producing, diffusing and distributing culture which is set up as a legitimate model, as the norm. It is, therefore, here a question of the hegemony of a U.S. model and of the alienating extent of the imagined nature of such a hegemony" ["la façon américaine-USA de produire, de diffuser et de distribuer de la culture qui est érigée en modèle légitime, en norme. Il est donc ici question de l'hégémonie d'un modèle étatsunien et de la portée aliénante de l'imaginaire qu'a une telle hégémonie"] (Lacroix 54–5). Even what may in effect be seen as a North American cultural style is increasingly a global cultural style rather than an American (i.e., United States) phenomenon that has affected the cultural identity of Quebec as well as of other nations and "imagined communities" (Sauvageau, "Paradoxes et ambiguïté" xxi, xxv; Serge Proulx 227). The anxiety remains, however: "We no longer speak of cultural imperialism, but of globalization: the anxiety remains the same, the fear of U.S. mass culture" ["On ne parle plus d'impérialisme culturel, mais de mondialisation: l'angoisse reste la même, la peur de la culture de masse étatsunienne"] (Bertrand 183). For Proulx (as for Bertrand), this fear is unfounded; today Quebec is pluricultural and in a permanent state of transformation; *américanité* as the spectre of U.S. cultural influence is only one source among many in the social construction of contemporary Quebec identity (228). As Lacroix points out both in narrative and in graphic form, there is a clear interaction of structural tendencies in the elaboration of cultural fields in Quebec, as well as in Canada: "Quebecization, Canadianization, Americanization/United States-ization; Continentalization; and Internationalization ["Québécisation; Canadianisation; Américanisation/étatsunisation; Continentalisation; et Internationalisation"] (37). Indeed, not everyone sees cultural globalization solely as Americanization (Legrain). On the level of concrete and popular culture, globalization has allowed Céline Dion to exploit on the international scene her identity as Canadian,

American, French, and international, while taking advantage of the "postmodern character of her Quebec identity" ["caractère postmoderne de l'identité québécoise"] (Dufour 179).

Similar influences and tendencies (without Céline) are apparent in Canada's ongoing search for its own identity vis-à-vis the United States. Although researchers seem to disagree as to which "nation" has a tougher time in relation to its powerful southern neighbour, all agree that there are different problems. One of the threads running through the essays in *The Beaver Bites Back*, for instance, is that living in North America with the United States is much more difficult for English Canada than for Quebec because of the common language and the similarity of the "cloth" from which both Americans and English Canadians have been cut. Ironically, Canada obsessively tries to maintain its identity as a "distinct society," much as Quebec has been trying to do within Canada. Frank Manning thus presents us with an intriguing analogy: "As Quebec is to Canada, Canada is to the continent" (25). Balthazar and Hero agree that francophone Québécois and anglophone Canadians both share the same apprehension regarding U.S. influence and domination but that they are almost never on the same wave length in resisting this Americanization (61). Canada has adopted nationalist policies to protect itself from the United States,[26] whereas Quebec, especially because it has the protection of its distinct language, has been more open to American influence – at least in the realm of popular and mass culture. Anglo-Canadians are obsessed with preserving their cultural identity against an invasion of American popular culture, whereas francophone Québécois are obsessed with the preservation of their identity but seek less to limit economic exchanges with the United States than to protect their language and culture within the North American context: "Thus, when Quebecers legislated their language, other Canadians reproached them for their protectionism. On the other hand, when these same Canadians were opposed to American penetration, as was the case in 1988 during an electoral campaign over the free-trade treaty, Quebecers did not appear to be willing to follow their lead" ["Ainsi, quand les Québécois ont légiféré sur la langue, les autres Canadiens leur ont reproché leur protectionnisme. Par contre, quand ces derniers se sont opposés à la pénétration américaine, comme ce fut le cas en 1988 à l'occasion d'une campagne électorale portant sur le traité de libre-échange, les Québécois ne se sont pas montrés disposés à emboîter le pas"] (51).

Linguistic protection for Quebec is also mentioned by Yvan Lamonde as proof that Americanization for Quebec is not as problematic, or at least presents different types of problems: "In counteracting Americans, English-speaking Canadians outnumber Quebecers, but this advantage disappears when one considers their common language; French-Canadians have the language differential, but it is compromised by their smaller numbers" ["Face aux Américains, les Canadiens anglais ont le nombre par rapport aux Québécois, mais cet avantage est annulé par la communauté de langue; les Canadiens français ont une langue différentielle, mais compromise par leur faiblesse numérique"] (*Ni avec eux* 81; see also Chassy, *L'Ambiguïté américaine* 189; Seymour 90–2). But it is precisely because of this differentiation that Bouchard sees Quebec's stance and situation in relation to the United States as more difficult and less successful to date. In his view, in order to ensure their survival and development, francophone Quebecers have preferred decentralization and even a separation from the Canadian nation-state; English Canadians, on the other hand, as protection especially against the United States, have tried to reinforce their national identity and have tried to integrate Quebec society and culture as part of the new multicultural Canadian mosaic (*Genèse* 238; see also Seymour 46–58). According to Bouchard's account, Canada has done quite well in counteracting the United States, as it has gained political sovereignty, whereas Quebec's neonationalism has only threatened to break up the Canadian federation. In addition, Canada has for a long time "found in its membership in the Empire a counterbalance to the threat from the United States" (329) ["trouvé dans son appartenance impériale un contrepoids à la menace étatsunienne"] (329). In Bouchard's view, it is more difficult for Quebec to live in North America.

These differences between Canada and Quebec, and the United States were also addressed during the North American Cultures round table already mentioned. Wiggers's initial question was: "Do the successes of Quebec diva Celine Dion and the acrobatic troupe Cirque du Soleil in both the U.S. and the wider global market indicate that French Canada has been able to develop a formula that actually turns the table on the apparent omnipotence of American pop culture?" (424). Diane Pacom saw no special formula at work, but rather a long-standing acceptance by Quebec of its "Americanity," especially by the urban masses, who viewed America's influence as a way to emancipate themselves from the conservative ideology of the past held by the rural masses and the traditional and intellectual elite: "This particular characteristic of Quebec's culture puts it in a different cultural space than the rest of Canada, which tries to build an identity to resist American cultural influence.

Contrary to Anglo-Canadian culture, which tries to insulate itself from its Americanity, Québécois society, especially since the 1950s, has accepted, integrated and, in many ways, bypassed this question, which continues to haunt Anglo-Canadian society and its elites" (441–2). For Pacom the "Quiet Revolution" ["La Révolution tranquille"] helped to create a new Quebec culture that celebrated its unique status and contributed to an awareness of "the triple nature of its Social Imaginary. It became not only French (*la Francité*), but also Québécois (*la Québecité*) and American (*l'Américanité*)" (445). This triple identity has matured even more recently into a new "hybrid" Quebec (446).

Reginald Stuart, at this same round table discussion, maintained that "far greater danger exists for Canada from the internal fault lines of historical solitudes, social changes, and the rise of the provinces as principal actors in the federal system than from the alleged perils of Amazon.com ... or the triumph of Wal-Mart in retailing" (431). Michael Seymour would probably agree with this assessment, although he also argues that Canada needs to accept Quebec as the sociopolitical nation that it has become and not simply as a cultural nation composed of people who are "linguistically fragile in North America" ["linguistiquement fragilisés en Amérique du Nord"] (*La Nation en question* 87–8, 118). Seymour believes that Canadians for the most part deny the existence of an Anglo-Canadian nation and thus refuse to accept the existence of a Quebec nation (133). Those who do recognize a Canadian nation do not, however, define it in terms of language – which he sees as a fundamental identity factor (138). Linguistic affiliation becomes important only when one is confronted with people who speak another language – like French. But since Canadians speak a language that is used throughout North America (Mexico and Latin America seem to get lost in these investigations), and one that has become international as well, they do not recognize this importance of language and maintain their cultural specificity simply as the "Canadian experience" ("l'expérience canadienne," 138–9). For Seymour, Canadian nationalism was born from Canadians' desire to see the country as different from the United States, as a distinctly North American civic nation (140).

Some of the most exciting work being done on issues of *américanisation* and *américanité* in reference to the relationship between Quebec and the United States has come from the Groupe interdisciplinaire de recherche sur l'Américanité (GRAM), which has become the Groupe interdisciplinaire de recherche sur les Amériques (GIRA), headed by

Donald Cuccioletta and comprising researchers from Quebec, the United States, and Mexico. Before moving to the specific results of their survey in Quebec on popular culture, it will be helpful to place their work in the broader context of North American cultures that I have been discussing.

L'Américanité et les Amériques, edited by Donald Cuccioletta, along with the more recent *Le Grand Récit des Amériques* edited by Cuccioletta, Côté, and Lesemann, presents an array of essays grouped into sections: "Intersecting Views of the Americas"; "Continental Integration, Liberalism, and Americanness"; "American Cultural Identities"; "Borders and Metropolises"; "Languages, Identities, Transculturalism"; and "Encountering the Other" ["Regards croisés sur les Amériques"; "Intégration continentale, libéralisme et américanité"; "Identités culturelles américaines"; Frontières et métropoles"; "Langues, identités, transculturalité"; "La Rencontre de l'autre"]. In the opening essay in the first collection, Côté refers to Quebec's American identity as a cultural complex that is not strictly "of the United States" ["étatsunienne"] but rather, designated as "Americanness" (*américanité*) (13). Louis Dupont, in his essay, calls *américanité* a prism that allows for a certain interpretation of Québécois society and Franco-Québécois culture, formed from its Canadian and French-Canadian past and linked to the geography and history of North America; it is a concept, a paradigm, and a problematic (47). He goes on to state that Quebec's "place" on the continent is simple: "What distinguishes Quebec to the Anglo-American eye is its Frenchness; what distinguishes it to the francophone eye is its *américanité*" ["Ce qui distingue le Quebec dans l'oeil de l'Anglo-Amérique, c'est la francité, ce qui le distingue dans l'oeil de la francophonie, c'est son américanité"] (48). Distinguishing even further an "Ameriquan" Quebec ("Quebec amériquain") different from the America of the United States,[27] Dupont believes that since 1980 it has been necessary and fruitful to "combine Frenchness and modernity with belonging to America" ["conjuguer francité et modernité avec appartenance à l'Amérique"] (49, 51). With "*américanité* as a means to counter Canadianization, that is to say Quebec in a Canada where Quebecers constitute only one cultural group among others" ["l'américanité étant un moyen de contrer la 'canadianisation,' c'est-à-dire du Québec dans un Canada où les Québécois ne constituent qu'un groupe culturel parmi d'autres"] (61), *américanité* offers the possibility of inscribing the past and the future of Quebec in "a continental experience with multiple singularities, the experience of the Americas" ["une expérience continentale aux multiples singularités, celle des Amériques"] (62).

This continental experience is further explored in *Le Grand Récit des Amériques*, which brings together material from a colloquium held in Montréal in 2001 on "the themes of transculturality, identity, Americanness and the role of metropolises in a context of continentalization" ["les thématiques de la transculturalité, de l'identité, de l'américanité et ... le rôle des métropoles dans un contexte de continentalisation"] to investigate questions related to the polyphony of cultural identities (Cuccioletta, Côté, and Lesemann, "Introduction" 4). Côté discusses this new "great story" ["grand récit"] of the Americas as a poetic history that recognizes cultural identity as a hybrid, constantly transformed by colonial, national, and U.S. contexts and attempting to define itself as continental ("Le Renouveau" 36–7). Cuccioletta's optimistic contribution to this collection speaks of a Pan-Americanism that includes the concept of a "citizenship of the Americas." Transculturalism will be the new humanism, with new social subjects, the emergence of mixed races, ("métis") and new continental identities based on a mutual recognition of alterity, of otherness, and of a cultural mix that "discards the dominant-dominated dichotomy" ("Towards a Citizenship" 48): "This emerging citizenship of the Americas should allow a link between the 'local' belonging and the 'continental' belonging. In other words, this citizenship should reflect a dynamic of the redistribution of the American identity and position itself in opposition against any cultural homogenization stemming from a presumed U.S.-style 'Americanization' of the continent. Questioning identities at a continental level makes it possible to have a critical approach to the dominant vision and representations resulting from the influence of the U.S. model" (49).

Gérard Bouchard sums up much of what the contributors advocated, as he proposes another option for the future: a world coalition of small and medium-sized nations ["les petites et moyennes nations"] with the goal of developing a platform of equals that would allow different voices to be heard, ensure that partners are more equitably included in the global network, preserve cultural diversity, and promote a new form of democracy. For Bouchard, if a "plan for identity, for inter-American solidarity" ["projet d'une identité, d'une solidarite interaméricaine"] were formulated, it could become a prototype for a larger coalition. Quebec's role would be essential, as "its hybrid character particularly singles it out for this type of rapprochement" (186] ["son caractère hybride le désigne particulièrement à ce genre de rapprochement" ("Une nouvelle frontière" 186).

Bouchard's perspective beautifully parallels the research that this interdisciplinary group has completed on *américanité* and Americanization in

Quebec public opinion, summarized in *Le Devoir* in 1998, partially published in 2000 in *Quebec Studies*, and then fully reported and analysed in 2001 in *L'Américanité et les Amériques.*

Québécois Self-Perception in Relation to Canada, the United States, and North America: The GIRA/GRAM Survey

As explained by Csipak and Héroux in their 2001 article, this survey was conducted in 1997 and consisted of 100 questions asked in a lengthy telephone questionnaire with 2,204 individuals throughout Quebec.[28] Among the questions were a number that dealt specifically with Quebec's distinctiveness: "What is *l'américanité* des Québécois?; Since the advent of the FTA and NAFTA, has Quebec's cultural distinctiveness decreased, remained the same, or decreased? Do Quebecers appear to be more Francophone than American or more American than Francophone? Is Quebec becoming a 'Francité Américaine?'" ("Nationalism, Liberalism and the *Américanité* of Quebecers" 107).

Responses to the overriding question about primary and secondary levels of identification are revealing: 54% of those surveyed identified themselves as Québécois, 19% as Canadian, 23% as French Canadian, and 2% as English Canadian; however, at a secondary level, 68% identified themselves as North American (Bernier 185; see also Csipak and Héroux, "Nationalism, Liberalism" 108–9). With 60% interpreting the definition of an American as being a citizen of the United States, 40% of the respondents considered the province where they lived as the primary geographic site of their belonging, and only 4% named North America in the first position. Secondarily, however, 53.6% named North America, as compared to Canada (20.5%) (Bernier 185). Breaking down these categories more precisely, Bernier reports that although very few Quebecers considered themselves to be primarily North Americans, a majority made this identification at a secondary level, especially those who identifed themselves first as Québécois rather than as Canadian or English Canadian (177–8). An initial identification with Quebec was also only rarely accompanied by a secondary identification with Canada. As Bernier points out: "For citizens of Quebec who call themselves *Canadians* first, this primary identification would tend to shield a wider feeling of belonging to North America, while for those who feel that they are *Quebecers* first, the identification with Canada would easily seem to be short-circuited to the benefit of a feeling of continental belonging" ["Pour les citoyens du Québec qui se disent d'abord

Canadiens, cette identification première aurait tendance à faire écran au sentiment d'appartenance plus large à l'Amérique du Nord tandis que pour ceux qui se sentent d'abord *Québécois*, l'identification au Canada semblerait facilement court-circuitée au profit d'un sentiment d'appartenance continentale"] (178; see also Bernier and Bédard 19).

Bernier and Bédard have also reported these levels of identification according to age categories. The younger the age group, the more likely was the primary self-identification as Québécois: 76% of those 18–24 years of age, 64% of those 25–34 years of age, 60% of those 35–44 years of age, 55% of those 45–54 years of age, 34% of those 55–64 years of age, 22% of those 65 years of age and older identify themselves in first place as Québécois (17). An identification of oneself as Québécois is of course particularly characteristic of the francophone population of the province, since only 6% of the Anglophones chose Québécois but 70% responded that they were, first of all, Canadians (Bernier and Bédard 17). A second level of identification as North American appears especially among those younger than fifty-four: 40.7% over 55; 56.6% between 45 and 54; 54.4% between 35 and 44; and 59.5% between 18 and 34 (Bernier and Bédard 18). It seems clear that younger Québécois are increasingly identifying themselves, at least secondarily, as North American.

But do these younger citizens of Quebec see themselves as similar to or different from their counterparts in the United States? Csipak and Héroux report that 56% of respondents perceived themselves as different ("Nationalism, Liberalism" 108). In reference to specific categories, however, the responses revealed that the perceptions of difference are interesting: 74% mention language; 62% food; 49% clothing; and 44% holidays (108, 122). The most surprising of these results, of course, is the perceived difference in clothing – and apparently U.S. fast food is not as widespread as one may have thought! In addition, Quebecers who identified themselves more locally with Quebec tended to be more focused on Quebec popular culture – listening more to Québécois music, reading more local news, and watching more local films – than those who identified themselves as Canadians, who listened to American music, watched U.S. television programs, read American fiction, and saw American films (Bernier 182–3). Quebecers also see similarities with the United States as well, however: 58% mention leisure, 47% family values, and 47% attitude toward work (108–9, 122). Interestingly, 60% of the respondents agreed that Quebecers were as individualistic as Americans (109). In addition, for every category except one,

Québécois reported that they felt that their situation was preferable to that of the United States: health care, quality of life for seniors, environmental quality, poverty, educational system, racism, and standard of living (job opportunities were seen as superior in the United States, however (109, 122). And finally, to the statement, "I would rather live in the United States than in Quebec," 89% mostly disagreed, while when asked whether they felt closer to English Canadians or Americans, 48% said English Canadians, and only 33% chose Americans (109).

Csipak and Héroux also provide the results of the survey about Québécois attitudes toward NAFTA. Perhaps the most relevant of these results for our purposes are those that concern NAFTA's impact on Quebec's cultural development. According to the survey, 51% of the respondents reported that the U.S. influence on Quebec's cultural development was generally "beneficial" ("NAFTA, Quebecers and Fear" 34). When asked if cultural products should be excluded from NAFTA, 40% of the respondents responded in the affirmative, while 54% disagreed – with younger respondents increasingly in disagreement and the most educated closely divided (34–5, 36). The researchers also concluded that Quebecers have a certain fear of Americanization (60%) and feel that Quebec should strengthen its ties to francophone countries in order to offset the impact of American culture (36–7). Surprisingly, in contrast to the historical situation I have mentioned above, whereas it was previously the elite who looked nostalgically toward France while the younger generations more openly embraced American culture, this contemporary survey reveals that it is now the youngest (63%), the least educated (69%), and the lowest income groups (65%) who are in greatest agreement with strengthening ties to France (36). Csipak and Héroux found, however, that when respondents were asked if Quebec should become a U.S. state if it had no ties to the rest of Canada, 62% responded negatively, and the youngest, the most educated, and those in the highest income brackets most strongly disagreed. Csipak and Héroux conclude from these data that "Quebecers feel 'distinct' from both Canada and the U.S., and that a strong majority of Quebecers do not fear Americanzation" (37). For these researchers, Quebec's present elite, in particular, does not fear the United States and the process of Americanization that is accompanying increased economic integration as a result of NAFTA (38–9).

What the results of the GRAM/GIRA survey seem to demonstrate is that, as Lesemann has pointed out, a Quebec mass culture oriented toward the continent is quite capable of participating fully in that North

American culture while at the same time articulating its linguistic and cultural specificity (Lesemann, *L'Américanité des Québécois* 53; Lesemann, "Le Rôle de l'État-providence" 155). For Léon Bernier: "This tends to show not only that *américanité* is not synonymous with acculturation to the United States, but rather that Quebecers' recognition of their Americanness could well come to take over any European reference by way of a counter-offensive implicit in 'Americanization' understood as a process of cultural *de*-differentiation as a result of the globalization of the U.S. cultural industry" ["Cela tend à montrer non seulement qu'américanité n'est pas synonyme d'acculturation états-unienne, mais que la reconnaissance, par les Québécois de *leur* américanité pourrait bien venir prendre le relais de la référence européenne à titre de contre-offensive implicite à 'l'américanisation' entendue comme processus de *dé*différenciation culturelle par effet de mondialisation de l'industrie culturelle étatsunienne"] (183). Finally, if the Québécois and *their* Americanness can become a continental "francophonie," envisaged by Van Schendel as a "de-Americanizing Americanness" (an "américanité 'désaméricanisante'") and defined as "franco-polyphonic" ("francopolyphonique") (221) in contact with other varieties of French, as well as with other linguistic and cultural universes – both anglophone and hispanophone (Van Schendel 198) – then new possibilities may arise:

> The Americanness of the francophone world would be characterized by the relative permeability of the French language and, more specifically in regard to Quebec, by the possibility of progressively greeting and integrating other sociolects, thanks to immigration ... The polyphonic francophone world is another possible dimension of this Americanness that we are speaking of, in that it gives evidence, through the hybrid expression of its language, of a plurality of points of view and, especially, to the extent that Americanness is seen as incarnating an experience other than that conveyed by Americanization, of a need to say things differently. [L'américanité de la francophonie se caractériserait par la perméabilité relative de la langue française et, en ce qui concerne plus spécifiquement le Québec, par la possibilité d'accueillir et d'intégrer progressivement, grâce à l'immigration, d'autres sociolectes ... La parole francopolyphonique est une autre dimension possible de cette américanité dont nous parlons, en ce qu'elle témoigne, à travers l'expression métissée de son langage, d'une pluralité de points de vue et, surtout, dans la mesure où l'américanité est vue comme incarnant une autre expérience que celle véhiculée par l'américanisation, d'un besoin de dire les choses autrement.] (199)

Toward a Quebec Identity

But can the Québécois succeed in defining themselves as this North American specificity that is increasingly open to a polyphony of francophone voices, all joining to form their own form of *américanité* (Americanness)? After all, the concept of *américanité* itself arose from concerns over Americanization and a need to reconsider Quebec identity in its entirety (Côté 10). Bouchard and Lamonde believe that Quebec is still trying to come to grips with its *américanité* because it is not a nation (169). And if Nancy Huston can call Canada an ambiguous country (32), then Morisset and Waddell can also state that "Franco-America will always have been an *in-between* adventure" ["La Franco-Amérique aura toujours été une aventure de l'*in-between*"] (22). "Too northern to be considered *Latinos*, too 'Frenchy' to be considered fully American, we belong to an America of the *in between*. We are in some way the reverse of the lost America. In short, an America that has not yet found itself and which, still unaware of its limits, continues to embody a promise for the future on the vast horizon" ["Trop nordique pour être considérés comme *latinos*, trop 'frenchés' pour être considérés comme pleinement américains, nous appartenons à une Amérique de l'entre-deux. Nous sommes en quelque sorte l'envers de l'Amérique perdue. Bref, une Amérique qui ne s'est pas encore trouvée et qui incarne toujours une promesse à venir au large d'un horizon ignorant toujours ses limites"] (276). These debates remain current in Quebec's attempts to define its identity.[29]

QUEBEC IDENTITY AS A GENDERED "NATION" IN NORTH AMERICA

Especially germane to this study is the question of how one becomes Québécois if one feels that national identity has always been predominantly masculine and if one sees current debate about nationhood and sovereignty as based on a language and a territory that belie a masculine project. It is interesting to note that, in the minds of certain feminist scholars, the long-standing metaphors of a masculine United States and a feminine Canada have been replaced by the proposition of a national, masculine Quebec that denies the perspective of women and specifically of feminists.

In her discussion of a potential postmodern, feminist Quebec, included in the collection *Malaises identitaires: Échanges féministes autour d'un Quebec incertain*, Chantal Maillé bases her argument on the performative image of the "nomadic subject," as developed by Rosi Braidotti. For Braidotti: "The nomadic subject is a myth, that is to say a political fiction, that allows [her or him] to think through and move across established categories and levels of experience" (Braidotti 4). The nomadic subject is also a linguistic polyglot who "practices an aesthetic style based on compassion for the incongruities, the repetitions, the arbitrariness of the languages she/he deals with" (Braidotti 15). As Maillé sees the feminist: "[She] is a nomad, neither migrant nor exiled. The nomadic conscience appears like a form of political resistance to hegemonic visions of subjectivity" ["La féministe est une nomade, ni migrante ni exilée. La conscience nomade apparaît comme une forme de résistance politique aux visions hégémoniques de la subjectivité"] (146). Indeed, the nomadic subject is the new symbol of fragmented postmodern identity (Maillé 152–3).

Maillé takes this fragmented image of the postmodern nomad and applies it to current debates in Quebec vis-à-vis a national identity; she does so with deep ambivalence about ethnicity, given the need to preserve the French language and Quebec culture in North America: "Quebec is uncomfortable with ethnicity" ["Le Québec est mal à l'aise avec l'ethnicité"] (153). She thus advocates new ways to think about Quebec national identity: "Notions such as hybridity, rhizome, and diaspora, which evoke heterogeneity, correspond even more to the human landscape that one meets there. If ... the exiled person is the new symbol of identity, redefined by the yardstick of postmodernity, racial and cultural identity becomes something fluid, extremely complex, reflecting the different journeys of a heterogeneous population" ["Des notions comme l'hybridité, le rhizome, la diaspora, qui évoquent l'hétérogène, correspondent davantage au paysage humain que l'on y rencontre. Si ... l'exilé-e est le nouveau symbole de l'identité repensée à l'aune de la postmodernité, l'identité raciale et culturelle devient quelque chose de flou, d'extrêmement complexe, reflétant les parcours différents d'une population hétérogène"] (160).

In an essay in this same collection (which she co-edited), "La Posture du fils," and in a subsequent critical monograph, *L'Amère patrie: Féminisme et nationalisme dans le Québec contemporain*, Diane Lamoureux agrees that Québécois society is presently confronted with a crisis of "identitary fragmentation" ["fragmentation identitaire"] (*L'Amère patrie* 131). But she pushes the analogy much further by interpreting the "trilogy" of language, culture, and institutions in search of a Quebec nation (*L'Amère patrie* 162), along with the current political debate itself, as a metaphor of the family (*L'Amère patrie* 123; see also "La Posture du fils" 38), in which the "son's stance" ["la posture du fils"] is the most significant issue ("La Posture du fils" 25–51).

The first stage of nationalist discourse, according to this analogy, is essentially the stage of decolonization, during which the national subject is the castrated male. The second stage focuses more on normalization; the Québécois try to prove that they are adults by contracting a marriage, represented by the attempt at sovereignty-association, but this modern/postmodern marriage is one in which the woman/Quebec risks losing her/its individuality in the process.[30] For Lamoureux, therefore, the 1982 patriation of the Constitution had the symbolic consequence of this loss of identity – subsumed under that of the family and its head, man ("La Posture du fils" 38–9). The third stage is thus characterized by divorce: The idea of national affirmation and accession to independence corresponds to the "virilization" of Quebec men, who desire to leave behind the role of son and become fathers and complete citizens ("La Posture du fils" 39). At the same time, Maillé continues the analogy by referencing the "real" back-drop of the status of women historically in the traditional Quebec family – perhaps with some power within the domestic arena, but without any power or authority politically or legally (*L'Amère patrie* 100).[31]

It is, therefore, a two-sided story of humiliation and affirmation: "Quebec appears, alternatively, either under a feminine mode or a masculine mode. Oppression places Quebec in a feminine posture, as a battered woman who needs a divorce. Affirmation, on the other hand, is a virile figure, that of Quebec, Inc., of performance and of mastery" ["Le Québec figure, alternativement, sous un mode féminin ou sous un mode masculin. L'oppression met le Québec en posture féminine, en femme battue qui a besoin du divorce. L'affirmation est, par contre, une figure virile, celle du Québec Inc., de la performance et de la maîtrise"] ("La Posture du fils" 41; see also *L'Amère patrie* 124, 94). In other words, oppression is declined in the feminine, while affirmation is declined in the masculine; oppression belongs in the private sphere reserved for the feminine, and affirmation enters the public sphere with its access to the virile nation-state (*L'Amère patrie* 123). Ceasing to be a minority within Canada and becoming a majority within Quebec means passing from the stage of childhood or womanhood to that of an adult, symbolically a man; it is a form of "revenge on the Other" ["une revanche sur l'Autre"] by moving from "we/us others" ("nous autres") to the future father who constructs his own future and his own nation ("L'Amère patrie" 125; "La Posture du fils" 42). The problem for Quebec women, of course, is that when Quebec men talk of the necessity of achieving this stance of affirmation and self-confidence, the language and the metaphors are always virile, always male. Where does that leave Quebec women who have the same stake in the future of their "nation"?

Lamoureux believes that there are many parallels between nationalism and feminism: the refusal of an assigned identity, the search for one's own identity, the need for coalition, militantism, and the call for community and openness, among others. The points of convergence are threefold: "a complete 'detraditionalization' ... a common work for the construction of the national welfare State ... the politicization of identity" ["La 'détraditionalisation complète' ... un travail commun de construction de l'État providence national ... la politisation de l'identité"] (*L'Amère patrie* 179). She calls for a political culture of rebellion among both nationalists and feminists in order to define and build a Quebec nation.

CANADIAN-QUEBEC CULTURAL POLICIES

Such a recommended political culture of rebellion within the nation of Quebec can ignore neither the current realities of living "inside" Canada and north of the United States, nor Canada's own ambiguous position and attitude vis-à-vis the United States – a point that I explored briefly at the beginning of this chapter. From the "hybrid" perspective of an Albertan, for example, Nancy Huston (who lives and writes in France) the Québécois, unlike Albertans, have benefited from centuries of traditions and transmissions of the stories of their ancestors. She, on the other hand, has experienced and continues to experience the "uncomfortable co-existence ... of two languages and two ways of being that make [her] the most profoundly *Canadian* ... [the two cultures] are fond of criticizing each other, of being sarcastic, of making jokes at each other's expense; in short they lay claim to all the ambiguity of their situation" ["Cette coexistence incomfortable ... de deux langues et de deux façons d'être qui [la] rend le plus profondément *canadienne* ... elles tiennent à se critiquer, à ironiser, à faire des blagues l'une aux dépens de l'autre; en somme, elles revendiquent toute l'ambiguité de leur situation"] (38). Clearly, although some Quebec critics also see a certain level of ambiguity on the part of Quebec toward the United States (Bouchard, *Genèse* 181), it is Canada that nationalistically and legally has perhaps felt a greater need to develop cultural policies to protect itself from its gigantic southern neighbour.[32]

To some scholars, such as Balthazar and Hero, the fact that Canada speaks on behalf of the entire country has denied the existence in Quebec of a different perspective toward the United States, causing some Quebecers to see a complicity between English Canada and the United States, both of whose citizens feel a closeness that is not replicated toward francophone Canadians (200–2). Although both English and francophone Canadians have long had a tacit agreement to reject the American model, at the same time as falling under its influence (Balthazar and Hero 46), English Canada, according to Balthazar and Hero, has both attempted to affirm itself as a distinct nation and constructed itself on the model that it had long repudiated: "In order to caricature both its own nation and population and America and its inhabitants, it made itself American the better to combat the Americans" ["Pour caricaturer, on s'est fait Américain pour mieux combattre les Américains"] (53). Ironically, as I shall show in subsequent chapters, the writers under consideration here also use caricatures of macho, violent American males in order to combat them – with their caricatured, macho, violent Québécois females.

The irony of this observation about English Canadians is all the more profound when one looks at the policies that Canada has promulgated to protect its own culture from the encroachment of the United States. Edelgard Mahant and Graeme Mount suggest that "Canadian efforts to protect and foster a national culture have been more successful than have those of the governments of many other developed countries" (449). By the end of the 1990s, for instance, there were at least five different types of measures in place to protect Canadian culture: the so-called Cancon (i.e., Canadian content) regulations governing broadcasters on radio and television stations; trade protection for magazines;[33] investments related to ownership and cultural performance; direct subsidies for such cultural entities as book publishing, films, readings, and art exhibits; and mixed and ad-hoc measures for specific issues (Mahant and Mount 460–1).

According to Kevin Mulcahy in his study of cultural imperialism and cultural sovereignty in regard to U.S. and Canadian cultural relations, debates about these measures and about issues of cultural exemption as protection from U.S. cultural imperialism have long been part of the Canadian discourse, in contrast to the United States where most Americans – with the exception of those in the entertainment industry and trade negotiators – barely pay attention and where the country can afford to have a "cultural open-door policy" since it has little to fear from foreign competition (181–2). In what he calls the "big nation, small neighbor syndrome" (183), Mulcahy documents the U.S. domination of Canadian culture: feature films (95% of screen time); music on radio stations (70%); book market (70%); and consumer magazines (83%) (184). As he ominously concludes: "Canadians have lost their ability to define themselves culturally" (184).

In contrast to the results noted above from the GIRA/GRAM survey on how Quebecers see themselves in relation to Canada, the United States, and North America, Mulcahy reports that one-third of Canadians believe that Canada and the United States will become one nation within the next twenty-five years; half of the Canadians surveyed thought that Canadians had become more like Americans over the past decade; and of those with this opinion, the strongest evidence of the Americanization of Canada was found to be related to the American media (84%), followed by U.S. investments (79%) and the Internet (75%) (Mulcahy 185–6). Given the distinction between U.S. culture, as defined by entertainment (a marketable commodity) and Canadian culture as an expression of national identity (a social or public good), it is not surprising that there is a misunderstanding between these two countries about an exempt status for cultural industries in free-trade agreements (Mulcahy 188–9). In other words, for Canada "cultural protectionism is the necessary guarantor of cultural sovereignty" (Mulcahy 190).[34]

The fact that Canada is the home of two major linguistic societies and that it is officially a bilingual country, however, causes additional and layered tensions in the development of cultural protectionism as a defence against U.S. cultural encroachment. It is clear that Americanization (greatly as a result of media influence) is seen differently within Quebec, since language tends to offer some insulation from the U.S. domination of its cultural industries (Mulcahy 191). Mulcahy reports that a 1993 survey of bestsellers in Montreal, for example, has shown that Quebec authors sell about 40% of all titles, with U.S. authors at 30%, French authors at 25%, English-language (mostly British) authors at 2.6%, and finally English-Canadian authors at less than 2% (191–2). These figures need to be seen in comparison to those in English-speaking Canada, where 70% of the books sold are American, 25% are Canadian (mostly textbooks, cookbooks, and the like), with less than 1% of the mass-market fiction by Canadian authors

(Mulcahy 191). Essentially because of language, one would assume, the English-Canadian book market is more dominated by the United States than is the Québécois book market: "Language provides Quebec with a modicum of protection against the penetration of American cultural products as part of a broader resistance to Anglophone hegemony in general" (Mulcay 198).[35]

QUEBEC IDENTITY THROUGH CULTURE AND LITERATURE

Theories of the nation and nationhood, especially as they relate to culture and literature and as they seek to define minority nations and cultural differences, have been on the front burner of intellectual discourse since the advent of postmodernism and postcolonialism. Increasingly, in addition, discussions about whether Quebec literature is postcolonial have preoccupied scholars, academics, and theoreticians. My intention here is not to reiterate what others have said about such issues – or even to add my commentary – but rather to contextualize the concept of Quebec's national identity as it has been developed through its culture and literature. I hope then to recontextualize it within the parameters of North America, and in particular, a violent and gendered North America.

Still one of the most highly regarded and cited texts in the fields of cultural studies and postcolonialism, *Nation and Narration* edited by Homi Bhaba, questions our concepts of the social and national context of cultural representation. Bhaba himself, in his opening essay, begins the investigation of what he nicely calls "this ambivalent margin of the nation-space," the "turning of boundaries and limits into the *in-between* spaces, through which the meanings of cultural and political authority are negotiated" ("Introduction: Narrating the Nation" 4). He indicates that the authors in this collection write from the narrative positions between cultures and nations, and seek to affirm and extend Frantz Fanon's revolutionary credo: "National consciousness, which is not nationalism, is the only thing that will give us an international dimension" (Bhaba 4) ["La conscience nationale, qui n'est pas le nationalisme, est la seule à nous donner [une] dimension internationale"] (Fanon 174; original French cited). It is this "*inter*national dimension both within the margins of the nation-space and in the boundaries *in-between* nations and peoples" that is the "crossroads to a new transnational culture. The 'other' is never outside or beyond us; it emerges forcefully, within cultural discourse" (Bhaba, "Introduction" 4). As I shall point out, this definition of an in-between nation-space at least partially defines the cultural space of Quebec and especially its gendered cultural space.

Timothy Brennan also pays homage to Fanon, as well as to Ricoeur's concept of the tension between universal civilization and national culture and Foucault's notion of the nation as a discursive formation. He shows how literature has been crucial in defining the nation as an "imagined community" (as in Anderson's term discussed above) and how contemporary fiction has served as a bridge between imaginative literature and other forms of cultural information and communication (63, 46, 48, 60). Simon During, looking at nationalism as the discursive and representational practices that define and legitimize a nation-state, deals specifically with "the feminization of society," which replaces the law of the father with autonomous subjects (139, 143). He also looks at postcolonial novels and novelists that use realism to fold the Imaginary into the real, work within a Global Imaginary, and set forth the interplay between subjectivity and representation (151–2).

In his essay "Dissemi-Nation: Time, Narrative, and the Margins of the Modern Nation," Homi Bhabha suggests that we need another time of writing (a non-sequential present that incorporates both the past and the future) in order to inscribe the ambivalent intersections of time and place that characterize the modern experience of the Western nation (293). By reading between the borderlines of nation-space, by a process of splitting, one can use this conceptual ambivalence of modern society as the site of writing the nation ("Dissemi-Nation" 297), as a place of "contentious *internal* liminality" from which to "speak of, and as, the minority, the exilic, the marginal, and the emergent" (300). From this liminal space emerges a minority discourse, and the nation begins to speak its "disjunctive narrative ... which disturbs the homogenizing myth of cultural anonymity" (311). These spoken and written cultural differences that re-articulate knowledge differently and elaborate a new logic of interpretation offer a frontier of hybridity that is "the perplexity of the living as it interrupts the representation of the fullness of life," and whose "sites of meaning open up a cleavage in the language of culture" (314).

Sherry Simon has developed Bhabha's concept of cultural hybridity as it pertains to Quebec in its language, culture, and nationhood.[36] She further explores the problematic of culture in "Espaces incertains de la culture," part of the edited collection *Fictions de l'identitaire au Québec*, where her goal is to work out how to think about the "uncertain borders of culture" ["les frontières incertaines de la culture" (17)] – sounding much like the explorations of Bhabha as just described. Acknowledging that Quebec culture is penetrated by American culture, Simon proposes five definitions of culture: "the site of competing tensions and visions"; "a surging collection of discourses and institutions"; "a conflicting space of discourses and representations"; "a juxtaposition of spaces, references, and beats" and "a conflicting field of discourses, interests, and allegiances" ["le site de tensions et de visions concurrentes" (18); "un ensemble mouvant de discours et d'institutions" (25); "un espace conflictuel de discours et de représentations" (24); "une juxtaposition d'espaces, de références, de pulsations" (45); "un champ conflictuel du discours, d'intérêts et d'allégeances" (48).]

Ratiba Hadj-Moussa similarly uses Bhabha's notion of a third space, as well as Appadurai's "scape" and Trinh's "postcolonial concept of difference" to think about identity as indetermination, belonging, and identification. She asks how one is to think about identity, alterity, and multiple identifications when one is transplanted into another culture (Hadj-Moussa 220). Like Simon, basing her views on Bhabha's concept of hybridity as a figure of language and not simply a mix of genres, as a form of mimicry that creates a double vision, Hadj-Moussa speaks of culture being located in this third space, "always in an in-between which refuses any transcendence from one pole to another. The notion of hybridity serves here to go beyond essentialisms ... permits the emergence of new positions" ["toujours dans un entre-deux qui refuse toute transcendance d'un pôle sur un autre. La notion d'hybridité sert ici à aller au-delà des essentialismes ... permet l'émergence de nouvelles positions"] (231). It is a decentred culture that allows one to avoid binaries. Although as a sociologist Hadj-Moussa is speaking here specifically about Muslim women in Canada, her remarks relate profoundly to a hybrid Quebec in search of its identity through an increasingly hybrid culture and literature. And specific to this study, the notion of a hybrid site of writing and telling that avoids binaries dovetails with the work that certain Quebec women writers have been undertaking as a fundamental element of a violent and gendered hybrid North American culture.

In her edited collection *Produire la culture, produire l'identité?* Andrée Fortin writes of culture as the product of social activity, of tradition and the future, of a vision of the world and a shared identity ("Présentation" xi). Culture has never been coherent and homogeneous, especially if one remains mindful of the tensions between elite/high and popular culture (Fortin xi). In Bouchard's view, this distinction has been at the source of Quebec's inability and incapacity to "concretize its great visions and ambitions" ["concrétiser ses grandes visions et ambitions"] and to "let its dreams into the too restricted space that it – Quebec as a minority collectivity – occupies on the continent" ["faire entrer ses rêves dans l'espace trop restreint qu'elle (le Québec comme une collectivité minoritaire) occupe sur le continent"] (*Genèse* 180). For Bouchard, the fault lies completely with high, elite, or learned culture ("la culture savante") in Quebec, which has difficulties, even today, with the New World and its *américanité*, since it continues to relate to France in the Old World: "High culture has reconciled itself with Americanness but it has ulterior motives that bring it back to French references" ["La culture savante s'est réconciliée avec l'américanité mais il lui vient des arrière-pensées qui la ramènent vers ses références françaises"] *(Genèse* 178).

Fortin proposes, however, that this tension between popular and elite culture no longer exists, but has been replaced by "an agonizing struggle among several. New cultural and identitary referents are superimposed on those of an inherited culture, that of the nation and its various classes" ["un écartèlement entre plusieurs. De nouveaux référents culturels et identitaires se superposent à ceux de la culture 'héritée,' celle de la nation et ses variantes de classes"] (xi). She then poses these important questions: Is there still a common, shared culture in this current period characterized by pluralism? Must society itself be dissolved at the same time as a common culture and a shared identity? (xii). If culture is a space of both convergence and difference, can art bring along with its aesthetic pluralism an "identitary pluralism" ["pluralisme identitaire"] by exposing and proposing a new and different vision of the world? (xiv, xvi):

> The geographic tearing apart of French America leads to tension between the local and the continental; in certain regions ... French culture and identity are no longer a matter for communities but for the individuals who bear them. The community ... inhabits an evanescent territory where the link to language is problematic. Looming up at the same time are questions of the de-territorialization of a culture and of an identity group, of tearing apart and of networking; in this context, does the notion of the boundaries of a group make any sense any more? What are the criteria for belonging to this group? In the absence of a "real" territory, what hold can one have on public space? Does identitary space then necessarily become "imaginary"? [L'écartèlement géographique de l'Amérique française induit une tension entre le local et le continental; dans

certaines régions ... la culture et l'identité française ne sont plus affaire des communautés, mais des individus qui la portent. La communauté ... habite un territoire évanescent où le rapport à la langue est problématique. Surgissent donc simultanément la question de la déterritorialisation d'une culture ou d'un groupe identitaire, de l'écartèlement et du réseau; dans ce contexte, la notion de frontière du groupe a-t-elle encore un sens? Quels sont les critères d'appartenance à ce groupe? En l'absence de territoire "réel," quelle prise peut-on avoir sur l'espace public? L'espace identitaire devient-il alors nécessairement "imaginaire"?] (xix)

Fortin continues to ask troubling questions. For those in francophone North America and in Quebec in particular, only some are descendants of the French. Does one speak, therefore, of a heritage or an invention, of a fabrication of memory? What is the role of mass media in the transmission of culture? In other words, does the inevitable opening up of culture in our postmodern world necessitate the risk of losing identity? (xix).

In 1997 and 1998, thirteen Québécois intellectuals were asked to speak on a Montreal radio station for fifteen minutes on their perception of Quebec culture at the beginning of the new millennium ["Quelle est votre perception de la culture au Québec à l'aube du XXIe siècle?"], and their responses were gathered into a collection by Yvon Montoya and Pierre Thibeault (Montoya and Thibeault, *Frénétiques*). The respondents' comments were depressing, whether they focused on Quebec culture in general or more specifically on the state of its language. In their prologue the editors define culture as a rupture with the order of things, the search for a new way of being and a new mode of expression, a distance from what is known, and an eternal rebeginning (21). If, however, North America – and Quebec as part of it – is an abstraction because it is geographically isolated from Europe, then how does one take advantage of this rupture in some sort of dialogue and prevent the current smothering of the emergence of a culture here (27, 21)?

Suzanne Jacob – whose novel of infanticide I shall study in chapter 4 – paints a picture that is as depressing as some of the other respondents' comments: Quebec (and, I take it, North American) culture at the end of the twentieth-century is bland, boring, and mechanical. It assumes that someone is taking care of everything, while we wait for something to happen, for someone to take a gun and shout out loud so that we can watch the "event" on the television news. And yet there are still certain voices, some individuals who will create music and art – something that will be experienced by others, by us. It is our only hope (Jacob, in

Frénétiques 69–74). Perhaps the (female) voices I shall be studying are also causing something to happen, as they write about guns and shouting – here in the hands and words of imaginary women.

Many of the intellectuals who responded to the question about Quebec culture at the turn of the century mentioned the impoverished state of French – echoing once again the split between high/elite and popular culture. Similarly, many writers since the Quiet Revolution have managed either to "folklorize" their language or create gratuitous linguistic complexities that have nothing to do with "the real" (Montoya and Thibeault 16). The tension between high and popular culture is likewise emphasized:

There are two languages in Quebec: the official language, the academic one, that is the French language, and the Quebec language, that of the street, oral and not written, which the electronic media try, however, to institutionalize and others try to "literalize" ... The culture of Quebec is in trouble ... Even in literalizing it, Quebec "spoken" speech cannot allow the emergence of a culture because it does not offer any valuable knowledge of different levels of meaning ... [The language] cannot evolve, since in so doing it would lose the sole "way of speaking" that allows Quebecers to express their identity. The literalization of the "spoken" language is stuck in the past, in a bygone sense of the past. [Il existe deux langues au Québec: la langue officielle, académique, c'est-à-dire la langue française, et la langue québécoise, celle de la rue, orale et non écrite, que les médias électroniques tentent pourtant d'institutionnaliser et d'autres de 'littéraliser," ... La culture du Québec est en difficulté ... Même en le littéralisant, le "parlé" québécois ne peut permettre l'émergence d'une culture parce qu'il n'offre pas de valeur de connaissances en rapport avec les différents niveaux de sens ... [La langue] ne peut évoluer puisqu'elle perdrait de ce fait le seul "parlé" permettant au Québécois d'exprimer son identité. La littéralisation du "parlé" est en enlisement dans le passé, dans un sens révolu du passé.] (Montoya and Thibeault 19)

Not everyone agrees with this assessment of the existence of two languages in Quebec, the impoverished state of French, or even the construction of identity through language. Lise Gauvin, for example, in her 2000 text *Langagement: L'Écrivain et la langue au Québec*, writes positively about contemporary writers who no longer worry about language as a symbol of identity politics ["l'identitaire"] because it is now a symbol of liberty, of experimentation, of the imaginary. Tracing the history of language and writing in Quebec, Gauvin states first that in the nineteenth century, writers described their language as one of exile; it soon became one of refuge. As of the 1960s writers perceived language as a symptom and a scar; later, for women especially, it was transformed into a laboratory and an expression of transgression. More recently, literary language has become passage and trace – an object of mourning, desire, and fascination. Speaking one's language was to venture into one's imaginary territory, the best place for experimentation (Gauvin 209–12). In the last decade of the twentieth century, however, in Gauvin's view, language in Quebec has been modified as a result of a new distribution of linguistic functions in Quebec society: "At the same time as language is re-territorializing itself, writing is de-territorializing itself and is distancing itself from the problematic of identitary politics" ["En même temps que la langue se reterritorialise, l'écriture se déterritorialise et prend des distances avec le problématique identitaire"] (Gauvin 212). The intervention of other languages has become possible, and plurilingualism is now experienced less as a form of tension than as a form of "verbal and textual polysemy" [("polysémie verbale et textuelle" Gauvin 212); (see also Van Schendel, "Un Québec francopolyphonique" and Marco Micone, *Speak What,* with an analysis by Gauvin).] The identification of a Québécois literature must still consider language, but it surpasses language, as well, becoming synonymous with freedom: "Language is then perceived as a fictional more than frictional space, as the best place for invention" ["La langue est alors perçue comme un espace de fiction plus que de friction, comme le lieu par excellence de l'invention"] (Gauvin 213). In Gauvin's view, today's Québécois writer possesses an awareness of language as a vast laboratory of possibilities: "Such is the *linguistic commitment [langagement]* that their works show" ["Tel est *langagement* dont témoignent ses oeuvres"] (213). As I shall show, many of these writers under discussion perceive their fiction as a form of this linguistic commitmenmt [*langagement*] with social and gendered cultures.

QUEBEC POPULAR CULTURE, MEDIA, AND LITERATURE – "ONE OF THE *AMÉRICANITÉS*"?

Much of my discussion in the previous section of this chapter has been focused on Quebec's elite culture, but Quebec's *américanité* (Americanness) is also a part of and greatly influenced by popular culture – by this hybrid culture, a "culture of interstices" ["culture des interstices"]

(Bouchard, *Genèse* 182) that lives in a "between place" ["entre-lieu"], an interstitial space ["un espace interstitiel"] (Bernd 25), much like Bhabha's "in-between spaces." If the Québécois is more of a "French-speaking American"than a "French person from America" or "a sort of failed *Yankee*" ["Américain francophone" ... "Français d'Amérique" (as cited in Lemelin 101) "une sorte de *yankees* manqués"] (Pierre Monette 160), and if the Québécois "are fundamentally North American in their values, tastes, and ways of life" (Hero and Balthazar, *Contemporary Quebec and the United States* 199), then one needs to consider contemporary Quebec culture as *une américanité* among several in North America. Its cultural fields must also be understood, as I have noted above, within the context of tensions created by "Quebecization," "Canadianization," "Americanization/United States-ization," "Continentalization," and "Internationalization" (Lacroix 37).[37]

Only fairly recently have critics been paying more attention to the influence of American culture (read U.S.) and the cultures of the Americas on Quebec's popular culture. In their 1999 *Le Québec dans l'espace américain*, for example, Balthazar and Hero briefly discuss the "invasion" of American popular culture on television, films, magazines and books, and music in Quebec. They state that as of the 1950s, when Anglo-Canadian public television devoted a certain portion of its programming to popular U.S. programs, the French-language network of Radio-Canada defied this televised assault and produced, as of 1952, complete daily Canadian, and indeed Québécois, programming. Although these initial steps into television were clearly influenced by American programs, "far from abandoning itself to Americanization, this pioneering work first signalled the cultural emancipation and the national affirmation of the francophones of Quebec" ["loin de s'abandonner à l'américanisation, cette oeuvre de pionniers a d'abord signalé l'émancipation culturelle et l'affirmation nationale des francophones du Québec"] (187). Although the Québécois did watch American programs either on the English-Canadian network of Radio-Canada or with strong antennas that enabled them to receive signals from across the border, they seemed to have greatly preferred their own productions (Balthazar and Hero 188).

The language barrier did not block the penetration of American television into Quebec, however, and as of the 1960s, dubbed versions of U.S. programs made their way onto Quebec television screens. Soon, the advent of cable television and Québécois advances in understanding English caused a major shift; as of the 1970s almost half of the French-speaking population of Quebec was watching American television (Balthazar and Hero 188). The situation changed, however, in the 1980s; between 1984 and 1987, the level of viewing for Canadian (predominantly Québécois) programs increased from 52% to 62% (Balthazar and Hero 188). As of 1991 the fifteen most widely viewed programs in Quebec were all Canadian, and by 1996 in Montréal, 23% of the francophone population watched Radio-Canada, with that figure at 28% for all of Quebec. According to a poll in 1998, the six most popular programs in Quebec were local productions (Balthazar and Hero 189). American influence continued, however, and in 1996, four of the twenty most popular television programs in Quebec were American, and PBS drew a larger viewing francophone audience than the French TV5. American films broadcast on television were equally popular: 61% in 1990, with 37% on Radio-Canada and 29% on Radio-Quebec (Balthazar and Hero 189). Finally, the majority of video-cassettes sold in Quebec have come from the United States (Balthazar and Hero 190).

According to Dave Atkinson, there are two types of Americanization at work on popular culture: content – by which process certain values are transferred – and commercialization (60). In the first instance, prosperous and materialistic U.S. culture as seen on television programs comes into conflict with more traditional and less developed societies, creating aspirations that are impossible to achieve in certain locales (61). Québécois born at the beginning of the 1960s, he reports, were deeply affected by American television programming on Saturday and Sunday mornings: cartoons, Walt Disney, *Batman, Hawaii 5–0, Mission Impossible, Kojak,* and *Little House on the Prairie*, among others. Atkinson wonders if these children and adolescents "suffered" from a form of Americanization that led to a loss of their "national" values (62). For Québécois who were born in the early 1980s and were adolescents in the 1990s, television programs were different: there were fewer programs specifically for children, fewer American programs, and more successful Quebec shows (Atkinson 62) – with the number of American series almost cut in half by the end of the decade/century (Atkinson 62–3).

The past decade, however, has seen an increase in "téléséries" in Quebec television programming; these have borrowed from commercial American television series by imitating their form of production and their themes, universal enough to find buyers on the international market (Atkinson 63–4). Talk shows (*L'Ecuyer*, which imitates the *David Letterman Show)*, entertainment shows (*Flash*, which imitates

Entertainment Tonight), infomercials, no-cost reruns – these are examples that Atkinson offers to support his finding that the Americanization of Quebec television is closely allied with an imitation of American methods of production and programming (65–6):[38] "Americanization must therefore be thought of at a much more general level. One can thus make the hypothesis that there is a wholescale Americanization of television, both in Canada and in Quebec, in that the notion that we have today of these media is increasingly different from what one had in the 1950s. It is our notion of television itself which is continuously being Americanized" ["L'américanisation doit donc être pensée à un niveau beaucoup plus général. On pourrait ainsi faire l'hypothèse qu'il y a américanisation de la télévision dans son ensemble, au Canada et au Québec, en ce que la conception que nous avons aujourd'hui de ce média diffère de plus en plus de celle qu'on s'en faisait dans les années 1950. C'est notre conception même de la télévision qui s'américanise sans cesse"] (67). Atkinson sees Americanization as a process that tends to make Quebec television a commercial sector and gradually denies the possibility of having it play any other role than that which is dictated by market forces and commercial regulations (71).

One of the most interesting studies on popular culture and the influence of American culture focuses on televised novels, known as "téléromans" and often similar to soap operas. Véronique Nguyên-Duy makes the interesting point at the outset of her study that if the Québécois prefer their own francophone programs to anglophone shows, they also prefer francophone Québécois productions to foreign productions translated into French (132–3). What she is emphasizing in this statement is that the thesis that linguistic specificity serves as a barrier to protect local Quebec culture from the onslaught of American culture (132) does not suffice to explain the "health" of Quebec culture on the North American continent. If, as others have pointed out, for every American product there exists a Quebec equivalent, how does one account for the high popularity of very specific Québécois television programming – the "téléromans" and the "feuilletons québécois" (Quebec serials) – which draw one out of every two Québécois to the television screen (Nguyên-Duy 133, 135)? Nguyên-Duy sees these dramas – even those that focus on the private spheres of love and family – as increasingly social and ideological, serving as social, educational, and even civic instruments, raising issues of public debate, constructing a collective identity, and linking the "nation's" past to its future (146–7).[39]

Can one point to this same cause for the popularity of Quebec films? Certainly much has been published recently on national cinemas in general and whether they can survive in this global world, whose screens are dominated by Hollywood, in which transnational issues are portrayed in numerous cinemagraphic versions and languages. Concerns have been raised more particularly about Canadian and Quebec cinema.[40] Can one even speak of a Quebec national cinema when one has to consider a range from the successful international film *The Red Violin* to the wildly successful local/regional films *Séraphin, un homme et son péché* and *Les Boys*, not to mention *Les Boys II*, *Les Boys III*, and *Les Boys IV*, subsequently imitated by the Canadian *Men with Brooms*? Most critics of Quebec film tend to agree that despite the fairly recent decline in the number of films produced in Quebec (Balthazar and Hero 190), both historically and currently the vibrant Quebec film industry has managed to forestall a "takeover" by the American film industry, often producing *auteur* films considered more "artsy" than commercial Hollywood productions.[41]

We should note, however, that even in 1996, 87% of Quebec box office receipts still went to American films, compared to 97% in the rest of Canada, 54.7% in France, and 77% for the European Union countries overall (Balthazar and Hero 191). And even the financial successes of *Les Boys* in 1998 and *Séraphin* in 2002 were still very small in comparison to the monies earned by Hollywood blockbusters.[42] As Balthazar and Hero observe: "The American method in a Quebec sauce has succeeded better on television where rapid action series, sprinkled with violence and sex [more about that in the next section], have earned the larger public's support and high ratings in terms of its share of listeners. It was perhaps a way for Quebecers to digest Americanization" ["La méthode américaine à la sauce québécoise a mieux réussi à la télévision où des séries à l'action rapide, saupoudrées de violence et de sexe ont gagné l'adhésion du grand public et atteint des sommets en termes de cotes d'écoute. C'était là peut-être pour des Québécois une façon de digérer l'américanisation" (193)]. There are, of course, certain films that, although Québécois, have been described as being anchored ["ancrés"] on the planet Earth – Robert Lepage's *Le Confessional,* François Girard's *Le Violon rouge*, and Michel Poulette's *Louis 19* and *La Conciergerie* (Poulette 166) – but by and large, critics see Quebec film as its own genre – popular but not as popular as American movies. More recently, however, this may have changed: first with the double success at the 2003 Cannes Film Festival of Denys Arcand's *Les Invasions barbares*, which earned awards for best screenplay and best actress (Marie-Josée Croze), was distributed in the United States by Miramax (Odile Tremblay, "Festival de Cannes"), garnered good critical reviews, was nominated for two Oscars (best foreign film and best original screenplay) at the American Academy Awards, and won the Oscar for best foreign film; and second, with Jean-François Pouliot's first feature film, *La Grande Séduction/Seducing Dr. Lewis*, which won the world cinema dramatic audience award at the 2004 Sundance Film Festival and was subsequently distributed in the United States.

It is comedies, however, that have been most popular among Quebec movie-goers, and not the *auteur* films on which many Québécois film-makers have staked their artistic reputations, and about which most film scholars write. In one sense these popular-culture comedies represent a distinct Quebec society – the way certain Québécois, at least, like to see themselves (as in the *Les Boys* films) – and yet in another sense, such films also share an interesting mix of Québécois francophone culture and North American/U.S. mass culture (as in the *Elvis Gratton* films). Both aspects of popular Quebec cinema have resulted in three of the four most commercially successful films in Quebec in the past forty years being Louis Saia's 1997 *Les Boys*, his 1998 *Les Boys II*, and the 1999 *Elvis Gratton 2 – Miracle à Memphis* by Pierre Falardeau (the fourth, as indicated above, was *Séraphin*) (Gauthier, chapter 3).

Images of U.S. culture have been part of Quebec cinema for some time now. Even in the 1964 feature film *Le Chat dans le sac*, the director, Gilles Groulx, underscored the dual influences of Europe and the United States on Quebec culture through the interests of the two main characters. Other examples are: Frantz Fanon (whose writings were, of course, very significant to Quebec nationalists); *Parti Pris* (influential in the coming Quiet Revolution); the music of Vivaldi (a clear example of the high culture of Europe, although not specifically of France); and John Coltrane (a quintessential American popular culture icon) (see Gauthier, chapter 3).

But there was/is perhaps no more powerful icon of American popular culture than Elvis Presley, who inspired the escapades of the Québécois Elvis Gratton, who dresses like the Memphis rock star in Falardeau's feature-length compilation of short films from 1981–1985, *Elvis Gratton: Le King des kings*, and in his 1999 *Elvis Gratton: Miracle à Memphis*. More recent is the Québécois spectacle *Elvis Story*, popular both at home and in France, where it premiered in November 2003. American cultural imperialism and Quebec national identity in North America here blend in a comedic fashion (see Gauthier, chapter 3). From Denys Arcand's *Le Déclin de l'empire américain,* and now its sequel, *Les Invasions barbares*, to the insertion of Alfred Hitchcock's *I Confess* in Robert Lepage's marvellous *Le Confessional* and American rock and roll music in Léa Pool's equally stunning *Emporte-moi/Set Me Free,*[43] Quebec filmmakers seem not to be afraid of incorporating U.S. popular culture in such a way as to celebrate their own francophone North American cultural identity.

This pronounced awareness of a hybrid North American popular culture, however, also has its "downside," in the eyes of a number of Québécois cultural critics, since it can become an excuse to play into the economics of filmmaking as dominated by the United States. The result of this cultural/financial consciousness has been the recent making of Quebec films in English – tantamount to high treason for certain Québécois. Highly regarded and successful filmmakers like Robert Lepage (*Possible Worlds* in 2000), Denys Arcand (*Stardom* in 2000), and Léa Pool (*Lost and Delirious* in 2001, and even her 2004 *Le Papillon bleu* – filmed in English and Spanish, dubbed into French, and starring the American actorWilliam Hurt) have sparked debate in Quebec and beyond about the seriousness and effects of making films in the language of the "Other," given the close link in many people's minds between language and national/provincial identity. At the time of the 2000 Toronto Film Festival, articles in both *Le Devoir* and *The New York Times* approached this issue, with the Montréal newspaper declaring: "The danger is of losing our best francophone actors in the ocean of the language of the other. Danger also of chosing anglophone projects while sweeping under the rug our national realities" ["Le danger, c'est de perdre nos meilleurs joueurs francophones dans l'océan de la langue de l'autre. Danger aussi de choisir des projets anglophones en balayant sous le tapis nos réalités nationales"] (Odile Tremblay, "Tourner en anglais" B3). The American newspaper responded that this is really not a controversy but rather, citing Robert Lepage on this debate, the outcome of the fact that Quebec is a young society, not yet assured of its own identity in North America (Whyte sec. 2:16). Of course the issue is essentially one of funding, the selection of actors, distribution, and the possibility of an international audience, and these filmmakers have assured those who have questioned their motives that their films remain Québécois – that is, both personal and universal. Yet the threat of encroaching Americanization (here in a commercial and financial vein), rather than *américanité* continues to frighten some Quebec cultural observers.

Balthazar and Hero also see an increasing Americanization of popular music in Quebec. U.S. rock, rap, and other popular groups find crowds at their concerts, and despite regulations of the Conseil de la radio et des télécommunications du Canada (CRTC), radio air waves are filled with American music. These two critics of Quebec culture, however, although seeing this influence as part of a "shared Americanness" and a process of Americanization, also see it in another light as a "phenomenon capable of contributing to the enrichment of Quebec culture [for] a culture is nourished with exchanges, borrowing and cross-breeding" ["un phénomène susceptible de concourir à l'enrichissement de la culture québécoise [car] une culture se nourrit d'échanges, d'emprunts et de métissages"] (195). Although Americanization has become a form of international standardization that could eventually destroy cultural diversity and specificity: "Quebec can well put up with American cultural influence if it is at liberty to temper this influence by others" ["Le Quebec peut fort bien s'accommoder de l'influence culturelle américaine s'il est loisible de tempérer cette influence par d'autres"] (Balthazar and Hero 195–6). What this statement seems to imply is that Quebec popular culture could safely become increasingly inter- and transnational – like other "small" cultures.

What can bridge the gap between popular culture and "high" literature? Interestingly, it appears to be the North American "bestseller." The formulaic plots of these popular novels, posits Denis Saint-Jacques, illustrate that "identity is a plot" (178). He notes that approximately a third of the bestseller titles listed in Quebec come from the United States (180). The same basic plot, although inherited from nineteenth-century European popular literature, is used in more than two-thirds of the Quebec bestseller market (185): one has to face adversity with strength so that success will eventually prevail, and all previous wrongs will be redressed; one needs to endure here on earth so that one can ultimately find fortune and happiness and reap their rewards. As Saint-Jacques aptly points out, this formula for the best seller novel – in Quebec as throughout North America – constitutes what we call "the American Dream" (186).[44]

Although I turn more specifically to the "North American" literature of Quebec in chapter 3, it is worth mentioning here some of the issues that both literary and cultural critics have been tackling for some time now. Many of these concerns and themes are reflected in *L'Identité et le littéraire dans les Amériques*, edited by Bernard Andrès and Zilà Bernd. Here, as the editors state, "identity invents itself," and their contributors attempt to understand varying conceptions of *américanité*, the multiple processes of Americanization, the conflicting feelings arising from belonging to three Americas, and a comparative literary and cultural approach that is, in the final analysis, interamerican (Andrès and Bernd, "Préface" 9, 12).

Referring to the interstitial nature of American literatures which break down the binary structure of identity – as I have pointed out above and shall study in subsequent chapters – the Brazilian critic Zilà Bernd characterizes these literatures as creolized, composite, hybrid, and polyglot, and as texts that use parody and irony in order to destabilize (20–7). Jocelyn Létourneau, more specifically oriented toward francophone Québécois identity, sees in such literatures both a desire to vanquish and a fear of losing the other – both suggesting a difficulty in projecting their future in a globalized world ("Sur l'identité québécoise francophone" 61). He describes three ways in which the Québécois conceive of their rapport with alterity: opening up toward the other while avoiding losing oneself in that same realm; taking charge of one's emancipation while remembering one's alienation; and redefining group identity without confusing its historic attributes (Létourneau 61).

Pierre Monette, who has characterized the Québécois as Yankees who couldn't quite make the grade ["Yankees manqués"] also views the Quebec "nation" as an example of Anderson's "imagined community" (Monette 147, 148, 160). For Monette, it is not the culture of Quebec that is fragile, as many have defined it, but rather its cultural industries; French itself is precarious because of its small North American market (Monette 153). Quebec, its language, and its culture are all major minorities confronting the North American hegemony of the English language (Monette 159). There is nothing homogeneous about this francophone culture, however: "Identity has nothing of unity. It is, rather, a functional diversity. And America is the best display window for such a reality" ["L'identité ... n'a rien d'une unité. Elle est plutôt une diversité fonctionnelle. Et l'Amérique est la vitrine par excellence d'une telle réalité"] (Laroche 257).

It is indeed through this window of North American cultural identity that many critics have been recently viewing contemporary Quebec fiction and poetry. Richard Saint-Gelais and his colleagues, for example, ask many astute questions in their introduction to *Roman contemporain et identité culturelle en Amérique du nord* in order to frame the issue of North Americanness itself and its relationship to representation: "Is there a North-American identity that transcends both traditional, 'national' barriers and ethnic, sexual, communal differences, or even individual barriers? Is there such a thing as 'North Americanness' based on an identifiable community? ... In addition ... there are questions of *representation* and of how it relates to any national identity. Do these representations reflect an identity that is already constituted, prior to them? To what extent do these representations play a *constitutive* role, making them to a greater or lesser degree a formative element for this identity? And what to think of the subversive character of certain representations that undermine established representations or bring out their fictive nature, without an unequivocal link to the empirical or cultural reality?" (17–18). If, as I have pointed out and as these editors make clear, *américanité* is, as Chassay expresses it, "a symptom, one that eventually reveals the place from which one can speak and that gives a meaning to cultural space" ["un symptôme, celui qui permet éventuellement de révéler le lieu d'où on parle, de donner sens à l'espace culturel"] (Chassay 18), this Americanness "continually renews and transforms itself, cutting right across the discourse *about* 'Americanness' which simultaneously produces what it discusses, in a way similar to the concept referred to as performative" (Saint-Gelais, Lintvelt, Verhoeven, and Raffi-Béroud 18).

In addition, the authors distinguish *representation* from the *context of utterance*: although works of fiction are embedded in a given sociocultural context, one cannot assume that works produced in North American space are concerned with the representation of that particular space. The context of utterance, the place from which one is speaking, allows one to analyse the geographical, cultural, and social context, while recognizing that one cannot necessarily be certain of any preexisting reality (Saint-Gelais et al. 19). If, therefore, the concept of American has been taken over by the United States, then one must question whom one is addressing and what that individual hopes to achieve by proclaiming his or her Americanness (Saint-Gelais et al. 20). These concepts are particularly significant when the (subversive) speaking subject (author and/or protagonist) is a female who is undoubtedly linking her utterances to a reframed cultural reality of gender.

Saint-Gelais and his co-authors/co-editors also acknowledge that the postmodern Quebec literary text is one of alterity and duality, generating only virtual Americas (21). If the North American text represents an errand, a quest, then there is no real essence to North Americanness, and its fiction, like the continent itself, epitomizes Baudrillard's concept of a simulacrum (Saint-Gelais et al. 21–2). Indeed Baudrillard refers to

America as an "absolute simulacrum" (104, 126), a "perfect simulacrum" (28), and a "total simulacrum" (70), although he does not make clear why America and its fiction should be more of a simulacrum than that of any other locale, or especially any other fiction.

In any event, North Americanness is seen in this volume as a quest for American identity rather than as an affirmation (Morency 161) and as the development of a new concept of regionalism that opens up the possibility of new (ironically, local rather than universal) hegemonies (Saint-Gelais et al. 24–5). As Bertens remarks, "all literature has in a sense become regional" (257), since the universality and homogeneity of modernity has given way to the "imagined communities" [to cite Anderson again] of postmodernity (255). Multiculturalism has also taken over the sphere of national identity, as postmodernism has done in the sphere of individual identity (D'haen 36). North American cultural identity is, ultimately, seen as being torn among the founding myths and their contemporary versions, as well as between the traditional hegemony of the Anglo-Saxon male and the heterogeneity of communities in America today (Saint-Gelais et al. 23, 24). Both of these perceptions are germane to my study.

In a similar vein, Pierre Nepveu, one of the most astute literary and cultural critics of Quebec today, asks how one can truly live in America and develop any semblance of an inner life, since even the name "America" conjures up images of space, the "Kerouacian" road, discovery, conquest, heroism, perpetual nomadism, and wild nature – as I mentioned at the beginning of this chapter (Nepveu, *Intérieurs du nouveau monde* 26–7). If these images suggest an anti-intellectual conception of America, how can subjectivity be granted a place from which it can elaborate a culture? How can this place generate the possibility of adventure – albeit a different kind of adventure? Or, as Nepveu asks: "How especially can literature, in its insatiable appetite for resistance, turn away from the grand myths of space in order to invent, some place in a room, a house, a city, another way of being in the New World?" ["Comment surtout la littérature, dans son insatiable appétit de résistance, se détourne-t-elle des grands mythes de l'espace pour inventer, quelque part, dans une chambre, une maison, une ville, une autre manière d'être dans le Nouveau Monde?"] (27). In other words, and for my purposes, how can this hybrid, francophone, North American literature create a fragile – and yet powerful – subjectivity turned in on itself and its intimate universe instead of turned outward toward an expansive adventure in the more acceptable and usual North American literary tradition? Or as Chassay phrases it, how can contemporary Quebec fiction invent its own America in the face of a stifling United States with whom it maintains a schizophrenic relationship and when America is "everywhere" on the world scene (*L'Ambiguité américaine* 24, 27, 188)? These queries, as we shall see, will become even more problematic for the women writers whose work I shall be examining, as they develop their protagonists from fragile female subjects to powerfully violent actors in a North American landscape, creating both an interior – perhaps more typically French and Québécois – universe and a more typically American violent "adventure."

VIOLENCE IN QUÉBÉCOIS POPULAR CULTURE AND LITERATURE

In the aftermath of the 1995 referendum on Quebec sovereignty, along with a "partnership" ["partenariat"] with Canada, Marc Brière gathered a representative group of twenty Québécois from a wide spectrum of the population. The group eventually proposed a declaration that affirmed a number of points relative to their "nation." Among them was "the rejection of all physical or verbal violence" ["le refus de toute violence physique ou verbale"] (Brière 19). Despite the sincerity of this laudable goal, most Québécois – and certainly most Canadians – also realize the difficulty of achieving it, especially given the power of violent images from the United States that filter across the border. As Reid Gilbert, in his excellent essay "Mounties, Muggings, and Moose: Canadian Icons in a Landscape of American Violence," asks: "How do the images of self that fill Canadian popular entertainment differ from those that present America to Canadians in the entertainments that flood across our long, peaceful, but highly porous border? What has been the effect on a contemporary Canadian sense of self of seeing the strong, urban, and often violent images that fill American film and television?" (178).

This concern about the effect of violent images from what Canadians and Quebecers perceive as a substantially more violent society to the south is not a recent issue. In the 1920s, for example, the dominant circle of Quebec nationalists led by Abbé Lionel Groulx and L'Action française condemned American journalism, cinema, vaudeville, fashion, advertising, and dance halls for "spewing forth a mental and moral poison that imperiled the health of the French-Canadian community" (Rutherford 268). Provincial governments throughout

Canada established boards of censors to ban offensive films or cut any scenes that portrayed pictures of crime, horror, excessive drinking, loose conduct, religious or racial ridicule, or undemocratic opinions (as cited in Rutherford 268). By the mid-1930s, a survey of opinion showed that the images of American life that continued to be prevalent in Canada upset many Canadians, leading them to believe that their society was superior to the childlike, money-crazed, lawless, corrupt, immoral, and less cultured citizens of the United States (as cited in Rutherford 270).

If Lionel Groulx and his colleagues specifically mentioned American journalism as a negative influence on French-Canadians, he was probably referring to the "new" American form of journalism, dubbed "yellow journalism," which had become popular in the United States as of the late nineteenth century and which did, indeed, influence newspapers in Quebec. Characterized as journalism that catered to its readers with striking and startling headlines, illustrations, and sensational stories of crime, tragedy, divorce, and personal drama, yellow journalism was popularized by such American newspaper giants as Joseph Pulitzer and William Randolph Hearst (Bonville 79–80). There was at that time – and still is today – a difference of opinion as to whether this U.S.-style newspaper journalism had penetrated Canadian and Québécois presses, although Bonville cites evidence to prove that yellow journalism affected only a minority of newspapers – both in the United States and throughout Canada – and was a phenomenon exclusively of large cities (82). Using the major Montréal dailies *Le Star* and *La Presse* as examples, Bonville shows that Quebec reporters did begin to imitate their U.S. counterparts, especially in their style of crime reporting, exploiting readers' emotions, including even the most minor details of dreadful crimes, and sensationalizing incidents with large type and frightening headlines: "The most horrible of murderers/The autopsy of the body of Antoine Séguin ... brings to light ghastly facts. Poignant scene at the coroner's inquest ... Horrible ... A young man is crushed between two cylinders ... The anguish of a poor mother ..." ["Le plus horrible des meurtriers/L'autopsie du corps d'Antoine Séguin ... met à jour des faits affreux. Situation poignante à l'enquête du coroner ... Horrible ... Un jeune homme se fait broyer entre deux cylindres ... L'angoisse d'une pauvre mère ..."] (Bonville 89). Even in 1909 complaints of this nature were heard: "One can say of our newspapers ... that they are American newspapers written in French" ["On peut dire de nos journaux ... ce sont des journaux américains écrits en français"] (Bonville 90).[45]

If tabloid journalism made its way into Canada and Quebec as of the end of the nineteenth century, one must look at the advertisers in these newspapers who were underwriting the product and therefore, insisting on newspapers that would interest the largest number of readers: "So, the greatest number prefer the story of a sordid crime to an editorial on free trade" ["Or, le plus grand nombre préfère le récit d'un crime sordide à un éditorial sur le libre-échange"] (Bonville 93). In Quebec in particular, newspaper editors had to convince advertisers that they were applying American business methods to French-language journalism and that despite the language difference, their newspapers would also sell to a wide group of readers who were thirsty for criminal and sensationalized reporting. According to Bonville, Montréal newspapers were run by the same market forces as newspapers throughout Canada and the United States, and the content – announced by striking and overblown headlines – was the most effective tool to attract increasing numbers of readers (Bonville 95). As explained in 1899 by the editor of *La Presse* in a letter to the Archbishop of Montréal who had requested that the newspaper stop running stories about crime: "[*La Presse*] continues to publish portraits of murderers and sensational stories ... For, as you know, people are hungry for these things" "[*La Presse*] continue de publier des portraits de meurtriers et des histoires à sensation ... Car, vous le savez, le peuple est avide de ces choses"] (as cited in Bonville 95).

American-style yellow journalism in its most lurid manifestations did wane somewhat, but many of its characteristics had simply been absorbed into most daily newspapers. It remains true to say, however, that the reading public – whether in the United States, in English-speaking Canada, or in Quebec – is "hungry for these things" ["avide de ces choses"]. Is this taste indicative of an American way of life and its obsession with glamorous and sensationalized violence that has poured across the border to create a glamorously and sensationalized violent North American culture or rather, as discussed in chapter 1, the widely experienced ambivalent abhorrence of and fascination with violence that is a characteristic of human nature?

What is clear is that throughout the rest of the twentieth and into the twenty-first century, a rather schizophrenic attitude toward the United States has emerged, oscillating between admiration and dislike, mimicry and snobism, as Canadians – and Québécois, although less so – have increasingly accepted U.S. reality and behaviour. With the caveat that many Canadians and Quebecers are currently not enamoured of a

United States which they view as domineering and militaristic in face of much of the world, it is useful to return to Reid Gilbert, who has noted that "as Canadians seek a more sophisticated cultural image, they [chillingly] appear ready to incorporate this treatment of [U.S. glamorous] violence into the complex of their self-perceptions" (Gilbert 191).[46]

In one sense the Québécois have consciously avoided imitating the violence glorified in much American popular culture, as witnessed in the absence of villains, of truly evil characters, in their successful "téléromans": "In Quebec territory, it's not so much the good guys versus the bad guys who are engaged in a fight to the finish, but rather action versus inaction, strong versus weak, hard versus soft, winners versus losers" ["En terre québécoise, ce ne sont pas tant les bons et les méchants qui s'opposent dans un combat à finir que l'action et l'inertie, les forts et les faibles, les durs et les mous, les gagnants et les perdants"] (Nguyên-Duy 143). In another sense, however, one has to consider what Claude Jean Bertrand calls "a format ... a type of publication or broadcast, in a broad sense, such as game shows on radio and television or half-hour comedy series. And in a narrow sense, it is the news magazine *Time* being imitated by *L'Express*, the game show *Wheel of Fortune* having become *La roue de fortune* or the sitcom *Steptoe & Son* (in Great Britain) being transformed into *Sanford & Son* (in the United States)" ["un format ... un type de publication ou d'émission, comme, au sens large, les jeux d'argent à la radio et à la télévision ou une série comique d'une demi-heure. Et, au sens étroit, c'est le newsmagazine *Time* imité par *L'Express*, le jeu *Wheel of Fortune* devenant *La roue de fortune* ou le sitcom *Steptoe & Son* (de Grande Bretagne) transformé en *Stanford* [sic] *& Son* (aux États-Unis)"] (Bertrand 185).

Although Bertrand has identified three different types of "formats," for my purposes, the third type – whereby a certain ideology and vision of either the world or of human life underlies the cultural production – is the most relevant (Bertrand 186). Bertrand includes in this category the obviously simplistic Manicheism of certain U.S. police dramas, the simultaneous Puritanism and pathological obsession with a perverse form of sexuality that pervades U.S. talk shows, and in particular, "violence as an outlet ... as a solution to conflicts, or as spice, in televised newspapers, added to the sauce of the world of spectacle" ["la violence comme exutoire ... comme solution aux conflits, ou comme piment, dans des journaux télévisés mis à la sauce du monde du spectacle"] (Bertrand 186). He sees some imitative formats as successful (certain reality shows – witness the wild success of *Star Académie* – as well as talk shows and police dramas), others as partially acceptable to audiences (erotic magazines, court television, and home-shopping networks), and still others rejected (pornographic weeklies and radio talk shows expressing views of the extreme right) (Bertrand 188). Mentioning both European and Latin American formats, as well, Bertrand goes on to state that certain imported formats, especially those from the United States, can be dangerous, creating a cultural shock and unreal economic and political aspirations, injecting values contrary to one's cultural heritage – such as hyperviolence (Bertrand 192). He concludes on an optimistic note, however: all cultures can benefit from hybridization and fertilization from other cultures, and in many instances, the imitation surpasses the original (Bertrand 193). Is he speaking here, therefore, simply about another aspect of inevitable globalization, or should the United States be blamed for having (negatively) Americanized the world – without necessarily equating globalization with Americanization?

Finally, and more recently, Guy Paquette and Jacques de Guise have tackled the issue of the increase of violence on Quebec and Canadian television, clearly identifying the United States as the origin of this problem. Documenting the number of violent acts on television as of 1993, Paquette and de Guise report that between 1993 and 2001, violent acts displayed went from 772 to 3,689, an astounding increase of 378% in eight years. More worrisome is their further observation that since 1998 this violence has increased an additional 25% (535). Private and francophone channels broadcast more violence than both public and English-language channels – indeed by a factor of two – but the cause may well be a preference on francophone channels for films that contain more violent scenes than television programs do (535–6). Unfortunately, 39% of these televised acts of physical violence are seen before 8:00 p.m. and 88% before 9:00 p.m., making them largely accessible to young viewers (536). Paquette and de Guise emphatically state that 83% of these acts of violence on television in Canada and in Quebec occur as part of U.S. programming, especially in films, where they are particularly brutal. In Canada, the Québécois produce fewer televised violent acts (2.1% of the total number of acts), as compared to 7% in English-speaking Canada (537). What is interesting, however, is that French-language programs show more psychological violence – at the same level as in the rest of Canada – stemming most likely from the popularity of the "gentle" "téléromans" discussed above (538). Paquette and de Guise speculate, however, that such violent programming on

Quebec television is not a direct cause of violence in real life: francophone television is more violent than anglophone television, and yet Quebec has lower crime levels than the rest of Canada (541). As I have indicated earlier in this study, although there is no simple and direct correlation between representational and real violence, the connections are there, adding to a general atmosphere of violence that frightens and repulses – and yet attracts viewers.

NEGATIVE ASPECTS OF *AMÉRICANITÉ*, OR THE AMERICANIZATION OF QUEBEC?

If Québécois culture has indeed been influenced by a United States culture and way of life that is perceived as more violent and more titillated by violence, and if Québécois culture has also imitated, absorbed, and made its own that very U.S. culture and way of life, can one speak of the violence evident in certain Quebec literary texts as its own brand of *américanité* or North Americanness? And can one really speak of a clear negative influence from the United States in reference to (male) violence on Canada and on Quebec? In some sense, the answer to both of these questions can be affirmative, since there are so many adaptations and variations of North American (i.e., U.S.) way of life, popular culture, and even high culture throughout both Canada and Quebec – and the world. Indeed, one could mention transnational cultures that blame, decry, and berate an internationalism/globalism (often greatly based on and influenced by the United States), and yet continue to watch, consume, and produce products teeming with violence, erotica, and sexuality – cultural products created both by men and, increasingly, by women.[47]

But can one say that the violent representations of life in American popular culture and on the streets of the United States, teaching that violence is a way to settle issues and provide justice, are direct negative influences on the artistic creators in Quebec, especially on the fictional women whom I shall discuss in novels created by women writers? Yes, there has been an increase in erotic, sexual, and violent fictional characters – perhaps after the violent representations of the North American landscape in such Quebec novels as Nicole Brossard's *Le Désert mauve* and Marie-Claire Blais's *Visions d'Anna*. But it is still difficult to understand why the number of violent female protagonists has increased. As suggested above, I believe that certain women writers have been influenced by, or are reflecting, the sensationalism of newspapers and the continual "breaking news" of the media in their outcry that there is a tremendous increase in actual violence by women and girls. As I shall emphasize, however, much of this literature is parodic – of such media events, of (particularly U.S.) male violence, and of the ensuing public moral panic, but novels about infanticide and filicide, as well as about serial killers, are not parodies; they are disturbingly serious literary texts. These texts, too, reflect our fascination with such cases that always make the news.

It is probably accurate to say, therefore, that this "high" literature that I shall analyse in the remaining chapters is in the process of creating – and indeed has already created – a metafiction of popular culture, influenced by mass media reporting that is preoccupied by – and often even obsessed with – issues of violence. I can add that when seen in the context of our simultaneous condemnation and fascination with violence and our lasting stereotypes about gender, as I have underscored in chapter 1, these literary texts, created by women writers who have "handed over" violence to their female protagonists, reflect and inform our very views of what it means to live on a globalized North American continent that is alive with shifting cultural boundaries, the meshing of popular and high cultures, the liberation from traditions, rules, and preconceived ideas, and especially the changing of gender roles, all of which contribute to the breaking apart of long-held binary constructions.

3

Who's the Subject Now? Female Imagination and Representations of Sex and Violence

THE SEXUALITY AND VIOLENCE OF FEMALE REPRESENTATION/THE REPRESENTATION OF FEMALE SEXUALITY AND VIOLENCE

"Re-vision," says Adrienne Rich in a 1971 essay,[1] has revolutionary potential. Re-vision can be revolutionary when understood as "the act of looking back, of seeing with fresh eyes, of entering an old text from a new critical direction ... an act of survival." Enriching the term even more, Rich calls it a "drive to self-knowledge ... more than a search for identity ... part of our refusal of the self-destructiveness of male-dominated society ... how we can begin to see and name – and therefore live – afresh" ("When We Dead Awaken: Writing as Re-Vision" 35). Linda Williams, borrowing a decade later from Rich's essay in her analysis of a recent and general revision of pornography made by and for women, extends this re-vision to "an actual *re-vision* of hard core by women authors" (232). For Williams, such a re-vision of old texts has developed into the notion that for women, within a traditionally male genre, "survival" means "transforming oneself from sexual object to sexual subject of representation" (232).

For my purposes, "re-vision" – both in Rich's original interpretations and in Williams's adaptation – is a particularly useful concept. It relates first to the visual image in the title of this study, in which re-visioning becomes a "re-framing" of gender – through new, bold, and unsettling texts – in contemporary cultures. Women's attempts to transform themselves from sexual and violent object-victims to sexual and violent speaking subjects of representation (see Irigaray 167) constitute another form of "re-vision," as I shall discuss here, expanding on my earlier discussion of the violence of representation and the representation of violence. This chapter will also continue the enquiry begun in the previous chapter into the literature of Quebec at the end of the twentieth and beginning of the twenty-first centuries, by focusing more specifically on this North American society as it is created and viewed by women writers. I shall pay particular attention to a novel by Hélène Rioux that forms a bridge between Quebec and the United States, while hinting at the transformation – at least in the female mind – from violated female object to violating dangerous subject. I then move to eroticism and graphic sexuality in the female imagination, analysing texts from Quebec and placing them in a more global (North American and French) context. An exploration of sexuality and cruelty/violence in woman-authored texts from Quebec (with references to the U.S., Britain, and France) will form the fourth section of this chapter. A discussion of overt female literary violence in a number of texts follows, leading to a conclusion that will, in turn, link to specific forms of violence – infanticide and serial killing – which I shall treat in the following two chapters.

Sociologist Judith Lorber has proposed that gender imagery is "the cultural representation of gender and the embodiment of gender in symbolic language and artistic productions that reproduce and legitimate gender statuses"; further, she suggests, "culture is one of the main supports of the dominant gender ideology" (Lorber 30–1). In this context, the female writers I bring forward here have recently been questioning and changing this cultural representation by trying to legitimate different gender statuses and break open our culture's dominant gender ideology. They are attempting to re-frame these cultures (or "dismantle the frame," as McPhersen calls it [10]) by co-opting and redefining both the violence of representation and the representation of violence.

In reviewing the investigations into issues of violence and representation – Ackley, Tanner, Armstrong and Tennenhouse, Kowalewski, and De Lauretis, among others – many of whom base their studies on earlier work by Bakhtin, Baudrillard, Foucault, and Derrida (see chapter 1), I wondered if artistic representations aestheticize violence by distancing the audience/viewer/reader (Prince 27–8), and I suggested that violent images are fundamentally "an artifact embodying ideological assumptions," leading to what was decried in the 1960s as a "pornography of violence" (Sharrett 10, 12). I mentioned the notion of gender as narrative (Tavris) and spoke about narrative as a site for political struggle (Daniels). It was confirmed for me that we are in the "season of the (textual) bitch" (Aguiar). In particular, I agree with Teresa De Lauretis when she states that the "representation of violence is inseparable from the notion of gender" and that "violence is en-gendered in representation" ("The Violence of Rhetoric" 240).

In discussing Hollywood and the woman killer, Christine Holmlund makes reference to a 1990 essay in which De Lauretis[2] argues that at any moment in time, "a 'standard frame of visibility' determines 'what can be seen, and eroticized' in both cinema and society." Yet, says Holmlund, this frame, which De Lauretis calls "representability," can and does change: "what is portrayed and what is perceived shift over time, according to who is looking, at whom, when and where" (Holmlund 130). Susanne Kappeler had in 1986 already made a similar observation in reference to "the pornography of representation," a concept I shall apply to the "sexual violence and violence of female representation." Kappeler finds that representation is too often interpreted merely as a reflection of reality, and people neglect to ask: "Who is holding the mirror, for whose benefit, and from what angle?" (2): "Representations are not just a matter of mirrors, reflections, key-holes. Somebody is making them, and somebody is looking at them, through a complex array of means and conventions. Nor do representations simply exist on canvas, in books, on photographic paper or on screens. They have a continued existence in reality as objects of exchange; they have a genesis in material production. They are more 'real' than the reality they are said to represent or reflect. All of these factors somehow straddle the commonsense divide between fiction and fact, fantasy and reality" (3).

Clearly echoing Foucault and others, Kappeler goes on to explain that "fiction wants no part *in* reality, it is the 'Other' to the real. It is the surplus of the real" (9).[3] As such, the structure of representation "extends to 'perceptions' and self-images"; it is fundamental to conceptualization and is centred on the subject: "Perception is the representation of something to oneself, a conflation of the author and the audience in one single subject" (32–3). Kappeler is speaking of pornography constructed primarily by men for men even if there is, at times, an attempt to privilege the female point of view. But what if the author is female and intends her feminine erotic, sexual, and violent representations for consumption by a female audience? Who then moves into the subject-position role?

Perhaps most germane to this potential subject-position in the form of a (sexually) violent woman created by a woman – and related to my earlier discussion of the "monstrous," especially as described by Halttunen and Halberstam (see chapter 1) – is what Mary Russo calls the risk, excess, and modernity of "the female grotesque." The grotesque is reminiscent of the cave, the "grotto-esque," the low, hidden, earthly, dark, material, visceral space that evokes the cavernous anatomical female body – a metaphor that valorizes traditional images of the earth mother, crone, witch, and vampire. It also encompasses the terror and revulsion of blood, tears, vomit, and excrement (Russo 1–2). Russo recounts that by the end of the nineteenth century, the grotesque had deepened from the carnivalesque (as in Bakhtin) and the uncanny (as in Freud) to the criminal – often associated with the outrageous, the hilarious, and even the comic (7).[4] It became a trope of the body: the carnivalesque lower stratum of the people; the degradation and filth of low culture. And it underwent a social transformation into repressed political consciousness (again see Bakhtin). The uncanny became associated with the deformed, the excessive, and the abject, in which female hysteria played the role of the out-of-bounds alien (again as created by Freud). And, as Julia Kristeva has shown us, the social and political potential of transgression, along with the linguistic transgression of norms, codes, and language structures, led to a fascination with the extreme, the derangement of identity, and the abject and horrorible (Kristeva 208).

Russo writes also of the grotesque as a deviation from the norm, invariably identified with the female: "The expression 'female grotesque' threatens to become a tautology, since the female is always defined against the male norm" (14). A space of risk and abjection, the grotesque defines and explains a number of associated codings: Medusa, crone, bearded woman, fat lady, tattooed woman, unruly woman, Hottentot Venus, starving woman, hysteric, and vampire (Russo 14). Although Russo refers to the criminal in the history of the grotesque, links historical associations of the grotesque with social and sexual deviances, and extends her definitions to include new technological and biomedical creatures such as Donna Haraway's simians and cyborgs, capable of monstrous metamorphoses (15), she does not explicitly list the sexual, the sexually violent, and the violent woman as categories. I do. These literary creations by women writers also emerge as a "deformation of the normal," suggesting "provisional, uncomfortable, even conflictual coalitions of bodies which both respect the concept of situated boundaries and refuse to keep every body in its place" (16). This is the new world of the sexuality and violence of female representation, and of the representation of female sexuality and violence that is characteristic of many writings by a number of women in Quebec as we begin a new millennium.

AMÉRICANITÉ /NORTH AMERICAN SOCIETY AT THE TURN OF THE MILLENNIUM: THE VIEWS OF QUEBEC WOMEN WRITERS

Il y a là, quelque chose d'une "révolution" beaucoup moins "tranquille" qu'on aurait cru, car le nihilisme québécois, au sein de l'écriture, se vit dans une violence radicale, à la limite du terrorisme. Violence qui est celle de la dégradation elle-même (du langage, de l'histoire, de l'être), violence du grotesque, violence du corps et de la matière impossibles à sublimer et à interpréter. Il faudra un certain temps pour que tout cela s'apaise.

[What we have here is something of a "revolution" much less "quiet" than one would have believed, for Quebec nihilism, at the heart of writing, is experienced in a radical violence verging on terrorism. Violence which is that of degradation itself (of language, history, and being), violence of the grotesque, violence of the body and of matter, all impossible to sublimate and to interpret. Some time will be needed before all this subsides.]

Pierre Nepveu, *L'Écologie du réel* 138–9

Pierre Nepveu's seminal *L'Écologie du réel*,[5] which focuses on Québécois poetry and fiction of the 1960s, 1970s, and especially the 1980s, provides a powerful backdrop and context for my study of texts from the mid-1980s to the early years of the twenty-first century. By privileging literary genres such as the burlesque, irony, humour, "ti-pop," violence, caricature, the demonic, hysterical, clownish, and apocalyptic, Nepveu allies himself with Russo in her investigation into the grotesque. He equates the failure of realism with the failure of representation and ultimately with the failure of Quebec itself (134–5). Referring to the novel's power to evoke the "suffering-pleasure of incompletion" ("souffrance-jouissance de l'inachèvement" 136), he puts contemporary Quebec fiction in the context of writings with an apocalyptic tone (see Derrida) – a rhetoric of disaster, a catastrophic subject, a fragmentary being, hyper-alterity, world theatricality, ritual and ceremony, hyper-stimulation, perpetual disorder, and neo- and pseudo-primitivism

(155–70). Drawing an interesting link to American popular culture, Nepveu states that recent Quebec women's literature (specifically in reference to Yolande Villemaire's *La Vie en prose*) consists of a strategy to live contemporary nihilism as psychic and energetic: "Not as a reconquest of the true, but as a Nietzschean affirmation of power, as an accession, simultaneously Dionysian and ludic, of superwoman, alias Wonder Woman"[6] ["Non pas comme reconquête du vrai, mais comme affirmation nietzschéenne de la force, comme avènement à la fois dionysiaque et ludique de la surfemme, alias Wonder woman"] (170). Through stages, from hedonism to a return to subjectivity and representation, to post-formalism and post-modernism, the contemporary "real" has become, for Nepveu, hyper-referential, hyper-real, and hyper-symbolic, as it simultaneously proclaims its hybridity, impurity, and alterity (177, 185, 208–9). Post-Québécois culture and literature, with its plurality of centres (219–20), has become Baudrillard's ritualistic and transgressive, and Kroker and Cook's excremental (212–14), reminiscent, once again, of Russo's concept of the grotesque.

But have the nihilism, radical violence, violent self-degradation, and violence of the grotesque and the body subsided since the 1980s in Quebec culture and literature, or are they alive and well? As we have seen in chapter 2, Nepveu himself, ten years later in *Intérieurs du nouveau monde,* wondered if it was even possible to create an inner, subjective life – a different type of adventure – in Quebec, given the anti-intellectual conception of America and its wild and heroic space of conquest (27). And as I have also wondered, can this hybrid, francophone, North American literature create a new form of subjectivity turned in on itself, or must it turn outward toward the more acceptable North American (i.e., U.S.) literary tradition with its myth of expansive – and frequently violent – adventure? More specifically, how do certain contemporary women writers of Quebec work to place their powerfully sexual and ultimately violent female subjects in the liminal, intersticial, "in-between nation-space" (Bhaba 4), and "third space" of both an interior North American francophone world and a more typically American (and even global) violent culture? Do they even desire to achieve the former?

As I have noted in chapter 2, much has been written about the literature and culture of Quebec, both as they oppose and incorporate U.S. culture and literary tradition, especially toward the end of the twentieth century, particularly in reference to language, the city, and "violent" literary texts by writers such as Jacques Godbout, Nicole Brossard,

Monique LaRue, and Madeleine Monette. Jules Tessier in particular, speaks of the dialectic between a dominant and a dominated language, the insertion of English in certain francophone texts, the "deterritorialization" of French, and the "deschizophrenialization" of writers (30–1). Sherry Simon sees in the strangeness of language a means by which one can deconstruct the fixed and highlight the "mixed" in textual innovation (*Le Trafic des langues* 20). Simon Harel contrasts the national text and the extra-territorial text (88). Gérard Bouchard and Yvan Lamonde discuss "l'américanophilie" ("Americanophilia") and the victory of popular/mass culture over elite culture (170–1). Jaap Lintvelt, Richard Saint-Gelais, Will Verhoeven, and Catherine Raffi-Béroud write of America as a novelistic world and the post-modern Quebec literary text as one that generates virtual ("imagined") Americas, the epitome of Baudrillard's simulacrum,[7] whereby cultural identity establishes itself in multiple sites at the intersection of invention and reinvention, and whereby it shapes – and is shaped by – novel writing (21–2, 27). Theo D'haen examines the issues related to the development of multiculturalism and postmodernism in the United States and Canada, stating that while they have spelled the death of the grand American narrative, "what passes as multiculturalism on the North-American continent goes by the name of postcolonialism in the rest of the anglophone world" (36, 38). Debates continue to rage over whether Quebec literature can be identified as postcolonial, but D'haen sees narratives based on race, ethnicity, class, and gender as essentialist in nature, substituting other scripts for the tyranny of the former grand master narrative (39). If, as Linda Hutcheon claims, Canadian novelists have – often through the use of parody – contested the canonical myths and forms of both European and American literatures (6), then, similarly, the Quebec women writers under consideration here are currently contesting – often through the use of parody – the canonical and tyrannical myths and forms of European/French, American, North American, and especially male literature.

Contested North American Space

A number of critics have tackled the concept of contested space and locale in their studies of Québécois literature within a North American context, often in reference to specific authors and texts. Hilligje Van't Land, for example, in her work on Jacques Godbout's *Une Histoire américaine*, defines novelistic space and discusses the rapport between this complex notion and character and ideology. She describes Godbout's Californian space as imprisoning and alienating, a space that soon lets fall its "heavenly mask to reveal its hellish face" ["masque paradisiaque pour dévoiler son visage infernal"] (254). The sunny yet dark California of drugs, rape, and murder continues to fascinate Godbout's Quebec protagonist, but he is expelled from it – back into what Godbout sees as the closed, restrictive, prison-like, and ultimately precarious and fragmented culture of Quebec (260, 262, 264).

Referring specifically to novels by Madeleine Monette and Monique LaRue, Jean-François Chassay relates how the American ambiguity of the Quebec novel is predicated on the image of the city, how the image of Montreal can be both deformed and transformed against an American reality of cities such as New York and San Francisco (168). New York, in particular in Monette's *Petites violences*, becomes a complex metaphor, a "mise en abîme," of violence, in which monstrous crowds of urban dwellers engender a powerful violence that in turn engenders urban chaos (170). Ironically in this novel, the violence of Montreal is the "real" one, whereas the violence of New York is the fictitious spectacle of academic conferences, the discourse of violence as mediated by the media (173–5). Similarly, the hyper-reality and the confusion between the original and the perfect copy that form the backdrop for LaRue's *Copies conformes* transform San Francisco into a fictitious American site[8] from which the novelist can explore connections among reality, memory, and history on the American continent (182–4). Chassay concludes by observing that these two novels attempt to make sense of the reality of a city like Montreal by invoking other urban spaces. Fearful of losing the Quebec metropolis, Monette and LaRue distance it just as it becomes increasingly important: "The city is precisely all that remains when reference points disappear" ["La ville, c'est justement tout ce qui reste quand les points de repère disparaissent"] (185). In his final comments on these novelistic urban landscapes, Chassay quotes Jim Morrison's lyrics – "Save us, city" – which prefigure a frightening North American world as viewed, or perhaps imagined, by a Québécois female protagonist created by a female novelist – Hélène Rioux's Éléonore.

In an earlier critical piece, Chassay lamented that contemporary Quebec was having a very difficult time inventing its own version of America because of its stifling and aggressive neighbour to its south ("Reflets des États-Unis" 15). Karen Gould, in her work on rewriting America, argues that the fiction works of Monette, La Rue, and Brossard, among others, have articulated a vision of Americanness that raises issues of gender, minority cultural status, and postmodernity. For Gould, these novelists, in extending their feminist critique of gender and gender relations to the entire North American continent, have broadened their scope of investigation ("Rewriting 'America'" 189). Examining violence, postmodernity, and parody in these novels, Gould maintains that: "Refiguring 'America' thus means rewriting the American story ... from the point of view of gender, francophone minority culture, and transculturalism" (189). The newer feminist writers under consideration in this study have also chosen to rewrite this story and to re-envision/re-vision/re-frame a gendered America as a contested space and the locale of sexuality, sexual violence, and violence by women.

Female Eroticism in a Shortened Form

Like many Quebec writers of fiction, a number of these women authors have a preference for short literary genres, for brief sequences that are easily visualized. Guy Poirier has pointed out that their fascination for "the short form and cultural snapshots" ["la forme brève et instantanés culturels"] (6) stems from a need to represent fragments of images visually and decode them rapidly. This medium – what he calls the "vidéosphère" – reinvents the parameters of the "logosphere," causes the disappearance of boundaries between genres that were so important to a "graphosphère," and replaces them with a new reign of senses and images (6). Many audiences today prefer the short clips, fast images, and hypertexts of videos, films, and television, and "my" women writers often appropriate the forms and images of tough, sexual, and violent women from popular-culture artifacts such as comic books and fringe-fandoms. The primacy of images, the visual instant, the "passage from the literary to the popularized media" ["le passage du littéraire au médiatisé"] (Poirier 7–8), the intrusion of the media into the symbolic, the imitation of coded language sound bites from television, and "humour capsules" ["des capsules d'humour"] (Poirier 10–11) – these characteristics of contemporary Quebec literature are all satisfying for today's readers who find that earlier texts simply had too many words. Referring *On Television*, the important work done by Pierre Bourdieu on the symbolic violence of television and its move toward voyeurism and exhibitionism exemplified by talk shows that privilege slices of life,[9] Poirier defines these postmodern cultural objects as "successions of images, texts, or filmed or acoustic sequences [that] bring about a compression of temporal unity and a condensation of mental activity ... according to a model of immediate or instantaneous gratification, freed from the mediation of written signs" ["successions d'images, de textes ou de séquences filmiques ou sonores [qui] amènent une compression de l'unité temporelle et une condensation de l'activité mentale ... selon un modèle de la jouissance immédiate ou instantanée, délivré de la médiation des signes de l'écriture"] (14). The short story has thus become, for Poirier, *the* literary form from which readers can glean one central, concentrated, and unified episode. The short story is synonymous with rupture, silence, interruption, the unsaid ["non-dit"], syncopated rhythms, and repetitive micro-unities, a genre that adapts well to the detective story (that stalwart of representative violence), science fiction, and erotic tales, and which constitutes the fragmented and vulnerable privileged form of a national minority that is Quebec (19–20, 22). Although a number of the short stories that I analyse below do fit into Poirier's framework, the female imagination creating them tends to push the erotic further and more deeply into uncharted realms.

One of the earliest critics to remark upon this tendency toward the erotic, as well as the recurrent use of urban themes, linguistic directness, humour and sarcasm, and more accessible prose, was Luise von Flotow. What is significant in von Flotow's observations (in addition to her analysis of the erotic, to which I turn in the third section of this chapter) is her insistence that this "post-feminist writing," perfected in the short story, highlights socio-political questions of poverty, sickness, drugs, immigrant life, urban life, and multiculturalism ("La Relève féminine" 57). This is a writing that is freer in language, written for a larger public, implicitly feminist but with interests that are less theoretical, less abstract, and sometimes fantastic (58). As von Flotow sees it, there is a certain feminist "engagement" in these short stories, but only as part of a larger struggle,[10] in which these women writers use language as their major weapon (58). In texts set primarily in urban Montreal or Paris, poverty is mostly female, and violence is familial; the murderous and insane rage of the female protagonist, according to von Flotow, is that of the abandoned and betrayed woman (58–9) – an observation that applies only to some of the texts that I shall consider. As well as using traditional forms, these postfeminist writers recount situations, life fragments, and fantasies in more readable and more accessible texts, such as "journaux intimes" (diaries) and inner monologues: "The female narrator, often in the first-person singular, recounts her situation in order to understand it herself ... in order to make life, circumstances, problems comprehensible" ["La narratrice, souvent à la première personne, raconte sa situation afin de la comprendre ... pour rendre compréhensible la vie, les circonstances, les problèmes"] (62–3). In von Flotow's analysis, these contemporary female Quebec writers desire to be read, to be readable, accessible – even popular – and to move a public by engaging them differently (64).

Metafeminism

Lori Saint-Martin, in her 1997 critical study *Contre-Voix: Essais de critique au féminin*, introduces her own concept of "métaféminisme." Echoing writers and critics as diverse as Suzanne Jacob and Lisa Duggan, Saint-Martin states up front that "writings do not evolve in some beyond with no relationship to the real" ["les écrits n'évoluent pas dans un quelconque au-delà sans liens avec le réel"] (10). She initially pays homage to earlier Quebec feminist writers such as France Théoret and Suzanne Lamy and to their recognition of the emergence of a feminine subject in language as specifically female and not as defined by men (45–7). Calling von Flotow's (and others') term "post-feminist" pernicious at best, Saint-Martin defines Quebec literature after 1980 as "a writing linked to what has been called 'modernity,' marked by experimentation, by narrative and formal ruptures" ["une écriture liée à ce qu'on a appelé 'la modernité,' marquée par l'expérimentation, par les ruptures narratives et formelles"] (236). She then introduces her concept of metafeminism as "after" feminism, ["après"], which goes beyond "post": it integrates the past rather than abandoning it; it does not announce the decline of feminism but rather accompanies and envelops it; and it suggests and signifies transformation, participation, and metamorphosis: "Thus, metafeminist texts affirm their rootedness as much as their difference, suggest that they go further while at the same time commenting, prolonging, and invigorating feminism rather than repudiating it" ["Ainsi, les écrits métaféministes affirment autant leur enracinement que leur différence, suggèrent à la fois qu'ils vont plus loin et qu'ils commentent, prolongent et vivifient le féminisme plutôt que de le renier"] (237).

Like voices of what is in the United States currently termed Third-Wave Feminism, these new metafeminist writers do not, according to Saint-Martin, use the word "feminism" – indeed, they keep their distance from it. Their stance says "yes to feminism in life, no to the enslavement of writing to a cause. Freedom of expression takes precedence over political commitment" ["oui au féminisme dans la vie, non à l'asservissement de l'écriture à une cause. La liberté d'expression prime l'engagement"] (238). They question the strategies of older feminists, but they integrate similar concerns into their fiction (239). Even though their writings are more intimate and accessible – and here Saint-Martin agrees with von Flotow – they still borrow from older feminist writers and demonstrate continuity rather than rupture, without actually speaking of collective feminism (240): "There is little question of feminism as a movement or as an ideology – unless it is cast in an ironic vein ... Gone are the collective struggles; gone are the calls for solidarity. Instead, personal experience is omni-present, the form more or less traditional ... the writing relatively accessible ... In general, the quest for a specifically feminine writing, for a female-writing, seems to have been abandoned" ["Il y est peu question du féminisme comme mouvement ou comme idéologie – sinon sur le mode ironique ... Finies les luttes collectives, finis les appels à la solidarité. Au contraire, l'expérience personnelle est omniprésente, la forme, plus ou moins traditionnelle ... l'écriture relativement accessible ... En général, la quête d'une écriture spécifiquement féminine, d'un langage-femme, semble abandonnée"] (241).

And yet this new metafeminist writing still questions and remains preoccupied with concerns associated with feminism: the place of women in culture, society, and language; the role of the feminine in history, literature, myth, and psychoanalysis; relationships between mothers and daughters, among women, and with men (241):[11] "Rather than crying revolt or calling out for an insurrection, metafeminist writings ask questions that destabilize and make one think" ["Au lieu de crier une révolte ou d'en appeler à l'insurrection, les écrits métaféministes posent des questions qui déstabilisent et font réfléchir"] (242). For Saint-Martin, metafeminist texts are less "committed" ["engagés"] than those of radical feminism; they are less serious and more playful, less hermetic and less dense, but more ambiguous and personal; they present historical, political, and discursive issues but treat them with the bias of a life and a voice; they prolong feminism rather than contesting it; they do not vacate feminism, but rather absorb it, interrogate it, and make it evolve (265–7). And, perhaps most pertinent to this study, in these metafeminist texts: "Not only has the woman appropriated the gaze until now reserved for the man ... but she has also opened up a real – and new – curiosity for the other" ["Non seulement la femme s'est-elle approprié le regard jusque-là réservé à l'homme ... mais perce une réelle – et nouvelle – curiosité pour l'autre"] (267). This newly appropriated female look, for many contemporary writers in Quebec and elsewhere, does indeed open up a new curiosity about the other. But it also turns its gaze upon the self, men, and children as the other, reframing and recreating a culture where the new female subject takes centre-stage both as an erotic, sexual, and violent voice of identity and power in control (McPherson 7) and as a person of agency.

Brossard, LaRue, and Monette

Before examining some lesser known but exemplary works of fiction that illustrate women's writing in the context of *américanité*, it will be helpful to mention three novels that have received substantial critical attention in this regard:[12] Nicole Brossard's *Le Désert mauve*; Monique LaRue's *Copies conformes*, and Madeleine Monette's *Petites Violences*.

Perhaps no other contemporary woman writer and no other contemporary feminist novel has garnered more deserved critical attention than Nicole Brossard with her 1987 *Le Désert mauve*. Highly regarded critics such as Chassay, Janet Paterson, Karen Gould, Alice Parker, and Karen McPherson have brought much insight to this experimental novel which, in Gould's words, "is a cross-border tale of creative resistance that speaks allegorically of the culturally sanctioned violence and intolerance that women and men must face," and in which there is "an effort to reinvent the American desert and transform a menacing cultural horizon so that life, not death, is painted there" (Gould, "Rewriting 'America'" 200). But America, as painted by Brossard, does not fare well in this novel. Janet Paterson's excellent essay "Fast So Fast: Dérives identitaires dans *Le Désert mauve* de Nicole Brossard," speaks of "the apocalyptic state of American culture" ["l'état apocalyptique de la culture américaine"] and of Baudrillard's hyperreality of America, "as if the novel proved the very essence of postmodern America" ["comme si le roman mettait en évidence l'essence même d'une Amérique postmoderne"] (45–6). Brossard's images – the nuclear space of the desert, the motel as a space of violence and a parody of home, the television as a simulacrum, television violence as the loss of the real and the supremacy of violence in the symbolic order, "Longman" ["l'homme long"] as the potential of violence, "a culture wounded by violence" ["une culture meurtrie par la violence"], the omnipresence of violence where revolvers are always cocked – all paint America as an alterity both spacially and linguistically, a postmodern America in ruins (45–6, 51–2).

I have mentioned how Monette, in *Petites Violences*, superimposes real violence on Montreal and fictitious, academic, violence on New York City – where the Quebec novelist has actually lived for many years. Karen Gould also maintains that Monette's novel encourages the reader to "consider the ways in which the circulation and proliferation of violent images in North American culture fuel the everyday violence ... that occurs in the private lives of contemporary couples" ("Rewriting 'America'" 195).

North America, and in particular the United States, fares no better in LaRue's novel, *Copies conformes*. There, California becomes the space and locale of impure forms and imperfect translations, and where the only hope for the future resides in a feminine discourse. Lucie Guillemette, in her essay "Formes impures dans *Copies conformes* de Monique LaRue: La Jonction du postmodernisme et du féminisme," points to what she sees as "the feminist declaration [that] problematizes the real and inscribes ... the female subject in a specific socio-cultural context" ["l'énoncé féministe [qui] problématise le réel et inscrit ... le sujet féminin dans un contexte socio-culturel spécifique"] (90) in a number of texts written by Québécois women since the beginning of the 1980s. For Guillemette, the presence of a United States' America opens up onto the feminine as a form of alterity and puts the place of women in both history and culture into question. If, as Derrida has pronounced, America is synonymous with deconstruction (*Mémoires. Pour Paul de Man* 41), then: "The discourse on America in female texts could pass itself off as a catalyst for women's speech from which symbolic values would be distorted and would divert, on the rebound, meanings constructed by patriarchal language" ["Le discours sur l'Amérique dans les textes féminins pourrait se poser comme catalyseur d'une parole de femmes à partir de laquelle les valeurs symboliques seraient défigurées et dériveraient, par ricochet, des significations construites par le langage patriarchal"] (Guillemette 90). Guillemette sees America as an imperfect translation that on the one hand decentres Europe and on the other hand "is articulated as an imaginary component capable of transforming the feminine Other" ["s'articule comme une composante imaginaire susceptible de transformer l'Autre féminin"] (91).

My question then becomes: what happens if and when this feminine "Other" becomes sexual, sexually violent, and especially violent in its own right – just like male America and most interestingly from a perspective outside the United States? More specific to LaRue's novel, Guillemette suggests that the representation of the feminine "I" produces a postmodern American simulacrum that in turn both becomes an amalgam of significant, impure forms (95) and proclaims the decline and decadence of values in a society that is in the process of disappearing (98). The most determined orientation of a postmodern autorepresentative discourse in this novel is thus defined as "the feminine statement, that of a mother" ["le dire féminin, celui d'une mère"] who maintains the narrative in its impurity and heterogeneity, suggesting new possible readings for women imagined in a Québécois context and "related to North American culture in its U.S. ramifications" ["relevant de la culture nord-américaine dans ses ramifications étatsuniennes"] (101–2). Applying and extending this notion to the writers considered here, once again one has to wonder what transformations could occur when the new feminine statement becomes that of a sexual, sexually violent, and especially violent female, who destroys those around her and defies the mother-child bond.

And Some Others Who Play with Imagined Reality and Fiction

Several lesser known novels and short stories also help form a bridge in this analysis to more sexual and violent literary transformations of Quebec women writers. One such text has been proposed by Saint-Martin as an example of "metafeminism": Anne Dandurand's *Un Coeur qui craque: Journal imaginaire* published in 1990. For Saint-Martin, Dandurand's novel integrates fantasy and politics, suggests new links between the essay and the novel, and – with its subtitle of "imaginary journal/diary" – helps to blur the boundary between fiction and reality (260). With a narrative that evokes a fin-de-siècle world of violence against women, self-defensive violence, global violence, and overt sexuality, this text achieves "an end-of-the-millennium tone, the voice of a woman, lucid but romantic" ["un ton ... de fin de millénaire, la voix d'une femme lucide mais romantique"] (260). It also can be read "like a quasi-parody of feminist discourse on female sexuality" ["comme une quasi-parodie du discours féministe sur la sexualité féminine"] (261) in a garden of realities and fantasies of female sexuality. Saint-Martin also believes that the narrator in this particular text stresses the troubling rapport between the real and the textual, as she puts this very relationship in question (263).

Dandurand has maintained, however, that her novel is not autobiographical and that her female protagonist is a liar, but that she purposely confuses the line between autobiography and fiction, and multiplies the many parallels between herself and her protagonist (Saint-Martin 263–4). Such statements, along with the bifurcated/fused sub-title, leads us to a double reading of the "fantastic, fantasmatic, and self-referential" ["fantastiques, fantasmatiques et auto-référentiels"] elements in that novel: "The more Dandurand's novel approaches a confession ... the more it affirms its status as pure fiction, and vice versa, in a never-ending ludic spiral ... a back-and-forth movement between fiction and reality which allows the insertion of another feminine reality into the text" ["Plus le roman de Dandurand se rapproche de la confession ... plus il affirme son statut de pure fiction, et vice versa, dans une spirale ludique sans fin ... un va-et-vient entre fiction et réel qui permet la mise en texte d'un autre réel féminin"] (264–5). Like other metafeminist texts of the late twentieth century, *Un Coeur qui craque* exemplifies "the intimate and the political, intersecting here in an unusual way" ["l'intime et le politique [qui] se croisent ici de manière insolite"] (265).

The more recent work of Kathleen Kellett-Betsos on Anne Dandurand and her "journal imaginaire" expands Saint-Martin's analysis of this particular text by defining the journal as a way of exploring the female condition, "a privileged form of writing," a daily record kept in a portable diary and on a computer disk and in which the personal and the fictional can mix (35, 36). Although deeply concerned with sincerity, the narrator can also lie and spin tales, reconciling with difficulty the fragmentary form of her honest "journal" and her spun literary work: "Dandurand creates the literary work from this discontinuous form of the diary" ["Dandurand crée l'oeuvre littéraire à partir de cette forme discontinue qu'est le journal intime"] in which the "exploding" subject creates an open text and examines the relationship between creation and the feminine condition in Quebec society (43, 45).[13]

A year after *Un Coeur qui craque*, Dandurand wrote a collection of stories entitled *Petites âmes sous ultimatum*, in which she included two stories that also illustrate the state of the world at the end of the twentieth century. "Le Courage est un bon poignard" is narrated by a fifteen-year old boy, Bruno, who writes a letter to a girl in his school. Presented entirely in italics, this letter rambles on about personal and world violence, real and imagined. Bruno imagines, for example, scenes in which the girl's brothers are assassinated by Israeli soldiers, she escapes to a refugee camp in Turkey, or that she originally came from Iraq but luckily was not poisoned by mustard gas. He imagines killing his mother to save her from her long-term depression. For Bruno, the wickedness of late twentieth-century urban and global life must be faced with the courage of a metaphorical (masculine) sword. He ends his letter on two personal notes: his addressee should not reveal his secret thoughts; and, now that the Berlin Wall has fallen, perhaps his mother will come out of her depression. With this blend of fact and fantasy, personal/local and global, Dandurand's adolescent male narrator offers a bleak and somber view of the world – and the mind – in the late twentieth century.

In a similar discontinuous vein, "La Dernière Journée du milk-shake" is recounted without resolution by a young girl who lives in a foster home run by an old punk woman from the previous short story in this collection. We are witness, through her first-person narrative, to personal, domestic, historical (slavery), and international (Vietnamese and Chinese) violence. She tells of her anger, her imagined violence, and her desire to harm her father physically. Her favourite breakfast is "Tigress Milk" (101) (milk, banana, egg, yogurt, and wheat germ), clearly a power drink for powerful, "animated" young women. She reads that twenty-seven students have been executed by the Chinese government, notes the names of her schoolmates in her diary, and gets ready to go back to her family for the holiday. With a very matter-of-fact attitude, this girl accepts and imagines the dangerous world that she lives in, dreaming of changing it by violent means (karate chops to her father – again echoing the popular actions of powerful female comic strip, video game, and televisions characters) when she grows up.

The postmodern urban world of Montreal is painted in Flora Balzano's *Soigne ta chute* from 1992: families are dysfunctional; mothers and daughters do not relate to each other; kids steal bikes, drugs, and designer clothes; and immigrants are treated like hybrid, verbally handicapped people. In a series of Balzacian vignettes of contemporary life, we meet in turn: a female writer bothered by the telephone and by a friend; a talking fish; a fifty-five-year-old woman who sees homeless couples on the television and wants to leave Quebec; Maria, who meets creepy men; and a narrator who is with a man who "doesn't get it." A young girl finds out that she is pregnant and introduces herself as a heroin addict. It is really only toward the end of the text that one realizes that the tales are being told by the same narrator – the fifteen/almost sixteen-year-old heroin junkie who is not Québécoise but most likely French, who commits violence against herself but loves to draw peaceful scenes. We are then suddenly thrown into scenes of child abuse – perpetrated by the mother against the narrator when she was younger: "Suddenly, she spreads my slit and stuffs crushed hot pepper into it. It burns ... Later, she unties me. I have trouble kneeling ... I have trouble walking, I have trouble sitting ... Outside, it's war, too. Everyone is getting killed. They explode, poof, their bodies all torn apart by grenades" ["Soudain, elle écarte ma fente et la remplit de piment broyé. Ça brule ... Plus tard, elle me détache. J'ai du mal à m'agenouiller ... J'ai du mal à marcher, j'ai du mal à m'asseoir ... Dehors aussi c'est la guerre. Tout le monde se fait tuer. Ils explosent, pouf, leur corps tout démantibulé par les grenades"] (111). Only in the epilogue does the narrator remember finding a paper heart on her pillow – a message either from her own daughter or to her mother – that speaks of her love for her mother even though she is "mixed up." Perhaps the note questions the "truth" about the mother/daughter violence; perhaps the daughter, despite the violence, reaches out for maternal love in the midst of a world of violence. It is this tension between the "real" and the imagination/lie in a number of Dandurand's works that characterizes the world – the literary world, at least – at the end of the twentieth century.

Lise Bissonnette's "L'Échafaud," in her 1997 collection of short stories *Quittes et doubles*, similarly plays with truth, storytelling, and the power of the imagination – all as related to sex and violence. In this instance the stakes are quite high, since the story is about a law court, a female prosecutor, a jury, and the outcome of the murder trial of an accused male serial killer. What is fascinating is the complexity of the narrative levels. It is narrated by a male juror who at times speaks for himself and at others speaks as a member of the jury. On one plane, the story moves seamlessly along: the juror listens to the words of the female prosecutor; imagines that she has exposed herself to him and the defendant; visualizes the images that she paints about the serial murders; enters into her imagination as she graphically describes what would happen to the defendant if he were condemned and if Canada had capital punishment; senses the "penetration" of her sexually violent words into all of the members of the jury; pictures her nude under her robes and subsequently copulating briefly with the defendant; relates the reaction of the media; and learns that from this indecent act in the court room a child was born. What ties this story to my study is the question not only of what is the truth and what is a lie, but also of what motivates and fuels the gory imagination of the female prosecutor. Her descriptions of the sexual torture and murder of the serial killer's victims and her elaboration of his potential ghastly death are infused with heightened sensuality and sexuality, as though she were "getting off" on this violent lifestyle herself. Ironically, the male defendant is acquitted on the charge of murder, but not on the charge of indecent exposure in a court of law; in prison, he becomes a poet – a man of imagination. As for the female prosecutor, her imaginative prosecution gets her disbarred.[14]

The world of junkies, drugs, prison, AIDS, self-violence, and the murder of prostitutes and drug addicts – all in the urban space of the children of survivors of the Holocaust – defines Emmanuelle Turgeon's 1998 novel *Les Beaux Survivants*. Entering into a detective story of sorts, the reader attempts, along with the narrator, to discover who has murdered these prostitutes and drug addicts: Hélène suspects Georges and kills him, but Georges' brother was actually the murderer. However, if everything about Georges was a lie, is he really innocent? The reader continues to wonder, therefore, who really killed the women. There is clearly no solution to the murders. There are no winners in any (national or urban) war, just survivors. Once again, the "truth" lies somewhere in the story, if one can even tell what is a story and what is real.

In Lynn Diamond's 1999 novel *Le Passé sous nos pas*, three narrators recount the story of a family that is reunited by the murder of one of the sisters and, in the telling, evoke the moral and social atmosphere of the second half of the twentieth century. In a series of short, fragmented points of view, we learn about many of the secrets and tensions in this family, witness the encroachment of U.S. culture into Quebec during the 1940s, along with the attraction of the United States as a better place to live. Another of the sisters, who had left Quebec fifteen years earlier and returns home to write a film about her family, is unaware that her sister has just been killed. She becomes a suspect because of her sudden return, but in typical fashion, we are given only insinuations, never learn the truth, and are left with an unsolved murder. Suspicious violence, instability, and a blurring of the lines between the real and the imaginary mark this novel as well.

Marie-Sissi Labrèche's first novel, *Borderline* (2000), is a powerful, funny and truly francophone North American text that is steeped in popular culture and includes several scenes of graphic sexuality. The English title of the novel refers both to the personal "issues" of the female protagonist and, more subtly, to the divided nature of Quebec/North American society and culture, a culture of *américanités* at the turn of the millennium. Sissi, the narrator, tells the reader that she has a borderline personality disorder, which she then defines in English directly from the DSM-IV diagnosic manual: "A pervasive pattern of instability of interpersonal relationship, self-image, and affects, and marked impulsivity beginning by early adulthood and present in a variety of contexts" (73). In chapters alternating between childhood and young adulthood, and with self-deprecating humour, Sissi gives us her self-diagnosis: "I have a sick personality. A personality with the flu. No, it's even worse: I have personality cancer ... I'm borderline. I have a problem with limits. I can't tell the difference between outside and inside. It's because my skin is inside out. It's because my nerves are hypersensitive. Everyone can see my insides, it seems. I'm transparent ... I'm so transparent that I have to shout for people to see me ... I smash into everything. My borders are too blurry. My reality is stretched out. I wander in a space that isn't filled with air, but with sex and beer. Nothing is for sure in my life" ["J'ai une personnalité malade. Une personnalité qui a la grippe. Non, pire, j'ai un cancer de la personnalité ... je suis borderline. J'ai un problème de limites. Je ne fais pas de différence entre l'extérieur et l'intérieur. C'est à cause de ma peau qui est à l'envers. C'est à cause de mes nerfs qui sont à fleur de peau. Tout le monde peut voir à l'intérieur de moi, j'ai l'impression. Je suis transparente. D'ailleurs, je suis tellement transparente qu'il faut que je crie pour qu'on me voie ... Je défonce tout. Les limites sont trop floues. Ma réalité se distend. J'erre dans une sphère qui n'est pas remplie d'air, mais de sexe et de bière. Rien n'est défini dans ma vie"] (77–8).

Labrèche's novel is infused with American (U.S.) popular culture and the "American way of life, Quebec version" (56), which is itself infused with imagined and real sexuality and imaginary violence: Disney, Sharon Stone in *Basic Instinct*, Fisher Price, Elvis Presley, Raison Bran, McDonald's, Big Macs, Annie Sprinkle, *Emmanuelle*, Barbie, Luke Skywalker, Lego, Smashing Pumpkins, Nine Inch Nails, Tori Amos, Peter Gabriel, Arnold Schwarzenegger, *Lost in Space*, the Empire State Building, *King Kong*, *The Exorcist*, *Little House on the Prairie*, and *The Simpsons*. It also evokes French texts; for example, "Dessine-moi un mouton" is the title of one of the chapters, referring, of course, to Saint-Exupéry's *Le Petit Prince*. As a child – with a mother who literally goes crazy in front of her and her schoolmates, a grandmother who teaches her to be afraid of just about everyone and everything, and schoolmates who make fun of both her (body-related) first and last names – Sissi undresses her Barbie doll in an imaginary brothel. She wants to be "a real Arnold Schwarzenegger [the movie star, not the politician] in a skirt" ["une vraie Arnold Schwarzenegger en jupon"] (119), destroying everything with her imaginary bazooka, like a popular-culture caricature. As an adult, she dreams of being Annie Sprinkle, and has sex like a prostitute; she complains that "as soon as a man takes control, I want to kill him, stick a big bread knife into his stomach and make zigzags" ["dès qu'un homme prend le contrôle, j'ai envie de le tuer, de lui planter un gros couteau à pain dans le ventre et de faire des zigzags"] (19). As in many other contemporary female texts, the narrator of *Borderline* plays on the boundaries between fact and fiction, the real and the imaginary, using "realism to fold the Imaginary into the real … and setting forth the interplay between subjectivity and representation" (During 151–2). She plays humorously with the reader; she is sexual; and she is imaginatively violent. Whether or not she has become the (bipolar) independent female subject, gazing upon herself and others remains a question.

A Male or Female Gaze? Hélène Rioux's Les Miroirs d'Éléonore

What is the distance between the face in the mirror and the mirror in front of the face where the boundaries blur? The real is the unreal … and I say I. But when I say I, I'm not the woman who is writing this very page. When I say I, I'm merely imagining myself. She is the one who is writing. And my face in the mirror? Who is it? Who is the woman who writes me? I know because I made her up … She has no I. She's the other. I am I … [S]he has no knowledge of her I. Done in by a single letter. In one letter I am I. And in my faces in the mirror. I?

Helena Parente Cunha, *Woman Between Mirrors*

Are you a lucky little lady in the city of light?/Or just another lost angel?

Jim Morrison, "L.A. Woman"

Girl, unhappy girl, left all alone playing solitaire.

Jim Morrison, "Unhappy Girl"

Music is your only friend/Until the end …

Jim Morrison, "When the Music's Over"

Some are born to sweet delight/Some are born to the endless night.

Jim Morrison, "End of the Night"

The future is uncertain/But the end is always near.

Jim Morrison, "Roadhouse Blues"

The killer awoke before dawn/And he put his boots on/
He took a face from the ancient gallery. …

Jim Morrison, "The End"

In her award-winning critical study *Écrire dans la maison du père*, Patricia Smart convincingly proposes that, in contrast to female voices being "other" as they are in Oedipal, omniscient, and culturally and ideologically structured texts written by men, women's texts are "born together" ("co-naître") and speak through an "unorganized texture" ["texture désordonnée"] that opens up to the reader as an invitation to share and exchange (29). In order to break out of the paternal house, to become free from both the Father and the Mother (to escape both the Oedipus and Electra myths), texts need women-subjects and men ready to listen to their words, even if the multiple, polyphonic female voices of desire write of a destructive act, as in Anne Hébert's *Les Fous de bassan* (255). To illustrate, Smart presents an analysis of France Théoret's works, in which violent and crude language projects the degradation, corporal alienation, and absolute non-mythical place of the woman in her victim status (300–1). Translating into precise words what is heard in certain pieces of vocal classical music, Théoret, in *Nous parlerons comme on écrit*, also cleverly plays with the use of the pronouns, "je," "elle," "on," and "nous" (308, 312). According to Smart, as female characters come to accept their own bodies, their own reflection in the mirror – as they oppose the murder of a woman by and in the house of the Father with the rhythmic dance of love, in Brossard's *Le Désert mauve* – they take the first step toward a network of reflections free from the gaze of the Father, the Male (334, 335).

Hélène Rioux, especially after 1986, has created a disturbing world of sex, violence, murder, rape, death, danger, stalking, macabre and morbid fantasies, macho and arrogant cruel men who dream of their perfect woman, and lonely, alienated, aging women who tell and retell the stories of their (perhaps) real or invented lives. Playing with post-modern techniques, she creates this world through the clever use of language that manipulates narrative structure and implicates the reader, narrator, and characters in the invention of the stories. Playing with feminist techniques, she places the female in a fragmented mirror of self where the woman seems to play the role of subject under a superficial overlay of elegant, elite classical music. The environment is consistently permeated, however, by the male, sexual, vagabond, drug culture of the 1960/70s, as represented by Jim Morrison's music and lyrics, which continued in the vein of Arthur Rimbaud and were subsequently revived in the films of Oliver Stone, and Morrison's rock music group, The Doors.

The composite and complex figure of Rioux's reccurring protagonist/possible narrator, Éléonore, was created in "Les Fantasmes d'Éléonore," the first short story of the 1986 *L'Homme de Hong Kong*. In it, questions of narrative structure, narrator identity, and the gendered gaze of characters and readers are almost immediately raised. Éléonore defines herself as an object, existing only under the gaze of others, rather than for herself. But, she asks, sensing the possibility of a freer identity: "What if I were my own public? I would then exist as a result of a relationship with myself. I would exist in my very own gaze" ["Si c'était moi, le public? J'existerais alors par mes rapports avec moi-même. Et dans mon propre regard j'existerais" (23–4).

In the 1992 novel *Chambre avec baignoire* Éléonore reappears in the process of writing a postmodern autobiography, while she sees her own story published first by another, Lorrie Moore – or is it "Mort"? She imagines herself as eight different characters – all of whom love danger, violence, and sex: she thinks of herself as a modern-day Judith or Salomé cutting off a man's penis (a postmodern Lorena Bobbitt), identifies with an assassin, and dreams of hurting her opera-loving companion by taking Jim Morrison (dead, of course) as her lover. In the short stories of the 1994 *Pense à mon rendez-vous* – portraits of young to old women, or perhaps different reflections of the same woman as seen in a broken mirror – the narrator ("je," "elle," "on," or "nous") exposes and destabilizes the creative/narrative process by implicating the reader in the creation ("imaginons," "disons," "peut-être"). Éléonore listens to the music of The Doors. Perhaps as Soledad, she loses her son, a Morrison fan. Potentially as a middle-aged woman, her rotting flesh creates disgusting odours. And ultimately, as old Marguérite, she dies when she enters/becomes the image of the other woman in the broken bathroom mirror: "Run to the mirror in the bathroom"; "The end ... my only friend," sings Morrison, in "The End."

The most complete picture of Éléonore appears in the 1990 novel/short story collection, *Les Miroirs d'Éléonore*, in which the image of each different (or the same?) woman is linked simultaneously to a mythological figure and preceded by lyrics by Morrison. The narrative text here offers a rich illustration of theories of gender, but it twists disturbingly, especially in the last mirror, in which the gender of gaze and narration – the autonomous, free voice of the female – is again called into question.

The female image on the novel's cover immediately unsettles the viewer/reader. Is Eléonore Black, Hispanic, Spanish, North African, or of mixed race? Significantly, the cover portrait gives one of the few clues that we have to the puzzling, composite character of Éléonore, in that she is portrayed as a painter. Reminding us of Narcissus on Morrison's "Crystal Ship" (like Rimbaud's "Bateau ivre" – referred to by both Éléonore and Morrison) in the first mirror, Eléonore inserts herself (in a semblance of freedom, but "tell me where [it] lies" chants Morrison) into every person she paints. It is a distinctive composite self-portrait: "She had imagined a system of mirrors allowing her to see herself from all angles at the same time ... her repeated, multiple reflections, from one mirror to another, from one reflection to an infinite number of them. Some of her poses were truly erotic ... She played all the roles – geisha, woman of the world ... Amazon, courtesan, empress, spy" ["Elle avait conçu un système de miroirs lui permettant de se voir sous tous les angles à la fois ... son reflet répété, multiplié, d'un miroir à l'autre, seule à l'infini. Certaines de ses poses étaient très érotiques ... Elle incarnait tous les rôles, geisha, femme du monde ... amazone, courtisane, impératrice, espionne" (*Miroirs* 36–7). Éléonore does more than paint, however; she also narrates and invents stories. She plays all the roles (the female roles, at least) in her stories – roles that are all affected by an undercurrent of violence: "She says there is always a killer at bay" ["Elle dit qu'il y a toujours un tueur aux abois"] (*Miroirs* 54). She hears of "the man from Hong Kong" and his filming of his torture victims as they die; she begins a story about the violent and voluptuous world of the harem; she refers to the constant violence on television news; she initiates her ongoing story of a visit to Torreblanca, where she makes love with Angel, an anarchist who loves violence (perhaps "just another lost angel," sings Morrison in subsequent lyrics of "L.A. Woman").

Éléonore narrates in a particular style and paints herself as a "fragile presence ... about to disappear" ["présence fragile ... sur le point de disparaître"] (*Miroirs* 19), as a mystery, a void whose reality is in question, since she exists only "where she was present one day, in that moment" ["là où elle fut présente un jour, en ce moment"] (*Miroirs* 42). She appears only conditionally, introduced by linguistic signposts such as "peut-être," "si," "c'est possible," "elle imagine." Most interestingly, she invents herself and is invented by others in a multitude of layers. We first meet her as she sits alone in a Vancouver bar: "What can we say about her? ... We look at her, we wonder ... let's say ... And what if we were to follow her in this dream? Our dream." ["Que dire d'elle? ... On la regarde, on se demande ... disons ... Si on la suivait dans ce rêve? Le nôtre"] (*Miroirs* 21–3). It is initially the narrator who tells/invents the story, implicating the reader as viewer, witness, and ultimately as collective narrator. We can imagine that the narrator/reader invents Éléonore speaking of herself to a man whom she has just met and to whom she admits that she herself has been making up these tales. She asks him to imagine with her and allows him (an American, although for her all men are alike) to invent her story, as well. The narrator/reader imagines that the man thinks Éléonore is sad but then reminds us that sadness exists in the viewer rather than in the person viewed.

We encounter, therefore, at least four levels of invention, with variations on all of them – the narrator, Éléonore, the reader/viewer, another character in the story – all imagined by the narrator, or by us, or by Éléonore, or by the American. Which version is "real," since reality is constructed by the observer/viewer in whose gaze everything else becomes "alive"? Is Éléonore in charge of her life, her past, her body, her reflection, her voice, as she speaks to a man who will listen to her, or is she being created by another/others? "We can imagine that they leave together ... But perhaps before all this can happen, she will have already fled ... We will have seen her disappear ... She will have been only just that – a woman who came to the old-fashioned hotel bar to have a drink. We will know nothing more" ["On peut imaginer qu'ils partent ensemble ... Mais peut-être qu'avant que tout cela ne se produise, aura-t-elle fui déjà ... On l'aura vue disparaître ... Elle n'aura alors été que cela, une femme venue prendre un verre au bar d'un hôtel désuet. On ne saura rien de plus"] (*Miroirs* 58). Initially the text seems to offer a perfect open ending, where it is the task of the narrator and reader to invent, but upon rereading, one can also see a perfect closure: the image/portrait/mirror opened when one first saw the woman at the bar; all that occurred in between was invented and imagined, and now the image has closed. Maybe she was just a woman alone drinking at a bar, and we will know nothing more.

Éléonore/Narcisse was, perhaps, a painter, perhaps a prostitute, Morrison's "lucky little lady in the city of light ... or just another lost angel" ("L.A. Woman") speaking to an American man in a Vancouver bar. In "Sisyphe," at a Montreal bar, she becomes fused with Jeanne, a Québécoise lawyer who was also in Torreblanca having her portrait done by Éléonore (who once again puts herself into the painting) and is the dream woman of the man now listening to Éléonore's story. The narrator/reader invents an entire life for this man: "His name could be Marc. Yes, Marc is a good name for him" ["Il pourrait s'appeler Marc. Oui, Marc est un prénom qui lui convient"] (*Miroirs* 65), as the woman listens to music by The Doors and to "Le Bateau ivre" sung by Ferré. Marc then begins to invent another version of Éléonore/Jeanne's trip to Torreblanca: this time, as he listens to "L.A. Woman," he sees her with her wild love of violent, obscene, drug-induced sex – or "perhaps not" ["ou rien de cela"] (*Miroirs* 78). He remembers having conquered Jeanne, as he murmured the name of Éléonore, the inaccessible object of his desires, the woman whom he would never possess. Marc needs to calm down and listen to his recordings of the *Brandenburg Concertos*. Everything appears to be under a pall of violence, sex, and death: Vancouver/Montréal/Torreblanca; Éléonore/Jeanne; the American/Marc; the narrator/the reader/Éléonore/the male character. If everything is interchangeable, which person is the free speaking subject, the listener/observer, and which version is "reality," if there is one?

If Narcissus is associated with the flowers and perfume of death, and Sisyphus remains in Hades, Persephone clearly lives in the same realm ("Well, I been down so very damn long," sings Morrison in "Been Down So Long"). Reducing the signposts given by the narrator to the implicated reader, this third mirrored woman (a barmaid on the Magdalen Islands) openly admits that the mirror has broken into many pieces. Like Penelope (of the fourth mirror), knitting and reknitting her shroud, Éléonore recounts different stories, transforming and reinventing them according to her current state of mind, paying no attention to contradictions: "She starts a new version of this never-ending story. We can say that in varying it this way to infinity, she is looking to make it unreal. She denies its existence ... She looks to lose herself in it ... in the maze of her story ... It was one, it was another. With her in the middle" ["Elle entreprend une nouvelle version de l'éternelle histoire. On dirait qu'en la variant ainsi à l'infini, elle cherche à la rendre irréelle. Elle lui nie son existence ... Elle cherche à se perdre ... dans les dédales de son histoire ... C'était l'un, c'était l'autre. Elle au centre"] (*Miroirs* 102). Éléonore appears here to be the spider, at the centre and in control of her story, telling tales of increasingly greater violence and sex, but this world of eroticism and death will soon be affected by the violence of the male gaze.

Admitting that her story about Torreblanca was imagined – thereby negating her story to the American and the memory of her in the mind of Marc – Éléonore proceeds to add another level of invention to her repertoire: she imagines that as an adolescent she played the role of a woman brutalized by a sultan in his harem. This adolescent/adult obsession with sex and mutilation moves to a frenzied level, as Éléonore recounts/invents her past life with the vulgar, sexually disgusting male, Jean-François Delarue, in a barrage of x-rated scenes of male fantasies, often with one male and several women at once – all men are alike, searching for the perfect woman, and Éléonore is several women in one – who are mirrored in the text. She reads, once again, about the man from Hong Kong who filmed the torture of his victims and compares him to Delarue, to people who love pornography and death.

A clear link is thereby established between the world of necrophilia and vampirism and the gaze or look of the other – in film, painting, and narrative. As a speaking subject, Éléonore "feared above all the gaze of the other, this rape" ["craignait par-dessus tout le regard de l'autre, ce viol" (*Miroirs* 91). Her self-regard is different from that of another, especially a male: "You don't see how ugly I am, no, you can't see it, you don't even have the same look ... you see nothing. And I love it that you don't see me" ["Tu ne vois pas combien je suis moche, non, tu ne peux pas le voir, tu n'as pas le même regard ... toi, tu ne vois rien. Et j'aime que tu ne me voies pas"] (*Miroirs* 118). To whom is she speaking? To him? To herself? In keeping with her statement in *L'Homme de Hong Kong* that if she were her own public, she would exist in her own gaze, Éléonore has chosen a special man to listen to and look at her: a deaf-mute. Is Hyacinthe another layer of herself? Is he another man whose dream girl has materialized in the image of Éléonore? Is he the male listener/observer who cannot hear what she is recounting and cannot speak of his own imagined tales? Is he the perfect reader/viewer – silent and controlled by the narrator or by an autonomous Éléonore (and therefore, not the perfect postmodern reader!)? Or is he the silent creator of these stories, allowing Éléonore to return from hell (like Persephone and the Éléonore in *Pense à mon rendez-vous*, "Celle qui revient de voyage")?

Penelope, Morrison's "unhappy girl, left all alone, playing solitaire" ("Unhappy Girl") is alone in a bar in (imagined) Torreblanca, perhaps waiting for her lover. We are not certain, especially since the linguistic signposts of doubt have returned to the text – the "on peut l'imaginer," "peut-être," "on jurerait," "ou" – without, now, any first-person plural imperatives implicating the reader. One can invent that she writes a love letter, a fragment of her diary, like each broken, fragmented mirror of the postmodern/feminist self, in which she carefully inserts references to characters mentioned/invented in other mirrors, along with further clues about herself (she smokes Camels, like a man). Her lover is clearly a revolutionary, a rebel (Angel, with his leather jacket), "on the road" like Rimbaud and Jack Kerouac, both of whom had an influence on Morrison's life and songs ("Roadhouse Blues," "Riders on the Storm"). Characters have become so related, confused, fused, invented, that they ask in this open ending of a fog, "Could we have bumped into one another without recognizing each other?" ["Nous serions-nous croisés sans nous reconnaître?"] (*Miroirs* 139).

Éléonore's Eros is of the type "born to the endless night" of the Morrison song ("End of the Night"), as she sits at a bar anywhere. As the décor has become vague and fused, like the characters/roles played and narrated/invented, Éléonore has become "an absence, having walked into the nothingness of the sea ... She could be transparent. Ethereal. Strollers walking by would pass right through her without noticing. She could be an empty memory" ["une absence, entrée dans le néant de la mer ... Elle pourrait être transparente. Immatérielle. Les promeneurs, alors, passeraient à travers elle sans s'en apercevoir. Elle pourrait être une mémoire vide"] (*Miroirs* 146). If she is the perfect, absent woman (the blank page of sexuality), any passerby can invent her to his/her liking, since "Everything happens in the mind of the voyeur" (*Miroirs* 148). But who is this voyeuristic observer/inventor with the violent gaze, who supposes that she listens to Morrison's "End of the Night," tells of her first brutal sexual encounter with an older man – in all its pleasure, pain, and blood – has her see Angel from a distance, and imagines her offering herself to the burning looks of men?

For the remainder of this erotic, x-rated mirror, someone invents that Éléonore dreams six different stories, with five variations of sub-stories about Soledad, the favourite of the sultan mentioned earlier. These tales of exotic, orientalized brutality against women are recounted in quotation marks, as though Éléonore is speaking to herself: she is narrator/inventor and listener/reader/viewer. Of course she plays all the female victim roles as she continuously goes back to the beginning and takes up the story again – Soledad initially drowns in a black pond (reminiscent of Ophelia) and then is strangled – all in a narrative exploding with danger, sex, and violence. Do we simply have here another example of women taking charge of their narratives, even if the text mirrors male-perpetrated violence? The answer must depend upon the gender of the narrator, protagonist, characters, and reader/viewer. Is there an answer in the last mirror, Thanatos, or perhaps in Morrison's Oedipal song "The End," which precedes that mirror?

To this day, there exists a cult around the figure of Jim Morrison, lead singer and lyrics writer for The Doors. The name of the rock music group was taken from a line by William Blake, which was later used by Aldous Huxley as the title of a novel, and which for Morrison represented the purpose of his work: "It's a search, an opening of one door after another (much like Éléonore's mirrors) ... It's a striving for metamorphosis. It's like a purification ritual in the alchemical sense" (cited in Fowlie 19–20). This reference to alchemy reminds us that Morrison, considering himself to be the poet of his generation – and who did compose poetry as well as rock lyrics – greatly fashioned himself after Rimbaud. His biographers confirm that he had studied Rimbaud's work and life and that his notebooks contain references to the French poet, along with verses steeped in Rimbaldian influences. In fact, the renowned critic Wallace Fowlie published a monograph, *Rimbaud and Jim Morrison: The Rebel as Poet*, which explores this relationship. Fowlie refers to Morrison as a *voyeur*, a dark figure obsessed with pain, violence, sex, death, revolt, disorder, chaos, evil, and music as a ritualistic, sexual exorcism, ultimately moving toward transcendance for these "angels" (as in Rimbaud's use of the term).

Morrison's lyrics sing that death and love simply happen and that human life is mere accident and chance.[15] His published poems are even more violent and sexual than his songs; the killer is forever lurking, awaiting the brutality of copulation. "The Hitchhiker: An American Pastoral," for example, written in the form of a film (one of Morrison's passions, along with music, poetry, and theatre), introduces us to Billy, who must keep moving from place to place because of his acts of sexual violence and murder – another "man from Hong Kong" on the road (Fowlie 114). Fowlie also refers to Morrison as an Oedipal figure, the erotic, narcissistic male who entered popular mythology especially because of his performances of "The End" (inspired by his reading of Nietzsche). It is, in fact, this trance-like song that Rioux has chosen to quote at the beginning of the sixth mirror of Éléonore. But she only quotes the first three lines. The complete ending of the song, however, is revealing: "The killer awoke before dawn,/He put his boots on,/He took a face from the ancient gallery,/And he walked on down the hal(lllll)./He went into the room where his sister lived/a(aaaaa)nd .../ Then he paid a visit to his brother,/And then he ... walked on down the hal(lllll)./And he came to a do(ooooo)r,/And he looked insi(ddddd)e,/ "Father?"/"Yes, son?"/"I want to kill you. Mother ... I want to/ FFFUUUUUUUCKKKK YOOOOOOOU!!"[16] This is the end, beautiful friend .../my only friend/No safety or surprise/Limitless and free/It hurts to set you free .../The end of laughter and soft lies."[17]

The sixth mirror opens quite differently from the previous ones – with the projected vague image of a man, a stranger walking on the beach in Torreblanca. The reader is there, too, with the narrator. From what we are told, from what is invented about this man, he could be – we have the impression ... we wonder ... we could believe ... he might be – a composite of all the men encountered in the other mirrors: Angel, the American, Marc, Delarue, even the man from Hong Kong. He lives on the edge of town (where danger lurks, sings Morrison in "The End"). The narrator/reader invents an entire possible background for him: born in a bombed-out town during the war; his mother dead in a home for neurasthenics; an austere, orphaned youth; no links, relationships with others; no sense of humour, nor sense of the tragic. In a word, we are being "set up" – "we" are inventing a portrait of a man who could easily be a potential killer, a stalker, at least an observer/watcher of violence and sex.

The plot thickens. This invented, composite man in an imagined Torreblanca stands before the Moorish palace of a sultan and murmurs the name of Soledad. From his readings about Arab harems, about women in chains, he remembers the story of Soledad, drowned (just as Eléonore had remembered/imagined the story):

Soledad, was it I who drowned you in the pool? ... But who was I, who were we? [composite man; narrator/reader; characters?] What were you doing in this palace where you didn't belong? [You belonged in Vancouver or Montreal.] They say a woman died ... That someone kept her head under the water. She struggled ... then she stopped struggling ... He had loved this woman once, [as one can only love Éléonore] he knows that ... His solitude, he calls it Soledad ... He plunges into her story. I was the sultan ... The other women were jealous ... They drowned her [first version] ... She cheated on me with a young Andalusian ... I drowned her [second version] ... She threw herself into the pond [third version – Éléonore had five versions of this story] [Soledad, est-ce moi qui t'ai noyée dans le bassin? ... Mais qui étais-je, qui étions-nous? Que faisais-tu dans ce palais auquel tu n'appartenais pas? Une femme serait morte ... On lui maintenait la tête sous l'eau. Elle se débattait ... puis elle cessait de se débattre ... Il avait aimé cette femme, un jour, il sait cela ... Sa solitude, il l'appelle Soledad ... Il se plonge dans son histoire. J'étais le sultan ... Les autres femmes étaient jalouses ... Elles la noyèrent ... Elle me trompa avec un jeune Andalou ... Je la noyai ... Elle se jeta dans l'étang.] (*Miroirs* 172)

Who is this unknown male, in/inventing the same story as Éléonore/ Soledad and therefore indistinguishable from her, much like the deaf-mute? To whom is he speaking?

He sees an artist on the stairs (Éléonore) and remembers a woman in a bar who was later found dead in a swimming pool (Jeanne): "Did he follow her ... Her head under the water. He doesn't know any more. Only Soledad [his dream girl] exists" ["L'avait-il suivie ... La tête sous l'eau. Il ne sait plus. Seule Soledad existe"] (*Miroirs* 173). He will go home and listen to the *Brandenburg Concertos*, just like Marc, the professor who, while making love with Jeanne, murmurs the name of Éléonore. The plot has become a puzzle, a mystery to solve.

The scene abruptly shifts, and we are back in Vancouver where Éléonore is with her lover François (as in Delarue?) and two new characters, Daniela and Rodrigue. They talk animatedly about Charles Ming, the man from Hong Kong, and his accomplice.[18] He is said to have crossed the border (just like Angel) and to be on the prowl in the area ("There's danger on the edge of town," in Morrison's "The End," and Éléonore likes to walk alone on the beach). While Éléonore simply listens and does not narrate, maintaining that she does not read newspapers, the threesome discusses Ming's filming (male gaze) of his tortured victims and the successful sale of these masterpieces of horror. Ming, in his black leather jacket (like Angel), has walked across the United States like a specialist in death (like the hitchhiker in Morrison's poem; as he sings in "Riders on a Storm": "There's a killer on the road") who concentrates on the victim's genitals and appears insensitive to tears and supplications (like the stranger at the beginning of this mirror).

The narrator inserts some observations: Éléonore tries to imagine the man from Hong Kong as "longiligne" (slender) – reminding us of "l'homme long/oblong" in Brossard's *Le Désert mauve* – and then superimposes the image of Rimbaud, that other vagabond rebel. While she is thus thinking, the three friends use their excited conversation about Ming as an opportunity to talk about the obvious – to them – links among sex, pleasure, orgasm, pain, torture, and death: "'They wonder if, having reached these paroxysms, pain is not related to sexual pleasure.' 'Death would then be a special kind of orgasm'" ["'On se demande si, arrivée à ces paroxysmes, la douleur ne s'apparente pas à la jouissance.' 'La mort serait un orgasme très particulier'"] (*Miroirs* 177). It seems that Ming only loves death (in *The Doors*, Morrison is portrayed the same way): "That insatiable lover," says Éléonore in her sole interjection into this conversation (*Miroirs* 178).

She then leaves the bar to walk on the beach: "Of course, who could know that the killer is panting, starving, this hunted beast ...? But from far away the beast sees the woman walking, it smells from afar the odour of this woman coming toward it ... the beast holds its breath, hunches up, ready to pounce. Its eye gleams in the dark" ["Bien sûr, qui pourrait savoir que le tueur halète, affamé, cette bête traquée ...? Mais la bête perçoit de loin le pas de la promeneuse, elle flaire de loin l'odeur de celle qui vient vers elle ... la bête retient son souffle, se recroqueville, prête à bondir. Son oeil luit dans le noir"] (*Miroirs* 178).

In this terrifying open ending, where we cannot know what will happen, where Éléonore is being stalked by a male beast (or at least as it is invented and narrated), the killer could take any "face from the ancient (Greco-Roman?) gallery" [the mask of any of the men in these mirrors: "The face in the mirror won't stop," sings Morrison in "When the Music's Over"] and "walk on down the hall" (beach). With a primal scream, he could violently rape his dream girl/mother and, with this birth of tragedy (toward which he has no sensitivity), kill the female. If death is the insatiable lover ("our love become a funeral pyre," in "Light My Fire"), then it could also be one's "only friend," "limitless and free," where there is "no safety or surprise" ("The End"). For, as Morrison sings at the beginning of Rioux's first mirror, "Tell me where your freedom lies" ("The Crystal Ship"), and as an introduction to all six mirrors, "The future is uncertain / but the end is always near" ("Roadhouse Blues").

It is possible that all of these stories have been imagined, invented, and narrated by a female (the "I" who says "I"; the woman who writes her; the faces in the mirror? – to paraphrase Cunha), perhaps Éléonore. She is, perhaps, a free subject using crude language to depict the continuing victim-status of women in a violent, sexual male world. But unlike the counteracting of male violence with female, lesbian, creative love in *Le Désert mauve*, there is no antidote in this text. The male gaze continues to dominate and control, in particular at the end. The Oedipal ending of Jim Morrison's song, as applied to the ending of the novel, brings us back to Smart's theory: in order to take the first step toward a network of reflections other than those under the male gaze of the Father, the female writer must break out of the Oedipal house. *Les Miroirs d'Éléonore* seems, rather, to bring us back into that dominant sphere, where Éléonore's transgression has only led her back to be encoded in a gendered role as a woman.

Rioux's novel was published in 1990. Since the 1980s, and especially as of the 1990s and now in the first decade of the twentieth century, however, other women writers of Quebec – as well as in the United States, France, and Great Britain – have been crafting texts, films, and a variety of forms in popular culture in which female protagonists have crossed into that dominant male hegemonic sphere, created their own "tough" female gaze, and taken control of their own sexuality and even the sexuality of others. In a progression of erotic, sexual/pornographic, sexually violent, and purely violent texts – often playing with the audience/reader in a game of "reality" *versus* "spun tales" and thus frequently assuming a parodic stance – the female imagination has begun to "re-frame" gender in what we have come to accept as North American (and increasingly global) cultures.

EROTICISM AND GRAPHIC SEXUALITY

Experiences aren't pornographic; only images and representations – structures of the imagination – are.

Susan Sontag, "The Pornographic Imagination"

L'imaginaire est le plus actif aphrodisiaque. Et le seul.
[The imaginary is the most potent aphrodisiac. And the only one.]

Claire Dé, "Comme un état de grâce." *Coup de foudre* (1993)

The Pornography Debate in the United States

Americans are divided on the issue of pornography. Even trying to define it causes confusion, and, as former U.S. Supreme Court Justice Potter Stewart once stated, pornography, although recognizable, may be indefinable: "I shall not ... attempt further to define [pornography] and perhaps I could never succeed in intelligibly doing so. But I know it when I see it" (Jacobellis v. Ohio, 378 U.S. 184 [1964]). In the United States, efforts to limit or criminalize pornography have led some to object that such measures would deny the First Amendment, giving all citizens the right to free speech. Others feel that pornography must be restricted because it is harmful to women and children. Feminists are quite split on these matters, and the resulting battle lines have been interestingly drawn: pro-pornography feminists allied with porn producers and distributors; anti-pornography feminists weighing in with allies across all political and social spectrums. The pro-porn camp is currently headed by feminist lawyer, professor, and president of the American Civil Liberties Union, Nadine Strossen, along with others such as performance artist Karen

Finley; and the anti-porn camp is headed by feminist lawyer and professor, Catharine MacKinnon and feminist theorists Andrea Dworkin and Robin Morgan. Both groups are battling against silencing women. Does pornography silence women by giving a voice solely to the men who produce it and whose fantasies and realities it reflects? Or does censoring pornography silence women who have a right to express themselves sexually? Either pornography robs women of their free speech (the anti-pornography view), or censorship robs women of their free speech (the pro-pornography stand). But whatever the stance, pornography is "big business" in the United States – as in the rest of the world. The existence of thousands of porn websites, the production of porn films, the popularity of strip shows, and even the launching in 2003 of a new television series entitled *Skin* demonstrate that pornography has a wide audience.

Pornography in Canada

In Canada the situation is similarly confusing, although the emphasis is somewhat different. An example is the case of R. *v.* Butler. Donald Butler, the owner of a Manitoba video store, had been convicted for the possession, sale, and distribution of hard-core videotapes, magazines, and sexual paraphernalia. In February 1992, the Supreme Court of Canada granted his appeal and ordered his case returned to the lower court for retrial. This constituted the first challenge to Canada's obscenity law, Section 163 of the Criminal Code. At issue was the consideration of whether Section 163 violated the freedom of expression guaranteed by Section 2(b) of the 1982 Canadian Charter of Rights and Freedoms. Although the case was found to violate the Charter, this violation was seen to be justified under Section 1 as a reasonable limit prescribed by law and informed by equal rights guaranteed in Sections 15 and 28. The Court upheld the constitutionality of these obscenity laws and set out a new test for determining whether representations are obscene. Sexually explicit representations that do not include violence, are neither degrading nor dehumanizing, and do not involve children were deemed to be not obscene. In other words, sexual explicitness was not condemned in and of itself (Cossman and Bell 3–4). Six weeks after the Butler decision was handed down, however, the Toronto Police brought criminal charges against a gay and lesbian bookstore for selling *Bad Attitudes*, an American lesbian, erotic fiction magazine. At the trial, the magazine was deemed obscene, and the bookstore was found guilty of selling lesbian sado-masochistic representations (Cossman and Bell 4).

According to Brenda Cossman and Shannon Bell, in their edited volume *Bad Attitudes on Trial: Pornography, Feminism, and the Butler Decision*, in the post-Butler era, straight, mainstream pornography is flourishing, but if there is even a hint of "alternative sexualities," such representations are scrutinized because they challenge conventional notions of sexuality: "What is on trial are so-called 'Bad Attitudes': the attitudes of sexual others" (4). In addition, Cossman and Bell, and the contributors to their volume, challenge the interpretation that the Butler decision was a feminist victory, arguing that there is no consensus on the meaning of pornography (we are back to Justice Stewart): "Multiple meanings reside in the same image, therefore the image can never be seen; it is and it is not" (9). Playing with these multiple meanings can challenge established sexual morality and practice and destabilize the distinction between the realms of high theory (i.e., philosophy) and low theory/culture (i.e., pornography) (9). What becomes even more interesting, in my view and for the purposes of this study, however, is what happens to these meanings and these images when they are created by women ostensibly for women?

Pornography and Socially Constructed Sexuality

In their essay "Porn Power: Sex, Violence, and the Meaning of Images in 1980s Feminism," the self-pronounced pro-porn feminists Kegan Doyle and Dany Lacombe maintain that sexuality is socially constructed, that pornography helps to construct sexuality, that social structures continually produce new subjectivities, and that meaning is consequently always a matter of context. To them, images are thus pornographic only if they negate women's autonomy and agency (190, 195, 196). In this same volume of essays on women, sex, and power in the nineties, Lillian S. Robinson speaks of the "Subject/Position": "This newest feminism announces itself as being about power and a fully realized female sexuality ... The current fashion in academic theory is ludic feminism, with its emphasis on *jouissance* and performative modalities and its universalizing assumptions about the relation between historical, psychological, and sexual situations" (182–3).

Judith Butler's important essay "The Force of Fantasy: Feminism, Mapplethorpe, and Discursive Excess," on the real (determined by the unreal), representation, and fantasy, as well as on feminism's relationship with pornography, takes these issues even further: when the phantasmatic assumes the status of the real, it exercises its power most effectively. Referencing both Jacqueline Rose and Foucault, Butler points out that fantasy postures as real, haunts and contests borders, and informs political discourse (106–8). For her, the narrator of a fantasy is, by definition, in the fantasy; the "I" contributes to and is the frame (109). In other words, the "I" has created or made up the entire fantasy and thus has to play a multiple and ever-shifting role in the scene. But if there is no subject in fantasy, only the proliferation of identities, then fantasy must be self-reflexive, its own subject of desire, suspending any claim of being real (110). Unlike many anti-porn feminists, Butler does not see pornography as restricting identity to one position (114). For her, the violence of regulation and prohibition, endorsed by such anti-porn activists as Dworkin, MacKinnon, and former U.S. Senator Jessie Helms, only produces and proliferates what she sees as binary (male, female; gay, straight) representational violence (119). Butler calls instead for replacement of the binary itself through the proliferation of "discursive excess." Her comments are pertinent to one of the major points raised in chapter 1: "In the production of a chaotic multiplicity of representations ... the authority and prevalence of the reductive and violent imagery ... will lose their monopoly" (121). Erotic, sexual, and pornographic texts by women also help break down those binaries, add even more excess to the discursive, and ultimately produce a rich and chaotic multiplicity of representational "I"s that need to be read with those of "real" female life.

Women's Theories of Pornography

These more contemporary investigations into issues of pornography and its relationship to women are prolongations of earlier critical work by historians and theorists such as Lynn Hunt, Angela Carter, Susan Griffin, Susan Sontag, Linda Williams, Susan Rubin Suleiman, and Susanne Kappeler. *The Invention of Pornography: Obscenity and the Origins of Modernity, 1500–1800*, for instance, is a highly cited work in which Hunt explores the link between male-created porn and democracy and attempts to explain why pornography has for so long been worrisome to so many. Quoting Peter Wagner, Hunt states: "'Porn is a written or visual presentation in realistic form of any genital or sexual behavior with a deliberate violation of existing and widely accepted moral and social taboos'"(Wagner 7, as quoted in Hunt 25). Refering to Cleland's *Fanny Hill* as well as the works of Sade, for example, Hunt defines certain pornography as a specialized form of the novel for which the reader's imagination is called upon to create the effect of real sexual activity. She calls this characteristic the "truth-telling trope of pornography," which uses a "language of transgression" (37):

> [An] obscene word played on [the] contrast between different social registers of language – crude and elegant, lower and upper class, masculine and feminine – in order to achieve its effect. To enact social transgression and a kind of hyper-realism, obscene language fetishizes certain words related to sex; the obscene word substitutes for the body part in question but, in the process, acquires the status of a fetish. As a consequence, the original emphasis on realism paradoxically devolves into a form of the grotesque where penises are always huge, vaginas multiply in number and sexual coupling takes place in a kind of frenzy that is hardly "realistic." This results in pornography that is imaginary and at times fantastic even though its effects on its readers are very real. (37–8)

Clearly related to Russo's concept of the female grotesque, Butler's explorations of fantasy, and Williams's "frenzy of the visible," Hunt's discussion also refers to Angela Carter's *The Sadeian Woman*, in which Carter proposes that pornography reinforces the tendency to think in the false universals of sexual archetype and has the "false simplicity of fables" (Carter 16; Hunt 39–40). Interestingly, early modern pornography, written by men for other men, often valorized female sexual activity, by displaying interchangeable bodies, thereby minimizing certain social and gender differences (Hunt 44). From the sixteenth to the eighteenth centuries, pornographic women's bodies were also offered as a focus of male bonding, creating a sort of male social levelling (Hunt 44). As of the eighteenth and especially the nineteenth centuries, "new biological and moral standards for sexual differences evolved [and] pornography seemed to become even more exotic and dangerous. It had to be stamped out" (Hunt 45). Our contemporary "issues" with pornography stem from this period and from such concerns. Unlike pornography written by men for other men, however, more recent female pornography (written by women presumably for other women) is seen as an attempt to break out of, transgress, liberate, and rewrite sexual archetypes and false universals. Many clearly consider it exotic and dangerous to suggest that women have agency, control, and power and that they are indeed refusing any biological and moral standards. How do such female sexual and pornographic texts "play" to audiences and readers when they move even further into the realms of sexual violence and representations of female violence as re-framed by women?

Not all critics see female-created pornography as a liberation for women. Susan Griffin in her *Pornography and Silence*, for example, describes pornography as "an expression not of human erotic feeling and desire, and not of a love of the life of the body, but of a fear of bodily knowledge, and a desire to silence eros" (1). She interprets Pauline Réage's *Histoire d'O*, perhaps the most famous pornographic (sexually violent) novel written by a woman for both male and female readers, as the representation of the destruction of the woman's body, and as a powerful example of sadomasochism and female non-being, rather than as a liberating proclamation of agency. A novel that she, like Susan Sontag, considers to be a work of art, *The Story of* O ends with the death of O, thereby promoting the negation of the self, the shell of a sexual quest, and the extinction of fulfillment as a sexual being (226). If this novelistic non-being is simply a fiction that exists only in male experience (229), and if "the pornographic mind is the mind of our culture" (3), then, says Griffin, "we have inherited an identity of nothingness from the pornographic culture" (232).

In "The Pornographic Imagination," Sontag also writes of "the emotional flatness of pornography" (219), although she views the obscene as a primal attribute of humanity: human sexuality "remains one of the demonic forces in human consciousness – pushing us at intervals close to taboo and dangerous desires, which range from the impulse to commit sudden arbitrary violence upon another person to the voluptuous yearning for the extinction of one's consciousness, for death itself" (221–2).[19] Expressing itself through a limited and crude emotional vocabulary, related to prospects of action, the totalizing pornographic universe in *The Story of* O abounds with religious metaphors as it denigrates "the range and seriousness of sexual experience that still rules this culture" (230). In our era pornography gives the imagination different choices, which have resonated with "this vast frustration of human passion and seriousness since the old religious imagination, with its secure monopoly on the total imagination, began in the late eighteenth century to crumble" (231). Sontag firmly believes that the pornographic imagination, although often degraded and emotionless,[20] is worth listening to as a: "spectacularly cramped form of the human imagination [with] its peculiar access to some truth ... (Everyone, at least in dreams, has inhabited the world of the pornographic imagination ... but only the full-time residents make the fetishes, the trophies, the art.) That discourse one might call the poetry of transgression is also knowledge. He [*sic*] who transgresses not only breaks a rule. He [*sic*] goes somewhere that the others are not; and he [*sic*] knows something the others don't know" (232). It is evident that such a potentially transgressive voyage, when imagined and artistically created by women, risks being seen as even more dangerous – especially if, given its female gaze and agency, the pornographic woman goes somewhere where the others are not and if she knows something the others don't (yet) know.

Linda Williams also explores this female pornographic imagination in "Sequels and Revisions: 'A Desire of One's Own,'" a chapter of her *Hard Core: Power, Pleasure, and the "Frenzy of the Visible."* With women now entering a sphere formerly identified as the domain of the male – as both consumers and creators of pornography – the difficulty lies in their having to use the dominant discourse in their own tentative speaking voices (230). Williams uses the model of Candida Royalle's predominantly female production company, Femme Productions, to explore the problem of what to do with the phallus, not just as a pattern of imagery, but also in relation to narrative structure. If heterosexual women's desire for a man and his sexual difference is focused on his penis, how does the female pornographer represent women's pleasure in pornography; how can it be represented other than as the envy of or the submission to the phallus that symbolizes phallic power and potency? "Is it possible," Williams asks, "to represent the penis so that it is not also the phallus, that is, so that the penis is not associated as the standard and measure of all desire?" (247). For Williams, the crux of the issue of hard-core power and the representation of desire and pleasure for women "is not simply a matter of subduing the phallus or curtailing its symbolization." Rather, she continues, quoting Jessica Benjamin in "A Desire of One's Own" (1986, 342), "it is a matter of replacing the monopoly on the sexual subjectivity that this phallus stands for, its monolithic symbolization of desire" (258). Again referring to Benjamin, as well as to Teresa De Lauretis, Williams posits that a woman's difficulty in owning desire is not caused by her lack of a penis but rather by her need to identify with a sexual agent, to articulate as a sexual subject of desire. The problem, therefore, is social. It is not a matter of replacing the power of the phallus with that of the vulva, as does Judy Chicago. It is not about the symbol itself but what it stands for – exciting movement to the outside, exploratory freedom and agency, all associated with sexual subjectivity. A female re-vision of pornography, therefore, must include both the exciting outside and the self-discovery of one's inside, the recognition of one's own sexual subjectivity and outward agency (258–62). My interest here, however, is this: what takes place when this form of pornography becomes sexually violent and this sexual violence turns into representations of female violence. What outer agency is then being proposed?

Linda Williams mentions the linguistic difficulties encountered by women empowering women in pornographic texts. Similarly, Susan Rubin Suleiman, in "The Politics and Poetics of Female Eroticism: 'Equal Rights, or, Telling It with Four-Letter Words,'" categorizes the use of obscene language in Erica Jong's *Fear of Flying* as a "self-conscious reversal of stereotypes, and in some sense a parody of the language of the tough-guy narrator/heroes" (121). The accumulative use of the word "fuck" in this novel, for example, must be interpreted as parodic[21] – a reversal of roles and of language whereby the objectified woman of male pornographic fiction usurps both the language and the way of looking at the opposite sex, as she exhibits self-irony and undercuts her predecessors (121). Additionally, the female protagonist, Isadora Wing, frequently couples the first-person pronoun with an obscene noun ("my cunt"), reminding one, as Suleiman cleverly tells us, of Claudine Herrmann's "female thieves of language" ["les voleuses de langue"][22] – women who invent "new structures, new words, a new syntax that will shake up and *transform* old habits of thought and old ways of seeing" (123).

I have already mentioned Susanne Kappeler's description of the (male for male) "pornography of representation" in which representations are more "real" than reality, serve as the "Other" to the real, and provide a perceived conflation of the (male) author and the (male) audience. According to Kappeler, pornography is not a special case of sexuality but a form of representation in which the debate has focused on "porn" at the expense of "graphy" (2). Pornography has come to mean obscene or violent sex, expressions of sexuality that most people do not approve of, do not particularly like, and do not want to see in "real" life (2). What some fear even more, of course, is such representation being created by a woman for other women – an imagined danger that could "spill over" into "reality." If "pornography exists in the symbiosis of Thanatos and Eros" (Kappeler 98), as I have shown in Hélène Rioux's Éléonore, writing becomes a surrogate pleasure for men (99) and the narrative becomes "the cultural archeplot of power" (104), a paradigm of domination, coercion, and degradation of the Other to object status (104–5) – with the subject/object positions reversed in pornographic and especially sexually violent and violent texts by certain female writers. For Kappeler, the male pornographic subject, imagined by the male writer of pornography, is on a quest for both sexual and writing subjectivity (142), especially if Butler's multiple "I"s contribute to and form the frame of the text. Given the meaning of the Greek origin of the word "porn" as "prostitution," this form of artistic representation emphasizes power and exchange of a commodity. And when the "commodities" take control of their own bodies and their own texts, as I shall demonstrate in the Québécoise Nelly Arcan's *Putain* and the French Catherine Millet's *La Vie sexuelle de Catherine M.*, for example, "everyone is running for the 'speaking function'" (Kappeler 199).

U.S. Popular Culture and Sexual Women

In the United States, the female speaking subject has for some time been highlighted in popular culture. Sherrie Inness's "tough girls," for instance, and more recently "action chicks," may not necessarily write or star in pornography for other women – although there is a growing female sex industry by women for women (Navarro) – but their physical, mental, and sexual strength is heightened in the female roles of comic books, the animated character of *Kim Possible*, the television stars of *Xena: Warrior Princess* and *Buffy the Vampire Slayer,* in post-apocalyptic films like *Terminator* and *Matrix*, and in outer space films such as *Aliens* and *Star Trek*. As Helen Birch has pointed out, however, the "usual" connections among toughness, danger, violence, and sexuality remain: the "deadly dolls" of Hollywood – for example, the killers of *Fatal Attraction* and *Thelma and Louise* – transgress into the formerly all-male world, all the while maintaining their sexy looks or subtly suggesting "alternative" sexual preferences (as I have noted in chapter 1). If these tough and sexual women cross boundaries and become speaking subjects, is it not expected – in fact feared – that their representations of pornographic, sexually violent, and violent behaviour will follow?

The mention of the popularity of *Star Trek* as a platform from which powerful women have sprung in U.S. popular culture brings me to another phenomenon that has influenced both American and global/western depictions of sexual and sexually violent women by women: "fringe-fandoms." As of the late 1960s, a significant number of women began writing explicitly erotic material, imbued with pain and violence, in the form of women's "zines" – "fringe-fandoms," fandoms, and SF (speculative fiction). Influenced by *Star Trek*, but greatly ignored by the men in fandom circles, these women's zines have become erotic, violent, sexual, angry, and increasingly sexually explicit since the 1970s (Bjorklund 255, 256, 259, 264). This underground women's erotica is mostly about men, often featuring heroic male partners in homoerotic love relationships – writing known as "slash" (Bjorklund 264). In addition to these texts by women for women another new creative female product has recently appeared: the underground video artform called the songtape, "homemade music videos, created by fans to tell entirely new 'stories' through providing collages of carefully chosen visual images" (Bjorklund 287). These songtapes are explicitly erotic, showing men in scenes of masturbation, fellatio, and anal penetration, and treating these images as if they were centerfold illustrations in *Hustler* and *Playboy* (Bjorklund 288–9). Clearly exposing and mocking the (violently) sexist and sexualized world, these underground erotic, pornographic, and sexually violent written, musical, and video images offer yet another form of subversion by women for women.

Female Pornography in France

But the United States by no means has the monopoly on pornography created by and for women, as the latest developments in France confirm. In a country that has given us Rabelais, the Marquis de Sade, and Laclos (and in 2003 even the launching of the magazine *Bordel*), among countless others, it was only a matter of time before women followed suit. What is surprising is how long it has taken this erotic and overtly pornographic literature to surface and to be noticed. Rachilde's (the pseudonym of Marguerite Eymery) *Marquise de Sade* and Pauline Réage's *Histoire d'O* notwithstanding, one would think that the first female pornographic French text to appear in print was Catherine Millet's *La Vie sexuelle de Catherine M.* in 2001. Perhaps it is the fact that the author is the recognized director of *Art Press*; perhaps it is that she recounts her sexual escapades with a crudeness and clarity that have astounded (and bored) some French. Millet may not (yet) be in the mainstream – unlike the powerfully sexual artwork by Sarah Lucas in Great Britain – but this novel has piqued the interest of and "worried" both critics and the reading public.

Indeed, journalist and literary critic Christian Authier, in his 2002 study *Le Nouvel Ordre sexuel*, uses the expressions "porno-chic" (7), "under the sign of "hard" (8), and "protesting neo-feminism" ["un néo-féminisme revendicatif"] (9) in his discussions of Millet's novel, Virginie Despentes' novel and film *Baise-moi*, Catherine Breillet's

Romance, Raffaela Anderson's *Hard*, Claire Legendre's *Viande*, Alice Massat's *Le Ministre de l'intérieur*, and Marie Nimier's *La Nouvelle Pornographie,* among other such texts. Assessing this literature and film in the context of and as examples of a new sexual order that has emerged only since the mid-1990s, Authier asks what is going on here. To him, these women have initiated a new wave of the body, sexuality, pornography, incest, and prostitution (13). *Baise-moi* has, according to Authier, become a rallying cry for a certain type of counter culture (14), while these authors' texts exhibit a "fascination for fluctuating identities and mutating bodies" – all in what he calls a new queer culture (141–2).[23] In a nice touch, Authier, disturbed, confused, sarcastic, and yet somehow proud, identifies "the French touch of Generation X" (23) – the Generation X of Kurt Cobain and Courtney Love – and states that this new women's pornography is authentic; it is to literature what reality shows are to television: "Direct. The author is no longer hidden. Masks are off. Not a novel, not fiction, but a memoir, an assigned memoir" ["Du direct. L'auteur ne se cache plus. Bas les masques. Pas de roman, pas de fiction, mais une mémoire, un devoir de mémoire"] (23). Interestingly relating some of this narcissism to the young "génération lyrique" in Québec, as defined by François Ricard (234), Authier maintains that the French have recently become "sex animals" (Authier 269), rather than Foucault's "confessing animals" (*History of Sexuality* 59) ["bêtes d'aveu"] (*Histoire de la sexualité* 80). Stay tuned for Authier's subsequent analysis of female sexual violence.

It Started Earlier in Québec

Christian Authier identifies this phenomenon of French female literary sexuality/pornography only as of the mid-1990s. In Canada, as early as 1977, John Moss wrote in his *Sex and Violence in the Canadian Novel* that contemporary and postmodern Canadian fiction, distinguished by its affinity for sex and violence as related to identity, has long constructed the female as the sexual aggressor (5,13). He also declares that there is less sex (and violence) in the Quebec novel because identity is not in question in Quebec; the Québécois know who they are (28–9).[24]

More familiar with Quebec, Lori Saint-Martin, in *Contre-voix,* devotes several pages to an analysis of politics and sexuality in reference to the figure of the prostitute in both canonical and more recent feminist Québécois literature. She cites examples from the 1970s and 1980s by such well known and highly regarded feminist writers as Brossard,

France Théoret, Denise Boucher, Josée Yvon, Carole David, and Francine Noel, and concludes that these works exhibit "a fascination for the prostitute, not in her otherness as in masculine texts, but in her similarity, even in her complicity. Victim or rebel, the prostitute, in these texts, is an exemplary feminine figure" who openly enjoys erotic pleasure ["une fascination pour la prostituée, non pas dans l'altérité comme dans les textes masculins, mais dans la ressemblance, voire la connivence. Victime ou révoltée, la prostituée, dans ces textes, est une figure féminine exemplaire"] (Saint-Martin 201).

As I mentioned earlier, one of the first critics to explore the growing literature of female eroticism written by women was Luise von Flotow. In "Tenter l'érotique: Eroticism in Contemporary Women's Writing from Quebec,"she extrapolates from a short story, "Histoire de Q" by Anne Dandurand, which appeared in the 1985 special issue of *La Vie en Rose* devoted to eroticism. Von Flotow's argument is based on the contrast between an essay by Audre Lorde, who sees female eroticism as a life force and a creative energy, and work by Georges Bataille – who sees the erotic as transgressive, death-oriented, and intimately connected to violence and murder. Dandurand's text, says von Flotow, with "its crude explicitness, its violence and rage, and its curious form of moralism," created much controversy, eliciting five pages of discussion and commentary in the same issue of the journal as to whether the story was a "cheap, gratuitous text in bad taste" or was indeed erotic (von Flotow 91). Recognizing that these controversies would undoubtedly not have arisen if the text had been written by a man and if the sexual aggressors had been male instead of female, Dandurand herself fanned the flames even further two years later by stating: "Eroticism in writing affects me like a drug; I always need to go further" ["l'érotisme en écriture me fait l'effet d'une drogue, il faut toujours aller plus loin"] (as cited in von Flotow 91; Dandurand, "Écrire ou mourir" 40).

For von Flotow, women writing the erotic are "writing their way out of a suppression of the erotic, and into a reassessment of the quality of all aspects of their lives. This *writing-out* must lead to confrontation" (93). It is difficult to express women's eroticism, since it has long been a cultural taboo, with the representation of the nude and the obscene entirely usurped by men. Some feminist theorists and writers, however, claim that women's erotic expression celebrates the woman as an active agent: "In the more recent scenario, the woman may still perceive herself as object ... but has simultaneously constructed herself as the subject of the erotic discourse. She takes on both roles, the traditionally passive female role as well as the active role of voyeur and sexual predator" (von Flotow 93). Women's erotic writing attempts to privatize the formerly public female body and to "re-inscribe an individual mode, a personal construct of the body, its feelings and functions" (95). But, in von Flotow's view, it is still only a tentative attempt (as in the French "tenter") to write on the edge, take risks, and confront a reading public (95). As we move from the mid-1980s to today's erotic/sexual writing coming out of Quebec, however, I shall make clear that this risk-taking has become increasingly bold.

Von Flotow remarks in her 1990 essay that there had been a baffling silence of critics writing about female eroticism, especially in Quebec. Indeed, it was a good eight years later before Jean Levasseur published "Le Féminisme québécois et la littérature sexuelle." After taking us through the history of early feminism, with its hatred of the male, Levasseur speaks of "the emergence, in the mid-1980s, of an erotic and heterosexual literature which represents a crucial stage in the evolution of Quebec feminism as much as of women's literature ... The woman dares to avow openly and publicly her interest in the male and in sex [in a] flowering of homo and heterosexual erotic-pornographic literature, where the principle of personal pleasure dominates all others" ["l'émergence, au milieu des années 80, d'une littérature érotique et hétérosexuelle [qui] représente une étape cruciale dans l'évolution autant du féminisme québécois que de la littérature féminine ... La femme ose avouer ouvertement et publiquement son intérêt pour le mâle et le sexe [dans une] floraison d'une littérature érotico-pornographique homo ou hétérosexuelle, où le principe du plaisir individuel domine tous les autres"] (976–7). In the mid-1980s, in the midst of feminist debates in the United States about the nature, dangers, and free expression of male pornography (see Dworkin, MacKinnon, and Strossen), Lorde wrote of the power of the erotic, Anne de Guise spoke of the "pornographic gaze" ("le regard pornographique"), which is innate in men but absent in women, and Elfriede Jelinek announced the feminist failure of porn/eroticism because men had so overexploited it that women writers couldn't help but fail to take it over (Levasseur 978–9).

Into this global context came the previously mentioned 1985 special issue of *La Vie en Rose* on eroticism, which included Dandurand's "Histoire de Q" and the commentaries and analyses of female pornography that it incited: these studies, writes Levasseur, "will cause the confrontation between a radical and aging feminism, which saw in this text a gratuitousness that shattered the utopia of a new matriarchal society, and a more open neo-feminism, which wanted to express freely its taste for sexuality, for all sexualities" ["feront s'affronter un féminisme radical et vieillissant, lequel voyait dans ce texte une gratuité qui brisait l'utopie d'une nouvelle société matriarcale, et un néo-féminisme plus ouvert qui voulait exprimer librement son goût de la sexualité, de toutes les sexualités"] (Levasseur 979). According to Levasseur, these texts used almost word for word all of the critiques that feminists before them had levelled against men and their pornography. In the same issue, as well as Anne Dandurand's "scandalous" short story, there appeared a piece by a writer soon to become one of the most popular heroines of Quebec female heterosexual eroticism, Diane Boissonneault, alias Lili Gulliver. Levasseur places these Quebec texts in the vein of a tendency already in vogue in the United States with Susie Bright, Lonnie Barbach, and the Kensington Ladies' Erotica Society (980).[25] Thus began, in Levasseur's view, an era of female empowerment: "'Neo-' or 'post-' feminism has thus chosen to free itself from the anti-male model imposed by the older generation and from now on has no more fear of being unworthy of 'Saint Kate Millet or Saint Andrea Dworkin'" ["Le 'néo' ou le 'post' féminisme a donc choisi de s'affranchir du modèle anti-mâle imposé par l'ancienne génération et ne craint plus désormais de ne pas être digne de 'sainte Kate Millet ou de sainte Andrea Dworkin'"] (Levasseur 981 and as quoted from Tramier 1). Citing writers such as Louise Anne Bouchard, Pauline Harvey, Lili Maxime, Brigitte Caron, Lise Bissonnette, as well as Lili Gulliver, Levasseur expands what I have maintained in chapter 2 in regard to Quebec's being influenced by its cross-border neighbour: "In the image of the United States, feminine Quebec itself has also produced many texts with unrestrained eroticism and with diverse and diversified sexual tendencies" ["À l'image des États-Unis, le Québec féminin a lui aussi produit une multitude de textes à l'érotisme effréné et aux tendances sexuelles diverses et diversifiées"] (981) – linking (somewhat unfortunately, in my view) to American conservative feminists like Katie Roiphe and Camille Paglia. He also prefigures my assessment that this "tidal wave" of female erotica moved across the Atlantic to France only at a later date (981).

The Parodic

"Pornography isn't a form that can parody itself," says Susan Sontag (217). And yet, she also suggests that pornography and parody are in one sense antithetical and in another sense one and the same. In my view, the two are interrelated, and any analysis of female erotic and pornographic texts – whether they are purely sexual or sexually violent (or even purely violent) – must include an attempt to understand the role that parody plays in many of them. Sontag continues: "It is the nature of the pornographic imagination to prefer ready-made conventions of character, setting, and action. Pornography is a theater of types, never of individuals. A parody of pornography, so far as it has any real competence, always remains pornography. Indeed, parody is one common form of pornographic writing" (217).

Canadian critic Linda Hutcheon considers parody to be the perfect postmodern form (*A Poetics of Postmodernism* 11). As a technique that has helped women take theory and move it into the "real" world and highlight the value of margins (16) rather than the central dominant discourse (as I have indicated in chapter 1), parody, "repetition with critical distance ... allows ironic signalling of difference at the very heart of similarity ... [and] enacts both change and cultural continuity" (26). It is a self-reflexive discourse that "allows an artist to speak *to* a discourse from *within* it, but without being totally recuperated by it." As such, it has become a form popular among those who have been marginalized by a dominant ideology to allow them both to distance and to involve the artist and her readers (35). Echoing Adrienne Rich and predating Linda Williams's use of the term "re-vision" and my use of the term "re-framing," Hutcheon sees postmodern difference as "always plural and provisional" (65) – and for my purposes here, always plural and "pro-visional" – before the vision, a tentative vision, a provisional vision, a positive and pro-active vision.

What these female writers of eroticism and pornography often do well is to take a male pornographic text – complete with its canonical images and discourse coded as male – open it up, and turn it on its head by means of what Hutcheon calls "parodic double-voicing" (67) and "parodic intertexts" (118), and (what I have touched on at the end of chapter 1) as witty punning, exaggeration, carnivalesque, or "camp," humorously rebelling, abusing, and transgressing all the way. It is in this sense that (female) postmodern parody puts "into question the authority of any act of writing" (Hutcheon 129), seemingly in opposition to certain of Lori Saint-Martin's "metafeminist" texts with their intimate and personal nature.

Of course women writers have been using different forms of humour for a long time, as Lucie Joubert shows us in *Le Carquois de velours:*

L'Ironie au féminin dans la littérature québécoise, 1960–1980. The texts she cites as examples are replete with ironic punctuation markings – parentheses, quotation marks, dashes, and capital letters (36). The authors mimic the vulgar and obscene terms used by men: "Taking back vulgarity in their own name, they nullify its humiliating potential and enslave it ... turning the meaning upside down in order to show just how far they can go" ["Reprenant la vulgarité à leur compte, elles en annulent le potentiel dévalorisant et l'asservissent ... renverser le sens, pour montrer jusqu'où elles peuvent aller"] (45). These female authors put misogynistic words into the mouths of men in order to denounce such attitudes (54), and they try, through irony, to take back a form of male derogatory discourse by using it as a tool of mockery ["récupérer par l'ironie une forme de discours dépréciatif des hommes que ces auteures emploient comme instrument de dérision"] (56). According to Joubert, some women writers show the stupidity of males and make use of both irony and sarcasm against male virility and the penis – not directly, but subtly making fun of it (136–8). Joubert has, of course, limited her study to texts written between 1960 and 1980. Since then, and especially since 1985, as I have mentioned, many women writers have stopped being so subtle and have become crude and obscene about the male body and especially the penis. Their mocking version of the world, and especially of the (male) North American world, as presented to their readers may have been different from what was expected of them between 1960 and 1980, but it has "matured" since those decades. Joubert's writers "are not looking to conquer power, but simply to occupy the space that is coming to them" ["ne cherchent pas à conquérir le pouvoir, mais simplement à occuper l'espace qui leur revient"] (202). The writers under consideration here want both to occupy their desired space and to conquer power.

1982–2002: Two Decades of an Imaginary World of Quebec Female Sexuality

Since the focus of this study remains the Quebec/North American female imagination and literary violence, and since the thrust of this chapter is to illustrate the move from the construction of the erotic/pornographic to the sexually violent and finally to the violent female protagonist, as imagined by women writers, I shall content myself with a brief and chronological textual analysis of representative female erotic and sexually graphic works of fiction that have appeared since 1982.

If Anne Dandurand has been "highlighted" a number of times already in this study, I need now to introduce her twin sister, Claire Dé, whose short stories and novels also help form a core of sexually transgressive fiction in the past two decades. One such early example is "La Causeuse orientale" (1982), a short story included in a collection of tales, *La Louve-garou*, written by Dé and Dandurand. Cleverly illustrated with black and white images that in themselves are worthy of analysis, this collection basks in the darkness of black humour, science fiction, and horror stories, for, as Dandurand says in a presentation to the volume, "Writing, accessible especially at night, and so cheap, inevitably opens its dangerous door to my ghosts" ["L'écriture, accessible surtout la nuit, et si bon marché, ouvre inévitablement sa dangereuse porte à mes fantômes"] (Dandurand, *La Louve-garou* 6).

A humorously recounted erotic reverie of multiple sexual partners, sexual aids, exotic food, and a pleasure-provoking and leisurely lifestyle in a hedonistic landscape, "La Causeuse orientale" tells the tale of the sexually aggressive Dumontine Millejours (rather than "millefeuilles"), her seductive Aunt Alexina, her "pick-up" Richard Beauséjour, and many of their acquaintances who spend a few lazy days together, prepping for sex, talking about sex, experimenting with sex, eating "seafood vol-au-vents, sausages in evocative shapes, and exotic fruit salads" ["des bouchées aux crustacés, des saucissons aux formes évocatrices, et des salades de fruits exotiques"], reading about the "*Sexual Habits of Molluscs/Whimps*" ["*Moeurs sexuelles chez les mollusques*"] (Dé, "La Causeuse" 108), and watching each other dress and undress in titillating strip-teases. The get-together comes to its so-called climax when they make a visit to another friend, Émilien, who offers to show the group "his famous automated curio" ["sa fameuse curiosité automate"], the suggestively titled "Oriental love seat/female conversationalist" ["causeuse orientale"].

An electric shiver ran through the guests. Led by the honorable Émilien, they ["ils et elles" – here no "elles" will be subsumed under "ils"] penetrated a room with walls of stretched, black Flemish rabbit. Nothing else. In the centre was enthroned the purple silk love seat, ten feet long and six feet deep. The silk had been finely worked into multiple creases, recreases, folds, nymphs, petals, lips. Thanks to a most complex electronic movement, everything undulated in suppleness, a gigantic carnation, a shell, a vulva. The honorable Émilien called for two partners. Dumontine's eyes took on an extraordinary brightness, Richard felt himself melting and getting hard as never before. She kissed him, he held her tightly against him. Forgetting the presence of the others, glued to each other, he and she buried themselves in the soft warm depths of the Oriental love seat. [Un frisson électrique parcourut les convives. Guidés par l'honorable Émilien, ils et elles pénétrèrent dans une chambre aux murs tendus de lapin des Flandres noir. Rien d'autre. Au centre trônait la causeuse en soie pourpre, longue d'une dizaine de pieds, profonde de six. La soie avait été travaillée en multiples plis, replis, bourrelets, nymphes, pétales, lèvres. Grâce à un mouvement électronique des plus complexes, tout ça ondulait en souplesse, un oeillet gigantesque, une coquillage, une vulve. L'honorable Émilien réclama deux partenaires. Les yeux de Dumontine prirent un éclat extraordinaire, Richard se sentit fondre et bander comme jamais. Elle l'embrassa, il la serra sur lui. Oubliant l'assistance, collés l'un à l'autre, il et elle s'enfouirent dans les profondeurs moelleuses de la causeuse orientale.] (Dé, "La Causeuse" 110)

After this suggestive but not graphically described sexual experience, Dumontine sensuously undresses and takes a hot bath. She then lies down on her bed and begins to caress herself, abandoning herself over and over to pleasure: "Especially tonight, when my daydreams carry me toward his caresses. How well he has learned, how well he brings me to orgasm. How thirsty I am, this evening, for his kisses, his mouth, his body, his hands. Thirsty for his penis" ["Surtout ce soir, alors que mes rêveries m'emportent vers ses caresses à lui. Comme il a bien appris, comme il me fait jouir. Comme j'ai soif, ce soir, de ses baisers, de sa bouche, de son corps, de ses mains. Soif de son sexe"] (Dé, "La Causeuse" 111).

When Gustave Courbet's painting *L'Origine du monde* appeared in 1866, it provoked outcries of obscenity, and the ensuing scandal led to its supposed and mysterious disappearance until 1995, when it came out of hiding to be part of the collection of the Musée d'Orsay (Courbet, *L'Origine du monde)*. What Courbet had created, of course, was the realistic "portrait" of a women's genitals/vulva as an object for all men to gaze upon and fantasize about. Commissioned by a Turkish diplomat (an "Oriental" of course), this representation of the female sex as the origin of the world (symbolism and humour notwithstanding), was viewed as obscene male pornography – the female sexual object desired by the male subject. Exemplifying what Hunt calls "the truth-telling trope" of pornography with its "language of transgression" and exaggeration, where penises and vaginas are super-sized and ubiquitous (Hunt 37–8), Claire Dé, in characteristic parodic style, has turned this sexual object upside down, so to speak. In her story the female vulva becomes an actual object – a piece of "Oriental" furniture with all the undulating layers of a vulva, draped in purple velvet, and open to engulf both men and women, themselves open to sex. It humorously chats and gossips like a woman while inviting sexual encounters.[26] As the enabler, it is in control, taking its creative role as "the origin of the world" quite seriously but with a light-heartedness that mocks male eroticism and pornography while placing itself in the female subject position. And it does all of this mechanically!

Five years after the appearance of Dé and Dandurand's collection *La Louve-garou*, Dandurand published her own collection of short stories, *Voilà, c'est moi: c'est rien, j'angoisse (Journal imaginaire)*, in which she presents several sexually graphic and sexually violent tales, including her scandalous, "Histoire de Q," which I shall study later in this chapter. I have noted that Kellett-Betsos calls Dandurand's "journal intime" a "discontinuous form," (43), a fragmentary structure through which she explores the relationship between creation and the female condition, and through which she confounds the reader with "truth" and lies. In a number of these stories, Dandurand creates an erotic, sexual landscape for her intimate, discontinuous tales: the woman is the graphically sexual aggressor ("Pour endormir ma mort"); women have created a new race by means of manipulation and mutation, and the men in that new world need to be touched by a woman in order to rediscover their identity ("Pour me consoler j'imagine que les bombes sont tombées"); lesbian sex is described in some detail ("Inès courage"); two best friends aggressively make love with one man and a vibrator ("Marc-André, sa blonde et blanche"). In "Dans la nuit les bruits, les cris et les parfums," couples have sex as an antidote to thinking about global horror, violence, and bombs much as the couples do in Dandurand's subsequent short story "Le Corps des saisons" in her 1991 collection *Petites âmes sous ultimatum*, where sex takes on a similar palliative role.

Dandurand's playful confusion between truth and fable becomes evident in "Les Muses cathodiques," where we meet a writer who sexually captures her desired man on her computer screen, graphically writing him into her real/unreal world of fiction. Similarly in "Montréal moite," the third-person female masturbates "with her vibrator-specially-developed-for clitoral pleasure" ["avec son vibrateur-spécialement-développé-pour-la-jouissance-clitoridienne"] (69) and, using a mirror, photographs her vulva – "parfaitement pornographique" (69) – much in the manner of Courbet's *L'Origine du monde*, but here for her eyes only. "She" is then described in some detail in a sexual encounter with "him" in a bar. But in what Kellett-Betsos calls "shifting pronouns" ["des glissements de pronoms"] in Dandurand's work (40), "she" announces at the end: "Almost none of this is true: I write it only to excite you, to seduce you, so that you will love me. And so that I can love you" ["Presque rien de tout cela n'est vrai: je ne l'écris que pour t'exciter, te séduire, pour que tu m'aimes. Et que je puisse t'aimer"] ("Montréal moite" 71). "She" has led us on in her imaginative sexual game, admitting only at the end that it was all made up – for "il" (him), for "tu" (you), and for us – underscoring, once again, the troubling rapport between the real and the textual.

Diane Boissonneault, whom Levasseur calls the most popular writer of Québécois heterosexual eroticism and great sex traveller (Levasseur 980), has ironically given herself the pen name of Lili Gulliver (parodying, of course, the "original" *Gulliver's Travels*, itself a great parody), and has to date published four "travel guides" to world sex, complete with her own star system that rates her sexual encounters by the number of "bites" (pricks): *L'Univers Gulliver I: Paris* (1990); *L'Univers Gulliver II: La Grèce* (1991); *L'Univers Gulliver III: Bangkok, chaud et humide* (1993); and *L'Univers Gulliver IV: L'Australie sans dessous dessus* (1999). Brimming with detailed narratives of the narrator's sexual exploits around the world, these parodic texts also reveal an interesting development: starting from a purely sexual travelogue in the first volume, Gulliver incorporates at least the semblance of a travel journal in the second and then moves toward including fewer sexual escapades and more travel notes, more reflection and commentary on herself, love, and life, more gender reversal (male strippers, a brothel of men for women), and even a pronounced search for love in addition to sex in the later "guides." What all of this means is open to interpretation, but at first glance, it does appear that the female sexual explorer – who illustrates beautifully Butler's narrative "I" who both contributes to and frames her self-reflexive fantasies (Butler 109–10) – has discovered that even with an encounter worthy of five "bites" she needs more than purely physical satisfaction. She wants to stay in control, in the subject position, but perhaps in a more equal relationship now that the twentieth century is over, and a new one has begun, hopefully with more shared sexual power.

But fictional women are still obsessed with getting enough sex, as Claire Dé reminds us in her 1991 collection *Chiens divers (et autres faits écrasés)*. In "Chevelure de flammes," a woman in her fifties leaves her husband because he refuses her sex on a Saturday night (he then burns down the house with himself in it). "Les Dessous" and "Le Téléphone" introduce us to women who are frank about and obsessed with male underwear and hard penises, as they suggest the eternal link between sexuality and death, Eros and Thanatos.

One of the most highly reviewed novels of the last decade of the twentieth century is Pauline Harvey's *Un Homme est une valse*, published in 1992. Beautifully written, this novel is an example of recent "mainstream" women's writing in Quebec that tells a good and complex story and speaks unabashedly in sexual terms: "the only truth is sexual" ["la seule vérité est sexuelle"] (44); "man's generosity is his sperm" ["la générosité d'un homme, c'est son sperme"] (61). Here the female ironically gazes upon men and decides – both in self-reflexive irony and with a sense of fatalism about the world and the sexes – that to be a woman is interesting and in effect, a full-time job: "There's really no point in being anything else but a woman" ["Ca ne vaut vraiment pas la peine d'être autre chose qu'une femme"] (63). A female intellectual, artist, writer, scientist – nothing is more interesting than simply being a woman. Besides, this is all that men care about, and once a woman realizes this, she will have everything she needs (63). In this novel have liberated women have taken a step backward, or have they decided that their sex is all-consuming?[27]

Another highly regarded writer, as well as journalist and administrator, is Lise Bissonnette, whose 1997 collection of short stories *Quittes et doubles* is equally concerned with issues of female sexuality, the male gaze, representation of female sexuality – all endowed with a female sense of humour. "Les Amants," one of the most erotic and clever stories in this volume, brings to mind the successful Quebec film *The Red Violin* and harks back to the "voyage" of Courbet's *L'Origine du monde*, as suggested in Dé's "La Causeuse orientale." Just as the main protagonist of François Girard's film is a hollow, "female" violin originally lovingly made in Italy and which travels around the globe from owner to owner until ultimately auctioned off to a black American (those powerful capitalists!), the narrator of Bissonnette's tale is an 1888 French painting – indeed a copy of Courbet's famous canvas. "She" arrogantly explains to us, however, that she is far more seductive than Courbet's masterpiece, with her beautiful exposed breast and her excited clitoris (111), for she is also "a superb ass" ["un superbe cul"] (116). In other words, she is a parody of pornography and therefore, as Sontag has remarked, still pornographic (217). With exquisite irony, the inanimate narrator who is, in effect, female sexuality, spins the tale of her journey through "life": "born" of the painter, Léon Burelle, but related to Courbet's painting, she ends up in religious Quebec, passed from male owner to male owner. Her photograph is reproduced in several sex manuals,[28] but she never makes it into a gallery or a museum, like her famous "cousin." The painting's narrative gives her the opportunity to comment amusingly on men and how they see women, that is, as representations/objects for contemplation strictly under the male gaze. When she reaches the age of one hundred, privately owned by a certain M. Marguillier, she is finally given the chance to make her public debut – albeit by means of violence. She alone witnesses the murder of her owner by a man who cleaned his house and had become enchanted with her as he dusted her each night, determined to keep her "clean" and beautiful: "When he severed the handsome boy's jugular vein, he forced him to look at me, he talked to him about the ferocious and fragile sex of a woman. And that he had to kill him before he really had gotten me, before I was placed under glass, *Untitled, red chalk drawing, Léon Burelle, 1888*. Which I am. Tomorrow, I move into a museum, I wipe out part of the inheritance taxes. I will have thousands of lovers, who will think of me as real, and whom I will deceive" ["Quand il a tranché la veine jugulaire du beau garçon, il l'a forcé à me fixer, il lui a dit la joie féroce et fragile d'un sexe de femme. Et qu'il devait le tuer avant qu'il ait ma peau, avant que je devienne, sous verre, *Sans titre, dessin à la sanguine, Léon Burelle, 1888*. Ce que je suis. Demain, j'entre au musée, j'efface une partie des impôts de la succession. J'aurai des milliers d'amants, qui me croiront vive et que je tromperai"] (118). She is, with wonderful irony, the female sex, female sexuality itself, who wants to be under the gaze of as many men as possible because she understands her power; she knows that she can control – deceive and be unfaithful to – men in their weaknesses, for they cannot even tell the difference between a real woman and an artistic representation. She, as artistic object, therefore, can be the ultimate representation of the female subject.

In 2000 there appeared a work that caused a stir in Quebec, much as Virginie Despentes's novel and film *Baise-moi* did in France around the same time. Indeed the work was then published by Éditions du Seuil in Paris in 2001 and is mentioned in Authier's critique of the "new sexual order in France." Nelly Arcan's "récit" *Putain* tells the first-person story of a university student's life in prostitution. Readers expecting to be titillated by graphic/pornographic scenes were most likely disappointed, for this text provides far less sex and far more philosophical musing on her family, life, and the people with whom she comes into contact (so to speak) than many had anticipated. A student of literature, the narrator writes neither an erotic nor a sexual exposé, but rather a memoir, her observations and reflections as a feminist. According to the narrator, prostitution does not prevent violence by men against women. In fact, it – and society in general – causes women like herself to hate themselves and often to hate all men. Sometimes she wishes she were a man in order to have all the male privileges. And yet she also tells us that she has imagined having a double, a sister, her "Wonder Woman," with whom she would live in a world of mothers, sisters, and daughters, all venerated by men wanting to be part of this "family where fraternity would be a sisterly matter" ["famille où la fraternité serait une affaire de soeurs"] (76). Since she feels it is too carnal to have a child, she imagines women being able to multiply by some magic formula and be happy: in order that "men no longer turn around to look at women in the street and women do away with their mirrors, there can be only one single sex" ["les hommes ne se retournent plus sur les femmes dans la rue et que les femmes se défassent de leur miroir, il faudrait qu'il n'y ait plus qu'un seul sexe"] (76). Pornography? Not quite! It will, indeed, be interesting to see how this novel is transformed into a feature-length film, anticipated for 2006 and to be produced by Nicole Robert of Les Films Séville and Go Films. The 2004 announcement of this project made it clear that the film would praise neither pornography nor prostitution. In fact since the publication of her novel, Nelly Arcan has denounced what she sees as the dangerous pervasiveness of pornography in our society, especially on the Internet (Montpetit B7).

Is there eroticism, sexuality, or pornography in Geneviève St-Amour's 2002 *Passions tropicales*? Even more so – from the rather obvious cover of the insides of a tropical fruit, gushing with pink seeds and dripping with viscous purple juice, to the sexy young woman on the back cover in her exotic clothing and pose – this "roman érotique" recounts the sexual escapades of Soana during two weeks as a tourist in Cuba, interspersed with her sexual fantasies of Amsterdam (as a prostitute), Istanbul (as an exotic dancer and "odalisque" – courtesan), Bali (as a "servant of love"), and Polynesia (as a goddess), as well as in India, Tunisia, Kenya, Marrakesh, Fez, Laos, Japan, and Saigon. Often more sensual than overtly sexual, Soana explains that she is acting like a contemporary courtesan, especially in Cuba, in contrast to her life (as a fiancée) in Montreal as a painter, writer, sculptor, and danser: "I don't do this in order to self-destruct – on the contrary – nor to discover something about myself. I do it just for myself, to glorify my senses and because I really want to. That's all! It's a present to myself" ["Je ne fais pas cela pour m'autodétruire – au contraire – ni pour découvrir quelque chose de moi-même. Je le fais seulement pour moi, pour glorifier mes sens et parce que j'en ai profondément envie. Voilà tout! C'est un cadeau que je m'offre"] (109–10). It seems as if Soana, the creative subject at home, wants to expand her subjectivity, multiply her "I"s, and transgress into the realm of the senses. Still in love with her fiancé, Dylan, Soana believes profoundly in the Sanskrit meaning of love – "to give freedom" (226). Arcan has given her readers the representation of a woman who appears to be self-confident, reflective, empowered, creative, and openly enjoying sex – thereby, in effect, reclaiming her own sexuality.

The same cannot be said about Véga, the female protagonist of Pauline Gélinas's 2001 novel *Le Sexe sale*. Like the narrator of *Putain*, who is a university student with a strong penchant for sex, and like Soana in *Passions tropicales*, who relishes her vacation affairs, Véga is a self-made sexual woman on summer break from her days as Sabrina, a student of philosophy. Unlike Soana, who searches for and enjoys sex seemingly without guilt, but more similar to Arcan's prostitute who performs sex without mixed feelings, Véga is also a woman of the North American popular culture, like Rioux's Éléonore, who dances in a bar to Jim Morrison's "L.A. Woman" and "becomes the music" just before her first sexual encounter with her summer lover (Gélinas 31).

The title of this novel clearly reveals Véga's attitude toward sex. Right from the first pages, she describes how she loved and feared sex from a very early age: "And never enough will power to resist this diabolical attraction. Sin. Evil. Filth. Shame. Shame. Shame ... I finally admitted to myself that I was perverted. Deranged. Crazy. Impure" ["Et jamais assez de volonté pour résister à cette diabolique attraction. Péché. Mal. Saleté. Honte. Honte. Honte ... je me suis finalement avouée perverse. Dérangée. Détraquée. Impure"] (13–14). She even has an orgasm in class: "I had come. And hard. In front of the class. In front of my executioner. In front of the nun. In front of this professor. My persecutor ... The shame of being perverted. I had only one way out: to leave my sexuality ... to take sexuality out of my body" ["J'avais joui. Et fort. Devant la classe. Devant mon bourreau. Devant la religieuse. Devant cette professeure. Ma persécutrice ... Honte d'être perverse. Il ne me restait plus qu'une seule issue: sortir de ma sexualité ... sortir la sexualité de mon corps"] (37). But she doesn't; on the contrary, she increasingly sees herself as a prostitute, goaded by her own mother's attitude: "My mother takes me for a whore. You can sense it in her voice. In her eyes, too. There's shame in her voice. I feel that I am dirtying her house. I am dirtying her name. Her image. Her conscience" ["Ma mère me prend pour une putain. Ça se sent dans sa voix. Dans ses yeux aussi. Il y a de la honte dans sa voix. Je sens que je salis sa maison. Je salis son nom. Son image. Sa conscience"] (112). And Sabrina is still an adolescent.

The refrain of being a "putain" echoes throughout the novel. At thirteen and fourteen she denies being one, since whores like sex, and she does not. She becomes increasingly obsessed with not being seen as a whore: "It's so disgusting, this word, "whore." So dirty. Whore even almost rimes with scorn. I am not a whore" ["C'est tellement répugnant, ce mot: putain. Tellement sale. Ça rime avec dédain. Je ne suis pas une putain"] (129). When she fashions herself as Véga, the purely sexual being who takes up with a mysterious stranger in the summer, he reminds her again and again that he likes whores, that he needs to treat her like one, that she loves being treated like a one, that she going to come like one, and ultimately that since he loves the whore in her, she should learn to accept it (51, 52, 55, 56, 154).

This "innate" role of prostitute that Véga constructs for herself and that is constructed for her by her lover is one of the most relevant components of the sexual fantasy world that the two of them build together. With mysterious, theatrical, and ritualistic planning and eventual action, Véga narrates for her readers some of the most graphically sexual scenes in "mainstream" literature. Their sexual escapades are also, from the beginning, fraught with violence and sado-masochistic actions, exhibiting what Kristeva has called our fascination with the derangement of identity and our interest in the abject (Kristeva 208). Vega's lover (Philippe) believes that all women desire to be raped. She agrees, but adds that this desire refers only to someone the woman knows (50). She tells him her violent sexual fantasies. He scarily tells her that he is going to make her fantasies real – and he does (50). They use leather, rope, and handcuffs; he brutally rapes her in his car. She knows that what she is doing is dangerous and that she should be afraid, but she deeply feels the need to explore even further. She feels that by doing so, she will somehow be able to rid herself of her past obsessions with filth and guilt: "To touch what goes beyond the forbidden. Beyond the censured. Beyond Evil ... To break taboos. To break guilt. To break shame. To break the anger of taboo. To break violence. To break my past. To break the violence of my past. The violence of shame. The violence of guilt. The violence of taboos" ["Toucher ce qu'il y a au-delà de l'interdit. Au-delà du censuré. Au-delà du Mal ... Casser les tabous. Casser la culpabilité. Casser la honte. Casser la colère du tabou. Casser la violence. Casser mon passé. Casser la violence de mon passé. La violence de la honte. La violence de la culpabilité. La violence des tabous"] (75). Such a "clipped" series of "neutral" infinitives mirrors Vega's mind and her desperate need to rid herself of socially and religiously learned notions, on a journey toward purety, absolution, and freedom.

But love (and a bit of silliness) conquers all. At the close of the novel, Véga has become Sabrina again, the philosophy student back in the university classroom. Her visiting professor of Nietzsche walks in, and (surprise!) he is none other than Philippe, her violent summer lover, who ultimately convinces her that he loves both Véga and Sabrina. Can he really love her other than as a "putain," she wonders? Ah yes, love has won out, and she can finally rid herself of her demons. She can walk, timidly, into "a world finally clean!" ["un monde enfin propre!"] (155). It is almost as if Gélinas originally intended to create a violently sexual woman – part object for the unknown male, part subject of the sex and violence – but at the last moment could not perpetuate the representation of such a "dirty" female in a Quebec society still divided into binary oppositions. Other female writers, however, will push the boundaries further.

SEXUALITY AND CRUELTY/VIOLENCE GO HAND IN HAND

La cruauté est un bonbon délicieux à sucer longtemps.
[Cruelty is a delicious piece of candy to be sucked for a long time.]

Anne Dandurand, *La Salle d'attente* 15.

Everyone has felt (at least in fantasy) the erotic glamour of physical cruelty and an erotic lure in things that are vile and repulsive. These phenomena form part of the genuine spectrum of sexuality.

Susan Sontag, "The Pornographic Imagination" 222.

Female Literary Sexual Violence in the United States, France, and Great Britain

I have already mentioned the U.S. phenomenon of female "fringe-fandoms" and speculative fiction (SF), begun in the late 1960s by women who created erotic zines about men for other women. Edi

Bjorklund describes some of this material as "get-em stories" (a variant of the "hurt-comfort story") in which "primary attention is devoted to inflicting pain on the protagonists" in order to "relish male vulnerability and ... to take unabashed pleasure in seeing *them* suffer for a change" (276; See also 268–9). In what has been called by several critics the "pornography of violence," these underground stories often contain sexually violent passages about sadomasochistic bondage between two men where one is feminized and thus "degraded" (278). With its repeated rape scenes, this form of women's erotic writing unsubtly reveals raw emotions: "Rape – and rage – have become major themes in women's underground fiction, often in combination with themes of physical enslavement and bondage" (279). Complete with explicit illustrations, or "illos," the stories glorify bondage of and domination over men, who are turned into objectified toys (280), much as women are in male pornography: "Substituting men for ourselves (and for other women, among them for zine readers as a group) and then turning them into objects for rape, enslavement, and violence of all descriptions is the archetypal significance of get-em stories. Do unto *them*, as it were, as they have done unto women" (280). Clearly, representations of these forms of sexual violence function as metaphors for the rage of some women who have experienced sexual cruelty and pain at the hands of men (286). In other words, these representations of sexual violence need to be read alongside "reality," as I have suggested in chapter 1 (See Duggan, Tanner, and Inness), since, as Kramer has pointed out, actual sexual violence is grounded in representation: "Sexual violence against men ... disturbs representation whenever it happens, with no exceptions. It is, in effect, violence against representation itself" (183).

In France, as I have noted, a siginificant group of female writers and filmmakers have also been moving in the direction of pornographic/sexual violence – albeit more recently than the underground writers in the United States. Authier calls this movement "*le french touch* de cette Génération X" (23) and "this new western handed over to cow-girls" ["ce nouveau western livré à des cow-girls"] (17), a "tongue-in-cheek" statement that links this artistic material to Americanization, whereby U.S. history, film, culture, and especially popular culture, have set a global "standard" that is seeping not only into other North Amercian regions, but also into France and Europe.

Authier focuses his critique largely on the works and comments of fiction writers and filmmakers such as Virginie Despentes, Claire Legendre, Claire Denis, Alice Massat, Christine Angot, Marie Nimier, and Catherine Breillat, among a number of others (including Catherine Millet and the Québécois Nelly Arcan). Calling all of these women rebels and audacious transgressors (207), he seems to be the most offended by Despentes, for whom, he says, "the acts of killing and screwing obey the same impulse and the same pleasure ... the dryness and the simplicity of the writing, just like the naturalness with which the heroines live their bloody wandering, reinforces the violence of the text" ["l'acte de tuer et celui de baiser obéissent au même élan et au même plaisir ... la sécheresse et la simplicité de l'écriture, comme le naturel avec lequel les héroines vivent leur errance sanglante, renforcent la violence du texte"] (17). Authier is speaking of the two female prostitutes-turned-actors-who-play-murderous-prostitutes (Raffaela Anderson and Karen Bach) in Despentes's film, *Baise-moi* (distributed in the United States as *Rape Me*, but more colloquially, "Fuck Me"), which hit Parisian cinemas in 2000 and is based on her 1994 novel of the same name. One wonders if the fight over this film, raising issues of censorship, X-ratings, and the like, would have occurred – at least so widely and openly in France and other countries – if this had been a film made by a male director and with male protagonists. It was not helped, however, by comments made by Despentes: "It gave me great pleasure to kill everyone ... I really like that idea, to go somewhere in order to fuck with everyone"; "It is time for women to become executioners, including the use of the most extreme violence" ["Ça me faisait plaisir de tuer tout le monde ... L'idée me plaît bien, d'aller quelque part pour baiser avec tout le monde"; "Il est temps pour les femmes de devenir les bourreaux, y compris par la plus extrême violence" (as quoted in Authier 206, 250). It was odd, she added, that there was this censorship in a country where one reads Sade and Genet (Authier 250–1). Is *Baise-moi*, the film, art, obscenity, pornography, or trash? It is, at the very least, a profoundly upsetting and brutal film, "proving" our fascination for horror and the abject (Kristeva 208).

But as a writer of fiction, Despentes is not alone in her sexually violent depictions of men and women. The female protagonist of Claire Denis's *Trouble Every Day* devours her lovers after orgasm (Authier 204). In Claire Legendre's *Viande*, a woman murders a man, eats parts of his body, and then takes his penis and rapes and kills her female friend (Authier 24–5) – thereby solving the problem of how women are to represent the phallus in their pornographic texts (Williams 247)! Neither men nor women are safe from this fury. The obsession with and phobia of the male body continues in Alice Massat's *Ministre de l'intérieur*, as well as in Christine Angot's *Inceste* and in *Baise-moi*, where the violently sexual female uses a revolver to sodomize a man: the woman may not have her own penis, but she can still sodomize (Authier 141–2) – especially with a male-associated weapon. As Authier puts it, such films use and subvert pornographic expressions, taking away anything that is glamorous or sexy about them; they reverse the classic male domination code and oppose it with "un *girl power* d'une violence radicale" (179)[29] Despentes and Catherine Breillat (in her film, *Romance*) agree in their aversion to eroticism: "Eroticism is the total humiliation of the woman. The idea that it is acceptable, because it's pretty. Pornography is ugly; as for me, I prefer ugly" ["L'érotisme, c'est l'humiliation totale de la femme. L'idée que c'est acceptable, car joli. La pornographie, c'est laid, moi je préfère le laid"] (Authier 179). As described by at least one female female-pornography actor, these films present "un féminisme pro-sexe" and "highbrow porn" ["l'intello de porno," Authier 184) – a comment one may accept or reject (see chapter 1). For Authier, these fictional texts and films, although certainly proposing a "*girl power* aesthetic à la Spice Girls/Lara Croft" ["esthétique *girl power* façon Spice Girls/Lara Croft"], cannot be blamed for any increase in violent crime, but they do contribute to a disturbing general climate (205–6). Breillat takes more credit: "'It's a war that we are declaring on men ... [Sex] calls for violence and desire, not for fusion but for murder, as the only outlet [for it's a good idea] to free ourselves from the arrogance of the erect member'" ["'C'est une guerre qu'on déclare aux hommes.' ... [Le sexe] 'appelle la violence et désir non de fusion mais de meurtre, comme la seule issue' [car il convient de] 'se libérer de l'arrogance du membre érigé'"] (as quoted in Authier 206–7). French writers may have started later, but their imagined sexual violence is now leading the way.

The situation does not seem to be any safer for men in Great Britain, if one considers the popularity of novels such as Helen Zahavi's 1991 *Dirty Weekend*, a delightfully funny depiction of female sexual violence: "This is story of Bella, who woke up one morning and realised she'd had enough" (1). A former whore who lives alone in a dark basement in Brighton and fears all men, Bella decides to take revenge against a stalker – "One small step for Bella, but a huge leap for womankind" (49) – as she bludgeons him to death "for all her silent sisters" (60). She wakes up the next morning thinking about guns, "the only phallus worth having" (67),[30] and starts on her one-woman crusade to rid the world of garbage, to clean up the mess (that is, of men who frighten and prey on women) (99). In this regard, as I shall show in chapter 5, Bella is a "sister" to the narrators/actors of Dandurand's "Maîtresse des hautes oeuvres/Underground Requiem" and Dé's "A tuer," who also become serial killers on missions to destroy bad and annoying people. Deliciously parodying the dichotomous stereotype of the woman, as I have described her in chapter 1, Bella sexually lures men into her lair and then laughs at them – before killing them: "If you're Bella, you can break all the rules. If you're Bella, and the adrenalin's pumping, you can throw back your head and point your finger and mock the phallic god that failed. But only if you're Bella, if you're *mad, bad Bella* [emphasis mine] and you're burning up inside" (109). At the end of her "dirty weekend,"[31] Bella meets a male serial killer who sexually assaults her before she stabs him in a "strangely intimate" manner (185). He spurts and gushes messily all over her. She could have whispered in his ear, she says, that if a man sees a woman walking and desires her sexually: "Think on. Don't touch her. Just let her pass you by. Don't place your palm across her mouth and drag her to the ground. For unknowingly, unthinkingly, unwittingly you might have laid your heavy hand on Bella. And she's woken up this morning with the knowledge that she's finally had enough" (187).

England is also the home of the extremely popular and controversial sexually violent art of Sarah Lucas and Tracey Emin. Lucas's first solo show, *Penis Nailed to a Board – in Sex Game*, which launched her famous and infamous career in 1992, is a prime example. With its crudeness and "in your faceness," Lucas's main focus was representations of gender – how people come up with the base and crude symbols that represent gender difference: "Visitors were impressed by Lucas's staging of brute, unsubtle content ... The individual works were symbols of modern attitudes to sex and gender. You could say the objects had two codes – a popular one and also a critical one that comes from feminism. The unifying element was a kind of crude, on-the-lap handicraft that disarmed you" (Collings 22). Sarah Lucas now has her own huge room in the Tate Modern Museum in London – evidence that, at least in Great Britain, the art of angry, critical, sexually violent, and cleverly mocking females has been mainstreamed.

Female Literary Sexual Violence in Quebec: Do Violent Sex and Black Magic Cause Gender Fusion?

Jean Levasseur remarks in his overview of Quebec feminism and sexual literature that there exists "a certain feminine sadism of virtue" ["un certain sadisme féminin de la vertu"] in the 1984 texts of the special issue of *La Vie en Rose* – not really female sexual violence but rather a level of being totally fed up with sexual patriarchy (979). Such an attitude would certainly run counter to any earlier feminist ideal that lesbian love was gentle, tender, and egalitarian (Levasseur 979), but there is also no reason to believe that it could not lead to more sexually violent texts by women – as I witness in several examples from the past two decades, especially by Anne Dandurand and, although to a lesser extent, Claire Dé.

Two years before the publication of "Histoire de Q," in *La Vie en Rose*, three short stories by Dandurand appeared in her collection with Dé, *La Louve-garou*, which highlight female sexual aggression, power over the male, gender identification, the supernatural, and above all, female ironic humour. What ties these stories together are the links among an almost demonic sexual lust, torture, and death, as well as the desired or resultant fusion of gendered identity and self. The accompanying design for "Danger: Désir de glace" is reminiscent of something out of Dante or Bosch – couples intertwined in an endless circle of tortured desire, itself represented as the head of a mythical-looking beast. The narrator is a female stalker who, with a little help from her friends' magical love potions, brings her male sexual object under her spell. After a scene of lovemaking described in graphic detail, she makes the mistake of laughing, thereby breaking the spell. The narrator had apparently not read Mary Russo's analysis of uncanny and grotesque female laughter and had thus forgotten that such "diablerie" (devilishness) scorns this sound:

An incredible stench spread between him and me, an infamous steeping mortification of cadaverous sweat. Our souls tortured, we heard the howls of lovers dead for centuries without having been loved. A horrible wrenching twisted my flesh, and our two entities fused together in pain. Ever since, incubus and succubus at the same time, together we torture those who are sleeping. He and I remain forever thirsty for voluptuous pleasures, forever united in our quest for bodies to assuage our thirst. Together for eternity, I laugh again. [Une puanteur renversante s'étala entre lui et moi, une macération infâme de sueurs cadavériques. L'âme écorchée, nous entendîmes les hurlements des amants morts depuis des siècles sans s'être aimés. Une déchirure horrible tordit ma chair, et nos deux entités se fusionnèrent avec douleur. Depuis, incube et succube[32] à la fois, nous torturons ensemble ceux qui dorment. Lui et moi sommes à jamais assoiffés de voluptés, à jamais unis dans notre quête des sources du corps. Ensemble pour l'éternité, je ris encore.] (44)

Here the violently sexual woman unsuspectingly enlists the aid of the male sexual object, as the fused being continues on its voyage between Thanatos and Eros.

Similarly, the female narrator of the ironically titled "Home Sweet Home" uses black magic to create havoc for the man she loves. She manages to make his house haunted with rats, falling plaster, and horrifying sounds so that he becomes a babbling idiot in the eyes of his mistress, who sees and hears none of this. Ultimately the narrator sets herself on fire, and the flames engulf the house and her desired lover, killing them both: "Ever since, forever bound together, we shout out the moans of those greatly burned by love, in the nightmares of passionate people" ["Depuis, liés à jamais, nous vociférons la plainte des grands brûlés d'amour, dans les cauchemars des passionnés"] (63). Once again, the violent, sexual female fuses with the male object of her love and wrath in order to torture others.

The female narrator of "La Porte en dessous" describes an encounter with a monster – most likely depicted in the accompanying drawing of a female/snail with antennae and crustacean-like breasts. The horror story, as told by the monster, again speaks of the dangers of violent sex and the resultant gender fusion. Constantly biting the inviting neck of her lover during sex, the "monster" notices that he is becoming increasingly calcified. To try to undo this encroaching metamorphosis, she rubs his oiled penis for hours and then in desperation mounts him, hoping for a wild and torrential orgasm. It doesn't work: the evil disease enters both of them, and by the next morning: "We were fused together, he behind and I in front. She (the female monster) eats and moves around for us. Hermaphrodism, and symbiosis" ["Nous étions soudés, lui derrière, elle devant. Elle mange et se déplace pour nous. Hermaphrodisme, et symbiose"] (85). Yet another female-male creature is born of violent sex initiated by the woman.

It is clear that in all of these stories, Dandurand has used the conventions of science fiction, horror tales, and parody to create an imaginary world where the woman is the tireless sexual aggressor, needs the aid of black magic (often associated with women), tends to go too far to get her man, and ultimately loses her individual agency and gender identification by becoming fused in some way with the male object. Her only recompense is to torture other lovers forever. Is Dandurand saying that women should be warned not to be so lustful and sexually violent, for they may well have to relinquish their own identities? Or is she simply having fun with her readers?

She is clearly having fun in "La Voleuse," published in 1987 as part of *Voilà, c'est moi: c'est rien, j'angoisse (Journal imaginaire).* In this story the nineteen-year-old narrator is "a stealer ... of kisses ... where the victims never complain" ["voleuse ... de caresses ... où les victimes ne se plaignent jamais"] (31). What she steals is sex, taking money only if the men are handsome and rich; the poor, tired, old, and ugly get a free service. She washes away her crimes by supporting the arts and would like to create a society of succubi (a favorite, ironically intended word of Dandurand's) with the goal of invading first the (male) public sphere, then the (traditionally female) private sphere, and finally the world (32). What role reversal – women attacking men for sex: invasive, trangressive, subversive, and aggressive – yes; humorous – certainly.

Dandurand's "Histoire de Q"

Even though Dandurand most frequently uses her wonderfully parodic style of writing to stand male pornography and cruel male agency on their heads, she can also imagine disturbing and truly sexually violent scenes. I have now referred several times to her clever parody of *Histoire d'O*, her "Histoire de Q," originally published in the special 1984 issue of *La Vie en Rose* and republished in 1987 as part of her collection *Voilà, c'est moi: c'est rien, j'angoisse (Journal imaginaire).* As Dandurand herself discloses her motive in the "prologue" to this special issue: "I wrote "The Story of Q" in order to torture my torturer. Should I have censored myself, shut myself up, been ashamed of my violence, of my wickedness, deny that yes, I felt murderous, sadistic urges?" ["J'ai écrit 'Histoire de Q' pour torturer mon tortionnaire. Est-ce que j'aurais dû me censurer, me taire, avoir honte de ma violence, de ma méchanceté, nier que oui, j'éprouvais des pulsions meurtrières, sadiques?"] (Dandurand, "Prologue" 37). And Levasseur picks up on the author's admission when he concludes that through the "heroine" of Dandurand's short story is born the image of "the female Conqueror, the feminine equivalent of the 'macho' male ... a being still for the most part brutal and insensitive" ["la Conquérante, l'équivalente féminine du 'macho' ... un être encore généralement brutal et insensible"], who sees the penis as an entertaining diversion, as isolated from its male possessor (982). Levasseur seems to be saying that little has changed in the binary world of the sexes; women have simply taken on the age-old actions and attitudes of men. Only in this case, they have managed to separate the penis from the phallus.

In "Playing with Gender, Playing with Fire" Lori Saint-Martin convincingly compares "Histoire de Q"[33] with Pauline Réage's earlier French novel that Sontag already sees as meta-pornography, a brilliant parody, despite her statement that pornography is not a form that can parody itself (Sontag 217). Saint-Martin makes the claim that Dandurand's playing with gender hierarchy challenges both the distribution of power and the literary tradition on which *Histoire d'O* is based and which it eptomizes (31). For this Québécois critic, women writing between eroticism and feminism are playing with fire, since so many feminists have argued against representations of this type (31). Although like Authier, Saint-Martin does not make a distinction among eroticism, pornography, and violent pornography – some feminists are against the third, but not necessarily the first or even the second – she does ask to what extent the use of parody allows us to revisit the traditional distributions of gender roles and power (32). For Saint-Martin, Dandurand's parodic intentions are explicit. She chooses the letter, "Q," instead of "O," in order to suggest the vulgar word, "cul," or ass/sex; "O" refers to the name of the French heroine,[34] while "Q" is not the name of the Québécois male in the story, but rather refers to sex itself: "Dandurand's first departure from 'Histoire d'O,' then, is to demystify it through vulgarity and humour, shifting the focus from a character (O) to sex and writing itself (Q)" (32). Using the past conditional as the dominant tense, thereby overdetermining her text with the earlier one, Dandurand ends her story with the sacrificial death of the male victim who has been taken away and violently and sexually tortured by his loved one – as the woman is in *Histoire d'O* (33). In a line worthy of Claire Legendre's *La Viande*, the final image of "Histoire de Q" is: "She then lies down on top of him and begins to devour him" ["Elle se couche alors sur lui, et commence à le dévorer"] (Dandurand 30). Quebec women writers have clearly led the way for the subsequent French gourmands!

Saint-Martin also points out that Dandurand changes both the meaning of the French tale and the effect that it has on readers by a reversal of gender roles – the male sexual object under the gaze and control of the female others. "Il" is reduced to the female position and subjected to all the "normal" trappings of male pornography applied to the female object: "All the old creaky accessories borrowed from *Histoire d'O* – chains, corsets, ritual body preparation such as shaving and tattooing – take on new and provocative social meanings simply because they are used on men, not women. They become truly *visible* again, and therefore shocking" (33). The story becomes destabilizing and unsettling for the reader, especially for male readers (33), who have internalized and accepted the expected roles of dominant male violent pornography. It is also a disturbing text, given its delight in using the crude language of the body, with its bodily functions and secretions (34) – perhaps even "over-using" obscene words, as Erica Jong does in *Fear of Flying*, in order to rattle the notion that men have a monopoly on such language. Dandurand's women of agency even get to the point of comically transforming the male sexual object into "a gingerbread man ... ready for tea time" ["bonhomme de pain d'épice ... prêt pour l'heure du thé"] (Dandurand 29). Once again, we have here a forerunner of the sexually gourmet French texts of Legendre and Claire Denis.

Saint-Martin interestingly sees Réage as the "good girl" of female porn and Dandurand as the proverbial "'bad girl' who enjoys violating the boundaries of literary genre and good taste as well as standard of behaviour – and writing – for women" (35). Dandurand questions our social constructs of anticipated female submission and male dominance, legitimizing woman's anger and rage, much in the way that certain French novelists and filmmakers have done more recently. Saint-Martin also aptly wonders if such a narrative strategy opens up new opportunities for "rewriting cultural scripts [for] the very fact that it shocks us also needs attention rather than silence" (35) – a query to which I would firmly answer in the positive.

But ultimately, Saint-Martin decides – and I concur – that Dandurand's use of role reversal inverts traditional roles rather than subverting them here: "While it pulverizes old stereotypes, role reversal remains within the same logic of domination and destruction: to escape her object status, a woman turns a man into the object rather than imagining two desiring subjects engaging with one another ... 'Histoire de Q' leaves the binary system itself intact" (35). In one sense one could say that Dandurand's earlier attempts at imagining sex and violence from a female perspective allowed her to dream about a new world order with one fused sex (perhaps with several genders, however), but in that model each sex loses any sense of individuality and remains eternally interwoven, (positively?) disturbing others as a joined incubus/succubus. In "Histoire de Q," the binary system, which is so restrictive and superficial (see chapter 1), may remain intact, but woman's anger is at least vented – a necessary stage perhaps on the voyage to Saint-Martin's dream of a subject-subject (or several gendered subjects?) world.

This vented anger is also in evidence in sections of Dé's 1993 novel *Sourdes amours*. One scene in particular needs to be underscored, not because the violence is perpetrated by a women whose husband has been such a cad (a form of female violence that I am not considering in this study, as I have explained in chapter 1), but rather because the scene is another example of a reversal of male pornographic sado-masochism. In this particular scene, the wife orders her husband to undress and then ties him up to the bed. She beats him with leather, causing zebra striping (reminiscent of the title of Jeanne Le Roy's novel). He gets excited: "Then. With a shoelace from my sandal. At the base: tied up, your erection. You're moaning? That's how I love you the most" ["Alors. Avec un lacet de ma sandale. A la base: garrottée, ton érection. Tu geins? Voilà comme je t'aime le plus"] (77). The sexually-aroused, masochistic male object-victim and the sadistic female-subject/dominatrix are highlighted here, thereby still keeping the sexual binary system alive.

Sexual Violence and Fractured Gender

Gender in a sexually violent mode, however, can be imagined in a more fluid and confused state, as Dandurand tells us in her complex 1994 *La Salle d'attente*. This miniature novel (61) recounts the long history of a relationship between "je" ("I") and "elle" ("she"), as told by "je." Whether these are two distinct beings or two parts of the same woman remains purposefully vague throughout much of the text, just as the boundary between the "real" and the "imagined" remains transgressively fluid. In four musically titled chapters that take place in the waiting room of a medical clinic, "je" either remembers, experiences, or imagines sexually graphic and fantasmagoric, violent moments that she then instills in the thoughts/mind of "elle," who is a part-time librarian and asthmatic and whom she has "known" for almost fifty years. When "je" speaks directly to "elle," Dandurand alerts us by using italics, as in one lengthy sado-masochistic lesbian scene where "je" is present with two women in their sixties ("elle" and "tu" – she and you) in a trinity of sexually violent love. At one point, "il" ("he") – a gigantic black man with a monstrous penis – enters and rapes "tu," who soon learns that "il" is her lesbian lover in disguise with a strap-on phallus (predating Legendre and others). The three of them form a libidinous triangle (16–20). In another scene "je" suggests to "elle" a bloody fantasy of men "torn apart by chains, their ankles crushed by Spanish gaiters, their wrists kept close to their necks in pillories" ["écartelés par des chaînes, aux chevilles écrasées par les guêtres espagnoles, aux poignets maintenus près du cou dans des piloris clochettes"] (27–8), as a result of which "she 'got off on' the frightful screams" ["elle se nourrissait de hurlements effroyables"] (28).

In some sort of truce, "elle" suddenly becomes "je"; finding her Voice, "je" can then become "JE" (capital "I"), thereby silencing the voice of "je" (lower-case "I"); this new "JE" thinks first only of sex (39–40). But this time the sexual being is even more powerful, since she becomes mythical, a woman living in the jungle with four jaguars, who captures a man, has sex with him seven times, picks up his male sexual odour, and then discovers that the jaguars have left her because of her smell (41–6). The initial "je" returns and again in italics claims the story, since she represents an infinite number of voices, with an infinite number of tales to tell (46). "Elle" (referred to by "je" as "tu") has/imagines sex with the doctor she has been waiting for, while outside (and always parenthetically noted as such in the text), everyone else seems to be having sex, as well. As the sex in the doctor's office becomes increasingly furious, so do the external sexual scenes – starting locally, moving further and further away (to Mexico, Tokyo, and Bangkok, for example), and ultimately turning violent because of the abrupt appearance of the sex trafficking of young girls, female genital mutilation, and then defibulation through sexual intercourse and incestuous rape by a father (50–7). The "coda" sums things up a bit too neatly: "elle/tu" (she/you) falls in love with the doctor (the sexual encounter in his office was real?), and he with her. A hundred and one "screws" later: "You will unburden yourself, confess to him in a low voice this weighty torture I have been subjecting you to for so long, these obsessions, this incessant counterpoint to your thought, this flood of couplings, debaucheries, orgies that I pour into your soul ... he will murmur: 'Why don't you write about this?' And then with your purple ink pen, you will enslave me. With all of your desires, oh my beloved" ["Tu te confieras, lui avoueras à voix basse ce pesant supplice auquel je te soumets depuis si longtemps, ces obsessions, cet incessant contrepoint à ta pensée, ce flot d'accouplements, de débauches, d'orgies que je déverse dans ton âme ... il murmurera: 'Pourquoi n'écris-tu pas cela?' Et alors, avec ta plume à l'encre violette, tu m'asserviras. A tous tes désirs, ô ma bien-aimée"] (60). "Elle" does finally become her own

"JE," her own sexually violent musical voice/counterpoint and imagination, and "je" can disappear as a separate part of her. If "everyone is running for the 'speaking function'" (Kappeler 199), the "total" woman wins out. The new "JE" can write this literary text and rid herself of the "demons" of gender confusion and sexual violence by speaking of them.

Female Adolescent Sex and Murder

Dandurand and Dé have each written a short story that provides a bridge between sexually violent and exclusively violent literary texts composed by women: Dandurand's "Les Étrennes," written in 1987 as part of her *Voilà, c'est moi: c'est rien, j'angoisse (Journal imaginaire)*; Dé's "L'Amour éternel" from her 1998 *Le Désir comme catastrophe naturelle*. With a similarly detached, dry, and ironic sense of humour, each of these two stories introduces us to a fifteen-year-old girl who moves from sex to violence rather effortlessly and seamlessly.

"I'm fifteen. Do you think it's easy to be fifteen? Not at all, especially when someone like me has a cold sore on her lips and a cadaver on her conscience. Warm, I loved him. Cold, he's more of a burden than I thought he would be" ["J'ai quinze ans. Vous croyez que c'est facile? Pas du tout, surtout quand comme moi on a un feu sauvage sur la lèvre et un cadavre sur la conscience. Chaud, je l'aimais. Froid, c'est plus pesant que prévu"] (Dandurand, "Les Étrennes" 37). Thus begins Dandurand's story of a show-business groupy who follows and seduces an older star, parodically and intertextually named (with the "nom de plume" of *Cyrano de Bergerac*) Panache Obstacle, with whom she has sex. He seems uncomfortable about her age but decides, ironically speaking in English: "*Just a groupy, why not?*" (39). The adolescent is insulted by this and decides to kill him out of revenge ("*Now or never*" 39) – a fairly easy plan to carry out: skipping geography class, she convinces her vicar to give her a gram of coke in exchange for sucking his "cock." She then buys some rat poison and mixes it with the drug. On New Year's Eve, "armed" with her present to him, she goes to Panache's truck and offers him the coke laced with rat poison. He accepts, sniffs, starts twitching, and dies: "I crammed Obstacle under a blanket. I got out of the truck. I threw my screaming green gloves through the window onto the driver's seat. I can't help leaving my signature" (40); a good serial killer always leaves "his" mark. ["J'ai tassé Obstacle sous une couverte. Je suis sortie du *truck*. Par la fenêtre j'ai tiré mes gants vert hurlant sur le siège du chauffeur. Je peux pas m'empêcher de laisser une signature"] (40). Her own New Year's present comes in the form of reports of the murder in several newspapers, although no one knows if it was murder or suicide. As for our young sexual killer, she cannot wait for the end of the Christmas holidays so that she can tell her friend (or is it her twin sister?) Claire, all about it. Her only regret is "not to have stuffed him. My art teacher's going to be very disappointed" ["de ne pas l'avoir empaillé. Ma professeure d'arts plastiques va être très déçue"] (41). She may even get a bad mark.

Dé's fifteen-year-old sex murderer is also a school girl; she is smart, wears thick glasses, and looks as if she is ten – no breasts and no pubic hair yet – and yet she is totally obsessed with sex. She tells us in the first sentence that she is not like her sister, Anne, who prefers established rock stars (and possibly kills them off – at least in her violent literary imagination). She falls in love with the ironically named Yves Courchesne (short oak/penis?) who makes her all wet, practically orgasmic, and with whom she is determined to have sex (again in English, "*Do it now, or die tomorrow*" 34). Echoing or imitating her sister, she sleeps with Yves once, but she will not let him sleep with her again unless he is in love with her. Adolescents have traditional high standards. She still asks to see him a second time and decides to pretend to strangle him just as he is ejaculating – guys like him are ready for anything that will give them an additional "kick" (35).

But this adolescent sex-pot is more curious, a serious scientist in her sex lab: "I strangled him for real, of course. It's funny, I had never read about this anywhere ... that the tongue swells up and comes out of the mouth, just at that moment, and that they keep their erection. I even put my glasses back on so that I could observe this phenomenon more closely: indeed, Courchesne wasn't losing his hard on, even dead. I'll have to talk to my bio prof about this one of these days" ["Je l'ai étranglé pour de vrai, bien entendu. C'est drôle, j'avais pas lu ça nulle part ... que la langue leur gonfle et leur sort de la bouche, à ce moment-là, et qu'ils conservent leur érection. J'ai même remis mes lunettes, pour observer le phénomène de plus près: en effet, Courchesne débandait pas, même mort. J'en toucherai un mot à ma prof de bio, un de ces jours"] (35). Not knowing what to do with the body, she empties her exotic fish aquarium and puts Yves in it. Always the conscientious and curious student, she goes to her chemistry teacher (rather than her biology teacher) and asks where to get some formaldehyde. People start to wonder where Yves, the famous harmonica player, is. But the narrator is happy: "Today my bio prof said people have successfully kept specimens in formaldehyde for a hundred years or more. That way, my pickled beloved, with his tongue hanging out and (sexually) at attention, will marinate in my aquarium for quite some time. That way, love is eternal" ["Aujourd'hui, ma prof de bio a déclaré qu'on réussit à entretenir des spécimens dans le formol un siècle et plus. Comme ça, mon amoureux confit, langue sortie et au garde-à-vous, va mariner dans mon aquarium un bon moment. Comme ça, l'amour est éternel"] (36). Another precursor to the French female literary, sexually violent gourmands, this Québécois adolescent manages to keep love "alive" with sex and murder – and a little chemical help. And if Pierre Nepveu is right in saying that Quebec fiction of the 1980s is ironic, humorous, demonic, caricatural, and clownish (*L'Écologie du réel* 20–1), then this young female narrator of the 1990s continues to exemplify her "nation's" text, while turning the tables on age and sex.

FEMALE LITERARY VIOLENCE

Il est temps pour les femmes de devenir les bourreaux, y compris par la plus extrême violence.
[It is time for women to become executioners, including using the most extreme violence.]

Virginie Despentes, *Le Journal du dimanche* (25 juin 2000).

Some Early Signs of Female Literary Violence in Quebec

In "La Violence dénoncée dans le roman féminin des années soixante," Anne Brown postulates that Quebec women novelists of the 1960s wrote about the reality of women in the home where they were raped, brutalized, and terrorized by controlling and sadistic husbands. Although the female characters in these texts did not actually rebel, by writing about such issues, they were, in a sense, speaking subjects, paving the way and taking the first step toward the real revolt and liberation in novels as of the 1970s (193–4). While Brown's statement is partially accurate, it does not take into account certain early texts in which the violent female protagonist makes her début.

Marie-Claire Blais's 1959 novel *La Belle Bête*, for example, is prefaced – at least in the 1968 version – by a quotation from Rosamond Lehman: "Creatures of terror ... are going to swell up and become monsters ... that no one has ever dreamed of, that no one has ever known what to do with, destructive monsters who live forever" ["Des créatures d'épouvante ... vont s'enfler et devenir des monstres ... dont personne n'a jamais rêvé, dont personne n'a jamais su que faire, des monstres destructeurs qui vivent à jamais"] (Blais 9). As Judith Halberstam has told us: "The monster/phantom ... never stands for a simple or unitary prejudice, it always acts as a 'fantasy screen' upon which viewers and readers inscribe and sexualize meaning" (10). Indeed, Blais's early novel has long been interpreted as a "tale of many meanings" (Green 8–14) – mythical, allegorical, sociohistorical, political, and psychoanalytical – but no one can forget that the female protagonist, the ugly and angry Isabelle-Marie, disfigures her brother, burns down the family farm with her mother inside, and throws herself under a moving train.

In Diane Giguère's 1961 *Le Temps des jeux*, the young Céline, who hates herself as much as she hates her mother, similarly describes herself as a monster, as evil: "Why this desire to push people to their destruction? ... From the depths of her being gushed an inaccessible, impenetrable sorrow ... as if she had suddenly chosen, in her madness, to be the monster that she was discovering in herself" ["Pourquoi cette envie de pousser les êtres à leur perte? ... Du fond de son être jaillissait une douleur inaccessible, insondable ... comme si elle avait soudain choisi, dans sa folie, d'être le monstre qu'elle découvrait en elle-même"] (Giguère 98). Céline is cruel, pushing her aging lover to kill his wife, threatening to commit infanticide against their as yet (and fictitious) unborn child, and sensing a great feeling of pride when she reads that her criminal wishes have come true.

Like Céline, Anne Hébert's Elisabeth d'Aulnières-Tassy-Rolland does not commit murder herself, but she is certainly the major force behind the bloody killing of her brutal husband, Antoine, by her American doctor lover, George Nelson, in Hébert's well known 1970 novel, *Kamouraska*. She is a good example of Brown's female speaking subject, but she soon wanders into the territory of Karen McPherson's guilty women, telling stories where, with great underlying tension, there exists "the constant potential for violence" (112). But McPherson also appropriately reminds us that Elisabeth ultimately refuses to cross the border of crime with George; her use of ellipses in the text covers the place of the crime and marks the place of trangression (128–9). However, such "narrative suspension attempts unsuccessfully to cover transgression, but actually ends up (re)producing it and leaving a thick residue of guilt" (129). Although Elisabeth, in McPherson's analysis, does not transgress – and even declares her innocence – her refusal to cross over "inarticulate boundary ... seems to mark her trespass and her transgression" (129). Moreover, she is haunted at the end of novel by the image of La Corriveau, the eighteenth-century woman who was hanged for murder and witchcraft and whose corpse was publically displayed by the British in a cage in Quebec.[35]

Female Literary Violence in Contemporary Quebec

As I noted in my first chapter, cultural critics such as Lisa Duggan reject "the separation of social life ('reality') from representations ('myth,' or 'stereotype')" (Duggan 4); I agree, like Laura Tanner, that the representation of violence emerges at the intersection of linguistic and material worlds" and that "the act of reading a representation of violence is defined by the reader's suspension between the semiotic and the real, between a representation and the material dynamics of violence which it evokes, reflects, or transforms" (Tanner 6); and I believe, like Sherrie Inness, that female heroes can, therefore, "rescript stereotypes about what it means to be a woman" (Inness 143), demonstrating that they, too, can be tough and even violent. But I have also noted that Inness and others question whether women should even want to be tough like men, especially since, when tough and violent women are thus represented, they are frequently reduced to being simply girls and women anyhow. Female killers – Holmlund's "deadly dolls," for example – remain erotic and sexy (135–6). They are judged, as I have discussed in chapter 1, to be mad or bad, seldom with any nuances between these categories.

When such women are deemed to be bad or evil, we are – as Karen Halttunen has suggested in reference to any form of horror – speechless because we fail to assign any single and clear meaning to this frightening transgression and end up placing "interpretive mayhem" onto the "monster" herself (Halttunen 2). What I am exploring in this study, therefore, is whether violent literary females – and especially those imagined by women writers – are seen as even more monstrous than their male counterparts because they have crossed over the boundaries of acceptable gender roles, even if they are using violence as "an instrument of criticism in the interest of a feminist *critique*" (Hanssen 213). How to interpret this female literary violence by women writers who are creating such representations in a postmodern North America still dominated by men who see this "other" as monstrous and alien? What we do know, as Halberstam has pointed out, and as I have agreed in chapter 1, is that contemporary monstrosity has become an "amalgam of sex and gender," indeterminate gender and sexuality, or perhaps all gender (6) – as I have already brought out in certain of Dandurand's characters. The body of the literary and filmic (violent female) monster has become what Halberstam calls a "meaning machine"(21); the reader or viewer can read whatever she or he wants to read into the narrative.

It is surprising that until now there has been so little written on the issue of contemporary representations of violent women and discursive violence – especially so in Quebec, as part of both the North American continent and the seemingly inevitable global encroachment of violent American popular culture. I have mentioned the critical work of Lori Saint-Martin, Luise von Flotow, Jean Levasseur, and Kathleen Kellett-Betsos on sexuality and sexual violence, and I shall refer to articles by Claudine Potvin, Francine Bordeleau, and Susan Ireland on violence in the works of particular authors, but beyond these critical writings, little else has appeared.

Part of what I am trying to illustrate in this and subsequent chapters is that there has been a noticeable change in this new/recent work by women: from expressions of eroticism and pornography, to sexual violence, to "pure," exclusive violence – all in the hands (and minds) of fictional women who question gender and its social roles, transgress into areas usually reserved for men, and ultimately play with and destroy former relations of power. The literary violence, as I shall show in the texts I shall study next, is at first directed primarily against men. As of chapter 4, we shall see that the violence is turned against the children of these female protagonists. The violence described in chapter 5 is directed against anyone, in sprees of serial killings. A now violent North America, the influence of U.S. society and its popular culture not only on Canada and Quebec but also, as I have shown, on countries such as Great Britain and France (where some female writers and filmmakers are "over the top" in their representations of sexual violence) – all of this forms a disturbing context and backdrop for the work of certain Québécois women writers and has disturbing implications for our future. In the "peaceable kingdom" of Canada and the even more peaceable "nation" of Quebec, some Québécois women writers have been leading the charge in re-framing gender through female literary violence for the past two decades.

Some Literary Women Get Back and Get Even

In several short stories by these women writers who create violent female protagonists, the female commits violent acts either in self-defence or as a result of abuse by a male. In a fairly traditional set-up, Christine Brouillet's Hélène of "Hélène et Hervé," for example, kills Hervé in a sexual ploy because he raped her friend. Claire Dé is more inventive: her 1982 "Un Cas de lycanthropie," for instance, is an amusing science fiction tale that plays with transformation, violence against women, murder, gender bending, and hyper-reality/alterity, to say the least. In a post–nuclear-disaster world, diseases reign, television has replaced religion, Americanism is triumphant, and lies replace truth. The local fish store that the female protagonist visits reeks of a "troubling culinary eroticism" (18) suggestive of forgotten pleasures – and French erotic gourmets. Hypnotized by a large blue-green lobster, she purchases it, brings it home, and prepares to put it into boiling water. She hesitates for an instant, and the lobster pinches her. She drops it into the water, and it dies. After eating the meat, she finds herself suddenly terribly thirsty and goes outside to drink the falling rain. It is dangerous for a woman to walk outside at night and, sure enough, she is assaulted. Rather quickly, she notices that she is being transformed into an enormous lobster, seriously ready to fight back in the passé simple: "The face of this unknown man became contorted in terror. This was his final feeling, the pincer cut him at the chin with a sound like a nut cracker. The other pincer, the right one, tore him in two, length-wise, starting with his genitals. The corpse jerked a little more, then collapsed in a gurgling heap. She fled with her giant lobster steps" ["Le visage de l'inconnu se révulsa de terreur. Ce fut son dernier sentiment, la pince le coupa au raz le menton avec un crac de casse-noisettes. L'autre pince, la droite, le disloqua en deux, dans le sens de la longueur, à partir du sexe. Le cadavre gigota encore un coup, puis s'affaissa en glougloutant. Elle s'enfuit à pas de homarde colossale"] (21). Unfortunately, she becomes pregnant (presumably from the rape that is only suggested), and gives birth to thousands of little human lobsters, "women lobsters and men lobsters ... known and recognized for their wisdom and their calm" ["les femmes homardes et les hommes homards ... connus et reconnus pour leur sagesse et leur calme"] (21). They work together for the return of nature and peace. As for the female killer, every night she is transformed back into a lobster and remains the mother of them all.

With a mischievous sense of humour, Dé seems to be suggesting that the murder of dangerous men by women is acceptable for the good of the world, but since society does not truly recognize the violent woman, she has to disguise herself and remain maternal, if only at night.

Dé's clever but darker irony also permeates her 1998 short story "Pot de colle" in *Le Désir comme catastrophe naturelle*, interestingly narrated by an omniscient narrator who may possibly be in the mind of the female victim/subject. Pierre Marmin hates his wife, Brigitte, a writer who "sticks to him like glue," repeatedly professes her love for him, is sickeningly sweet, and has a voracious sexual appetite. Against a backdrop of world violence, he decides that he must kill her and slowly poisons her with arsenic (rat poison). But: "Brigitte Marmin kept on decomposing. Kept on writing. Kept on wanting to make love" ["Brigitte Marmin continuait de se décomposer. Continuait d'écrire. Continuait de vouloir faire l'amour"] (49). He triples the dosage. He has yet another affair, tells his wife, and thinks of different ways to kill her more quickly. In the end, it is so easy to do: he suffocates her with a pillow. In his car, on the way to dispose of her body, he surprisingly hears a radio play written by Brigitte, entitled *Accident*. Suddenly, his car hits a curve; the brakes fail; the car turns over and bursts into flames, incinerating Pierre. It had all been arranged between his wife and the garage mechanic and in fact subtly announced to Pierre in advance: "What irony. What bitterness. What exhaustion. Pierre Marmin thinks about Brigitte Marmin. About her mouth, about her sex ... So she would always stick to his body. To his soul. In a few instants ... Attached to him all the way to hell. And forever" ["Quelle ironie. Quelle amertume. Quelle fatigue. Pierre Marmin pense à Brigitte Marmin. À sa bouche, à son sexe ... Elle lui collerait donc toujours au corps. À l'âme. Dans quelques instants ... Attachée à lui jusqu'en enfer. Et pour l'éternité"] (57). In a cunning twist of fate – or more likely in a carefully planned murder – she kills him after he has killed her. They are both dead, but who is the victim-object, and who is the more clever perpetrator/subject?

Dandurand's Gallery of Violent Women: In the Mind

Anne Dandurand's witty and violent imagination "serves up" four categories of violent women. I have already introduced female characters who thrive on erotic and sexual violence. Others explore violence, sex, and gender ambiguity. Still others are in control, masterminding plots and killings – like the adolescent groupy in "Les Étrennes" (and her "sister" in Dé's "L'Amour éternel"), and others who shall soon make their appearance. And finally, there are those who thrive in a violent world of their imagination – on paper or on the computer screen – much like the protagonists in "Les Muses cathodiques" and "Montréal moite," who prefer their sex imagined rather than real.

Some critics have spoken of the use of the third-person as alienating to women in erotic and sexual (and, I would add, violent) narratives, since, in these instances, the woman remains an object rather than a subject (Dardigna 104). Nancy Huston argues in *Mosaique de la pornographie* that women usually do write pornographic works in the third person, since using the first-person would only imply their submission and self-destruction (62). Saint-Martin notes, however, that in texts such as Jeanne Le Roy's *La Zébresse*, the female characters appropriate the narrative act, steal their own stories and language (as in Claudine Herrmann's term, "les voleuses de langue"), and thus "speak, narrate, control what is happening to them" (Saint-Martin, "Playing with Fire" 37). Kellett-Betsos points out that certain of Dandurand's female characters use doubles and what she calls "shifting pronouns" ["glissements de pronoms"] to emphasize the tension between the narrating "I" and the narrated "I," where the existence of a given character is put in doubt and the identity of the narrating and narrated subject begins to flounder (40). Such characters also use distancing techniques, such as the past conditional tense, in order to maintain the space between the text and any referentiality and to create a sense of unreality (von Flotow, "Tenter l'érotique" 95–6). And some female characters purposefully work against realism and emphasize the links between stories rather than links between stories and reality; they focus on how the story is told, repeating and multiplying the tales (Saint-Martin, "Playing with Fire" 38–9).

By applying these techniques to the creation of some of her violent female characters, Dandurand highlights the importance of writing, the written word, and language in the creation of volence on paper and in the mind's eye/imagination – much like Rioux's Éléonore. Dandurand's "Le Chagrin," included in *Voilà, c'est moi: c'est rien, j'angoisse (Journal imaginaire)*, for example, is divided into three short parts. "Avant," which shifts among the conditional, past conditional, "passé compose," and present tenses, is narrated by a female, "Je," who speaks to her lover (real or not, we do not know) about what her life could have been (living as a writer with her porcelain dolls, listening to heavy rock music) and is (living with her cat and Inès Courage, the lesbian lover in another short story of the same name). She – who would like to be called Ruth – admits that these are dreams that help her survive and while awaiting her lover's departure, flight, or death. In the meantime, she asks him to abandon his "big shadowy body," which she is "inventing ... from caresses, for want of the universe" ["grand corps d'ombre," qu'elle "invente au moins des caresses, à défaut d'univers"] (44). In "Pendant," the lover has left her; at least she (as "elle") has written this, before the actual fact. In the final "Après" – where "je" slips into "elle" in the imperfect and "passé simple"– she is desolate, listening to her Walkman, and ultimately deciding to write to console herself: "Which story to invent in order to detoxify myself? Serve him up as food to the hungriest Malaysian tiger? Drown him in the Arctic ocean? Give him a urinary tract infection through poisoning? It was so simple. In a single stroke of the pen, she erased him from her life as if he had never lived other than on paper"["Quelle histoire inventer pour se désintoxiquer? Le servir en pâture au tigre de Malaise le plus affamé? Le noyer dans l'océan Arctique? Lui infliger, par empoisonnement, la pollakiurie? Ce fut si simple. D'un seul trait de plume, elle l'effaça de sa vie comme s'il n'avait jamais vécu ailleurs que sur le papier"] (45). As "Je" she could only dream, be in control of her imagination. As "elle" at the end, however, she kills her lover on paper, thereby banishing him (real or imagined?) from her life. "Je" reflects Lashgari's claims that "language *is* loaded and has the power to kill" (13).

Fantasy continues to posture as the real (Butler 106–8), when the same female character (presumably) moves back and forth between being the "je-narrant" (narrating "I") and the "je-narré" (narrated "I") as "elle" in Dandurand's "Les Sentiers d'Agathe," also in *Voilà, c'est moi*. This time, told in a sequence of months from June through October, the story continues with her attempts at killing off this lover on paper. She is completely obsessed with thoughts of killing him in a bloody murder – to the point of taking back her identity from "elle" to "Je" and throwing it in the faces of subsequent lovers: "My name is Agathe, beware of finding my leg necklace around your necks. With one spark, I could singe your face" ["Je me nomme Agathe, prenez garde au collier de mes jambes autour de vos cous. D'une étincelle je pourrais vous flamber au visage"] (60). Singed by these sexually crude acts or language, by entering either between her thighs or into her words, her lover/men will become her prey (60), the prey of a dangerous woman who still lives with her collection of dolls as "je." Her lover leaves her, and she falls back into "elle." August brings her back to "je" for the most part, in which role she tells/writes of graphic sexual experiences, but she ends in her usual depth of anger, preparing her poisons (63). "Elle/je" meets (a different?) man in September and again has wild sexual encounters. But ... "She awakens ... By what magic could she push this man off the paper so he can be embodied in life?" ["Elle s'éveille ... Par quelle magie pourrait-elle pousser cet homme hors du papier afin qu'il s'incarne dans la vie?"] (65). In October she turns to her female friends (Jeanne Couteau, for one, whom the reader has met in other stories) and in the present tense "writes" of Violon, who ultimately also leaves her. She is bitter and angry, establishing a link between her (imagined) sex life, her murderous tendencies, and the world of torture in South America, apartheid in South Africa, and bombs endangering all of us. But with characteristic furor, followed by Russo's uncanny and grotesque laughter of a woman, "Je" hears the sounds of the battle for light: "Here I am. Here are my forces. Finally" ["Me voici. Voici mes forces. Enfin"] (67). "Je" has at last become the narrating "I" of her own repetitve tales of sex and especially of the killing of men.

Echoes of the same character abound in Dandurand's "L'Assassin de l'intérieur," title story of her 1988 collection; here, however, she has no semblance of control or victory –not until the end, at least, and then only partially. The title (of the collection and first story), translated by Luise von Flotow as "The Inside Killer," conjures up murderous detective tales that take place inside one's (female or male?) head and/or psyche, inside homes, apartments, offices, businesses, hairdresser salons, morgues, and the like – all figuring in the stories – as we continue to meet up with those recurring "spooky" porcelain dolls, Walkmen, and North American rock music.

On the surface, the story is simple: "Je"/the narrator/Blanche Bellemare lives alone with her beloved collection of porcelain dolls; she is sexually harassed by her boss, Robert Lalancette, at work; she is being stalked by someone who enters her apartment while she is away; Lalancette is found strangled; she is reminded of her former lover, Jean-Pierre, who suddenly left eight years ago with her house key; she sees a crossdresser on the street who bothers her; she buys another porcelain doll; the crossdresser is found strangled; someone tries to burn down her neighbour's house; she buys implements to attempt to catch the stalker if he dares enter her apartment again; she is found dead, either as a result of murder or of suicide. But the simplicity stops there.

Kellett-Betsos interprets the short story by placing the "journal intime" that the narrator is writing at the centre. For her, this diary is an outlet for the narrator's complaints about her sexual harrasment at work and an alibi for both the murders and her encroaching double personality/gender (37–8, 41). When Blanche's boss is strangled, the reader begins to question Blanche's story, and when the crossdresser becomes the second victim, we begin to wonder about the possibility of double gender, since the transvestite asks the narrator: "Hey, Réal, so you're dressing like a woman nowadays?" ["Hé, Réal, tu t'habilles en femme, astheur?"] (Dandurand, "L'Assassin de l'intérieur" 18). In other words, is Blanche really a man or transgendered, cross-dressing like a woman? Perhaps the stalker/intruder into her life and apartment is not Jean-Pierre, or perhaps "il" is the same as the female "je" (Kellett-Betsos 37), suggesting once again the "glissement de pronoms" I have mentioned. When the narrator is found dead in her own trap – electrocuted, wearing men's clothing, surrounded by her dolls, her burned notebook near her body, Kellett-Betsos identifies the dolls as witnesses to the victory of Blanche over the masculine identity of Jean-Pierre, which had tried to take over her true being (38). Whether Blanche, the female narrator, was aware of her male former lover as a psychological projection of herself, or whether she was blind to her real nature (Kellett-Betsos 41) remains an unanswered question.

Let me also fill in some details regarding the violent nature of "Je"/ Blanche Bellemare/"il"/Jean-Pierre. If everything recounted in this story is the product of the female narrator's imagination, then she is undoubtedly prone to visions/frames of violence. Entering her apartment, for example, she sees her black silk stockings "hanging up by garters … arranged like the open legs of a woman" ["accrochés à des jarretières … disposés comme les jambes ouvertes d'une femme"] (Dandurand, "L'Assassin de l'intérieur" 13). The stalker/Jean-Pierre/her masculine double has carefully positioned the female as a sexually violated object. Robert Lalancette is later strangled with a single black silk stocking – a symbolic victory of the female sex (or at least of female sexual "trappings") over the male – and with apparent lucidity, the narrator announces, "Clearly, I only have one single black stocking" ["Évidemment, je n'ai plus qu'un seul bas noir"] (14). As if in revenge, the narrator's porcelain doubles are then subjected by "il" to gruesome violence: "My three *Bye-Lo* dolls are hanging by their feet, with a piece of string. My little *Brue* doll, so cute with her flowered hat, is floating in the toilet. The *Frozen Charlotte* dolls are lined up like slices of bacon in the frying pan" ["Mes trois *Bye-Lo* sont pendues par les pieds, avec une ficelle. Ma petite *Brue*, si mignonne avec son chapeau à fleurs, flotte dans la toilette. Les *Frozen Charlotte* sont alignées comme des tranches de bacon dans la poêle à frire"] (16–17). Even her eighteen Pierrots have been drowned in the garbage can: clown dolls have ambiguous sex – and gender. Her favourite doll merchant mutters in Spanish: "*You have the smell of death, my beautiful*" ["*tu hueles a la muerte, mi bella.*"] (18), as she cradles her new purchase like a talisman against the violence. With great parodic humour, the frightening intruder who next attempts arson is seen dressed in a black cloak and hat – mimicking both the feared killer and the detective.The narrator decides to buy an electric cable, a large water bassin, alligator clips, a small square rug, and a long copper pipe – all to fashion a "stalker trap." She falls into her own trap and is electrocuted: "And what's more, the policeman gets lost in conjectures about the male clothing that the dead woman was wearing, in particular a cape and a black hat, and about the collection of dolls, seated as if at a show right on the beaten earth cellar floor." ["De plus, le policier se perd en conjectures sur les habits d'homme que portait la morte, en particulier une cape et un chapeau noir, et sur la collection de poupées, assises comme au spectacle à même la terre battue de la cave"] (21). Thus ends this marvellous gender-bending violent and darkly comic tale.

As Kellett-Betsos has reminded us, Dandurand's narrators are very good at what they do: with their diaries they claim sincerity and yet they are adept at spinning tales and inventing lies (42). They do not necessarily even worry about the link between the created/imaginary and the real world but tend to emphasize the connections between stories that speak to one another (Saint-Martin, "Playing with Fire" 38–9). Accordingly, porcelain dolls, stalkers, murders and suicides, rock music, Walkmen, Jeanne Coteau, policemen, detectives, hairdressing salons – and eery laughter – all reappear and prance throughout the remaining stories of *L'Assassin de l'intérieur.*

In "L'Ex au max," Nina – who of course listens to rock music on her Walkman – stalks her former lover and neighbour, Christophe. She kills his (or her?) cat and places it on his bed; she calls him frequently in the night. When she screams for him to help her one night, he arrives, brandishing a knife, only to find her furniture turned over, and her dolls broken into pieces: "She is alone, naked, and seriously wounded: all over her skin are the designs of musical staffs covered with notes. Nina is a great fugue stabbed in the throat, in her sex. She whispers to him: 'Good-bye my love, you won't be able to get away from me any more.' And her laughter fades away into a ghastly gurgling" ["Elle est seule, nue, et grièvement blessée: partout sur sa peau sont dessinées des portées de musique couvertes de notes. Nina est une grande fugue poignardée à la gorge, au sexe. Elle lui souffle: 'Adieu mon amour, tu ne pourras plus m'échapper.' Et son rire s'éteint dans un affreux gargouillis"] (Dandurand, "L'Ex au max" 27). Christophe, of course, becomes the major suspect in this "murder," especially after the police find photographs of Nina in pornographic poses, along with a letter stating that she will no longer give him money and no longer cares what he does with the pictures; but why did he kill her cat? The police also discover that she has been depositing money into Christophe's bank account. Her friends swear that she had been afraid of him. After an initial "male bonding" that allows the policeman, Marc Mongeau, to continue to believe in Christophe's innocence, it is discovered that the musical markings etched into Nina's skin were an exact copy of the third movement of one of Christophe's compositions. He is tried and convicted for her murder. He knows that she set everything up so that they could remain together: in his cell for life, Nina is always with him; they talk and embrace; Nina is happy and laughs; he is called "le craqué" (33) (the crazy guy); but he doesn't care, since he has fallen in love with Nina again. In this story, it is clear that Nina/"elle" (like Dé's Brigitte) – if truth were told – is the mastermind behind her own suicide/murder, working out every detail in order to incriminate and regain the lost love of a man. It is her grotesque laughter – as in other short stories already considered – ringing in her gurgling/death rattle, that has taken the stereotype of a woman and turned it into an empowered (dead but eternal) agent.

The same policeman, Marc Mongeau, enters the morgue, investigating the death of three men, all electrocuted in "Le Salon des coeurs perdus." Their three wives/partners/lovers all have solid alibis but seem rather relieved by these deaths. The only connection among them is that they go to the same hairdresser! Marc goes to the salon and falls madly in love with the owner, Adrienne, while remarking how curious her place of business is – with its wigged heads, each with a different face (40). One might think of its resemblance to a morgue – except that this room also has a machine for duplicating keys. After a frightening dream in which he is devoured by a large cat, Marc goes to visit Adrienne, only to find to real spiders and webs throughout her apartment. She explains that she loves the fact that they produce the strands of their web from their stomachs, and when Marc reminds her that they also devour their males,

Adrienne smiles: "'Only those who don't give them presents.' Marc Mongeau lights up, he now knows, he has a feeling that it is Adrienne who has committed these murders ... she was able to copy the three women's keys ... then she went to the houses of the three men ... three perfect crimes he'll never be able to prove" ["'Seulement ceux qui ne leur font pas de cadeaux.' Marc Mongeau s'illumine, il sait maintenant, il pressent que c'est Adrienne qui a commis les meurtres ... elle a pu reproduire les clés des trois femmes ... puis elle s'est rendue chez les trois hommes ... trois crimes parfaits qu'il ne pourra jamais prouver"] (42), Marc understands that Adrienne was only trying to help her customers, who had complained about their men to her while they were getting their hair done. So – what would be the point in trying to convict Adrienne? Instead – with great gendered humour intended – Marc quits his job as police inspector and becomes a hairdresser, working for the murderous Adrienne! The male moves from a stereotypical male profession to a stereotypical female job and becomes subservient to the violent female in charge of this establishment. The role reversal is complete, but, as Saint-Martin has noted in reference to Dandurand's "Histoire de Q," the binary system still remains intact ("Playing with Gender" 35).

Female Violence and Class

A "natural" link between the sexually violent females of "Danger: Désir de glace" and "Home Sweet Home" and the female serial killers of Dandurand's "Maîtresse des hautes oeuvres/Underground Requiem," "La Louve-garou" and Claire Dé's "A tuer" (which I look at in chapter 5) is Dandurand's "Des milliers de minotaures" from her 1991 collection *Petites âmes sous ultimatum.* This short story interestingly brings in the issue of class; the female killer is a woman who originally cleaned the bathrooms of a youth detention home, lives in the urban underworld of drug dealers and addicts in order to track and find a serial killer, and uses a weapon from that world – a dirty hyperdermic needle – to kill. Having heard that a young woman whom she had befriended in the youth detention home had been murdered, "elle," a forty-year-old widow, leaves her former life and pursues what turns out to be a serial killer who lures, sexually tortures, and kills young women. She discovers his torture chamber, complete with surgical tools, chains, and handcuffs, finds a young girl who has just been disembowelled, and sees the serial killer ejaculating on the dead body. She strikes him with a bed lamp but continues in her violence and rage. Using her scarf as a tourniquet, "she takes the syringe from her pocket. Fills it with air. She sticks the vein, drives the air toward the heart. She removes the valve, puts it back in, pushes the air again. Four or five times. The man gives a start. Shrivels up in a final spasm" ["elle prend la seringue dans sa poche. L'emplit d'air. Elle pique dans la veine, chasse l'air vers le coeur. Elle ôte le piston, le remet, pousse l'air à nouveau. Quatre ou cinq fois. L'homme tressaille. Se crispe dans un spasme final"(Dandurand, "Des Milliers de minotaures" 61). Yes, this middle-aged woman has killed once – and has rid the world of a dangerous male serial killer – but the ending of the story suggests that she will kill again, if need be: "There you go. One minotaur down. How many thousand to go?" ["Voilà. Un minotaure de moins. Combien de milliers encore?"] (61). Her mission will be to destroy these male mythical beasts/predators who prey on young girls. The woman has become the avenging angel, dangerous in her own right, and powerful enough to begin to create a balanced world for the new millennium.

The theme of getting one's way at this end of the millennium is also strong in "Le Vol de Jacques Braise" from the same collection (Dandurand 76). Here, rather than a "run of the mill" murder committed by a woman, we have the theft of a man's body and soul – everything a woman can hope for in this day and age. With an exemplary use of science fiction, black magic, horror, and dark humour, "Je," with the wonderful name of Jacinthe-Pierre O'Bamsawé, part Haitian and part Cree (and fully Irish from the "bombs-away" family) fixes up her mother's recipe (how typically female) for a brew consisting of strands of her love-object's hair, mandragore, ancestral ashes, part of a sanitary napkin soaked with menstrual blood, and rat saliva. After thirteen hours in a slow boiler, the potion is ready to be poured into Jacques Braise's beer. The potion works like a charm. He slumps over, and she transfers his soul into a wine decanter (gourmets, all of these women), which she immediately buries in her cellar. With a new potion, she brings him back to "life," as her "love zombie" (von Flotow, *Three by Three* 25) ["zombi d'amour"] (Dandurand 75), now in her power and the object of her adoration – much like adored female-objects placed on a pedestal to view. She writes his journalistic essays for him/takes over his profession. He rests in her arms at night – "unfortunately not with body and soul" (von Flotow, *Three by Three* 25; Dandurand 76). But at least, through a form of violence, she has created her own male (though not porcelain) doll.

Warrior Princesses and Slayers in a Post-Apocalyptic World

Sherrie Inness tells us that "in the often barbaric and excessive world of the post-apocalyptic narrative, women are freer to act tough and be independent because it is evident that the world has been turned topsy-turvy" (123). In comic books, for example, "the female hero can rescript stereotypes about what it means to be a woman. Just by *being*, she suggests that the male stranglehold on the heroic can be subverted. The woman hero serves as a bold, new role model for women and girls" (143). She adds that the tough female hero who has great physical power and confidence appeals to women because she gives them a sense of empowerment (Inness 135). Characters like Xena: Warrior Princess and Buffy the Vampire Slayer are new versions of the superhero, who challenges and defeats evil-doers. Unfortunately, these female superheroes also perform in what Inness calls the "safe space" of "camp," which "reveals the artificiality of things we accept as the norm (such as gender roles)" (173). Consequently, in some sense, they are identified as make-believe, rather than as "normal and real" women.

What if these new female "action figures" are not those who protect the world from evil forces? What if they are, themselves, tough, powerful and violent, performing as part of Nepveu's hyper-alterity (*L'Écologie du réel* 158) and in Hunt's hyperreal and yet grotesque world (37–8)? Dandurand's disturbing and yet intriguing short story "Après la bombe N," part of *La Louve-garou*, her 1982 collection co-authored with Dé, is prefaced by a grotesque drawing. Bald, animalistic figures hang from a cross above a large, bare-breasted woman. This story clearly takes place in a post-apocalyptic world where a female narrator, accompanied by her seemingly semi-unconscious male lover, can barely speak, since fear has killed all language. One morning, a huge blond woman appears, dragging a bald woman along with her: "She kills everything that is being devoured, the cruel Blond" ["Elle tue tout ce qui se dévore, cruelle Blonde"] (142).The bald female sidekick decides that the narrator's male companion must be killed: she will make up the plan, and the blond will carry it out. In order to protect her lover, the female narrator lies down on him and covers him in a sexual pose: "They wait, inexorable. I am moaning, terrified. He doesn't understand anything, gets excited, screws me. The Blond coldly smiles. As for him, he sacrifices himself to pleasure. The Blond pounces and strangles him. Their voices tear into each other with rapture and horror. The Blond holds on tightly. Underneath her, the face of death with a swollen tongue" ["Elles attendent, inexorables. Je me lamente, affolée. Il ne comprend rien, s'excite, m'enfile. La Blonde sourit avec froideur. Lui s'immole à son plaisir. La Blonde bondit et l'étrangle. Leurs voix se déchirent de ravissement et d'horreur. La Blonde tient bon. Visage sous elle de la mort à la langue gonflée"] (143).

Who is this powerful, unemotional, and violent blond woman, the antithesis of the dumb, sexy blond? Is she a new sort of post-apocalyptic, comic-book Eve, a female warrior who, unlike other violent female characters I have presented and shall analyse in chapter 5, does not rid the world of unsavoury and dangerous men, but rather kills indiscriminately, even while sex is being used by another woman as a protective covering for the male? In this rendition of a topsy-turvy world, Dandurand's superhero is, rather, a super-evil-doer herself – not "camp," not humorous, but an unsettling mirror image of the violent super-male.

"La Blonde" is also the cousin of a host of unsavoury, subversive female characters who rule in the violent, hyper-realistic, and pornographic world (Potvin 197–8) imagined by Josée Yvon as of 1976 in *Filles-Commandos Bandées*, in her 1980 *Travesties-Kamikaze*, her 1982 *Danseuses-mamelouk*, her 1986 *Maîtresses-Cherokees*, and her 1993 *La Cobaye*, published a year before her death in 1994. Perhaps because of the excessive "in-your-face" nature of Yvon's writing and filmic scenes, there has not been much critical appraisal of her work. Francine Bordeleau, in one of the few studies, calls Yvon a "female warrior, missile girl, and kamikaze woman writer" ["guerrière, fille-missile, et écrivaine-kamikaze"] who doesn't hold back from violating language in order to present her Amazons, prostitutes, dancers, and transsexuals (92). In this violent, comic-strip, pop culture world, the body is abject – subjected to blood, feces, crucifixion, mutilation, sadism, and masochism (Bordeleau 92). Women are primitive and spend their lives oozing alcohol, sex, and drugs: "Nauseating women who make war in an America of chaos. Nightmarish women bathing in their blood and in their excrement ... exposed in their overly full nature as if to rout out the dream woman of masculine discourse. The provocative violence of these women is indefensible, unbearable, their cruelty is demonic" ["Femmes à vomir qui vont faire la guerre dans l'Amérique du chaos. Femmes cauchemardesques baignant dans leur sang et leurs excréments ... exposées dans leur trop-plein de nature comme pour mettre en déroute la femme de rêve du discours masculin. La violence provocatrice de ces femmes-là est insoutenable, insupportable, leur cruauté est démonique"] (Bordeleau 92).

Let me introduce some of the more outrageous characters of Yvon's *La Cobaye*, for example, who are reminiscent of certain fictitious female characters born of recent French literary female imaginations, who push and transgress the boundaries of gender identity and "performance," who parody female and male U.S. popular culture heroes, and who thus represent the "daughters" of the sexual, violent, chaotic, and primitive North American culture of this change of millennium.

In the wild-west American town of Big Red Rock/[Grosse Roche Rouge] (and sometimes in Quebec) lives the sheriff, Emma, an adventurer, former security guard and mercenary – a job she got from an advertisement in the now-defunct U.S. paramilitary magazine, *Soldier of Fortune* – who enjoys capturing, torturing, and killing others. A female Charles Ming (of Rioux's world, inhabited by Éleonore), Emma is known for her "fabulous experiences of composure, her degrees in jiu-jitsu and her Herculean stature" ["fabuleuses expériences de sang-froid, ses diplômes de jiu-jitsu et sa stature herculéenne"] (Yvon, *La Cobaye* 18), which ironically define her "feminine condition." This larger-than-life "boy-girl" ["fille-garçon"] (22) sees Jessica, one of two young girls on display in cages in a club where they are publicly humiliated, tortured, and sexually abused in a Foucauldian spectacle of violence – since "cruelty is an act of compassion" ["la cruauté est acte de compassion"] (41) in this upside-down world. Emma then begins her sadistic physical and sexual abuse of Jessica (and of herself), linking torture, sex, orgasm, and guns. With kindness abruptly turned to sadism, Emma penetrates Jessica's orifices with different objects, "just to see how they ooze or drip. The game turns into madness: she photographs her when she is rearing up and when the suffering cuts through her, she films her and shudders. One evening, she gets carried away, goes too far and opens her stomach with a knife" ["juste pour voir comment ils jutent ou coulissent. Le jeu tourne à la folie: elle la photographie quand elle se cabre et quand la souffrance la transperce, elle la filme et frémit. Un soir, elle s'emporte, va trop loin et lui ouvre le ventre avec un couteau"] (59). Emma (frequently referred to in mythical terms as Hecate and Sisyphus – like Rioux's Éléonore) says that she loves young girls and adores torturing and killing them either with her knives or with her collection of guns, toward which she displays a ritualistic religiosity (70). The North American "Emma half of the night, Emma rock-and-roll, Emma Baby" ["Emma demi-du-soir (ironically like the caricature of a demi-mondaine), Emma rock-and-roll, Emma Baby"] (88) is also French/American: "She is an Other. And much more" ["Elle est une

Autre. Et bien plusse"](87), a female rebel of the likes of Rimbaud (and of Rambo) who has gone even further into the land of the Other, into Nepveu's hyper-alterity (*L'Écologie du réel* 58).

Then there is Threesa "Doubleshot," an old drunk who loves her vibrator, makes Molotov cocktails, listens to Jimmy Hendrix, Eric Clapton, Hot Chili Peppers, Talking Heads, Prince, the Sex Pistols, James Brown, and Van Morrison – but not Sinead O'Connor – and whose three husbands have all died violent deaths. Wanted for armed robbery, Threesa loves her weapons: "six submachine guns (three Stens, one Baretta, an MP 40, a Mini-Uzi); eight automatic pistols (two Colt .45's, a Parabellum P. 08, a Browing 9mm, various 7.65's), three revolvers (a Colt Python, a Smith and Wesson .357 Magnum, a Taurus), as well as three pump-action shotguns from the U.S.A., one of which, not commercialized, carries the instruction *For law enforcement only*" ["six pistolets-mitrailleurs (trois Sten, un Beretta, un MP 40, un mini-Uzi); huit pistolets automatiques (deux Colt .45, Parabellum P.08, Browing 9mm, divers 7.65), trois revolvers (un Colt Python, un Smith and Wesson .357 Magnum, un Taurus), ainsi que trois fusils à pompe en provenance des USA, dont l'un, non commercialisé, porte l'indication *For law enforcement only*"] (89). She also prides herself on knowing the most unexpected and treacherous ways to kill. Human genius in this arena knows no limits (84).

At one point in her life, Threesa forms a group of female robbers and meets up with Tava, a poet who wants to write about Threesa's life: on one side "action woman" who does not believe in anything, and especially in writing; on the other side, a woman writer "who is desperately looking for a plausible, original feminine subject" ["qui cherche désespérément un sujet féminin plausible, original"] (96). As if Yvon has not already been parodying everything that she has learned in North America, here she truly "has a field day." Threesa and her four robber friends spend the winter with Tava, who is so involved with her writing that she does not even notice that slowly these women are stealing everything she owns. Spring arrives, and Ghostbuster, one of the group, decides that she has had enough: "So she liquidates all of Tava's bank accounts, drags her into the parking lot and in between two cars, simply breaks her neck" ["Alors elle liquide tous les comptes de banque de Tava, l'entraîne dans le parking et entre deux voitures lui tord le cou, tout simplement"] (100). Tava dies like a good character in a dated folk song – with all of the spasms and contorsions of a transe. But writing is victorious: after the murder, either Threesa buys a copy of *Soldier of Fortune* and sees a poem by Tava about her own death, or the escapade just described terminates with a poem about these "heroes of the night" ["héros de la nuit"] (101).

And finally, readers meet Amélie, an androgynous or hermaphroditic eight-year-old who tortures and kills animals, sets fire to Threesa's hotel, and ends up in prison. Caught between dream and reality (like everyone else in her world), Amélie, "l'androgyne future" (106), and probably the narrator of this story, leaves reform school and returns to her lovely village where she no longer knows anyone. Everything has changed: the local Sioux population has opened boutiques to sell souvenirs to tourists. She becomes a street child, a homeless person who ultimately finds two of Threesa's guns and then Emma herself – alone in a house surrounded by an overgrown garden of "special archduchess seringes, the drum packed with guns and machetes" ["les seringues spéciales archiduchesses, le tambour tassé de carabines et de machettes"] (111), in a final bestial and non-linguistic state.

What does all of this mean? Claudine Potvin describes Yvon's imaginary world this way:

> Waste matter appropriate to a civilization seen as ugliness ou horror, their (these female characters') subversive practices do not assume anything less than the overturning of the principle of beauty as defined by an ethic and a social code equally based on a simulacrum [see Baudrillard]. Out-laws and "outside-language," Yvon's "female rippers" always position themselves on the border of a territory limited on one side by the grotesque bodies of young girls and old women represented in pornographic scenes, and on the other side, by the screen circumscribed by male sperm ... The realization of desire, accentuated by the violence of the lighting, the rhythmn of the movie camera, the magical projection of film, illusion, only opens up into an artificial, simulated climax. [Déchets propres à une civilisation dite de la laideur ou de l'horreur, leurs pratiques subversives n'en supposent pas moins un renversemenet du principe de la beauté défini par une éthique et un code sociaux également basés sur le simulacre. Hors-la-loi et hors-la-langue, ces "éventreuses" de Yvon se positionnent toujours à la frontière d'un territoire délimité d'un côté par le corps grotesque des fillettes et des vieilles femmes représenté dans la scène pornographique, et de l'autre, par l'écran circonscrit par le sperme des mâles ... [L]'actualisation du désir, accentuée par la violence des éclairages, le rythme de la caméra, la projection fantasmatique du film, l'illusion, ne débouche que sur une jouissance factice, simulée.] (198)

Potvin then examines three axes of Yvon's writing: the resistant body; the pornographic scene; and the grotesque/abject in America. Starting with the obvious meaning of the titles of Yvon's books – all of which underscore the marginality of her characters – and the monstrous, obscene, and shocking paratextual nature of the covers of these texts, Potvin uses Russo's concept of the grotesque to posit that Yvon's female bodies are, in fact, freak bodies, that resist at the level of the abject any "normal" construction of the feminine (Potvin 201–2). Her pornographic scenarios play with Kappeler's "cultural archeplot of power" (Kappeler 104), since her characters' transgressions represent the transvestite in all of us (Potvin 206) whereby, as Baudrillard has noted, everything is makeup, theatre, and seduction (*De la séduction* 23), and spectacle becomes the manifestation of hyperreality (*De la séduction* 45, 50; Potvin 207).

Perhaps more to the point of the current study, Potvin identifies the *américanité* of Yvon's work (a phenomenon I have discussed in chapter 2 and at the beginning of this chapter). Let us remember Baudrillard's description of America: "America is neither dream nor reality. It is a hyperreality. It is a hyperreality because it is a utopia which has behaved from the very beginning as though it were already achieved ... It may be that the truth of America can only be seen by a European [or by any outsider, hence also by a Québécois], since he [she] alone will discover here the perfect simulacrum – that of the immanence and material transcription of all values. The Americans, for their part, have no sense of simulation. They are themselves simulation in its most developed state, but they have no language in which to describe it, since they themselves are the model" (Baudrillard, *America* 28–9). To Potvin, Yvon's texts present the ugly side of *américanité*: "*Américanité* is here the exploded self ... It is a dirty, cruel, inhumane America with sharp knives ... A reactionary and conservative America ... Bodies to put in the garbage can, in the ditch, in the ravine, in a cage, in the cellar, in a plastic bag" ["L'américanité, c'est ici le moi éclaté ... C'est une Amérique sale, cruelle, inhumaine, aux couteaux tranchants ... Amérique réactionnaire et conservatrice ... Corps à mettre à la poubelle, dans le fossé, dans le ravin, dans une cage, dans la cave, dans un sac de plastique"] (Potvin 208). Her androgynous creatures, cross-dressers, lesbians, and transsexuals belong to "a universe of disgust, spasms, vomiting and stain" ["un univers du dégoût, de spasmes, de vomissements et de souillure"] (Potvin 209), to what Kroker and Cook have called "excremental culture." With "the zoom of a vicious, nosy, perverse camera, pointed at false sexes, at appearances" ["le zoom d'une caméra vicieuse, fouineuse, perverse, braquée sur de faux sexes, des apparences"]

(Potvin 210) in a "re-framing" of gendered North American life, Yvon's degraded and publicly exposed bodies question, resist, and upset our notions of the geographies of power and the concept of male and female space. I now wonder if it is from such characters in such an inhospitable (North) American space that even more violent female characters are born.

On Patricide, Castration, and a New World Order

Domestic life at the end of one millennium and at the beginning of another does not necessarily correspond to the brutal and primitive world imagined by Josée Yvon, but in the minds of many Québécois women writers, it has its equally violent side. Domestic violence in all countries is overwhelmingly caused by boyfriends, lovers, husbands, and fathers, and some of the female characters in the fiction created by these women, are simply fed up with it. If the decolonized Quebec national subject could be seen as a castrated male, the "new" national subject who affirms an independent stance is the virile male (Lamoureux, "La Posture du fils" 39, 41; *L'Amère patrie* 123), whom the female must then castrate in order to take power into her own hands.

"Pourquoi les marmottes," Claire Dé's short story from her 1991 collection *Chiens divers (et autres faits écrasés)*, is narrated by Alexia in the form of a diary. From the very first entry – beautifully illustrating Cerulo's argument that it is the "point of entry" into a story of violence that provides the specific lens to guide the reader through the sequences (Cerulo 7) – she tells her diary about her controlling, alcoholic, and physically and sexually abusive father and her unhappy mother. When Alexia begins to menstruate, her mother explains that she can now have children: "'Even with Daddy?' Mommy's face became totally grey ... It's then that she said this unbelievable thing: 'I'm gonna kill him'" ["'Même avec papa?' Le visage de maman est devenu tout gris ... C'est alors qu'elle a dit cette chose incroyable: 'Je vais le tuer'"] (58). At a "war council" of the family (mother and her three children), Alexia announces that she will eliminate her father, but her mother calmly responds that she will overdose him with sleeping pills. "J Day" arrives; everything goes as planned; Alexia has never seen her mother so happy. But the father keeps on breathing. Narrating in a very matter-of-fact tone, Alexia explains how she, her brother, and mother then attack and beat him with their fists. He keeps on breathing, and the mother can't understand why. When her son, Damien, suggests using a kitchen knife, mother objects: after all, he is her husband. Alexia calmly goes back upstairs to the bedroom: "I put the barrel against the nape of his neck ... It's funny, dear Diary, I had never noticed the nape of his neck. While his skin is like cured leather, his hands rough like bark, I paid enough to know that ... the skin on the nape of his neck is totally pale, almost the skin of a Gentleman. I was surprised, and this almost stopped me. But I closed my eyes, I thought about the marmots" ["J'ai appuyé le canon contre sa nuque ... C'est drôle, cher Journal, je n'avais jamais remarqué sa nuque. Alors qu'il a la peau comme du cuir boucané, les mains rudes comme de l'écorce, j'ai assez payé pour le savoir ... celle de sa nuque est toute pâle, presque une peau de Monsieur. J'ai été surprise, ça a failli m'arrêter. Mais j'ai fermé les yeux, j'ai pensé aux marmottes] (61). In a thought characteristic of victims of child abuse, the narrator does not focus on the child abuse as her reason for shooting her abusive father, but rather on the memory that he used to shoot and kill nice marmots who did harm to no one.[36] Of course the reader never knows if the narrator actually murders her father, but the ending suggests that she aims and pulls the trigger on the pale, gentlemanly nape of his neck.

The obese female protagonist narrator of Lise Tremblay's 1999 novel *La Danse juive* also calmly commits patricide by stabbing her father in the neck with her boyfriend's Swiss Army knife: "I cut, there, where I see veins. Blood gushes out. My father is surprised ... I stick the knife in again ... My father falls onto the floor ... The smell of blood in my grandmother's house and my grandfather's gaunt body come to mind. I pick up the cookie tin and start to eat some" ["Je tranche, là où je vois les veines. Le sang surgit. Mon père est étonné ... Je replonge le couteau ... Mon père tombe sur le plancher ... L'odeur de sang de la maison de ma grand-mère et le corps décharné de mon grand-père me viennent à l'esprit. Je ramasse la boîte de biscuits et je commence à en manger"] (142). In this case, however, the patricide does not come after a long history of abuse. As Lori Saint-Martin has pointed out, this murder is all the more shocking because it is so sudden and so out of character for the narrator ("The Other Family Romance" 182). The narrator has always been obsessed with bodies – her own obese body, the thin bodies of the dancers who train at the ballet school where she works, her mother's slim body, the obese bodies of her father's family, and especially her father's no longer fat body that has become a public icon on television and in magazines. She has always hidden her emotions in her fat, admitting that she is an embarrassment to her father, whom she rarely sees. The act of patricide, therefore, in Saint-Martin's interpretation, is precipitated by the narrator's hatred of her father's genes, which have caused her obesity, and by her desire to destroy the paternal body, which represents not necessarily patriarchal law, but, rather, patriarchal pretensions (Saint-Martin, "The Other Family Romance" 182). The act of patricide is committed, as well, in rebellion and anger against a patriarchal society that glorifies slimness as beauty and places women into predefined boxes as sexual objects.

In *L'Écho du silence* (1997), one of the darkest and most powerful novels to come out of Quebec in the past decade, Gabrielle Gourdeau creates a multiple split narrative, in which each daughter in the Desmarais family narrates her own particular story of sexual abuse at the hands of their rich, successful father. These are echoed by a similar tale told by their mother, who finally finds her voice from a deep coma. Against this backdrop of the multiple "re-visioning" and "re-framing" of their sexual abuse, each female narrator expresses her violent anger and is thus "set up" as a potential perpetrator of the ultimate criminal act against the father – ritual castration. As Susan Ireland has noted: "The father is represented above all by his sexual organ, which is clearly equated with paternal authority and, from the daughters' perspective, with the abuse of power that has destroyed their lives ... As a tool of inscription and the primary symbol of the patriarchal order, the father's phallus underscores the relationship between the body and the law" (Ireland, "The Daughter's Revenge" 187–8).

The oldest daughter, Nathalie, a lesbian and a nurse, is filled with anger and rage and finally threatens her father that there will be justice one day for what he has done to all of them (Gourdeau 140). Isabelle, who is a prostitute and a juvenile delinquent and has had a child by her father, is constantly planning, plotting, and threatening to kill her father, foreshadowing the crime that will ultimately be committed: "I want to plant death between your legs" ["Je veux te planter la mort entre les jambes"] (61–2). She cries out that times have changed: patriarchal justice is over, female silence is over, women have been called to action, and will take over justice for themselves (Gourdeau 70). Thirteen-year-old Véronique has displaced her resultant psychoses elsewhere – into history and sexual denial. She is obsessed with World War II, lives through an imaginary Blitzkrieg, and self-mutilates in order to become a "real" soldier in the war. She also refuses to be a woman – or a man:

> I told you, diary ... When I'm legally old enough ... I will be operated on ... I will have these horrible lumps removed, lumps that disfigure my chest that is

growing like it had a mind of its own ... The hideous sack where children are hatched will be removed from my body. The eggs will be cut out. No more ovaries. No more ova. No more vagina. No more vulva. No more lips ... My hole will be sown up. Finally. And then, in its place – nothing. I don't want any hair, penis, testicules, breasts. Just peace. A free mind in a neutral body (Ireland 194–5 in part). [Je te l'ai dit, journal ... Quand j'atteindrai l'âge ... je me ferai opérer ... Je ferai enlever ces horrible bosses, qui défigurent ma poitrine à la va-comme-je-pousse ... On videra mon abdomen de l'affreux sac où sont complotés les enfants. On sectionnera les oeufs. Plus l'ovaires. Plus l'ovules. Plus de vagin. Plus de vulve. Plus de lèvres ... On coudra mon trou. Enfin. Et puis, à la place, rien. Je ne veux ni poils, ni pénis, ni testicules, ni seins. La paix. Un esprit libre dans un corps neutre. (Gourdeau 114–15)

But the most moving "testimony" comes from five-year-old Julie, who often daydreams about poisoning her father, cutting out the tongue of the man who rapes and sodomizes her with his "big fat finger-mushroom" ["gros doigt-champignon"] (Gourdeau 166). She transfers her pain and shame onto a double – her doll, Lise – in whom she cuts three orifices like hers and whom she eventually kills in order to save her from the same sexual fate. Julie wants Isabelle to kill Papa so that she won't have to bleed anymore from her "mouths" down there; but then again, it isn't nice to kill one's papa: "'Kill Daddy but don't hurt him because after all, he's still my daddy'" ["'Tue papa mais fais-lui pas mal parce que c'est mon papa quand même'"] (Gourdeau 159). Perhaps she will kill him herself. She knows how to poison a person: she has seen it in the movies. Then she can tell everyone what he has done to her. She's not afraid because she is already dead – there – in all of her "mouths" (Gourdeau 167–8).

Remaining silent because of her own history of sexual abuse, Maman eventually and silently watches Nathalie, Isabelle, Véronique, and Émilie (Nathalie's lesbian lover) drug her husband and place him upon the kitchen table. In ritualistic and transgressive fashion [again à la Baudrillard], Nathalie avenges them all and cuts off their father's penis: "Good-bye, damned member. Hemostatic pincers. Most of all, preserve the life of this monster. Keep him alive, him too. Find the urethra. Be careful not to tie off the urethra. We want him alive. From now on he'll have to piss like a girl, sitting on the toilet" ["Adieu, membre maudit. Pinces hémostatiques. Surtout, conserver la vie au monstre. Le laisser pour vivant, lui aussi. Identifier l'urètre. Faire attention de ne pas ligaturer l'urètre. On le veut vivant. Il devra désormais pisser comme une fille, assis sur la cuvette"] (Gourdeau 186). In this carefully planned crime against the abusive penis and symbolic phallus, the women leave the mutilated body of their father on the side of a road and call for an ambulance to pick up this man who is missing a little something. The mother only wishes that she had been the one to castrate her husband, and she exhorts all abused daughters to follow the example of her children (Gourdeau 187).

Ireland underscores the carnivalesque nature of this transgressive act, which liberates the daughters by their performance of what Jane Gallop calls "dephallicizing the father" (Gallop, *The Daughter's Seduction* XV; Ireland 199). In a macabre and ritualistic revenge fantasy, the daughters assume the negative role of castrating women (Ireland 199) – once again maintaining the binary system of male and female and the binary view of women as purely good or purely evil or as mad or bad. But Ireland notes that this castration also suggests the "parallel dismantling of the paternal order. In this sense, the knife wielded by the daughters, a symbol of agency and inscription, writes a new daughter-oriented script on the father's body ... The daughters appropriate the means to shape their own recovery and, by extension, to reconfigure the social body" (Ireland, "The Daughter's Revenge" 199).

As I have shown, this reconfiguration of the social body has led to imaginative creations of erotic, sexual, pornographic, sexually violent, and violent acts by women who have become empowered enough to take control from and over men and at times, over the world – well, at least to re-vision and to re-frame gender in Quebec and North America. By parodying male pornography and violence and making them their own, these women writers have cleverly imagined females who have usurped traditionally male roles and actions and transformed themselves from sexual and violent object-victims to sexual and violent speaking subjects of representation. They will not stop there.

4

Public and Private Violence: The Novels of Infanticide/Filicide of Aline Chamberland and Suzanne Jacob

She picked at her head until she scratched bald spots on her scalp.
Her blackest depressions left her mute and catatonic, unable to recognize any semblance of hope. She tried to commit suicide in June 1999 and berated herself for failing. She thought, as a nurse, she should at least know how to kill herself.

And barely a month after the first suicide attempt, Andrea Yates tried to slash her own throat before her husband grabbed the knife.

Later she admitted: "I had a fear I would hurt somebody. I thought it better to end my own life and prevent it. There was a voice, then an image of the knife. I had a vision in my mind, get a knife, get a knife."

These details of a woman tormented by periods of psychosis and depression emerge in more than 1,000 pages of medical records ... filed in court by lawyers for Mrs. Yates, the mother who has admitted drowning her five young children one by one in a bathtub in their home in the Clear Lake section of Houston.

Jim Yardley, *The New York Times* 7 September 2001

Le monde est un livre qui espère de chaque naissance qu'elle ajoute une page à son histoire.
[The world is a book that hopes, with each birth, to add a page to its story.]

Suzanne Jacob, *La Bulle d'encre* (20)

INFANTICIDE AND FILICIDE: LEGAL DEFINITIONS, OCCURRENCES, AND PATHOLOGIES

Although it is common to refer to the killing of any child – newborn or older – by either parent as infanticide (as I shall do in this study), current legal definitions of infanticide and filicide are precisely defined and are quite country-specific. According to *Black's Law Dictionary* as used in the United States legal system, infanticide is: "1. The act of killing a newborn child, esp. by the parents or with their consent. In archaic usage, the word referred also to the killing of an unborn child. – also termed *child destruction; neonaticide*. 2. The practice of killing newborn children. 3. One who kills a newborn child" (781) (a usage I also adopt here). Other American legal experts have specified infanticide as the term generally used when referring to the killing of infants or children. Infanticide itself has also been more precisely defined by distinguishing between the killing of an infant within twenty-four hours of birth (neonaticide) and the killing of an infant or child older than twenty-four hours (filicide) (Dvorak 2). The Canadian legal system uses a much narrower – and yet more widespread – definition: "A female person commits infanticide when by a wilful act or omission she causes the death of her newly born child, if at the time of the act or omission she is not fully recovered from the effects of giving birth to the child and by reason thereof or of the effect of lactation consequent on the birth of the child her mind is then disturbed" (Consolidated Statutes of Canada. Criminal Code, Part VIII. 233).

In the case of Great Britain, the history and reasons behind such legal definitions are particularly revealing. The British *Infanticide Act* of 1922 reduced the charge of infanticide from murder to manslaugther on the basis of insanity. This change was premised upon the belief that a woman who commits infanticide may do so because "the balance of her mind [is] disturbed by reason of her not having fully recovered from the effect of giving birth to the child" (Meyer, Oberman et al. 11, 171, 183; see also Pearson 80). This statute was revised in 1938 and extended the age of infanticide victims from "newly born" to "under the age of 12 months," citing specifically the "effect of lactation" on a woman's mind (Pearson 80; Morris and Wilczynski 204). This *Infanticide Act* has been replicated in slightly varying forms in at least twenty-two nations around the world, including Canada.[1] James Dvorak notes that the majority of neonaticide/infanticide statutes in these countries make the crime a lesser offence than homicide and that, although countries may define infanticide differently, the most common elements include a mother who kills her infant after the child has been born because the mother had not fully recovered from the effects of giving birth (Dvorak 5). The statute in effect links infanticide to mental illness, thereby medicalizing the crime and limiting the defendant's culpability to manslaughter rather than murder (Meyer, Oberman et al. 11, 13, 183). The United States has not followed suit.

According to Alison Morris and Ania Wilczynski, British Criminal Statistics report that the age group most at risk of death by homicide are those under one year old: three-quarters of these homicides are listed as filicides; that is, they involve children who were killed by their parents, including step-parents and cohabitees (200). These published statistics, however, provide information only on the number of parents who kill their children and not on their sex. It has been left to specific studies – at least in Great Britain – to show that over half of these child-killings are committed by mothers (201). Indeed, a large number of women originally suspected of filicide – the murder of a child or children – are subsequently convicted of the lesser offence of infanticide, a crime that, by definition, can be committed only by women (Morris and Wilczynski 202).[2]

Criminologist Coramae Richey Mann reports in *When Women Kill* that, of victims killed by women in the United States, 10.9% are their own children (165). She also cites a 1986 U.S. study showing that females account for 56.8% of child fatalities (6). Defining the word "infanticide" as the generic term for child murder and "filicide" as the murder of one's own child,[3] Mann cites evidence to show that homicide is one of the five leading causes of early childhood death in the United States; the country has the second-highest child homicide rate in the world. Although limited research on child murder has been undertaken, what has been done identifies women, primarily mothers, as the predominant killers in the United States (Mann 70). Since male children continue to be more valued than female children, more girls are victims of infanticide than boys. Mann also cites a Canadian study that found that 57% of the infanticides involved female victims. In Mann's study in the United States, female infants constituted 64.3% of the victims under the age of one and 54.5% of those between two and five (Mann 73–4).

One of the most significant issues related to child homicide is the rough positive correlation between one's "best guess" as to the "reality" of these crimes, as documented in government data, and what the public perception is, as reported and fuelled by the media. I shall report on the "reality" first. As illustrated by Figures 10 and 11, taken from Statistics Canada reports on homicide between 1999 and 2003 (the last of which includes data from between 1993 and 2003), the total number of child victims under the age of twelve has not varied dramatically from year to year. The same is true if one looks at the number of child victims killed by their parents and the number of these homicides as a percentage of the total number of solved murders in Canada during these years. As for the differing numbers of children killed either by a father (or step-father) or mother (or step-mother), generally more fathers were accused – and in some years significantly more men – with the exception of one year (1997), when one more mother than father was accused. Data are far more difficult to obtain for homicides of children under the age of one, with small numbers and no data available (at least governmental data) for certain years.[4] This last issue probably relates to the suggestion made by Fedorowycz in one report that infant homicides "may still be under-reported since some claims of accidental childhood deaths such as falls or 'sudden infant deaths' could actually be due to child abuse" (Fedorowycz 2000, 11).

Again, in looking at Figures 10 and 11, it is interesting to note that there was a small "spike" in the number of child victims, the number of child victims killed by their parents, and parent-child homicides as a percentage of all solved homicides in Canada in 1997, which dropped somewhat in 1998 and dropped even lower for the following years until 2003, the most recent data available. It is this observation that provides evidence for the claim of a rough positive correlation between the "reality" of data and public perception as reported in the news media regarding child homicides – whether labelled infanticide or not.

Probably reacting to data for 1996 released in 1997, ironically the year before the spike in the number of child homicides and the percentage of those murders committed by parents, some Canadian news items between 1997 and 1999 reveal a public concern about child deaths and interestingly specifically in Quebec. On 31 July 1997, for example, the *Calgary Herald* reported that not long after the slaying of a battered toddler shocked Quebecers, a four-year-old girl and her three-year-old brother were stabbed to death in their home in suburban Varennes – the latest in a series of domestic killings that had taken the lives of eight children since April 1997. In this case, the twenty-seven-year-old mother

Figure 10
Child Homicide in Canada, 1993–2003

	Under 12 Years of Age					*Under 1 Year of Age*			
YEAR	*Total number of child victims (under 12 years old) [Series 1]*	*Number of child victims killed by parents (under 12 years old) [Series 2]*	*Number killed by father or step-father [Series 3]*	*Number killed by mother or step-mother [Series 4]*	*Parent-child homicides as a percentage of all solved homicides [series 5]*	*Number killed*	*Number of children killed by parents*	*Number killed by father*	*Number killed by mother*
1993	46	32	17	14	6.4				
1994	59	43	24	19	8.8				
1995	53	36	21	13	7.4				
1996	53	41	26	15	8.2				
1997	65	53	23	24	11.4				
1998	55	47	26	17	10.6				
1999	36	26	16	9	6.3	11	9	5	4
2000	39	27	15	9	6.5	20	13		
2001	39	30	14	12	6.8	12	12	4	8
2002	44	31	18	9	6.8	13	8	4	4
2003	33	23	13	11	5.7	14			

(Data derived from Dauvergne, *Homicide in Canada* 2003, 19, Table 10; Fedorowycz 1999, 6, 11; Fedorowycz 2000, 11; Dauvergne 2001 12; Savoie 2002, 8, 9, 17, Table 9; Dauvergne 2003, 9)

Figure 11
Child Homicide in Canada, 1993–2003

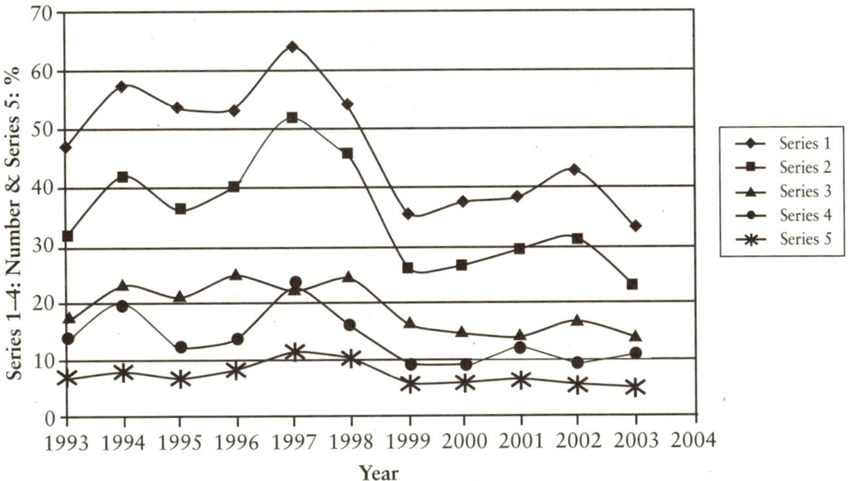

(Data derived from Dauvergne, *Homicide in Canada 2003* 19, Table 10)

was found hanged in the house. This article accurately indicated that for all of Canada, there were fifty-three homicides of children under the age of twelve in 1996, compared to an average of fifty-five a year since 1986. But the article also reported that in 1996 parents were responsible for 85 per cent of the killings, not a significantly higher proportion than in the previous decade – but inaccurate according to Statistics Canada, whereby in 1996, 41 out of the 53 child homicides were committed by parents (that is 77% of those crimes). The news report then goes on to state: "The proportion of infanticides committed in the Québec-Ontario region compared to the rest of the country increased significantly in 1996, to 80 percent; the 10-year-average is 63 per cent" (15). Interestingly, the news item mentions that depression is a common factor in such murder-suicides and that difficult economic times may predispose individuals to more family violence. Was a trend toward increased infanticides occurring, wondered the news reporter (15)? Among other articles, *The Montreal Gazette* reported additional infanticide cases in Quebec, and *The Edmonton Sun* in 1999 reported that a team of experts looking into the deaths of more than 400 children under the age of five in the Montreal and Quebec City regions had found that some may have been cases of infanticide. This "suspicion" echoed an earlier study that revealed that between 1985 and 1994 in Quebec, cases of infanticide were twice as high as coroner reports indicated (28).[5] It also again supports the suggestion in the Fedorowycz report cited above that infant homicides may still be under-reported by parents (Fedorowycz 2000, 11). Whatever the "reality" of the level of child homicide/infanticide in Quebec during those years, the news reporters must have moved on to other "breaking stories."

Most research on infanticide in both Britain and the United States has been fairly recent. Cheryl Meyer, Michelle Oberman, and their colleagues, in their book *Mothers Who Kill Their Children,* review studies by a number of researchers and focus on those published by Wilczynski in 1997 in her *Child Homicide,* which were based on samples of child killers in Britain and Australia. In that study, Wilczynski identified ten categories of alleged motives.[6] The only classification system based exclusively on a sample of U.S. cases was presented by Michelle Oberman in 1996.[7] The research undertaken by Meyer, Oberman, and their colleagues and presented in their 2001 text offers five categories or types based not on motive or intent but rather on the patterns associated with filicides from the perspective of social, cultural, environmental, and individual variables. The researchers identify: filicide related to an ignored pregnancy; abuse-related filicide; filicide due to neglect; assisted/coerced filicide; and purposeful filicide where the mother acted alone (36–8). This last category is especially pertinent to the novelistic cases studied in this chapter, as they underscore the link between representation and "reality" (along with the public perception of that "reality") and the need to read them together.

No matter which definition one uses and no matter what the statistics may be, however, a significant question in infanticide and filicide cases is why the murder occurred and what triggered this homicidal action on the part of a mother. As Morris and Wilczynski note, North American and British criminal justice systems support the belief that "such an action cannot be the act of a *normal* woman. She cannot have been fully responsible for her actions; she must need help of treatment. The clearest example of this assumption of the underlying pathological nature of mothers who kill their children is the very existence of the infanticide charge. It is based on the notion that maternal child killing is due to puerperal psychosis" (206).

As Patricia Pearson points out, references to maternal instinct and the assumption that there is an immediate bond between a mother and a child are remnants of the sentimental nineteenth-century view of mothers and motherhood (76). When that presumed bond is broken, then the label of "diminished responsibility" is applied to the woman, whereby she is seen as having been suffering from such an abnormality of mind as to impair her mental responsibility for the crime (Morris and Wilczynski 202). Although "diminished responsibility" is a legal term, it also underscores two assumptions about women. First, although the American Psychiatric Association's *Diagnostic and Statistical Manual of Mental Disorders* has no listing for "postpartum psychosis,"[8] it does cite "postpartum onset" as the cause for certain mental illnesses such as bipolar disorder and clinical depression (Pearson 81), thereby suggesting the assumed pathological nature of new mothers. According to Pearson, it was the British legal system that first used "postpartum insanity" as a legal defence, presumably forgetting that "postpartum psychosis was widely used in nineteenth-century England as a reason why women shouldn't vote. British criminologist Nigel Walker calls the laws that govern infanticide in his nation 'myth-making by legislation'" (91).

The second assumption made about women as a result of infanticide cases relates to the underlying dichotomous belief about all women – here with a maternal twist – that all women are "naturally" good and "naturally" good mothers; all women are potentially bad or mad as women and as mothers at certain times in their lives. Focusing on the potential pathologies of women, however, disallows the reality that any "normal" woman could kill her children if and when confronted with the "overabundance" of reality that sets in after childbirth or when faced with severe social and economic circumstances. As Morris and Wilcyznski point out: "Treating women's filicide as pathological diverts attention from the social conditions which are conducive to its occurrence: poverty, inordinate childcare responsibilities, social isolation, lack of support, the myths surrounding motherhood and cultural standards of 'good' (i.e., perfect) mothers" (216). Meyer and Oberman agree: "Infanticide may be seen as a response to the societal construction of and constraints upon mothering ... The crime of infanticide is committed by mothers who cannot parent their child under the circumstances dictated by their unique position in place and time. These circumstances vary, but the extent to which infanticide is a reflection of the norms governing motherhood is a constant that links seemingly disparate crimes" (2, 169).

In fact, one of Meyer and Oberman's major points is that the U.S. legal system (more so than those of Britain, Canada, and many other countries) continues to use the dichotomy of "mad" or "bad," sane or insane. When Meyer and Oberman initially developed their fifth category of purposeful filicide, killings in which the mother acted alone, they examined cases that were to be divided into purposeful filicide with mental illness and purposeful filicide without mental illness. When they tried to come up with definitions for these sub-categories, however, they could not decide how to define mental illness – using legal, mental health, or societal/cultural standards. The dichotomy became meaningless (Meyer and Oberman 70). In the U.S. legal arena, the question of a defendant's mental status relates either to the person's competence to stand trial or to the mental state at the time of the offense, with the first competency issue invoked most frequently. Mental status at the time of the offense is most commonly used for the insanity defense – for which each state has its own definition or test (Meyer and Oberman 70–1).[9] Unlike the dichotomous legal system, mental health professionals classify disorders as either clinical or personality disorders. On the basis of the cases they investigated, in which the defendants were, with one exception, all legally found to be "bad," the researchers' fifth category of purposeful filicide, in their view, appeared to be part of a continuum rather than a dichotomy (73): "These women did not easily fit into a dichotomy (i.e., 'mad versus bad') but represented a diverse continuum, covering the entire spectrum of mental illness, ethnic and cultural group distinctions, and socioeconomic strata. Ultimately the 'mad versus bad' dichotomy fails to accurately classify these mothers because it does not take into account the varying contextual, legal, and psychological factors which contributed to their emotional states and decision to kill their children" (93).

However, this dichotomy between the "good" and the "bad" mother and woman is maintained in the legal system – especially in the United States – and as I have mentioned, in the mindset of much of our society, since it acts as a method for controlling and reinforcing the boundaries of behaviour considered appropriate for all women and mothers. The assumptions, myths, and stereotypes of women that I discussed in chapter 1 here become the screen behind which murders take place, since infanticide – or filicide – is what Pearson entitles her third chapter: "The Problem That Still Has No Name." It is as if Andrea Yates had met the protagonists of the novels I shall be looking at.

INFANTICIDE AND FILICIDE: HISTORICAL, CULTURAL, AND NOVELISTIC CONSIDERATIONS

In seventeenth- and eighteenth-century North America, execution sermons delivered by members of the clergy stressed the role of original sin, of universal, innate depravity. Consequently, sermons and trials relating to infanticides focused not on the act of murder itself, but rather on its "uncleanness" (Halttunen 14), not on its criminality, but rather on the sin of having covered up a dirty deed of sex – if the infanticide were an unwed mother (136) – or an act of adulterous depravity within the privacy of the home (144). Women convicted of infanticide were severely punished – usually publicly hanged – because their crime was seen to violate divine authority. Such women were said to have mocked religion, broken civil law, and scorned patriarchal leaders; servants and slaves, in particular, scoffed at their masters, civil authorities, and God (Jones 50–1). At the executions of women convicted of infanticide, ministers "warned them against the sins of lying, secrecy, anger, disobedience, hypocrisy, sullen discontent, idleness, and 'gadding about' with other women. In a political context, these 'sins' amount to resistance, rebellion, subversion, sabotage, coalition, and conspiracy" (Jones 52). As religious authority gave way to secular authority, however, infanticide became less heinous a crime. By the nineteenth century, juries seldom sentenced infanticides to hang, since the murder of a child seemed less serious than the murder of an adult: "Among the lower classes infanticide was considered a necessary evil, while within certain high-ranking circles it became merely the unfortunate sequel to a sexual peccadillo. Lawyers ... handled 'everything' for women of high rank; courts did not require the women to appear, and newspapers did not print their names" (Jones 62). Such thinking has played into a historical and contemporary view that verdicts are really determined by the "worth" of the person who was killed – by the significance of the victim and the value that society places on him or her, rather than by the crime itself (as I have noted in chapter 1 in reference to the longer prison terms typically accorded women who kill men rather than other women).

Similarly, in nineteenth-century Paris, an increase in crimes of infanticide was portrayed as a symptom of the rise of the working class and of urban decay; in other words, as an aspect of social custom in certain sectors of the population (Shapiro 22, 24, 84). In contrast to the increased use of medical or legal discourse on the diminished mental capacity of female criminals in other cases, such medical rhetoric was completely absent in infanticide cases.[10] Ironically, nevertheless: "Outcomes in infanticide trials did not differ greatly from outcomes in other criminal categories: in both situations, juries ... granted high acquittal rates to female defendants, regardless of whether the court emphasized reason or unreason. What is noteworthy about infanticide cases, however, is an absence of the kind of medical discussion about women's reproductive instability that was such a large part of the narrative repertoire of ... gynecologists" (Shapiro 133). By the 1890s what these women were charged with, interestingly, was "egoism," while infanticide was described as "une terreur égoiste" (Shapiro 131, 212–13).

In Canada, from Confederation until 1948 when infanticide became a non-capital offence, capitally condemned women were the least likely to be executed, except for women who seemed particularly "cold-hearted." Women who killed their own babies were treated most leniently. During this period none of the ten women sentenced for killing their infants was executed: "Infanticide, under a death penalty regime, was widely considered to be a form of murder that did not call for the full severity of the law. Women were not executed because Canadians generally agreed that their crimes were motivated more by distress than by malevolence ... From the second half of the nineteenth century onward, cabinets did not impose the death penalty for women who killed their infants" (Strange 3).

Characterizing infanticide as an egotistical act relates to the premise that murder is the most narcissistic crime, the taking of someone else into oneself. As Lynda Hart paraphrases Jacques Lacan: "The ultimate act of aggressive incorporation is murder, a profoundly relational act" (Hart 37). In a psychoanalytical and anthropological vein, Françoise Couchard maintains that the sacrifice of children, especially of girls, occurs in all religions. Maternal cannibalism and the dual orality of the female, reincorporating the child as a thing must be tied to the reintegration of the child into the self" (Couchard 41–2, 42–6, 156).

Lori Saint-Martin's work[11] on Aline Chamberland's *La Fissure* and Suzanne Jacob's *L'Obéissance* raises several important points: "The emergence of infanticide in the Quebec novel is contemporaneous with the articulation of a mother's point of view in literature" ("Les Deux Femmes" 196); the textual devices of fragmentation and repetition that shatter the novelistic form in these works mirror the maternal violence that "breaks the daughter's sense of self into a thousand pieces" ("Les Deux Femmes" 198); "the infanticidal mother obeys a suicidal impulse" ["la mère infanticide obéit à une impulsion suicidaire"] (*Le Nom de la mère* 90), thereby killing her beloved and hated daughter – who can also be seen as taking her own life – and herself; and "society in general and fathers in particular are the accomplices, if not the cause, of maternal violence against daughters" ("Les Deux Femmes" 210).

Placing Chamberland's and Jacob's novels in a historical, legal, sociological, and criminological context – in addition to the psychological – as they relate to both public and private issues and to links among private criminal acts, public trials and public reporting, voyeuristic private reading, and novelistic narratives will show that infanticide is even more complex than initially described and that acquitting the two mothers of responsibility for their acts supports society's stereotypes of women.

Attempting to analyse the multi-layered and intense relationships between mothers and daughters, as well as with fathers, lovers, lovers' wives, siblings, friends, lawyers, social workers, psychiatrists, imagined characters, and other selves, in *La Fissure* and *L'Obéissance* is a little like attempting to (re)create entire fields of psychology or psychiatry. Jacob herself has recently admitted: "After *L'Obéissance*, I had to go back to the beginning even in writing" ["Après *L'Obéissance*, il me fallait remettre le compteur à zéro dans l'écriture même, quoi"] (*La Voix de l'au-delà* 1). Even Lori Saint-Martin's incisive interpretations could be supplemented by additional books in this vein. But since the focus of the analysis here is not on the psychological, I shall simply lay a psychological foundation for my study of novelistic public and private female criminality.

In Chamberland's *La Fissure*, Élaine kills her young daughter, Ève-Lyne, with a kitchen knife, as the child lies asleep on her belly. Élaine, unmarried when she became pregnant, had not wanted this child and had never felt any maternal instinct: "I didn't have it in my blood, it wasn't coming on its own. It had never come" ["Je n'avais pas ça dans le sang, ça ne venait pas tout seul. Ça n'était pas venu"] (57). There is little doubt throughout the novel, however, that she loved her daughter greatly and continues to love her in death. Two major points must be made about this fictional infanticide. In an incantatory, lyrical, and repetitive litany or lullaby, as Saint-Martin illustrates ("Les Deux Femmes" 203; *Le Nom de la mère* 96), Élaine explains the killing of her daughter by her desire to protect her from the violence of the outside world and from her own family. It is a case of what can be called "altruistic infanticide," a variation of what Toni Morrison describes in *Beloved*:[12] "'Liars, thieves, traitors, it's dangerous, Ève-Lyne, they're everwhere, hidden, well disguised, they're everywhere but don't be afraid, we're going to go away, we're going to hide ourselves, we're going to be just fine, just the two of us ... come Ève-Lyne, come my baby'" ["'Des menteurs, des voleurs, des traîtres, c'est dangereux,

Ève-Lyne, il y en a partout, dissimulés, bien déguisés, ils sont partout mais n'aie pas peur, on va s'en aller, on va se cacher, on va être bien, rien que nous deux ... viens Ève-Lyne, viens mon bébé'"] (Chamberland 139). She also wants to prevent her daughter from growing up like her – becoming her as a new Eve. This last excuse leads to the second point: as Saint-Martin has proposed, in killing the daughter, the mother is killing part or all of herself, especially since Élaine repeats that she wishes to go away with Ève-Lyne (but interestingly does not kill herself). Such an interpretation also dovetails with the testimony that Luc, Élaine's psychiatrist, will offer at her trial, but it does not take into account the confusion that reigns in Élaine's mind as she contemplates and continually relives/rewords the murder. In effect, Élaine consistently confuses Ève-Lyne with her dead cat, Pluche, along with the embryo/fetus growing inside of her lover, Julien's, wife (and possibly the fetus in her sister's womb) – with which she is clearly obsessed. All are objectified, as Élaine herself has been objectified in her traditional female and maternal role. It makes the killing easier.

This same objectification/"chosification" ("thingification"), linked to judgment, lies at the root of the infanticide in Jacob's *L'Obéissance*; however, its mother-daughter relationships are much more difficult to analyse psychologically. When Florence, who hates her mother and all females (and men), gives birth to Alice (her "accomplice")as a result of marital rape, she no longer feels alone: "She feels the need to talk to someone for the first time in her life ... she repeats the same things to her ... it's you, it's me, it's me, it's you. She looks at her as if it were herself who had just arrived on earth and been given a new chance" ["[Elle] éprouve le besoin de parler à quelqu'un pour la première fois de sa vie ... elle lui répète les mêmes choses: ... c'est toi, c'est moi, c'est moi, c'est toi. Elle la contemple comme si c'était elle-même qui venait d'arriver sur la terre avec une nouvelle chance"] (Jacob 70). Alice is Florence's Eve. But this sun- rather than moon-child (Jacob 71) soon exerts her independence and at the age of three, breaks the television screen – so essential to Florence, whose "reality" has been formed by it for three to four hours a day – with her "wimpish" brother's hammer.[13] Florence flies into a rage and begins her persistent, cruel punishment of her daughter immediately. These emotions and abusive actions reach their climax the night that Alice unwittingly sees her mother, a former nude dancer – but a virgin at marriage – dancing naked in front of Alice's father, Hubert: "Florence wants to escape, flee Alice's gaze. Hubert makes her keep going. He holds her. He forces her. He has seen

Alice. He gets even more excited" ["Florence veut s'échapper, fuir le regard d'Alice. Hubert la force à continuer. Il la tient. Il l'oblige. Il a vu Alice. Il s'est excité davantage"] (Jacob 179). The next morning Florence waits for Alice after school, and the two of them go down to the river, where Alice walks into the water and drowns. As Florence later explains to Marie, her lawyer: "'He took me like an animal. Alice saw me. Alice was looking at me ... He forced me to stay there, bent over, until he had finished. Alice judged me'" ["'Il m'avait prise comme une bête. Alice m'a vue. Alice me voyait ... Il m'a forcée à rester là, pliée, jusqu'à ce qu'il ait fini! Alice m'a jugée'"] (Jacob 180). After judging Alice all of her young life, Florence cannot allow herself to be judged, to be objectified by her daughter, especially when she has already been objectified by her husband.

Alice instinctively understands these complex emotions. She tries to please her mother, but even when she obeys her, she is accused of "monkeying around" ["singerie"] and judging. She reacts in a way that is consistent with what many studies of child abuse tell us: she begins to live in a fantasy world, creating imaginary beasts who receive punishment and inventing another self as a playmate, another Alice. Alice and Alice also become friends and talk to one another: "'Mommy cries that we are judging her. It's hard, it's very hard to understand. Look closely. Listen to Mommy's voice when she says we are judging her ... Now, Alice, maybe you can answer me. Are you suffering?' 'I'm not suffering, because I'm not hurting,' answers Alice. 'I'm proud of you,' sighs Alice ... 'How,' Alice asks Alice, 'how to look at Mommy without her suffering?'" ["'Maman crie que nous la jugeons. C'est difficile, c'est très difficile de comprendre. Regarde bien. Écoute bien la voix de maman dire que nous la jugeons ... Maintenant, Alice tu peux me répondre, peut-être. Est-ce que tu souffres?' 'Je ne souffre, parce que je n'ai pas mal,' répond Alice. 'Je suis fière de toi,' soupire Alice ... 'Comment,' demande Alice à Alice, 'comment regarder maman sans qu'elle sente la souffrance?'"] (Jacob 99–100). Neither Alice nor Alice may realize that there is no answer to this question, but what "they" do know is that Alice will never grow up because "things" do not grow up and because "they" have heard Florence tell her husband that their daughter will never grow big enough not to be under the control of her mother. For as Marie has clearly understood from her conversations with her client, "Alice died because she was growing up! Alice died because growing up means disobeying, laughing at the world. Alice would have had to stop growing up!" (Jacob 213). ["Alice est morte parce qu'elle grandissait! Alice est morte parce que grandir, c'est désobéir, c'est rire du monde! Il aurait fallu qu'Alice cesse de grandir!"] (Jacob 213).

Speaking of the power of the law and the obeying subject, Michel Foucault states: "All the modes of domination, submission, and subjugation are ultimately reduced to an effect of obedience" (*The History of Sexuality* 85) ["Tous les modes de domination, de soumission, d'assujettissement se ramèneraient finalement à l'effet d'obéissance"] (*Histoire de la sexualité* 112–13). Suzanne Jacob's novel of infanticide is a powerful illustration in fiction of Foucault's words. Florence, in effect, tells Alice to walk into the river and drown herself because she wants to teach her to obey. According to Marie, "Florence is tormented – and fascinated – by Alice's obedience. On the one hand, she hates Alice's perfection and she believes that Alice is making fun of her by obeying her. On the other hand, she wonders how far her daughter can go without rebelling" ["Florence est tourmentée par l'obéissance d'Alice, et fascinée. D'un côté, elle déteste la perfection d'Alice et elle croit qu'Alice se moque d'elle en obéissant. De l'autre, elle se demande jusqu'où sa fille peut aller sans se révolter"] (Jacob 217). Indeed, the entire novel is encapsulated by the title, as it relates to mother-daughter relations: Marie's mother used to hold her head under water every Saturday to teach her not to rebel;[14] Muriel, the "potential" lover of Jean, Marie's husband, hid her pregnancy and gave up her baby girl in order to obey her mother, and she still suffers from her actions. "Obéissance" (obedience/submission) is also the key to the broader world that so obsesses Marie's best friend, Julie, (and that will come into my discussion of public violence): parents who bleed their children to death (Marcos, Duvalier, and others) and the children who allow this to happen; adolescents who free themselves from obeying their parents but then as adults, join the silent complicity with torture and violence; the abused child who does not speak because of having been "sewn shut": "They sew up vulvas in other places, why not the mouth here?" ["On coud bien des vulves ailleurs, pourquoi pas la bouche ici?"] (Jacob 18).

In all these examples, submission – and even infanticide – is demanded by the mother, but it can also be blamed on a fear of the father and of the male in general.[15] As in the case of the abused child mentioned above, the torture that mothers inflict on their daughters can go as far as a metaphorical or an actual act of female genital mutilation.[16] Yvonne, Florence's mother, had Florence sewn shut in order to protect her from sex with her own husband and three sons – and later from other men; it is purposely left unclear whether this infibulation was real or symbolic (Jacob 48–9). When Alice is born, this "new Eve" has the effect of "un-sewing" her mother. But metaphorically, Florence infibulates her daughter by silencing her natural chatter and curtailing her freedom to grow up. And Alice's death is the ultimate female mutilation. All of her orifices are blocked by water.

Indeed all of *L'Obéissance* moves between the violence of silencing, or metaphorical FGM, and the outpouring of what Saint-Martin calls a "book of confessions" ["livre d'aveux"] (103). It is a fictional representation of what Foucault calls a "confessing animal" (*The History of Sexuality* 59) ["bête d'aveu"] (*Histoire de la sexualité* 80) or a "confessional discourse" (*The History of Sexuality* 62) ["discours de l'aveu"] (*Histoire de la sexualité* 83). But confessing publicly to the crime of infanticide may be such a private matter, whereby the family becomes such "a site of dark mysteries and unspeakable horrors" (Halttunen 169), that the title of another work of fiction about infanticide, a short story by Claire Dé, may sum up the tension between public and private female violence: "Ce n'était pas de nos affaires" – it was none of our business.

Some analysis of this interesting 1991 piece is worthwhile, given its link to the two novels in question.[17] In the Dé short story, the narrator is identified only as "on" ("one/they/we"), a pronoun that presents an anonymous, generalized, formal, and yet inclusive stance or perspective on the story. "On" guides the reader, from the initial point of entry, through the sequences leading up to the murder (Cerulo 7). "On" is also clearly connected to the "nos" ("our") of the title – a point that becomes obvious at the end of the story. In addition, "on" narrates in the past tense – after the event – and alerts the reader to this fact not only by the use of the present perfect and imperfect tenses, but especially through the use of parentheses at the beginning of the story, in reference to the (future) trial of the female protagonist. We know, therefore, that something criminal has occurred. Although this is a serious piece involving the killing of one's child, Dé characteristically still cannot resist interpolating some humour: a young social worker who arrives briefly on the scene is described as being unable to suggest to the sex-driven mother that she become a prostitute or join a harem because her traditional curriculum does not teach such applications!

Yes, the female protagonist and infanticide is a sexually driven mother of eight who comes from a dysfunctional family and had her first child at eighteen. She is presented as a stereotype of the lustful female harpy, with the operatically seductive name of Carmen: she has the eyes of a trapped animal; the body of a sexually obsessed being who masturbates in public, rubs herself wherever and whenever she can, pulsates with desire between her thighs, demands constant sex from her husband, threatens to kill herself and their children if he does not comply, and falls into a spiral of depression when he does not. Her eighth child is the "spitting image" of her husband, who pays her even less attention after the birth. She follows through on her threat: "Carmen Trempe threw her three-year old little boy out of the window from the fourth floor. Killing him instantly. Ten years of imprisonment with labour" ["Carmen Trempe a défenestré son garçonnet de trois ans du haut de son quatrième étage. Le tuant net. Dix ans de réclusion criminelle"] (31). (I shall show toward the end of this chapter how this reflects the sentences that women in Canada receive for infanticide and filicide, as well as the outcomes of the fictional trials in the two novels in question.)

The story concludes with a reference to the "on" of the narration and the "nos" of the title: "Her family, neighbours, social services, we all knew that something bad would happen. We knew, but we didn't do anything" ["Ses proches, les voisins, les services sociaux, on savait tous qu'il arriverait malheur. On le savait, mais on n'a rien fait"] (31). People close to the mother and the social institutions created to help her did nothing, for it was "none of 'our' business." As a result of this lack of action on the part of a now guilty society (precisely the responsible society whom Julie, of *L'Obéissance*, chides for sitting back, witnessing, and letting violence happen), the child is dead, and the mother is serving time in prison.

PUBLIC *VS.* PRIVATE SPACE AS A BACKDROP FOR THESE TWO NOVELS

La frontière entre la famille et la société est devenue très floue, car les liens du sang sont plus rares qu'autrefois.
[The border between the family and society has become very fluid, for the bonds of blood are more rare than in the past.]

Suzanne Jacob, *La Voix de l'au-delà*

The infanticide cases in these novels test the boundaries of public and private space, not only within the private home and in subsequent media accounts and courtroom scenarios, but also insofar as they are foiled by the presence of violent international events of a massive proportion, which, in *La Fissure*, obsess Élaine's husband, Bruno, and her social worker, Marcelle, and, in *L'Obéissance*, Marie's best friend, Julie.

Defining the boundaries between public and private spheres has become an increasingly difficult and perhaps fruitless task, since, as Shapiro points out, such boundaries are permeable (216), and such categories are themselves inadequate and rhetorical, actually informing one another (219–20). In America before the late eighteenth century, for example, crime, punishment, and death were more public, with public hangings and execution sermons pronounced by the clergy (and in France with what Foucault calls "gallows speeches" (*Discipline and Punish* 65) ["discours d'échafaud"] (*Surveiller et punir* 78) given by the condemned person.[18] With the rise of prisons, anaesthesia, private funerals, burials, cemeteries, and undertakers, death became more private, but the public retained a prurient interest in the horror of crime, obscenity, punishment, and death, as reflected in the simultaneous growth in the popularity of Gothic novels, detective fiction, and newspaper accounts of crimes (Halttunen 64–6). Reading this horror literature was, and still is, a private activity, an interiorization of a taboo toward which one experiences both attraction and revulsion (Halttunen 82).

At the same time, in late-nineteenth-century Paris, the "social" (as in social physiology, social photography, and the founding of criminology) became an intermediary ground between formerly separate public and private arenas, a space in which new sociological categories ("women," the "feminist," the "working class," the "criminal") were defined, dehistoricized, and opened to remedial intervention (Shapiro 18). Criminology and criminals' stories "entertained" audiences with discussions of public questions such as depopulation, urban decay, the working class, prostitution (now rendered personal), and crime "dramas" of "real-life" criminals, which made issues of private life attractive to public attention (Shapiro 47–8). There emerged an imbrication of private and official worlds through the criminal story and a collaboration between the accused and the accuser: stories in tension with other stories became arenas of exchange between the private and the public (Shapiro 50–1). The private lives of female criminals – that is, narratives pieced together from various sources – were made public for newspaper readers, and the "non-pathologizing reading" (Savage 104) about a given crime was done in a space between the public and the private (Jones 255–6; Priest, Jenefsky, and Swenson 104). Indeed, women at this time began to challenge the presumptions that had separated public and private spheres, while professionals (criminologists, legal experts, and psychologists) sought and found scientific explanations for gender differences (e.g., the hysteric) which might forestall these challenges (Shapiro 122). Crimes of passion, for instance, carried domestic struggles from the private to the public arena (Shapiro 137), questioning the view that women were not supposed to be in the male public world, but in a private and nurturing domestic space; women moving into the public arena were, therefore, a threat (Jones 110).

Crimes of passion can thus be seen as social texts that indicated unsettled ideas about how to address issues that crossed between public and private spheres, issues that revealed the convergence of intimate stories of domestic life with public developments related to women's place and rights, the disruption of the equilibrium in relations between men and women, and evidence that direct and private action was substituting for public policies and legal remedies that did not adequately address women's problems (Shapiro 165–6). Both feminists and female criminals broke down the distinction between public and private space, and this conflation of the feminist and the criminal woman suggested their joint role in weakening an otherwise ordered opposition of binary spheres (Shapiro 210, 212–13).

If the eighteenth and nineteenth centuries in North America and Europe saw changes in definitions of and interactions between public and private realms, thanks to the growing availability of newspapers, the twentieth century – especially its latter years – and the early days of the new century, have witnessed a major erosion of these former boundaries with the rise of mass media, popular culture, and technology. Events such as the Persian Gulf War, famine in Africa and India, civil strife on the African continent and central and eastern Europe, religious clashes and terrorist organizations in the Middle East, the aftermath of the Oklahoma City bombing, the Montreal massacre, the O.J. Simpson and the Susan Smith trials, the destruction of the World Trade Center buildings, the plane crashes at the Pentagon and in Pennsylvania, the anthrax scare, the war against the Taliban and Al Qaeda in Afghanistan, the war against Saddam Hussein in Iraq, the continued war in Iraq, the war against world terrorism, the Madrid metro bombings, suicide bombers, the effects of the SARS virus, avian flu, the Asian tsunami, and the London underground bombings are all brought to us in the privacy of our homes by television, radio, newspapers, magazines, mass-market paperbacks, and the Internet. And of course the advent of "reality or voyeur television" and web sites in Europe and North America allows us publicly to view the deeply private lives of "ordinary" people who are willing participants in variations of the *Truman Show*.

Against this backdrop of national and international violence – which provides leit-motivs in many of the texts considered in this study – and as made public in the media, the private narratives of domestic violence/infanticide in both *La Fissure* and *L'Obéissance* are revealed. Chamberland's novel opens (or rather, we enter the novel) with a scene of private violence made locally public and then contrasted with world violence, all narrated – or scripted – by the female infanticide to be: Élaine finds her cat, Pluche, dying on the street with its stomach ripped open.[19] She brings Pluche home, to find her husband, Bruno, characteristically sitting in front of the television set:

> He was listening to the television; there was a report on El Salvador (violent words and images, torn-up bodies, guts, blood), I had not spoken of the cat, I had sat down with him and I had looked; disappearances, tortures and murders in El Salvador, all this was added to, was mixed up with the cat on edge of the sidewalk, all this was filled with disemboweled corpses around her, disappearances, tortures, murders, here, there, everything was all muddled up, what to do? what to do? [Il écoutait la télévision; il y avait un reportage sur le Salvador (paroles et images violentes, corps déchiquetés, tripes, sang), je n'avais pas parlé de la chatte, je m'étais assise avec lui et j'avais regardé; disparitions tortures assassinats au Salvador, ça s'ajoutait, se mêlait à la chatte au bord du trottoir, ça se remplissait de cadavres éventrés autour d'elle, disparitions, tortures, assassinats, ici, là-bas, tout s'embrouillait, quoi faire? quoi faire?] (Chamberland 8–9)

In fact Bruno does nothing much more at home than listen to and watch violence on the television news every night at 6:00 – unless (ironically) he is watching a hockey game or reading about the latest outbreak of violence in the newspapers.

This obsession with public violence as reported in the media becomes a barrier to private communication: when Élaine attempts to talk to her husband about Pluche, her state of mind, or their relationship, either she feels that she is interrupting him and has chosen a bad time to talk, or he does not listen to what she then characterizes as unimportant, "babbling just like Ève-Lyne in her sled" ["du babillage comme en faisait Ève-Lyne dans son traîneau"] (Chamberland 61). Élaine is trying to analyse her private, inner violence, and Bruno, not able to screen out the public media, allows public words, images, and the actual newspaper to block his awareness and understanding:

> "It's tough in El Salvador, did you read that? all the inhabitants of a village massacred, there's some real 'beautes' down there," said Bruno, looking at me

from under the newspaper he had begun to read when he got home ... once again he had picked up the newspaper and I couldn't see him any more. (I had imagined that moment all afternoon, he would come home ... and I would speak to him, I had to talk to him today ... tell him: "It's no longer possible, to go on like this, (we're) deaf, mute, strangers, it's not possible ..."). "There's some real 'beautes' down there," he had said, looking at me from under the newspaper, and immediately afterward he had disappeared, there was nothing but the paper, and me ... incapable of making happen what I had prepared all afternoon." ["Ça fait dur au Salvador, t'as lu ça? tous les habitants d'un village massacrés, il s'en passe des belles là-bas," disait Bruno, me regardant par-dessous le journal qu'il s'était mis à lire en rentrant ... il avait de nouveau relevé son journal et je ne le voyais plus. (J'avais imaginé ce moment-là tout l'après-midi, il allait rentrer ... et je lui parlerais, il fallait lui parler aujourd'hui ... lui dire: "Ça n'est pas possible, continuer comme ça, sourds, muets, étrangers, ça n'est pas possible ..."). "Il s'en passe des belles là-bas," avait-il dit, me regardant par-dessus le journal, et tout de suite après il avait disparu, il n'y avait plus que du papier, et moi ... incapable de faire venir ce que j'avais préparé tout l'après-midi."] (Chamberland 115–16)

Private and public spheres are even more clearly delineated but also enmeshed when we see Élaine in her private domestic moments while the reporting of public violence invades her home. She rocks Ève-Lyne in the kitchen rocker, while Bruno watches a hockey game. She retreats to her bedroom upstairs, "closed in, almost barricaded so as not to hear the television downstairs, its din, its racket, not to hear all of those cries of anger or of triumph that came out of the television ... I didn't know if the noises were still coming from downstairs or from me, from my tired head" ["enfermée, barricadée presque pour ne pas entendre la télévision en bas, son tapage, son vacarme, ne pas entendre tous ces cris de colère ou de triomphe qui sortaient de la télévision ... je ne savais pas si les bruits venaient encore d'en bas ou de moi, de ma tête fatiguée"] (Chamberland 15). Bruno is so oblivious to his familial surroundings that in the midst of his wife's growing depression, her thoughts of "removing" Ève-Lyne from this dangerous and violent world, and her ongoing affair with Julien, he suggests that they have a second child.

The narrative of *La Fissure* moves back and forth among events leading up to the infanticide, the analysis of Élaine's thoughts prior, during, and after the killing, the reliving of the criminal act, and her life during and after her arrest and public trial. In none of these time zones can she escape the world of international violence, as if, ironically, the private violence in her head and in the home that result in her killing her child must continually be seen in the context of massive public murders and the publicity and newspaper accounts of her own trial.

When she is acquitted of her crime, it is with the proviso that she receive psychological treatment and live with a social worker, Marcelle. As though fated, Marcelle is even more obsessed than Bruno with international torture and crimes against humanity. In fact the novel's chapters often alternate between Élaine's thoughts and her life with Marcelle, who is constantly angry about the situation in El Salvador and the neutrality of the Canadian government, and who demonstrates and signs petitions to help victims of dictatorships and other violence. While Élaine purports an inability to distinguish among the different stories of politics, war, and power – and is seen by Marcelle as a silent witness to these crimes – Marcelle who "sees especially the weapons, the blood, and the dead" ["voit surtout les armes, le sang et les morts"] (131), watches the news on television, reads newspapers, talks agitatedly about violence on a massive scale, and spends much of her life working to prevent it – as an activist and as a social worker in an intervention program to help female criminals like Élaine.

If *La Fissure* begins with the scene of the nearly dead cat lying in the street, the opening section of *L'Obéissance* includes a similarly significant encounter. Julie, a friend of Marie, the attorney defending Florence, who is accused of having killed her daughter, Alice, and through whose lens we enter the narrative is a woman as obsessed with world violence as Marcelle. Julie sees an abused little girl on the street, with cigarette burn marks on her palms. She decides to get involved and contacts the Child Protection Agency. She acts for several reasons: "The child from the sandbox will have become a child in general, a global child, a concept of a mutilated child, and there will no longer be anywhere to dress her wounds, since it is hard to spread an analgesic balm and a real antibiotic on the conceptual wounds of a child deemed to be a class rather than an individual" ["L'enfant du carré de sable sera devenue une enfant en général, une enfant globale, un concept d'enfant mutilée, et il n'y aura plus lieu de panser ses plaies, étant donné qu'il est difficile d'étendre un baume analgésique et antibiotique réel sur des plaies conceptuelles d'une enfant considérée comme sa classe plutôt que comme individu"] (Jacob 21). This individual and private case must be seen in a public, class, and global context. Secondly, Julie is concerned not only with international violence,[20] but also with what she sees as collective amnesia, silence, and thus guilt (as in Dé's "Ce n'est pas de nos affaires"): "This type of pact of silence that allows the setting up of grand dictatorships, that authorizes locking people up, executions, torture" ["Ce genre de pacte du silence qui permet la mise en place des grandes dictatures, qui autorise les enfermements, les mises à mort, la torture"] (Jacob 28). We witness worldwide violence and torture on television, and yet, like Élaine, we remain silent. The children of these dictators stand by and let their parents abuse others. As children, we obey our parents who abuse us. Prefiguring the infanticide case that Marie will defend – or rather, has defended, since we learn at the end of this powerful narrative that Julie has this rush of thoughts at Marie's funeral – Julie decides that it only takes the action of one or two individuals in a private case of violence to begin to end the suffering of many. If she can act to help this one abused girl, then others may spontaneously join in and put an end to private violence made public. This initial melding of private and public spheres of violence sets the tone for the rest of the text.

In fact *L'Obéissance* is a cross between the "livre d'aveux" ("book of confessions"), as Lori Saint-Martin describes it, and the "ce n'est pas de nos affaires" ("it's none of our business") of the Claire Dé short story about infanticide. Julie, Marie, Jean, Florence, Alice, and others spill out their confessions (some real, some imagined, some dreamed) about private matters, about private violence done to them or that they have done to others. And yet, this is also a novel of masks (see Jack): the hiding of private criminal acts and violent pasts behind successful public personae; the public faces of marriage and family that privately mask what society does not want to see; couples publicly and privately living their lives as though actors in a film; an infanticide who prefers the "reality" of television to the reality of rage that she exhibits in her own home; an eloquent public voice that is "amputated" in private life. There is no single "truth" to any of these confessions or to the meaning of any of these acts, since they – both public and private – are all constructed narratives.

STORIES IN TENSION: PRIVATE CRIMINAL ACTS, PUBLIC TRIALS, AND PUBLIC REPORTING; VOYEURISTIC PRIVATE READING AND NOVELISTIC NARRATIVES

Ce récit général de notre passé commun de texte-visage à déchiffrer possède autant de versions qu'il y a d'êtres humains ... Il y a des versions terrifiées par la haine où le regard vous lit comme une page à supprimer et vous supprime,

comme on en a été *témoin* à l'occasion des plus récents génocides. Des versions où la mort ... ne s'éloigne pas ... Des versions où le visage qui donne le lait est distrait, absent ou effacé par la dépression ou la maladie. Toutes les versions racontent ... comment c'est par la lecture que s'effectue notre entrée dans le monde et que c'est par elle que nous nous y installons pour y demeurer. Nous habitons le monde par l'activité ininterrompue de lecture que nous en faisons et c'est cette activité même qui rend le monde habitable.
[This general story of our common past of text-face to decipher has as many versions as there are human beings ... There are versions terrified by hatred in which the gaze reads you like a page to suppress and suppresses you, as if one has been *witness* to the most recent genocides. Versions where death ... does not go far away ... Versions where the milquetoast face is distracted, absent or erased because of depression or sickness. All the versions recount ... how it is by reading that our entrance into the world takes place and that it is by this reading that we are placed in the world to live. We live in the world by the uninterrupted activity of the reading that we make of it, and it is this very activity that makes the world livable.]

Suzanne Jacob, *La Bulle d'encre* (21)

L'art accomplit sa fonction en proposant des versions, des fictions diversifiées du monde.
[Art accomplishes its function by proposing versions, diversified fictions of the world.]

Suzanne Jacob, *La Bulle d'encre* (36)

These novels by Chamberland and Jacob present a complicated web of public and private spheres and the spaces occupied between them. The private domestic crime of infanticide is put into public view in a public trial – itself a constructed narrative – and in the public forum of the news media – clearly a narrative construct. These public accounts are read privately by others, who view this private "text" made public and internalize it, judging it according to their own private experiences. And finally, we, as yet another audience, read these carefully constructed novels about constructed narratives. Courtroom narratives and the private reading of accounts of crimes are both embedded in these novelistic fictions and need to be read alongside the historical and legal scholarship that has recently been published on these issues. From the use of expert witnesses to the roles of the lawyers, from the defendants' own narratives to the ultimate acquittals in both of these fictional infanticide cases, both Chamberland and Jacob have captured

– albeit with greater complexity – the very nature of the public and the private in female criminality, clearly reading fiction/representation and reality together and treating the representation of these violent crimes and trials at the intersection of the linguistic and material worlds (see again, Duggan, Tanner 6, 9, 10, 12, and Inness 4).

If, as Hayden White has observed, every narrative account is an artificial construct (23), then "any story of murder involves a fictive process which reveals much about the mental and emotional strategies employed within a given historical culture for responding to serious transgression in its midst" (Halttunen 2). The problem at hand, therefore, is the issue of authority: who interprets the criminal act (Shapiro 39)? Shapiro has shown that in fin-de-siècle Paris, social issues were raised, and questions were asked by criminal stories – questions such as the relation between classes and sexes, problems of unmarried mothers and seduced and abandoned women, adultery, the rights of women in marriage, and unregulated sexuality (Shapiro 44). Female criminality "became the material and discursive site" where one could address the problem of mass culture, and where politics turned into stories (Shapiro 47). Women charged with infanticide and abortion, in particular, produced a discourse that paralleled public discussions of depopulation and promoted links to laws that prohibited women from initiating paternity suits (Shapiro 47). Crime dramas thus mobilized popular sentiment around issues of private life that were attracting public attention (Shapiro 48). Shapiro analyses personal, criminal stories that have both different tellings and different interpretations as "the move, rhetorical and social, from trifles and sexual affairs through falsehoods, idle stories, and tales to the writing of a history, to making sense of experience" (49).[21] Since "culture is an arena of exchange," and storytelling is an "interactive process among differently positioned people," these narratives exist in tension with other narratives and expose the "deeply patterned activity of legal storytelling, the ways that the ideology of dominant groups pass for neutrality" (Shapiro 50–1).

If "the psychological and social function of a public trial is to restore a feeling of order, to make the public feel that chaos has been held at bay" (French 35), then we must recognize the "storytelling potential of law" (Stanko and Scully 58), the fact that even "the legal system shapes the stories which are told" (Myers and Wight xii): "Criminal trials are organized around storytelling, the construction of clear, 'commonsense' narratives which assist jurors ... which cut through the confusion generated by trial testimony to achieve narrative clarity" (Halttunen 101). As

Suzanne Jacob has commented, "The good version is the most plausible version, the most believable for a jury made up of twelve people sufficiently normal– there are tests to evaluate this normality – to assume the representation of the convention of the reality of a given society at a given moment in its history" ["La bonne version est la version la plus plausible, la plus vraisemblable pour un jury composé d'une douzaine de personnes suffisamment normales – il y a des tests pour évaluer cette normalité – pour assumer la représentation de la convention de réalité d'une société donnée à tel moment de son histoire" (*La Bulle d'encre* 43). In the past – as today – "like melodramas, courtroom proceedings recited a dramatic story, fueled by emotional hyperbole, that sought to make the moral universe visible ... Criminal stories became, in effect, exemplars – morality tales that weighed the rights and worth of each party and commented on appropriate gender roles and expectations" (Shapiro 163).

It is precisely these "appropriate gender roles and expectations" that are at issue in public courtroom trials – historically, contemporaneously, and fictitiously – and which "my" female writers and protagonists are refuting, tearing apart, and re-framing, as I have already shown. A number of feminist legal and historical scholars have pointed out that "a woman's conformity to the stereotype of femininity crucially affects how she fares in the courts" (Myers and Wight xiii). Given the limited subject positions available to women, they are judged in court – not at all surprisingly – according to their profile as mad, or bad, or as stereotypical women (often seen as victims) (Ballinger 2). While female violence may be seen as intolerable, alien, and even monstrous, exceptions are made for "proper" female courtroom behaviour, defined as "extra-feminine, extra-helpless, extra-naïve" (Grindstaff and McCaughey 149).[22] With these several set discourses around female behaviour and conduct in court, there has been little space for the creation of new discourses and knowledge about violent women (Ballinger 22).

Given the common belief that women are emotional, irrational, and therefore unreliable – especially when testifying on their own behalf, when telling their own story of the crime – since the nineteenth century it has been the prosecuting and defence lawyers, along with medical, psychological, criminological, and legal experts, who have shaped courtroom narratives. Halttunen explains that in the United States, "in the story lines set out by attorneys, murder trials achieved their greatest degree of narrative coherence" (101): "both attorneys shape chaos into plotted narrative," acting like "dueling storytellers" (102–3); Duggan calls the prosecuting and defence lawyers "sparring interpreters" who present "competing" or "clashing master narratives" (74, 68). Enter the medical/psychological expert, the "author-ities" (Horvitz 110), who, using fixed assumptions about women, portray them as weak and hysterical by nature. Indeed in late nineteenth-century France, medical experts were called upon by defence counsel in order to obtain acquittals for female criminals. Couched in "new" scientific and criminological terms and language, their testimonies continued to confirm women's incapacity – often for biological reasons – to commit "real" violence (Shapiro 112–13). As Foucault noted in a lecture given at the Collège de France in 1975: "The evidence given by psychiatric experts in criminal courts has three qualities: (a) It has, or may have, the power of life and death; (b) It functions as a discourse of truth, being scientific – it is given by people qualified within scientific institutions; (c) When one reads the transcripts, they make one laugh. Such testimonies are an integral part of the daily juridical discourse" (as quoted in Duggan 87).[23]

When women have dared to "resist the mad/bad categories by presenting their own logical and rational explanations of their violent crimes, they are [often] disqualified as speakers – their accounts become 'muted' by dominant 'expert' ... knowledge constructions around violent women" (Ballinger 3). Indeed only sixty years ago, women in many societies were not even authorized to represent the convention of reality and could not "according to the logic of the dominant fictions of this period" (Jacob, *La Bulle d'encre* 43) either testify or serve as members of a jury. What follows is a "nondialogue," "an ongoing contest over meaning ... between accused and accusers" (Shapiro 90). Such narrative disjunctions – only later co-opted and transformed into violently angry and transgressively disjointed and fragmented literary texts – have silenced female criminals, making them unable "to speak through the rigidly dichotomous representations of deviant women preserved in the culture: feminine/virile; maternal/sadistic; hysterical/cunning; responsible/irresponsible" (Shapiro 90). Such "stories in tension" become "moments of cultural construction and cultural dissonance" because of the attempt to push female-narrated stories toward a homogeneity that emphasizes the division between the female narrators and their listeners of a different class and sex (Shapiro 93). Shapiro has found that "women traditionally have had a problematic relation to their own violence and incorporate this ambiguous positioning into their self-presentation as perpetrators of crime" by the "use of received story lines" (Shapiro 86).[24] With acquittals of women on grounds of mental incapacity, the court could then discount their alternative stories and assume their repentance even when it could not be publicly elicited (Shapiro 90). Such a perspective on the female criminal plays into the status of the woman as a weak victim, not responsible for her crime – even if the crime is infanticide.

In *La Fissure* and *L'Obéissance*, public trials, with their attendant legal and psychological experts, judges, and jurors, figure prominently, although always filtered – either through the lens of Élaine's disjointed mind[25] or through Julie's intense memory of Marie's account and interpretation. In Chamberland's novel, even prior to the public trial, Élaine is silenced and treated like an incapable, weak, and irrational woman who needs someone else to speak for her. Her lawyers construct their version of the crime, and, although Élaine objects, she does nothing to change their version of the events:

> "I don't want him to go on, he's going to tell lies, a story of his own invention, I'm afraid, these are no longer the calm images, a little hazy, in my mind, it's something else, words, the words from outside, the words in the mouth of this man, I'm afraid ..." I get up, I want to, I'm going to hit him, a punch in the mouth, but he grabs me, holds my wrists, I want to hit him, if only he'd shut up, I struggle, he holds my wrists, continues to talk ... I began to cry, hunched up on the bed, cry without being able to stop. ["Je ne veux pas qu'il continue, il va me raconter des mensonges, une histoire de son invention, j'ai peur, ce ne sont plus les images tranquilles, un peu floues, de ma tête, c'est autre chose, des mots, les mots du dehors, les mots dans la bouche de cet homme, j'ai peur ..." je me lève, je veux, je vais le frapper, coup de poing sur la bouche, mais il me saisit, me tient les poignets, le frapper, qu'il se taise, je me démène, il me tient les poignets, continue à parler ... Je m'étais mise à pleurer, recroquevillée sur le lit, pleurer sans pouvoir m'arrêter.] (Chamberland 66)

Élaine's trial is frequently referred to as theatre, drama, spectacle, a game, and at one point a church mass and sermon. Like a good Catholic, Élaine sits silently before the judge, another male symbol of the law.[26] Knowing she is guilty of this crime of infanticide, she awaits his condescending smile, since with all the proof in front of him, he will certainly not be moved by the testimony of Luc, the psychologist and expert witness called in to answer questions on her behalf. The men speak about her and her "drama" as if she is not in the courtroom or does not understand what is happening and what they are saying: "I didn't like what Luc was saying, what he was now telling all these strangers quite openly, in the same neutral and detached tone as the doctor before him, he had no right" ["Je n'aimais pas ce que Luc disait, ce qu'il disait maintenant sans réserve à tous ces inconnus, du même ton neutre et détaché que le médecin avant lui, il n'avait pas le droit"] (Chamberland 48). Luc did not have the right to display in public so many details about her private life: "What got into Luc to say these things, to reveal these confidences in the middle of a room filled with strangers?" ["Qu'est-ce qui prenait à Luc de dire ces choses, de faire ces confidences au beau milieu d'une salle pleine d'inconnus?"] (Chamberland 126).

Élaine has her own story to tell, but she will not be telling it in public. Instead, she will absent herself from the trial by appearing distracted: "The same impression as being totally outside what was being said there: they weren't talking about me, they were talking about other people, other things, things far away and a little mysterious that didn't concern me but that I had to listen to anyhow" ["La même impression d'être tout à fait étrangère à ce qui se disait là: on ne parlait pas de moi, on parlait d'autres gens, d'autres choses, de choses lointaines et un peu mystérieuses qui ne me concernaient pas mais qu'il me fallait écouter quand même"] (Chamberland 125–6). The story that Luc tells over and over again in court is that Élaine did not kill her daughter. His testimony is never completed in the narrative that Élaine remembers and which we receive from her, but disjointed and significant parts of it reappear as a leit-motiv that we, as readers of this narrative, can piece together: "She was disorganized. She didn't kill her daughter. She destroyed the part of herself that she didn't like" ["Elle était désorganisée. Elle ne tuait pas sa fille. Elle détruisait la partie d'elle-même qu'elle n'aimait pas"] (Chamberland 33, 48, 125, 126, 141, 150, 151).

Élaine is completely manipulated by the men who represent her private thoughts and actions and make them public. Moreover, what appears in her courtroom trial may be public, but what really influences the outcome is the private "behind-the-scenes" bargaining that goes on among the lawyers, the medical and psychological experts, and the judge. She is acquitted without ever having presented her own story publicly – at least not until this novel.

In Jacob's *L'Obéissance* most of the public trial revolves around the role of Marie, the defence counsel for Florence, rather than around the defendant – or even the crime. Indeed, we never hear from Florence directly, but rather we learn about the infanticide – if it is infanticide – through Marie's recounting of Florence's confession to Julie. We are not even certain whether this confession is recounted by Marie herself or played out in Julie's mind and memory. Once again, the trial is referred to as theatre, much as the trials of international defendants such as the Ceaucescu and the Duvalier couples were a "judicial ritual" prefiguring that of Florence (Jacob 10). Marie likewise compares Florence to international figures in a tirade about the dilemma of legal responsibility: "So it's come to that: is it because Florence Chaillé's mind was distraught that she is any less responsible? Oh sure! Pinochet, Ceaucescu, Barbie, all distraught minds, legally incapable? ["Voilà où nous en sommes: est-ce parce que l'esprit de Florence Chaillé s'est égaré que Florence Chaillé est moins responsable? Mais alors, Pinochet, Ceaucescu, Barbie, tous des esprits égarés, irresponsables?"] (Jacob 213). According to Julie, the law is arbitrary and relative. It can change in different countries and at any time. For Marie, Florence and Alice have shaken up the law that would eventually have questioned Alice's mental state: after all, she did walk into the river and drown herself.

Marie is here speaking as the defence counsel who is trying to get her client acquitted – or is she? Since meeting Florence and taking on her case, Marie, this "old little girl lawyer" ["vieille petite fille avocate"] (Jacob 179) has become obsessed with her and what has become a famous trial case:

> "Ever since the morning I agreed to defend Florence Chaillé, my heart stopped working properly ... Until that morning, I was entirely Marie Cholet. Ever since then, I've been in pieces. I am made up of a certain number of pieces that do not function so as to forget their separate existence as pieces. I have become an object for myself, an object made up of different pieces that are angry with one another so that I can't possibly reconcile them ... My voice plays a role, as if we had become actors, she and I. We are separate from one another. We no longer make a single Marie. There's Marie and there's Marie's voice ... The embarassing truth: I have begun to live Florence's life so that I can get to her ... I won a trial which has worn me out and from which I shall never recover. I am defeated." ["Depuis cette matinée où j'ai accepté de défendre Florence Chaillé, mon coeur s'est déréglé ... Jusqu'à cette matinée, j'étais tout entière Marie Cholet. Depuis, je suis morcelée. Je suis une certaine quantité de morceaux qui n'arrivent pas à fonctionner de manière à faire oublier leur existence séparée de morceaux. Je suis devenue un objet pour moi-même, un objet composé de divers morceaux qui sont fâchés les uns avec les autres, qu'il m'est impossible de réconcilier les uns avec les autres ... Ma voix joue un rôle comme si nous étions devenues des comédiennes, elle et moi. Nous sommes séparées.

Nous ne formons plus une seule Marie. Il y a Marie et il y a la voix de Marie … L'inavouable: je me suis mise à vivre la vie de Florence pour pouvoir avoir accès à Florence … J'ai gagné un procès qui m'a abattue, dont je ne me relève pas. Je suis défaite."] (Jacob 173–5)

Although a speaking subject in the public eye, Marie sees herself as an object – a victim of her own inability to separate herself from either of her clients. Her own narrative reveals that she identifies with Florence, but as a child who was abused by her own mother, she also identifies with Alice. As such, she does not actually want her own client to be acquitted; Florence should be condemned as an example to all parents who have tortured their children. But then again, Marie tries to understand her parents, especially her mother, and she wants to defend Florence as she would defend her own family. She plays both sides: she has an affair with the prosecutor and explains her strategy for him to win the case and tells him how he should argue the case for the deceased Alice against Florence. But he does not follow her advice. Marie wins; Florence is acquitted; and Marie, although a bit "heady" from the success, is broken up and defeated: "I can only see little Alice … I can't stop seeing Alice walking into the water. I myself cannot breathe. I betrayed her. I betrayed Alice" (Jacob 176). ["Je ne vois que la petite Alice … Je ne cesse pas de voir Alice entrer dans l'eau. Je manque d'air à mon tour. Je l'ai trahie. J'ai trahi Alice"] (Jacob 176). Who is Marie in all of this? She is a successful lawyer, an adulterous lover (with a purpose), a wife who does not want a child and who becomes pregnant and then dies; she is lawyer who wants to lose and yet wins; she is an abused daughter; she is Alice; she is Florence. It is her words that make Florence's private life and crime public, that confuse private and public space, as they relate to her own life. It is her words that reverberate in the mind of her friend Julie, who narrates (and possibly interprets) her version to us.

Further complicating the tension between private stories and these courtroom events is the public account of a trial and of a crime – making the private act increasingly public in the course of the trial and even more public as it captivates a mass audience in newspaper accounts, while fictional accounts of crimes and criminals are created in mystery, detective, murder, and Gothic horror literature. As of the eighteenth-century in America, for example, newspapers afforded "ordinary" readers the opportunity to become voyeurs – to read accounts of murderers and murderesses as bad people, as monstrously immoral aliens.

Mid-nineteenth-century America also saw the birth of accounts of fictional murderesses – accounts that readers were supposed to read as cautionary tales (Jones 111–12). Today we read press reports of crimes and trials; we read crime novels and murder mysteries; we watch court television; we devour "real" and violent television programs, films, and world-wide-web sites. Much of this "reporting" of crime and especially of female criminals assumes and helps maintain stereotypical views of gender differences (not to mention racial, ethnic, religious, and sexual-preference prejudices). And we, as the reading public, accept and validate these societal constructs, as we remain both outside and inside the criminal world portrayed on the page and on the screen: we privately and intimately visualize, reconstruct, vicariously participate in, and judge private acts that have become public. In other words, we are repelled by and attracted to horror and violence, as Kristeva, Halttunen, and Halberstam, among others, have reminded us.

Chamberland's Élaine is horrified by what the newspapers have written about her and her crime. She is described as a terrible mother, a monster. Her crime and trial are sensationalized for the benefit of readers who thrive on the latest murder or frightening criminal: "A mother killed her child, carried, brought into the world, nursed and cared for for two years, she killed her in cold blood, it was all there, printed in black and white on page one: 'LITTLE TWO-YEAR-OLD GIRL STABBED TO DEATH BY HER MOTHER,' and there was even a little photo of the child in between the words, STABBED TO DEATH" ["Une mère tuait son enfant, portée, mise au monde, nourrie et soignée pendant deux ans, elle la tuait de sang-froid, c'était là, imprimé en toutes lettres sur la première page: 'FILLETE DE DEUX ANS POIGNARDÉE À MORT PAR SA MÈRE,' et il y avait même une petite photo de l'enfant entre les mots POIGNARDÉE À MORT"] (Jacob 103). On a bus, Élaine overhears people talking about her and the infanticide, saying that she needs to be locked up for the protection of others. She sees herself as a wounded animal – a reference to a natural history documentary she has seen on television – pounced on by animals stronger than her. Clearly paranoid, she gets off the bus and begins to run, imagining other passengers running after her. She must get to safety and hide from these readers of newspapers. She runs to the office of her psychiatrist, Luc, the expert witness at her trial.

In *L'Obéissance* the role of newspapers is less prominent, but Jacob's Marie nevertheless sees murder trials as responsible for the creation of many jobs, including those in the media. The media attention given to such events also makes the career of lawyers, as witnessed by her own rising success and reputation that give her a feeling of near euphoria, accompanied by exhaustion. Such attention can also invent new personalities for the "real" person: "When the newspapers ran the headline: 'Miracle lawyer: kill your children, Marie Cholet will get your case dismissed,' I knew that things weren't going the way she wanted them to" ["Quand les journaux ont titré: 'Une avocate miracle: tuez vos enfants, Marie Cholet vous fera absoudre,' j'ai su que ça n'allait pas du tout comme elle voulait"] (Jacob 244–5).

While late nineteenth-century France saw an enormous growth in the popular press, serialized novels ["romans feuilletons"] published in newspapers also participated in the development of a discourse of mass literary popular culture. Foucault speaks of that period's "whole aesthetic rewriting of crime ... the discovery of the beauty and greatness of crime; [of] the literature of crime [where] the struggle between two pure minds – the murderer's and the detective's – will constitute the essential form of the confrontation" (Foucault, *Discipline and Punish* 68–9) ["réécriture esthétique du crime ... la découverte de la beauté et de la grandeur du crime [de] la littérature policière [où] la lutte entre deux purs esprits – celui de meurtrier, celui de détective – constituera la forme essentielle de l'affrontement"] (*Surveiller et punir* 82). Literature in general, long seen as poisonous, presented crime as the product of the imagination, possibly promoting copy cat crimes" (Shapiro 26–9).[27] Women, in particular, once again characterized as impressionable – within a socially defined and accepted intertextuality for both the popular press and for novels of crime – were seen as the "wrong" readers of crime stories (Shapiro 30–4).

Acknowledging Todorov's work in this area, Lynda Hart states that in classic crime stories and detective fiction there are always two murders, two narratives – the story of what really happened and the detective's own tale (Hart 80). In fact, one might say there are several narrative levels, or layers, to an actual crime: the crime itself (first narrative, private), which is publicly tried in a courtroom (second narrative, typically with a number of interpretations in tension with one another), reported in the newspapers and in other media (third narrative, again with different perspectives), and then made into a novel, film, or television drama or series (fourth, multiple and intertextual narrative). The reading of any of these narratives – and especially with horror and crime literature – is a private activity of illicit desires, the triumph over taboos and the "spectacle of murder" (Halttunen 82–3).

Readers and viewers, as voyeurs, visualize the scene as in a private performance (Halttunen 85, 86), watching and participating in the crime, coming closer to the violence, while heightening the need to vilify the killer in an effort to reassert a reassuring moral distance from evil (Halttunen 90). This dynamic returns us to the concept of the powerful, but comforting, screen from behind which we can witness the aestheticized violent text (Tanner 14; Kowalewski 47), "substitutionary violence" (Reineke 2), and substitute abstraction (Ackley 175–6) discussed in chapter 1.

The reader, then, becomes both an active juror and a detective crafting his or her own narrative (Halttunen 116, 117). Reading newspaper accounts of crimes and trials, detective fiction, Gothic horror stories, or, in this instance, novels about female infanticide allows the reader, often in the privacy of his or her home, to visualize and reconstruct the crime in its hidden mystery where there is no moral closure or truth, and where the reader is both distanced and involved (Halttunen 121–5, 131, 133). A relation is formed between the murderer and the reader; the killer walks among us, and we, as "ordinary" citizens, put ourselves in his or her position (Halttunen 245–6). As readers, therefore, we vacillate between distancing ourselves from and identitying with this evil "alien" and his or her crime.

Do we, as readers, distance ourselves from or identify with the narratives of Élaine and Florence, as well as the stories told by Alice and Marie? The narratives of these characters mirror their state of mind, whether as the distraught – or angry – mother who kills her child, the obedient daughter, or the composite lawyer, and we need to make some judgment on their actions in order to agree with or condemn the ultimate acquittals of these female crimes.

Lori Saint-Martin writes that the murder of Ève-Lyne creates a "narrative rupture, a 'crack' in Élaine's story, as the novel's title has it, which determines nearly all aspects of its narrative form" ("Les Deux Femmes" 202), and that this "break in the narrative thread" ["brisure dans la trame narrative"] this "hole," is reflected in the text by the use of both fragmentation and repetition (*Le Nom de la mère* 94). Building on this interpretation, one can also speak of "une fissure" (a crack/split) in characterization: between Julien and Élaine, between Bruno and Élaine, ultimately between Ève-Lyne and Élaine, and especially between Élaine's different selves – Élaine and "reality"; her private and publicly constructed personae; her private domestic self and her courtroom self; her private, silenced inner self and the self that cries out to be heard. Élaine mentions that at the end of her affair, Julien still tries to "fill the crack with his words" ["combler la fissure avec ses mots"] (Chamberland 118), but she realizes that the relationship has ended. Indeed, "the "fissure" in this novel can be seen as the split between private and public selves, where the infanticide (and here Élaine) can attempt to fill in the "cracks" by narrating, speaking, writing, painting what it is that we are reading. The narrative would of course be fragmentary and repetitive, since it reflects the instability of the otherwise silenced mother who is suffocating, and explosive.

This split narrative also reflects the fact that the authorship is both confusing and multiple. Once again, whose story is being constructed and told (a puzzle that would make it difficult to follow Cerulo's concept of sequencing and scripting)? Even if Élaine tries to tell her own story, she is constantly being pushed into another "version." In his office, Luc listens to her and asks her questions she doesn't like and to which she gives answers he doesn't like. He wants to delve further into her mind for a motive for killing her child:

"Are you sure, Élaine? Sure you're not feeling something else? Yes yes, you felt helpless, but that's not enough, that's not everything, there must be something else, dig even deeper, look further ... what don't you want to feel? what stops you from feeling? what's underneath? what's so dangerous underneath this helplessness?' And I felt ... lost, I'm lost; no way to retreat, he corners me with his eyes, his voice, what to do? ... and for a moment, I was about to raise my voice, me too, like him, more than him, to shout ... to cry out to him: It's none of your business! leave me alone! it's me, nothing but me! Mind your own business! thief, thief!" ["Es-tu sûre, Élaine? sûre que tu ne ressentais pas autre chose? oui oui il y avait l'impuissance, mais ce n'est pas assez, ce n'est pas tout, il devait bien y avoir autre chose, creuse encore, va voir plus loin ... qu'est-ce que tu ne veux pas ressentir? qu'est-ce que tu t'empêches de ressentir? qu'est-ce qu'il y a là-dessous? qu'est-ce qu'il y a de si dangereux sous cette impuissance?' Et je me sentais ... perdue, je suis perdue; plus moyen de reculer, il me coince avec ses yeux, sa voix, quoi faire? ... et pendant un instant, j'étais sur le point de hausser le ton moi aussi, comme lui, plus que lui, de crier ... lui crier: C'est pas de tes affaires! laisse-moi la paix! c'est à moi, rien qu'à moi! mêle-toi de tes affaries! voleur, voleur!"] (Chamberland 62–3)[28]

But Luc does "steal" her words, her story, especially when he testifies on her behalf in court before lawyers who themselves, not content with her own version, have had to construct her case carefully: "Every time I answer him [one of her lawyers], he gets mad; his tone becomes harsh, as if I were tricking him or were hiding something important from him on purpose, and he protests: That makes no sense, what you're telling me ... we'll never get anywhere this way ... how do you expect me to defend you with so little? ... you'll have to decide to help me more than this, otherwise ..." ["Chaque fois que je lui réponds ça, il se fâche; il prend un ton sévère, comme si je rusais ou je faisais exprès de lui cacher quelque chose d'important, et il proteste: Ça n'a pas de sens, ce que tu me dis ... on n'arrivera jamais à rien de cette façon-là ... comment veux-tu que je te défende avec si peu? ... il va falloir que tu te décides à m'aider plus que ça, autrement ..." (Chamberland 65) It is no wonder there is frequent repetition throughout the novel, since we, as readers, are hearing many different accounts of the same crime and many versions of the confused mind of the female criminal.

Even when we do hear from Élaine herself, we – and she – are still not certain of the authenticity of her words. Through the use of parentheses, Élaine seems to be recounting different versions of past events. At times she is going even further into the past; at others, she offers additional information or an explanation to herself, to Luc, or to the readers. She even uses parentheses within other sets of parentheses when, in talking about the past, she recounts another event in the more distant past and then adds commentary or a brief thought.[29]

Such narrative techniques underscore the isolation, paranoia, and the split between private and public selves that plague and yet define Élaine. She worries about the public image of her as a mother that appears in the media; she is, as we have seen, afraid that others are chasing her as though she were a monster or a wounded animal; she feels alone and scared even when surrounded by her family at home; she hides in the kitchen, convinced that the others are complicitly talking negatively about her. She is aware that something, some other self, is growing inside her: "It was there, I knew it now, it was there, I didn't know when it started, how long it had been there, I didn't even know what it was exactly but it was there, and it was dangerous, I had to make sure the others didn't find out about it, I had to keep my mouth shut. (It was there almost all the time, well, all the time, but especially at night, it was the worst at night, it was growing inside my head, it was taking up all the space" ["C'était là, je le savais maintenant, c'était là, j'ignorais depuis quand, pour combien de temps, j'ignorais même ce que c'était au juste mais c'était là, et c'était dangereux, il ne fallait pas que les autres l'apprennent, il ne fallait pas que j'ouvre la bouche.

(C'était là presque tout le temps, alors, tout le temps mais surtout le soir, c'était le pire le soir, ça grossissait dans ma tête, ça prenait toute la place."] (Chamberland 71–2). A feeling, a need, a desire to kill, a desire to speak, a need to be her true self – we do not know what or who is growing inside of Élaine, although whatever it is does mimic the fetus that was growing ("grossissait") inside Julien's wife (and inside her sister) and with which we know Élaine is obsessed. All Élaine knows at this point in time is that she must not open her mouth, for to do so might reveal the confusion that she is feeling about "le ventre" (stomach, belly, uterus) that she would like to make go away: her own past unwanted pregnancy and current lack of maternal instinct; Julien's wife's pregnant belly; her sister's pregnant belly that will prove her to be a wonderful mother; the disemboweled belly of her cat; and the belly on which her daughter sleeps – specifically when she is stabbed by her rather drunk mother.

Élaine is split at home with Ève-Lyne and Bruno, with her lover,[30] with her lawyers, with her psychiatrist, and especially in the public courtroom. She separates from herself and thinks to herself, as she-moves from one self to another: "And the accused smiled ... And I ... And since they were not in the process of talking about her, as if she didn't understand very well what was going on, the accused smiled" ["Et l'accusée souriait ... Et je ... Et comme on n'était pas en train de parler d'elle, comme si elle ne comprenait pas très bien ce qui se passait, l'accusée souriait"] (Chamberland 17, 34). She cannot relate to what is being said about her in court, so she "tunes out," just as she had done the day before in Luc's office, focusing on the colours and lines of a painting. The men in the trial do not know her and should not, but do, speak for her, as they make her into a woman for public consumption only, turning her private acts and self/selves into someone she does not recognize. So why should she pay attention?

There is, however, another "truer" private self that Élaine acknowledges but suppresses or is suppressed by others. She realizes that if she were to begin speaking, she would not be able to stop: "As soon as I started speaking, it would all come out by itself, I would try to speak and it wouldn't be words, not their words, all the same, monotonous, I would open my mouth and it would all come out in spite of myself. It would shout, it would scream, wildly, uncontrollably. It was too dangerous, here in this house, better to hide myself, to hide myself and keep quiet" ["Aussitôt que je commencerais à parler, ça sortirait tout seul, j'essaierais de parler et ce ne seraient pas des mots, pas leurs mots égaux, monocordes, j'ouvrirais la bouche et ça viendrait malgré moi. Ça crierait, ça hurlerait, sauvage, incontrôlable. C'était trop dangereux, ici dans cette maison, mieux valait me cacher, me cacher et me taire"] (Chamberland 73). Whatever private self lives inside of her comes out either as a scream, a cry, exploded language (Irigaray 177), or an explosive act of murder – made public. She was never able to speak to Bruno; he would not listen to her. She spoke to her cat instead. She spoke silently to Ève-Lyne, repeating her litany of love and death. Even after the infanticide, she plays a game in Luc's office as part of her therapy and ends up screaming and crying out loud, all the while encouraged by her psychiatrist: "'It's there inside of you, still alive, go for it, show them, scream! With all of your strength! Scream!' ... I screamed. I suddenly sat bolt upright, terrified but determined to defend myself, to resist to the end, and I began to scream, a huge cry suddenly escaped from me, a rib-breaking scream" ["'C'est là en toi, encore chaud, vas-y, montre-leur, crie! De toutes tes forces! Crie!' ... je criais. Je m'étais redressée soudain, terrorisée mais résolue à me défendre, à résister jusqu'au bout, et je m'étais mise à crier, il y avait un immense cri tout à coup sorti de moi, un cri à me fendre la poitrine"] (Chamberland 108–9).

When Élaine does finally speak/remember, she is honest about her feelings: how she hated being pregnant, hated her enormous, monstrous stomach (now, as I have shown, confused in her mind with all stomachs), hated the little, useless thing inside of her, and the "puny little helpless thing, dirty little red thing" ["petite chose chétive et impuissante, petite chose rouge, sale"] that was born (Chamberland 56). She remembers how she would speak to herself at home and how the sound of her own voice was such a comfort to her:

> This voice, my voice still warm and alive in the silent room, this voice that used to come from me and wrap me up when I was alone in the afternoon ... I used to sit in the same place, near the empty arm chair, and I used to speak: "Not even able to draw, I used to say, that doesn't make any sense ..." And I used to complain: "I'm tired, I've had enough ..." And I used to threaten: "If this keeps up ..." I wasn't afraid of speaking, of saying this very loudly in the silent house, it was already more bearable with this voice that wrapped around me, that filled the room. [Cette voix, ma voix encore chaude et vivante dans la pièce silencieuse, cette voix qui venait de moi et m'enveloppait quand j'étais seule l'après-midi ... je m'assoyais encore à la même place, près du fauteuil vide, et je parlais encore: "Même pas capable de dessiner, disais-je, ça n'a pas de bon sens ..." Et je me plaignais: "Je suis fatiguée, j'en ai assez ..." Et je menaçais:

"Si ça continue ..." Je n'avais pas peur de parler, de le dire tout haut dans la maison silencieuse, c'était déjà plus supportable avec cette voix qui m'enveloppait, qui remplissait la pièce.] (Chamberland 121–2)

And she continues to speak to herself alone even while living with her social worker, Marcelle: "It happens that I speak all alone when Marcelle isn't there ... a word that comes out loudly, a word that emerges from the dance of images in my head, swells up, feels confined, pushes and finally comes out ["Ça doit m'arriver de parler toute seule quand Marcelle n'est pas là ... un mot qui sort tout haut, un mot qui émerge de la danse des images dans ma tête, qui enfle, qui est à l'étroit, qui pousse et finit par sortir"] (Chamberland 120) – clearly a birthing image. Ultimately Élaine does give us her private story – trying to become a speaking subject –along with all of the other public and falsified versions of her life and criminal act. She tries to fill in the "fissure" within herself and among the other narratives. She reads a book on design and plans to write this book/novel about her own private violence, while Marcelle reads her book about the torture of a woman in El Salvador – and will ultimately finish her thesis: "'Hey, your book, how's it coming along?' 'Not very quickly.' I hear the water starting to boil. 'If I finish mine fairly soon, I'll be able to read yours so that I can give you a summary,' she says, laughing. 'I'm not sure it would interest you,' says Élaine to Marcelle. 'Me either,' she says, coming back into the room, holding her cup of coffee" ["'Toi, ton livre, ça avance?' 'Pas très vite.' J'entends l'eau qui commence à bouillir. 'Si je finis le mien assez tôt, je pourrai lire le tien pour t'en faire un résumé,' dit-elle en riant. 'Je ne suis pas sûre que ça t'intéressait,' 'Moi non plus,' dit-elle en revenant dans la pièce, sa tasse de café à la main"] (Chamberland 69). Clearly, even if Élaine can overcome the crack in her own self, the space between the public and the private cannot be bridged.

The narrative styles in *La Fissure* mirror Élaine's intimate state of mind, in tension with the public stories told about her and for her. *L'Obéissance*, on the other hand, presents the reader with textual material that reflects both private and public discourses of female criminality in general, infanticide in particular, motherhood, childhood, the legal profession, international violence, marriage, and friendship. This complex and beautifully written novel opens with a suffocating outpouring of Julie's thoughts in a flood of serious ideas that guide the reader through images of both personal and international, public violence. Julie's obsession with these issues is mirrored in a smothering discourse of long, repetitive sentences and "if" clauses that blur the boundaries between the real and what can be called "what if's" – confusing the real and the imaginary much as several of Dandurand's female protagonists do (see chapter 3). This overwhelming and difficult narrative concludes with the depiction of Julie at Marie's funeral, where she says she is about to break the complicitous silence and betray Marie's secret – not revealed until the end of the novel when we, as readers, are not even certain which secret has been betrayed. Whether Julie is ultimately the narrative voice of the entire novel is intentionally never made clear, but the opening section captures the reader in that ambiguous space between the private and the public, confusing the two and creating tremendous tension, even before we read about and witness the infanticide to come.

There is a remarkable shift from the intense first-person narrative of the "Dit Julie" to the detached, third-person narrative of the second section, "Un Fait divers," where the actual murder (or suicide) occurs, where we learn about Florence, Yvonne (Florence's mother), Hubert, Alice, and Rémi, and where, by the end of the section, Alice and Rémi are dead, Florence is on trial, and Hubert seems to have disappeared from view. Virtually everything in these pages betrays the most private of people's lives and minds, as we enter the histories, daily lives, and inner thoughts of the characters, recounted by an omniscient third person, who manages to make public for our private, prurient interests an amazing amount of information in a relatively short space.

Indeed, we never hear directly from Florence, except through this third person – who may be Julie – and toward the end of the novel when we learn more about the crime, the motive, and Florence's confession to Marie – through the words of her lawyer, again possibly recounted by Julie. What we do learn in "Un Fait divers" is that Yvonne Vézina, Florence's mother, is "l'origine de tout" ["the origin of everything"] (Jacob 38) – reminding us again of Courbet – a cruel and unloving woman whom Florence hated passionately but who attempted, literally or metaphorically as I have noted, to protect her daughter from all men: "Her mother infibulated her so as to protect her from her husband and her brothers" ["Sa mère l'a infibulée à force de la protéger contre son mari et ses frères"] (Jacob 48). Florence arrives on her wedding night not able to do much about the "sewing that kept her closed up" ["couture qui la tient fermée"], but still a "false virgin" ["fausse vierge"], since her mother continued to doubt her virginity (Jacob 48, 37). As voyeurs we are witness to the most intimate of details about

Florence and Hubert – in simple and dry language: "He takes Florence. As soon as he comes, she stops wriggling, she is stretched out on the sheets, dead ... He sleeps. The TV lights up his sullen face ... She doesn't sleep. It was okay. It was what it was ... When her spirit reenters her body, she gets up without a sound. She goes into the bathroom to wash up" ["Il prend Florence. Dès qu'il y est, elle ne grouille plus, elle est étendue dans les draps, morte ... Il dort. La télé éclaire son visage boudeur ... Elle ne dort pas. C'était bien. C'était ça ... Lorsque son esprit réintègre son corps, elle se lève sans bruit. Elle va se laver dans la salle de bains"] (Jacob 50–1).

Continuing in this same punctuated style, the narrator shows us how angry, potentially violent, insecure, and emotionally and psychologically unstable Florence really is. She imagines hurting people and believes that they want her dead: "For a very long time she had understood, deep down, that for other women, like for her mother Yvonne, it would be better if she no longer existed, or rather if she were like an empty ping-pong ball, empty and forever empty" ["Il y avait bien longtemps qu'elle avait compris, au fond d'elle-même, que pour les autres femmes, comme pour sa mère Yvonne, il valait mieux qu'elle n'existe plus, ou alors comme une balle de ping-pong vide, vide, et encore vide"] (Jacob 57). Indeed, Florence is symbolically empty like a ping-pong ball; her very thoughts and motives are narrated by others, who speak on her behalf and try to interpret her private self, made public in a trial and in the press.

This same detached narrative style is used to relate the complex and explosive relationship between Florence and Alice. Unlike her mother, Alice is talkative and tries to make her needs and wishes known publicly, but she, too, is sewn shut by the anger, silence, and punishments of her mother who isolates her daughter in her room and gives her ice-cold showers. As Lori Saint-Martin has pointed out, the cruel actions of Florence toward Alice are painful for both, and "the time for a mother-daughter reconciliation has not yet come" ["le temps d'un rapprochement mère-fille n'est pas encore venu" (*Le Nom de la mère* 112). Reminiscent not only of Gabrielle Roy's *Bonheur d'occasion* but also of Marie-Claire Blais's *Visions d'Anna*, the relationship between Florence and Alice stops short of any communication and hurts them both:

The two women, the little one and the big one, faced each other in silence, entrenched, both of them, behind a heartache of love deprived of expression, which could have been called betrayal, later, much later, if they had been given time to name their story. But time was not given to them, just as it is not given to most young girls, even to very old little girls, nor to most mothers, even mothers who sometimes live to be a hundred, for each of them to talk it over ... Florence stiffened, congratulating herself on not having given in to emotion. She did not have to give in ... Alice stretched her arms toward her mother to ask for forgiveness. It was too late. [Les deux femmes, la petite et la grande, se faisaient face en silence, retranchées l'une et l'autre derrière une peine d'amour privée d'expression, qui aurait pu s'appeler trahison, plus tard, beaucoup plus tard, si le temps leur avait été donné de nommer leur histoire. Mais le temps ne leur fut pas donné, comme il n'est pas donné à la plupart des petites filles, même aux très vieilles petites filles, ni à la plupart des mères, même aux mères qui vivent parfois jusqu'à l'âge de cent ans, de s'expliquer entre elles les unes aux autres ... Florence se raidit, se félicitant de n'avoir pas cédé à l'émotion. Elle ne devait pas fléchir ... Alice tendit les bras vers sa mère pour demander pardon. Il était trop tard.] (Jacob 76)

If words are missing in this relationship, they become the cause of tragedy soon thereafter. At school a boy taunts Alice and Rémi, saying that their mother dances nude. Alice, so furious that she cannot even speak, physically assaults the boy and strikes him, significantly, in the mouth with a stone. The schoolmate picks on the weaker opponent, Rémi, and pushes him down onto the sidewalk. When Florence hears about this incident, she finally communicates out loud: "Never had anyone heard Florence scream. Never had Florence raised her voice. Florence always spoke very slowly, very sweetly, because of the ghost that she didn't want to awaken" ["Jamais on n'avait entendu hurler Florence. Jamais Florence n'avait encore élevé la voix. Florence parlait toujours très lentement, très doucement, à cause du fantôme qu'elle ne voulait pas réveiller"] (Jacob 93). Rémi dies a short while later from an internal hemorrhage – caused by the fall – as the victim of both silence and words, turned into physical pain and death. Without her brother, and lacking any communication with her mother, Alice, as mentioned, creates another Alice with whom she has a dialogue. This imaginary split narrative mirrors Alice's own persona, which finds a way to survive her abusive childhood.

Her method does not work. Alice cannot survive the lack of words, the seething silence with which her mother abuses her. She can never be perfect enough to obey Florence in all she asks. And Florence can never accept Alice's perceived refusal to obey her, her perceived judgment, and her attempt to grow up. The daughter walks into the water:

"'Mommy, help me, I'm going to drown myself.' The moon pushes the water, the water pushes the little girl, causes her to lose footing, carries her off, fills her up, her mouth, nostrils, throat, all the way to her lungs"[31] ["'Maman, aide-moi, je vais me noyer.' La lune pousse l'eau, l'eau pousse la petite fille, lui fait perdre pied, l'emporte, la remplit, bouche, narine, gorge, jusqu'au fond, des poumons"] (Jacob 105). As Saint-Martin aptly interprets: "The water that enters Alice's body and blocks up all its orifices recalls both the cold showers Florence forces upon Alice and the 'infibulation' both have undergone" ("Les Deux Femmes" 213). Both Alice and Florence have now lost the chance to tell their own stories. But their most private of stories is soon to become a public narrative, in tension with its reintegration into the private world of Florence's defence lawyer, Marie.

The rest of the novel is largely devoted to our getting to know Marie and the people who inhabit her world. Foucault's "confessing animal" is particularly at work in these sections, as we learn in both in dialogue and in third-person narrative form – possibly in the mind and memory of Julie – about a number of troubled individuals: Marie's husband, Jean, a selfish man, who is upset with Marie when she reveals that she has had a lover, all the time he was in Rome with his new potential lover, Muriel; Muriel, who tells her own story and then accuses Jean of being a weak and impotent woman because he cannot commit to any woman; Aglaé and an unnamed man who confess a lot about their own lives (including a possible infanticide), who are confused in Marie's mind with Florence, Alice, and herself, and who are ultimately revealed as characters in one of Marie's dreams; Julie, about whom there are vague and accusatory lesbian references by Jean in regard to her friendship with Marie; and of course Marie herself, who is increasingly seen as troubled, confused, and even paranoid. The initial narrative between Marie and Jean is interesting in that it reveals different levels of dialogue, from the private inner thoughts of Jean while Marie sleeps, to Marie's own private thoughts, to their actual dialogue, and a third-person perspective. The dream sequence is likewise disguised as a fairly public conversation on a train, but despite the sub-title, "Un Voyage de rêve," the reader does not know until the end that the entire scene has taken place in Marie's mind – just as the entire novel may have taken place in Julie's thoughts at Marie's funeral.

But it is Marie who is the major focus of this lengthy section of *L'Obéissance:* Marie, the lawyer; Marie, the private wife, who had an abortion and who now becomes a future mother; Marie, the legal confessor to whom Florence tells her story (repeated in Marie's words, however); Marie, who identifies both with Florence and Alice; and especially Marie, who must relive the past events, must recount the tale of the infanticide, and must tell others and herself about herself in order to survive. She is not successful.

Marie announces that she is not sure who is speaking when she does speak: "I hear the intonations of my voice, its attitudes, its games. My voice plays a role as if we had become actors, she and I. We are separate from one another. We no longer make a single Marie. There is Marie and there is Marie's voice" ["J'entends les intonations de ma voix, ses attitudes, ses jeux. Ma voix joue un rôle comme si nous étions devenues des comédiennes, elle et moi. Nous sommes séparées. Nous ne formons plus une seule Marie. Il y a Marie et il y la voix de Marie"] (Jacob 174). As I have already mentioned, Marie is a speaking subject in the public arena, but in some sense her own objectified voice in her own private space. In a barrage of words, reminiscent of Julie's narrative at the beginning of the novel, and spoken perhaps in her own mind, to Jean, or to Julie, Marie spills out her thoughts about Florence and Alice, their relationship, her own identification with both mother and daughter, her refusal to become a mother, and her own guilt at having defended Florence successfully against the charge of murdering Alice: "My mouth fills with hatred. I am here for no good reason. I have never hated. I have lived without hate. I have always wanted to make peace everywhere ... My mouth was entirely myself, pure and without lies, like Alice's mouth. My mouth has become the tool of the worst hypocrisy" ["Ma bouche s'emplit de haine. Je n'y suis pour rien. Je n'ai jamais haï. J'ai vécu sans haine. J'ai toujours voulu faire la paix partout ... Ma bouche était entièrement moi-même, pure et sans mensonge, comme la bouche d'Alice. Ma bouche est devenue l'instrument de la pire hypocrisie"] (Jacob 177). She obtained the most intimate details of the private life of Florence, and she used them to win the case publicly – all but one secret that she swore to Florence she would never reveal: the scene where Alice witnessed her mother dancing nude before her father and being forced to have sex with him. And now – perhaps – Marie has told that secret to Julie.

At one point, in a feverish state and ironically soon to be "with child," Marie recounts the entire story of Florence and Alice to Julie, under Julie's authoritative urging. Marie seems to improve as each word of the tale enters a space between the private world of Florence and Alice and the public world of the courtroom and the newspapers:

"As soon as she began to tell the story, Marie was transformed. Power, energy, intelligence rushed into her through this story of Choinière that she claimed to hate more than anything. The story nourished her, gave her life, kept her entirely captivated and captive, although Marie did not stop repeating that it was only an obscure news item, a pathetic anecdote of no interest ... When the cold November water filled Alice's boots, Marie had regained all of her vitality and her radiance" ["Dès qu'elle eut commencé à raconter, Marie fut métamorphosée. La force, la verve, l'intelligence affluèrent en elle par le canal de cette histoire de Choinière qu'elle prétendait haïr par-dessus tout. L'histoire la nourrissait, lui redonnait vie, la tenait tout entière captivée et captive bien que Marie ne cessait de répéter qu'il ne s'agissait que d'un obscur fait divers, d'une anecdote minable et sans intérêt ... Lorsque l'eau froide de novembre pénétra dans les bottes d'Alice, Marie avait repris toute sa vitalité et son éclat"] (Jacob 211). Telling this tale of infanticide is cleansing and life-giving to Marie. She desperately needs to explain herself: "I just want to make myself clear, to make myself clear again to myself and hear myself making myself clear" ["Je veux seulement m'expliquer, m'expliquer à nouveau moi-même et m'entendre m'expliquer"] (Jacob 216).

This narrative is so lifegiving, in fact, that Marie changes her mind about motherhood and soon becomes pregnant. She hopes that the child will be a girl, and she and Jean seem to be reconciled. Then, in a rather melodramatic twist, she learns that she has a brain tumour and that the cancer has spread. At first she wants the child to survive so that Jean can raise her, and then suddenly she wants to die quickly and take the child with her. In a return to Julie's thoughts and memory in the final section of the novel, we learn that Marie had already had one abortion about which Jean knew nothing: "She refused to give birth to a child who would be unwittingly threatened with drowning. 'I gave birth to her in another world where she will be blessed among all women,' she had said. It was the lightest of secrets between us, the existence of 'her daughter' in another, more serene dimension of the universe" ["Elle refusait de mettre au monde un enfant qu'on menace de noyer à son insu. 'Je l'ai mise au monde dans un autre monde où elle sera bénie entre toutes les femmes,' avait-elle dit. C'était le secret le plus léger entre nous, l'existence de 'sa fille' dans une autre dimension plus sereine de l'univers"] (Jacob 242).[32] Marie's identification with Alice is likewise based on her own childhood abuse – her mother held her head held under the water in the bathtub every

Saturday – an additional secret that she has revealed only to Julie, who promises never to tell. Bringing us full circle to the blurring of boundaries between the public and the private, Julie confuses what Marie sees as her own personal "atrocities" – either from her own abusive childhood, as a future mother/parent, or in her terminal cancer – which she does not want to pass on to her daughter, and the atrocities rampant in the violent world at large, into which she would not want to bring another child.[33]

In their last conversation before Marie's death, Marie takes Julie's hand and sadly says: "'I'm trying to bring her back to life, but I won't be able to do it. Oh! Julie, I won't be able to, I'll have to start all over again!' 'Your daughter?' 'Oh no, Julie, my mother'" ["'J'essaie de la remettre au monde, je n'y arriverai pas. Oh! Julie, je n'y arriverai pas, il faut tout recommencer!' 'Ta fille?' 'Oh non, Julie, ma mère'"] (Jacob 250). In a twist reminiscent of Roy in the title story of *La Route d'Altamont*, in which the daughter gives (re)birth to her mother and grandmother through her narrative text,[34] Marie dies before giving (re)birth to her mother. But luckily we have Julie, who holds several of Marie's private secrets: Alice's witnessing Florence dancing nude before and forced into sex by her husband; Marie's own abusive childhood at the hands of her mother; Marie's abortion in order to send her child to a safer place; Marie's dying and, like Élaine, taking her child away from the world of both private and public violence. And, as we have mentioned, all the private stories, all Jacob's versions, are now made public for private reading in the form of a novel.

FEMALE INFANTICIDE, ACQUITTALS, AND GENDER STEREOTYPES

In 1831 Lucretia Chapman was charged in Pennsylvania with the murder of her husband. The prosecution melodramatically portrayed her as a woman with "masculine intelligence and habits" and an outrage to the ideal of true womanhood, while the defence presented her as a devoted wife, mother, and teacher who had been seduced by the wiles of another man (see chapter 1). Given the choice between these two stories, the jury found her not guilty because they were unable to accept the vile narrative of a demonic woman and preferred the tale of a helpless victim (Halttunen 152–4; see chapter 1). Playing into the perceived duality of women's nature, female defendants' "proper" courtroom behaviour, and prejudices against the poor, working class, and women of colour,[35] juries have historically acquitted females on criminal charges, infanticide in particular, in the United States, France, and Canada.

Foucault's study of late nineteenth-century legal psychiatry in France suggests that medical opinion about criminals resonated with social theory (as cited in Shapiro 134). For female defendants, as I have noted, acquittals were often justified on the grounds that the women on trial demonstrated a certain level of mental incapacity (Shapiro 90). Basing their decisions on medical discourse, juries expressed sympathy for female criminals as unstable and disabled, pointing to a "syndrome of femininity that underlined women's disequilibrium, grounded on their biological sex," suggesting their need for the tutelary support both of the court system and of the medical profession (Shapiro 134–5). Some juries were accused of being "feminized" because they had acquitted female defendants (Shapiro 170). Others caused an increasing societal anxiety over the leniency shown to women criminals, whom they saw as menacing figures, examples of a new "despotism of women," rather than as inexperienced victims created by the popular press (Shapiro 112–13). And finally, linking female criminals and late nineteenth-century French feminists, some interpreted the high acquittal of women charged with crimes as a victory for women in the greater war of the sexes (Shapiro 113).

In Canada commutations in infanticide cases rarely elicited public criticism. The pool of public sympathy for mothers who killed their newborns was so deep that prosecutors preferred to prosecute under the charge of "concealment of birth" in order to secure a conviction (Strange 5). The case of Viola Thompson, convicted of murdering her baby girl in 1919 in rural central Ontario, provides illuminating historical information on Canada's treatment of infanticide cases. The Crown argued that Thompson had suffocated her one-week-old daughter and had tossed her from a moving train. Her attorney presented her at trial as a distressed woman, delirious from the effects of childbirth and unmindful of the nature and consequences of her act. The jurors found her criminally responsible and yet were reluctant to have her convicted and sentenced to the mandatory death sentence. Convinced by the judge, the jury rendered a guilty verdict but added a strong recommendation for mercy – with which the judge and the remissions officer agreed. The executive considered the case and commuted her death sentence to life imprisonment. Petitions poured in, however, from neighbours, family, religious groups, and her own children – letters revealing Thompson's terrible home life and her love for her children. Ultimately she was released on "Ticket-of-Leave," an early form of parole, and quietly placed in her mother's care in 1926 (Strange 3–6).

According to Carolyn Strange's review of Canadian (maternal) infanticide cases in light of the 2001 conviction of Robert Latimer in Saskatchewan for the 1993 murder of his twelve-year-old daughter, who suffered from cerebral palsy,[36] by the early twentieth century, cabinets were so ready to commute the death penalty in infanticide cases that the pronouncement of the death sentence "became something of a farce" (6). In 1948 a bill was introduced that created a sub-category of homicide for which a penalty of three years would apply; the penalty was raised to five years in 1954. Strange interprets this legal and political move as an acknowledgment of "the cultural inclination towards lenience for the women convicted of murdering infants," as well as the shoring up of "respect for the rule of law" (6). What the 1954 Criminal Code did was to formalize what was already an informal historical practice: "It introduced a gender-specific, physiological rationale ... to replace the customary practices of under-charging, jury nullification, and automatic commutations. And it left the legality of the mandatory death penalty for all other forms of murder unchallenged" (Strange 6). In effect, the new statute underscored what I have noted as the presumed underlying pathological nature of mothers who kill their children.

More recently, especially in the United States as I have noted (see chapter 1), women who kill are still categorized as mad or bad, or alternately as pathetic and harmless victims. In Mann's study of the offender in criminal justice history and processing in the United States, for women who killed intimate relations, including their offspring, she found that women who had killed their children tended to be assessed significantly higher bonds than those who had killed sexual intimates: $76,249 for the infanticide as compared to $20,066 for killing a husband or lover (Mann 147). In addition: "Women who were convicted of killing their offspring were just as likely to receive prison sentences as women who killed those with whom they were sexually intimate; and, on average, their prison sentences were longer. Filicide offenders were twice as frequently given twenty to forty years in prison as women who killed their sexual intimates (4.1 percent). The mean number of years in prison for women who killed their children was 7.4 years, a year longer than the average of 6.4 years allocated to female killers of husbands and lovers ... women who killed their offspring were more frequently given the more severe probation sentences of five to 10 years (64.3 percent)" (Mann 150).

According to Meyer and Oberman, such offenders are tried and sentenced in wildly disparate ways because of the "incoherent and arbitrary case law that characterizes U.S. infanticide jurisprudence" (174). No distinction is made between killing an infant/child and a non-infant/child; nor do courts generally use the terms "infanticide" or "neonaticide" in their opinions. The charges against an individual for killing her infant range from first degree murder to manslaughter (Dvorak 4). As I have already indicated, in the two most recent "celebrated" cases in the United States of mothers having killed their children, Susan Smith is currently serving a life sentence in South Carolina for the murder of her two sons; and in the Andrea Yates case in Texas, the prosecution, after having declared that it would seek the death penalty, agreed to life imprisonment for this mother, found guilty of the murder of three of her five children (see note 9). In the United States, at least, although one must make a distinction between lighter sentences given in infanticide cases and more stringent sentences given in filicide cases, it does appear that as of fairly recently, some women are no longer "getting away with the murder" of their offspring (again see note 9 regarding the Laney case of 2004).

In Britain the *Infanticide Act* allows for a more consistent and lenient sentence in infanticide cases – providing for probation with counselling (as in *La Fissure)* – while heavier sentences are given in filicide cases (Meyer and Oberman 171–2). In particular, many "women "found guilty of infanticide may avoid a custodial sentence altogether providing they agree to receive medical and/or psychiatric treatment" (Ballinger 2). Morris and Wilczynski report on one sample in England that showed that women given prison sentences tended to be those viewed as having acted in ways inconsistent with traditional conceptions of female behaviour. They were seen as bad women and bad mothers – selfish, cold, negligent, uncaring, and sexually active (212–13) (again see chapter 1). In another British study of 395 parents suspected of murdering their child between 1982 and 1989, 44 percent were mothers: "Almost half of the mothers (although less than a third of the fathers) were given hospital orders specifying psychiatric treatment in a mental hospital ... and more than two fifths of the mothers (though only just over 10 percent of the fathers) were given probation orders ... Although half of the mothers ... were given prison sentences, virtually all the fathers were. Conversely, a much greater proportion of the mothers were given probation" (203).

In Canada, the punishment for infanticide is determined by the Criminal Code: "Every female who commits infanticide is guilty of an indictable offence and liable to imprisonment for a term not exceeding five years" (Consolidated Statutes of Canada, Part VIII. 237). The possibility of acquittal is also clearly spelled out: "No acquittal unless act or omission not wilful. Where a female person is charged with infanticide and the evidence establishes that she caused the death of her child but does not establish that, at the time of the act by which she caused the death of the child, (a) she was not fully recovered from the effects of giving birth to the child or from the effect of lactation consequent on the birth of the child, and (b) the balance of her mind was, at that time, disturbed by reason of the effect of giving birth to the child or of the effect of lactation consequent on the birth of the child, she may be convicted unless the evidence establishes that the act or omission was not wilful" (Consolidated Statutes of Canada, Criminal Code, Part XX. 663). In laypersons' terms: a woman who is charged with infanticide may be convicted if sections (a) and (b) are not established. Otherwise, she can be acquitted.

According to Strange, once death penalty moratoria were introduced in Canada in 1967 and renewed until 1976, when the penalty was formally abolished,[37] a new era of inflexibility and greater harshness in sentencing occurred. Women found guilty of infanticide remained subject to lesser penalties for murder, but all other persons convicted of first- or second-degree murder faced a new mandatory life sentence (7). A person found guilty of manslaughter received a minimum of four years to life imprisonment, whereas, as noted, a mother guilty of infanticide can be imprisoned for a maximum of five years. Although the Canadian statute allows for this prison term of up to five years, "the case law indicates that convictions are difficult to obtain. Furthermore, if convicted, the maximum sentence is rarely issued or upheld" (Dvorak 6).

Annette Ballinger (in some sense echoing Patricia Pearson) believes that until recently, many feminists showed a reluctance to deal with female violence, and when they "addressed the issue of violent women, they too have been inclined to portray the perpetrators as victimized individuals reacting to a particular set of circumstances" (Ballinger 2–3). In order to avoid using the image of victim for the purpose of rendering women seemingly weak and incapable – thereby supporting juries who acquit women and instead provide them with medical and/or psychiatric treatment – some feminists have limited studies of female violence to instances when an abused strikes back at her abuser or when certain women challenge dominant ideologies and prejudices about female behaviour (Ballinger 2–3) – the latter forming the corps of "my" female fictional characters. As Ballinger argues, we need to create new discourses in order to explore and analyse "the differences between how such women view themselves and the circumstances which led up to their crimes, and the way in which their accounts are mediated and 'translated' in the court-room, the media and the public mind" (Ballinger 3). Once again the question is: whose private story will be made public, told and accepted by a jury; who will ultimately be judged responsible for the crime, here, of infanticide?

Élaine's acquittal for the murder of her daughter perfectly dovetails with both historical and contemporary cases of infanticide in Canada (although Ève-Lyne is two years old, and the crime is thus not legally an infanticide but a filicide). Élaine does not speak for herself but allows others – the medical and legal experts – to tell her story on her behalf. Luc, her psychiatrist, repeats that she did not kill her child but that she killed a part of herself, that she was "désorganisée," painting a portrait of a woman detached from her real self, depressed, confused, vulnerable, mentally impaired, pathetic, and tragic – similar to Andrea Yates in certain ways. Élaine plays that role beautifully in the courtroom. Unbeknownst to her, plea bargaining also occurs behind the scenes, and her luck continues with the appointment of an understanding and sympathetic judge who can rule on her case without the presence of a jury in this bench trial. Her defence attorney takes full advantage of this: "'We have even heard here the opinion of the psychologist, who has confirmed to us that a prison sentence would be harmful to the accused ... would be harmful to the recovery of her independence ... we are not in the presence of a criminal case, nor of a threat to society ... so why imprisonment?' he asked the judge, who didn't bother to answer, knowing like everyone that the question wasn't addressed to him, that it didn't call for a response, was only one sentence, one element like others in a long speech ... 'That's why, Your Honour, I am recommending for my client the issuance of a ruling of probation'" ["'Nous avons entendu ici même l'avis du psychologue, qui nous a affirmé qu'une sentence d'emprisonnement nuirait à l'accusée ... nuirait au recouvrement de son autonomie ... nous ne sommes pas en présence d'un cas criminel, ni d'une menace pour la société ... alors pourquoi l'emprisonnement?' demandait-il au juge qui ne se donnait pas la peine de répondre, sachant comme tout le monde que la question ne lui était pas adressée, qu'elle n'appelait pas de réponse, n'était qu'une phrase, un élément comme les autres du long discours ... 'C'est pourquoi, Votre Honneur, je recommande pour ma cliente l'émission d'une ordonnance de probation'"] (Chamberland 94–6).

Although initially and naively believing that she could simply go back home, Élaine is surprised and confused by the judgment: "I don't understand why it happened like this, why the judge decided to ..." ["je ne comprends pas pourquoi ça s'est passé comme ça, pourquoi le juge a décidé de ..."] (Chamberland 150). She is acquitted on provision that she live with a social worker, continue to receive psychiatric care twice a week, and go back either to her art studies or to work. Of course she is not a threat to the rest of society, and a prison sentence does not seem appropriate, but she did commit a crime and must in some way be held responsible. It is significant, however, that it was the men in her legal and medical life who managed to obtain her acquittal by presenting/objectifying her as a victim of herself, as a weak and powerless woman who, despite the murder, is not really capable of violence. Whether she will benefit from the book she is writing (and that we are reading) about the case is not, of course, explored in that very book!

Florence, too, is acquitted as a result of the successful defence that Marie presents in the court room, although we do not know if the acquittal was based on diminished responsibility or insanity, and we do not know if counselling was a mandated part of the acquittal. A lawyer who will go as far as to entice a judge sexually if her actions can keep one of her clients out of prison, Marie seduces the prosecutor, in this case in order to persuade him of a strategy that would condemn Florence and win the case for the deceased Alice. When he does not follow her advice, she moves forward with her defence, referring to her client as mildly retarded ["débile légère"] and a scapegoat – of whom we do not know (Jacob 212). Understanding the history of female criminals and their tendency to be acquitted as mad, bad, or weak, she would have preferred not to paint such a picture of Florence and does react negatively to the persistent questioning of reporters who want to know if she is going to try to win by proving a "dérèglement mental" [mental derangement] for her client (Jacob 139). To Marie, it is a question of responsibility (i.e., pathologically – Florence could not have been responsible for her act). In order to obtain a judgment of guilty for Florence, the prosecutor should have tried to convince the jury that Florence was responsible for the murder of her daughter: "I would have done it, I would have! I would have dared, and Florence would have been found guilty. I would have said: 'So it's come to that: is it because Florence Chaillé's mind was distraught that Florence Chaillé is less responsible? Oh sure! [sounding very much like Julie] Pinochet, Ceaucescu, Barbie, all distraught minds, legally incapable? Are we going to allow psychology to undermine the legal system forever?'" ["Je l'aurais fait, moi! J'aurais osé, et Florence aurait été condamnée. J'aurais dit: 'Voilà où nous en sommes: est-ce parce que l'esprit de Florence Chaillé s'est égaré que Florence Chaillé est moins responsible? Mais alors Pinochet, Ceaucescu, Barbie, tous des esprits égarés, irresponsables? Allons-nous laisser éternellement la psychologie miner l'édifice de la loi?'"] But Marie was the counsel for the defendant and as such, had to play the legal game of defending her client as both mad and a victim: "Marie says that it was all theatrics, that one shouldn't dig oneself into a hole over it" ["Marie dit que c'était du théâtre, qu'il ne fallait pas se creuser"] (Jacob 213). Marie played her part so well in public before the jury that Florence was acquitted, but Marie died.

Who is responsible for these two infanticides, and should Élaine and Florence have been acquitted, as many such women have been in actual cases? Are they "monster women," as Linda Chavez has called such women (as quoted in Meyer and Oberman 168), in keeping with society's assumptions about transgressive women (see chapter 1)? And should we treat their cases not as legal infanticide (Alice was neither a newborn nor under one year of age; Ève-Lyne was two years old) but rather as filicides/child homicides – or suicide in the case of Alice – in which case, they should have received, under Canadian law, harsher sentences? One possible argument is that they should not be held responsible as violent mothers, since society in general and fathers in particular are the accomplices, if not the cause, of maternal violence against daughters (Saint-Martin, "Les Deux Femmes" 210). In other words, these aquittals suggest that the two women's actions "do not violate the Father's Law but rather reinforce it" (Saint-Martin "Les Deux Femmes" 214). In a purely psychological interpretation, this argument makes sense – and is one way of looking at the novels in question. But in a more historical, sociological, criminological, and legal context, the acts of infanticide, the narratives of mother, daughter, friend, lawyer, courtroom expert, press and public – and the novels that we, as readers, are privately reading and interpreting – are far more problematic and play into real and other fictional cases of female infanticide and female violence. As a subscriber to the critical method that "refuses the separation of social life ('reality') from representation ('myth' or 'stereotype')" (Duggan 4), I agree with Suzanne Jacob's statement: "When real-life enters the novel, it enters into another time where everything is still to be lived, where nothing has yet been lived. The novel will open up this space where plausibility, veracity, fidelity will be submissive only to the illumination that language gives to it" ["Lorsque le vécu entre dans le roman, il entre dans un autre temps où tout est encore à vivre, où rien n'a encore été vécu. Le roman va lui ouvrir cet espace où la vraisemblance, la véracité, la fidélité ne seront plus soumises qu'à l'éclairage que la langue lui donnera"] (*La Bulle d'encre* (44–5). It seems, therefore, that Chamberland's and Jacob's novels must be read in the context of historical and cultural gender assumptions that foreground binary oppositions between men and women and thereby deny the complexities that must be applied to female violence, whether real or artistically created.

Note: As this book was going to press, the Texas Court of Criminal Appeals refused, on 9 November 2005, to reconsider a lower court's decision to overturn Andrea Yates's capital murder convictions. The First Court of Appeals in Houston had overturned those convictions in January 2005 because of false testimony by a forensic psychiatrist. As a result, the Yates case will be retried or a plea bargain will be considered. On 12 November 2005, however, Andrea Yates, through her attorney, stated that she did not want to go through another trial.

5

Regendering and Serial Killing in the Fiction of Hélène Rioux, Anne Dandurand, and Claire Dé

Murder is negative creation, and every murderer is therefore the rebel who claims the right to be omnipotent.

W.H. Auden, *The Dyer's Hand*

BOUNDARIES AND REPRESENTATION

When Northrop Frye wrote his concluding essay for the 1965 *Literary History of Canada*, he pointed out that Canadians, historically, have had significant respect for law and order in the face of mammoth, threatening, and somewhat monstrous wilderness. Although Frye uses European existentialism and the Russian Revolution as examples of differing social structures and philosophies, the underlying comparison he draws throughout the essay is between Canada and the United States. Assuming Canada's overriding mythology to be pastoral, Frye found it an easy step to emphasize that Canada, unlike the United States with its history of revolution and technological productivity, is on a "quest for the peaceable kingdom" (249). Historians such as William Kilbourn have extended Frye's assertion. In an essay entitled "The Quest for the Peaceable Kingdom," Kilbourn suggests that the *British North America Act* of 1867 "sets up objectives of peace, order and good government" (49) and, further developing the assumed contrast between Canada and the United States, argues that "in a masculine world of the assertive will and the cutting edge of intellect, a certain Canadian tendency to the amorphous permissive feminine principle of openness and toleration and acceptance offers the possibility of healing" (53), as I have raised in chapter 2.

Both Frye's emphasis on peace and the willingness of Kilbourn to gender North America so casually have been roundly and understandably debunked. Contemporary theorists and critics rightly point to the absurdities inherent in such stereotyped generalities and place more emphasis on irony, mentioned but developed only peripherally by Frye in terms of Canada. For example, Linda Hutcheon suggests that Canadians (and I include here the Québécois) have made the border a marginal, postmodern space from which they can effectively use parody and irony on both themselves and their southern neighbours.[1] People living in Canada and in Quebec continue, with or without irony, to contrast their society with that of the United States, not only emphasizing Canada's careful gun laws and unwillingness to subject its population to the more bizarre results of mass reporting frenzies, but also somewhat smugly, pointing to the general stability and safety of her cities (see the urban crime statistics reported in chapter 2).

It stands to reason, then, that Canadians and Québécois may well have a particular "paranoia about boundaries" (Halberstam 36) and thus be invested in keeping theirs intact, perhaps most seriously because, as the editors of the preface to *The Beaver Bites Back* note, one of the more recurrent contemporary symbols of Canadian identity is "the sense of an uncertain, ironic, ambivalent, and self-contradictory identity" (xii). Writers are not confined to borders, however. As the Canadian mass media become increasingly influenced by the culture of the United States (as I have discussed in chapter 2), violence has become daily fare on television in both Canada and Quebec, in films from the United States, and even in the news reported throughout Canada.

In this chapter I again focus on the ways in which Québébois women writers imagine and create female violence – in this case, the extreme of serial killing. Also, returning to the gendering – even if debunked – of Canada, and Quebec within it, as feminine "nations," I look at how these women writers in particular unsettle any assumed causal links between fact and fantasy. In "The Force of Fantasy," Judith Butler discusses the power of the real to limit and fix interpretation. Writers create fantasy, however, and it is at the level of fantasy, according to Butler, that the proliferation of identities prohibits the postulation of singular identities: "The fixed subject-position of 'women' functions within the feminist discourse in favor of censorship as a phantasm that suppresses multiple and open possibilities for identification, a phantasm, in other words, that refuses its own possibilities ... as fantasy through its self-stabilization as the real. Feminist theory and politics cannot regulate the representation of 'women' without producing that very 'representation'; and if that is in some sense a discursive inevitability of representational politics, then the task must be to safeguard the open productivity of those categories, whatever the risk" (120).

This chapter moves through a discussion of serial killing in general and female serial killing in particular, an analysis of the appearance of serial killing in Québécois fiction, ways in which gendered border-crossing illustrates the national/provincial dilemma of being overrun by the American media, the effort to disconnect gender identity from real bodies, and finally, the proposal that Québécois women writers actively participate in dismantling both gender and national/provincial categories in their attention to violence. Like Butler, I argue that we cannot regulate the representations of women, as we try to keep open the national and provincial categories that are at stake.[2]

SERIAL KILLING AND MONSTROUS RECONSTRUCTIONS

Monstrosity (and the fear it gives rise to) is historically conditioned rather than a psychological universal.

Judith Halberstam, *Skin Shows: Gothic Horror and the Technology of Monsters* (6)

The subject of serial killing has dominated the American, more than the Canadian or the Québécois, imagination. In spite of reports of serial killings in most Canadian provinces – with the possible sixty-three murders by Robert Pickton in Port Coquitlan, British Columbia, the most horrific, and the mass (rather than serial) killing of fourteen women known as the "Polytechnique," the "Montreal Massacre," or the "December 6 Massacre" in 1989 having had the greatest effect – in order to theorize the subject at all, one needs to refer at some length to the topic of serial killing as it has impregnated the American imagination. Although constituting only 1–2 percent of all homicides in the United States, serial killings occupy the public's mind because of the often gruesome nature of the crimes and their exploitation in popular films, television documentaries, and true crime novels – making legendary the likes of Charles Manson, Jeffrey Dahmer, or the fictitious larger-than-life Hannibal Lecter. Especially in the twentieth and twenty-first centuries, they are also the "stuff" of white, middle class paranoia and moral panic: the domain of the ordinary white, suburban male, the Ted Bundy who, intelligent, has a morbid fascination with college co-eds, or the BTK (Bound, Tortured, and Killed) serial killer who preyed on his neighbours over a thiry-year period. As a recent article on true-crime novels has pointed out: "Serial killers, pedophiles, and the like are the suburbs' heavily overworked bogeymen. We choose to pay attention to them because of their quality, not their quantity ... it is evidence of a society more and more terminally bored, coddled and protected from real threat, distant from living death ... Never in the history of the great white American suburb has so much murder been committed for so many by so few" (Ross 77).

Halberstam also points out that "serial murders have something of a literary quality to them – they appear with a predictable (serial) regularity and each new one creates an expectation; they involve a plot, a consummate villain, and an absolutely pure (because randomly picked) victim; they demand explanation; they demand that a pattern be forced onto what appears to be 'desperately random'[3] ... Serial killings, like chapters in a periodical, stand in need of interpretation and their interpreters (like the police, the tabloids, the public, the detective, the psychologist, the critic) produce the story that the bodies cannot tell ... Telling does not mean finding a story in the unconscious that fits, it means inventing the unconscious, and inventing the unconscious so that it can lie well enough to keep up with the fiction of everyday life" (172). In other words, real-life and fictional serial killings and killers mutually reinforce each other, escalating both public fear and moral panic.

When we think of serial killers, we usually think of the murderers as men, the victims as women. In his *Serial Killers: The Insatiable Passion*, David Lester proposes that "the modern serial killer is a failed bourgeois who stalks university women and other middle-class victims" (34). Joel Norris, in *Serial Killers: The Growing Menace*, links such killing to domestic and social violence. The feminist sociologist Jane Caputi stresses gender in interpreting sex crimes and, in "American Psychos: The Serial Killer in Contemporary Fiction," gender in serial killing in particular. Taking Jack the Ripper as the quintessential (and thus male) serial murderer, Caputi argues that this killer's appearance at the end of the nineteenth century coincided "not only with a powerful movement of Western Feminism, but also with the rise of the popular press and mass media, the invention of the camera, the mass production and distribution of pornography, the medical inventions of gynecology and psychoanalysis, and the technologizing of weapons" (*Sex Crime* 12). Caputi thus links what are often presented as extraordinary crimes (singular in that serial killing emphasizes a single murderous figure) with broad social changes, with crime formulas, as practised by the media, for example, and with the world of mechanical reproduction.

Caputi is not so naive as to argue for any simple correlation between representation and reality. Nonetheless, in "American Psychos" she proposes that in contemporary fiction, the "border between representation and reality is more porous than conventional thought allows" (101).[4] Like other murder analysts, Caputi suggests that the figures mythologized by society represent deeply buried cultural desires and fears. She believes that the serial killer is one such figure, its mythic representations (for example, as "the preternatural, enigmatic, eternal genius" 102) designed specifically to terrify women. The appearance of the serial killer figure in films, novels, and short stories, according to Caputi, offers a certain legitimacy to "misogyny and femicide" (102), the latter term coined by Caputi to isolate the killing of women because of their gender. Caputi's association between misogyny and serial killing connects, too, to the contemporary backlash against feminism. Her statistics suggest that approximately 74 percent of the world's serial killers are located in the United States where feminism is well ensconced, and the backlash against it is particularly severe. This association even has links with what Caputi and others call "ecocide," the "characteristic eroticization of domination" (104), which leads to the cannibalizing of the natural world. "Patriarchal culture," she claims, "does indeed require the ritual sacrifice of women, sometimes called witches, sometimes prostitutes, sometimes even feminists" (108).

Indeed, some of the current critical literature on serial killers – in criminology, sociology, history, cultural studies, film studies, and gender studies – frames its discussion around the public's view of these repetitive murderers as monsters, wild beasts, vampires, sadists, stalkers – in short, "as totally other as can be imagined" (Jenkins 111). Although there are instances of female serial killers (Aileen Wuornos being the most infamous (see chapter 1), the stereotype almost always includes the qualifier "male." The mythologizing of the serial killer through popular culture, moreover, is most commonly accomplished by male crime fiction writers, novelists, screenwriters, and film directors. From *Helter Skelter* to *American Psycho* and from *Silence of the Lambs* (and its sequel and prequel) to the novels of Stephen King, men frequently create images of male serial murderers who stalk, torture, kill, and even eat female (or young homosexual male) victims – the latter action interestingly "copied" by certain recent Quebec and French women writers about violence.

More recently, however, there has been a new interest in female serial killers – most likely as a result of some of the gender assumptions and media frenzies discussed in chapter 1 on the contextualizing of violence and gender – not in an attempt to show that the number of women who kill in a serial manner comes even close to that of men, but rather to point out that women can be violent, have, and do commit multiple murders. In addition to telling and retelling Aileen Wuornos's story – to which I shall briefly return – these researchers have been attempting to shed some light on the prevalence and the nature of serial crimes committed by women.

Michael and C.L. Kelleher, in their *Murder Most Rare: The Female Serial Killer*, point out that serial killing is increasing in the United States, although it remains rare. Despite the fact that there are different types of serial murder, the common definition used by law enforcement agencies is rather narrow: "the act of murdering three or more individuals in a period of thirty days or more" (4). The authors prefer their own definition: "the murder of at least three individuals in which each lethal act was separated from the next by a discrete cooling-off period" (5–6).

According to Kelleher and Kelleher, female serial killers are more successful than their male counterparts: "Female serial killers are able to carry out their crimes for a median duration of over eight years before the killing is stopped – double that of the male serial killer. For a variety of reasons, the female serial murderer is much more successful at avoiding apprehension than her male counterpart. Her choice of weapons, generally careful selection of victims, and methodical planning of the crime, combined with a strong social bias that denies the likelihood of a female serial killer, make this criminal significantly more successful than the male serial murderer" (7).

Female serial killers are rarely involved in sexual homicide – the typical motivation for male serial killers. They prefer to victimize children, the elderly, a lover, or a spouse. Rarely do they attack an adult stranger – a point that runs counter to what I shall bring out in the short stories discussed here. When a woman teams up with a partner in killing, however, she can perform as a sexual predator. Of course, regardless of the nature of these crimes, they are usually underreported because of the social bias that maintains certain assumptions and stereotypes about women, as seen above and discussed in my first chapter (Kelleher and Kelleher 8).

Kelleher and Kelleher have identified different categories of female serial killers and killings – a listing that is extremely interesting. Without giving the lengthy descriptions of each type, it suffices to list their classifications: black widow (as discussed in chapter 1); angel of death; sexual predator; revenge; profit or crime; team killer; question of sanity; unexplained; unsolved (11; see also Skrapec 243–4). Using this classification system, they examined nearly a hundred cases of serial murder committed by women, half of whom were American. They found a wide age range within which a female claimed her first victim – from fourteen to fifty-five. The typical female serial killer began killing at the age of twenty-five, however. The average number of years during which the woman killed varied according to her motive and method; those who killed for profit killed for a longer period of time, and sexual predators tended to kill over very short periods of time (13–14).

With nicknames such as Queen Poisoner, Lady Bluebeard, Mrs. Bluebeard, Giggling Grandma, Beautiful Blonde Killer, Suicide Sal, Lonely Hearts Killer, and Black Widow – names that connote a less lethal form of violence, as contrasted with the more violent names used for male serial killers[5] – these female serial killers were most successful when motivated by reasons other than sex and when operating alone: "In such a scenario, the perpetrator is usually mature (in her mid-twenties or older) and carefully plans each crime. She is most likely to use a weapon or killing technique that is difficult to discern (such as poison, lethal injections, simulated accidents, or suffocation), and she may exhibit rather long cooling-off periods between attacks. Unlike the male serial killer ... the female perpetrator who operates alone will usually target victims with whom she has some relationship or who are dependent on her for care ... [She] will usually attack her victims in her home or place of work" (Kelleher and Kelleher 15–16). She is most likely a "quiet killer," methodical, in a position of trust and responsibility, careful, deliberate, socially adept, highly organized, and secretive. And yet – most important – she has no reliable profile (Kelleher and Kelleher 16–17).

Taking aim at feminists and what she sees as their co-opting of female serial killers into concerns about violence against women, the controversial Patricia Pearson has nonetheless written a fascinating chapter, "Woman as Predator," in her *When She Was Bad*, in which she highlights a number of important points. Basing her study initially on the case of Dorothea Puente of Sacramento, California, who, dubbed as the "Arsenic and Old Lace Killer," was convicted in the late 1980s of murdering eight boarders at her rooming house – victims whose cheques and benefits she had been collecting for two years – Pearson goes on to echo much of what Kelleher and Kelleher had highlighted, as well as to provide additional information about female serial killers. She notes that 17 percent of known American serial killers are women (a figure that appears in other studies, as well, although other researchers have used 10–15 percent as the more appropriate figure: see Jenkins 151) and that at least twenty-five of them have been arrested and convicted since 1972. However, in our "collective amnesia" (Pearson 156), "they failed to take hold in our collective psyche as monstrous, and therefore as resonant. No female serial killer has the mythic force of the classic predator. We find it impossible to perceive of them as frightening creatures. There is no Jane the Ripper" (153). As I have already noted in other chapters, even when a woman is tough or violent, she is often deemed to be not as tough or as violent as a man (see Inness, 65–73; chapter 1 of this study).

Films warn us that female predators choose men as their victims, men who are led astray by their lust for smooth and clever, sexually dangerous women[6] – and Aileen Wuornos does fit in here, at least as having been sexually dangerous. But in reality, it is the young, old, disabled, and lonely who are usually the victims of these female murderers (Pearson 155). These women killers are place-specific, operating in their own homes, in hospitals, in boarding houses, and in nursing homes. One study of the victims of twenty-two solo female serial killers in the United States between 1972 and 1992 found that 43% of their victims were in their killer's custodial care, 57% were poisoned, 29% were smothered, and 11% were shot (Pearson 154).

Noting that the FBI's Behavioral Science Services Unit (of *Silence of the Lambs* fame) is responsible for having defined the crime of serial killing in the United States in 1978 and for having developed certain profiles of serial killers, Pearson notes that this psychological profiling has failed to develop a profile for the place-specific serial murderer. There are consequently, according to this FBI unit, no female serial killers, since the overwhelming majority of such killers are place-specific criminals who remain in what is referred to as their "comfort zone":[7] "Until recently, women have had much more constricted geographic mobility in both their routine activities routes and their comfort zones. As a result ... female predators are 'trappers' rather than 'stalkers'" (Pearson 160; see also Skrapec 258, 260–1). As I shall show below in my discussion of two short stories, even fictional female serial killers operate in their own local territories, although neither at home nor at work. These protagonists also (ironically and humorously) reflect the belief that some female serial killers cultivate a sense of themselves as moral creatures who are killing in order to do good (Pearson 169) or ridding the world of those who are bothersome or too demanding (Skrapec 253) – not too different from some female infanticides who confess that they killed their children in order to save them from the mean world (much like Élaine in *La Fissure*) or because they heard a divine call to save their offspring from the devil (echoing Andrea Yates). After all, society tells them that women are supposed to help others and make the world a better place.

As Pearson interestingly concludes:

> The marked difference in public response to male and female serial killers reflects the difference in our archetypes of gender, but it also speaks to the effect on our sensibilities of their modus operandi. The violence they do is less visible, less offensive to us, somehow ... If they mutilate a body, it's usually for purposes of disposal, not for display. They rarely engage in sexual assault. Yet their crimes are equally expressive of their politics. The female serial killer's version of sexual defilement will either be robbery or the sabotage of intellectual and political authority, because that is how she conceives of masculine power. Aileen Wuornos robbed all the men she killed in "self-defense" ... [Others] profited from insurance policies, bank account transfers, the sale of their victims' possessions ... No less than with male killers, these women seem to be commenting contemptuously on staples of power – intellectual, financial – that society has hitherto denied them. They are vandalizing men's temples of prestige. (170–1)

Alternatively, as Candace Skrapec suggests, if the crimes of female serial killers seem unrelated to considerations such as monetary gain, the key to understanding a woman who kills repeatedly may be "the recognition that by killing, she experiences herself as someone who matters, as the agent of some substantial happening and, by inference, as powerful" (263). In this perspective, these "real" violent women are similar to the female writers I have been discussing, analysing, and trying to understand. Through the textual lens of their fictional female characters, they are taking life and death into their own hands by imitating, subverting, transgressing, tearing apart, and completely re-framing the world in which they live.

As noted in chapter 1, however, society still has a difficult time seeing a woman as powerful in her own right: she may be powerful as the nurturing mother and Madonna; she may be powerful in her (dis)guise of evil, sexual whore. But these roles are consistently defined in reference to men, and any gender "border crossing" is labelled alien and monstrous, and is severely punished. Such complexities of gender played into the media representation of the Aileen Wuornos serial killing case, for example. Kelleher and Kelleher point out that Wuornos, persistently and mistakenly portrayed in the media as the first American female serial killer, could indeed be the first American female sexual serial killer who acted alone in committing her crimes, "if one discounts the possibility that she acted in self-defense when she murdered seven men in Florida in 1989 and 1990" (75). Of course it is precisely this plea that was rejected by the court that sentenced her to death, since her jurors could see only the dichotomous stereotype of any woman and not this masculinized female who was a prostitute and yet had a serious same-sex relationship. They could look beyond her long history of abusive encounters with men, but not hear the woman who cried out: "'If I didn't kill them, you know, of course, I mean I had to kill them ... or it's like retaliation, too. It's like, you bastards, you were going to hurt me'" (as quoted in Kelleher and Kelleher 82). What they saw, instead, was a woman who had transgressed all cultural constructions of the passive female to become a monstrous sexual predator and serial killer, coded as a lesbian. Indeed the title of the 2003 feature-length film made about Wuornos is *Monster*, referring both to people's belief that any serial killer is monstrous and to the "extremely monstrous" nature of a female serial killer in particular.[8]

NATIONAL AND GENDER ALTERNATIVES

> Canadians import and eagerly consume American cultural products but reconstitute and recontextualize them in ways representative of what consciously, albeit ambivalently, distinguishes Canada from its powerful neighbour.
>
> Frank Manning, "Reversible Resistance: Canadian Popular Culture and the Canadian Other" (8)

Bombarded and invaded by the mass media and popular culture of the United States, Canada and Quebec frequently succumb to the influence of American icons (chapter 2). In addition, like Labrèche's Sissi in *Borderline* and Yvon's Threesa in *La Cobaye*, for example, they are enamoured of American rock and roll, and other aspsects of mass culture (chapter 3). In my analysis of *Les Miroirs d'Éléonore* I emphasized that despite writing in French, Hélène Rioux has integrated the music and the cult following of Jim Morrison and The Doors into a number of her works. We know that one of her major – and recurring – fictional characters, Charles/Leonard Ming, passes freely from the United States to Canada, carrying his violence to the north, and is described as a former American Marine in Vietnam. Such content and imagery contrast dramatically with Canada's persistent (and yet mythical) reputation as a "peaceable kingdom" and with a long history of metaphors referring to its relative passivity: note even the term used by historians and political scientists for Quebec nationalism in the late '60s and early '70s – the "Quiet Revolution." But the reality of American violence and our fascination with it seem increasingly to be winning, as Quebec's (female) authors (and some other Canadian writers, as well – Margaret Atwood for one in *The Robber Bride* and *Alias Grace*) write about violence and violent crimes and about female murderers and female serial killers.

For some of Quebec's women writers in particular, such national gendering provokes satire, irony, and parody (chapter 3). How better to evoke such forms of humour than to appropriate – and perhaps regender – the most potent and violent of American cultural icons, the male serial killer? By feminizing the monstrous, some Quebec women writers are creating female (and male) serial killers who stalk, torture, and kill both male and female victims. Their work, permeated by extreme paranoia and terror, often plays with the sexual conventions, subtle irony, and punning of Gothic horror: Hélène Rioux's Eléonore and Charles/Leonard Ming in several of her short stories and novels; Anne Dandurand's female metro murderer; and Claire Dé's betrayed wife turned serial killer are prime examples.

Of course one can argue that there has been a long history of violence in Quebec literature – violence sometimes even committed by women or at least instigated by them (as analysed in chapter 3). But here I am speaking of serial killing, brutal male and female killers, and "serious" gender crossing. Some of these characters have mysterious motives; others kill almost for sport. What I have been trying to determine, is whether interest in this subject is a result of certain women writers picking up on a general trend or whether it is simply a fad on the part of these particular writers. As I have been asking throughout this study: has violence infiltrated all world cultures and cultural output as economics and demographics change; has gender become so confused and diffused that it is leading to violent acts; or are some women simply beginning to mimic the violence traditionally associated with men?

There is some tension between sociological and psychological approaches to serial killing, particularly in discussions of its representation in literature. Michelle Massé, in *In the Name of Love: Women, Masochism and the Gothic*, addresses the intersections between the sociological and psychological dimensions of violence which are connected with the national and individual regendering that is being considered here. She mentions that women "do not merely reflect" systems of sado-masochism but also help to shape them since, by internalizing "its values, they potentially remain victims or accomplices" (5). Massé asks a question certainly relevant to the fictions I am discussing: how did women come to interweave love and pain? How is it, she asks, that women are so often depicted– as in many Gothic fictions, for example – as desiring the position of victim? As many critics of the position of women in Gothic structures have done, Massé analyses the Bluebeard story, a highly eroticized and evocative story to which women writers such as Margaret Atwood are drawn. Broadly, Massé relates masochism as a psychological mechanism to reflections and representations of "cultural patterns of domination and subordination" (239), linking psychological and social constructions most notably demonstrated in Gothic form.

Such connections occur in Rioux's portraits of the serial killer Charles (changed to Leonard in a subsequent novel) Ming,[9] and correspond most closely to the views of the public, the media, and crime enforcement officials of such a "human beast." Rioux manipulates the reader's perception with her layered narratives, ambiguous speakers, and the introduction of a female translator in a later novel. Throughout the short story "L'Homme de Hong Kong," which introduces us to him, Ming is stereotypically described as a former street child, a child thief influenced by stories of Charles Manson and by American music, a torturer of animals, and an aficionado of slaughter houses.[10] As an adult "enemy number one," he is compared to several wild animals, with a "natural instinct"[11] to stalk, victimize, torture, and kill – "getting off" on the vampiristic pleasure of blood, in a classic case of sexual or lust murder (Skrapec 246).

As shown in chapter 3, the literary construction of Ming becomes increasingly complex as it is intertwined with images of other potentially homicidal men (and perhaps women) who stalk, brutalize, rape, and kill women because of their own austere, orphaned childhood, love of necrophilia and vampirism, and monstrous association of sexuality/orgasm and death. Here, with the exception of Ming himself, the serial killers are ordinary men turned monsters, the "monster at home" (Halberstam 15), who, like the real-world killer John Wayne Gacey, appear normal and ordinary in the rest of their lives. As for Ming, he is fused with the bestial world: "The killer is panting, starving, this hunted beast ... But from far away the beast sees the woman walking, it smells from afar the odour of this woman coming toward it, musk, lily of the valley, the beast holds its breath, hunches up, ready to pounce. Its eye gleams in the dark" ["Le tueur halète, affamé, cette bête traquée ... Mais la bête perçoit de loin le pas de la promeneuse, elle flaire de loin l'odeur de celle qui vient vers elle, musc, muguet, la bête retient son souffle, se recroqueville, prête à bondir. Son oeil luit dans le noir"] (*Miroirs* 178).

In her later novel *Traductrice de sentiments*, Rioux focuses entirely on Leonard Ming through the role of a female translator who struggles with the translation from English into French of Ming's autobiography, written while on death row before he is put to death in the electric chair. Constructed by his self-reflective gaze, which is supplemented by the gaze of the translator and public/media attention, Ming's persona exudes evil, sadism, and bestiality; he is shown as a virtual caricature of serial killers, as popular culture constructs them. Nourished by his Rambo-like years as a Marine in Vietnam, Ming calls himself a warrior, a hunter, and lures men, women, and children into his "bunker" for subsequent slow torture and murder, like Charles Ng. He is James Gibson's "New Warrior," gone astray since the U.S. defeat in Vietnam.[12] Most significantly, Ming has labelled himself "Wolfman" which the translator wants to make "Thanatos," although her editor insists on "Homme-loup"[13] (Wolfman). As someone who knows how to "transform himself into a beast," this "black angel, ninja" ["ange noir, ninja"] (*Traductrice* 87) identifies with a lone wolf, following the law of the jungle, and has had tattooed on his left biceps a wolf head with enormous fangs. Mythomaniac" ["fait tatouer sur son biceps gauche une tête de loup aux crocs démesurés. Mythomane"] (*Traductrice* 87). Is he a maniacal mythmaker, a pathological liar who invents his own unconscious in his published autobiography, with the ability to "lie well enough to keep up with the fiction of everyday life" (Halberstam 172)?

As early as 1982 Anne Dandurand published the title story in *La Louve-garou*, a collection with Claire Dé about a female serial killer – clearly using the feminized version of a "Wolfman" or a "Homme-loup" – here a female werewolf or "bogeywoman."[14] We are alerted – perhaps – but also deceived by the opening illustration, which depicts a man and three women seated at a table, with the arms/wings of a female mulatto "creature" serving them drinks and "embracing" them. In the narrative, however, it is not the female mulatto server who is the killer. In fact, the reader knows the sex of the serial killer only by the title of the story. Tension begins with the opening line: "I had been waiting for several victims for almost an hour" ["J'attendais quelques victimes depuis bientôt une heure"] (11). The killer first spies on a couple and other guests in a café, creating an image of dangerous sensuality in the man (unusually identified as a cobra, generally paired with a female image), who enjoys imagining the woman naked under her clothes and having women fall to their feet before him; she then stalks the couple. This connection between sensuality and stalking widens to include sexuality, with a graphically described scene of love making. Linking sex and orgasm with violence and death, the killer shoots the two lovers at their orgiastic moment: "Orgasm and blood. They passed away without losing their climax" (13) ["L'orgasme et le sang. Ils s'éteignirent sans perdre leur joie"] (13). The epilogue comes in the form of a jolting newspaper report that informs the reader that we are dealing with a female serial killer: "MONTRÉAL-MATIN, July 15, pages 2 and 3: The she-werewolf has struck again. Two lovers staying in a rooming house. Thirteenth and fourteenth inexplicable murders" ["La louve-garou a encore frappé. Deux amants descendus dans une maison de chambres. Treizième et quatorzième meurtres inexplicables"] (13) Dandurand here mixes fiction, folklore, gender-crossing, and reality in her story of sex and serial murder. Most significantly, she turns upside down the defined characteristics of a male serial killer and of violent men in general and grafts them onto a woman.

In analysing the technology of monsters, Halberstam focuses on the "man next door," who becomes the wild, monstrous, homicidal beast in Gothic tales and in films such as *Silence of the Lambs*. But what of the "female next door," who, like a vampire – or she-werewolf/bogey-woman – kills serially?[15] Some of these female fictional characters who "live next door" turn to serial murder for more specific reasons, such as responding to a divine call or to avenge marital infidelity. In the wonderfully interesting short stories "Maîtresse des hautes oeuvres/ Underground Requiem" by Anne Dandurand and "À Tuer/Kill" by Claire Dé, for instance, no reference whatever is made to the animal or monster world as their two female murderers go about their killing sprees. They don't stalk; they don't torture; they don't even seem to get much pleasure out of their murders. Dandurand's metro killer, in fact, is seen as a protector of harmed people and, in one case, almost as a female Dr. Kevorkian who puts a drug-addicted/HIV positive young man out of his misery. And the aggrieved wife in Dé's story goes only as far as to describe herself as manic-depressive, haggard and unkempt – certainly not the vampire/wolf of Ming's jungle or even the female werewolf of Dandurand's "La Louve-garou." Has serial monstrosity here been feminized by female writers in their construction of the female serial killer? Or are these killers perhaps not seen as monsters/beasts because their murders are either moralized or warranted, as both Pearson and Skrapec have noted: either they murder people who prey on weaker humans or they eliminate the "nasty" people of the urban metropolis – the meter maid, the exploitative shop keeper – even the baker of lousy croissants.

Such victims, who seem to be chosen in a "desperately random" fashion – to borrow, once again, from the terminology of *Silence of the Lambs* – are inevitably part of a pattern created by the serial killer and only later understood by law enforcement officials. According to some studies: "While in actual cases, serial killers' victims are predominantly women, children, or young men [with the seven men killed by Aileen Wuornos clearly an exception], in film, serial killer characters' victims are adults and equally distributed between the sexes" (Epstein in Ferrell and Sanders 70–1). In other words, if Jack the Ripper, the Green River Killer, Gary Ridgeway, and Robert Pickton preferred prostitutes, Ted Bundy liked college coeds with long, brown hair, and John Wayne Gacey and Jeffrey Dahmer lusted after young boys, the religiously inspired killer in Dandurand's short story kills only adult men, and the female murderer in Dé's story makes no distinction between men and women. Charles/Leonard Ming, with his sidekick, Gary Sheldon (aka Leonard Lake), seems to have desired the slow torture and death of small groups, often families, so that the mother could watch the murder of her spouse and the rape and murder of her child, after which she might have own her nipples, breasts, and feet cut off.

The association between sexual pleasure, orgasm, torture, and death is explicitly stated in all of Rioux's depictions of Ming and Sheldon, whereas no such relationship exists in the serial killings of Dandurand and Dé – reflecting studies that show that female serial killers are not motivated by sexual desires. Dandurand's underground female killer does, however, have a pattern in her choice of victims: those who harm harmless others, within her 150 kilometres and 3,600,000 square metres of metro tunnels – her fairly extensive "comfort zone." Dé's female murderer also remains local and place-specific as she rids her neighbourhood of the types of annoying people that bother all of us on some days. Although neither of these female killers appears to start out with the idea of harming any specific sex, Dandurand's killer ends up murdering only men who harm women – with the same purpose as Bella in *Dirty Weekend* – while Dé's killer has a wider range. After killing an Arab shopkeeper, she worries: "I hope it won't be peddled as a racist crime. For me it's not the Arab. It's humanity in general" ("Kill" 27) ["J'espère qu'ils ne colporteront pas que c'est un crime raciste. Moi, ce n'est pas les Arabes, c'est l'humanité en général"] ("À tuer" 27).

The victims cannot talk to us. We get their story only through its construction by the killer, omniscient narrator, or translator, just as in real life we hear from the journalist, the television reporter, and the enforcement official: we – that is, readers of gruesome tales, viewers of snuff films, the "audience" of spectacles of torture and death on the public square. Reams of psychological, sociological, and media papers have been published about voyeurism, a dark side of human nature – what it is that makes many want to view violence, get high on catastrophes, applaud at fight scenes, and laugh nervously at horror movies.[16] In "Consuming Cannibals: Psychopathic Killers as Archetypes and Cultural Icons," John Grixti links our attraction to portraits of killers such as Jeffrey Dahmer with contemporary culture's "consuming interest in the subject of murder." Indeed, he maintains, "we all carry a destructive beast beneath our skins" (95).

Such voyeurism on the part of many people comes, however, not only from "beneath the skin" of individuals but also from a clear purpose on the part of governments and those in power. As noted in the previous chapter, until the nineteenth century public executions in America were exploited as opportunities to harangue citizens on the dangers of sin (see Halttunen 14, 136, 144; Jones 50–1). As Michel Foucault reminds us, the guillotine may have shortened the amount of time needed for a public execution, but the Revolution also granted it the status of a theatrical ritual (*Surveiller et punir* 22). As Foucault states, the role of the people in such spectacles is double-edged: "People were summoned as spectators: they were assembled to observe public executions and *amendes honorables* ... Not only must people know, they must see with their own eyes. Because they must be made to be afraid; but also because they must be the witnesses, the guarantors, of the punishment, and because they must to a certain extent take part in it" (*Discipline and Punish* 58) ["Il est appelé comme spectateur: on le convoque pour assister aux expositions, aux amendes honorables ... Il faut non seulement que les gens sachent, mais qu'ils voient de leurs yeux. Parce qu'il faut qu'ils aient peur; mais aussi parce qu'ils doivent être les témoins, comme les garants de la punition, et parce qu'ils doivent jusqu'à un certain point y prendre part"] (*Surveiller et punir* 70).

Richard Rhodes[17] speaks similarly of the use of torture and death as a public spectacle, including the complex roles of those in charge and those watching: "So hangings, brandings, whippings, blindings, amputations, beheadings, garrotings, scorchings by fire, breaking with hammers, breakings on the wheel before or after death, throat slashings, drawings and quarterings ... became dual-purpose public events: They reminded locals of who was in charge, while the resulting corpses, left exposed on gibbets ... along the roads leading into the district until they rotted away, offered a warning to strangers happening by" (226).

In the United States in the late twentieth and early twenty-first centuries, however, how can one account for the continuing popularity and financial success of Hollywood westerns, World War II and Vietnam war films, the novels of Stephen King, slasher/splatter films when the very same public that is riveted by them is filled with paranoia and panic about the crime rate and global terrorism? Even in Canada, as Reid Gilbert demonstrates, "Canadian culture is constituted by a 'double iconography': a split between an external [American] set of images appearing in current Canadian popular entertainment and an often inarticulate internal set of images kept private and coded" (18).

Rioux's Ming goes to great length to give us an answer, in "his" short story and two novels: the audience's love for the public spectacle of horror and violence – in Ming's view – is also motivated by the heightened sense of sexuality and orgasm that it arouses, for the "audience" as well as for the person tortured and eventually killed:

> He also emphasizes that executioners have existed in all periods, all over the world ... In his autobiography, he lingers over these torments and their refinements ... the public has always enjoyed the spectacle of torture. His argument goes like this: cruelty can also be respected, practised like an art. All one has to do is open a newspaper, no matter what newspaper, to get a measure of how thirsty people are for this type of sensual pleasure ... He adds that one only has to note the success of horror films and pornographic magazines, the infatuation for chains, whips, handcuffs and other such accessories. His videos, he says, have given spectators, men and women, their wildest orgasms ... And his autobiography, he was convinced, would become a bestseller, would be translated

into all languages. Death, cruel death, is a powerful aphrodisiac. With his wealth of experience, he affirms this as well: the tortured body reaches an undreamed of sexual pleasure. [Il fait aussi valoir que les bourreaux ont existé à toutes les époques, dans tous les lieux du monde ... Dans son autobiographie, il s'attarde sur ces tourments et leurs raffinements ... [L]e public s'est toujours régalé du spectacle des supplices. Son argumentation repose sur ceci: la cruauté peut aussi être considérée, pratiquée comme un art. Il suffit d'ouvrir un journal, n'importe lequel, pour mesurer combien le peuple a soif de ce genre de volupté ... Il ajoute qu'il suffit de constater le succès de films d'horreur et des revues pornographiques, l'engouement pour les chaînes, les fouets, les menottes et autres accessoires. Ses vidéos, dit-il, avaient donné aux spectateurs, hommes et femmes, leurs orgasmes les plus sauvages ... Et son autobiographie, il en était convaincu, deviendrait un best-seller, serait traduite dans toutes les langues. La mort, la mort cruelle, est un puissant aphrodisiaque. Fort de son expérience, il affirme également ceci: le corps torturé accède à une jouissance incoupçonnée.] (*Traductrice* 191–2)

Serial killings and killers sell: even Dandurand's metro murderer gets her computer-portrait in the newspaper. Dé's disturbed killer knows that her estranged husband will read about her exploits the next day in the society column (the "women's pages") of *Le Monde*: "A crazed woman executes several people in the first arrondissement (Dé, "Kill" 66) ["'Une forcenée exécute plusieurs personnes dans le 1er arrondissement'"] (Dé, "À tuer" 31). This is the "stuff" of mass media, public relations, legend/myth making, pulp fiction, crime/detective fiction bestsellers, snuff films, and Hollywood blockbusters.

Charles/Leonard Ming painstakingly filmed the bestial torture and slow death of his victims – as did the real-life Charles Ng – and lucratively sold these "real" snuff films to people who paid large sums of money to watch scenes of "authentic" horror. He also created his own legend by writing and selling a million copies of his autobiography, complete with photographs, which detailed (or created) the events of his murderous life. It is, in effect, a tabloid self-portrait of a serial killer, to be translated into fourteen languages, and soon to come to Hollywood-financed theatres in local neighbourhoods. Unfortunately, Ming deposited all of his hard-earned monies from filmmaking into a bank account that he could not touch while "on the road," and the revenue from his best selling autobiography will not help him after a seat in the electric chair. But the myth will go on, aided by translators such as Eléonore.

TRANSGENDERING

If transvestism offers a critique of binary sex and gender distinctions, it is not because it simply makes such distinctions reversible but because it denaturalizes, destablizes, and defamiliarizes sex and gender signs.

Marjorie Garber, *Vested Interests: Cross-Dressing and Cultural Anxiety* (147)

This very myth invites multiple interpretations, given the complex and sometimes contradictory portraits of serial killers we have seen and read about and the intriguing power these monstrous criminals hold over many of us. To add to this complexity, in the recent criticism on serial homicide, horror and Gothic literature and film, and cultural criminology (see Jenkins, Clover, Halberstam, and Ferrell and Sanders), the serial monster is frequently referred to and analysed as a border crosser, an ambiguous figure who passes through boundaries between rationality and savagery (Jenkins 110), breaks down gender and genre, and defines the subject as at least partially monstrous (Halberstam 23, 27): "The monster always represents the disruption of categories, the destruction of boundaries, and the presence of impurities and so we need monsters and we need to recognize and celebrate our own monstrosities" (Halberstam 27). Such statements suggest that the serial killer – real and fictional – is both human and beast (or neither), male and female, real and fictitious, narrator and protagonist, gazer and gazed, constructor and constructed, writer and translator, murderer and victim, subject and object, and audience/reader/viewer and killer. The serial murderer needs to be interpreted as part of the darkest – and perhaps non-gendered or ambiguously gendered – side of each one of us.

The confusions and boundary crossings that I have been studying are particularly striking in the works under examination here. Who effects such transformations, for example, in Rioux's fictional world of translation and murder? If serial killing is usually committed by men against women or young boys, and their fictional counterparts are usually constructed by male writers and film makers, whose narratives does the female writer construct? Who assumes the gaze while writing about violence?

I have argued in chapter 3 that, even though the layered stories of Rioux's *Les Miroirs d'Eléonore* may be imagined, invented, and narrated by a female free subject, the male gaze continues to dominate and control. In *Traductrice de sentiments* the construction of the male serial killer is accomplished by Ming himself in his videos and published autobiography, by the media, and by the female translator who, in a certain sense, becomes the male killer's accomplice or co-conspirator. Ironically a former translator of Harlequin-type romance novels ("romans de *bons* sentiments" – novels of good feelings) for a female audience when she never used "je" because she could remain outside as an "ironic" witness, Eléonore (perhaps the same as in *Les Miroirs*, perhaps her mirror-image) has agreed to translate Ming's autobiography in order to try to understand how someone can torture and mutilate people, especially children. Her own daughter died when very young, after having been adopted by others, and Éléonore has often imagined her possibly violent death. Indeed, Éléonore herself reveals her very violent imagination even before "meeting" Ming – although in stereotypical scenes in which the female remains the victim of the violent male (*Traductrice* 25, 30–1, 41, 60, 133, 137).

With a constant sense of guilt at being a part of something monstrous, however, the narrator/translator begins to move into Ming's violent world, as she imagines her own actively violent scenes, now associated with torture and sex (albeit in the conditional tense): "A man's cock that I suck into my mouth. I think that I could bite; with my teeth, I could sever, I could cause a lot of pain, force my victim to implore, to scream, to promise ... I could continue to bite ... feel my mouth fill up with blood ... Orgasm is close to death. Go all the way. *No kill, no thrill*" ["Le sexe d'un homme que j'aspire dans ma bouche. Je pense que je pourrais mordre; avec mes dents, je pourrais sectionner, je pourrais faire très mal, obliger ma victime à implorer, à crier, à promettre ... je pourrais continuer à mordre ... sentir ma bouche se remplir de sang ... L'orgasme est proche de la mort. Aller jusqu'au bout. *No kill, no thrill*"] (*Traductrice* 142). In another imagined scene, Éléonore even becomes sexually involved with Ming, referencing both Jim Morrison's "Crystal Ship" and Rimbaud's "Le Bateau ivre," as she personifies the latter's "I is Another" ["Je est un Autre"]: "I dance with him. *Cristal* [sic] *Ship* is playing very loudly, I drift on a fragile vessel, I dance in the arms of death, I dance dance in his arms, his deathly sex gets hard against my stomach. He invites me to his place, I listen to the call of death, I am that call" ["Je danse avec lui. *Cristal Ship* joue à tue-tête, je vogue sur un vaisseau fragile, je danse dans les bras de la mort, je danse danse dans ses bras, le sexe de la mort se durcit contre mon ventre. Il m'invite chez lui, j'écoute l'appel de la mort, je le suis"] (*Traductrice* 151).

The major translation issue for Éléonore is that she must use "je" if she is going to lend her voice to Leonard Ming, find words in French that will accurately translate his words in English: "I can't stay on the surface any more. I enter him, our identities blend together. Between him, dead, and me, alive, a terrifying intimacy is created" ["Je ne peux plus rester à la surface. J'entre en lui, nos identités se mêlent. Il se crée entre lui mort et moi vivante une terrifiante intimité"] (*Traductrice* 139). Making this symbiosis even more ambiguous, Eléonore also begins to identify with at least one of Ming's female victims, as described, of course, by Ming himself: "I have the killer's voice, but I am the victim" ["J'ai la voix de l'assassin, mais je suis la victime"] (*Traductrice* 151).[18] She has assumed both the speaking/active violent subject-position and the object-victim-position in this new "roman de *mauvais* sentiments" (novel of bad feelings), turning the Harlequin romance on its head.

She ultimately fuses with the killer, with the victim, with death:

> I write this, the words burn me, I become Nancy tied up to the chair, urine runs between my thighs, my body, stiff with pain, I close my eyes ... I scream, I feel the blade, but I don't die, I am Nancy naked and torn apart on a wooden table, blood streams between my legs, [in a ritualistic act of female genital mutilation, since excising the clitoris makes some men hard (152)] chains fit tightly around my wrists ... I continue to write, I write "I," all forms of torture, I inflict them, I am at the same time the tormentor and the victim, my right eye runs down my cheek, I am that eye, I beg and I inflict at the same time ... I am Leonard Ming ... I implore my executioner to finish me off and I am the executioner, I am Gary Sheldon who spits, I am Leonard Ming who ejaculates on Nancy's face, and I am that face. [J'écris cela, les mots me brûlent, je deviens Nancy attachée sur la chaise, l'urine coule entre mes cuisses, mon corps, raide de souffrance, je ferme les yeux ... je crie, je sens la lame, mais je ne meurs pas, je suis Nancy nue et écartelée sur une table de bois, du sang ruisselle entre mes jambes, des chaînes enserrent mes poignets ... Je continue à écrire, j'écris "je," toutes les tortures, je les inflige, je suis à la fois le tourmenteur et la victime, mon oeil droit coule sur ma joue, je suis cet oeil, je supplie et j'inflige en même temps ... je suis Leonard Ming ... j'implore mon bourreau de m'achever et je suis le bourreau, je suis Gary Sheldon qui crache, je suis Leonard Ming qui éjacule sur le visage de Nancy et je suis ce visage.] (*Traductrice* 152–3)

Such fusion is common in genres that, like the Gothic, play with borders. In this instance, however, the female becomes so fused with the male serial killer that she metaphorically ejaculates on the face of the female victim (with whom she continues to identify). She has achieved a horrifying level of phallic appropriation.[19]

Rioux has created a female writer and a female narrator and yet constructs a male serial killer. But with the introduction of a female translator of female romance novels, gender becomes confused, the gaze becomes ambiguous, and the feminized monster becomes part of the dead male murderer, his popularized legend, his female translator, the "ordinary" reader – of both the English and the French versions of his story – and by extension, all of us. As Halberstam suggests, the monster is a "meaning machine" that can "represent any horrible trait that the reader feeds into the narrative," representing gender, race, nationality, class, and sexuality. It is a narrative technology that produces "the perfect figure for negative identity" (Halberstam 21–2) – much like Auden's "negative creation" with which I began this chapter.

It is not always easy to decipher the gender of some serial killers, just as the gender of Buffalo Bill in *Silence of the Lambs* is purposefully and frighteningly ambiguous. Rioux's clearly seem androgynized. In Dé's and Dandurand's serial killing world, however, both narrator and killer are female – a woman has assumed the gaze as she writes about violence in a narrative of her own voice, which relates her own serial killing activities. What is one to make of these monsters? And does the reader, especially the female reader, identify (or negatively identify) with these murderers?

Luise von Flotow has argued that such texts focus essentially on the current human condition, as many live with poverty, violence, drugs, and death (58–61), while Philip Jenkins, basing his comments on sociological and criminological studies, states that "the bizarre and violent actions of killers are seen as a reflection of social tendencies: modernization, urbanization, industrialization," in short, dehumanization (134–5). Clearly, Dé's and Dandurand's short stories document a frenetic and violent modern urban life where a money card and a knife are the signs of a new religion or the mark of our era (Dandurand, "Maîtresse des hautes oeuvres" 29; "Underground Requiem" 28).

At the root of the complex interwoven love letter at the core of Dé's story, Dandurand's requiem, and Rioux's romance-novel-turned-male-serial-killer-translation lies humour, a black ironic stance that underscores Reid Gilbert's belief that "Canadian culture is consciously ironic, parodic, and self-satiric" (19). The objects of the sarcastic attacks are indeed modern urban life, along with men, women, religion, ritual, sexuality, serial killing, all cultural patterns of domination and subordination, and national and personal gender stereotypes. In addition, some studies have shown that when depressed men and women experience deep anger and hatred, depressed men often use outwardly directed violence and depressed women turn that violence inward onto themselves (James). Rioux's translator has suffered the death of her own child. Similarly, Claire Dé's female narrative "I" is depressed, as she writes a letter/diary entry to her lover/husband, "For you. My sweet love" (Dé, "Kill" 49) ["Pour toi. Mon cher amour"] (Dé, "À tuer" 19) – thereby parodying the "typically female" epistolary form and style and the "common" use of the "journal intime" by women. Initially she plays the role of the discarded woman and reacts in a "normal" way: "I'm laying into everybody. Five in the morning. The hour of despair. They said so. Yesterday. On TV" (Dé, "Kill" 49) ["Je bute tout le monde. Cinq heures du matin. L'heure des désespérés. Ils ont dit ça. Hier. À la télévision"] (Dé, "À tuer" 19)] – presumably on one of those daytime talk shows for women, with "experts." She is also under medical treatment and has been identified as manic-depressive, according to the stereotypical path of a depressed and angry female.

But then parodying the serial actions of some angry, depressed men, and even using their typical weapons, she decides to commit premeditated murder in the form of "serial revenge" (Caputi) against her male partner, who has taken a mistress, and against herself in a self-deprecating fashion, replaying in her mind the scenes that led to her discovery of this other woman. She uses sex to confuse her victims: she wears only underwear under her raincoat; the elderly pawnbroker dies with an erection; she opens her coat in front of a policeman and then shoots him in the mouth. She puns; she jokes; she smiles; she continues to kill. She easily strangles a meter maid dressed in baby blue (a colour for baby boys) by confusing the victim, who is taken unaware because she is being attacked by another woman (no one expects women to be violent). She finally encounters the ultimate male authority figure – the policeman. But she is disappointed with her murder of him: "It spurts. But not as nicely as with Alain Delon. In *Three Men to Kill*. In that one it sprayed across a mirror. A dazzling red. Here it's his acne-covered face. His gelatinous brain. Everything. That splatters me. That's the pain. At the movies. Death is always prettier. Like things on TV" (Dé, "Kill" 65).[20] ["Ça gicle. Mais pas en aussi joli qu'avec Alain Delon. Dans *Trois hommes à abattre*. Là, ça arrosait un miroir. Un éblouissement de rouge. Ici, c'est tout son acnéique physionomie. Sa gélatineuse cervelle. Tout. Qui m'éclabousse. C'est ça aussi qui est pénible et pernicieux. Au cinéma. La mort toujours jolie. Ou n'importe quoi à la télé"] (Dé, "À tuer" 30). Confusing fiction/film with reality, her parody attacks and subverts the ways in which American mass culture dominates the Canadian/Quebec (and French) imagination.

But then she feels that she is going to crack; she hates herself for having known about her husband's affair and denying it; she has lost confidence in everyone, including herself. After her male-like killing spree, she turns her anger back onto herself .

> Let's hope they don't take too long. And don't hesitate to use their guns. If I have to, I'll kill some more. Anyone within my reach. So the cops will use. Their guns. On me. Forgive me my love. You won't have your croissants this morning ... I couldn't resign myself. To you no longer touching me. No longer making love to me. I couldn't resign myself. To leaving you. To killing you. Or to killing myself. Desperate. From always hoping. From still hoping. Every moment. That you love me, love me, love me. (Dé, "Kill" 65–6) [Pourvu qu'ils ne tardent trop. Et qu'ils n'hésiteront pas à se servir de leur arme de service. S'il le faut j'en abattrai d'autres. Tous ceux qui passeront à ma portée. Que les gendarmes se servent. Contre moi. De leur arme de service. Pardonne-moi mon amour. Tu n'auras pas tes croissants ce matin ... Je ne me résignais pas. À ce que tu ne me touches plus. À ce que tu ne me fasses plus jamais l'amour. Je ne me résignais pas. À te quitter. À te tuer. Comme à me tuer. Désespérée. D'espérer toujours. D'espérer encore. À chaque instant. Que tu m'aimes, que tu m'aimes, que tu m'aimes.] (Dé, "À tuer" 31)

Ultimately, she cannot "pull it off," and she reverts to being the stereotypical female object-victim.

With her wonderful parodic killing spree (killing three or more individuals in a thirty-day or longer period of time, but without a discrete cooling-off period in between murders), has Dé's serial monster been feminized, or with her pathetic cry at the end, has she simply returned to a feminine stance, unlike her literary sister, Bella, from Zahavi's *Dirty Weekend*? Dé's narrator, it seems, has learned much from the popular legends and representations of American male serial killers and yet has remained in her female skin and mind. This female serial killer is violently slashing, shooting, and strangling because of rejection by a man. But also like many male serial and mass murderers, who either commit suicide at the end of their rampage or allow themselves to be killed, she prays for an end to her misery – at the hands of the local authorities. She has confused film and reality, the public and the private, and fused depressed male and female criminals.

As for the female narrator, serial killer, of Dandurand's "Maîtresse des hautes oeuvres"/"Underground Requiem,"[21] she obeys what she feels is a divine call to abandon her comfortable life and move to the metro in order to commit murder. As I have shown above and as Jenkins also argues: "It is quite common for acts of extreme violence to have as their goal some imagined religious motive, such as a response to a divine commandment. Receiving orders from supernatural forces is a common manifestation of paranoid schizophrenia, a condition believed to be present in a number of multiple homicide cases" (Jenkins 205). But this female serial killer, in a parody of the male religiously inspired murderer, is quite practical (and charitable) before becoming a murderer: she kills her old cat, gives away her winter clothes to the homeless, and deposits two suitcases of clean laundry in the lockers of the bus station above the Berri-UQAM metro station (Dandurand, "Maîtresse des hautes oeuvres" 29; "Underground Requiem" 27). She is also cautious about changing her line of work too quickly – at first living in hotels while working below (rather than on) the streets.

She still assumes the guise of the sexual predator (she dresses like a hooker) to lure her victims into her grasp, but she then adds "a woman's touch," placing her cardigan sweater under the head of a rapist she has just murdered. Using a wide range of religious terminology when she documents her life and her crimes,[22] she becomes the good Samaritan and the stereotypical protective mother figure – not only ridding women of their assailants but ridding the world of yet another male gaze: "I shot forward like a hawk, grasped the guy by the hair and put out his eyes with precise strokes, pushing the knife in just far enough to not touch his brain. One second, the gaze of a maniac, two seconds, streaming eyeballs" (Dandurand, "Underground Requiem" 32) ["Je courus comme un râle, agrafai le quidam par les cheveux et lui crevai les yeux avec précision, en enfonçant la pointe du couteau sans toucher le cerveau. Une seconde, le regard d'un déséquilibré, deux secondes, des orbites coulantes"] (Dandurand, "Maîtresse des hautes oeuvres" 32). And after her mercy killing of the HIV-positive drug addict, the final scene that she presents to the reader is her return to the stereotypical nurturing mother figure – singing an ancient lullaby until the young man dies. For Anne Dandurand, the serial monster has finally – and parodically – been feminized, transgendered.

PARANOIA AND GENDERED ASSUMPTIONS

Fear, as we know it, is gendered … I want to reread the case histories of paranoia in order to unhinge monstrosity from masculine power and fear from feminine victimhood.

Judith Halberstam, *Skin Shows: Gothic Horror and the Technology of Monsters* (108)

It is evident that writers such as Hélène Rioux, Anne Dandurand, and Claire Dé are fascinated by gendered violence and crime. In addition, they will not allow the United States to hold a monopoly on violence and glorify the masculinization of a country that stereotypes victims as women, as it can at times stereotype as feminine the less violent country of Canada and the "nation" of Quebec.[23] This genre of literary fascination seems to be increasing: Margaret Atwood's novel *Alias Grace* for example, is based on a nineteenth-century murder case in which a young servant woman is arrested for the murder of her employer. Like their English-Canadian counterpart, Rioux, Dandurand, and Dé all refuse to leave murder in the hands of men (American, Canadian, French, or Québécois). Even though homicide files indicate that violent murders – including serial killings – are much more frequently committed by men than by women, and male writers and filmmakers (with some recent notable exceptions) most often position women as victims rather than perpetrators, it seems apparent that the resulting dichotomy keeps gender roles in place. Jane Caputi, in her essay "American Psychos," suggests that the eroticization of domination and subordination creates just such divisions. It is certainly true that in our collective imaginations women, especially mothers, are not associated with killing, because such an association is too frightening. Does patriarchal culture try to keep the "right" to kill and the power of death out of the hands of women? Is it that women, who control birth, are prevented from controlling death? Fiction writers, of course, are free to experiment with all our fears and desires. Caputi observes that women's serial revenge is "an increasingly prevalent theme in fiction authored by women" (108). What might be gained by such fictional revenge? All the writers discussed are transgressing borders, particularly the borders within which we lead our gendered lives – once again making the link between the real and the imaginary – and they often do so with viciously sarcastic and wickedly humorous language and form, as well as with frightening detail.

The serial killers of Rioux, Dandurand, and Dé are all gender border-crossers, taking life and death into their own hands, and tending to "slip into [their] opposite," thereby trying to alter the familiar binary codes of their fictional worlds (Halberstam 179). These are not your typical neighbourhood monsters. Nonetheless, they oblige us to question violence, with its gendered categories, to investigate the rationale of paranoia, and to think about how victims – and perpetrators – become constructed. They focus on the connection between violence as it is reported and violence as it is fictionalized. They shock us by altering our expectations, and then they expose the gendering of our own assumptions.

CONCLUSION

Women Imitating Men or the Feminization of Violence? Re-Framing Gender in North American Cultures

In *Sexing the Self*, Elsbeth Probyn tells us that "in the name of ... connecting (or at least acknowledging) the crevices within and between the previous chapters," she would try to proceed "'en guise d'une conclusion' (which roughly translates as 'in the manner of a conclusion,' although [she likes] the idea of being 'disguised as a conclusion' better)" (165). Given the complexity, breadth, and timeliness of my topic, such a stance seems most appropriate: to present here "in the manner of a conclusion," some disguised concluding remarks. Let me state at the outset that I see the questions that I have raised and continue to raise as among the most interesting aspects of my research, especially since there are no simple and comprehensive answers to them and since they set forth, "en guise de conclusion," my efforts to approach significant societal and literary issues.

I shall begin with one U.S. view of Canada, current at the time of writing, at least. In my final note for chapter 5, I speculated that "with the advent of the George W. Bush Republican administration and especially since the United States commenced a war in Iraq – with many countries worldwide, including Canada, against this military action – the United States has indeed been seen by many as particularly 'macho' and 'cowboy-like,' in the finest Texan sense. In a gendered comparison, therefore, Canada (like France) has been seen by some Americans as less virile, less tough, and by extension, more feminine."

I hasten to add, however, that more recently, the American view of Canada – and even its worldwide reputation – has been changing, not only because of international events (former prime minister Jean Chrétien's refusal to back the United States in its war in Iraq, for example) but also because Canada has increasingly been seen as a socially progressive nation, with its move toward the legalization of same-sex marriage (Massachusetts notwithstanding) and the use of marijuana for medicinal purposes. If Canada is now being seen as a "hippy nation," with its opening up of social questions, then, as Antoine Robitaille points out, Quebec has the most radical of positions on these issues – positions in opposition to those of many Americans today (61). Suddenly it seems to many that the formerly "boring" Canada is in the forefront of the postmodern world, with Quebec in the lead.

But if journalists like Jean Dion[1] are even only partially accurate in their assessment of (some of) the world's continued opinion that Canada is boring, unexciting, and virtually invisible, then why should I even consider these Quebec women writers and their imagined violent female protagonists as being able to offer new perspectives on gender in North American cultures? As I elaborated in my Introduction:

> The literature of this postcolonial, francophone, North American society provides a fruitful case study. At the crossroads of a French theoretical, cultural, and linguistic tradition, an English-Canadian dominance, a British presence, and especially a powerful and sometimes smothering U.S. popular culture and media, Quebec society and the literature that reflects and helps create it constitute an interesting laboratory for broad scholarly investigation. Canada is perceived as, and indeed *is*, a far less violent country than the United States (although not as peaceful as one commonly thinks, according to crime statistics), and within Canada, Quebec is one of the least violent provinces. Quebec, in its own right, is not in an "and/or" polarity, not in a binary opposition – hence my second link. In its own search for identity and self-determination, it is on the decentred margins, at the boundaries, but its form of violence, of revolution, has always been quiet – a war of words and political stances, often in reaction to constitutional experiments by the Canadian federal government. Its literature similarly provides experimental representations that go beyond defined genres, refusing to be limited by the binary.

In this study, I have been speaking about Quebec, Canada, the United States, North America – and indeed the world – in reference to sex, gender, and violence, and their representations in literary form.

Second, I have been speaking about gender stereotypes and assumptions that are also global in nature and in acceptance. "My" writers and their creative imaginations are in the privileged, postmodern and postcolonial position (without getting into the discussions about the use of these terms in Quebec and Canada) of speaking from the margins, from a certain distance, from a safer and less violent space. If I "read" representation and "reality" together, the perspectives of these writers can offer important and helpful insights for our quest to understand our cultures better.

It might be beneficial to keep in mind the questions I have been posing throughout this study, some of which I now restate as suggested answers or guideposts, as I see them. I can then offer some possible "causes" for such violent female imaginations, along with some (disguised) conclusions – that will perhaps remain unanswerable or go forward as questions for further study. My first set of re-stated and answered questions regards North America. I have asked, for instance, if the literary texts studied here can be read in conjunction with a debunking of the myth of Canada as a "peaceable kingdom," given an acknowledged rise in violence in Canada, and especially with the feared resemblance with what Canadians see – rightfully in many instances – as a far more violent United States. I contend not only that these texts can be thus studied but also that they need to be. If it is possible to read certain Quebec literary texts that depict lethal violence perpetrated by women in conjunction with a Québécois society in one of the least violent Canadian provinces – as I have tried to do in this study – can it be said that U.S. violence and crime have moved north and in some way influenced Quebec as well as the rest of Canada? Although any answer to this question cannot be definitive and "proven," it seems impossible that the violence of U.S. society and culture has not, again in some way, influenced Quebec and Canada, as it has the rest of the world. As I have suggested above and in response to a question raised in my study, certain women writers in Quebec do seem able to provide different perspectives and narratively re-frame gendered cultures, precisely because they can distance themselves more easily from their more violent neighbour to their south, even though they are also inevitably influenced by the powerful popular culture and life style of the United States. By so doing, these women writers have clearly transformed at least some of their protagonists from fragile female (objectified) subjects into powerful and violent actors in a North American landscape, creating both an interior – perhaps more typically Québécois – universe and a more typically American violent "adventure." And if Québécois culture has been influenced by an American culture and lifestyle that are perceived as more violent (and indeed more enthralled by violence), and if Québécois culture has also imitated, absorbed, and made its own that U.S. culture and way of life, can we speak of the violence evident in certain Quebec literary texts as its own brand of *américanité* or North Americanness? Perhaps unfortunately, this appears to me to be at least one recent aspect of Quebec's literary Americanness.

Second, I have been concerned with female violence and the effect of media reports of an increase in such crime. I have noted that there has indeed been an increase in female crime both in the United States and throughout Canada, but I have also stressed that the base numbers remain small and that the major bulk of this increase comes from property crime (although there has been an increase in aggravated assault – not in homicide – in the United States and a small increase in homicide among younger females in Canada, but not in Quebec). There has also been an increase in the number of female gangs and women inmates, but I have noted that the larger number of female prison inmates, in particular, has primarily been the result of law authorities' growing willingness to prosecute women. It remains true, however, that the *public perception*, fuelled as it has been by the media, is that rates of female violence are rising in Quebec, as well as throughout Canada and the United States. It seems, therefore, that these women writers may well have been influenced by North American media, "buying into" widely held – although inaccurate – popular convictions and public moral panics. But can one say that the representation of violent life in fiction (and especially in popular culture), and the belief in violence as a viable option for settling issues and providing justice have been negative influences on the artistic creators in Quebec, especially on these fictional women? Once again, no direct link or simple cause and effect can be proven here, although one cannot deny the powerful attraction of representations of violence. Indeed, as I have mentioned, there are transnational cultures that, at the same time as decrying and berating U.S.-stimulated internationalism/globalism, continue to watch, consume, and produce cultural products rife with erotica, sexuality, and violence – products that are increasingly created by women. Can one say, therefore, that the "high" literature that I have brought forward here is likewise in the process of collapsing into or of creating – indeed has perhaps already created – a metafiction of popular culture, influenced by sensationalized mass media reporting that is at the same time anxious about and obsessed with issues of violence? I believe so.

I have also – and most prominently – been concerned with the question of gender and its representation. Are these literary women protagonists, as envisioned by female writers, merely imitating males in the more recent outward direction of their anger and hostility? Are these violent literary protagonists/subjects with agency "really" violent, or are they simply postmodern versions/objects of the typical female as traditionally constructed in the male gaze – the age-old dangerous, desirable, and yet grotesque whore, vamp, vampire, Eve, and seductive sex kitten? They are certainly perceived as even more monstrous than their male counterparts because they have crossed over the boundaries of acceptable gender roles, even if they are using violence as "an instrument of criticism in the interest of a feminist *critique*" (Hanssen 213).

So why, then, have these women writers imagined and created such female subjects, who transgress and thus re-envision and re-frame gender in North American cultures? Even more troubling are the possible interpretations of what I see as a noticeable progression in this new and recent work by women: from expressions of eroticism and pornography, to sexual violence, to indiscriminate violence – all in the hands (and minds) of women who question gender and its social roles and who ultimately play with and destroy former power hierarchies. Questioning gender and desiring female agency as expressed in the form of eroticism and pornography may be understandable, but why do these representations then move into realms of violence? These are the questions at the core of my research, and to which I have attempted to provide some plausible answers throughout this book. Other people's perspectives on violence and gender and on gender relations will undoubtedly result in differing views.

I have also dealt with some of the methods that Quebec's women writers have used in their efforts to reverse, subvert, transgress – and indeed annihilate – these power relationships: character development, language, form, narrative, intertextuality, and tone. Some of the female characters they have created are deadly serious, and as such their murderous actions reflect the complexity of their intimate lives, the status of women and girls, and their anger toward an unjust societal system. Others get their point across with wickedly dark humour. With their biting irony and parody, are these "tough, action" girls/women mimicking and mocking the sexuality and violence of traditionally expected and accepted male attitudes, roles, and actions through their own feminine/feminist "macho" exploits of sexuality and violence – even when their actions result in (serial) murder? In my view, there is little doubt about this. Or is it that these literary works are reflecting the reality that gender has just become so confused and diffused in our current world that it is erupting indiscriminately in violent acts, with both men and women exhibiting their frustrating experiences with (post)modern life? I believe that this is true as well.[2]

In other words, I offer the view that violence – and even "gender-bending" at some level – has infiltrated most of the world's cultures and cultural output as economics and demographics have changed. Is this literary violence a trend among certain women writers or is it simply a passing interest or fad? Or is it a stage that needs to be gone through in order for women writers to express their anger toward and retaliate against a still hegemonic patriarchy that tries to keep the (literary) "right" to kill and the power of death out of the hands of women? As I noted at the end of my last chapter, fiction writers are free to experiment with all of our fears and desires. What stands to be gained by such fictional revenge? Can it effect any positive change? Ultimately, have these women writers imagined and created violent female characters in order to "feminize" violence, re-gender violence, go beyond gender toward the non-binary oppositions and boundaries between the self and the other, as they attempt to re-envision and re-frame gender in the violent cultures of North America? These are some of the questions that I present as needing further investigation and study.

Now that I have actually come to the point where some might expect me to offer solutions or at least intelligible, if not probing concluding remarks, Probyn's (no pun intended) "en guise d'une conclusion" becomes strikingly appropriate. I have raised a number of what I believe are significant and crucial questions, and I hope that my analyses of some of these literary texts offer some clues to what, in my view, is redefining gender in much of our (North American) cultures. By way of underscoring my "conclusions," let me reiterate my observations. It seems clear to me that an increasingly violent North American culture has influenced the mindset of some contemporary women writers from Quebec. Similarly, these women must be reacting to and reflecting the assumption that there has been a major increase in female criminal activity, as reported and sensationalized in the media, especially since their literary texts, in some sense, are to be "read" as being incompatible with the "reality" of female crime in Quebec. In addition, virtually no one can be isolated from the influence of American and global popular culture, which now often portrays women, at least on the surface, as tough, strong, and at times deadly (or at least as "deadly dolls"). Perhaps these violent literary women are indeed part of a fad or a needed "stage" that allows certain female writers to reflect and create a space for the expression of understandable anger and frustration with a society that is still not changing rapidly enough. Or perhaps such representations of violent women will remain with us. We cannot know.

Depictions of changing and more fluid gender roles have also penetrated the popular mind; however, I do not think that these writers have created violent women in order to imitate men. That would be too frightening, and besides, why would they want to be like those who are so violent, as Sherrie Inness has asked (*Tough Girls* 180)? Violence is not justified, in my view, under (almost) any circumstances, and it would indeed be unfortunate if female agency had to be achieved in such a manner. Instead, these writers can create characters and plots in such a way as to make fun of men in fictional form, without imitating them in real life. But they do want to appropriate (phallic) power in some sense and try to have men – and other women – understand better the complexities of their lives, their sexual desires, and even their sometimes aggressive tendencies. By doing so, perhaps they will be able to induce men – those in authority and those on the domestic front at home – to recognize more openly their own "tough guise" – to realize that being male does not require one to be invulnerable, mean, abusive, or violent. As Jackson Katz has so eloquently and effectively shown in his documentary *Tough Guise*, strong and "real" men are also vulnerable, just like women.

I also certainly do not think there is any basis for a "blame-it-on-feminism" cause for female violence – whether that violence is "read" separately as real or fictional or whether the two are seen in conjunction with one another. There is clearly some link between the real and the imaginary, however, and these women writers are valiantly using their texts to demonstrate it. Both real and fictional women are exploring, sharing, and needing to transgress in order to experience for themselves and to express the power of agency (if even in the imagination), formerly and still in the hands of men, so that they can then work with men and women to make that shared livable space more equitable.

From the "in-between," "third," or liminal space of a less violent society on the North American continent and with the outlook and standpoint of strong, "tough," and feminist women, these literary females can provide the rest of us with an important perspective on the violence of our continent and our world, as well as on the gender divisions that in great part cause this violence. Through their creative imaginations, these women writers of Quebec are making us take a step back, think more deeply and honestly, and perhaps do something about the gendered violence that plagues us all. They have stopped at nothing short of re-framing gender in North American cultures.

Notes

INTRODUCTION

1 Sadly and ironically, since these opening sentences were originally composed, one wonders if the world has not reverted to a binary system, an "us *vs.* them" mentality – especially in the minds of many U.S. citizens in the wake of September 11, 2001, global terrorism, and the war in Iraq. For a number of politicians – as well as for a number of radical groups – the world is divided into the Judaeo-Christian West, dominated by the United States, and the proponents of certain forms of Islam. Despite this view of an inevitable "clash of civilizations," as old as the Crusades, I continue to believe that binary systems are dangerously simplistic and that indeed the only way for people to come to terms with differences is to study, understand, and appreciate the constructed borders that separate us.

2 As early as 1993, however, Elsbeth Probyn spoke of "feminists with attitude," in her text, *Sexing the Self* (138).

CHAPTER ONE

1 All these issues will be treated in later chapters on novelistic representations of infanticide and serial killers, along with the work of other scholars such as Karen Halttunen, Ann-Louise Shapiro, Ann Jones, and Richard Rhodes.

2 A day after that editorial appeared, another article in *The New York Times* revealed that a number of U.S. states had been quietly rolling back some of

their most stringent anti-crime measures, including those imposing mandatory minimum sentences and forbidding early parole (Butterfield). And five days later, *The Washington Post* reported that executions were down sharply across the United States for the second year in a row, with dramatic declines in the leading death-penalty states of Texas and Virginia (Masters).

3 Boisnard is guided in his interpretation by both Theodor Adorno and Jean-François Lyotard, along with Jacques Sivan.

4 Figures for 2003 were reported in October 2004.

5 See UCR 2003, Section 4, Table 42.

6 See UCR 2003, Section 7, Appendix 1, Methodology.

7 See UCR 2003, Section 4, Appendix 1, Methodology; Table 29, Persons Arrested. One person may of course be arrested several times during the year for the same or different offences.

8 See UCR 2003, Section 4, Persons Arrested.

9 These figures are based on *Preliminary Semiannual Reports*, January–June 2004. (13 December 2004).

10 Wallace, *Crime Statistics in Canada 2003*, 17, Table 1.

11 For example, the United States does not use the category of sexual assault in its listings and does not include sex offences, except for forcible rape and prostitution, under violent crimes. It does not, in addition, include possession of stolen goods and fraud in its category of property crimes. Canada does not include arson under property crimes.

12 Wallace *2003*, 19, Table 3.

13 This was the first substantial increase in over a decade and was driven by a 72% increase in counterfeiting and an increase in property crime.

14 Wallace, *Crime Statistics in Canada 2003*, 1, 19, Table 3.

15 Wallace *2003*, 5.

16 Wallace *2003*, 17, Table 1; 19, Table 3.

17 Wallace *2003*, 6.

18 Logan, *Crime Statistics in Canada 2000*, 6.

19 Savoie, *Crime Statistics in Canada 2001*, 1.

20 Wallace *2002*, 18, Table 3.

21 Wallace *2003*, 19, Table 3.

22 Wallace *2003*, 6.

23 Wallace *2003*, 7, 19, Table 3; Dauvergne, *Homicide in Canada 2003*, 1.

24 Data from UCR 2003, Section 4, Table 42; UCR 2002, Section 4, Table 42.

25 Wallace *2003*, 25, Table 9.

26 See Wallace *2002*, 22, Table 7.

27 See Wallace *2002*, 22, Table 7; Savoie, *Crime Statistics 2001*, 19, Table 6.

28 Logan, Table 6.
29 Mann bases her work on the Uniform Crime Reports (UCR), the National Center for Health Statistics (NCHS), prison studies, anecdotal studies, city studies, studies from the United States and Canada from 1958 to 1996, as well as her own six-city study.
30 UCR 2002, Section 4, Table 33.
31 UCR 2002, Section 4, Table 33.
32 UCR 2001, Section 4, Table 33.
33 UCR 2002, Section 4, Table 33.
34 UCR 2002, Section 4, Table 33.
35 UCR 2003, Section 4, Table 33.
36 UCR 2002, Section 4, Table 33.
37 UCR 2002, Section 4, Table 33.
38 UCR 2002, Section 4, Table 33.
39 UCR 2002, Section 4, Table 33; UCR 2003, Section 4, Table 33.
40 UCR 2003, Section 4, Table 33.
41 UCR 2003, Section 4, Table 33.
42 UCR 2003, Table 42.
43 UCR 2003, Section 4, Table 33.
44 UCR 2003, Section 4, Table 33.
45 Logan 12.
46 Dauvergne, *Homicide in Canada 2003*, 9.
47 Savoie, *Homicide in Canada 2002*, 9.
48 Dauvergne, *Homicide in Canada 2001*, 13.
49 Fedorowycz, *Homicide in Canada* 2000, 12.
50 Dauvergne *2003*, 20, Table 12.
51 Savoie *2002*, 18, Table 12.
52 Dauvergne, *Homicide in Canada 2001*, 14.
53 Fedorowycz 2000, 13.
54 Fedorowycz 2000, 13.
55 I shall return to this issue in chapter 5 on female serial killing.
56 For an interesting discussion of "Methods of the Multiple Murderess," see this chapter in Patricia Pearson's *When She Was Bad: Violent Women and the Myth of Innocence*. For an equally interesting, although quite biased, view of women and firearms, see Mary Zeiss Stange and Carol K. Oyster's *Gun Women: Firearms and Feminism in Contemporary America*. In this second study the authors present the issue in a manner similar to the pornography and censorship debate among feminists. Believing that the anti-gun stance of second-wave feminists has provided an image of women as inept and

unstable, Stange and Oyster agree with women who are fighting back and refusing the "good girl" and victimhood labels. But, as I shall discuss, this portrait of armed women also plays into the stereotype of the "bad girl."

57 I shall be considering the figures on infanticide in chapter 4.

58 Once again, figures for infanticide will be treated in chapter 4.

59 DeKeseredy cautions, however, that these figures must be read with the understanding that they are founded on very small base figures.

60 Women as killers do make news when it is a question of infanticide or serial killing.

61 The relationship to causes of domestic violence here is evident.

62 In French the *Larousse* Dictionary defines "l'uxoricide" as the murder of a wife by the husband. Interestingly, there is no specific term to refer to the murder of a husband by a wife. The term, "maricide" (matricide), or the expression, "homicide conjugal féminin" [female conjugal homicide] is used, therefore, in a series of articles in a 1996 issue of the Quebec journal *Criminologie*, in which these issues are explored. According to Sylvie Frigon, "maricide" was historically severely punished as a crime of "little treason" ["petite trahison"] and as "the crime of the century" ["le crime du siècle"] by women, considered outside penal logic – in contrast to men who fit neatly into established criteria of jurisprudence (Frigon, "Editorial" 4, 5). In a subsequent article in the same issue, Frigon also discusses two specific cases: the long-celebrated and even now folklorized case of Marie-Josephte Corriveau, condemned to death in 1763 for "maricide" and whose body was suspended in a cage in the public square in Lauzon, Quebec for one month; the case of Angélique Lyn Lavallée who was acquitted in 1990 in the first case tried in Canada under the defence of "Battered Woman's Syndrome" and whose outcome caused what Frigon sees as a "rupture épistémologique" since legal defences were finally seen through the woman's perspective (Frigon, "L'Homicide conjugal féminin" 14, 17).

63 Some chapter titles in the 2004 translation are slightly different.

64 Joanne Bernier and André Cellard wrote a "fun" article in the 1996 special issue of *Criminologie* in which they trace some court records of the "syndrome de la femme fatale" [the "femme fatale" syndrome] in "maricide" (matricide) court cases in Quebec between 1898 and 1940. They see the historical representation of the criminal woman in Quebec, a strongly patriarchal society, as particularly interesting since "in murdering or in participating in the murder of her husband, she threatened the very foundation of society" ["en assassinant ou en participant au meurtre de son époux, [elle] menaçait les fondements mêmes de la société"] (30). In what the authors describe as a court spectacle, they give evidence of judges and

magistrates who consistently used inflammatory and stereotypical language to refer to the defendants and their crimes, thereby reflecting popular indignation, itself reflected in newspapers: "an odious murder, the most brutal, the most horrible, the most abominable, an enormous scandal ... with terror and disgust, the most complete act of treason, almost unbelievable, the terrible act ... that would make a good subject for a sensational novel, a horrible struggle ... in front of the crucifix hanging on the wall, society ... outrageously violated, before the crucifix and religious images, the accused ... indifferent ... cold ... with a heart of stone ... impassive ... and even smiling at times ... calculating ... inhuman ... Machiavelian, a tigress" ["un meurtre odieux," "le plus brutal," "le plus atroce," le plus abominable," "un scandale énorme ... avec terreur et dégoût," "l'acte de trahison le plus complet," "presque incroyable," "l'acte terrible ... qui ferait bien le sujet d'un roman à sensation," "une lutte atroce ... en face du crucifix pendu à la muraille," "la société ... outrageusement violée," "en face du crucifix et des images saintes," "l'accusée ... indifférente ... froide ... avec un coeur de pierre ... impassible ... et même parfois souriante ... calculatrice ... inhumaine ... machiavélique," "une tigresse"] (33–42).

65 As Myers and Wight have entitled their collection of essays, *No Angels: Women Who Commit Violence.*

66 For example, "Women who kill are in. Women who whine are out" (Scholder 165).

67 She cites the FBI Uniform Crime Reports for 1992 as her sources for these figures, although it is unclear how she was able to include the 124% increase from 1986 to 1995.

68 See James Oliver.

69 Since the 1980s there have been a number of studies conducted on lesbian sexual violence, as reviewed by Lori Girshick in her own 2002 study, *Woman-to-Woman Sexual Violence.* Girshick reports that "prevalence of lesbian domestic violence is estimated to approximate that in heterosexual relationships, between one-fourth and one-half of all relationships. The American Bar Association estimates the prevalence of domestic violence among gay and lesbian couples as between 25 and 33 percent. It claims that each year, between 50,000 and 100,000 lesbians are battered" (Girshick 13). Girshick claims in her own work that homophobia and biphobia are closely linked to the problem of woman-to-woman sexual violence (19).

70 I shall return to the issue of female serial killers in chapter 5.

71 I can, of course, update these images with the ironic and stereotypical image of violent and tough women in the Oscar-winning film *Chicago*, with the two films about Lara Croft, with the successful revival of *Medea* on

Broadway in 2003 (see Brantley, "The Attack of the Killer Moms on Broadway"), and with the widely viewed television productions of *Buffy The Vampire Slayer* (where women rule the world) and *Oz*, where women are cast in the roles of powerful and at times violent security prison guards and whose viewing audience is heavily female (see Dilday).

72 One recent example is Elana Gomel's *Bloodscript: Writing the Violent Subject*, published in 2003, in which the author analyses "how violence interacts with narrative to generate identity" (xiv).

73 Similar to what Greg Forter calls "compositional violence" (7).

74 Horvitz cites Cathy Caruth's work, among others, on psychoanalytic and trauma theories.

75 One cannot forget that in French romantic literature, there existed an aesthetic of crime, criminals, and murder. One can find literary violent women and women who kill in works by, for example, Stendhal, Balzac, Mérimée, and Dumas, and later in Flaubert, Gauthier, Baudelaire, and Huysmans. These women, of course, were created and seen through male eyes (Marcandier-Colard, 10, 73–94).

Mireille Dottin-Orsini has added to Dijkstra's inventory of the representation of evil women at the end of the nineteenth century in *Cette femme qu'ils disent fatale*. Mentioning the heroines of Rachilde's novels who are presented as male depictions of female evil and the monstrous, even though created/ imagined by a woman, Dottin-Orsini goes on to document specific authors and works: Jules Lermina's popular illustrated novel, *Les Hystériques de Paris*; Octave Mirbeau's *Le Jardin des supplices* ["The most horrible crimes are almost always the work of a woman ... She is the one who imagines, plans, prepares, and directs them" ["Les crimes les plus atroces sont presque toujours l'oeuvre de la femme ... C'est elle qui les imagine, les combine, les prépare, les dirige"] (40, as cited in Dottin-Orsini 252); *Assassin, espoir des femmes*, a play written by the painter Kokoschka; and the refrain of the necessity of killing dangerous women as found in Zola, Wilde, and Jean Lorrain's *Crimes de Montmartre et d'ailleurs* and *Le Métier de femme*.

76 Both Dijkstra and Gibson have written about harpies and black widow women, as I have noted. This connection between women's violence and their heightened sexual appeal to men has recently been popularized and parodied in song in the successful musical comedy and subsequent film *Chicago*.

CHAPTER TWO

1 UCR 2003, Section 4, Persons Arrested, Table 42.

2 Wallace, *Crime Statistics in Canada 2003*, 16, Table 1.

3 Wallace *2003*, 19, Table 3.
4 Wallace *2003*, 7, 19, Table 3; Dauvergne, *Homicide in Canada 2003*, 1.
5 Dauvergne *2003*, 3, Table 1.
6 Wallace *2003*, 5.
7 Gartner, "Homicide in Canada," 196, Table 7.3.
8 Fedorowycz, *Homicide in Canada 2000*, Figure 2, Table 2.
9 Dauvergne *2001*, Figure 2, Table 2.
10 Savoie, *Homicide in Canada* 2002, 4, Figure 2.
11 Savoie, *Homicide in Canada* 2002, 1, 4, Figure 2; Wallace, *Crime Statistics in Canada* 2002, 1.
12 Dauvergne, *Homicide in Canada 2003*, 3, Figure 2.
13 Gartner, *Homicide in Canada* 209, Table 87.11.
14 Dauvergne *2001*, Table 3.
15 Savoie *2002*, 13, Table 3.
16 Dauvergne *2003*, 14, Table 3.
17 Gartner 210, Table 7.12.
18 Savoie, *Homicide* 2002, 16, Table 8.
19 Dauvergne, *Homicide* 2003, 17, Table 7.
20 Gartner 210, Table 7.12.
21 Gartner 210–11.
22 Dauvergne *2001*, Table 1.
23 Savoie *2002*, 3, Table 1.
24 Dauvergne *2003*, 3, Table 1.
25 It should be noted that violent urban crime, especially homicide, decreased in the United States in the early to mid-1990s but then increased slightly toward the end of the decade and into the twenty-first century (UCR 2002, Section 4, Table 36).

The 2000 Statistics Canada report on homicide also adds a new paragraph on youth homicide that relates to my study: "Youth homicide victimization trends similar in Canada and the United States: Although homicide victim rates in the United States are three to four times higher than in Canada, homicides against children and youth (under 18 years) in both countries share similarities in their trends. In the early 1980s, the trend in homicide rates for males and females in this age group in Canada and the United States was quite similar. However, the American homicide rate for males increased dramatically from 1985 to 1993. Most of this increase can be attributed to males aged 14–17 years and the increased use of firearms in homicides. American females, on the other hand, were homicide victims at a consistent rate over this time period. Since 1993, the homicide rate for American males has declined sharply while Canada's homicide rate for males has been consistent" (Fedorowyz 2000, 13–14, Figure 10). In the 2001 Statistics Canada report on homicide, the section on youth homicide states that homicide committed by youths is the lowest since 1969, with the sharp decline driven by a decrease in the number of males accused of homicide. Males still continue to account, however, for 83% of homicide committed by youth (Dauvergne 14). 2002 saw an increase after three consecutive annual declines of youths charged with homicide, but that number is still lower than the past ten-year average. However, "although most youth homicides were still committed by males, the proportion of females was higher for youth accused (21%) than for adults accused (10%) (Savoie, *Homicide 2002*, 9–10).

And most interestingly, it was reported in January 2003 that "Quebec is perhaps one of only two Canadian provinces still to give its support to the federal registry of firearms, but it is in this province that citizens conform the least to the requirements of the law. In fact, it is in Quebec that the proportion of firearm owners not having a license to carry a gun is the highest. At least 27.4% of people possessing a firearm have not obtained a license" [Le Québec est peut-être une des deux seules provinces canadiennes à encore accorder leur appui au registre fédéral des armes à feu, mais c'est dans cette province que les citoyens se conforment le moins aux exigences de la loi. En effet, c'est au Québec que la proportion de propriétaires d'armes à feu n'ayant pas de permis de possession est la plus élevée. Pas moins de 27.4% des gens possédant une arme n'auraient pas obtenu un permis de possession"] (Buzzetti).

26 The level of Canadian nationalism and patriotism is, however, in dispute (see Millard, Riegel, and Wright; Brody) and more recently has decreased (see "Le Patriotisme est à la baisse au Canada").

27 In a note Dupont explains: "The term 'Amériquan' is used to denote the continental U.S. experience, generally called 'American'; it was proposed by the Quebec geographer Jean Morisset" ["Le terme amériquain est utilisé pour démarquer l'expérience continentale de l'expérience étatsunienne, généralement appelée 'américaine'; il a été avancé par le géographe québécois Jean Morisset"] (1984).

28 It is important to know more from this survey about who was at home to answer a twenty-two minute survey. In addition, one needs the breakdown of people asked per region of Quebec, as the proportion of the total population of the province. As reported in the 13 March 2002 edition of *Le Devoir*, the 2001 census figures indicate that the total 2001 population of Quebec was 7,237,479. Although, bizarrely, there was no listing in this report of the population of Montreal (although it is the second most populous

city in Canada, after Toronto), the populations for the other large cities were: Quebec (682,757), Ottawa-Hull (257,568), Sherbrooke (153,811), and Trois-Rivières (137,507). Statistics Canada reports that the 2001 population of Quebec was 7,410,504 (Savoie 16, Table 3). Earl Fry, in an article about Quebec's relationship with the United States, makes reference to the fact that Montreal represents 44% of the provincial population (Fry 333). This figure would make the population of Montreal between 3,260,621 and 3,184,490 at the time.

29 I shall not review these debates in this study since they are much broader than my chosen scope. References to them, however, can be found in my Works Cited and Consulted. See, in particular, texts by Bouchard, Simon, Seymour, Mathieu, Létourneau, Brière, Morin, Sarra-Bournet, Nielsen, and articles in *Le Devoir* on "Penser la nation québécoise" by Taylor, Bouchard, Jacques, Bourque, Chevrier, Baum, Delâge, Jenson, Létourneau, Cantin, Gagné, and Juteau. In addition, I would like to thank Jennifer Gauthier, who was helpful in discussing this series of articles with me.

30 Others have repudiated this metaphor of Quebec as female and Canada/United States as male.

31 One can also add that perhaps some of today's Quebec women writers have changed this situation to an extreme by writing about violence, erotica, sex, and violent women.

32 This action is similar to the cultural protection policies put into place in other countries such as France.

33 See Acheson and Maule for a more in-depth review of what is referred to as "the mystery of magazine policy."

34 Once again, a full discussion of Canadian and Quebec cultural policies vis-à-vis the United States, and especially in regard to television and film, goes well beyond the gendered scope of my study. See, however, in my Works Cited and Consulted references to texts by Sands, Mulcahy, Gauthier, and Odile Tremblay. I would like, once again, to thank Jennifer Gauthier for having keyed me into the history of Canadian and Quebec film policies as they link to the issue of nationalism.

35 The mention of language as a protective barrier brings up the issue of language as a marker of cultural and national identity and ultimately of sovereignty. Especially in reference to Quebec (and France), it also raises the issue of language laws, viewed by some as essential for protection and by others as dictatorial for members of other language groups. See, in my Works Cited and Consulted, references to texts by Apter, Latouche, and Sarra-Bournet. Concerns over the language of immigrants continues in Quebec, especially in light of a report released in February 2003 by Statistics

Canada, based on the 2001 census, that since 1980 the proportion of immigrants coming to Quebec who use French at work has decreased. Between 1976 and 1980, 56% of immigrants to Quebec used French in the workplace (as contrasted with 29% using English). Since then, the proportion has continually declined, "reaching 49% among immigrants who arrived between 1996 and 2001" ["pour atteindre 49% chez les immigrants arrivés entre 1996 et 2001"] (Boileau A1). This percentage includes immigrants whose native language is French.

36 See her *Hybridité culturelle* as well as her article "L'Appartenance hybride" in Lamoureux, Maillé, and de Sève's *Malaises identitaires*.

37 See the excellent article by Paul Rutherford, "Made in America: The Problem of Mass Culture in Canada," in Flaherty, David H. and Frank E. Manning, eds. *The Beaver Bites Back?*

38 A recent example of another imitation of U.S. television programming in Quebec is the extremely successful *Star Académie*.

39 "The televised novel has permanently come out of the kitchen and has landed with both feet in the domain of the social. The societal televised novels (are) the perfect mix of entertainment, information, education and commercialization" ["Le téléroman est définitivement sorti de sa cuisine pour entrer de plein-pied dans le social. Le téléroman sociétal [est] ce parfait mélange de divertissement, d'information, d'éducation et de commercialisation"] (Nguyên-Duy 151). These television dramas are, however, increasingly inspired by and based on an American model (147, 153), while maintaining their Québécois specificity: "Indeed, if the televised drama distinguishes itself little from American models in terms of generic characteristics, one can see however significant differences in terms of its content, what is open to the translation, fabrication and repetition of a distinct imaginary based on appropriate norms and values. Moreover, it is in the union of the proposed imaginary and its impact on the social that the televised novel is at its most original" ["En effet, si le téléroman se distingue peu des modèles américains en termes de caractéristiques génériques, on note cependant des différences significatives en termes de contenu, ce qui est susceptible de traduire, forger et réitérer un imaginaire distinct, fondé sur des normes et des valeurs propres. Plus encore, c'est dans la conjonction de l'imaginaire proposé et de son impact sur le social que le téléroman est véritablement original"] (Nguyên-Duy 154). One can also regard this televised entertainment as Homi Bhaba's other time/space of writing that is done in the present and yet incoporates the past and the future.

40 See Works Cited and Consulted.

41 This perspective, of course, implies that the American independent film industry (the "indie" that is also in decline in the U.S.) and once again, commercial successes like *Séraphin, un homme et son* péché and *Les Boys* series are not significant. See Gauthier, "Split Screen."

42 *Séraphin* in fact overtook *Les Boys* as the most popular Quebec film ever and was at least partially responsible for an increase from 9.6% in 2001 to 12.5% of the market for Quebec cinema in 2002 (Odile Tremblay "Une Année extraordinaire"). This film, along with *Les Invasions barbares* and *La Grande Séduction*, was also responsible for a huge increase in Canadian dollars in box office receipts.

43 One cannot forget the powerful interplay, as well, with Jean-Luc Godard's *Vivre ma vie* and the music of Marie Laforêt and Serge Gainsbourg in this film.

44 One can add to this discussion of the bestseller in Quebec the huge popularity of the children's novelist, R.L. Stine, whose worldwide success – including translations of his hundreds of books into French – has made him a publishing phenomenon, producing far more volumes than does J.R. Rowling, the author of another global success in children's publishing, the Harry Potter series.

45 This refers back to what I have discussed in chapter 1 concerning the United States at this same time. See Karen Halttunen's *Murder Most Foul*. Such "loud" headlines will also be found in the reporting of the infanticide in Chamberland's *La Fissure*, analysed in chapter 4.

46 Although Reid Gilbert is speaking here of Canadians in general, the prime example on which he bases his argument comes from Quebec: Lauzon's film *Un Zoo, la nuit*. Gilbert reminds us that the film was "touted as a breakthrough in Canadian cinema [and] juxtaposed pure American violence with highly sentimental and self-satirizing icons of Canadian life" (191). The underworld of Montreal is painted as "typically" American: drugs; rock music; muggings; corrupt cops; motorcycles; misogyny; homophobia; and male violence. The contrasting world of the protagonist's father is "typically" Canadian: innocence; wilderness escapes; northern lakes; old cars; heterosexuality. At one point in the film, the Québécois protagonist asks for help from his American cellmate in order to murder a policeman, killed in a "sleazy sex hotel without a French name but with filmic connections to every evil Chinatown in U.S. cinema" (Gilbert 191). After the murder is brutally committed, the American "assures the Canadian protagonist: 'Remember, you always have an American friend'" (Gilbert 191). At the same time, the relationship between the American-style gangster son and

the Québécois-style father further highlights the relationship between U.S. and Québécois ways of living and national values. Here the killing that is portrayed is that of a moose in the wild, with father and son – the latter in leather and chains – sitting in a canoe, in contrast to the violent urban inner city (Gilbert 191–2). Later in the film, the son brings an old eight-millimetre projector to his dying father's hospital room, and the two of them, in male bonding, watch a movie of moose-hunting – again in contrast to the high tech world of America. Gilbert concludes his analysis by referring to a series of images of Quebec life and true love, as the younger male lies naked and cuddles his nude dead father. As Gilbert concludes: "It is expressly because the audience can laugh at the falsity of the nostaligic moose-hunting and because Canadians visit their zoos to view more exotic animals that it understands what it is to be a Canadian" (Gilbert 192). It may be accurate to state that Canadians and Québécois understand who they are, but it is equally important to note that the laughter directed at the Canadian/ Quebec scenes and characters implies a self-deprecation and an awareness of the more seductive way of life in the violent United States.

47 Witness the recent, albeit controversial, popularity of such texts as *Baise-moi* in France and *Putain* in Quebec, both of which I shall discuss in chapter 3.

CHAPTER THREE

1 Rich's 1971 essay "When We Dead Awaken: Writing as Re-Vision" was republished in *On Lies, Secrets, and Silence: Selected Prose 1966–1978* (New York: W.W. Norton and Company, 1979).

2 "Gorillas in the Midst" 12.

3 Kappeler's claims are also substantiated by Armstrong and Tennenhouse in their description of violence as the provenance of the other (16).

4 I shall, of course, soon analyse the extension of the criminal to the horror and monstrosity of the female sexual and violent being.

5 *L'Écologie du réel* was originally published in 1989 and revised in 1998.

6 The mention of Wonder Woman brings to mind comic-book-like "tough girls."

7 See Baudrillard 28, 70, 104, 126.

8 This is possibly an example of Baudrillard's simulacrum.

9 See Bourdieu, *On Television* 16, 55.

10 As I shall note below, von Flotow's claim is later contested by Lori Saint-Martin.

11 This last concern is what Saint-Martin calls "the other family romance" in her study of daughters and fathers in Quebec women's fiction of the nineties. See Saint-Martin, "The Other Family Romance" 169–85 and Saint-Martin, "Les Espaces impossibles de la relation père-fille" 391–411.

12 Not to forget Marie-Claire Blais's powerful and depressing *Visions d'Anna*, which I have chosen not to include in this study; see Gilbert, "From Shattered Reflections" and Green, *Marie-Claire Blais*.

13 I shall have more to say about these creative confusions later in reference to Dandurand's more violent *L'Assassin de l'intérieur*.

14 The female prosecutor's imaginative prosecution will also link to the issue of "legal storytelling" as I shall discuss in chapter 4. She can likewise be compared to Rioux's translator of a serial killer's journals, who "gets into the head" of the male murderer, as I shall treat in chapter 5.

15 In Oliver Stone's fictionalized film of Morrison's life with The Doors, it is stated that the rock singer felt that the audience really only wanted his death, the chance to tear him to pieces.

16 Here, on the recording, Morrison lets out a sort of primal scream; in a Los Angeles concert he covered his eyes, singing "fuck you mama all night long"; in the film, *The Doors*, he repeats this line very clearly, dancing frenzily with the microphone, and then collapses, exhausted.

17 In the Los Angeles concert, he continues with: "The end of nights we tried to die."

18 This is the first time the killer is named in any of the Rioux texts. I shall have more to say about him in chapter 5.

19 Sontag's observation provides a wonderful link between my current discussion of female pornography/sexuality, leading to female-imagined sexual violence, and finally to representations of female violence and murder, as the ultimate taking into oneself of the other, often described as the ultimate relational act. See the discussion of infanticide in chapter 5.

20 Let us not forget that Sontag is writing here of the male pornographic imagination.

21 I shall return to this point as I analyse certain Quebec texts.

22 Isadora Wing is clearly an ironic name that reminds one of the female protagonist's "flying." Suleiman's reference to "female thieves of language" ["voleuses de langue"] similarly reminds readers of the transgressive ballet dancer "in flight": Isadora Duncan, worthy ancestor of the younger Isadora.

23 Interestingly, in Paris bookstores the works of these pornographic and sexually violent female authors do not appear in the section devoted to

erotic literature or eroticism, but rather simply under "literature," along with more "mainstream" authors. In these same bookstores, there is often a separate section for erotic works – and several authored by women – but I am not dealing with those texts.

24 I shall not attempt to dispute these claims but refer the reader back to chapter 2 on Quebec identity and to the rest of this study on Québécois literary sex and violence.

25 These white female writers were not long thereafter joined by critics of black erotica. See *Érotique noire/Black Erotica*, a 1992 collection edited by Miriam DeCosta-Willis, Reginald Martin, and Roseann P. Bell.

26 It is interesting how this large vulva chats. One cannot help but think of Eve Ensler's recent stage phenomenon, *The Vagina Monologues*, where multiple vaginas tell their formerly private stories in public.

27 For an interesting analysis of this novel, see Karin Egloff's "It Takes Two to Tango."

28 The painting is like a centrefold model in the scientific version of *Playboy* and *Hustler*.

29 The weakness in Authier's argument here stems from his comparison of male pornography with female *violent* pornography, as if male *violent* pornography did not exist. In "Pornography: Its Consequences on the Observer," for example, Edward Donnerstein and Neil Malamuth, both social psychologists and authorities on sexual aggression, pornography, and violence against women, offer an extensive review of the research studies and literature on erotica and on sexually aggressive pornography. They conclude that pornographic materials that lack aggressive/violent images seem to have little or no effect upon observers. Aggressive/violent pornography, however, can influence a whole range of harmful attitudes and behaviours toward women: "The evidence to date does suggest that long-term attitudes about rape, women, and violence can be both reinforced and shaped by exposure to material that combines sexual and aggressive images of women" (Donnerstein and Malamuth 45). It would make sense, therefore, to say that aggressive and violent female pornography can similarly influence harmful attitudes and behaviours toward men. Once again, women would have reversed what Kappeler calls "the cultural archeplot of power" through use of violent pornography that suggests a paradigm of degradation of the other (104–5).

30 I return here to Williams and the issue of women representing the phallus, not as the penis, but as power (Williams 247).

31 Is it the sex – as for Gélinas – or the murders that are dirty?

32 The incubus is a folkloric male demon who has sexual intercourse with sleeping women, and the succubus is a folkloric female demon who has

sexual intercourse with sleeping men, not surprisingly also referred to as an evil spirit in general.

33 In the same article, Saint-Martin also analyses Jeanne Le Roy's *La Zébresse* – which I shall not be considering here – as a second, even more transgressive, parody of the French "classic."

34 Sontag calls "O" a cartoon of her sex, standing for a zero and for all women (220).

35 This early example of female violence has remained in the popular imagination in Quebec, as shown by the 2004 filming and 2005 release of *Nouvelle France*, directed by Jean Beaudin (of the psychological thriller *Souvenirs intimes* co-written with Monique Proulx) and starring Noémie Godin-Vigneau, David La Haye, Gérard Dépardieu, and Tim Roth in a Quebec, French, and British co-production. Interestingly, this film is produced by Richard Goudreau, the producer of the successful *Les Boys* films.

36 Dé is probably here also playing on the meaning of the word "marmotte." In French, this is indeed a marmot, a little animal. But the word "marmot," as one would translate it into English, also means a "little kid." In other words, as she kills her father, Alexia could be thinking either of the animals which her father did shoot, as well as the little children of the family (herself included) who were abused by him.

CHAPTER FOUR

1 The *British Infanticide Act* of 1938 has been interpreted fairly liberally in England and in other countries with similar legislation, such as Hong Kong and Australia (Morris and Wilczynski 207).

2 Further definitions – at least in Great Britain – indicate that the term "neonaticide" refers to the killing of a baby within twenty-four hours of birth. Any filicide (and certainly infanticide) is also sometimes referred to as "battered baby syndrome" (Morris and Wilczynski 210–11).

3 In *Mothers Who Kill Their Children*, Cheryl Meyer, Michelle Oberman, et al. note the 1970 definitions made by psychiatrist Peter Resnick, who was the first to attempt to provide a typology for child murder. Resnick defines neonaticide as the killing of a newborn on the day of its birth or within twenty-four hours of birth. Filicide is the act of killing one's own child (see Meyer, Oberman 186). Infanticide is such a loaded term that anti-abortion advocates have also used it to strengthen their position. In 2003, for instance, it was used in the Commonwealth of Virginia to gain attention to and support for a bill – which eventually passed – that bans what anti-abortion advocates usually call "partial-birth abortion." The new law in

Virginia bans this procedure as "partial-birth infanticide." In addition, the United States Congress passed, in March 2004, the *Unborn Victims of Violence Act* stating that an attack on a pregnant woman is to be regarded as two distinct crimes: an attack on the woman and an attack on her fetus, whatever its stage of development. Pro-choice activists are claiming that making it a federal offense to harm a fetus, distinct from the crime of attacking the pregnant woman, is an attack on abortion rights masquerading as law enforcement.

4 According to Statistics Canada, reports Orest Fedorowycz, no actual infanticides (in this case, killings of a newborn child by a mother because of the effects of childbirth or lactation) took place in Canada in 1999, for the first time since 1974 when these data were initially collected (Fedorowycz 1999, 6). However, thirty-six children under the age of twelve were killed in 1999, and almost 80 percent by their parents. (The actual number of accused parents in 1999 was sixteen fathers and seven biological mothers.)

Looking back, from 1974 to 1983, slightly more mothers than fathers were accused of killing their children, whereas from 1984 to 1993, slightly more fathers were accused in such incidents. Since 1994, however, the ratio of accused fathers to mothers has been increasing (Fedorowycz 1999, 11). The number of infants under one year of age who were killed by parents decreased to eight in 1999 (as reported in 1999): five fathers and four mothers were accused (in one case, both parents).

In 2000 thirty-nine children under the age of twelve were murdered. Taking into account that some of these incidents involved multiple-accused and multiple-victims, the actual number of accused parents in 2000 was fifteen fathers and nine biological mothers (Fedorowycz 2000, 11). The number of infants under one year of age who were killed that year increased from eleven in 1999 (as revised in 2000) to twenty in 2000, two-thirds of whom were killed by their parents (Fedorowycz 2000, 11).

In 2001 thirty-nine children under the age of twelve were murdered; twenty-five of these cases were parent-child homicide incidents; the actual number of accused parents was fourteen fathers and twelve mothers (Dauvergne, *Homicide in Canada 2001*, 12). The number of infants under the age of one who were killed decreased from twenty in 2000 to twelve in 2001, although infants were still at the highest risk of being victims of homicide. In 2001 parents were responsible for all of the infant homicides (eight mothers and four fathers), most commonly by shaking and beating (Dauvergne, *Homicide 2001*, 12).

The latest figures for 2002 show that the number of mothers accused of homicide (eight) fell to its lowest level since 1965 (Savoie, *Homicide 2002*, 8, 17, Table 9). Forty-four children under the age of twelve were murdered in 2002, three-quarters of whom were killed by their parents: there were twenty-five parent-child homicide incidents involving thirty-one child victims; fourteen fathers, four step-fathers, and seven mothers were accused (Savoie, *Homicide 2002*, 8). For the second year in a row, the number of infants under the age of one (13) who were homicide victims remained lower than the ten-year average of eighteen; parents (four mothers and four fathers) were responsible for eight infant homicides (Savoie, *Homicide 2002*, 8–9).

Figures for 2003 show that homicides perpetrated against children under the age of twelve declined to their lowest point in more than twenty-five years. There were thirty-three such homicides in 2003, with fourteen infants killed. Parents continued to be the most likely perpetrators of child homicide, with thirteen fathers (including four step-fathers) and eleven mothers (including one step-mother) accused (Dauvergne, *Homicide 2003*, 9, 19, Table 10).

5 I note that these newspaper reports use the term "infanticide" generally for all child homicides.

6 Wilczynski identified ten categories of alleged motive: retaliatory killings; jealousy of or rejection by the victim; the unwanted child; disciplinary; altruistic; psychosis in the parent; Munchausen Syndrome by Proxy; killings secondary to sexual or ritual abuse of the victim or another person; no intent to kill or injure; cases of unknown motive (Meyer and Oberman 29).

7 "Oberman classified cases into two categories which included neonaticide and infanticide. Infanticide was further subdivided into infanticide and postpartum psychosis, infanticide by mothers with chronic mental disabilities, infanticide as a manifestation of an affective disorder with postpartum onset, and addiction-related infanticide" (Meyer and Oberman 31).

8 It was "postpartum psychosis" that was used as the defense in the Andrea Yates murder case, often referred to as infanticide, even though four of her children were older than newly born – seven, five, three, and two. The youngest child in this murder was six months old, qualifying its murder, at least under British law, as infanticide. One "benefit" deriving from both the Susan Smith and the Andrea Yates cases – and especially the latter – is that the U.S. media began to publish articles and cite research on postpartum depression and psychosis. Subsequent infanticide and filicide cases have made

it into the news, but the coverage has not been as extensive. Stereotypes, however, do die hard; some media framing of motherhood cast these women into the role of a "modern Medea."

9 A common test for insanity is the M'Naghten test, which states: "To establish a defense on the ground of insanity, it must be clearly proved that, at the time of the committing of the act, the party accused was laboring under such a defect of reason, from disease of the mind, as not to know the nature and quality of the act he was doing; or, if he did know it, that he did not know what he was doing was wrong" (Meyer and Oberman 71). Interestingly Susan Smith, although clearly depressed and suicidal for much of her life, did not plead insanity. She may have met the criteria for mental illness, but this would not have satisfied legal standards. The jury still considered her mental health as a mitigating factor – perhaps agreeing that the death penalty would not serve justice (Meyer and Oberman 71–2). Smith is serving a life sentence in prison. In Andrea Yates's case, it was determined that she was legally competent to stand trial, although, as indicated above, a postpartum psychosis defence was used. She was found guilty but spared the death penalty. She is currently serving a life sentence in a Texas prison. The case of Deanne Laney, who killed her two sons and wounded a third in 2003 in Texas, went to trial in early 2004, and the jury, somewhat surprisingly, found her not guilty by reason of insanity.

10 This use of medical and legal discourse often led – then as now and in the two novels in question – to acquittals or guilty verdicts, with no custodial sentence, provided the woman agreed to medical and/or psychiatric treatment. I shall explore this issue later in this chapter.

11 Saint-Martin's interpretation is substantially based on Couchard's work.

12 The situation in Morrison's novel is, of course, much more serious in that the mother murders her daughter in order to protect her from eventual slavery. In Chamberland's novel, the evil world into which the daughter has been born is more remote, although it appears to the mother to be encroaching increasingly on their lives.

13 The sexual and gender role reversal here is quite evident.

14 Florence would hold Alice's head under the ice-cold shower.

15 For some, I suspect that Marie's two unborn children – one by abortion and one who dies with her – would be seen as victims of infanticide. We do not know what became of Julie's child.

16 After all, it is mothers and grandmothers who continue the practice of FGM and perform many of the operations throughout the world.

17 In addition, Lori Saint-Martin has characterized Ying Chen's novel *L'Ingratitude* as a novel of infanticide. I have not thought of this text as a

novel of infanticide, but Saint-Martin's discussion can be read in her "Infanticide, Suicide, Matricide, and Mother-Daughter Love: Suzanne Jacob's *L'Obéissance* and Ying Chen's *L'Ingratitude*."

It is also rather interesting to compare the female protagonist in the Dé short story to Catherine Breillat's young female lead in her film *Romance*. In the controversial French film, the young woman – who is not initially a mother – is equally disturbed and indeed obsessed with the fact that her male partner does not want to have sex with her. She consequently becomes a female porn star in her own movie, searching for and finding sex wherever she can. Her form of striking back at her unsexual lover, however, is to kill *him* off (by turning on the gas in their apartment), just around the same time as she is giving birth to their child – in the presence of her sado-masochistic boss and lover. I will make no attempt here to analyse the actions of this violent female character in regard to the differences between Québécois and French cultures!

18 See Foucault's *Surveiller et punir* for a discussion of the public nature of punishment at public executions in his chapter "L'Éclat des supplices" (41–83); [*Discipline and Punish*, "The Spectacle of the Scaffold" (32–69)].

19 Even though one learns fairly soon that it is a cat that has a collar around its neck ["le collier autour du cou"], the use of the pronoun "elle" does prefigure the death of her daughter (Chamberland 7).

20 Julie talks suffocatingly and repeatedly about the crimes of Marcos, Duvalier, Ceaucescu, and Kim Il-Song.

21 Shapiro also quotes here from Restif de la Bretonne in his 1777 *Les Gynographes*: "There is in female murderers in general a thoroughly delightful mixture of poetry and arsenic, of sentimentalism and rat poison."

22 A good example of the result of such behaviour and presentation in court is the Lorena Bobbitt case and outcome.

23 See also Foucault's discussion of non-legal experts in trials in his *Surveiller et punir* (28–30); *Discipline and Punish* (21–2).

24 Shapiro has based her own study on Nathalie Zemon Davis's work on sixteenth-century French pardon tales.

25 Élaine's narrative is quite reminiscent of Elisabeth's in Anne Hébert's *Kamouraska*.

26 It is perhaps unusual that there is no jury in Élaine's trial, although we are not told if she herself chose a bench trial.

27 Copy cat crimes are, of course, an issue in today's violent world, as well.

28 Élaine's cry, "C'est pas de tes affaires!" ["It's none of your business!"] again echoes the title of Claire Dé's short story.

29 An example of this technique occurs on page 30 of the novel where, in the midst of remembering an early encounter with Julien (narrated within parentheses), Élaine suddenly adds (within a second set of parentheses) "(si Bruno ...)" (Chamberland 30).

30 Julien is the lover for whom she invents herself as a painter, with a potential "strident witch's laugh" ["rire strident de sorcière"] (Chamberland 40).

31 It must be remembered that Alice was always the sun-child.

32 Marie's identification of her unborn child as a girl, "blessed among all women" ["bénie entre toutes les femmes"] refers, of course, to the Hail Mary.

33 Once again, to some, Marie's abortion might be seen as another infanticide. In addition, her not wanting to bring a child into such a violent world reminds us of Élaine's decision to kill her daughter in order to protect her from outside cruelty. In this view, Marie's abortion would be another instance of "altruistic infanticide."

34 See Paula Ruth Gilbert (Lewis), "Trois générations de femmes."

35 Of the approximately 400 female offenders executed in the United States since 1632, 60 percent were women of colour; interestingly, representations of female killers are predominantly white (Hart 107–8).

36 As a father, rather than as a mother who could have been charged as an infanticide, Robert Latimer was convicted and received the mandatory minimum sentence for murder. He must spend ten years in prison before being eligible for parole. The Supreme Court of Canada upheld this conviction and sentence after eight years of trials, appeals, and retrials (Johnson 2).

37 After ten-year-old Holly Jones was murdered and dismembered in May 2003 in Toronto, there were calls for a reinstitution of capital punishment in Canada, but there has been no "official" discussion.

CHAPTER FIVE

1 I have underscored this point in my literary analyses in chapter 3; see also a discussion of Hutcheon on parody in Gilbert, "The Daughter Below" (512–14).

2 I would like to thank Lorna Irvine for much of the language in this opening section (and in other sections throughout this chapter), since it was originally part of a co-authored article of ours that discussed female serial killing in Rioux, Dandurand, and Dé, as well as in texts by Margaret Atwood, especially *The Robber Bride*. (See Gilbert and Irvine, "Pre- and Post-Mortem").

3 The expression "desperately random" comes from the film *Silence of the Lambs*.

4 I have emphasized these concepts in the critical work of Duggan, Tanner, and Inness, as well in my own analyses of fictional texts.

5 Some of the monikers attributed to male serial killers include: The Torture Doctor, The Cannibal, The Gorilla Murderer, Tacoma Ax Killer, Sex Beast, The Thrill Killer, The Boston Strangler, Coed Killer, The Mad Biter, Killer Clown, Skid Row Slasher, Son of Sam, Stocking Strangler, The Ripper, Sunday Morning Slasher, Night Stalker (Kelleher and Kelleher 15), and, as already mentioned, BTK, the nickname that Dennis Rader gave to himself.

6 Pearson uses the films *The Last Seduction*, *A Kiss Before Dying* and *Basic Instinct* as examples of these fictitious female predators. If one considers Thelma and Louise to be serial killers, then neither the weapon nor the places where the murders are committed, as defined by Pearson, holds true for these filmic female protagonists. Similarly, the French film *Baise-moi* portrays the two prostitute serial killers as employing "male" weapons and as moving about in order to murder their victims. In both of these films, however, the victims are men.

7 Pearson also notes that when Paul Bernardo was committing serial rape before his marriage, he stalked the streets from his childhood in Scarborough, Ontario. When he escalated to killing, with Karla Homolka, the venue changed to their home in Ontario, as the new comfort zone (159).

8 Wuornos's conversion to being a born-again Christian while in prison also did not sway the authorities, who denied her appeals. Complicated "clues" into the life, personality, and psyche of Wuornos can be seen in the two documentaries based on interviews with her in 1992 and 2002, the latter covering the period up until her execution by lethal injection in October 2002. See Works Cited and Consulted under "Aileen" for information on these documentaries.

9 Even though Rioux's Charles/Leonard Ming is said, in her fiction, to have been influenced by Charles Manson, the most obvious comparison to a "real-life" serial killer is to Charles Ng – with a number of similarities that will be made clear, as I discuss the fictional serial murderer and the imagined "fusion" with his female translator. Ng and his side-kick, Leonard (note the composite name of Charles/Leonard for Rioux's serial killer) Lake, delighted in a two-year sexual fantasy during which they abducted and tortured men, women, and children as their sexual slaves. None of these victims survived. What we know of Ng comes from the videotapes that he and Lake made of their "fun." Both carried cyanide pills with them in the event of capture. Ng was finally apprehended in Calgary and immediately

began a campaign to stall his case in Canada and to fight extradition to the United States. While in prison for six years in Canada, he studied law. He was finally extradited to California by order of the Canadian Supreme Court and in September 1999 was charged in a California court with twelve counts of murder. He then began flooding the courts with legal paperwork, replaced his lawyers, and attempted to confuse the system by complaining about his treatment in the U.S. prison – all in order to avoid the death penalty. After the longest and most costly trial in California history – during which members of the jury were said to experience fear and were haunted by the two videotapes of torture they had to watch – Ng was found guilty of first-degree murder and sentenced to death. A journalist who interviewed him reported that Ng admitted that he had enjoyed himself during his sexually violent killing spree and that he had especially loved the psychological control that he had over others during that time. He was described as a mild-mannered and shy man who showed no remorse and would say nothing to the families of his victims. Charles Ng remains on death row. See the following websites for further information on his case:
http://www.apbnews.com/newscenter/majorcases/ng/1999/06/30/ng0630_01.html
http://www.crimelibrary.com/serial/ng/3.html

10 Studies show that many adult homicidal men loved this form of torture as children. One should also recall that the "abattoir" was at the centre of the childhood nightmare of Agent Starling – Jody Foster – in *Silence of the Lambs.*

11 The use of the term, "natural instinct," comes from the popular film, *Natural Born Killers.*

12 The "New Warrior" is the term coined by James Gibson in his *Warrior Dreams: Violence and Manhood in Post-Vietnam America.*

13 "Wolfman" of course reminds one of Freud's case study of that name. In addition, Gibson's new warrior often wears a wolf or a wild man's mask during his paintball war games (see Gibson 129). And finally, one of Patricia Cornwall's more recent popular crime novels is entitled *Wolfman.*

14 One cannot help being reminded of the popular and legendary figure of the "loup-garou" in Quebec folklore. Here it seems evident that both Dandurand and Dé are having fun with this feminized version of that character.

15 Serial killers, furthermore, reappear serially, as contemporary scions of young adult horror, Christopher Pike and R.L. Stine, understand so well. Serial killing leads to serial fiction.

16 I can apply Kristeva's statement about the powers of horror and the abject to those of violence: "The abject is not an ob-ject facing me, which I name or imagine. Nor is it an ob-jest ... The abject has only one quality of the object – that of being opposed to *I* ... what is *abject*, on the contrary, the jettisoned object, is radically excluded and draws me toward the place where meaning collapses. A certain 'ego' that merged with its master, a superego, has flatly driven it away" (*Powers of Horror* 1–2) ["L'abject n'est pas un ob-jet en face de moi, que je nomme ou que j'imagine. Il n'est pas non plus cet ob-jeu ... De l'objet, l'abject n'a qu'une qualité – celle de s'opposer a *je* ... l'*abject*, objet chu, est radicalement un exclu et me tire vers là où le sens s'effondre. Un certain 'moi' qui s'est fondu avec son maître, un sur-moi, l'a carrément chassé"] (*Pouvoirs de l'horreur* 9).

17 Rhodes bases his observations on Pieter Spierenberg's 1984 *The Spectacle of Suffering.*

18 This identification with both the killer and the victim reminds one of Marie in *L'Obéissance*, who identified with both Florence, the possible infanticide, and Alice, the victim.

19 One is reminded here of the scene in the American film *G.I. Jane* in which the female, Navy Seal, has become so masculinized that she yells out, "Suck my dick." It is interesting to note, as well, that the director of this film, Ridley Scott, also directed *Thelma and Louise.*

20 This spurting of blood is associated more with the spurting of sperm in Helen Zahavi's *Dirty Weekend*: "He spurted in the way she made men spurt. He gushed all over her, without restraint. He blooded her and then he fell" (186).

21 The original French version of this short story, "Maîtresse des hautes oeuvres," was unpublished for a long time and the story was available only in an English translation by Luise von Flotow. In 1999 it finally appeared as part of Dandurand's *Les Porteuses d'ombre.*

22 Dandurand uses religious words such as "couvent" (convent), "cloître" (cloister), "monastère" (monastery), "noviciat" (noviciate), "sacrilège" (sacrilege), "rigoureuse ascèse" (rigorous ascetic), "voeux perpétuels" (eternal vows), "moniale anonyme" (anonymous monastic), "soulagement divin" (divine relief), "officier" (officiate), "béatitude" (beatitude), "ordination" (ordination), "lourd sacerdoce" (onerous holy orders)] to illustrate the metro killer's sense of divine calling.

23 With the advent of the George W. Bush Republican administration and especially since the United States commenced a war in Iraq – with many countries worldwide, including Canada, against this military action – the United

States has indeed been seen by many as particularly "macho" and "cowboy-like," in the finest Texan sense. In a gendered comparison, therefore, Canada (like France) has been seen by some Americans as less virile, less tough, and by extension, more feminine.

CONCLUSION

1 The 31 May and 1 June 2003 issue of *Le Devoir* presented "À la canadienne" a clever "tongue-in-cheek" column by Jean Dion, beautifully illustrating the ironic, self-deprecatory stance that many Canadians take in reference to their own country, as I have noted in chapter 2. Dion explains that a dangerous and tenacious myth is circulating around the globe: that Canada is a boring country. He is not alone in spreading this myth; Canada is doing this itself. Humorously paraphrasing this attitude, Dion states: "The entire world finds us unexciting. Americans in particular find us unexciting. At least the French, they hate them and scorn them. As for us, it's as though we didn't exist" ["Le monde entier nous trouve plates. Les Américains en particulier nous trouvent plates. Au moins, les Français, ils les détestent et les méprisent. Nous, c'est comme si on n'existait pas"] (Dion B2).

I have speculated that some Americans may see today's Canada as stereotypically feminine – that is, as indecisive and non-tough; Dion sees a neutral/neutered land – that is, asexual, non-gendered, androgynous, lacking, or simply not there.

2 Witness the unfortunate revelation in spring 2004 that three of the seven American soldiers charged with posing for photographs in acts of humiliating and torturing Iraqi prisoners in the Abu Ghraib prison were women. In addition, the officer in charge of sixteen military prisons in Iraq, including Abu Ghraib, was a woman who considers herself to be the "fall guy" in these accusations. Already, a few days after the publication of the first of these photographs, Linda Chavez stated on U.S. Fox news that the integration of women into this male military unit had affected its cohesion and had brought it down, thereby causing the violence against the prisoners on the part of both men and women (7 May 2004).

Works Cited and Consulted

Abescat, Michel. "Le Polar au féminin." *Le Devoir* 26–27 juillet 1997: D1, D2.

Acheson, Keith and Christopher Maule. *Much Ado about Culture: North American Trade Disputes*. Ann Arbor: University of Michigan Press, 1999.

– "No Bite, No Bark: The Mystery of Magazine Policy." *The American Review of Canadian Studies* 31.3 (Autumn 2001): 467–81.

Ackley, Katherine Anne, ed. *Women and Violence in Literature: An Essay Collection*. New York: Garland, 1990.

Adam, Ian and Helen Tiffin, eds. *Past the Last Post: Theorizing Post-Colonialism and Post-Modernism*. Calgary: University of Calgary Press, 1990.

Adler, Freda. *The Incidence of Female Criminality in the Contemporary World*. New York: New York University Press, 1981.

– *Sisters in Crime: The Rise of the New Female Criminal*. New York: McGraw-Hill, 1975.

– and Rita Simon, eds. *The Criminology of Deviant Women*. Boston: Houghton Mifflin, 1979.

Aguiar, Sarah Appleton. *The Bitch is Back: Wicked Women in Literature*. Carbondale: University of Illinois Press, 2001.

Aileen: Life and Death of a Serial Killer. Dirs. Nick Broomfield and Joan Churchill. Lafayette Films, Lantern Lane Entertainment, Ltd., 2003.

Aileen Wuornos: The Selling of a Serial Killer: The 1992 Interviews. Dir. Nick Broomfield. Lafayette Films for Channel Four, 1992.

Aldama, Arturo. *Violence and the Body: Race, Gender, and the State*. Bloomington: Indiana University Press, 2003.

Alder, Christine and Anne Worrall. *Girls' Violence: Myths and Realities.* Albany: State University of New York Press, 2004.

Alien. Dir. James Cameron. Perf. Sigourney Weaver. Videocassette. Fox Video, 1979.

Aliens. Dir. James Cameron. Perf. Sigourney Weaver, Michael Biehn. Videocassette. CBS Fox Video, 1986.

Alien³ Dir. David Fincher. Perf. Sigourney Weaver. Videocassette. Fox Video, 1992.

Allemagne, André d'. *Une idée qui somnolait: Écrits sur la souveraineté du Québec depuis les origines du RIN (1958–2000).* Montréal: Comeau & Nadeau, 2000.

Alper, Donald K. and David Biette. "Introduction: Weathering the Storm: The State of the Canada-U.S. Relationship, 2003." *The American Review of Canadian Studies* 33.1 (spring 2003): 1–4.

Alvi, S. *Youth and the Canadian Criminal Justice System.* Cincinnati: Anderson, 2000.

American Psychiatric Association, Diagnostic and Statistical Manual of Mental Disorders. 4th ed. Washington, D.C.: American Psychiatric Association, 1994.

Anderson, Benedict. *Imagined Communities: Reflections on the Origin and Spread of Nationalism.* London and New York: Verso, 2000.

Anderson, Curt. "Crime Rate Continues to Drop: 2002 Levels are Lowest in 30 Years, Justice Department Says." *The Washington Post* 25 August 2003. Section 1.

Anderson, Raffaella. *Hard.* Paris: Grasset, 2001.

Andrès, Bernard et Zilà Bernd, eds. *L'Identitaire et le littéraire dans les Amériques.* Montréal: Les Éditions Nota Bene, 1999.

– "Préface." In *L'Identitaire et le littéraire dans les Amériques.* Eds. Bernard Andrès et Zilà Bernd. Montréal: Les Éditions Nota Bene, 1999. 7–13.

Angenot, Marc. "Littérature et nationalisme." In *L'Identitaire et le littéraire dans les Amériques.* Eds. Bernard Andrès et Zilà Bernd. Montréal: Les Éditions Nota Bene, 1999. 243–7.

Angier, Nathalie. *Woman: An Intimate Geography.* Boston and New York: Houghton Mifflin, 1999.

Angot, Christine. *L'Inceste.* Paris: Stock, 2000.

Appadurai, Arjun. *Modernity at Large: Cultural Dimensions of Globalization.* Minneapolis: University of Minnesota Press, 1996.

Appiah, Anthony K. "Identity, Authenticity, Survival: Multicultural Societies and Social Reproduction." In *Multiculturalism: The Politics of Recognition.* Eds. Charles Taylor and Amy Gutman. Princeton: Princeton University Press, 1992. 149–63.

Applebaum-Hébert Report. (Report of the Federal Cultural Policy Review Committee). Ottawa: Minister of Supply and Services, 1982.

Apter, Emily. *Continental Drift: From National Characters to Virtual Subjects.* Chicago: University of Chicago Press, 1999.

Arcan, Nelly. *Folle.* Paris: Éditions du Seuil, 2004.

– *Putain.* Paris: Éditions du Seuil, 2001.

Arcand, Denys, dir. *Les Invasions barbares.* Perfs. Marie-Josée Croze, Rémy Girard, Stéphane Rousseau. Alliance Atlantis Vivafilm, 2003.

Arendt, Hannah. *On Violence.* New York: Harcourt Brace Jovanovich, 1970.

Armstrong, Nancy and Leonard Tennenhouse. "Introduction: Representing Violence, or 'How the West Was Won.'" In *Violence of Representation: Literature and the History of Violence.* Eds. Nancy Armstrong and Leonard Tennenhouse. New York: Routledge, 1989. 1–26.

Artz, Sibylle. *Sex, Power, and the Violent School Girl.* Toronto: Trifolium Books, Inc. 1998.

Ashcroft, Bill, Gareth Griffiths, and Helen Tiffin. *The Empire Writes Back: Theory and Practice in Post-Colonial Literatures.* London: Routledge, 1989.

Assiter, Alison and Carol Avedon, eds. *Bad Girls and Dirty Pictures: The Challenge to Reclaim Feminism.* London: Pluto Press, 1993.

Atkinson, Dave. "L'Américanisation de la télévision: qu'est-ce à dire?" In *Variations sur l'influence culturelle américaine.* Ed. Florian Sauvageau. Sainte-Foy, Québec: Les Presses de l'Université Laval, 1999. 59–72.

Attack of the 50-Foot Woman. Dir. Nathan Hertz. Perfs. Allison Hayes, William Hudson, Yvette Vickers. Videocassette. Allied Artists/Warner Brothers, 1958.

Atwood, Margaret. *Alias Grace.* New York: Nan A. Talese/Doubleday, 1996.

– *Cat's Eye.* Toronto: McClelland and Stewart, 1988.

– *The Robber Bride.* New York: Nan A. Talese/Doubleday, 1993.

– "Spotty-Handed Villainesses: Problems of Female Bad Behaviour in the Creation of Literature." 1994. <http://web.net/owtoad/vlness.html>

Auden, W.H. *The Dyer's Hand.* New York: Vintage, 1990.

Authier, Christian. *Le Nouvel Ordre sexuel.* Paris: Bartillat, 2002.

Bakhtin, Mikhail. *The Dialogic Imagination.* Ed. Michael Holquist. Trans. Cary Emerson and Michael Holquist. Austin: The University of Texas Press, 1981.

– *L'Oeuvre de François Rabelais et la culture populaire au moyen âge et sous la renaissance.* Trans. Andrée Robel. Paris: Gallimard, 1970.

– *Problems of Dostoevsky's Poetics.* Ed. and Trans. Caryl Emerson. Minneapolis: University of Minnesota Press, 1989.

– *Speech Genres and Other Late Essays*. Trans. Vern W. McGee. Eds. Caryl Emerson and Michael Holquist. Austin: University of Texas Press, 1986.

Ballinger, Anette. "The Guilt of the Innocent and the Innocence of the Guilty." In *No Angels: Women Who Commit Violence*. Eds. Alice Myers and Sarah Wight. San Francisco: Pandora, 1996. 1–28.

Balthazar, Louis and Alfred O. Hero. *Le Québec dans l'espace américain*. Montréal: Québec/Amérique, 1999.

Balzano, Flora. *Soigne ta chute*. Montréal: XYZ Éditeur, 1991.

Bammer, Angelika, ed. *Displacements: Cultural Identities in Question*. Bloomington: Indiana University Press, 1994.

Barbach, Lonnie, ed. *Pleasures: Women Write Erotica*. New York: Doubleday, 1984.

Barbes, Jean. "Anne Dandurand: la chair des mots." *Lettres Québécoises* 60 (1990–91): 11–13.

Barry, Donald. "Chrétien, Bush, and the War in Iraq." *The American Review of Canadian Studies* 35.2 (summer 2005): 215–45.

Barthes, Roland. *Le Degré zéro de l'écriture*. Paris: Seuil, 1953.

Basic Instinct. Dir. Paul Verhoeven. Perfs. Michael Douglas and Sharon Stone. Caralco Pictures, 1992.

Bataille, Georges. *L'Érotisme*. Paris: Minuit, 1957.

Baudrillard, Jean. *AMERICA*. Trans. Chris Turner. London and New York: Verso, 2000.

– *L'Amérique*. Paris: Éditions Grasset, 1986.

– "The Ecstasy of Communication." In *The Anti-Aesthetic: Essays on Postmodern Culture*. Ed. Hal Foster. Port Townsend, Washington: Bay Press, 1983.

– *De la séduction: L'Horizon sacré des apparences*. Paris: Éditions Galilée, 1979.

– *Simulacre et simulation*. Paris: Galilée, 1981.

Baum, Gregory. "Nationalisme et mouvements sociaux contre l'hégémonie du marché." In "Penser la nation québécoise." *Le Devoir* le 17–18 juillet 1999: A9.

Bélanger, Louis. "The Domestic Politics of Quebec's Quest for External Distinctiveness." *The American Review of Canadian Studies* 32.2 (summer 2002): 195–214.

Bélanger-Campeau Commission. *Rapport sur l'avenir politique et constitutionnel du Québec*. Gouvernement du Québec, 1991.

Bell, Shannon. *Reading, Writing and Rewriting the Prostitute Body*. Bloomington: Indiana University Press, 1994.

Benjamin, Jessica. *The Bonds of Love: Psychoanalysis, Feminism and the Problem of Domination*. New York: Pantheon, 1988.

Benjamin, Walter. "Critique of Violence." In *Reflections: Essays, Aphorisms, Autobiographical Writings*. Trans. Edmund Jephcott. New York: Schocken, 1986. 277–300.

Bennington, Geoffrey. "Postal Politics and the Institution of the Nation." In *Nation and Narration*. Ed. Homi K. Bhaba. London: Routledge, 1990. 121–37.

Bernd, Zilà. "Identités composites: Écritures hybrides." In *L'Identitaire et le littéraire dans les Amériques*. Eds. Bernard Andrès et Zilà Bernd. Montréal: Les Éditions Nota Bene, 1999. 17–29.

Bernier, Ivan. "Politiques culturelles et commerce international." In *Variations sur l'influence culturelle américaine*. Ed. Florian Sauvageau. Sainte-Foy, Québec: Les Presses de l'Université Laval, 1999. 231–60.

Bernier, Joanne et André Cellard. "Le Syndrome de la femme fatale: 'Matricide' et représentation féminine au Québec, 1898–1940." *Criminologie* 29.2 (automne 1996): 29–48.

Bernier, Léon. "L'Américanité ou la rencontre de l'altérité et de l'identité." In *L'Américanité et les Amériques*. Ed. Donald Cuccioletta. Sainte-Foy: Les Presses de L'Université Laval, 2001. 176–92.

– et Guy Bédard. "Américanité-Américanisation des Québécois: Quelques éclairages empiriques." *Québec Studies* 29 (spring/summer 2000): 15–24.

Bersianik, Louky. *La Main tranchante du symbole: Textes et essais féministes*. Montréal: Les Éditions du Remue-Ménage, 1990.

– et al. *La Théorie, un dimanche*. Montréal: Les Éditions du Remue-Ménage, 1988.

Bertens, Hans. "The Return of the Vanished Narrative: Cultural Identity and Postmodern Fiction." In *Roman contemporain et identité culturelle en Amérique du nord/Contemporary Fiction and Cultural Identity in North America*. Eds. Jaap Lintvelt, Richard Saint-Gelais, Will Verhoeven et Catherine Raffi-Béroud. Montréal: Éditions Nota Bene, 1998. 245–59.

Bertrand, Claude Jean. "Les 'Modèles' étatsuniens: Rien à craindre." In *Variations sur l'influence culturelle américaine*. Ed. Florian Sauvageau. Sainte-Foy, Québec: Les Presses de l'Université Laval, 1999. 183–94.

Bhaba, Homi K. "DissemiNation: Time, Narrative, and the Margins of the Modern Nation." In *Nation and Narration*. Ed. Homi K. Bhaba. London: Routledge, 1990. 291–322.

– "Introduction: Narrating the Nation." In *Nation and Narration*. Ed. Homi K. Bhaba. London: Routledge, 1990. 1–7.

– *The Location of Culture*. New York: Routledge, 1994.

–, ed. *Nation and Narration*. London: Routledge, 1990.

Birch, Helen. "Introduction." *Moving Targets: Women, Murder and Representation*. Ed. Helen Birch. Berkeley: University of California Press, 1994. 1–6.

Bissonnette, Lise. "Les Amants." In *Quittes et doubles: Scènes de réciprocité.* Montréal: Boréal, 1997.

– "L'Échafaud." In *Quittes et doubles: Scènes de réciprocité.* Montréal: Boréal, 1997.

– *Quittes et doubles: Scènes de réciprocité.* Montréal: Boréal, 1997.

Bizier, Hélène-Andrée. *Crimes et châtiments: La Petite Histoire du crime au Québec.* Tome I. Montréal: Libre Expression, 1982.

Bjorklund, Edi. "Attraction and Rage: Pain and Violence in Women's Recent Underground Fiction." In *Women and Violence in Literature: An Essay Collection.* Ed. Katherine Anne Ackley. New York: Garland, 1990. 255–89.

Bjorkqvist, Kaj and Pirkko Niemela, eds. *Of Mice and Women: Aspects of Female Aggression.* New York: Academic Press, 1992.

Black Widow. Dir. Bob Rafelson. Perf. Debra Winger, Theresa Rusell. Videocassette, 1987.

Blais, Marie-Claire. *La Belle Bête.* Montréal: Le Cercle du Livre de France, 1968.

– *Visions d'Anna.* Montréal: Stanké, 1982.

Blanchot, Maurice. *L'Entretien infini.* Paris: Gallimard, 1969.

Blue Steel. Dir. Kathryn Bigelow. Perf. Jame Lee Curtis, Ron Silver, Louise Fletcher. Videocassette. Metro-Goldwyn-Mayer, 1990.

Blunt, Alison and Gillian Rose. *Writing Women and Space: Colonial and Postcolonial Geographies.* New York: The Guilford Press, 1994.

Boileau, Josée. "L'Anglais, langue de travail des arrivants." *Le Devoir* 12 février 2003: A1, A16.

– "Le Québec fait du surplace." *Le Devoir* 13 mars 2002: A1+.

Boisnard, Philippe. "Violence et littérature." *Le Philosophoire: La Violence.* No. 13 (hiver 2001): 134–69.

Bok, Sissela. *Mayhem: Violence as Public Entertainment.* Reading, Massachusetts: Perseus Books, 1998.

Bonville, Jean de. "Le 'Nouveau Journalisme' américain et la presse québécoise à la fin du XIXe siècle." In *Variations sur l'influence culturelle américaine.* Ed. Florian Sauvageau. Sainte-Foy, Québec: Les Presses de l'Université Laval, 1999. 73–100.

Bordeleau, Francine. "Les Cris du corps: France Théoret, Josée Yvon et Monique Proulx." In *Le Roman québécois au féminin (1980–1995).* Montréal: Éditions Triptyque, 1995. 89–94.

Bordo, Susan. *Unbearable Weight: Feminism, Western Culture, and the Body.* Berkeley: University of California Press, 1993.

Boritch, H. *Fallen Women: Female Crime and Criminal Justice in Canada.* Toronto: Nelson, 1997.

Bouchard, Gérard. *Genèse des nations et cultures du nouveau monde: Essai d'histoire comparée.* Montréal: Boréal, 2000.

– "Identité collective et sentiment national dans le nouveau monde." In *L'Identitaire et le littéraire dans les Amériques.* Eds. Bernard Andrès et Zilà Bernd. Montréal: Les Éditions Nota Bene, 1999. 63–83.

– "Manifeste pour une coalition nationale." In "Penser la nation québécoise." *Le Devoir* le 4–5 septembre 1999: A13.

– "Une Nation, deux cultures: Continuités et rupture dans la pensée traditionelle (1840–1960)." In *La Construction d'une culture. Le Québec et l'Amérique française.* Eds. G. Bouchard [et] S. Courville. Sainte-Foy: Les Presses de l'Université Laval, 1993. 49–69.

– *La Nation québécoise au futur et au passé.* Montréal: VLB Éditeur, 1998.

– "Le Québec, les Amériques et les petites nations: Une Nouvelle Frontière pour l'utopie?" In *Le Grand Récit des Amériques: Polyphonie des identités culturelles dans le contexte de la continentalisation.* Eds. Donald Cuccioletta, Jean-François Côté, et Frédérique Lesemann. Saint-Foy, Québec: Les Presses de l'Université Laval, 2001. 179–89.

– "Le Québec comme collectivité neuve. Le Refus de l'américanité dans le discours de la survivance." In *Québécois et Américains: La Culture québécoise aux XIXe et XXe siècles.* Eds. Yvan Lamonde et Gérard Bouchard. Montréal: Fides, 1995. 15–60.

Bouchard, Louise Anne. *Cette Fois, Jeanne.* Montréal: VLB Éditeur, 1987.

– *La Fureur.* Montréal: VLB Éditeur, 1993.

Boucher, Marc. "L'Évolution de l'image du Québec aux États-Unis." *Politique et Sociétés* 18 (1999): 156–8.

Bourdieu, Pierre. *Distinction: A Social Critique of the Judgement of Taste.* Trans. Richard Nice. Cambridge: Harvard University Press, 1984.

– *La Domination masculine.* Paris: Éditions du Seuil, 1998.

– *On Television.* Trans. Priscilla Parkhurst Ferguson. New York: The New Press, 1998.

Bourque, Gilles. "Pour un nationalisme ouvert à la citoyenneté pluraliste." In "Penser la nation québécoise." *Le Devoir* le 3–4 juillet 1999: A11.

Bowling for Columbine. Dir. Michael Moore. DVD. United Artists. 2003.

Boyd, Neil. *The Last Dance: Murder in Canada.* Scarborough, Ontario: Prentice-Hall, 1988.

Les Boys. Dir. Louis Saia. Perfs. Rémy Girard, Marc Messier, Patrick Huard. Videocassette, 2001; DVD, 2002. Cinepix/Lion's Gate, 1997.

Les Boys II. Dir. Louis Saia. Perfs. Marc Messier, Patrick Huard, Rémy Girard. DVD, 1999; Videocassette, 2002. Cinepix/Lion's Gate. 1998.

Les Boys III. Dir. Louis Saia. Perfs. Patrick Huard, Marc Messier, Rémy Girard. Cinepix/Lion's Gate, 2001.

Bradley, Hannah, ed. *Defining Violence: Understanding the Causes and Effects of Violence*. Aldershot: Avebury, 1996.

Braidotti, Rosi. *Nomadic Subjects: Embodiment and Sexual Difference in Contemporary Feminist Theory*. New York: Columbia University Press, 1994.

Brantley, Ben. "Attack of the Killer Moms on Broadway." *The New York Times* 1 June 2002. Section 2: 1,14.

Breillat, Catherine. *Pornocratie*. Paris: Denoel, 2001.

– *Romance*. Perf. Caroline Ducey, Sagamore Stévenin, François Berléand, Rocco Siffredi. DVD. Trimark, 1999.

Brennan, Timothy. "The National Longing for Form." In *Nation and Narration*. Ed. Homi K. Bhaba. London: Routledge, 1990. 44–70.

Brière, Marc. *Point de départ! Essai sur la nation québécoise*. Montréal: Hurtubise, 2000.

Bright, Susie. *Totally Herotica*. New York: Quality Paperback Book Club, 1995.

Broadcasting Act. <http://laws.justice.gc.ca/en/B–9.01/index.html>.

Brooks, Peter. *Body Work: Objects of Desire in Modern Narrative*. Cambridge: Harvard University Press, 1993.

– *Troubling Confessions: Speaking Guilt in Law and Literature*. Chicago: University of Chicago Press, 2001.

Brooks, Stephen. "Comments on 'Here's Where We Get Canadian: English-Canadian Nationalism and Popular Culture.'" *The American Review of Canadian Studies* 32.1 (spring 2002): 35–40.

Brossard, Nicole. *L'Amèr ou le chapitre effrité*. Montréal: Quinze, 1977.

– *Le Désert mauve*. Montréal: L'Hexagone, 1987.

Brown, Anne. "La Violence dénoncée dans le roman féminin des années soixante." In *Trajectoires au féminin dans la littérature québécoise (1960–1990)*. Ed. Lucie Joubert. Montréal: Éditions Nota Bene, 2000. 175–96.

Brown, Richard Maxwell. *No Duty to Retreat: Violence and Values in American History and Society*. New York: Oxford University Press, 1991.

Browne, Angela. *When Battered Women Kill*. New York: Free Press, 1987.

Brûlé, Michel. *La DGCA: D'où elle vient et où elle va*. Québec, 1979.

– *Vers une politique du cinéma au Québec: Document de travail*. Québec: DGCA, 1978.

Brulotte, Gaetan. "Une Décennie de nouvelles québécoises: 1980–1990." *The French Review* 65.6 (1992): 963–77.

Brush, L.S. "Violent Acts and Injurious Outcomes in Married Couples: Methodological Issues in the National Survey of Families and Households." In *Violence against Women: The Bloody Footprints.* Ed. P.B. Bart. Newbury Park, California: Sage, 1993. 240–51.

Burbank, Victoria. "Female Aggression in Cross-Cultural Perspective." *Behavior Science Research* 21 (1987): 70–100.

Burnett, H. Sterling. "More People in Prison, Less Crime on the Streets." *The Washington Post* 1 September 2001: A29.

Buss, David M. and Neil Malamuth, eds. *Sex, Power, and Conflict: Evolutionary and Feminist Perspectives.* New York: Oxford University Press, 1996.

Butler, Judith. *Bodies That Matter: On the Discursive Limits of "Sex."* New York: Routledge, 1993.

– *Excitable Speech: A Politics of the Performative.* New York: Routledge, 1997.

– "The Force of Fantasy: Feminism, Mapplethorpe, and Discursive Excess." *Differences* 2.2 (1990): 105–21.

– *Gender Trouble: Feminism and the Subversion of Identity.* New York: Routledge, 1999.

Butterfield, Fox. "States Ease Laws On Time In Prison." *The New York Times* 2 September 2001: A1, A16.

Buzzetti, Hélène. "Armes: Les Québécois défient la loi." *Le Devoir* 20 janvier 2003: A8.

Cabrera, Natasha J. "Violence by and against Children in Canada." In *Violence in Canada: Sociopolitical Perspectives.* Ed. Jeffrey Ian Ross. Don Mills: Oxford University Press Canada, 1995. 126–52.

Campbell, Anne. *The Girls in the Gang.* Cambridge: Basil Blackwell, 1991.

– *Men, Women, and Agression.* New York: Basic Books, 1993.

–, Steven Muncer, and Daniel Bibel. "Female-female Criminal Assault: An Evolutionary Perspective." *Journal of Research in Crime and Delinquency* 35.4 (November 1998): 413–28.

Canadian Heritage. *From Script to Screen: New Policy Directions for Canadian Feature Film.* Minister of Public Works and Government Services, 2000.

Cantin, Serge. "Pour sortir de la survivance." In "Penser la nation québécoise." *Le Devoir* le 14–15 août 1999: A9.

Cantos, A.L., P. Neidig, and K.D. O'Leary. "Injuries of Women and Men in a Treatment Program for Domestic Violence." *Journal of Family Violence* 9 (1994): 113–24.

Caputi, Jane. *The Age of Sex Crime.* Bowling Green, Ohio: Popular Press, 1987.

– "American Psychos." *Journal of American Culture* 16 (1993): 101–12.

– *Goddesses and Monsters: Women, Myth, Power, and Popular Culture.* Madison: University of Wisconsin Press, 2004.

Carlen, Pat, ed. *Criminal Women: Autobiographical Accounts, Diana Christina, Jenny Hicks, Josie O'Dwyer, Chris Tchaikovsky and Pat Carlen.* Cambridge: Polity Press, 1985.

Cario, Robert. *Femmes et criminelles.* Toulouse, France: Éditions Erès, 1992.

Caron, Brigitte. *La Fin du siècle comme si vous étiez.* Montréal: XYZ Éditeur, 1995.

Carrington, Kerry. *Offending Girls: Sex, Youth and Justice.* St. Leonards, New South Wales: Allen and Unwin, 1993.

Carter, Angela. *The Sadeian Woman: An Exercise in Cultural History.* New York: Pantheon, 1978.

Carter, Cynthia, Gill Branston, and Stuart Allan. *News, Gender, and Power.* New York: Routledge, 1998.

Caruth, Kathy. *Unclaimed Experience: Trauma, Narrative, and History.* Baltimore: Johns Hopkins University Press, 1996.

Cascardi, M. and D. Vivian. "Context for Specific Episodes of Marital Violence: Gender and Severity of Violence Differences." *Journal of Family Violence* 10 (1995): 265–93.

Cerulo, Karen A. *Deciphering Violence: The Cognitive Structure of Right and Wrong.* New York: Routledge, 1998.

Chamberland, Aline. *La Fissure.* Montréal: VLB Éditeur, 1985.

Chamberland, Paul. "Deux Nationalismes: Le Bon et le mauvais." In *L'Identitaire et le littéraire dans les Amériques.* Eds. Bernard Andrès et Zilà Bernd. Montréal: Les Éditions Nota Bene, 1999. 253–4.

Charest, Danielle. *L'Étouffoir.* Montréal: Librairie des Champs-Élysées, 2000.

Chassay, Jean-François. *L'Ambiguité américaine: Le Roman québécois face aux Etats-Unis.* Montréal: XYZ Éditeur, 1995.

– "Littérature et américanité: La Piste technoscientifique." In *Québécois et Américains: La Culture québécoise aux XIXe et XXe siècles.* Eds. Yvan Lamonde et Gérard Bouchard. Montréal: Fides, 1995. 175–93.

– "Reflets des États-Unis dans le roman québécois: Une Version de l'Amérique." *Urgences* 34 (1991).

Le Chat dans le sac. Dir. Gilles Groulx. National Film Board of Canada, 1964.

Chatterjee, Partha and Pradeep Jeganathan. *Community, Gender and Violence.* New York: Columbia University Press, 2001.

Chavez, Linda. "The Tragic Story of Medea Still Lives." *Denver Post* 3 December 1995: E04.

Chen, Ying. *L'Ingratitude.* Montréal, Leméac, 1995.

Chesler, Phyllis. *Woman's Inhumanity to Woman.* New York: Thunder's Mouth Press/Nation Books, 2001.

Chesney-Lind, Meda. *The Female Offender: Girls, Women, and Crime.* Thousand Oaks, California: Sage, 1997.

– "Foreword." [In] *Women, Crime and the Canadian Criminal Justice System.* Ed. Walter DeKeseredy. Cincinnati: Anderson Publishing, Co., 2000. iii–v.

– "The Meaning of Mean." Rev. of *Odd Girl Out*, by Rachel Simmons, *The Secret Lives of Girls*, by Sharon Lamb, and *Queen Bees and Wannabes*, by Rosalind Wiseman. *The Women's Review of Books* 20.2 (November 2002): 20–2.

– "Women and Crime: The Female Offender." *Signs* 12.1 (1986): 78–96.

– and J. Koroki. *Everything Just Going Down the Drain: Interviews with Female Delinquents in Hawaii.* Hawaii: University of Hawaii Youth Development and Research Center Report, 1985.

– and Jocelyn Pollock. "Women's Prisons: Equality with a Vengeance." In *Women, Law and Social Control.* Eds. A. Merlo and Jocelyn Pollock. Boston: Allyn and Bacon, 1995. 155–77.

– and R. Shelden. *Girls' Delinquency and Juvenile Justice.* 2nd edition. Belmont, California: West/Wadsworth, 1998.

Chevrier, Marc. "Notre République en Amérique." In "Penser la nation québécoise." *Le Devoir* le 10–11 juillet 1999: A11.

Chicago. Dir. Rob Marshall. Perfs. Renée Zellweger, Catherine Zeta-Jones, Richard Gere. DVD. Miramax, 2003.

Chodorow, Nancy J. *Femininities, Masculinities, Sexualities: Freud and Beyond.* Lexington: University of Kentucky Press, 1994.

– *Feminism and Psychoanalytic Theory.* New Haven: Yale University Press, 1989.

– *The Power of Feelings: Personal Meaning in Psychoanalysis, Gender, and Culture.* New Haven: Yale University Press, 1999.

Clastre, Pierre. *Archeology of Violence.* Trans. Jeanine Herman. New York: Semiotext(e), 1994.

Cleland, John. *Memoirs of a Woman of Pleasure (Fanny Hill).* Ed. Peter Sabor. Oxford: Oxford University Press, 1985.

Clover, Carol. *Men, Women, and Chain Saws: Gender in the Modern Horror Film.* Princeton: Princeton University Press, 1992.

Collings, Matthew. *Sarah Lucas.* London: Tate Publishing, 2002.

Collins, Richard. *Culture, Communication, and National Identity: The Case of Canadian Television.* Toronto: University of Toronto Press, 1990.

La Conciergerie. Dir. Michel Poulette. Perfs. Serge Dupire, Tania Kontayanni. Videocassette. 1999.

Condit, Celeste Michelle. "The Rhetorical Limits of Polysemy." *Critical Studies in Mass Communication* 6.2 (June 1989): 103–22.

Le Confessional. Dir. Robert Lepage. Perfs. Lothaire Bluteau, Patrick Gavette. Videocassette, 1996. Alliance Atlantis/ Alliance Vivafilm, 1995.

Consolidated Statutes of Canada. Criminal Code. Part VIII Offences against the Person and Reputation. Murder, Manslaughter and Infanticide. Infanticide. R.S.C. 1985, c.C–46, s. 233.

– Criminal Code. Part VIII Offences against the Person and Reputation. Murder, Manslaughter and Infanticide. Punishment for Infanticide. R.S.C. 1985, c. C–46, s. 237.

– Criminal Code. Part XX Procedure in Jury Trials and General Provisions. Verdicts. R.S.C. 1985, c. C–46, s. 663.

Cook, Ramsay. *Canada, Quebec, and the Uses of Nationalism*. 2nd ed. Toronto: McClelland & Stewart, 1996.

Cook, Sandy and Susanne Davies, eds. *Harsh Punishment: International Experiences of Women's Imprisonment*. Boston: Northeastern University Press, 1999.

"Cops Call Off Search for Baby: But Sûreté Still Investigating Bizarre Case." *The Montreal Gazette* 16 April 1998. <http://www.lexis-nexis/news>.

"Cops Search for Baby: Couple Questioned After Pregnancy Mysteriously Ends." *The Montreal Gazette* 15 April 1998. <http://www.lexis-nexis/news>.

Cornell, Drucilla. *Transformations: Recollective Imagination and Sexual Difference*. New York: Routledge, 1993.

Corriveau, Hugues. "Josée Yvon, kamikaze." *Lettres Québécoises* 75 (1994): 16.

Corse, Sarah M. *Nationalism and Literature: The Politics of Culture in Canada and the United States*. Cambridge: Cambridge University Press, 1997.

Cossman, Brenda, Shannon Bell, Lise Gotell, and Becki L. Ross. *Bad Attitudes on Trial: Pornography, Feminism, and the Butler Decision*. Toronto: University of Toronto Press, 1997.

Côté, Jean-François. "L'Identification américaine au Québec: De processus en résultats." In *L'Américanité et les Amériques*. Ed. Donald Cuccioletta. Sainte-Foy: Les Presses de L'Université Laval, 2001. 6–27.

– "Le Renouveau du grand récit des Amériques." In *Le Grand Récit des Amériques: Polyphonie des identités culturelles dans le contexte de la continentalisation*. Eds. Donald Cuccioletta, Jean-François Côté, et Frédérique Lesemann. Sainte-Foy: Les Presses de l'Université Laval, 2001. 9–37.

Couchard, Françoise. *Emprise et violence maternelles: Étude d'anthropologie psychanalytique*. Paris: Dunod, 1997.

Cournut, Jean. *Pourquoi les hommes ont peur des femmes*. Paris: Presses Universitaires de France, 2001.

Cowan, Gloria. "Women's Hostility toward Women and Rape and Sexual Harassment Myths." *Violence against Women* 6.3 (2000): 238–46.

–, C. Neighbors, J. DeLaMoreaux, and C. Behnke. "Women's Hostility toward Women." *Psychology of Women Quarterly* 22 (1998): 267–84.

A Cry in the Dark. Dir. Fred Schepisi. Perf. Meryl Streep, Sam Neill. Videocassette. Warner Bros., 1988.

Csipak, James and Lise Héroux. "NAFTA, Quebecers, and Fear (?) of Americanization: Some Empirical Evidence." *Québec Studies* 29 (spring/summer 2000)[:] 25–42.

– "Nationalism, Liberalism and the *Américanité* of Quebecers: From Fear to Embrace?" In *L'Américanité et les Amériques*. Ed. Donald Cuccioletta. Sainte-Foy: Les Presses de L'Université Laval, 2001. 103–36.

Cuccioletta, Donald, ed. *L'Américanité et les Amériques*. Sainte-Foy, Québec: Les Presses de l'Université Laval, 2001.

– "Introduction." In *Le Grand Récit des Amériques: Polyphonie des identités culturelles dans le contexte de la continentalisation*. Eds. Donald Cuccioletta, Jean-François Côté, et Frédérique Lesemann. Saint-Foy, Québec: Les Presses de l'Université Laval, 2001. 1–6.

– "Towards a Citizenship for the Americas." In *Le Grand Récit des Amériques: Polyphonie des identités culturelles dans le contexte de la continentalisation*. Eds. Donald Cuccioletta, Jean-François Côté, [et] Frédérique Lesemann. Saint-Foy, Québec: Les Presses de l'Université Laval, 2001. 41–50.

–, Jean-François Côté, et Frédéric Lesemann. *Le Grand Récit des Amériques: Polyphonie des identités culturelles dans le contexte de la continentalisation*. Saint-Foy, Québec: Les Presses de l'Université Laval, 2001.

– and Albert Desbiens. "L'Americanité, the Dual Nature of the Québécois Identity." *Québec Studies* 29 (spring/summer 2000): 3–14.

Cunha, Helena Parente. *Woman Between Mirrors*. Trans. Fred P. Ellison and Naomi Lindstrom. Austin: University of Texas Press, 1989.

Currie, D. and Valerie Raoul. *The Anatomy of Gender*. Ottawa: Carleton University Press, 1992.

Dagenais, Huguette, ed. *Pluralité et convergences: La Recherche féministe dans la francophonie*. Montréal: Les Éditions du Remue-Ménage, 1999.

Dandurand, Anne. "Après la bombe N." In *La Louve-garou*. Montréal: Éditions de la Pleine Lune, 1982. 141–3.

– "L'Assassin de l'intérieur." In *L'Assassin de l'intérieur/Diable d'espoir.* Montréal: XYZ Éditeur, 1988. 11–21.
– *L'Assassin de l'intérieur/Diable d'espoir.* Montréal: XYZ Éditeur, 1988.
– "Le Chagrin." In *Voilà, c'est moi: c'est rien, j'angoisse (Journal imaginaire).* Montréal: Triptyque, 1987. 43–45.
– *Un Coeur qui craque: Journal imaginaire.* Montréal: VLB Éditeur, 1990.
– "Le Corps des saisons." In *Petites âmes sous ultimatum.* Montréal: XYZ Éditeur, 1991. 29–37.
– "Le Courage est un bon poignard." In *Petites âmes sous ultimatum.* Montréal: XYZ Éditeur, 1991. 79–89.
– "Danger: Désir de glace." In *La Louve-garou.* Montréal: Éditions de la Pleine Lune, 1982. 41–4.
– "Dans la nuit les bruits, les cris et les parfums." In *Voilà, c'est moi: c'est rien, j'angoisse (Journal imaginaire).* Montréal: Triptyque, 1987. 73–4.
– "La Dernière Journée du milk-shake." In *Petites âmes sous ultimatum.* Montréal: XYZ Éditeur, 1991. 93–102.
– "Écrire ou mourir." Interview. XYZ Éditeur (hiver 1987): 40.
– "Les Étrennes." In *Voilà, c'est moi: c'est rien, j'angoisse (Journal imaginaire).* Montréal: Triptyque, 1987. 37–41.
– "L'Ex au max." In *L'Assassin de l'intérieur/Diable d'espoir.* Montréal: XYZ Éditeur, 1988. 23–33.
– "Histoire de Q." In *Voilà, c'est moi: c'est rien, j'angoisse (Journal imaginaire).* Montréal: Triptyque, 1987. 23–30.
– "Home Sweet Home." In *La Louve-garou.* Montréal: Éditions de la Pleine Lune, 1982. 59–63.
– "Inès courage." In *Voilà, c'est moi: c'est rien, j'angoisse (Journal imaginaire).* Montréal: Triptyque, 1987. 21.
– "The Inside Killer." Trans. Luise von Flotow. *Exile, A Literary Quarterly* 11.3 (winter 1986).
– "La Louve-garou." In *La Louve-garou.* Montréal: Éditions de la Pleine Lune, 1982. 11–13.
– "Maîtresse des hautes oeuvres." In *Les Porteuses d'ombre.* Montréal: Planète Rebelle, 1999.
– "Marc-André, sa blonde et blanche." In *Voilà, c'est moi: c'est rien, j'angoisse (Journal imaginaire).* Montréal: Triptyque, 1987. 33–6.
– *La Marquise ensanglantée.* Montréal: XYZ Éditeur, 1996.
– "Des milliers de minotaures." In *Petites âmes sous ultimatum.* Montréal: XYZ Éditeur, 1991. 49–61.
– "Montréal moite." In *Voilà, c'est moi: c'est rien, j'angoisse (Journal imaginaire).* Montréal: Triptyque, 1987. 69–71.

– "Les Muses cathodiques." In *Voilà, c'est moi: c'est rien, j'angoisse (Journal imaginaire)*. Montréal: Triptyque, 1987. 47–9.

– *Petites âmes sous ultimatum*. Montréal: XYZ Éditeur, 1991.

– "La Porte en dessous." In *La Louve-garou*. Montréal: Éditions de la Pleine Lune, 1982. 83–5.

– *Les Porteuses d'ombre*. Montréal: Planète Rebelle, 1999.

– "Pour endormir ma mort." In *Voilà, c'est moi: c'est rien, j'angoisse (Journal imaginaire)*. Montréal: Triptyque, 1987. 13–15.

– "Pour me consoler j'imagine que les bombes sont tombées." In *Voilà, c'est moi: c'est rien, j'angoisse (Journal imaginaire)*. Montréal: Triptyque, 1987. 19–20.

– *La Salle d'attente*. Montréal: XYZ Éditeur, 1994.

– "Le Salon des coeurs perdus." In *L'Assassin de l'intérieur/Diable d'espoir*. Montréal: XYZ Éditeur, 1988. 35–43.

– "Les Sentiers d'Agathe." In *Voilà, c'est moi: c'est rien, j'angoisse (Journal imaginaire)*. Montréal: Triptyque, 1987. 59–67.

– "Story of Q: A Dirty Story." Trans. Luise von Flotow. *Three by Three*. Ed. Luise von Flotow. Montréal: Guernica Editions, 1992. 35–46.

– "The Theft of Jacques Braise." Trans. Luise von Flotow. *Three by Three*. Ed. Luise von Flotow. Montréal: Guernica Editions, 1992. 11–25.

– "Underground Requiem." Trans. Luise von Flotow. *Three by Three*. Ed. Luise von Flotow. Montréal: Guernica Editions, 1992. 27–34.

– *Voilà, c'est moi: c'est rien, j'angoisse (Journal imaginaire)*. Montréal: Triptyque, 1987.

– "Le Vol de Jacques Braise." In *Petites âmes sous ultimatum*. Montréal: XYZ Éditeur, 1991. 65–76.

– "La Voleuse." In *Voilà, c'est moi: c'est rien, j'angoisse (Journal imaginaire)*. Montréal: Triptyque, 1987. 31–2.

– et Claire Dé. *La Louve-garou*. Montréal: Éditions de la Pleine Lune, 1982.

Daniels, Helen. "Truth, Community, and the Politics of Memory: Narratives of Child Sexual Abuse." *"Bad Girls"/"Good Girls": Women, Sex, and Power in the Nineties*. Eds. Nan Bauer Maglin and Donna Marie Perry. New Brunswick: Rutgers University Press, 1996.

Dardigna, Anne-Marie. *Les Châteaux d'Éros ou les infortunes du sexe des femmes*. Paris: Maspero, 1981.

Dasgupta, Shamita D. "Just Like Men? A Critical View of Violence by Women." In *Coordinating Community Response to Domestic Violence: Lesson from the Duluth Model*. Eds. E. Pence and M. Shepard. Thousand Oaks, California: Sage Publications, Inc., 1999. 195–222.

– "Towards an Understanding of Women's Use of Non-lethal Violence in Intimate Heterosexual Relationships." VAWnet *Applied Research Series* (2001). http://www.vawneet.org/VNL/Library/general/ARwomviol.html.

Dauvergne, Mia. *Homicide in Canada, 2001. Juristat* 22.7 (2002). Ottawa: Statistics Canada. Canadian Centre for Justice Statistics, 2002.

– *Homicide in Canada, 2003. Juristat* 24.8 (2004). Ottawa: Statistics Canada. Canadian Centre for Justice Statistics, 2004.

Davies, Miranda, ed. *Women and Violence.* London: Zed Books, 1994.

Davis, Don. *Hush Little Babies: The True Story of a Mother who Murdered her own Children.* New York: St. Martin's Press, 1997.

Dé, Claire. "L'Amour éternel." In *Le Désir comme catastrophe naturelle.* Grenoble: Glénat, 1989. 33–6.

– "À tuer." In *Le Désir comme catastrophe naturelle.* Grenoble: Glénat, 1989. 19–31.

– *Bonheur, oiseau rare: Roman pointilliste.* Montréal: XYZ Éditeur, 1996.

– "Un Cas de lycanthropie." In *La Louve-garou.* Montréal: Éditions de la Pleine Lune, 1982. 17–22.

– "La Causeuse orientale." In *La Louve-garou.* Montréal: Éditions de la Pleine Lune, 1982. 105–11.

– "Ce n'était pas de nos affaires." In *Chiens divers (et autres faits écrasés).* Montréal: XYZ Éditeur, 1991. 27–31.

– "Chevelure de flammes." In *Chiens divers (et autres faits écrasés).* Montréal: XYZ Éditeur, 1991. 35–43.

– *Chiens divers (et autres faits écrasés).* Montréal: XYZ Éditeur, 1991.

– *Le Désir comme catastrophe naturelle.* Grenoble: Glénat, 1989.

– "Les Dessous." In *Chiens divers (et autres faits écrasés).* Montréal: XYZ Éditeur, 1991. 91–4.

– "Kill." Trans. Luise von Flotow. *Three by Three.* Ed. Luise von Flotow. Montréal: Guernica Editions, 1992. 49–66.

– "Once upon a Time." Trans. Luise von Flotow. *Three by Three.* Ed. Luise von Flotow. Montréal: Guernica Editions, 1992. 69–74.

– "Pot de colle." In *Le Désir comme catastrophe naturelle.* Grenoble: Glénat, 1989. 43–57.

– "Pourquoi les marmottes?" In *Chiens divers (et autres faits écrasés).* Montréal: XYZ Éditeur, 1991. 53–61.

– *Sourdes amours.* Montréal: XYZ Éditeur, 1993.

– "Le Téléphone." In *Chiens divers (et autres faits écrasés).* Montréal: XYZ Éditeur, 1991. 97–104.

Le Déclin de l'empire américain/The Decline of the American Empire. Dir. Denys Arcand. Perfs. Dominique Michel, Dorothée Berryman. Videocassette, 1986. MCA Home Video, 1987.

DeCosta-Willis, Miriam, Reginald Martin, and Roseann P. Bell. *Érotique Noire/Black Erotica*. New York: Doubleday, 1992.

De Guise, Anne. "Quels regards pornographiques." *La Vie en Rose* (janvier 1984): 7.

DeKeseredy, Walter S. "Woman Abuse in Dating Relationships: A Critical Evaluation of Research and Theory." *International Journal of Sociology of the Family* 18 (1988): 79–86.

– *Women Abuse in Dating Relationships: The Role of Male Peer Support*. Toronto: Canadian Scholars' Press, 1988.

– *Women, Crime and the Canadian Criminal Justice System*. Cincinnati, Ohio: Anderson Publishing Co., 1999.

– and Desmond Ellis. "Intimate Male Violence against Women in Canada." In *Violence in Canada: Sociopolitical Perspectives*. Ed. Jeffrey Ian Ross. Don Mills: Oxford University Press Canada, 1995. 97–125.

– and Ronald Hinch. *Woman Abuse: Sociological Perspectives*. Toronto: Thompson Educational Publishing, 1991.

– and Martin Schwartz. *Measuring the Extent of Woman Abuse in Intimate Heterosexual Relationships: A Critique of the Conflict Tactics Scales*. VAWnet Applied Research Forum paper. 1998. http://www.vawnet.org/vnl/library/general/AR_ctscrit.pdf.

– *Women Abuse on Campus: Results from the Canadian National Survey*. Thousand Oaks: Sage, 1998.

Delâge, Denys. "Les Trois peuples fondateurs du Québec." In "Penser la nation québécoise." *Le Devoir* le 24–25 juillet 1999: A9.

De Lauretis, Teresa. *Alice Doesn't: Feminism, Semiotics, Cinema*. Bloomington: Indiana University Press, 1984.

– "Gorillas in the Midst: Women's Cinema and the 80s." *Screen* 31.1 (spring 1990): 6–25.

– *Technologies of Gender: Essays on Theory, Film, and Fiction*. Bloomington: Indiana University Press, 1987.

– "The Violence of Rhetoric: Considerations on Representation and Gender." In *Violence of Representation: Literature and the History of Violence*. Eds. Nancy Armstrong and Leonard Tennenhouse. New York: Routledge, 1989. 239–58.

Delisle, Jeanne-Mance. *La Bête rouge*. Montréal: Éditions de la Pleine Lune, 1996.

– *Nouvelles d'Abitibi*. Montréal: Éditions de la Pleine Lune, 1998.

Denby, David. "Killer: Two Views of Aileen Wuornos." *The New Yorker* 26 January 2004. 84–6.

Denfeld, Rene. *Kill the Body, The Head Will Fall: A Closer Look at Women, Violence, and Aggression*. New York: Warner Books, 1997.

Densmore, John. *Riders on the Storm: My Life with Jim Morrison and The Doors*. New York: Delacorte Press, 1990.

Derrida, Jacques. *Mémoires. Pour Paul de Man.* Paris: Galilée, 1988.

– *Of Grammatology.* Trans. Gayatri Chakravorty Spivak. Baltimore and London: Johns Hopkins University Press, 1976.

– "Violence et métaphysique." In *L'Écriture et la différence.* Paris: Éditions du Seuil, 1967.

– *Writing and Difference.* Trans. Alan Bass. Chicago: The University of Chicago Press, 1978.

Descôteaux, Bernard. *Coup de foudre.* Montréal: XYZ Éditeur, 1993.

Despentes, Virginie. *Baise-moi.* Paris: Éditions J'ai Lu, 1999.

– *Le Journal du dimanche.* 25 juin 2000.

– and Coralie Trinh Thi, co-dirs. *Baise-moi.* Perfs. Raffaela Anderson and Karen Bach. DVD. Pan-Européenne Productions, Remstar, 2000; Videocassette. Filmfixx/Remstar Distribution, 2001.

D'haen, Theo. "Post-scripts: Postnational Identities in Contemporary North-American Fiction." In *Roman contemporain et identité culturelle en Amérique du nord/Contemporary Fiction and Cultural Identity in North America.* Eds. Jaap Lintvelt, Richard Saint-Gelais, Will Verhoeven et Catherine Raffi-Béroud. Montréal: Éditions Nota Bene, 1998. 29–44.

Diamond, Lynn. *Le Passé sous nos pas.* Montréal: Tryptique,1999.

Diamond, Stephen A. *Anger, Madness, and The Daimonic: The Psychological Genesis of Violence, Evil, and Creativity.* Albany: State University of New York Press, 1996.

Di Cecco, Daniela. *Entre femmes et jeunes filles: Le Roman pour adolescentes en France et au Québec.* Montréal: Les Éditions du Remue-Ménage, 2000.

Dijkstra, Bram. *Evil Sisters: The Threat of Female Sexuality and the Cult of Manhood.* New York: Alfred A. Knopf, 1996.

– *Idols of Perversity: Fantasies of Feminine Evil in Fin-de-Siècle Culture.* New York: Oxford University Press, 1986.

Dinnerstein, Dorothy. *The Mermaid and the Minotaur: Sexual Arrangements and Human Malaise.* New York: Harper & Row, Publishers, 1977.

Dion, Jean. "À la canadienne." *Le Devoir* 31 mai et 1 juin 2003: B2.

Dion, Robert. *Le Moment critique de la fiction: Les Interprétations de la littérature que proposent les fictions québécoises contemporaines.* Montréal: Nuit Blanche, 1997.

"Divers, Dogs Join Search for Baby." *The Montreal Gazette* 17 April 1998. <http://www.lexis-nexis/news>.

Doane, Janice and Devon Hodges. *From Klein to Kristeva: Psychoanalytic Feminism and the Search for the "Good Enough" Mother.* Ann Arbor: University of Michigan Press, 1992.

– *Nostalgia and Sexual Difference: The Resistance to Contemporary Feminism.* New York: Methuen, 1987.

Dobash, R. E. and R.P. Dobash. *Women, Violence, and Social Change.* New York: Routledge, 1992.

Doherty, Thomas. *Cold War, Cool Medium: Television, McCarthyism, and American Culture.* New York: Columbia University Press, 2003.

– "Cultural Studies and 'Forensic Noir'" *The Chronicle of Higher Education* 24 October 2003. B14–B15.

Donaldson, Laura E. *Decolonizing Feminism: Race, Gender, and Empire-Building.* Chapel Hill: University of North Carolina Press, 1992.

Donnerstein, Edward and Neil Malamuth. "Pornography: Its Consequences on the Observer." In *Sexual Dynamics of Anti-Social Behavior.* Eds. L.B. Schlesinger and E. Revitch. Springfield, Illinois: Charles C. Thomas, 1997. 30–49.

The Doors. Dir. Oliver Stone. Perf. Val Kilmer and Meg Ryan. Videocassette. Warner Bros., 1991.

The Doors Live at the Hollywood Bowl. 5 July 1968. Doors Video Company; MCA Home Video, Inc., 1987.

Doran, Charles F. and John H. Sigler, eds. *Canada and the United States: Enduring Friendship, Persistent Stress.* Englewood Cliffs, New Jersey: Prentice Hall, 1985.

Dottin-Orsini, Mireille. *Cette femme qu'ils disent fatale: Textes et images de la misogynie fin-de-siècle.* Paris: Bernard Grasset, 1993.

Doyle, Kegan and Dany Lacombe. "Porn Power, Sex, Violence, and the Meaning of Images in 1980's Feminism." In *"Bad Girls"/"Good Girls": Women, Sex, and Power in the Nineties.* Eds. Nan Bauer Maglin and Donna Marie Perry. New Brunswick: Rutgers University Press, 1996. 188–204.

Dragiewicz, Molly. "The Batterer's Voice: Equal Protection, Gender, and Domestic Violence Discourse." Diss. George Mason University, 2005.

Dufour, Christian. "Mondialisation et question identitaire: Réflexions à partir du cas du Québec." In *Variations sur l'influence culturelle américaine.* Ed. Florian Sauvageau. Sainte-Foy, Québec: Les Presses de l'Université Laval, 1999. 167–80.

Dufour, Valérie. "L'Exode régional se confirme." *Le Devoir* 13 mars 2002: A3.

Duggan, Lisa. *Sapphic Slashers: Sex, Violence, and American Modernity.* Durham: Duke University Press, 2000.

Dumont, Fernand. *Genèse de la société québécoise.* Montréal: Boréal, 1993.

– *Raisons communes.* Montréal: Boréal, 1995.

Dumouchel, Paul, ed. *Comprendre pour agir: Violence, victimes et vengeances.* Sainte-Foy, Québec: Les Presses de l'Université Laval; Paris: L'Harmattan, 2000.

–, ed. *Violence and Truth: On the Work of René Girard.* Stanford: Stanford University Press, 1988.

Du Plessis, Rachel Blau. *Writing Beyond the Ending: Narrative Strategies of Twentieth-Century Women Writers.* Bloomington, Indiana: Indiana University Press, 1985.

Dupont, Louis. "L'Américanité québécoise: Portée politique d'un courant d'interprétation." In *L'Américanité et les Amériques.* Ed. Donald Cuccioletta. Sainte-Foy: Les Presses de L'Université Laval, 2001. 47–63.

Dupré, Louise, Jaap Lintvelt, et Janet Paterson. *Sexuation, espace, écriture: La Littérature québécoise en transformation.* Montréal: Éditions Nota Bene, 2002.

During, Simon. "Literature – Nationalism's Other? The Case for Revision." In *Nation and Narration.* Ed. Homi K. Bhaba. London: Routledge, 1990. 138–53.

Dvorak, James. J. "Neonaticide: Less Than Murder?" *The Northern Illinois University Law Review* (fall 1998). <http://www.lexis-nexis/legal>.

Dworkin, Andrea. *Pornography: Men Possessing Women.* New York: Perigee Books, 1981.

Early, Frances and Kathleen Kennedy, eds. *Athena's Daughters: Television's New Women Warriors.* Syracuse: Syracuse University Press, 2003.

Egloff, Karin. "It Takes Two to Tango: Pauline Harvey's *Un Homme est une valse.*" In *Doing Gender: Franco-Canadian Women Writers of the 1990s.* Eds. Paula Ruth Gilbert and Roseanna L. Dufault. Madison & Teaneck, New Jersey: Fairleigh Dickinson University Press; Cranbury, New Jersey, London, & Mississauga, Ontario: Associated University Presses, 2001. 130–41.

Elliott, Michelle, ed. *Female Sexual Abuse of Children: The Ultimate Taboo.* New York: John Wiley & Sons, 1993.

Ellis, Havelock. *The Criminal.* New York: AMS Press, 1972.

Elvis Gratton: Le King des kings. Dir. Pierre Falardeau. Perfs. Julien Poulin and Denise Mercier. Videocassette and DVD, 1999. Lion's Gate, 1981–85.

Elvis Gratton: Miracle à Memphis. Dir. Pierre Falardeau. Perfs. Julien Poulin and Yves Trudel. DVD, 1999; Videocassette, 2001. Lion's Gate, 1999.

Emporte-moi/Set Me Free. Dir. Léa Pool. Perfs. Karine Varnasse, Pascal Buissières, Miki Manojlovic. Videocassette. Merchant Ivory Productions, 1998.

Ensler, Eve. *The Vagina Monologues.* New York: Villard Books, 1998.

Epstein, Su C. "The New Mythic Monster." In *Cultural Criminology.* Eds. Jeff Ferrell and Clinton R. Sanders. Boston: Northeastern University Press, 1995. 66–79.

Fahrenthold, David A. "Homicide Count Up 12% This Year: D.C., Pr. George's Post Biggest Increases." *The Washington Post* 29 December 2002: C1.

Fairstein, Linda A. *Sexual Violence: Our War against Rape.* New York: Berkley Books, 1995.

Faith, K. "Media, Myths and Masculinization: Images of Women in Prison." In *In Conflict with the Law: Women and the Canadian Justice System.* Eds. E. Adleberg and C. Currie. Vancouver: Press Gang. 174–211.

Fanon, Frantz. *Les Damnés de la terre.* Paris: François Maspero, 1982.

Fatal Attraction. Dir. Adrian Lyne. Perfs. Michael Douglas and Glenn Close. Paramount, 1987.

Fawcett, Barbara et al., eds. *Violence and Gender Relations: Theories and Interventions.* London: Sage, 1996.

Fedorowycz, Orest. *Homicide in Canada, 1999. Juristat* 20.9 (2000). Ottawa: Statistics Canada. Canadian Centre for Justice Statistics, 2000.

– *Homicide in Canada, 2000. Juristat* 21.9 (2001). Ottawa: Statistics Canada. Canadian Centre for Justice Statistics, 2001.

Feminist Majority Foundation, Domestic Violence Information Center. "Domestic Violence Facts." http://www.feminist.org/other/dv/dvfact.html.

La Femme Nikita. Dir. Luc Besson. Perfs. Annie Parillaud and Marc Duret. Videocassette and DVD, 2000. MGM/UA Studios, 1991.

Ferrell, Jeff and Clinton R. Sanders. *Cultural Criminology.* Boston: Northeastern University Press, 1995.

Fiebert, M. S. and D.M. Gonzalez. "Women Who Initiate Assaults: The Reasons Offered for Such Behavior." *Psychological Reports* 80 (1997): 583–90.

Film Industry Task Force. *Canadian Cinema: A Solid Base.* Ottawa: 1985.

Finley, Karen. "It's Only Art." In *Shock Treatment.* San Francisco: City Lights, 1990. 69–74.

First Blood. Dir. Ted Kotcheff. Perf. Sylvester Stallone and Richard Crenna. Videocassette. Carolco Pictures; Avid Home Entertainment, 1982.

Flaherty, David and Frank Manning eds. *The Beaver Bites Back? American Popular Culture in Canada.* Montreal: McGill-Queen's University Press, 1993.

Flannery, D.J., C.R. Huff, and M. Manos. "Youth Gangs: A Developmental Perspective." In *Delinquent Violent Youth: Theory and Interventions.* Eds. T.P. Gullotta, G.R. Adams, and R. Montemayor. Thousand Oaks, California: Sage Publications, 1998. 175–204.

Flotow, Luise von. "Legacies of Quebec Women's 'Écriture au féminin': Bilingual Transformances, Translation Politicized, Subaltern Visions of the Text of the Street." *Revue d'Études Canadiennes* 30.4 (hiver 1995–96): 88–109.

– "La Relève féminine au Québec: Une Écriture autrement engagée." *Québec Studies* 15 (1992–93): 57–65.

– "'Tenter l'érotique': Eroticism in Women's Texts from Québec." *Québec Studies* 10 (1990): 91–7.

Forbes, Jill and Michael Kelly, eds. *French Cultural Studies: An Introduction.* New York: Oxford University Press, 1995.

Forter, Greg. *Murdering Masculinities: Fantasies of Gender and Violence in the American Crime Novel.* New York: New York University Press, 2000.

"For the record, the text of the National Film and Video Policy." *Cinema Canada* (July/August 1984): 42–5.

Fortin, Andrée. "Présentation." In *Produire la culture, produire l'identité?* Ed. Andrée Fortin. Sainte-Foy, Québec: Les Presses de l'Université Laval, 2000.

– *Produire la culture, produire l'identité?* Sainte-Foy, Québec: Les Presses de l'Université Laval, 2000.

Foster, Thomas, Carol Siegel, and Ellen Berry. *Bodies of Writing, Bodies in Performance.* New York: New York University Press, 1996.

Foucault, Michel. *Discipline and Punish: The Birth of the Prison.* Trans. Alan Sheridan. New York: Random House/Vintage Books, 1979.

– *Histoire de la sexualité: I. La Volonté de savoir.* Paris: Éditions Gallimard, 1976.

– *The History of Sexuality. Volume I: An Introduction.* Trans. Robert Hurley. New York: Vintage Books, Random House, 1980.

– *I, Pierre Rivière, Having Slaughtered My Mother, My Sister, and My Brother ...: A Case Study of Parricide in the 19th Century.* Lincoln: University of Nebraska Press, 1975.

– "The Subject and Power." In *Michel Foucault: Beyond Structuralism and Hermeneutics.* Eds. Hubert L. Dreyfus and Paul Rabinow. Chicago: University of Chicago Press, 1983.

– *Surveiller et punir: Naissance de la prison.* Paris: Gallimard, 1975.

Fournier, Claude. *Deux femmes en or.* Canadian Film Development Corporation. 1970.

Fowlie, Wallace. *Rimbaud and Jim Morrison: The Rebel as Poet – A Memoir.* Durham and London: Duke University Press, 1994.

Fox, Richard L. and Robert W. Van Sickel. *Tabloid Justice: Criminal Justice in an Age of Media Frenzy.* Boulder, Colorado: Lynne Rienner Publishers, 2000.

French, Sean. "Partners in Crime: Defending the Female of the Species." In *No Angels: Women Who Commit Violence.* Eds. Alice Myers and Sarah Wight. San Francisco: Pandora, 1996. 29–43.

Frigon, Sylvie. "Éditorial." *Criminologie* 29.2 (automne 1996): 3–9.

– *L'Homicide conjugal au Canada. Criminologie* 29.2 (automne 1996). Montréal: Les Presses de l'Université de Montréal, 1996.

– "L'Homicide conjugal féminin, de Marie-Josephte Corriveau (1763) à Angélique Lyn Lavallée (1990): meurtre ou légitime défense? *Criminologie* 29.2 (automne 1996): 11–27.

Fry, Earl H. "Quebec's Relations with the United States." *The American Review of Canadian Studies* 32.2 (2002): 323–42.

Frye, Northrop. "Conclusion to a *Literary History of Canada.*" In *The Bush Garden: Essays on the Canadian Imagination.* Toronto: Anansi, 1971. 213–51.

Fuery, Patrick and Nick Mansfield. *Cultural Studies and the New Humanities: Concepts and Controversies.* Melbourne: Oxford University Press, 1997.

Gagné, Gilles. "Libre-échange, souveraineté et américanité: Une nouvelle trinité pour le Québec?" *Politique et sociétés* 18.1 (1999): 99–107.

– "Un Projet d'État pour contrer le capital libéralisé." In "Penser la nation québécoise." *Le Devoir* le 21–22 août 1999: A9.

Gagnon, Dominique, Louise Laprade, Nicole Lecavalier, Pol Pelletier. *À ma mère, à ma mère, à ma mère, à ma voisine.* Montréal: Les Éditions du Remue-Ménage, 1979.

Gagnon, Madeleine. *Les Femmes et la guerre.* Montréal: VLB Éditeur, 2000.

Gallays, François. *La Nouvelle au Québec.* Montréal: Fides, 1996.

Gallop, Jane. *The Daughter's Seduction: Feminism and Psychoanalysis.* Ithaca: Cornell University Press, 1982.

– *Reading Lacan.* Ithaca: Cornell University Press, 1985.

Gammon, Mary A.B. *Violence in Canada.* Toronto: Methuen, 1978.

Garber, Marjorie. *Vested Interests: Cross-Dressing and Cultural Anxiety.* New York: Harper Perennial, 1992.

Garde, Roger de la, William Gilsdorf, and Ilja Wechselmann, eds. *Small Nations, Big Neighbour: Denmark and Quebec/Canada Compare Notes on American Popular Culture.* London: John Libbey, 1993.

Garner, Bryan A., ed. in chief. *Black's Law Dictionary.* 7th edition. St. Paul, Minnesota: West Group, 1999.

Gartner, Rosemary. "Homicide in Canada." In *Violence in Canada: Sociopolitical Perspectives.* Ed. Jeffrey Ian Ross. Don Mills: Oxford University Press Canada, 1995. 186–222.

Gauthier, Jennifer. "Split Screen: National Cinemas, Cultural Policy, and Identity in Canada." Diss. George Mason University, 2003.

Gauvin, Lise. *Langagement: L'Ecrivain et la langue au Québec.* Montréal: Boréal, 2000.

Gélinas, Pauline. *Le Sexe sale.* Montréal: Les Éditions des Intouchables, 2001.

Gendron, Pierre. "L'Avenir du Québec et la vertu des petites nations." In *Le Pays de tous les Québécois: Diversité culturelle et souveraineté*. Ed. Michel Sarra-Bournet. Montréal: VLB Éditeur, 1998. 69–76.

Genette, Gérard. *Narrative Discourse*. Trans. J. Lewing. Ithaca: Cornell University Press, 1980.

Gibson, James William. *Warrior Dreams: Violence and Manhood in Post-Vietnam America*. New York: Hill and Wang, 1994.

Gibson, Pamela C. and Roma Gibson, eds. *Dirty Looks: Women, Pornography, Power*. London: British Film Institute Publishing, 1993.

Giguère, Diane. *Le Temps des jeux*. Montréal: Pierre Tisseyre, 1976.

G. I. Jane. Dir. Ridley Scott. Perf. Demi Moore and Viggo Mortensen. Videocassette. Caravan Pictures/Hollywood Pictures Home Video, 1997.

Gilbert, Paula Ruth. "The Daughter Below: Double Parody of Mother-Daughter Bonding in Michèle Mailhot's *Béatrice vue d'en bas*." *The American Review of Canadian Studies* 22.4 (Winter 1992): 511–32.

– "Discourses of Female Criminality: Suzanne Jacob's *L'Obéissance*, A Novel of Infanticide/Filicide." *Québec Studies* 32 (2001–02): 37–55.

– "Discourses of Female Violence and Societal Gender Stereotypes." *Journal of Violence against Women* 8.11 (2002): 1271–1300.

– "'The Killer Awoke before Dawn': The Multiple Mirrors of Hélène Rioux's Éléonore." *Québec Studies* 20 (1995): 56–65.

– "Neurotic Disorders: Gendered Inner Violence in Selected Short Stories by Monique Bosco and Hélène Rioux." *Québec Studies* 29 (spring/summer 2000): 115–27.

– "Public and Private Violence: A 'Mise en discours de la violence' in Aline Chamberland's *La Fissure*." *The American Review of Canadian Studies* 31.3 (Autumn 2001): 359–83.

– and Roseanna L. Dufault, eds. *Doing Gender: Franco-Canadian Women Writers of the 1990s*. Madison & Teaneck, New Jersey: Fairleigh Dickinson University Press; Cranbury, New Jersey, London, & Mississauga, Ontario: Associated University Presses, 2001.

– and Kimberly K. Eby, ed. *Violence and Gender: An Interdisciplinary Reader*. Englewood Cliffs, New Jersey: Prentice Hall, 2004.

– and Lorna Irvine. "Pre- and Post-Mortem: Regendering and Serial Killing in Rioux, Dandurand, Dé, and Atwood." *The American Review of Canadian Studies* (spring 1999): 113–33.

Gilbert, Reid. "Mounties, Muggings, and Moose: Canadian Icons in a Landscape of American Violence." In *The Beaver Bites Back?* Eds. David Flaherty and Frank Manning. Montreal: McGill-Queen's University Press, 1993. 178–96.

Gilligan, Carol. *In A Different Voice: Psychological Theory and Women's Development.* Cambridge: Harvard University Press, 1982.

Gilligan, James. "The Deadliest Form of Violence is Poverty." In *Violence: Our Deadly Epidemic and Its Causes.* New York: G.P. Putnam's Sons, 1996. 191–208.

– "How to Think about Violence." In *Violence: Our Deadly Epidemic and Its Causes.* New York: G.P. Putnam's Sons, 1996. 89–102.

– *Preventing Violence.* New York: Thames and Hudson, 2001.

– "Shame: The Emotions and Morality of Violence." In *Violence: Our Deadly Epidemic and Its Causes.* New York: G.P. Putnam's Sons, 1996. 103–36.

– *Violence: Our Deadly Epidemic and Its Causes.* New York: G.P. Putnam's Sons, 1996.

Girard, René. *La Violence et le sacré.* Paris: Grasset, 1972.

Giroux, Henry A. *Fugitive Cultures: Race, Violence, and Youth.* New York: Routledge, 1996.

Girshick, Lori B. *Woman-To-Woman Sexual Violence: Does She Call It Rape?* Boston: Northeastern University Press, 2002.

Gladwell, Malcolm. "The Tipping Point." *The New Yorker* 3 June 1996: 32–8.

Godbout, Jacques. *L'Écran du bonheur.* Montréal: Boréal, 1995.

– *Le Murmure marchand.* Montréal: Boréal Compact, 1989.

Goffman, Erving. *Stigma: Notes on the Management of a Spoiled Identity.* Englewood Cliffs, New Jersey: Prentice Hall, 1963.

Goldstein, Jeffrey H., ed. *Why We Watch: The Attractions of Violent Entertainment.* New York: Oxford University Press, 1998.

Gomel, Elana. *Bloodscripts: Writing the Violent Subject.* Columbus: The Ohio State University Press, 2003.

Gomme, Ian McDermaid. *The Shadow Line: Deviance and Crime in Canada.* Toronto: Harcourt Brace Jovanovich, 1993.

Gorer, Geoffry. "The Erotic Myth of America." *Partisan Review* (July-August 1950).

Gould, Karen. "Madeleine Monette, 'Otherness,' and Quebec Cultural Criticism." In *Women by Women: The Treatment of Female Characters by Women Writers of Fiction in Quebec since 1980.* Ed. Roseanna Lewis Dufault. Cranbury, New Jersey: Fairleigh Dickinson Press/Associated University Presses, Inc., 1997. 241–52.

– "Rewriting 'America': Violence, Postmodernity, and Parody in the Fiction of Madeleine Monette, Nicole Brossard, and Monique LaRue." In *Postcolonial Subjects: Francophone Women Writers.* Eds. Mary Jean Green et al. Minneapolis: University of Minnesota Press, 1996. 186–209.

– *Writing in the Feminine: Feminism and Experimental Writing in Quebec.* Carbondale and Edwardsville: Southern Illinois University Press, 1990.

Gourdeau, Gabrielle. *L'Echo du silence.* Trois Pistoles, Québec: Éditions Trois-Pistoles, 1997.

Gourmont, Rémy de. *The Natural Philosophy of Love* [1903]. New York: Collier Books, 1961.

Gouvernement du Québec. "Loi sur le cinéma/Cinema Act." 1975, 1979, 1983, 1991, 1992, 1994.

– "Loi sur la Société de développement des industries culturelles." 1994.

– "Règlement sur la reconaissance d'un film comme film québécois." *Loi sur le cinéma.* 1983, 1988, 1992, 1997, 1998, 1999.

Government of Canada, Minister of Supply and Services. *Vital Links: Canadian Cultural Industries.* Ottawa: 1987.

–, Secretary of State. *Tompkins Report: The Film Industry in Canada.* Ottawa: 1976.

La Grande Séduction/Seducing Dr. Lewis. Dir. Jean-François Pouliot. Perfs. Germain Lesage, David Boutin, Rita Lafontaine. Max Films Productions/Wellspring Media, 2004.

Green, Mary Jean. *Marie-Claire Blais.* New York: Twayne Publishers, 1995.

– et al., eds. *Postcolonial Subjects: Francophone Women Writers.* Minneapolis: University of Minnesota Press, 1996.

Greenwood, F. Murray and Beverly Boissery. *Uncertain Justice: Canadian Women and Capital Punishment, 1754–1953.* Toronto: Dundurn Press, Ltd., 2000.

Grewal, Inderpal and Caren Kaplan, eds. *Scattered Hegemonies: Postmodernity and Transnational Feminist Practices.* Minneapolis: University of Minnesota Press, 1994.

Griffin, Susan. *Pornography and Silence: Culture's Revenge against Nature.* London: The Women's Press Limited, 1981.

Grindstaff, Laura and Martha McCaughey. "Re-membering John Bobbitt: Castration Anxiety, Male Hysteria, and the Phallus." In *No Angels: Women Who Commit Violence.* Eds. Alice Myers and Sarah Wight. San Francisco: Pandora, 1996. 142–60.

Grixti, John. "Consuming Cannibals: Psychopathic Killers as Archetypes and Cultural Icons." *Journal of American Culture* 18 (1995): 87–96.

Group SECOR. "Evaluation of Telefilm Canada Feature Film Fund – Executive Summary." June 1991.

Guénette, Françoise. "Histoire de prologue." *La Vie en Rose* (juillet–août 1985): 37.

Gulliver, Lili. *L'Univers Gulliver!* Montréal: VLB, 1990.

– *L'Univers Gulliver II: La Grèce.* Montréal: VLB, 1991.
– *L'Univers Gulliver III: La Thailande.* Montréal: VLB, 1992.
– *L'Univers Gulliver IV: L'Australie sans dessous dessus.* Trois Pistoles, Québec: Victor-Lévy Beaulieu, 1999.
Gurik, Robert. *The Trial of Jean-Baptiste M.* Trans. Allan Van Meer. Vancouver: Talonbooks, 1974.
Gurr, Ted Robert. "Foreword." In *Violence in Canada: Sociopolitical Perspectives.* Ed. Jeffrey Ian Ross. Don Mills: Oxford University Press Canada, 1995. viii–xvii.
– and Hugh David Graham, eds. *The History of Crime.* Newbury Park, California: Sage Publications, 1989. Vol. 1 of *Violence in America.* 2 vols.
– and Hugh David Graham, eds. *Protest, Rebellion, Reform.* Newbury Park, California: Sage Publications, 1989. Vol. 2 of *Violence in America.* 2 vols.
Gustave Courbet: L'Origine du monde. Dir. Jean-Paul Fargier. Paris: Musée d'Orsay, Ex Nihilo, La Sept/Arte, RMN, 1996.
Hadj-Moussa, Ratiba. "Indétermination, appartenance et identification: Penser l'identité." In *Produire la culture, produire l'identité?* Ed. Andrée Fortin. Sainte-Foy, Québec: Les Presses de l'Université Laval, 2000. 219–43.
Halberstam, Judith. *Female Masculinity.* Durham: Duke University Press, 1998.
– *Skin Shows: Gothic Horror and the Technology of Monsters.* Durham: Duke University Press, 1995.
Halttunen, Karen. *Murder Most Foul: The Killer and the American Gothic Imagination.* Cambridge: Harvard University Press, 1998.
Hamberger, L.K. "Female Offenders in Domestic Violence: A Look at Actions in their Contexts." *Journal of Aggression, Maltreatment, and Trauma* 1.1(1997): 117–29.
– and C.E. Guse. "Men's and Women's Use of Intimate Partner Violence in Clinical Samples: Toward a Gender-Sensitive Analysis." *Journal of Violence against Women* 8 (2002).
Hamerton Kelly, ed. *Violent Origins: Walter Burkert, René Girard, and Jonathan Z. Smith on Ritual Killing and Cultural Formation.* Stanford: Stanford University Press, 1987.
Hamilton, Susan, ed. *Criminals, Idiots, Women, and Minors: Victorian Writing by Women on Women.* Ontario, Canada: Broadview Press, 1995.
Hampton, Blanche. *Prisons and Women.* Kensington, New South Wales: New South Wales University Press, 1993.
The Hanging Garden. Dir. Thom Fitzgerald. Perfs. Kerry Fox and Chris Leavins. Cineplex Odeon Films, 1998.
Hanssen, Beatrice. *Critique of Violence: Between Poststructuralism and Critical Theory.* New York: Routledge, 2000.

Harel, Simon. *Le Valeur de parcours: Identité et cosmopolitisme dans la littérature québécoise contemporaine.* Montréal: Le Préambule, 1989.

Harraway, Donna. "A Manifesto for Cyborgs: Science, Technology, and Socialist Feminism in the 1980s." *Socialist Review* 15.2 (1985): 65–108.

– *Simians, Cyborgs, and Women: The Reinvention of Nature.* London: Free Association Books, 1996.

Harris, Laura and Elizabeth Crocker. *Femme: Feminists, Lesbians, and Bad Girls.* New York: Routledge, 1997.

Hart, Lynda. *Fatal Women: Lesbian Sexuality and the Mark of Aggression.* Princeton: Princeton University Press, 1994.

Harvey, Frank P. "Canada's Addiction to American Security: The Illusion of Choice in the War on Terrorism." *The American Review of Canadian Studies* 35.2 (summer 2005): 265–94.

Harvey, Pauline. *Un Homme est une valse.* Montréal: Les Herbes Rouges, 1992.

Hasian, Marouf, Jr. and Lisa A. Flores. "Mass Mediated Representation of the Susan Smith Trial." *The Howard Journal of Communications* 11.3 (July/September 2000): 163–78.

Heavenly Creatures. Dir. Peter Jackson. Perf. Melanie Lynskey, Kate Winslet, Sarah Peirse, Diana Kent. Videocassette. Miramax, 1994.

Hébert, Anne. *Les Enfants du sabbat.* Paris: Éditions du Seuil, 1975.

– *Les Fous de bassan.* Paris: Éditions du Seuil, 1982.

– *Héloise.* Paris: Éditions du Seuil, 1980.

– *Kamouraska.* Paris: Éditions du Seuil, 1970.

– *Le Torrent.* Montréal: Éditions HMH, 1974.

Hekman, Susan J. *Gender and Knowledge: Elements of a Postmodern Feminism.* Cambridge, England: Polity Press, 1990.

Hendin, Josephine Gattuso. *Heartbreakers: Women and Violence in Contemporary Culture and Literature.* New York: Palgrave Macmillan, 2004.

Herman, Judith Lewis. *Trauma and Recovery: The Aftermath of Violence.* New York: Basic Books, 1992.

Hero, Alfred, Jr. and Louis Balthazar. *Contemporary Quebec and the United States, 1960–1985.* Lanham, Maryland: University Press of America, 1985.

Herrmann, Claudine. *Les Voleuses de langue.* Paris: Éditions des femmes, 1976.

Hester, Marianne, Liz Kelly, and Jill Radford. *Women, Violence, and Male Power: Feminist Activism, Research, and Practice.* Philadelphia: Open University Press, 1996.

Higgins, Lynn A. and Brenda R. Silver, eds. *Rape and Representation.* New York: Columbia University Press, 1991.

Higham C.L. and David N. Biette. "Introduction: Canada-U.S. Relations: Important Topics." *The American Review of Canadian Studies* 35.2 (summer 2005): 211–13.

Hirsch, Marianne. *The Mother/Daughter Plot: Narrative, Psychoanalysis, Feminism.* Bloomington: Indiana University Press, 1989.

Hite, Molly. *The Other Side of the Story: Structures and Strategies of Contemporary Feminist Narratives.* Ithaca: Cornell University Press, 1989.

Hjort, Mette and Scott Mackenzie, eds. *Cinema and Nation.* New York: Routledge, 2000.

Holmlund, Christine. "A Decade of Deadly Dolls: Hollywood and the Woman Killer." In *Moving Targets: Women, Murder and Representation.* Ed. Helen Birch. Berkeley: University of California Press, 1994. 127–51.

Hooper, M. "When domestic violence diversion is no longer an option: What to do with the female offender." *Berkeley Women's Law Journal* 11 (1996): 168–81.

Hopkins, Jerry and Danny Sugerman. *No One Here Gets Out Alive.* New York: Warner Books, Inc., 1980.

Horvitz, Deborah M. *Literary Trauma: Sadism, Memory, and Sexual Violence in American Women's Fiction.* Albany: State University of New York Press, 2000.

Hoskins, Colin, Adam Finn, and Stuart McFadyen. "Television and Film in a Freer International Trade Environment: U.S. Dominance and Canadian Responses." In *Mass Media and Free Trade: NAFTA and the Cultural Industries.* Eds. Emile G. McAnany and Kenton T. Wilkinson. Austin: University of Texas Press, 1996.

Houle, Michel. "Report on the Production and Distribution of Canadian Feature Films – Issues Paper." July 1997.

Howlett, Jana and Rod Mengham, eds. *The Violent Muse: Violence and the Artistic Imagination in Europe, 1920–1939.* Manchester: Manchester University Press, 1994.

Hunt, Lynn, ed. *The Invention of Pornography: Obscenity and the Origins of Modernity, 1500–1800.* New York: Zone Books, 1993.

Huston, Nancy. *Mosaique de la pornographie.* Paris: Denoel/Gonthier, 1982; Payot, 2004.

– *Pour un patriotisme de l'ambiguité: Notes autour d'un voyage aux sources.* Montréal: Fides, 1995.

Hutcheon, Linda. *The Canadian Postmodern: A Study of Contemporary English-Canadian Fiction.* Toronto: Oxford University Press, 1988.

– "'Circling the Downspot of Empire': Post-colonialism and Postmodernism." *ARIEL* 20.4 (1989): 149–75.

– *Narcissistic Narrative: The Metafictional Paradox*. New York: Methuen, 1984.
– *A Poetics of Postmodernism: History, Theory, Fiction*. New York: Rutledge, 1988.
– *The Politics of Postmodernism*. New York: Rutledge, 1989.
– *A Theory of Parody: The Teachings of Twentieth-Century Art Forms*. New York: Methuen, 1985.
Imbert, Patrick. "Hybridités discursives dans les Amériques." In *Le Grand Récit des Amériques: Polyphonie des identités culturelles dans le contexte de la continentalisation*. Eds. Donald Cuccioletta, Jean-François Côté, et Frédérique Lesemann. Saint-Foy, Québec: Les Presses de l'Université Laval, 2001. 85–101.
"Infanticide Experts Examining Slayings." *Calgary Herald* 31 July 1997. <http://www.lexis-nexis/news>.
"Infanticides Undetected, Report Says." *The Edmonton Sun* 7 February 1999. <http://www.lexis-nexis/news>.
Inness, Sherrie A. *Tough Girls: Women Warriors and Wonder Women in Popular Culture*. Philadelphia: University of Pennsylvania Press, 1999.
– ed. *Action Chicks: New Images of Tough Women in Popular Culture*. New York: Palgrave Macmillan, 2004.
Les Invasions barbares. Dir. Denys Arcand. Perfs. Rémy Girard, Stéphane Rousseau, Dorothée Berryman, Louise Portal, Marie-Josée Croze. Buena Vista Home Video, 2004.
Ireland, Susan. "The Daughter's Revenge: Father-Daughter Incest in Gabrielle Gourdeau's *L'Écho du silence*." In *Doing Gender: Franco-Canadian Women Writers of the 1990s*. Eds. Paula Ruth Gilbert and Roseanna L. Dufault. Madison & Teaneck, New Jersey: Fairleigh Dickinson University Press; Cranbury, New Jersey, London, & Mississauga, Ontario: Associated University Presses, 2001. 186–202.
Irigaray, Luce. "Any Theory of the 'Subject' Has Always Been Appropriated by the 'Masculine.'" In *Speculum of the Other Woman*. Trans. Gillian C. Gill. Ithaca: Cornell University Press, 1985.
– "Toute théorie du 'sujet' aura toujours été appropriée au 'masculin.'" In *Speculum de l'autre femme*. Paris: Les Éditions de Minuit, 1974. 165–82.
Itzin, Catherine, ed. *Pornography: Women, Violence, and Civil Liberties*. London: Oxford University Press, 1992.
Jack, Dana Crowley. *Behind the Mask: Destruction and Creativity in Women's Aggression*. Cambridge: Harvard University Press, 2001.
Jacob, Suzanne. *La Bulle d'encre*. Montréal: Les Éditions du Boréal, 2001.

– *Écrire: Comment, pourquoi*. Paroisse Notre-Dame-des-Neiges, Québec: Éditions Trois-Pistoles, 2002.

– *L'Obéissance*. Montréal: Les Éditions du Boréal, 1993.

– *La Voix de l'au-delà*. Interview with Stanley Péan. *Librairie Pantoute*. 2001. <http://www.librairiepantoute.qc.ca/magazine/rencontres/jacob.asp>.

Jacobellis *v.* Ohio, 378 U.S. 184 (1964).

Jacques, Daniel. "La Fin des deux solitudes passe par une fondation réussie." In "Penser la nation québécoise." *Le Devoir* le 26–27 juin 1999: A9.

James, Oliver. "Gender: The Outwardly-Directed Violence of Depresssed Men and the Inwardly-Directed Violence of Depressed Women." In *Juvenile Violence in a Winner-Loser Culture*. London and New York: Free Association Books, 1995: 75–92.

Jardine, Alice A. *Gynesis: Configurations of Woman and Modernity*. Ithaca: Cornell University Press, 1985.

Jeffords, Susan. *The Remasculinization of America: Gender and the Vietnam War*. Bloomington: Indiana University Press, 1989.

Jelinek, Elfriede. "Der Sinn des Obszönen." *Frauen und pornographie*. Ed. Claudia Gehrke. Tübingen: Verlag Claudia Gehrke, 1988.

Jenkins, Philip. *Using Murder: The Social Construction of Serial Homicide*. New York: Aldine de Gruyter, 1994.

Jenson, Jane. "De la nation à la citoyenneté." In "Penser la nation québécoise." *Le Devoir* le 31 juillet–1 août 1999: A9.

Johnson, Rebecca. "Perspectives on the Latimer Trial: Confronting the Bogeyman: Latimer, and Other Fearful Tales of Murderous Fathers and Monstrous Children." *Saskatchewan Law Review* (2001). <http://www.lexis-nexis/legal>.

Jones, Adam, ed. *Gendercide and Genocide*. Nashville: Vanderbilt University Press, 2004.

Jones, Ann. *Next Time, She'll Be Dead: Battering and How to Stop It*. Boston: Beacon Press, 1994.

– *Women Who Kill*. New York: Holt, Rinehart, and Winston, 1980.

Jones, Jennifer. *Medea's Daughters: Forming and Performing the Woman Who Kills*. Columbus: The Ohio State University Press, 2003.

Jones, Richard Glyn. *Women Who Kill*. Edison, New Jersey: Castle Books, 2004.

Jong, Erica. *Fear of Flying*. New York: Signet, 1996.

Joubert, Lucie. *Le Carquois de velours: L'Ironie au féminin dans la littérature québécoise 1960–1980*. Montréal: L'Hexagone, 1998.

–, ed. *Trajectoires au féminin dans la littérature québécoise (1960–1990)*. Montréal: Éditions Nota Bene, 2000.

Ju Dou. Dir. Zhang Yi-Mou and Yang Fen Liang. Perf. Gong Li, Li Bao-Tian, and Li Wei. Videocassette. Miramax, 1991.

Juteau, Danielle. "Une Collectivité québécoise multinationale et multiethnique." In "Penser la nation québécoise." *Le Devoir* le 28–29 août 1999: A9.

Juvenile Delinquency in Canada. The Report of the Department of Justice Committee on Juvenile Delinquency. Ottawa: Crown Copyrights, 1967.

Kappeler, Susan. *The Pornography of Representation*. Cambridge, England: Polity Press/Oxford, England: Blackwell, 1986.

Kappeler, V.E., M. Blumberg, and G.W. Potter. *The Mythology of Crime and Criminal Justice*. 2nd ed. Prospect Heights, Illinois: Waveland, 1996.

Kashak, Ellyn. "No Safe Spaces." Review of *Woman-to-Woman Sexual Violence*, by Lori B. Girshick and *No More Secrets*, by Janice Ristock. *The Women's Review of Books* 20.4 (January 2003): 20–1.

Kashi, Raija, Kathleen Kells, and Louise Forsyth, eds. *Les Discours féminins dans la littérature postmoderne au Québec*. San Francisco: EMT Press, 1993.

Katz, Jackson and Sut Jhally, dirs. *Tough Guise*. Video Documentary. Northampton, Massachusetts: Media Education Foundation, 1999.

Kelleher, Michael D. and C.L. Kelleher. *Murder Most Rare: The Female Killer*. Westport, Connecticut: Praeger, 1998.

Kennedy, Leslie and Robert A. Silverman. *Deadly Deeds: Murder in Canada*. Scarborough, Ontario: Nelson, 1993.

Kensington Ladies' Erotica Society. *Ladies Home Erotica*. Berkeley, California: Ten Speed Press, 1984.

Keough, Peter, ed. *Flesh and Blood: The National Society of Film Critics on Sex, Violence, and Censorship*. San Francisco: Mercury House, 1995.

Kerouac, Jack. *On The Road*. New York: Penguin Books, 1991.

Kilbourn, William. "The Quest for the Peaceable Kingdom." *Canadian Writing Today*. Middlesex, England: England, 1970. 46–53.

Kilmartin, Christopher. *The Masculine Self*. New York: Macmillan, 1994.

King, Neal and Martha McCaughey. "What's a Mean Woman Like You Doing in a Movie Like This?" In *Reel Knockouts: Violent Women in the Movies*. Eds. Martha McCaughey and Neal King. Austin: University of Texas Press, 2001. 1–24.

Klein, Dorie. "An Agenda for Reading and Writing about Women, Crime, and Justice." *Social Pathology* 3.2 (summer 1997): 81–91.

Kowalewski, Michael. *Deadly Musings: Violence and Verbal Form in American Fiction*. Princeton: Princeton University Press, 1993.

Kozol, Wendy. "Fracturing Domesticity: Media, Nationalism, and the Question of Feminist Influence." *Signs: Journal of Women in Culture and Society* 20.31 (1995): 646–67.

Kramer, Lawrence. *After the Lovedeath: Sexual Violence and the Making of Culture*. Berkeley: University of California Press, 1997.

Kristeva, Julia. *Pouvoirs de l'horreur: Essai sur l'abjection*. Paris: Éditions du Seuil, 1980.

– *Powers of Horror: An Essay on Abjection*. Trans. Leon S. Roudiez. New York: Columbia University Press, 1982.

Kroker, Arthur and David Cook. *The Postmodern Scene: Excremental Culture and Hyper-Aesthetics*. Montreal: New World Prespectives, 1986.

Kuribayaski, Tomako and Julie Thorp, eds. *Creating Safe Space: Violence and Women's Writing*. Albany: State University of New York Press, 1998.

Kwaterko, Józef. *Le Roman québécois et ses (inter)discours*. Montréal: Éditions Note Bene, 1998.

Labrèche, Marie-Sissi. *Borderline*. Montréal: Boréal, 2000.

– *La Brèche*. Montréal: Boréal, 2002.

Lacan, Jacques. *Écrits I*. Paris: Éditions du Seuil, 1966.

– *Écrits II*. Paris: Éditions du Seuil, 1971.

Lacombe, Dany. *Blue Politics: Pornography and the Law in the Age of Feminism*. Toronto: University of Toronto Press, 1994.

Lacroix, Jean-Guy. "Les Politiques culturelles et de communication au Canada devant la tendance à l'américanisation: Au mieux, un succès mitigé; dans les faits, un échec dramatique." In *Variations sur l'influence culturelle américaine*. Ed. Florian Sauvageau. Sainte-Foy, Québec: Les Presses de l'Université Laval, 1999. 33–58.

Lalonde, Michèle. *Speak White*. Montréal: Les Éditions de l'Hexagone, 1974.

Lamb, Sharon. *The Secret Lives of Girls: What Good Girls Really Do – Sex Play, Aggression, and their Guilt*. New York: The Free Press, 2001.

Lamonde, Yvan. "L'Ambivalence historique du Québec à l'égard de sa continentalité: circonstances, raisons et signification." In *Québécois et Américains: La Culture québécoise aux XIXe et XXe siècles*. Eds. Yvan Lamonde et Gérard Bouchard. Montréal: Fides, 1995. 61–84.

– *Ni avec eux ni sans eux: Le Québec et les États-Unis*. Montréal: Nuit Blanche Éditeur, 1996.

– et Gérard Bouchard, eds. *Québécois et Américains: La Culture québécoise aux XIXe et XXe siècles*. Montréal: Fides, 1995.

Lamont, Michele. "Most of my Friends are Refined: Keys to Cultural Boundaries." In *Money, Morals, and Manners: The Culture of the French and the American Upper-Middle Class*. Chicago: University of Chicago Press, 1992. 88–128.

Lamoureux, Diane. *L'Amère patrie: Féminisme et nationalisme dans le Québec contemporain*. Montréal: Remue-Ménage, 2001.

– "La Posture du fils." In *Malaises identitaires: Echanges féministes autour d'un Québec incertain*. Eds. Diane Lamoureux, Chantal Maillé, et Micheline de Sève. Montréal: Les Éditions du Remue-Ménage, 1999. 25–51.

– Chantal Maillé et Micheline de Sève, eds. *Malaises identitaires: Échanges féministes autour d'un Québec incertain*. Montréal: Les Éditions du Remue-Ménage, 1999.

Lampron, Pierre. *État de la situation de la contribution publique dans le financement du cinéma et de la production télévisuelle (Lampron Report)*. SODEC: November 1999.

Lamy, Suzanne. *D'elles*. Montréal: L'Hexagone, 1979.

– *Quand je lis je m'invente*. Montréal: L'Hexagone, 1984.

– *Textes: Écrits et témoignages*. Montréal: L'Hexagone, 1990.

Langlois, Simon et Jean-Louis Roy, eds. *Briser les solitudes: Les Francophonies canadiennes et québécoises*. Montréal: Note Bene, 2003.

Laplanche, Jean and J.B. Pontalis. *Formations of Fantasy*. London: Methuen, 1986.

– *Fantasme originaire*. Paris: Hachette, 1985.

Lara Croft: Tomb Raider. Dir. Simon West. Perf. Angelina Jolie. DVD. Paramount Home Video, 2001.

Laroche, Maximilien. "L'Élogie de l'Île." In *L'Identitaire et le littéraire dans les Amériques*. Eds. Bernard Andrès et Zilà Bernd. Montréal: Les Éditions Nota Bene, 1999. 255–8.

LaRue, Monique. *Copies conformes*. Montréal: Éditions Denoel, 1989.

Lashgari, Deirdre, ed. *Violence, Silence, and Anger: Women's Writing as Transgression*. Charlottesville: University Press of Virginia, 1995.

Latouche, Daniel. "Pour en finir avec la loi 101." In *Le Pays de tous les Québécois: Diversité culturelle et souveraineté*. Ed. Michel Sarra-Bournet. Montréal: VLB Éditeur, 1998. 99–107.

– "Quebec in the Emerging North American Configuration." In *Identities in North America: The Search for Community*. Eds. Robert L. Earle and John D. Wirth. Stanford: Stanford University Press, 1995.

Laurin, Danielle. "Josée Yvon, femme de personne." *Voix et Images* 8.16 (1994): 27.

Lecercle, Jean-Jacques. *Violence and Language*. New York: Routledge, 1990.

Ledbetter, Mark. *Victims and the Postmodern Narrative, or, Doing Violence to the Body: An Ethic of Reading and Writing*. New York: St. Martin's Press, 1996.

Lefkowitz, Bernard. *Our Guys: The Glen Ridge Rape and the Secret Life of the Perfect Suburb*. New York: Vintage Books, 1997.

Legaré, Anne. *Le Québec otage de ses alliés: Les Relations avec la France and les États-Unis*. Montréal: VLB Éditeur, 2003.

Legendre, Claire. *Viande*. Paris: Grasset, 1999.

Legrain, Philippe. "Globalization is not Americanization." *The Chronicle of Higher Education: The Chronicle Review*. 49.35 (9 May 2003): B7. <http:// www.chronicle.com/weekly/v49/i35/35b00701.htm>.

Leland, John. "I Am Woman. Now Prepare to Die." *The New York Times* 19 October 2003. Section 9: 1,11.

Lelièvre, Sylvain. "Entre Elvis et Félix: Le Jeu du risque." In *Variations sur l'influence culturelle américaine*. Ed. Florian Sauvageau. Sainte-Foy, Québec: Les Presses de l'Université Laval, 1999. 121–9.

Lemelin, Bernard. "Au-delà de l'américanisation culturelle: Les Influences politiques et économiques des États-Unis sur le Canada et le Québec, 1867–1988." In *Variations sur l'influence culturelle américaine*. Ed. Florian Sauvageau. Sainte-Foy, Québec: Les Presses de l'Université Laval, 1999. 101–17.

Leonard, Elizabeth Dermody. *Convicted Survivors: The Imprisonment of Battered Women Who Kill*. Albany: State University of New Press, 2002.

Le Roy, Jeanne. *La Zébresse*. Montréal: Les Herbes Rouges, 1994.

Lesemann, Frédéric. "L'Américanité des Québécois passe par un rôle actif de l'État-providence." *Québec Studies* 29 (spring/summer 2000): 43–53.

– "L'Américanité des Québécois: Le Rôle de l'État-providence dans l'expression de leur identité." In *L'Américanité et les Amériques*. Ed. Donald Cuccioletta. Sainte-Foy: Les Presses de L'Université Laval, 2001. 137–73.

Lester, David. *Le Livre noir du Canada anglais*. Montréal: Les Intouchables, 2001.

Lester, David. *Serial Killers: The Insatiable Passion*. Philadelphia: Charles Press, 1995.

Létourneau, Jocelyn. "Assumons l'identité québécoise dans sa complexité." In "Penser la nation québécoise." *Le Devoir* le 7–8 août 1999: A9.

– "The Current Great Narrative of Québécois Identity." In *Nations, Identities, Cultures*. Ed. V.Y. Mudimbe. Durham: Duke University Press, 1997.

– *Passer à l'avenir: Histoire, mémoire, identité dans le Québec d'aujourd'hui*. Montréal: Boréal, 2000.

– "Sur l'identité québécoise francophone." In *L'Identitaire et le littéraire dans les Amériques*. Eds. Bernard Andrès et Zilà Bernd. Montréal: Les Éditions Nota Bene, 1999. 51–62.

Levasseur, Jean. "Le Féminisme québécois et la littérature sexuelle." *The French Review* 71 (1998): 971–84.

Lever, Yves. *Histoire générale du cinema au Québec*. Montréal: Boréal, 1988.

Lévesque, A. *La Norme et les déviantes, des femmes au Québec pendant l'entre-deux guerres*. Montréal: Les Éditions du Remue-Ménage, 1989.

Lévesque, René. *La Solution: Le Programme du Parti Québécois*. Montréal: Éditions du Jour, 1970.

Levinas, Emmanuel. *Difficult Freedom: Essays on Judaism*. Trans. Seán Hand. Baltimore: Johns Hopkins University Press, 1990.

(Lewis), Paula Gilbert. *The Aesthetics of Stéphane Mallarmé in Relation to His Public*. Cranbury, New Jersey and London: Fairleigh Dickinson University Press; Associated University Presses, 1976.

– "From Shattered Reflections to Female Bonding: Mirroring in Marie-Claire Blais's *Vision d'Anna*." *Québec Studies* 2.1 (1984): 94–104.

–, ed. *Traditionalism, Nationalism, and Feminism: Women Writers of Quebec*. Westport: Greenwood Press, 1985.

– "Trois Générations de femmes: le rapport mère/fille dans quelques nouvelles de Gabrielle Roy." *Voix et Images* 10.3 (1985): 165–76; rpt. in *Women Writing in Quebec: Essays in Honor of Jeanne Kissner*. Eds. Paula Ruth Gilbert, Mary Jean Green, Jane Moss, and Lee Thompson. Plattsburgh: Center for the Study of Canada, 2000. 74–85.

– and Lorna Irvine, dirs. *Voice Vision Violence*. Videocassette. Canadian Film Distribution Center, 1994.

Lintvelt, Jaap, Richard Saint-Gelais, Will Verhoeven et Catherine Raffi-Béroud, eds. *Roman contemporain et identité culturelle en Amérique du nord/ Contemporary Fiction and Cultural Identity in North America*. Montréal: Éditions Nota Bene, 1998.

Lionnet, Françoise. *Postcolonial Representations: Women, Literature, Identity*. Ithica: Cornell University Press, 1995.

Lipset, Seymour Martin. *Continental Divide: The Values and Institutions of the United States and Canada*. New York: Routledge, 1990.

Loach, Loretta. "Bad Girls: Women Who Use Pornography." In *Sex Exposed: Sexuality and the Pornography Debate*. Eds. Lynne Segal and Mary McIntosh. New Brunswick: Rutgers University Press, 1993.

Loftus, Elizabeth. "The Repressed Memory Controversy." *American Psychologist* 49 (May 1994): 443–5.

Logan, Ron. *Crime Statistics in Canada, 2000. Juristat* 21.8 (2001). Ottawa: Statistics Canada. Canadian Centre for Justice Statistics, 2001.

Lombroso, Cesare and William Ferrero. *The Female Offender* [1893]. New York: D. Appleton and Co., 1895; London, England: T. Fisher Unwin, 1895.

– and Guglielmo Ferrero. *Criminal Woman, the Prostitute, and the Normal Woman*. Trans. and Intro. Nicole Hahn Rafter and Mary Gibson. Durham and London: Duke University Press, 2004.

Loranger, Françoise. *Mathieu*. Montréal: Le Cercle du Livre de France, 1967.

Lorber, Judith. *Paradoxes of Gender.* New Haven: Yale University Press, 1992.

Lorde, Audre. "Uses of the Erotic: The Erotic as Power." In *Sister Outsider.* Freedom, California: The Crossing Press, 1982.

Lorena Bobbitt. Videocassette. Blue Sky Productions, 1994.

Lost and Delirious. Dir. Léa Pool. Perfs. Piper Perabo, Jessica Paré, Mischa Barton. DVD and Videocassette. Studio Home Entertainment, 2001.

Louder, Dean, Jean Morisset, and Éric Waddell. *Vision et visages de la franco-Amérique.* Sillery, Québec: Septentrion, 2001.

Louis 19, le roi des ondes. Dir. Michel Poulette. Perfs. Martin Drainville and Michel Dominiq. Videocassette, 1996. Malofilm Video Dimedia.

Lovell, John. *Insights from Film into Violence and Oppression: Shattered Dreams of the Good Life.* Westport: Praeger, 1998.

Lowry, Beverly. *Crossed Over: A Murder, A Memoir.* New York: Alfred Knopf, 1998.

Lyon, A. D. "Be Careful What You Wish For: An Examination of Arrest and Prosecution Patterns of Domestic Violence Cases in Two Cities in Michigan." *Michigan Journal of Gender and Law* 5 (1999): 253–99.

Lyotard, Jean-François. *La Condition postmoderne: Rapport sur le savoir.* Paris: Les Éditions de Minuit, 1979.

Mac Kendrick, Karmen. *Counterpleasures.* Albany: State University of New York Press, 1999.

MacKinnon, Catharine. *Feminism Unmodified: Discourses on Life and Law.* Cambridge: Harvard University Press, 1987.

– *Only Words.* Cambridge: Harvard University Press, 1993.

– *Towards a Feminist Theory of the State.* Cambridge: Harvard University Press, 1989.

– and Andrea Dworkin. "Statement Regarding Canada Customs and Legal Approaches to Pornography." 20 August 1994.

MacLatchie, James. M. *Violence in Contemporary Canadian Society.* Toronto: John Howard Society, 1985.

Maglin, Nan Bauer and Donna Marie Perry, eds. *"Bad Girls"/"Good Girls": Women, Sex, and Power in the Nineties.* New Brunswick: Rutgers University Press, 1996.

Mahant, Edelgard E. and Graeme S. Mount. "The U.S. Cultural Impact upon Canada." *The American Review of Canadian Studies* 31.3 (autumn 2001): 449–65.

Maillé, Chantal. "Matériaux pour penser un Québec féministe postmoderne." In *Malaises identitaires: Échanges féministes autour d'un Québec incertain.* Eds. Diane Lamoureux, Chantal Maillé, et Micheline de Sève. Montréal: Les Éditions du Remue-Ménage, 1999. 145–65.

Malette, Louise and Marie Chalouh, eds. *The Montréal Massacre*. Charlottetown, Prince Edward Island: Gynergy Books, 1991.

Mallarmé, Stéphane. *Oeuvres complètes*. Paris: Gallimard, 1945.

Mandate Review Committee. *Making Our Voices Heard*. The Juneau Report, 1996.

Mandell, Nancy, ed. *Feminist Issues: Race, Class, and Sexuality*. Scarborough: Prentice Hall Canada, 1995.

Mann, Coramae Richey. *When Women Kill*. Albany: State University of New York Press, 1996.

Manning, Frank. "Reversible Resistance: Canadian Popular Culture and the Canadian Other." In *The Beaver Bites Back?* Eds. David Flaherty and Frank Manning. Montreal: McGill-Queen's University Press, 1993. 3–28.

Marcandier-Colard, Christine. *Crimes de sang et scènes capitales: Essai sur l'esthétique romantique de la violence*. Paris: Presses Universitaires de France, 1998.

Marcus, Stephen. *The Other Victorian: A Study of Sexuality and Pornography in Mid-Nineteenth-Century England*. New York: Basic Books, 1974.

Marshall, Pat Freeman and Marthe Asselin Vaillancourt. *Changing the Landscape: Ending Violence; Achieving Equality: Final Report*. Ottawa: Canadian Panel on Violence against Women, 1993.

– *The Community Kit*. Ottawa: Canadian Panel on Violence against Women, 1993.

– *Executive Summary: National Action*. Ottawa: Canadian Panel on Violence against Women, 1993.

– *"Without Fear": A Facilitator's Guide*. Ottawa: Canadian Panel on Violence against Women, 1993.

Martin, M.E. "Double Your Trouble: Dual Arrest in Family Violence." *Journal of Family Violence* 12.2 (1997): 139–57.

Mason, Gail. *The Spectacle of Violence: Homophobia, Gender, and Knowledge*. London and New York: Routledge, 2002.

Massat, Alice. *Le Ministère de l'intérieur*. Paris: Denoel, 1999.

Massé, Michelle. *In the Name of Love: Women, Masochism and the Gothic*. Ithaca and London: Cornell University Press, 1992.

Massey-Lévesque Report (Report of the Royal Commission on National Development in the Arts, Letters, and Sciences, 1949–1951). Ottawa: Edmund Cloutier, 1951.

Masters, Brooke A. "Executions Decrease for the 2nd Year." *The Washington Post* 6 September 2001: A1, A10.

Mathews, Robin. *Canadian Literature: Surrender of Revolution*. Toronto: University of Toronto Press, 1978.

Mathieu, Geneviève. *Qui est québécois? Synthèse du débat sur la redéfinition de la nation.* Montréal: VLB Éditeur, 2001.

Maugey, Axel. *De la francophonie québécoise à la francophilie internationale.* Ville de Brossard, Québec: Humanitas, 2001.

Maule, Christopher. "State of the Canada-U.S. Relationship: Culture." *The American Review of Canadian Studiess* 33.1 (spring 2003): 121–42.

Maxime, Lili. "Ether et musc." *Moebus* 56 (printemps 1993): 89–93.

Maxwell, Marilyn. *Male Rage, Female Fury.* Lanham, Maryland: University Press of America, 2000.

Mayer, Jane. "Rejecting Gina." *The New Yorker* 5 June 1995: 43–51.

Mayné, Gilles. *Pornographie, violence obscène, érotisme.* Paris: Descartes & Cie, 2001.

McCaughey, Martha and Neal King. *Reel Knockouts: Violent Women in the Movies.* Austin: University of Texas Press, 2001.

McCormack, Thelma. "American Popular Culture and the Canadian State: The Case of Pornography." In *The Beaver Bites Back?* Eds. David Flaherty and Frank Manning. Montreal: McGill-Queen's University Press, 1993. 281–92.

McKenna, Andrew J. *Violence and Difference: Girard, Derrida, and Deconstruction.* Urbana: University of Illinois Press, 1992.

McKinney, Devin. "Violence: The Strong and the Weak." *Screening Violence.* Ed. Stephen Prince. New Brunswick: Rutgers University Press, 2000. 99–109.

McMahon, Stephanie, ed. *Women, Crime and Culture: Whores and Heroes.* Toronto: Canadian Scholars' Press, 1998.

McPherson, Karen S. *Incriminations: Guilty Women/Telling Stories.* Princeton: Princeton University Press, 1994.

Men with Brooms. Dir. Paul Gross. Perfs. Paul Gross, Leslie Nielsen, Connor Price, Molly Parker. DVD. Artisan (Fox Video), 2002.

Mendel, Arthur P. *Vision and Violence.* Ann Arbor: University of Michigan Press, 1992.

Mendelsohn, Daniel. "The Melodramatic Moment." *The New York Times Magazine.* 23 March 2003: 40–3.

Merleau-Ponty, M. *Phenomenology of Perception.* Trans. Colin Smith. London: Routledge and Kegan Paul, 1962.

Meyer, Caroline and Fiona Clark. *Victims, Perpetrators and Actors: Gender, Armed Conflict, and Political Violence.* London: Zed Books, 2001.

Meyer, Cheryl L., Michelle Oberman, Kelly White, Michelle Rone, Priya Batra, and Tara Proano, contributors. *Mothers Who Kill their Children: Understanding the Acts of Moms from Susan Smith to the "Prom Mom,"* New York: New York University Press, 2001.

Meyers Helene. *Femicidal Fears: Narratives of the Female Gothic Experience*. Albany: State University of New York Press, 2001.

Michaelsen, Scott and David E. Johnson, eds. *Border Theory: The Limits of Cultural Politics*. Minneapolis: University of Minnesota Press, 1997.

Michaud, Andrée A. *Le Ravissement*. Québec: L'Instant même, 2001.

Michaud. Yves. *La Violence apprivoisée*. Paris: Hachette, 1996.

Micone, Marco. *Speak What*. Montréal: VLB Éditeur, 2001.

Miedzian, Myriam. *Boys Will Be Boys: Breaking the Link between Masculinity and Violence*. New York: Anchor Books, 1991.

– "Boys Will Be Boys." In *Boys Will Be Boys: Breaking the Link between Masculinity and Violence*. New York: Anchor Books, 1991. 41–76.

Millard, Gregory, Sarah Riegel, and John Wright. "Here's Where We Get Canadian: English-Canadian Nationalism and Popular Culture." *The American Review of Canadian Studies* 32.1 (spring 2002): 11–34.

Miller, S. L. "Expanding the Boundaries: Toward a More Inclusive and Integrated Study of Intimate Violence. *Violence and Victims* 9.2 (1994): 183–94.

– "The Paradox of Women Arrested for Domestic Violence: Criminal Justice Professionals and Service Providers Respond." *Journal of Violence against Women* 7.12 (2001): 1339–76.

Millet, Catherine. *La Vie sexuelle de Catherine M*. Paris: Éditions du Seuil, 2001.

Milot, Louise et Jaap Lintvelt, eds. *Le Roman québécois depuis 1960: Méthodes analyses*. Sainte-Foy: Les Presses de l'Université Laval, 1992.

Minh-Ha, Thi. "Not You/Like You: Postcolonial Women and the Interlocking Questions of Identity and Difference." In *Dangerous Liaisons: Gender, Nation and Postcolonial Perspectives*. Ed. A. McClintock et al. Minneapolis: University of Minnesota Press, 1997. 415–19.

Mi Vida Loca: My Crazy Life. Dir. Allison Anders Perf. Angel Aviles, Seidy Lopez, Jacob Vargas, and Panchito Gomez. Videocassette. Cineville Partners, 1993.

Monette, Hélène. *Crimes et chatouillements*. Montréal: Boréal, 2000.

Monette, Madeleine. *Le Double suspect*. Montréal: Éditions Typo, 1996.

– *Petites Violences*. Montréal: Éditions Typo, 1994.

Monette, Pierre. "*Yankees* manqués. Esquisse d'un questionnement sur le devenir-américain de la culture québécoise." In *L'Identitaire et le littéraire dans les Amériques*. Eds. Bernard Andrès et Zilà Bernd. Montréal: Les Éditions Nota Bene, 1999. 147–73.

Monster. Dir. Patty Jenkins. Perfs. Charlize Theron and Christina Ricci. Newmarket Films, DVD Dej Productions, 2003.

Montoya, Yvon and Pierre Thibeault. *Frénétiques: Treize intellectuels québécois répondent à la question: Quelle est votre perception de la culture au Québec à l'aube du XXIe siècle?* Montréal: Triptyque, 1999.

Montpetit, Caroline. "Le Roman *Putain* de Nelly Arcan en film: L'Enjeu de l'apparence." *Le Devoir* 7 avril 2004: B7.

Moore, Michael. Public Lecture. Oxford Union, Oxford University. November 2002.

Morency, Jean. "Les Modalités du décrochage européen des littératures américaines." In *Québécois et Américains: La Culture québécoise aux XIXe et XXe siècles*. Eds. Yvan Lamonde et Gérard Bouchard. Montréal: Fides, 1995. 159–93.

– *Le Mythe américain dans les fictions d'Amérique. De Washington Irving à Jacques Poulin*. Québec: Nuit Blanche Éditeur, 1994.

Morin, Jacques-Yvan. "Préface en forme de postface." In *Le Pays de tous les Québécois: Diversité culturelle et souveraineté*. Ed. Michel Sarra-Bournet. Montréal: VLB Éditeur, 1998. 7–18.

Morisset, Jean and Éric Waddell. *Amériques: Deux Parcours au départ de la Grande Rivière du Canada*. Montréal: L'Hexagone, 2000.

Morris, Allison and Ania Wilczynski. "Rocking the Cradle: Mothers Who Kill Their Children." In *Moving Targets: Women, Murder, and Representation*. Ed. Helen Birch. Berkeley: University of California Press, 1994. 198–217.

Morrissey, Belinda. *When Women Kill: Questions of Agency and Subjectivity*. London and New York: Routledge, 2003.

Morrison, Jim. "Been Down So Long." Rec. April 1971. *L.A. Woman*. Elektra Records, 75011, 1971.

– "The Crystal Ship." Rec. January 1967. *The Doors*. Elektra Records, 74007, 1967.

– "The End." Rec. January 1967. *The Doors*. Elektra Records, 74007, 1967.

– "End of the Night." Rec. January 1967. *The Doors*. Elektra Records, 74007, 1967.

– "The Hitchhiker." In *The American Night*. New York: Wilderness Publications, 1990.

– "L.A. Woman." Rec. April 1971. *L.A. Woman*. Elektra Records, 75011, 1971.

– "Light My Fire." Rec. April 1967. *The Doors*. Elektra Records, 74007, 1967.

– "Riders on a Storm." Rec. April 1971. *L.A. Woman*. Elektra Records, 75011, 1971.

– "Roadhouse Blues." Rec. February 1970. *Morrison Hotel*. Elektra Records, 75007, 1970.

– "Unhappy Girl." Rec. October 1967. *Strange Days*. Elektra Records, 74014, 1967.

– "When the Music's Over." Rec. October 1967. *Strange Days*. Elektra Records, 74014, 1967.

Morrison, Toni. *Beloved*. New York: Alfred A. Knopf, 1987.

– *Paradise*. New York: Knopf, 1998.

Mortal Thoughts. Dir. Alan Rudolph. Perf. Demi Moore, Glenne Headly, Bruce Willis, Harvey Keitel. Videocassette. RCA/Columbia Pictures, 1991.

Moser, Caroline O.N. and Fiona Clark. *Victims, Perpetrators or Actors?: Gender, Armed Conflict and Political Violence*. London: Zed Books, 2001.

Moss, John. *The Ancestral Present: Sex and Violence in the Canadian Novel*. Toronto: McClelland & Stewart, 1977.

Mulcahy, Kevin V. "Cultural Imperialism and Cultural Sovereignty: U.S.-Canadian Cultural Relations." *The American Review of Canadian Studies* 30.2 (summer 2000): 181–206.

Murray, J. Alex, ed. *Alienation and Violence in the North-American Community*. Windsor, Ontario: University of Windsor Press, 1972.

Myers, Alice and Sarah Wight, eds. *No Angels: Women Who Commit Violence*. San Francisco: Pandora, 1996.

Myre, Suzanne. *J'ai de mauvaises nouvelles pour vous*. Montréal: Les Éditions Marchand de Feuilles, 2001.

Naffine, Ngaire. *Feminism and Criminology*. Philadelphia: Temple University Press, 1996.

Natural Born Killers. Dir. Oliver Stone. Perf. Woody Harrelson and Juliette Lewis. Videocassette. Warner Bros., 1995.

Navarro, Mireya. "Women Tailor Sex Industry to their Eyes." *The New York Times/nytimes.com* 20 February 2004.

Nelson, Mariah Burton. *The Stronger Women Get, The More Men Love Football*. New York: Harcourt Brace & Co., 1994.

Nepveu, Pierre. *L'Écologie du réel: Mort et naissance de la littérature québécoise contemporaine*. Montréal: Boréal, 1988.

– *Intérieurs du nouveau monde: Essais sur les littératures du Québec et des Amériques*. Montréal: Boréal, 1998.

Neroni, Hilary. *The Violent Woman: Femininity, Narrative, and Violence in Contemporary American Cinema*. Albany: State University of New York Press, 2005.

Neuman, Shirley and Smaro Kamboureli, eds. *Amazing Space: Writing Canadian Women Writing*. Edmonton: Longspoon/NeWest Press, 1986.

New, William H. *Dreams of Speech and Violence: The Art of the Short Story in Canada and New Zealand*. Toronto: University of Toronto Press, 1987.

Newman, Peter C. *The Canadian Revolution (1985–1995): From Deference to Defiance*. Toronto: Viking, 1995.

Ng, Charles. http://www.apbnews.com/newscenter/majorcases/ng/1999/06/30/ng0630_01.html.

– http://www.crimelibrary.com/serial/ng/3.html

Nguyên-Duy, Véronique. "Le Téléroman et la volonté d'une télévision originale." In *Variations sur l'influence culturelle américaine*. Ed. Florian Sauvageau. Sainte-Foy, Québec: Les Presses de l'Université Laval, 1999. 131–57.

Nicholson, Linda J., ed. *Feminism/Postmodernism*. New York: Routledge, 1990.

Nielsen, Kai. "Un Nationalisme culturel, ni ethnique ni civique." In *Le Pays de tous les Québécois: Diversité culturelle et souveraineté*. Ed. Michel Sarra-Bournet. Montréal: VLB Éditeur, 1998. 143–59.

Nimier, Marie. *La Nouvelle Pornographie*. Paris: Gallimard, 2002.

Nkunzimana, Obed. "Le Débat postcolonial et le Québec." *Québec Studies* 35 (spring/summer 2003): 63–87.

Norris, Joel. *Serial Killers: The Growing Menace*. New York: Doubleday, 1988.

Nouvelle France. Dir. Jean Beaudin. Perfs. Noémie Godin-Vigneau, David La Haye, Gérard Dépardieu, and Tim Roth. Chrystal Films, Melanny Productions, 2005.

O'Malley, Suzanne. *Are You There Alone? The Unspeakable Crime of Andrea Yates*. New York: Simon & Schuster, 2004.

Once Were Warriors. Dir. Lee Tamahori. Perf. Rena Owen, Temuera Morrison, Mamaengaroa Kerr-Bell. Videocassette. Fine Line Features, 1995.

O'Neill, Kate. "How Two Cows Make a Crisis: U.S.-Canada Trade Relations and Mad Cow Disease." *The American Review of Canadian Studies* 35.2 (summer 2005): 295–319.

Ostry, Bernard. "American Culture in a Changing World." In *The Beaver Bites Back?* Eds. David Flaherty and Frank Manning. Montreal: McGill-Queen's University Press, 1993. 3–28.

Pacom, Diane. "Being French in North America: Quebec Culture and Globalization." *The American Review of Canadian Studies* 31.3 (autumn 2001): 441–8.

Paquette, Guy et Jacques de Guise. "La Violence augmente à la télévision." *L'Annuaire du Québec, 2004*. Ed. Michel Venne. Montréal: Éditions Fides, 2003. 535–46.

Pascal, Gabrielle, ed. *Le Roman québécois au féminin (1980–1995)*. Montréal: Éditions Triptyque, 1995.

Pascal, Rollande. "Correspondance litigieuse." *Le Devoir* 10 janvier 2003: A4.

Paterson, Janet M. "Fast So Fast: Dérives identitaires dans *Le Désert mauve* de Nicole Brossard." In *Roman contemporain et identité culturelle en Amérique du nord/Contemporary Fiction and Cultural Identity in North America*. Eds. Jaap Lintvelt, Richard Saint-Gelais, Will Verhoeven et Catherine Raffi-Béroud. Montréal: Éditions Nota Bene, 1998. 45–57.

– *Moments postmodernes dans le roman québécois*. Ottawa: Les Presses de l'Université d'Ottawa, 1990.

"Le Patriotisme est à la baisse au Canada." *Le Devoir* 27 mai 2003. A4.

Pearson, Patricia. *When She Was Bad: Violent Women and the Myth of Innocence*. New York: Viking, 1997.

Pease, Donald, ed. *National Identities and Post-Americanist Narratives*. Durham and London: Duke University Press, 1994.

Perret, Jean-Marie. "Ontologie de la violence." *Le Philosophoire: La Violence*. No. 13 (hiver 2001): 37–49.

La Petite Aurore, l'enfant martyre. 1951.

Le Philosophoire: La Violence. No. 13 (hiver 2001).

Pichette, Jean and Michel Venne. "Comment vivre ensemble?" In "Penser la nation québécoise." *Le Devoir* le 19–20 juin 1999: A1.

Poirier, Guy and Pierre-Louis Vaillancourt. *Le Bref et l'instantané: À la rencontre de la littérature québécoise du XXIe siècle*. Orléans, Québec: Les Éditions David, 2000.

Poizat, Jean-Claude. "Éditorial." *Le Philosophoire: La Violence*. No. 13 (hiver 2001): 3–7.

– "La Violence ou la déréliction du pouvoir." *Le Philosophoire: La Violence*. No. 13 (hiver 2001): 31–6.

Poliquin, Daniel. *Le Roman colonial*. Montréal: Boréal, 2000.

Pollock, Jocelyn. *Criminal Women*. Cincinnati, Ohio: Anderson Publishing Co., 1998.

Possible Worlds. Dir. Robert Lepage. Videocassette. 2000.

Potvin, Claudine. "L'Hyper-réalisme de Josée Yvon: La Scène pornographique." In *Trajectoires au féminin dans la littérature québécoise (1960–1980)*. Ed. Lucie Joubert. Montréal: Éditions Nota Bene, 2000. 197–212.

– *Pornographies*. Québec: Les Éditions L'Instant Même, 2002.

Poulette, Michel. "Culture, divertissement, commerce: Des produits américains sous étiquettes nationales?" In *Variations sur l'influence culturelle américaine*. Ed. Florian Sauvageau. Sainte-Foy, Québec: Les Presses de l'Université Laval, 1999. 159–66.

Presdee, Mike. *Cultural Criminology and the Carnival of Crime*. London/New York: Routledge, 2000/2001.

Priest, Patricia J., Cindy Jenefsky, and Jill D. Swenson. "Phallocentric Slicing: 20/20's Reporting of Lorena and John Bobbitt." In *No Angels: Women Who Commit Violence*. Eds. Alice Myers and Sarah Wight. San Francisco: Pandora, 1996. 101–12.

Prince, Stephen. "Graphic Violence in the Cinema: Origins, Aesthetic Design, and Social Effects." In *Screening Violence*. Ed. Stephen Prince. New Brunswick: Rutgers University Press, 2000.

–, ed. *Screening Violence*. New Brunswick: Rutgers University Press, 2000.

Probyn, Elspeth. *Sexing the Self: Gendered Positions in Cultural Studies*. London and New York: Routledge, 1993.

Prosser, Jay. *Second Skins: The Body Narratives of Transsexuality*. New York: Columbia University Press, 1998.

Proulx, Serge. "L'Américanité serait-elle ancrée dans les dispositifs techniques?" In *Variations sur l'influence culturelle américaine*. Ed. Florian Sauvageau. Sainte-Foy, Québec: Les Presses de l'Université Laval, 1999. 209–30.

Quarles, Mike. *Down and Dirty: Hollywood's Exploitatious Filmmakers and their Movies*. Jefferson, North Carolina: McFarland, 1993.

Rachilde (Marguerite Eymery). *La Marquise de Sade*. Paris: Gallimard, 1996.

– *Monsieur Vénus*. Paris: Flammarion, 1977.

Radford, Jill and Diana E.H. Russell, eds. *Femicide: The Politics of Woman Killing*. New York: Twayne Publishers, 1992.

Raise the Red Lantern. Dir. Zhang Yimou. Perfs. Gong Li, Ma Yingwu, He Caifei, Cao Cuifen, Jin Shuyuan. Videocassette. Orion, 1992.

Rambo: First Blood, Part II. Dir. George P. Cosmatos. Perfs. Sylvester Stallone and Richard Crenna. Videocassette. Carolco Pictures; Avid Home Entertainment, 1988.

Rathjen, Heidi and Charles Montpetit. *December 6: From the Montreal Massacre to Gun Control: The Inside Story*. Toronto: McClelland & Stewart, 1999.

Réage, Pauline (Dominique Aury). *Histoire d'O*. Précédé de *Le Bonheur dans l'esclavage* par Jean Paulhan. Paris: Pauvert, 2002.

– *Story of O*. Trans. Sabine d'Estrée. New York: Grove Press, 1965.

The Red Violin/Le Violon rouge. Dir. François Girard. Perfs. Samuel Jackson, Greta Scacchi, Jason Fleming, and Don McKellar. Videocassette. Universal Studios, 1998.

Reineke, Martha Jane. *Sacrificed Lives: Kristeva on Women and Violence*. Bloomington: Indiana University Press, 1997.

Rekers, George. *Susan Smith: Victim or Murderer*. Lakewood, Colorado: Glenbridge Publishing Ltd., 1996.

Renan, Ernest. "What Is A Nation?" In *Nation and Narration*. Ed. Homi K. Bhaba. London: Routledge, 1990. 8–22.

Renaud, Yann. "Donner des coups: La Construction du lien social." *Le Philosophoire: La Violence*. No. 13 (hiver 2001): 96–117.

Renzetti, C. M. "On Dancing with a Bear: Reflections on Some of the Current Debates among Domestic Violence Theorists." *Violence and Victims* 9.2 (1994): 195–200.

Revue des deux mondes: Que veulent les jeunes écrivains? (mars 2001).

Rhodes, Richard. *Why They Kill: The Discoveries of a Maverick Criminologist*. New York: Vintage Books, 2000.

Ricard, François. *La Génération lyrique*. Montréal: Les Éditions du Boréal, 1992.

Rich, Adrienne. *Of Woman Born: Motherhood as Experience and Institution*. New York: Bantam Books, 1976.

– "When We Dead Awaken: Writing as Re-Vision." In *On Lies, Secrets, and Silence: Selected Prose 1966–1978*. New York: W.W. Norton and Company, 1979.

Richards, Marvin. "Corralling the Wild Ponies: Correspondences between Quebec and the Postcolonial." *Québec Studies* 35 (spring/summer 2003): 133–51.

Rickman, John, ed. *A General Selection from the Works of Sigmund Freud*. New York: Doubleday, 1957.

Ricoeur, Paul. "Civilization and National Cultures." In *History and Truth*. Evanston, Ilinois: Northwestern University Press, 1965.

– *Soi-même comme un autre*. Paris: Éditions du Seuil, 1990.

– *Time and Narrative 1*. Trans. K. McLauglin and D. Pollover. Chicago: University of Chicago Press, 1981.

Rimbaud, Arthur. *Oeuvres*. Paris: Garnier, 1964.

Rioux, Hélène. *Chambre avec baignoire*. Montréal: Québec/Amérique, 1992.

– *Le Cimetière des éléphants*. Montréal: XYZ Éditeur, 1998.

– *L'Homme de Hong Kong*. Montréal: Québec/Amérique, 1986.

– "The Man from Hong Kong." Trans. Luise von Flotow. *Three by Three*. Ed. Luise von Flotow. Montreal: Guernica Editions, 1992. 77–90.

– *Les Miroirs d'Eléonore*. Montréal: Éditions Lacombe, 1990.

– *Pense à mon rendez-vous*. Montréal: Québec/Amérique, 1994.

– *Reading Nijinsky*. Trans. Jonathan Kaplansky. Montréal: XYZ Éditeur, 2001.

– "Sisyphus." Trans. Luise von Flotow. *Three by Three*. Ed. Luise von Flotow. Montreal: Guernica Editions, 1992. 91–103.

– "Thirteen Chrysanthemum Avenue." Trans. Luise von Flotow. *Three by Three*. Ed. Luise von Flotow. Montreal: Guernica Editions, 1992. 103–9.

– *Traductrice de sentiments*. Montréal: XYZ Éditeur, 1995.

Rioux, Marcel. *Une Saison à la Renardière*. Montréal: L'Hexagone, 1988.

Ristock, Janice. *No More Secrets: Violence in Lesbian Relationships*. New York: Routledge, 2002.

Robert, Martin. "La Conscience et son ombre." *Le Philosophoire: La Violence*. No. 13 (hiver 2001): 50–64.

Robinson, Lillian S. "Subject/Position." In *"Bad Girls"/"Good Girls": Women, Sex, and Power in the Nineties*. Eds. Nan Bauer Maglin and Donna Marie Perry. New Brunswick: Rutgers University Press, 1996. 177–87.

– *Wonder Woman: Feminisms and Superheroes*. New York: Routledge, 2004.

Robitaille, Antoine. "Les Québécois, pacifistes ou pacifiques? *L'Annuaire du Québec, 2004*. Ed. Michel Venne. Montréal: Éditions Fides, 2003. 53–64.

Rose, Jacqueline. *Sexuality in the Field of Vision*. London: Verso, 1986.

Ross, Alex. "The Shock of the True: Crime and Why We Can't Stop Reading about It." *The New Yorker* 19 August 1996: 70–7.

Ross, Jeffrey Ian. "Violence in Canada: An Introduction to its Sociopolitical Dynamics." In *Violence in Canada: Sociopolitical Perspectives*. Ed. Jeffrey Ian Ross. Don Mills: Oxford University Press Canada, 1995. 1–9.

–, ed. *Violence in Canada: Sociopolitical Perspectives*. Don Mills: Oxford University Press Canada, 1995.

Rostand, Edmond. *Cyrano de Bergerac*. Paris: Fasquelle Éditeurs, 1930.

Roussel, Stéphane. "Canadian-American Relations: Time for Cassandra?" *The American Review of Canadian Studies* 30.2 (summer 2000): 135–57.

Roy, Gabrielle. *Bonheur d'occasion*. Montréal: Beauchemin, 1973.

– *La Route d'Altamont*. Montréal: Éditions HMH, 1966.

The Royal Commission on Violence in the Communications Industry. *Interim Report*. Toronto, 1976.

Royle, Nicholas. *The Uncanny*. New York: Routledge, 2003.

Russell, Diana E.H. *Rape in Marriage*. Bloomington: Indiana Press, 1990.

Russell, Sue. "More of a Monster than Hollywood Could Picture." *The Washington Post* 8 February 2004. B03.

Russo, Mary. *The Female Grotesque: Risk, Excess, and Modernity*. New York: Routledge, 1995.

Rutherford, Paul. "Made in America: The Problem of Mass Culture in Canada." In *The Beaver Bites Back?* Eds. David Flaherty and Frank Manning. Montreal: McGill-Queen's University Press, 1993. 260–80.

Said, Edward W. *Culture and Imperialism*. New York: Vintage, 1994.

– *Orientalism*. New York: Vintage, 1979.

– *The World, the Text, and the Critic*. Cambridge: Harvard University Press, 1983.

Saint-Exupéry, Antoine de. *Le Petit Prince*. Paris: Gallimard, 1946.

Saint-Gelais, Richard. "L'Amérique virtuelle de la science-fiction québécoise." In *Roman contemporain et identité culturelle en Amérique du nord/ Contemporary Fiction and Cultural Identity in North America*. Eds. Jaap Lintvelt, Richard Saint-Gelais, Will Verhoeven et Catherine Raffi-Béroud. Montréal: Éditions Nota Bene, 1998. 141–53.

–, Jaap Lintvelt, W.M. Verhoeven, et Catherine Raffi-Béroud. "Introduction." In *Roman contemporain et identité culturelle en Amérique du nord/ Contemporary Fiction and Cultural Identity in North America*. Eds. Jaap Lintvelt, Richard Saint-Gelais, Will Verhoeven et Catherine Raffi-Béroud. Montréal: Éditions Nota Bene, 1998. 5–28.

Saint-Jacques, Denis. "The Basic Plot of the North-American Best Seller." In *Roman contemporain et identité culturelle en Amérique du nord/ Contemporary Fiction and Cultural Identity in North America*. Eds. Jaap Lintvelt, Richard Saint-Gelais, Will Verhoeven et Catherine Raffi-Béroud. Montréal: Éditions Nota Bene, 1998. 177–88.

Saint-Martin, Lori. "L'Amour et la rivière: *L'Obéissance* de Suzanne Jacob." In *Le Roman québécois au féminin (1980–1995)*. Ed. Gabrielle Pascal. Montréal: Éditions Triptyque, 1997. 162–74.

– *Contre-Voix: Essais de critique au féminin*. Montréal: Nuit Blanche Éditeur, 1997.

– "'Les Deux Femmes, la petite et la grande': Love and Murder in the Mother-Daughter Relationship." In *Women by Women: The Treatment of Female Characters by Women Writers of Fiction in Quebec since 1980*. Ed. Roseanna Lewis Dufault. Cranbury, New Jersey: Fairleigh Dickinson Press/ Associated University Presses, Inc. 1997. 195–220.

– "Les espaces impossibles de la relation père-fille." In *Sexuation, espace, écriture: La Littérature québécoise en transformation*. Ed. Louise Dupré, Jaap Lintvelt, et Janet Paterson. Montréal: Éditions Nota Bene, 2002. 391–411.

– "Infanticide, Suicide, Matricide, and Mother-Daughter Love: Suzanne Jacob's *L'Obéissance* and Ying Chen's *L'Ingratitude*." *Canadian Literature* 196 (2001): 60–83.

– *Le Nom de la mère: Mères, filles et écriture dans la littérature québécoise au féminin*. Montréal: Éditions Note Bene, 1999.

– "The Other Family Romance: Daughters and Fathers in Quebec Women's Fiction of the Nineties." In *Doing Gender: Franco-Canadian Women Writers of the 1990s*. Eds. Paula Ruth Gilbert and Roseanna L. Dufault. Madison & Teaneck, New Jersey: Fairleigh Dickinson University Press; Cranbury, New Jersey, London, & Mississauga, Ontario: Associated University Presses, 2001. 169–85.

– "Playing with Gender, Playing with Fire: Anne Dandurand's and Jeanne Le Roy's Feminist Parodies of *Histoire d'O.*" *Nottingham French Studies* 40.1 (2001): 31–40.

– "Writing (Jumping) off the Edge of the World: Metafeminism and New Women Writers of Quebec." In *Postcolonial Subjects: Francophone Women Writers.* Eds. Mary Jean Green et al. Minneapolis: University of Minnesota Press, 1996. 285–303.

Salmon, Catherine and Donald Symons. *Warrior Lovers: Erotic Fiction, Evolution and Female Sexuality.* New Haven: Yale University Press, 2004.

Sanders, William B. *Gangbangs and Drive-bys: Grounded Culture and Juvenile Gang Violence.* New York: Aldine de Gruyter, 1994.

Sands, Christopher. "A Chance to End Culture Trade Conflict between Canada and the United States." *The American Review of Canadian Studies* 31.3 (autumn 2001): 483–99.

Sarra-Bournet, Michel. "Comment devient-on Québécois?" In *Le Pays de tous les Québécois: Diversité culturelle et souveraineté.* Ed. Michel Sarra-Bournet. Montréal: VLB Éditeur, 1998. 237–49.

– "Introduction: À la poursuite d'un destin commun." In *Le Pays de tous les Québécois: Diversité culturelle et souveraineté.* Ed. Michel Sarra-Bournet. Montréal: VLB Éditeur, 1998. 19–35.

–, ed. *Manifeste des intellectuels pour la souveraineté* suivi de *Douze essais sur l'avenir du Québec.* Montréal: Fides, 1995.

–, ed. *Les Nationalismes au Québec du XIXe au XXIe siècle.* Sainte-Foy, Québec: Les Presses de l'Université Laval, 2001.

–, ed. *Le Pays de tous les Québécois: Diversité culturelle et souveraineté.* Montréal: VLB Éditeur, 1998.

Saunders, D.G. "Other 'Truths' about Domestic Violence: A Reply to McNeely and Robinson-Simpson." *Social Work* 32 (1988): 179–83.

– "The Tendency to Arrest Victims of Domestic Violence: A Preliminary Analysis of Officer Characteristics." *Journal of Interpersonal Violence* 10.2 (1995): 147–58.

– "When Battered Women Use Violence: Husband-Abuse or Self-Defense?" *Victims and Violence* 1.1 (1986): 47–58.

– "Wife Abuse, Husband Abuse, or Mutual Combat?" In *Feminist Perspectives on Wife Abuse.* Eds. K. Yllo and M. Bogard. Beverly Hills, California: Sage, 1988. 90–113.

Sauvageau, Florian. "Présentation: Paradoxes et ambiguités." In *Variations sur l'influence culturelle américaine.* Ed. Florian Sauvageau. Sainte-Foy, Québec: Les Presses de l'Université Laval, 1999. xi–xxviii.

–, ed. *Variations sur l'influence culturelle américaine*. Sainte-Foy, Québec: Les Presses de l'Université Laval, 1999.

Sauvé, Mathieu-Robert. "Le Québec, *yes Sir!*" In *Le Pays de tous les Québécois: Diversité culturelle et souveraineté*. Ed. Michel Sarra-Bournet. Montréal: VLB Éditeur, 1998. 49–58.

Savoie, Josée. *Crime Statistics in Canada, 2001. Juristat* 22.6 (2002). Ottawa: Statistics Canada. Canadian Centre for Justice Statistics, 2002.

– *Homicide in Canada, 2002. Juristat* 23.8 (2003). Ottawa; Statistics Canada. Canadian Centre for Justice Statistics, 2003.

Scarce, Michael. *Male on Male Rape: The Hidden Toll of Stigma and Shame*. New York: Plenum, 1997.

Scarpetta, Guy. *L'Impureté*. Paris: Grasset, 1986.

Scarry, Elaine. *The Body in Pain: The Making and Unmaking of the World*. New York: Oxford University Press, 1985.

Schissel, B. *Blaming Children: Youth Crime, Moral Panics and the Politics of Hate*. Halifax: Fernwood, 1997.

Schlesinger, Arthur, Jr. *Violence: America in the Sixties*. New York: Signet, 1968.

Schlesinger, Philip et al. *Women Viewing Violence*. London: BFI Publishers, 1992.

Schneider, Elizabeth. *Battered Women and Feminist Lawmaking*. New Haven: Yale University Press, 2000.

Scholder, Amy, ed. *Critical Condition: Women on the Edge of Violence*. San Francisco: City Lights Books, 1993.

Schor, Naomi. *Reading in Detail: Aesthetics and the Feminine*. New York and London: Methuen, 1987.

Schudson, Michael. "How Culture Works: Perspectives from Media Studies on the Efficacy of Symbols." *Theory and Society* 18 (1989): 153–80.

Schwartzwald, Robert. "Rush to Judgment? Postcolonial Criticism and Quebec." *Québec Studies* 35 (spring/summer 2003): 113–32.

Scott, Chris. *Jack: A Novel about Jack the Ripper*. Toronto: Macmillan of Canada, 1988.

Seiler, Robert M. "Selling Patriotism/Selling Beer: The Case of the 'I AM CANADIAN!' Commercial." *The American Review of Canadian Studies* 32.1 (spring 2002): 44–66.

Seltzer, Mark. *Serial Killers: Death and Life in America's Wound Culture*. New York: Routledge, 1998.

Sen, Mala. *India's Bandit Queen: The True Story of Phoolan Devi*. New Delhi: HarperCollins India, 1993.

Serial Killers. Videocassette. Wavelength Video Productions, 1994.

Sève, Micheline de. "Les Féministes québécoises et leur identité civique." In *Malaises identitaires: Echanges féministes autour d'un Québec incertain.* Eds. Diane Lamoureux, Chantal Maillé et Micheline de Sève. Montréal: Les Éditions du Remue-Ménage, 1999. 167–84.

Seymour, Michel. *La Nation en question.* Montréal: L'Hexagone, 1999.

– "Pour un Québec multiethnique, pluriculturel et multinational." In *Le Pays de tous les Québécois: Diversité culturelle et souveraineté.* Ed. Michel Sarra-Bournet. Montréal: VLB Éditeur, 1998. 219–35.

– "Le Problème de la nation québécoise n'est pas son existence mais sa (non) reconnaissance." In "Penser la nation québécoise." *Le Devoir* le 11–12 septembre 1999: A11.

Shapiro, Ann-Louise. *Breaking the Codes: Female Criminality in Fin-de-Siècle Paris.* Stanford: Stanford University Press, 1996.

Sharrett, Christopher, ed. *Mythologies of Violence in Postmodern Media.* Detroit: Wayne State University Press, 1999.

Sheley, Joseph F. and James D. Wright. *In the Line of Fire: Youth, Guns, and Violence in Urban America.* New York: Aldine de Gruyter, 1995.

Sherman, Cindy, dir. *Office Killer.* Perf. Carol Kane, Molly Ringwald, Jeanne Tripplehorn. Videocassette. Buena Vista/Dimension, 1997.

Silence of the Lambs. Dir. Jonathan Demme. Perfs. Jodie Foster, Anthony Hopkins, Scott Glenn. Videocassette. Orion, 1991.

Silverman, Robert A. and Leslie Kennedy. "Women Who Kill Their Children." *Violence and Victims* 3 (1988): 113–27.

Simmons, Rachel. *Odd Girl Out: The Hidden Culture of Aggression in Girls.* New York: Harcourt, 2002.

Simon, Rita. *Women and Crime.* Lexington, Massachusetts: DC Heath, 1975.

Simon, Sherry. "L'Appartenance hybride." In *Malaises identitaires: Échanges féministes autour d'un Québec incertain.* Eds. Diane Lamoureux, Chantal Maillé et Micheline de Sève. Montréal: Les Éditions du Remue-Ménage, 1999. 133–44.

– *Hybridité culturelle.* Montréal: L'Île de la Tortue, 1999.

– *Le Trafic des langues.* Montréal: Boréal, 1996.

–, Pierre L'Hérault, Robert Schwartzwald et Alexis Nouss, eds. *Fictions de l'identitaire au Québec.* Montréal: XYZ Éditeur, 1991.

Sinha, Niraj. *Women and Violence.* New Delhi: Vihas Publishing House, 1989.

Skrapec, Candice. "The Female Serial Killer: An Evolving Criminality." In *Moving Targets: Women, Murder, and Representation.* Ed. Helen Birch. Berkeley: University of California Press, 1994. 241–68.

Slotkin, Richard. *Gunfighter Nation: The Myth of the Frontier in Twentieth-Century America.* New York: Harper Perennial, 1992.

Smart, Carol. "Disruptive Bodies and Unruly Sex: The Regulation of Reproduction and Sexuality in the Nineteenth Century." In *Regulating Womanhood: Historical Essays on Marriage, Motherhood and Sexuality*. London: Routledge, 1992.

– *Women, Crime, and Criminology: A Feminist Critique*. London: Routledge and Kegan Paul, 1977.

Smart, Patricia. *Écrire dans la maison du père: L'Émergence du féminin dans la tradition littéraire du Québec*. Montréal: Éditions Québec/Amérique, 1988.

Smith, Paul. *Discerning the Subject*. Minneapolis: University of Minnesota Press, 1988.

Sofsky, W. *Traité de la violence*. Paris: Gallimard, 1998.

Solanas, Valerie. *SCUM Manifesto*. Edinburgh, Scotland/San Francisco: AK Press, 1997.

Soldier of Fortune. www.sofmag.com; www.soldier-of-fortune.com.

Sontag, Susan. "The Pornographic Imagination." In *A Susan Sontag Reader*. New York: Vintage Books, 1983. 205–33.

Span, Paula. "The Failing Light." *The Washington Post Magazine* 15 February 2004. 17–21, 31–7.

Spencer, Suzy. *Breaking Point*. New York: St. Martin's Press, 2002.

Spergel, Irving. *The Youth Gang Problem: A Community Approach*. New York: Oxford University Press, 1995.

Spierenberg, Pieter. *The Spectacle of Suffering*. Cambridge: Cambridge University Press, 1984.

Spivak, Gayatri Chakravorty. "Can The Subaltern Speak?" In *Marxism and the Interpretation of Culture*. Eds. Cary Nelson and Lawrence Grossberg. Chicago: University of Illinois Press, 1988. 280–1.

– *A Critique of Postcolonial Reason: Toward a History of the Vanishing Present*. Cambridge: Harvard University Press, 1999.

– *In Other Worlds: Essays in Cultural Politics*. New York: Methuen, 1987.

Stange, Mary Zeiss and Carol K. Oyster. *Gun Women: Firearms and Feminism in Contemporary America*. New York: New York University Press, 2000.

Stanko, Elizabeth and Anne Scully. "Retelling the Tale: The Emma Humphreys Case." In *No Angels: Women Who Commit Violence*. Eds. Alice Myers and Sarah Wight. San Francisco: Pandora, 1996. 57–71.

Stardom. Dir. Denys Arcand. Perfs. Jessica Paré, Dan Aykroyd, Robert Lepage, Frank Langella. DVD and Videocassette, 2001. Universal Studios, 2000.

Statistique/Statistique Canada. Ministère de la Justice. <http://www.statcan.ca/english/Pgbd/State/justic.htm#cri>

Stets, J.E. and M.A. Straus. "Gender Differences in Reporting Marital Violence and Its Medical and Psychological Consequences." In *Physical Violence in American Families: Risk Factors and Adaptations to Violence in 8,145 Families*. Eds. M.A. Straus and R.J. Gelles. New Brunswick, New Jersey: Transaction Publishers, 1990. 151–70.

Stiles, Kristine. "Shaved Heads and Masked Bodies: Representations from Cultures of Trauma." In *Talking Gender: Public Images, Personal Journeys, and Political Critiques*. Eds. Jean O'Barr, Nancy Hewitt, and Nancy Rosebaugh. Chapel Hill: University of North Carolina Press, 1996. 36–64.

Stille, Alexander. "Did Knives and Forks Cut Murders?" *The New York Times on the Web* 3 May 2003. <http://www.nytimes.com>.

Strange, Carolyn. "Perspectives on the Latimer Trial: Mercy for Murderers? A Historical Perspective on the Royal Prerogative of Mercy." *Saskatchewan Law Review* (2001). <http://www.lexis-nexis/legal>.

Straus, M.A. "The Controversy over Domestic Violence by Women: A Methodological, Theoretical, and Sociology of Science Analysis." In *Violence in Intimate Relationships*. Eds. X.B. Arriaga & S. Oskamp. Thousand Oaks, California: Sage Publications, 1999.

– "Physical Assaults by Wives: A Major Social Problem." In *Current Controversies on Family Violence*. Eds. R.J. Gelles and D.R. Loseke. Newbury Park, California: Sage Publications, 1993. 67–87.

– "Physical Assaults by Women Partners: A Major Social Problem." In *Women, Men and Gender: Ongoing Debates*. Ed. M.R. Walsh. New Haven: Yale University Press, 1997. 210–21.

Strossen, Nadine. *Defending Pornography: Free Speech, Sex, and the Fight for Women's Rights*. New York: Scribner, 1995.

Stuart, Reginald C. "Death of the Nation-State? Global Mass Culture in the Twenty-First Century: A Roundtable Discussion." *The American Review of Canadian Studies* 31.3 (autumn 2001): 427–40.

Suleiman, Susan Rubin, ed. *The Female Body in Western Culture: Contemporary Perspectives*. Cambridge: Harvard University Press, 1986.

– "Pornography, Transgression, and the Avant-Garde: Bataille's *Story of the Eye*." In *The Poetics of Gender*. Ed. Nancy K. Miller. New York: Columbia University Press, 1986. 117–36.

– *Subversive Intent: Gender, Politics, and the Avant-Garde*. Cambridge: Harvard University Press, 1990.

Swidler, Ann. "Culture as Action." *American Sociological Review* 51.2 (1986): 273–86.

Tal, Kali. *Worlds of Hurt: Reading the Literatures of Trauma*. New York: Cambridge University Press, 1996.

Talbot, Emile. Rev. of *Critique de l'Americanité*, by Joseph-Yvon Thériault. *The French Review* 76.6 (May 2003): 1291–2.

Talbot, Margaret. "Girls Just Want to be Mean." *The New York Times Magazine* 24 February 2002, late ed., sec. 6: 24+.

Tanner, Laura E. *Intimate Violence: Reading Rape and Torture in Twentieth-Century Fiction.* Bloomington: Indiana University Press, 1994.

Tarentino, Quentin, dir. *Kill Bill: Vol 1.* Perfs. Uma Thurman, Chiaka Kuriyama, Lucy Liu, Daryl Hannah, David Carradine. Miramax, 2003.

–, dir. *Kill Bill: Vol 2.* Perfs. Uma Thurman, Lucy Liu, David Carradine. Miramax, 2004.

Tavris, Carol. *The Mismeasure of Woman.* New York: Simon and Schuster, 1992.

Taylor, Charles. "De la nation culturelle à la nation politique." In "Penser la nation québécoise." *Le Devoir* le 19–20 juin 1999: A13.

Taylor, Joelle and Tracey Chandler. *Lesbians Talk Violent Relationships.* London: Scarlet Press, 1995.

Tessier, Jules. *Américanité et francité: Essais critiques sur les littératures d'expression française en Amérique du Nord.* Ottawa: Le Nordir, 2001.

Thelma and Louise. Dir. Ridley Scott. Perfs. Susan Sarandon and Geena Davis. Videocassette. MGM/UA, 1991.

Théoret, France. *Entre raison et déraison.* Montréal: Les Herbes Rouges, 1987.

– *Nous parlerons comme on écrit.* Montréal: Les Herbes Rouges, 1982.

Thériault, Joseph Yvon. *Critique de l'américanité: Mémoire et démocratie au Québec.* Montréal: Québec Amérique, 2002.

Thernstrom, Melanie. *Halfway Heaven: Diary of a Harvard Murder.* New York: Doubleday, 1997.

Thompson, John Herd. "Playing by the New Washington Rules: The U.S.-Canada Relationship, 1994–2003." *The American Review of Canadian Studies* 33.1 (spring 2003): 5–26.

– and Stephen J. Randall. *Canada and the United States: Ambivalent Allies.* Athens: University of Georgia Press, 1994.

Torrance, Judy and Margaret Curtis. *Public Violence in Canada 1867–1982.* Kingston: McGill-Queen's University Press, 1986.

Tramier, Sylvie. "Le Nouveau Féminisme." *Le Devoir* 8 mars 1994: 1.

Tremblay, Lise. *La Danse juive.* Montréal: Leméac, 1999.

Tremblay, Odile. "Agnès Maltais s'inquiète de la politique fédérale du long métrage." *Le Devoir* 7 October 2000: A6.

– "Une Année extraordinaire!" *Le Devoir* 15–16 février 2003: H1, H2.

– "Diane Lemieux dévoile sa politique du cinéma." *Le Devoir* 12 mars 2003: B10.

– "Festival de Cannes: Doublé pour *Les Invasions*." *Le Devoir* 26 mai 2003: A1, A8.

– "Le Nouveau Visage du cinéma québécois." *Le Devoir* 20–21 octobre 2001: C1, C4.

– "Un Tarentino 'irréel' où le sang gicle en quasi-permanence." *Le Devoir* 12 octobre 2003. Section E: 12.

– "Tourner en anglais au Québec." *Le Devoir* 10–11 juin 2000: B1, B3.

Trexler, Richard C. *Sex and Conquest: Gendered Violence, Political Order, and the European Conquest of the Americas.* Ithaca: Cornell University Press, 1995.

The Truman Show. Dir. Peter Weir. Perf. Jim Carey. Videocassette. Paramount Pictures, 1998.

Turgeon, Emmanuelle. *Les Beaux Survivants.* Outremont, Québec: Lanctôt, Éditeur, 1998.

Twitchell, James B. *Preposterous Violence: Fables of Aggression in Modern Culture.* New York: Oxford University Press, 1989.

United States Census Bureau. <http://www.census.gov>.

– *U.S. Census Bureau News.* 18 December 2003.

United States Department of Justice, Federal Bureau of Investigation. *Crime in the United States, 1999. Uniform Crime Reports,* 2000.

– *Crime in the United States, 2000. Uniform Crime Reports,* 2001.

– *Crime in the United States, 2001. Uniform Crime Reports,* 2002.

– *Crime in the United States, 2002. Uniform Crime Reports, 2003.*

– *Crime in the United States, 2003. Uniform Crime Reports,* 2004.

– *Crime Index, 2000 Preliminary Figures, 2001.*

– *Preliminary Semiannual Uniform Crime Report, January–June 2002. 16 December 2002.*

– *Preliminary Semiannual Uniform Crime Report, January–June* 2004. *13 December* 2004.

– *Preliminary Uniform Crime Report, 2002. 16 June 2003.*

Vance, Carol, ed. *Pleasure and Danger: Exploring Female Sexuality.* London: Routledge and Kegan Paul, 1989.

Van Gelder, Lindsay. "Attack of the 'Killer Lesbian.'" *Ms.* 2.4 (Jan./Feb. 1992): 80–2.

Van Schendel, Nicolas. "Un Québec francopolyphonique: La Langue française parmi d'autres." In *Le Grand Récit des Amériques: Polyphonie des identités culturelles dans le contexte de la continentalisation.* Eds. Donald Cuccioletta, Jean-François Côté, et Frédérique Lesemann. Saint-Foy, Québec: Les Presses de l'Université Laval, 2001. 149–62.

Van't Land, Hilligje. "L'Espace américain et l'emprisonnement de l'écriture: *Une Histoire américaine* de Jacques Godbout." In *Le Roman québécois depuis 1960: Méthodes, analyses.* Eds. Louise Milot et Jaap Lintvelt. Sainte-Foy: Les Presses de l'Université Laval, 1992. 249–68.

Vasil, Normande. *J'accuse la violence.* Chicoutimi, Québec: Les Éditions JCL, 1999.

Venne, Michel, ed. *L'Annuaire du Québec, 2004.* Montréal: Éditions Fides, 2003.

–, ed. *Justice, démocratie et prospérité: L'Avenir du modèle québécois.* Montréal: Québec-Amérique, 2003.

La Vie en rose. Juillet–août 1985.

Villeneuve, Paul. "Canada, Québec and North American Continental Integration." *Recherches sociographiques* 39.2–3 (1998): 393–416.

Vivre sa vie/My Life to Live. Dir. Jean-Luc Godard. Perfs. Anna Karina, Sady Rebbot. Videocassette and DVD, 1998. Fox Lorber, 1962.

Voronoff, Serge. *The Conquest of Life.* New York: Brentano's, 1928.

de Vries, Hent and Samuel Weber, eds. *Violence, Identity, and Self-Determination.* Stanford: Stanford University Press, 1997.

Wagner, Peter. *Eros Revived: Erotica of the Enlightenment in England and America.* London: Secker and Worburg, 1988.

Wallace, Marnie. *Crime Statistics in Canada, 2002. Juristat* 23.5 (2003). Ottawa: Statistics Canada. Canadian Centre for Justice Statistics, 2003.

– *Crime Statistics in Canada, 2003. Juristat* 24.6 (2004). Ottawa: Statistics Canada. Canadian Centre for Justice Statistics, 2004.

Warren, Karen J. and Duane Cady, eds. *Bringing Peace Home: Feminism, Violence, and Nature.* Bloomington: Indiana University Press, 1996.

Weil, Eric. *Logique de la philosophie.* Paris: Vrin, 1967.

Weinberger-Thomas, Catherine. *Ashes of Immortality: Widow-Burning in India.* Chicago: University of Chicago Press, 1999.

Welcome to the Dollhouse. Dir. Todd Solondz. Perfs. Heather Matarazzo and Christine Brucato. Columbia Tristar Home Video, 1996.

Welsh, Jennifer M. "Is A North-American Generation Emerging?" *ISUMA, Canadian Journal of Policy Research* 1.1 (spring 2000): 86–92.

Wernick, Andrew. "American Popular Culture in Canada: Trends and Reflections." In *The Beaver Bites Back?* Eds. David Flaherty and Frank Manning. Montreal: McGill-Queen's University Press, 1993. 293–302.

West, Candace and Don H. Zimmerman. "Doing Gender." *Gender and Society* 1 (1987): 125–51.

White, Hayden. "The Value of Narrativity in the Representation of Reality." In *On Narrative.* Ed. W.J.T. Mitchell. Chicago: University of Chicago Press, 1981.

White, J.W. and R.M. Kowalski. "Deconstructing the Myth of the Nonaggressive Woman: A Feminist Analysis." *Psychology of Women Quarterly* 18 (1994): 487–508.

Whitmer, Barbara. *The Violence Mythos*. Albany: State University of New York Press, 1997.

Whyte, Murray. "Where Films Made in English Can Seem a Cultural Betrayal." *The New York Times* 17 September 2000, sec. 2: 16.

Wieviorka, M. *Violence en France*. Paris: Éditions du Seuil, 1999.

Wiggers, Richard Dominic. "Introduction: SHAFR 2000 and North American Cultures." *The American Review of Canadian Studies* 31.3 (autumn 2001): 423–6.

Wilczynski, Ania. *Child Homicide*. New York: Oxford University Press, 1997.

Williams, Linda. *Hard Core: Power, Pleasure, and the "Frenzy of the Visible."* Berkeley: University of California Press, 1999.

–, ed. *Porn Studies*. Durham: Duke University Press, 2004.

– "Sequels and Revisions: 'A Desire of One's Own.'" In *Hard Core: Power, Pleasure, and the "Frenzy of the Visible."* Berkeley: University of California Press, 1999. 229–64.

Winderbank, Janice J. and Renate Gunther, eds. *Violence and Conflict in Modern French Culture*. Sheffield: Sheffield Academic Press, 1994.

Wiseman, Rosalind. *Queen Bees and Wannabes: Helping Your Daughter Survive Cliques, Gossip, Boyfriends, and Other Realities of Adolescence*. New York: Crown, 2002.

Woroby, Tamara M. "Should Canadian Immigration Policy be Synchronized with U.S. Immigration Policy? Lessons Learned at the Start of Two Centuries." *The American Review of Canadian Studies* 35.2 (summer 2005): 247–64.

Worrall, Anne. *Offending Women: Female Lawbreakers and the Criminal Justice System*. London: Routledge, 1990.

Wrangham, Richard and Dale Peterson. *Demonic Males: Apes and the Origins of Human Violence*. New York: Houghton Mifflin, 1996.

Wright, Robert. "The Biology of Violence." *The New Yorker* 13 March 1995: 68–77.

Wuthnow, Robert. *Meaning and Moral Order*. Berkeley: University of California Press, 1987.

Yardley, Jim. "Andrea Yates." *The New York Times* 7 September 2001.

Yvon, Josée. *La Cobaye*. Montréal: VLB Éditeur, 1993.

– *Danseuses-mamelouk*. Montréal: VLB Éditeur, 1982.

– *Filles-commandos bandées*. Montréal: Les Herbes Rouges, 1976.

– *Maîtresses-cherokees*. Montréal: VLB Éditeur, 1986.

– *Travesties-kamikaze*. Montréal: Les Herbes Rouges, 1980.

Zahavi, Helen. *Dirty Weekend*. London: Cleis Press, 2000.

Zerubavel, Eviatar. *The Fine Line: Making Distinctions in Everyday Life*. Chicago: University of Chicago Press, 1991.

Zizek, Slovoj. *Metastasies of Enjoyment: Essays on Women and Causality*. New York: Verso, 1994.

Zola, Émile. *Nana*. Paris: Fasquelle, 1971.

Un Zoo, la nuit. Dir. Jean Claude Lauzon. Perfs. Gilles Maheu, Germain Houde. 1987.

Index